sengoídelc

OLD IRISH FOR BEGINNERS

Irish Studies

JAMES MACKILLOP, *Series Editor*

David Stifter

sengoídelc

Old Irish for Beginners

SYRACUSE UNIVERSITY PRESS

This book was published with the assistance
of a grant from the University of Vienna.

All cartoons courtesy of Theresa-Susanna Illés.

Stylized Old Irish "Sengoídelc" on front cover and title page
courtesy of the Board of Trinity College Dublin.

∞The paper used in this publication meets the minimum
requirements of the American National Standard for Information Sciences—Permanence of Paper for Printed Library
Materials, ANSI Z39.48-1992.

For a listing of books published and distributed by
Syracuse University Press, visit our website at
SyracuseUniversityPress.syr.edu.

ISBN: 978-0-8156-3072-2

Library of Congress Cataloging-in-Publication Data
Stifter, David.
    Sengoidelc: Old Irish for beginners / David Stifter.—
        1st ed.
        p .cm— (Irish studies)
    Includes bibliographical references and index.
    ISBN 0-8156-3072-7 (pbk. : alk. paper)
    l. Irish language—To 1100—Grammar. I. Title. II. Series:
Irish studies (Syracuse, N.Y.)
PB1218.S75 2006
491.6'282421—dc22   2006045014

Manufactured in the United States of America

 DAVID STIFTER holds a Ph.D. in Indo-European
linguistics and Celtic studies from the University
of Vienna. He is a lecturer at the Institut für
Sprachwissenschaft at the University of Vienna and chair of
the Austrian Society for Celtic studies. He has taught Old
Irish for almost ten years.

Contents

Introduction/Remrád

When I started teaching Old Irish at the University of Vienna in 1996, I soon realized that the existing handbooks of and introductions to Old Irish did not meet the requirements of late 20th and early 21st century university teaching. With the rapid decline of Latin in modern schools and with the number of students who have had their fair share of classical languages ever dwindling, it has become practically impossible to explain the peculiarities of Old Irish by simply referring to similarities with or differences to Latin (not to mention Greek or Sanskrit). At the same time, because the number of students who take interest in Old Irish is ever growing, I found it necessary to write a beginners' course of Old Irish that is self-explanatory without making reference to a classical language. It has been my aim to compile a book that ideally allows even an absolute beginner to learn the language on his or her own, without the guidance of a teacher. This is not to say, of course, that tutorial guidance should not be sought in the first place!

To avoid the rather dull presentation of introductory courses not only in Irish but also in most old languages, I have chosen an approach that is still more at home in modern language teaching than in the instruction of so-called dead languages. Humorous ovine illustrations serve to emphasize grammatical points or help to give the students a bit of relief when the difficulties of the Old Irish language become too hard to bear. Odd as it may seem to scholars of traditional upbringing, it has been my own experience over the years that the students react very positively to the illustrations and that these help very much to keep the interest in the language alive.

The book is divided into 58 lessons. Each lesson again consists of several smaller paragraphs that are devoted to particular elements of Old Irish grammar. I have been careful not to pack too much material into the lessons at once. Instead a slow pace, proceeding step by step, has been chosen. Topics from nominal morphology, the verbal complex, and the syntax alternate with each other. After every two or three lessons an additional lesson has been inserted that is exclusively devoted to exercises and to the repetition of the newly learned material. These exercises partly consist of tests that aim at the recognition of verbal and nominal forms. But their most important part is comprised of translations of Old Irish sentences.

The translations go in two directions. First you will find 20 sentences in Old Irish that have to be translated into English. Then 20 sentences in English, using the same words and grammatical structures as the corresponding Old Irish ones, although with slight variations, which then have to be translated into Old Irish. Although the latter may seem an unnecessary task, it has been my personal experience when learning Old Irish that the language is best acquired by forming sentences in it by oneself. I have put much effort into finding as many authentic Old Irish sentences as possible for the exercises. This has not been possible for the first lessons, however, where the students have been exposed to too little grammar, and therefore I have had to invent those sentences myself. But in the later lessons I could largely rely on authentic material, gathered both from the glosses and from more secular literature. Nevertheless I have taken the liberty of interfering with the Old Irish texts to whatever extent seemed appropriate to me in order to avoid too complicated grammatical structures that would ask too much of the students.

A single asterisk * before a sentence indicates that it builds on authentic Old Irish material but that I have changed some elements in the sentence (e.g., the tense, persons, etc.). A double asterisk ** indicates that the following sentence is authentic Old Irish. But even in these latter cases I have sometimes silently adapted the orthography or slightly changed grammatical features so that they conform to standard grammar. Sometimes I have used Middle Irish texts and 'palaeo-hibernicized' them in order to accord with the standards of Old Irish. My own translations of Irish sentences, both in the exercise sections and in the corresponding solutions, may not always sound like good, idiomatic English, but this is intentional. I have tried to follow the wording of the Old Irish sentences as closely as possible, without doing too much violence at the same time to English syntax.

In all exercises and in most other paragraphs I have added phonological transcriptions of the Old Irish texts. Old Irish phonology and spelling are notoriously difficult, and it has been my experience while teaching that the rules of orthography cannot be repeated often enough. I hope that with many transcriptions I can offer guidelines to beginners of Old Irish that help them come to terms with the sounds and alphabet of this language.

Where it seemed necessary or advisable, I have made reference to grammatical features in modern languages that are similar or dissimilar to constructions in Old Irish. The primary reference language for that purpose has been English, but because the book was originally written for a German-speaking audience, examples from this language have also been included. I have added at the end of the book various appendixes, including a basic bibliography, a glossary containing the words used in the exercises, and solutions for all exercises, which may be useful to those using this text as their first stepping stone to mastering the Old Irish language.

My heartfelt thanks go to Jürgen Uhlich and Dennis King for many corrections and suggestions, to Melanie Malzahn for the special fonts, to my many students in Vienna from 1996 to 2004 for their unwitting service as guinea pigs in the book's development and for their unceasing encouragement, to the staff of Syracuse University Press for their patience and assistance in preparing the final version of the manuscript, and of course to my teachers Kim McCone, Heiner Eichner, and Helmut Birkhan to whom I owe all that has been put into this book and who supported me through all stages of its production. Last but most certainly not least, I thank Theres Illés for the wonderful sheep illustrations.

It gives me special pleasure that a provisional draft of this course has been completed in time for the 150th anniversary of the publication of Johann Kaspar Zeuss' *Grammatica Celtica*.

I hope you will enjoy learning Old Irish grammar as much as I enjoyed creating this course.

David Stifter, April 2006

At táu i mo šessam for gúailnib rošuad rošruithe.

To make it easier for users of this book to make suggestions, corrections, requests, etc., a special Web site has been set up at http://www.univie.ac.at/indogermanistik/sengoidelc.cgi, where entries can be made online.

sengoídelc

OLD IRISH FOR BEGINNERS

Lesson 1

1.1. The Celtic languages in the context of the Indo-European language family

Old Irish is part of the Celtic language family, which itself forms one of the twelve attested branches of the Indo-European linguistic family. The ancestor language called Proto-Indo-European (PIE) (German: *Urindogermanisch*) originated most probably in the 4th or 3rd millennium B.C. in the area north of the Black Sea (modern Ukraine). But by the end of the 3rd millennium B.C. at the latest PIE had begun to split up into different branches, which must have been mutually understandable as dialects at the beginning, but developed into separate languages in the course of time.

The Celtic branch shares some common traits with other Western Indo-European branches like Germanic or Italic. One of the most notable traits is the merger of the PIE velar and palatal consonants in one velar set ('*kentum*-languages').

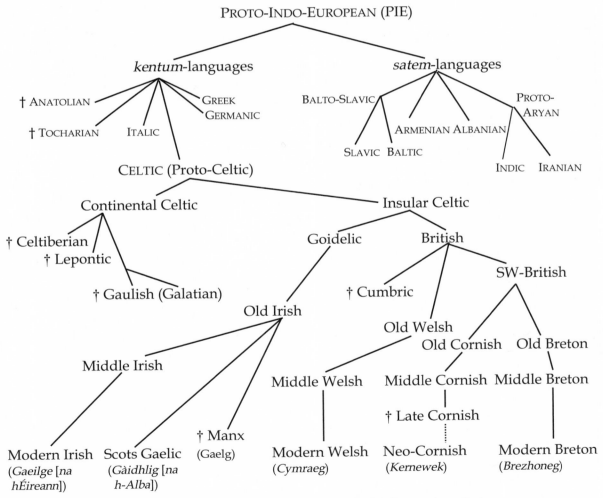

Illustration 1.1: The Celtic languages and the Indo-European family tree; † = extinct

1.2. The classification of the Celtic languages

The classification of the attested Celtic languages in relation to one another is somewhat problematic. The Celtic languages used to be grouped into p-Celtic (Gaulish and British) and q-Celtic (Goidelic) languages, depending on the reflex of the PIE phoneme *k^u (PIE *k^uétụores '4': Gaul. *petuar-*, Cymr. *pedwar*, OIr. *cethair*). This resulted in a clear-cut differentiation between the western-most group (Goidelic) and the rest. But with the deciphering of the Iberian script in the 1920s, the discovery of the Celtiberian language in the 1950s and the discovery that it, too, like Goidelic had kept PIE *k^u unchanged (e.g., Cib. *nekue* 'and not,' cp. Latin *neque*) a new picture started to emerge. Today scholars tend to stress the non-trivial morphological, morphonological and syntactical similarities between Goidelic and British, grouping them together under the label 'Insular Celtic languages,' with Lepontic, Gaulish and Celtiberian on the other hand forming a loose group of 'Continental Celtic languages' (the change *k^u > p in Lepontic, Gaulish and British is now viewed as a trivial common innovation in the central area of Celtic languages[1]). In effect, at the moment two competing models of the Celtic languages' family tree exist side by side (see illustration 1.2). It must, however, be noted that, since the Continental Celtic languages are only attested in ancient times (from the 6th century B.C. to approximately the 3rd or 4th century A.D.), whereas the Insular Celtic languages are attested from early medieval times until today, once existing linguistic correspondences between individual languages may have been obscured by this chronological divergence, or once minor differences may have intensified, so that in the end both models are built on a considerable amount of uncertainty.

Karl Horst SCHMIDT's model:

Kim MCCONE's model:

Illustration 1.2: The two models of the Celtic family tree (from: Kim MCCONE, *Towards a Relative Chronology of Ancient and Medieval Celtic Sound Change*, Maynooth 1996, p. 67 and 104). Reprinted by permission of the author

You will have noticed that I basically followed MCCONE's model in my family tree (ill. 1.1). This is not to say that this model is the 'correct' one: it only means that at the moment MCCONE's approach seems to account best for the given linguistic facts. But it may easily be that in the future new material (for example in the form of Continental Celtic inscriptions) will be discovered that will radically alter the situation. Maybe a completely different model will then be necessary.

Family trees are a rather superficial means of describing the relationships between languages, because it is not possible to express mutual influences between languages. On maps, as in illustration 1.3, these interrelations can be more easily represented.

---

[1] It is noteworthy that in Gaul itself not all areas seem to have undergone the sound change *k^u > p: cp., for example, the ethnic names *Sequani* and *Quariates*, which at least superficially show the sound k^u.

1.3. The Continental Celtic languages and their attestation

The map below illustrates the maximum extent of the Celtic speaking world in antiquity. The following ancient Celtic languages are known to have been spoken at the time:
1. Celtiberian, 2. Transalpine Gaulish, 3. Cisalpine Gaulish, 4. Galatian, 5. Lepontic, 6. Lusitanian ('para-Celtic'), 7. British, 8. Goidelic, 9. Pictish (perhaps British).

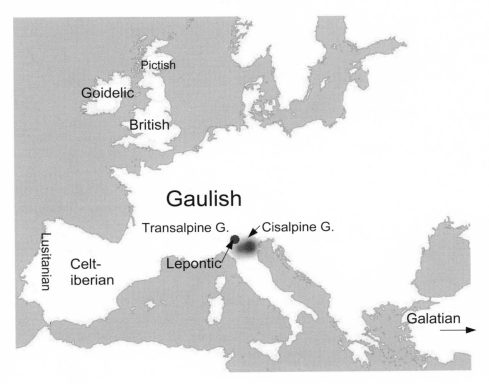

Illustration 1.3: Ancient Celtic languages

The attestation of these languages extends over a period of roughly a thousand years:

	-600	-500	-400	-300	-200	-100	0	+100	+200	+300	+400
Lepontic											
Gaul. (Gr.)											
Gaul. (Etr.)											
Gaul. (Lat.)											
Galatian											
Celtiberian											

Illustration 1.4: The Continental Celtic languages

1.3.1. Lepontic

Lepontic inscriptions come from an area of about 50 km around the Swiss town of Lugano. Lepontic is often considered to be an early variant of Gaulish. But despite the extreme scarcity of Lepontic inscriptions, it can be demonstrated to be an independent language, and the archaeological evidence suggests that Lepontic may have separated from the other Celtic languages even as early as the 13th century B.C.

Lepontic and cisalpine Gaulish (called *Gaulish (Etr.)* in table 1.4) are written in the North Italian so-called *Lugano alphabet*, which had been taken over from the Etruscans. This alphabet makes no distinction between voiced and voiceless consonants.

Illustration 1.5: Lepontic inscription on an urn from Ornavasso, Lugano alphabet to be read from right to left. Reprinted from *Latomus* 46 (1987), 498 by permission of the editor

transcription:
LATUMARUI ⋮ SAPSUTAI : PE ⋮ UINOM ⋮ NAŠOM
'for Latumaros and Sapsuta — Naxian wine'

1.3.2. Gaulish and Galatian

Gaulish was the language spoken in most of ancient Gaul ('transalpine Gaulish') and, after the invasion of the Apennine Peninsula at the beginning of the 4th century B.C., in Northern Italy ('cisalpine Gaulish'). Many inscriptions have been found so far, some of the longest and most valuable only in the past decades (e.g., Chamalières, Larzac, Châteaubleau). The writing systems used for Gaulish are the Greek, the Etruscan or North-Italian and the Roman alphabets. Little is known about the Celtic languages in Central Europe, but it is assumed that they were dialects of Gaulish and probably mutually intelligible. At least the personal and local names from these areas are similar to those of Gaul.

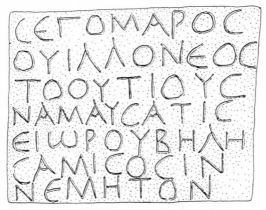

Illustration 1.6: Dedicatory inscription from Nîmes in the Greek alphabet. Reprinted from Wolfgang MEID, *Gaulish Inscriptions*, Budapest 1992, by permission of the author

transcription:	phonological transcription:
segomaros	segomāros
ouilloneos	u̯illonii̯os
tooutious	tou̯tii̯os
namausatis	namau̯satis
eiōroubēlē	i̯ou̯rū
samisosin	belesamī
nemēton	sosin
	nemeton

translation:

Segomāros ('big in victory'), son of Uillū, citizen (?) of Namausos, dedicated this sanctuary for Belesamā

Illustration 1.7: Lugano-alphabet, from a Latin-Gaulish bilingual dedicatory inscription from Vercelli. Reprinted by permission of CNRS Éditions

AKISIOS.ARKATOKO{K}
MATEREKOS.TOŠO
KOTE.ATOM.TEUOX
TONION.EU

translation:

Akisiịos Argantomăterekos ('silver measurer'?), gave this area (?) for gods and humans

phonological transcription:

akisiịos argantomăterekos
totsokonde (?) antom (?)
dēụoγdoniịon eu

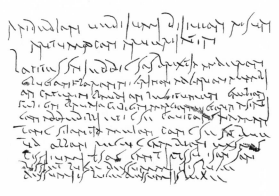

Illustration 1.8: Lead plate with magical inscription from Chamalières (Puy-de-Dôme), excavated 1971. Reprinted by permission of CNRS Éditions

Illustration 1.9: Facsimile of the Chamalières inscription by R. MARICHAL in Latin cursive. Reprinted by permission of CNRS Éditions

1 andedíon uediíumí diíiuion risun
2 artiu mapon arueriíatin
3 lop/tites sníeððic sos brixtía anderon
4 c lucion floron nigrínon adgarion aemilí
5 on paterin claudíon legitumon caelion
6 pelign claudío pelign marcion uictorin asiatí
7 con aððedillí etic se coui toncnaman
8 tonc siíontío meíon ponc se sit bue
9 tid ollon reguc cambion exsops
10 pissíiumí tsoc cantírissu ison son
11 bissíet luge dessumm iíis luge
12 dessumíis luge dessumíís luxe

attempt at translation (very doubtful!):

I pray with the (written?) force of interior (?) and sky gods to the son (or Maponos) of Aruernia ... us and them with the magic of the underworld (?, or women): C. Lucius Florus Nigrinus, the advocate, Aemilius Paterinus, Claudius Legitumus, Caelius Pelignus, Claudius Pelignus, Marcius Victorinus Asiaticus son of Aθθedillos and they who swear this oath. What was small will be whole, I will straighten the crooked, blind I will see. ... Swear at my right (??), swear at my right, swear at my right.

Until the conquest by C. IULIUS CAESAR in the years 58–51 B.C. the Greek alphabet was used for all writing purposes in Gaul. With some slight modifications (e.g., *tau Gallicum*) it was on its way to develop into a national alphabet (see ill. 1.6). After the incorporation of Gaul into the Roman Empire the Greek alphabet slowly went out of use for Gaulish and was ultimately replaced by the Roman alphabet (ill. 1.8 and 1.9).

Galatian was spoken in Asia Minor (today Central Turkey). Because of its geographical remoteness it is often taken as a language of its own, though from all that we know it must have been a dialect of Gaulish, brought to Asia Minor by Celtic invaders in the 3rd century B.C. No Galatian inscriptions have been found and we only know about the language from personal names and odd references to isolated Galatian words in the works of Greek and Latin authors. Apparently Galatian was never put to writing by native speakers.

1.3.3. Celtiberian

Lepontic and Gaulish (Galatian) share many features that make them look rather similar. *Celtiberian* on the other hand looks phonetically and morphologically decisively different. It seems to have separated from the other Celtic languages at an early stage. Celtiberian was recognized to be a separate language only after its decipherment in the 40s of the 20th century. Some of the most important inscriptions were found in the past 30 years. As an example of a Celtiberian text you can see below side A of the bronze tablet number 1 from the Spanish town of *Botorrita* (Celtiberian and Latin: *Contrebia Belaesca*), usually just called *Botorrita I* (ill. 1.10). It probably deals with legislation concerning a temple district in Contrebia Belaesca. Under the picture you will find a transcription of side A in Roman letters. Occlusives are transcribed by means of the 'archigrapheme,' which means that *Ta* stands for /tă/ or /dă/, etc.

Illustration 1.10: Celtiberian inscription on a bronze tablet, Botorrita I, found 1970; side A. Reprinted by permission of Museo de Zaragoza

(1) ti-r-i-ka-n-ta-m : be-r-ku-n-e-ta-ka-m : to-ko-i-to-s-ku-e : s-a-r-n-i-ki-o (:) ku-e : s-u-a : ko-m-ba-l-ke-z : n-e-l-i-to-m /
(2) n-e-ku-e [:] to-[u]-e-r-ta-u-n-e-i : l-i-to-m : n-e-ku-e : ta-u-n-e-i : l-i-to-m : n-e-ku-e : m-a-s-n-a-i : ti-z-a-u-n-e-i : l-i-to-m : s-o-z : a-u-ku / (3) a-r-e-s-ta-l-o : ta-m-a-i : u-ta : o-s-ku-e-z : s-te-n-a : u-e-r-z-o-n-i-ti : s-i-l-a-bu-r : s-l-e-i-to-m : ko-n-s-ki-l-i-to-m : ka-bi-z-e-ti / (4) ka-n-to-m [:] s-a-n-ki-l-i-s-ta-r-a : o-ta-n-a-u-m : to-ko-i-te-i : e-n-i : u-ta : o-s-ku-e-z : bo-u-s-to-m-u-e : ko-r-u-i-n-o-m-u-e / (5) m-a-ka-s-i-[a?]-m-u-e : a-i-l-a-m-u-e : a-m-bi-ti-s-e-ti : ka-m-a-n-o-m : u-s-a-bi-tu-z : o-z-a-s : s-u-e-s : s-a-i-l-o : ku-s-ta : bi-z-e-tu-z : i-o-m / (6) a-s-e-ka-ti : [a]-m-bi-ti-n-ko-u-n-e-i : s-te-n-a : e-s : u-e-r-ta-i : e-n-ta-r-a : ti-r-i-s : m-a-tu-s : ti-n-bi-tu-z : n-e-i-to : ti-r-nˡ-ka-n-ta-m / (7) e-n-i : o-i-s-a-tu-z : i-o-m-u-i : l-i-s-ta-s : ti-ta-s : z-i-z-o-n-ti : s-o-m-u-i : i-o-m : a-r-z-n-a-s : bi-o-n-ti : i-o-m : ku-s-ta-i-ko-s / (8) a-r-z-n-a-s : ku-a-ti : i-a-s : o-z-i-a-s : u-e-r-ta-to-s-u-e : te-m-e-i-u-e : r-o-bi-s-e-ti : s-a-u-m : te-ka-m-e-ti-n-a-s : ta-tu-z : s-o-m-e-i / (9) e-n-i-to-u-z-e-i : i-s-te : a-n-ki-o-s : i-s-te : e-s-a-n-ki-o-s : u-z-e : a-r-e-i-te-n-a : s-a-r-ni-ki-e-i : a-ka-i-n-a-ku-bo-s / (10) n-e-bi-n-to-r : to-ko-i-te-i : i-o-s : u-r-a-n-ti-o-m-u-e : a-u-z-e-ti: a-r-a-ti-m-u-e : te-ka-m-e-ta-m : ta-tu-z : i-o-m : to-ko-i-to-s-ku-e / (11) s-a-r-n-i-ki-o-ku-e : a-i-u-i-z-a-s : ko-m-ba-l-ko-r-e-s : a-l-e-i-te-s : i-s-te : i-r-e-s : r-u-z-i-m-u-z : a-bu-l-u : u-bo-ku-m /

For the greatest part Celtiberian inscriptions are written in the *Iberian script*. This script has alphabetic letters for vowels, sonorants and sibilants, but only syllabic signs of the type *Consonant + Vowel* for occlusives, without a distinction between voiced and voiceless consonants. From the time of the Roman occupation inscriptions in the Roman alphabet exist as well.

Lusitanian, a language known from a few inscriptions in the Roman alphabet in Portugal, is generally not considered to be Celtic, but at best para-Celtic.

	vowel	b	k	t		
a	Р	I	Λ	X	l	Γ
e	Ł	ⵝ	‹	◇	r	ⵕ
i	ᚱ	Ⲅ	⌠	Ⴤ	m	Ⱳ
o	H	✳	ⵅ	Ⱳ	n	Ⲅ
u	↑	□	◇	Δ	s	M
					z	⳵

Illustration 1.11: The characters of the Iberian script

1.4. The Insular Celtic languages and their attestation

The Insular Celtic languages are attested from the early and high Middle Ages onwards (not counting personal and local names in ancient Latin and Greek sources).

	300	400	500	600	700	800	900	1000	1100	1200	1300	1400	1500	1600	1700	1800	1900
Prim. Irish																	
Irish			Early Old Ir.		Old Irish			Middle Irish				Class. Mod. Irish			dialectal	Mod.	Irish
Scot. Gaelic																	
Manx																	
Welsh						Old Welsh			Middle	Welsh					Mod. Welsh		
Cornish							Old	Cornish			Middle	Corn.		Late Corn.			Neo-C
Breton						Old	Breton			Middle	Breton				Modern	Breton	

Illustration 1.12: The Insular Celtic languages

The map to the left illustrates the areas in Western Europe where Celtic languages were spoken at the end of the 19th century. In the meantime these areas have shrunk dramatically.

Key to the map:

1. Irish, 2. Scots Gaelic, 3. Manx, 4. Welsh, 5. Cornish (not spoken anymore at that time), 6. Breton

Illustration 1.13: The modern Celtic languages around 1900

1.4.1. The Gaelic languages

· *Primitive Irish* is an archaic stage of Irish, written in the peculiar Ogam alphabet. As the Ogam alphabet was in use during a decisive period of the development of Irish, a lot of sound changes are directly observable on Ogam inscriptions. That is, in older inscriptions inflectional endings ultimately going back to PIE are still written, whereas in later inscriptions these endings have been lost. Ogam inscriptions practically only consist of personal names in the genitive case.

Illustration 1.14: Panceltism

Irish, Scottish Gaelic and *Manx* form the *Goidelic* branch of Celtic. All three languages are 'Gaelic.' To avoid confusion it is best to refer to every language by its individual name. Up until late medieval times there existed only one literary standard. After Ireland had fallen under English dominion Scottish Gaelic and Manx started to develop standards of their own. The orthography of Scottish Gaelic is very similar to that of Irish, but Manx is written with English orthography! This can obscure important phonological distinctions of the language (e.g., the distinction between palatalized and non-palatalized consonants).

All Goidelic languages are minority languages in their respective countries and are in a very weak and vulnerable state. Despite being the first official language of Ireland, Irish as an everyday language is spoken only in a few remote areas, mainly on the west coast of the island. Approximately 2% of the Irish population regularly speaks Irish. Only in the last years has Irish become available on modern mass media like television. Scottish Gaelic is spoken mainly on the north western islands off the Scottish mainland. About 1% of the Scottish population speaks Gaelic. In Nova Scotia (Canada) a few Gaelic speaking villages used to exist, but the language has now ceased to be spoken. Manx was spoken on the Isle of Man and died out in the 1960s. Today efforts are made to revive the language.

1.4.2. The British languages

Welsh (Cymric), Cornish and Breton make up the *British* branch of Celtic. All three are closely related to one another, with Cornish and Breton being especially close. Cumbric, which died out some time in the Middle Ages, was spoken in North England and South Scotland and must have been very close to Welsh. Nearly nothing has come down to us of Cumbric. Perhaps Pictish, a language known from a handful of unintelligiable, early medieval inscriptions from Scotland, was a British language as well, but this is absolutely unclear.

Illustration 1.15: Fest-Noz Brezhoneg

All British languages are minority languages in their respective countries. Welsh has about 600,000 speakers, a quarter of the population of Wales. In recent years it has been possible to halt the former rapid decline of speakers and the numbers have started to rise slightly again. Welsh is also spoken in a few villages in Patagonia (Argentina). Despite being situated on the European continent, Breton is called an Insular Celtic language, because the language was brought to Brittany by refugees from Britain in the early middle ages. Breton has about 250,000 speakers, most of whom are over 60 years of age. Because of France's francocentric language policy Breton is doomed to death in a few decades. Cornish died out in the late 18th century. This century efforts have been made to revive the language. A few hundred people speak it as their everyday language, several hundred more know the language, but they are divided into three different standards.

1.5. What is Old Irish?

The period of the 8th and 9th centuries in Irish language history is called Old Irish. Our first extant manuscripts containing Irish language material date from ca. the end of the 7th century and the beginning of the 8th century. The Irish literary tradition probably started at least a century earlier, but no manuscripts from that time have come down to us. Those texts written in the 7th century that have survived (e.g., many law texts like *Críth Gablach*) are to be found in much later manuscripts from the early modern times.

The earliest Old Irish texts in contemporary manuscripts have mainly survived not in Ireland, but in monasteries on the European continent. For the most part these texts do not contain narrative or poetic literature, but consist of very short interlinear glosses and translations of Latin texts: the Pauline epistles (*Wb.* = *Würzburg glosses*, middle of the 8th century), a commentary on the psalms (*Ml.* = *Milan glosses*, beginning of the 9th century) and the Latin grammar of Priscianus (*Sg.* = *St. Gall glosses*, middle of the 9th century). From Vienna stem two very short collections of glosses on the Easter calculation (*Vienna Bede*) and on Eutychius. In the library of the monastery of St. Paul im Lavanttal the very famous *Reichenau Codex*[2] (9th century) is kept, which contains five Old Irish poems, among them the popular poem on the scholar and his cat *Messe ocus Pangur Bán*. All these texts are collected in the *Thesaurus Palaeohibernicus* (*Thes.*). Rudolf THURNEYSEN's *Grammar of Old Irish* (GOI), which is the foundation of all modern hand-

---

[2] This codex can be found online at: http://www.rz.uni-potsdam.de/u/lingtri/schulheft/index.html

books of Old Irish, is based on the language of the Old Irish glosses. This is basically the language you will learn in this course.

Because even in that corpus linguistic variation can be observed, the language of basically the 8th century is called *Classical Old Irish*, while that of especially the end of the 9th century *Late Old Irish*. The language prior to that period, that is from the 7th century or perhaps even earlier, shows decisively older linguistic traits and is therefore called *Early Old Irish*. The period from the 10th to the 12th century is labelled *Middle Irish*. The language of that period shows a great amount of grammatical simplification in comparison to Old Irish, but also an amount of linguistic variation, which points to the state of a language in transition to a different grammatical system. *Modern Irish* then (ca. from 1200 onwards) is again a language with a fixed and standardized grammar.

The language encountered in Old Irish texts shows a surprisingly high degree of uniformity, with hardly any dialectal distinctions discernible, although these certainly must have existed at the time. From this it would seem that Old Irish was a literary language whose standard was taught to the Irish 'men of writing' in school, much as standardized Latin was taught to Continental pupils as a language of literary communication, long after Classical Latin had ceased to be a spoken language of the people. One may wonder if Classical Old Irish was ever spoken as such, or whether it was solely a written standard.

What makes the study of Old Irish maybe a bit more difficult than that of other languages? Apart from the intricacies of the grammar (e.g., it is sometimes hardly possible to recognize the underlying word in a given grammatical form), there are other factors that contribute to the difficulties one encounters when reading Old Irish texts. Most of the texts are not to be found in manuscripts of the time they were originally composed, but in much later copies. Copying, on the one hand, always leads to orthographic mistakes. On the other hand, the language of the scribes was younger than that of the texts they were copying; this often lead to 'automatic corrections,' when the scribes replaced older, obsolete grammatical forms with more familiar ones. Thus the texts changed over the course of time, and often they show an intricately intertwined mixture of Old, Middle and Modern Irish grammatical forms. Additionally, the orthography of Irish changed over the course of time, too, so that you may find in a manuscript one word written in Old Irish, the next in Modern Irish spelling and the third in a completely odd attempt at combining different standards.

You won't, however, encounter difficulties of the latter type in the present book. What I will be using is an idealized grammar of Old Irish in a purity that probably never existed in reality, spelled in a normalized orthography, that today is usually used for modern editions. But you should be aware of the fact that as soon as you start to work with real Irish texts and with manuscripts, you will meet with trouble.

Lesson 2

2.1. The writing of Old Irish

In the course of history three different writing systems were used for Irish:

1. the *Ogam* alphabet
2. the *Cló Gaelach* ('Irish type' — a variant of the Roman alphabet)
3. and the Roman alphabet.

2.2. Ogam

The oldest writing system is *Ogam* (Modern Irish spelling *Ogham*), most probably developed in Ireland itself or in the multicultural environment of southwest Britain during the later centuries of Roman rule. Ogam is a monumental script consisting of strokes and notches engraved on the edges of standing stones (*Ogam stones*). The extant inscriptions either served a funeral function or denoted land possession. Maybe Ogam was also used on wooden sticks for other purposes but nothing of that sort has remained in the archaeological record and the odd references in Irish sagas to that practice need not necessarily be taken at face value. Ogam was in use from the 4th to the 6th/7th century. Occasional references in popular books to Ogam inscriptions from North America are pure phantasy.

In medieval manuscript tradition names for the Ogam letters have come down to us. Often tree names are used for the names, but many of these arboreal identifications are more than dubious (a detailed discussion in MCMANUS 1991: 36 ff.). Not all original phonological values of the Ogam letters are absolutely clear; values given in brackets in ill. 2.1 represent the certain or possible original value (cf. MCMANUS 1991: 1–41).

Group I		
⊤	B	Beithe (Birch)
⊤⊤	L	Luis (Rowan-tree)
⊤⊤⊤	F (V)	Fern (Alder)
⊤⊤⊤⊤	S	Sail (Willow)
⊤⊤⊤⊤⊤	N	Nin (Ash-tree?)

Group II		
⊥	H (P/J?)	hÚath (Whitethorn, Fear?)
⊥⊥	D	Dair (Oak)
⊥⊥⊥	T	Tinne (Holly?)
⊥⊥⊥⊥	C	Coll (Hazel)
⊥⊥⊥⊥⊥	Q	Cert (Bush?)

Illustration 2.1a: The Ogam alphabet

Group III		
╱	M	Muin (Vine)
╱╱	G	Gort (Ivy)
╱╱╱	NG (Gᵘ)	nGétal (Killing)
╱╱╱╱	Z (ST?)	Straif (Sulphur)
╱╱╱╱╱	R	Ruis (Elder-tree)

Group IV		
•	A	Ailm (Pine-tree)
••	O	Onn (Ash-tree)
•••	U	Úr (Heath)
••••	E	Edad (Aspen?)
•••••	I	Idad (Yew Tree?)

Illustration 2.1b: The Ogam alphabet

Ill. 2.2 gives a typical example of an Ogam inscription, found at the northwest end of Mount Brandon (Dingle Peninsula, Co. Chiarraí) [CIIC 145, p. 140]. The Ogam inscription reads as follows (from left to right):

In Roman transliteration (Ogam inscriptions are always transliterated in uppercase!):

QRIMITIR RON[A]NN MAQ COMOGANN
'of the priest Rónán, the son of Comgán'

Since the inscription shows linguistically young, i.e., Archaic Irish forms (loss of final syllables, raising of *e* > *i* before a following *i*, loss of *g* between vowel and *n* with compensatory lengthening), it must be from a relatively late date, perhaps the later 5th or 6th century, but no absolute dating is possible. In earlier inscriptions the mentioned sound changes would not have taken place yet; at a Primitive Irish stage the inscription would probably have looked like *QREMITERI RONAGNI MAQI COMAGAGNI. Into classical Old Irish the inscription would translate as *cruimthir Rónáin maicc Comgáin.

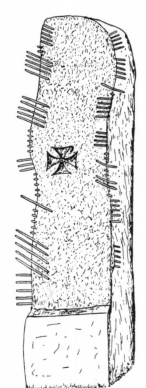

Illustration 2.2: Ogam stone, CIIC 145. Reprinted by permission of Four Courts Press

2.3. Cló Gaelach

In medieval times a special Irish writing style developed from the Roman semi-uncial scipt. At the early modern period with the invention of the printing press this Irish type was standard-ized as *Cló Gaelach* 'Irish type' for the printing of the Irish language. The *Cló Gaelach* is basically identical with the Roman alphabet, except for the shapes of a few letters (*g*, lowercase *r* and *s*). The *Cló Gaelach* was in use until the 1950s. In secondhand book shops you can find many books in this type, and the type is still often used to give public inscriptions a kind of old Irish flair. Older editions of Old Irish texts, especially from the 19th century, are also printed in *Cló Gaelach*.

ᴀ	b	c	ᴅ	e	f	ᵹ	h	ı
a	b	c	d	e	f	g	h	i

ʟ	m	n	o	p	R, r	S, r	τ	u
l	m	n	o	p	r	s	t	u

Illustration 2.3: Cló Gaelach, the basic set of letters

The *Cló Gaelach* is a reduced variant of the Roman alphabet and basically consists of 18 letters. But in addition some of the letters can be combined with the diacritics <´>[1] and <·>. Moreover there is one special sign <7> for 'and.' The diacritic <´> marks the length of a vowel, never the word accent (which in Old Irish basically is fixed on the first syllable). The name for the length mark in Irish is *síneadh fada*. The diacritic <·> is the lenition mark, which in modern ortho-graphy is expressed by an <h> following the letter. The transliteration below is in modern Irish orthography.

Á	ḃ	ċ	ḋ	É	ḟ	ġ	Í	ṁ
á	bh	ch	dh	é	fh	gh	í	mh

ó	ṗ	S, ṙ	ṫ	ú	7			
ó	ph	sh	th	ú	agus			

Illustration 2.4: The diacritics of the *Cló Gaelach*

---

[1] '<' and '>' are the brackets used to indicate *graphemes*, i.e., the basic, distinctive written signs.

This is a detail of page 113 of the famous manuscript *Book of Leinster* (*Lebor Laignech* or LL = TCD MS 1339), written in the 12th century. You'll find the complete page at: http://www.isos.dcu.ie/tcd/tcd_ms_1339/jpgs/113.jpg

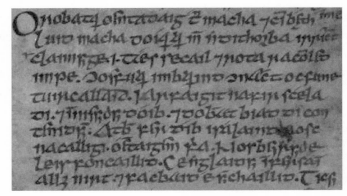

Illustration 2.5: portion of LL 20^b. Reprinted by permission of the library of Trinity College Dublin

2.4. The Roman alphabet

Since the introduction of literacy into Ireland in the early Middle Ages Irish was, apart from Ogam inscriptions, written in the Roman alphabet, though in a special character that gradually developed into the *Cló Gaelach*. In the course of the reform of 1953, when a new Irish standard language ('*An Caighdeán Oifigiúil*') was created, the *Cló Gaelach* was abolished as the official Irish script and the standard Western European Roman alphabet with certain adaptations was again adopted. Old Irish texts have been printed using the Roman alphabet since last century.

The orthographic conventions for Irish (Old and Modern) are very different from 'usual' writing rules for European languages and will be dealt with in the following lesson.

Lesson 3

3.1. The phonological system of Old Irish in comparison

Phonemes are the basic sounds of a language that make distinctions between words. Thus it is easily comprehensible that the difference between the two German words <haus> 'house' and <maus> 'mouse' lies in the two initial sounds /h/[1] and /m/, which proves that the two are independent phonemes. But often phonemes of one language are not perceived as different sounds in another. For example /s/ and /z/ are two different phonemes in English, i.e., they make lexical distinctions: /su:/ (spelled <sue>) is something other than /zu:/ (spelled <zoo>), whereas in German they are merely variants of one another: /sone/ and /zone/ are only different pronunciations of the same word <sonne> 'sun.' In this case we say that /s/ and /z/ are allophones in German. The phonological system of a language is the whole complex of its phonemes and their interrelations. Traditionally these phonemes are grouped according to certain phonetic features. Every language, and even every dialect of a language, has its own, individual phonological system that distinguishes it from other languages. Old Irish possesses an extremely high number of phonemes in comparison to other European languages. Old Irish has an especially high number of consonantal phonemes.

In nearly no alphabetically written language is there a correspondence in the number of phonemes and graphemes. In most cases the number of phonemes exceeds the number of graphemes by far. But there is hardly another language where the difference between phonemes and graphemes is as blatant as in Old Irish. Eighteen letters are used to express 66 sounds, which means that on an average every letter has more than 3 meanings, depending on the position in the word or sentence and depending on the surrounding letters.

In the following table (illus. 3.1) a few languages are compared as regards the numbers of their phonemes and the numbers of letters used in their respective orthographic systems. The phonemes are further separated into consonants, vowels and diphthongs. Sometimes letters may have both consonantal and vocalic values, as in English where <y> can be a consonant as in <year> or a vowel as in <by>. This is indicated by a number after a '+' in the fourth column.

Note:

1. If graphemes for long vowels marked with the *síneadh fada* (which is not obligatory in Old Irish) are counted separately from short vowel graphemes, one arrives at 23 graphemes (13/10). If one adds the letters with the *punctum delens*, which was not used in the earliest Old Irish period and prevailed only in Modern Irish, one arrives at 32 graphemes (22/10).

2. In THURNEYSEN's phonological system of Old Irish (GOI 96 ff.), which has velarization ('u-quality') as a third series of consonantal quality beside palatalization and non-palatalization, and gemination as a further mutation beside lenition, nasalization and aspiration, there is a record number of nearly 100 phonemes in Old Irish. A phoneme system of that type is typologically very improbable, however, and THURNEYSEN's system is generally not used any more today.

---

[1] Two slashes '/ /' indicate phonemes. I will make heavy use of phonological transcriptions in this book.

language	phonemes total	cons. / vowels / diphthongs	letters total	consonant / vowel graphemes
Old Irish	66	42 / 11 / 13	18	13 / 5
Modern Irish	52	37 / 11 / 4	18	13 / 5
Scottish Gaelic	67	38 / 19 / 10	18	13 / 5
North Welsh	54	26 / 13 / 15	22	14+2 / 5+2
Russian	51	40 / 6 / 5	33	21+2 / 10
English	44	24 / 12 / 8	26	20+1 / 5+1
German	40	22 / 15 / 3	30	21 / 9
Latin	31	17 / 10 / 4	23	17+2 / 4+2
PIE	40	25 / 11 / 4	-	-

Illustration 3.1: The phonological system of Old Irish in comparison with other European languages

3.2. The phonological system of Old Irish

The following illustration lists all phonemes of Old Irish. At the same time it presents the phonological transcription of Old Irish that I will use in this book.

1. vowels: 1.1. short vowels   1.2. long vowels

      i   u   ī   ū

       e   ə   o   ē   ō

          a   ā

1.3. diphthongs: ai̯   au̯ (ou̯)   āu̯ (ōu̯)

                  oi̯   eu̯   ēu̯

               (ui̯)   iu̯   īu̯

                   ia   ua

2. consonants:

2.1. sonorants:

    2.1.1. unlenited, non-palatalized: m   n   ŋ   r   l

    2.1.2. unlenited, palatalized: m'   n'   ŋ'   r'   l'

    2.1.3. lenited, non-palatalized: μ   ν   ρ   λ

    2.1.4. lenited, palatalized: μ'   ν'   ρ'   λ'

2.2. occlusives (and fricatives):

    2.2.1. unlenited, non-palatalized: b   d   g   p   t   k

    2.2.2. unlenited, palatalized: b'   d'   g'   p'   t'   k'

    2.2.3. lenited, non-palatalized: β   δ   γ   f/φ   θ   χ

    2.2.4. lenited, palatalized: β'   δ'   γ'   f'/φ'   θ'   χ'

2.3. sibilants (and aspirates):
    2.3.1. unlenited, non-palatalized: s
    2.3.2. unlenited, palatalized: s'
    2.3.3. lenited, non-palatalized: h
    2.3.4. lenited, palatalized: h'

Illustration 3.2: The phonological system of Old Irish

3.2.1. Vowels

3.2.1.1. The vowels are pronounced with their classical European quality, not with their English quality.

3.2.1.2. /ə/ *schwa* is a murmured sound without a distinct quality that in Old Irish appears only in unaccented syllables. Short vowels are sometimes marked by a special diacritic, e.g., /ă/.

3.2.1.3. Sometimes you can find long vowels represented by the vowel followed by a colon, e.g., /i:/. Early Old Irish apparently had two allophones of long *e*, namely closed /ẹ/ and open /ɛ̣/, which behaved differently in certain contexts. But for simplicity's sake I will render both with /ē/ in my phonological transcriptions.

3.2.1.4. My rendering of the diphthong system draws an idealized picture valid only for the earliest period of Old Irish. Already in Classical Old Irish /ou̯/ and /au̯/ had mostly developed into monophtongs. If /ui̯/ ever existed as a separate diphthong different from /oi̯/, the two must have merged very early. The /ai̯/ and /oi̯/ merged during the Old Irish period and eventually developed into a mid high monophthong which in modern orthography is spelled <ao> and <aoi>. The only Old Irish diphthongs still extant in Modern Irish are /ia/ and /ua/. All the other modern diphthongs, very numerous in modern Gaelic languages, developed later from other sound clusters.

The sign /i̯/ represents English consonantal <y>, German <j>, as in *year* or *jahr*. The /u̯/ represents English <w> as in *water*.

3.2.2. Consonants

Every Old Irish consonant (with the exception of /ŋ/) can appear in four different forms, depending on the presence or absence of the two features *palatalization* and *lenition*. The difference that the various possibilities make can be demonstrated with some examples: /bal/ 'member,' /bal'/ 'members,' /baλ/ 'situation (nom.),' /baλ'/ 'situation (acc.);' or /rōd/ 'road,' /rōd'/ 'roads,' Early Old Irish /rōδ/ 'fierce (sg.),' Early Old Irish /rōδ'/ 'fierce (pl.).'

3.2.2.1. *Palatalization* means the pronunciation of a sound with the back of the tongue raised towards the palate (roof of the mouth). If you try to pronounce a /i̯/ immediately following a consonant you produce its palatalized variant. Non-palatalization, on the other hand, is the 'normal' neutral pronunciation. In phonological transcriptions palatalization is usually marked by an apostrophe <'> after the palatalized consonant; non-palatalization remains unmarked. The Modern Irish term for non-palatalized consonants is *leathan* 'broad,' while palatalized consonants are called *caol* 'slender.'

In Irish the opposition between palatalized vs. non-palatalized extends to all consonants. In other languages (e.g., Romance and many Slavic languages) only some consonants are subject to this opposition (e.g., in Spanish the opposition between <n> and <ñ>). Another language where the palatalization opposition extends to almost the whole system is Russian. In consequence the number of consonantal phonemes in Russian is nearly as high as in Old Irish (see illus. 3.1).

3.2.2.2. *Lenition* is a complex phenomenon in Old Irish (and in Insular Celtic as a whole), but basically it means the 'relaxed' pronunciation of a consonant. In Old Irish lenition means that the place of articulation of the consonant in question more or less stays the same, but in contrast to the unlenited pronunciation no perfect occlusion is reached during the articulation: the mouth is left open a little bit. In the end this can result in sounds that differ markedly from their unlenited variants.

3.2.2.3. /k p t/ are pronounced, more or less like in English or Standard German, as voiceless stops with a slight aspiration. /b d g f m h/ are pronounced as in English and German, /β φ/ like English <v> and <f>. /s/ is pronounced as in English and German, but palatalized /s'/ is pronounced like English <sh> or German <sch>. /s/ and /s'/ are always voiceless in Irish. It is a matter of dispute if a palatalized variant of /h/ existed, but I set it up in this book for systematic reasons. /ŋ/ is the product of nasalization of /g/, and in Old Irish it is always followed by /g/. It is pronounced like <ng> in English <king>, but unlike in English or German the /ŋ/-sound can also appear at the beginning of a word, e.g., *a ngothae* /a ŋgoθe/ 'their voices.'

3.2.2.4. For the transcription of the lenited sounds I use Greek letters.

/μ/ is pronounced like /β/, but with a nasal quality. In other publications you may find this sound transcribed as /ṽ/.

/ν/[2] is more or less pronounced like German or English single <n>. The unlenited Old Irish /n/, on the other hand, is pronounced somewhat stronger, probably taking a bit more time. In other publications you may find the unlenited sound transcribed as /n:/ or as /N/, with /n/ being used for the lenited variant.

/ρ/[3] is pronounced with one flap of the tip of the tongue. The unlenited Old Irish /r/ on the other hand is pronounced with a sequence of trills of the tongue. This opposition is similar to the one in Spanish between <r> in <pero> 'but' and <rr> in <perro> 'dog.' In other publications you may find the unlenited sound transcribed as /r:/ or as /R/, with /r/ being used for the lenited variant.

/λ/ is more or less pronounced like a German or English single <l>. The unlenited Old Irish /l/ on the other hand is pronounced somewhat stronger, probably taking a bit more time. In other publications you may find the unlenited sound transcribed as /l:/ or as /L/, with /l/ being used for the lenited variant.

/β/ is a labial sound as in Latin *Vergilius*. In other publications you may find this sound transcribed as /v/.

/δ/ is pronounced somewhat like the English voiced <th> in <this, that, father>.[4] In other publications you may find this sound transcribed as /ð/.

---

[2] This sign is a Greek <ν> 'ny'; do not confuse it with Latin <v> 've'!
[3] This sign is a Greek <ρ> 'rho'; do not confuse it with Latin <p> 'pe'!
[4] Maybe, however, the tip of the tongue did not rest between the two rows of the teeth, but rather on the base of the upper teeth (alveols).

/γ/ is pronounced like <g> in Dutch, Modern Greek or Ukrainian, like <g> intervocally in Spanish or <gh> in Arabic, that is, it is the voiced counterpart to German <ch>. Palatalized /γ'/ is close to /i̯/.

/φ/ is actually the same sound as /f/. It is only used sometimes for systematic reasons to represent *ph*, that is, lenited *p*.

/θ/ is pronounced somewhat like the English voiceless <th> in <thick, thin>.

Unpalatalized /χ/ is pronounced like German <ch> in <ach, Bach>; palatalized /χ'/ is pronounced like German <ch> in <ich, dich>. Sometimes /x/ is used to represent this sound.

3.3. Pronunciation rules

Until now we have been talking only about the abstract phonological system of Old Irish. Now we are turning our attention to the actual graphematic realization, that is the orthography and the pronunciation of written Old Irish.

The pronunciation rules of Old Irish are very complex. The pronunciation of vowels depends on whether they stand in accented or unaccented syllables, or whether they are simply used as markers for the palatalization or the non-palatalization of consonants, in which case they are not pronounced at all. The pronunciation of consonants is determined by their position at the beginning or inside the word, whether they stand in a consonant cluster or not, and by the quality of the preceding or following vowel. Moreover the syntactical position within the sentence has an impact on the realization of *anlauting*[5] consonants as well. But step by step now (from now on I won't put Old Irish graphemes between < > brackets any more, but I will print them in italics):

3.3.1. *c p t*

1. *c, p, t* are pronounced as voiceless stops /k p t/ in *anlaut*, with some aspiration as in English and standard German, which, however, I won't mark in the phonological transcription: *cor* /koρ/ 'the putting,' *poll* /pol/ 'hole,' *tol* /toλ/ 'wish.' *Anlauting p* appears only in loan words.

2. Between vowels and in *auslaut* after vowels they are pronounced as voiced stops /g b d/: *bucae* /buge/ 'softness,' *boc* /bog/ 'soft,' *popul* /pobuλ/ 'people,' *op* /ob/ 'refusal,' *fotae* /fode/ 'long,' *fot* /fod/ 'length.' In most consonant clusters in the interior of words they represent voiced sounds as well, but no absolute rule can be given for that: *ecnae* /egve/ 'wisdom,' ·*eipret* /eb'ρ'əd/ 'they say,' *cétnae* /k'ēdve/ 'the same.'

3. After *r, l, n* in the interior or in the *auslaut* of a word no rule can be given: *derc* /d'erk/ 'hole,' but *derc* or *derg* /d'erg/ 'red,' *olc* /olk/ 'bad,' *delc* or *delg* /d'elg/ 'thorn;' *certa* /k'erta/ 'rights,' *cartae* /kaρde/ 'they who love,' *daltae* /dalte/ 'fosterling,' *celtae* /k'elde/ 'they who hide,' *anta* /anta/ 'staying (gen. sg.),' *antae* /ande/ 'they who stay.' Take special note of pairs such as the following: *altae* /alte/ '(s)he was reared' and *altae* /alde/ 'they who rear.'

4. When written double *c, p, t* most often mean voiceless /k p t/ in the interior or in the *auslaut* of words. Unfortunately *c, p, t* may be written with single letters in these cases as well: *mac(c)* /mak/ 'son,' *boc(c)* /bok/ 'he-goat,' *at(t)* /at/ 'the swelling,' *at(t)ach* /atəχ/ 'refuge, the praying,' *sop(p)* /sop/ 'wisp, tuft.' And even more unfortunately *cc, pp, tt* may mean voiced /g b d/ as

---

[5] Note the following terms: *anlaut* means absolute word-initial position, *inlaut* is word-interior position, and *auslaut* is absolute word-final position.

well: *macc* /mak/ 'son' and *bratt* /brat/ 'coat' have /k t/, but *becc* /b'eg/ 'small' and *brott* /brod/ 'goad, whip' have /g d/.

3.3.2. *b d g*

1. *b, d, g* are pronounced as voiced stops /b d g/ in *anlaut*: *gel* /g'eλ/ 'bright,' *bun* /buv/ 'ground, base,' *dul* /duλ/ 'the going.'

2. Between vowels and in *auslaut* after vowels they are pronounced as voiced fricatives /β δ γ/: *togu* /toγu/ 'choice,' *mug* /muγ/ 'slave,' *dubae* /duβe/ 'sadness,' *dub* /duβ/ 'black,' *mod* /moδ/ 'manner, mode,' *bádud* /bāδuδ/ 'the drowning.' In most word interior consonant clusters they are pronounced as voiced fricatives as well, although, as can be seen from the examples in 3.3.1.3, they can also stand for /b d g/, especially after *r, l, n.*

3. If written double *bb, dd, gg* mean voiced stops /b d g/, e.g., *abb* /ab/ 'abbot.'

4. After certain proclitic elements and in certain syntactical constructions initial *b, d, g, p, t, c* don't have their *anlaut* values, but those of word interior position. More will be explained about this in the chapter about mutations in lesson 4.

3.3.3. *ch ph th*

1. *ch, ph, th* are the voiceless fricatives /χ φ θ/; *ph* is identical in pronunciation with *f*: *ech* /eχ/ 'horse,' *oíph* /oi̯φ/ 'beauty,' *áth* /āθ/ 'ford,' *a chatt* /a χat/ 'his cat,' *in phían* /iv φiav/ 'the pain,' *mo thech* /mo θ'eχ/ 'my house.'

3.3.4. *f*

1. *f* is the voiceless fricative /f/: *féil* /f'ēλ'/ 'feast-day,' *léicfid* /l'ēg'f'əδ/ 'he will let.' In certain syntactic constructions it means /β/ in *anlaut*: *a féil* /a β'ēλ'/ 'their feast-day.' *ḟ* (often, especially in old texts, also *f* without the *punctum delens*) represents the 'non-sound' / /: *a ḟéil, a féil* /a ēλ'/ 'his feast-day,' *neimḟírinnech, neimfírinnech* /n'eμ'ī̆r'ən'əχ/ 'untruthful.'

3.3.5. *s x*

1. *s* is the voiceless sibilant /s/: *sail* /saλ'/ 'willow,' *leis* /l'es'/ 'with him.' In word-internal position especially after short vowels, /s/ can be written with double *ss*: *leiss* = *leis* /l'es'/ 'with him,' *cossa* = *cosa* /kosa/ 'feet.' *ṡ* (often, especially in old texts, also *s* without the *punctum delens*) represents /h/: *a ṡíl, a síl* /a h'ī̆λ'/ 'his seed, his offspring,' *drochṡúil, drochsúil* /droχhū̆λ'/ 'evil eye;' *x* and *chs* represent the consonant cluster /χs/: *foxal, fochsal* /foχsəλ'/ 'abduction.'

3.3.6. *r l n*

1. In *anlaut r, l, n* are pronounced as strong /r l n/: *rún* /rūv/ 'secret,' *lebor* /l'eβəр/ 'book,' *not* /nod/ 'note.' The same is true for double *rr, ll, nn*: *corr* /kor/ 'crane,' *coll* /kol/ 'hazel,' *cenn* /k'en/ 'head,' *a llibuir* /a l'iβuр'/ 'her/their books,' *a rríge* /a r'ī̆γ'e/ 'the/her/their kingdom,' *cenna* /k'ena/ 'heads.' The same pronunciation is true most of the time for the position before *t, d, s, l, r, n* and after *s, l, r, n.*

2. Between vowels and in *auslaut* after vowels single *r, l, n* are pronounced as lenited /ρ λ v/: *torad* /toрəδ/ 'fruit,' *tola* /toλa/ 'desires,' *cona* /kova/ 'dogs (acc. pl.),' *cor* /koρ/ 'contract,' *col*

/koλ/ 'sin,' *son* /sov/ 'sound.' The same is true for *anlauting r, l, n* when preceded by leniting words: *mo lebor* /mo λ'eβəρ/ 'my book,' *dond noí* /dond voi̯/ 'to the boat.'

3.3.7. *m*

1. *m* in *anlaut* represents /m/: *marb* /marβ/ 'dead.'

2. In the interior of words and in *auslaut m* is pronounced as the bilabial, nasal fricative /μ/: *dáma* /dāμa/ 'companies,' *dam* /daμ/ 'ox, stag.' The same is true for *anlauting m* when preceded by a leniting word: *a máthair* /a μāθəρ'/ 'his mother.'

3. Double *mm* always represents /m/: *móraimm* /mōρəm'/ 'I praise,' *lomma* /loma/ plural of *lomm* /lom/ 'naked,' *a mmáthair* /a māθəρ'/ 'her/their mother.' Unfortunately, all these cases can be written with a single *m* as well: *móraim* /mōρəm'/ 'I praise,' *loma* /loma/ plural of *lom* /lom/ 'naked,' *a máthair* /a māθəρ'/ 'her/their mother.'

3.3.8. *nd mb*

1. In early Old Irish *nd* and *mb* stood for /nd/ and /mb/ (also in the beginning of words). But from late Old Irish onwards they were pronounced as /n/ and /m/ and are freely interchangeable with *nn* and *mm* in the manuscripts.

3.3.9. *h*

1. In the earliest sources of Old Irish *h* seems to be an empty letter, which means that it stands for nothing (except in the digraphs *ch, ph, th*, where it marks lenition). One theory says that the letter *h* before vowels in the *anlaut* of short words was used to make the word look bigger: e.g., *hi* /i/ 'in,' *hí* /ī/ a deictic particle, *húair* /uaρ'/ 'hour, because.' Phonetic /h/ that results from lenition of *s* is written *ṡ* or *s*: *a ṡúil, a súil* /a hūλ'/. Phonetic /h/ that results from aspiration ('h-mutation') is usually not written: *a ech* /a h'eχ/ 'her horse,' *inna Éirenn* /ina h'ēρ'ən/ 'of Ireland.'[6] In later texts and manuscripts, however, written *h* usually does represent the sound /h/, though instances of cases like *hi* for /i/ also occur frequently.

3.3.10. Vowels

1. The short vowels *a, e, i, o, u* are pronounced with their own quality only in stressed syllables and in absolute *auslaut*, that is in the last syllable if no other consonant follows: *dam* /daμ/ 'ox, stag,' *fer* /f'eρ/ 'man,' *fir* /f'iρ'/ 'men,' *tola* /toλa/ 'desires,' *subach* /suβəχ/ 'happy,' *túatha* /tuaθa/ 'tribes, nations,' *céile* /k'ēλ'e/ 'client,' *céili* /k'ēλ'i/ 'clients,' *inna súlo* /ina sūλo/ 'of the eye,' *a firu* /a iρu/ 'oh men!'

2. In Old Irish all nouns and adjectives are stressed on the first syllable.[7] Only some adverbs, e.g., those starting with *in-*, are stressed on the second syllable. Where necessary, the accent in

---

6 For a different opinion on the nature of Old Irish *h* in the earliest sources see: Peter SCHRIJVER, 'On the Nature and Origin of Word-Initial *H-* in the Würzburg Glosses,' *Ériu* 48 (1997), 205–227.

7 This definition only holds true from a modern point of view of Old Irish parts of speech under the assumption that articles, prepositions and other particles are separate words of their own. It seems, however, that in earliest times Irish men of letters had a different concept of 'words.' Judging by the spellings found, for example, in the Old Irish glosses, it would emerge that anything that fell under one stress was conceived to belong to a single word. In the following two examples the stressed vowels have an understroke: 'he imitates my manners' was spelled with two orthographic words in *Wb.* 9a15 *insamlatharside mobésusa*, whereas we would today write *in·samlathar-side mo bésu-sa*; or *tresinfuil storidi adoparar cachdia forsindaltoir* (*Wb.* 20d13) 'through the spiritual blood which is offered every day

phonological transcriptions is represented by the acute < ´>: *indíu* /in'd'íu̯/ 'today,' *innuraid* /in*u̱*p̱əð/ 'last year,' *alaile* /aλá̱λ'e/ 'the other, some.' Some word classes like prepositions, possessive pronouns and articles are unstressed. In compound verbs, which means verbs that consist of more than only the verbal root plus ending, at the beginning of the sentence the stress falls on the second element; in fact the second element is treated as the beginning of the word also in other respects. In this book the second element in the 'verbal complex' will be marked by a preceding mid-high dot <·>;[8] the stress falls immediately after the dot: *as·beir* /as·b'ép̱'/ 'he says,' *condid·nderoímed* /kond'əð·n'd'ép̱oi̯µ'əð/ 'so that he should protect him.'

3. In non-final unstressed syllables all short vowels except for *u* represent /ə/ 'schwa,' that is a short, murmured sound without full vocalic quality. How this *schwa* is spelled is determined by the quality of the surrounding consonants:[9]

3.1. /CəC/: <CaC>

If both surrounding consonants are non-palatalized, *schwa* is spelled with *a*: *tabart* /taβərt/ 'the giving.'

3.2. /CəC'/: <CaiC> or <CiC>

If the preceding consonant is non-palatalized and the following is palatalized, *schwa* is spelled with *ai* or *i*: *formait* or *formit* /formǝd'/ 'envy.'

3.3. /C'əC/: <CeC>

If the preceding consonant is palatalized and the following is non-palatalized, *schwa* is spelled with *e*: *epert* /eb'ərt/ 'the saying.'

3.4. /C'əC'/: <CiC>

If both consonants are palatalized, *schwa* is spelled with *i*: *baitsid* /bat's'əð/ 'he baptizes.' Note the possibility of confusion with case 3.2.

Etymological spellings can overrule these rules. In the vicinity of labial sounds (*m, b, p*) *schwa* can be represented by *o* or *u*, e.g., the personal name *Conchobor* /koṽχəβəp̱/. Where *u* is found in an unstressed, non-final syllable it means that /u/ and not /ə/ *schwa* is the sound to be pronounced in this syllable; *iu* in unstressed syllables stands for /u/ after a palatalized consonant, e.g., *fothugud* /foθuγuð/ 'the establishing,' *léiciud* /l'ēg'uð/ 'the letting.'

4. The long vowels *á, é, í, ó, ú* are pronounced longer than their short counterparts. They always retain their own quality, irrespective of their position. For /ē/ sometimes *æ* or *ǽ* is written. Sometimes, especially in early texts, the length of a vowel can be indicated by the double spelling of the vowel, e.g., *rii* or *ríi* /r'ī/ 'king.' It seems as if at no stage of medieval Irish history the marking of vowel length by the *síneadh fada* < ´> was obligatory; it could always be left out, leaving the vowel length orthographically unexpressed.

5. Diphthongs (not to be confused with the vocalic digraphs, see 3.3.10.6 below!) always retain their own quality. In normalized editions the diphthong /oi̯/ is written *oí* and *óe*, the diphthong

---

upon the altar' would break up into the following eight words *tresin fuil storidi ad·oparar cach dia forsind altōir* in modern editions. If we based our phonological analysis of Old Irish accent rules on these spelling conventions, things would become much more complicated and we could in no way speak of regular initial stress in Old Irish.

[8] A hyphen <-> is used by some scholars to indicate the same thing. In many Old Irish text editions, however, and of course in the manuscripts themselves, the pre-accentual part of the verb may be separated from the accented part by a space, or the position of the stress may be not indicated orthographically at all: the verbal form is written as one word.

[9] In this course C is used as cover symbol for all consonants.

/ai̯/ is written *aí* and *áe* (note the position of the *síneadh fada*!): *lóech, loích* /loi̯χ/ 'warrior,' *maíl, máel* /mai̯λ/ 'shorn, bald.' *áe* and *óe* can only be used before non-palatalized consonants. The variants *oí* and *aí* stand mostly before palatalized consonants, but they may also be used before non-palatalized consonants.

The diphthongs /ōu̯/ and /āu̯/ are written *óu* and *áu, áo* in normalized editions: *báo* /bāu̯/ genitive singular of 'cow.'

The diphthong /ēu̯/ is written *éo, éu*, the diphthong /īu̯/ is written *íu*, the diphthong /ui̯/ is written *uí*: *béo, béu* /b'ēu̯/ 'alive,' *indíu* /in'd'íu̯/ 'today,' *druí* /drui̯/ 'druid.'

The diphthongs /ia/ and /ua/ are written *ía* and *úa*: *grían* /g'r'iav/ 'sun,' *trúag* /truaγ/ 'sad.'

Never mistake a manual for real life! In the manuscripts the use and the position of the *síneadh fada* varies freely. To avoid confusion with the vocalic digraphs and with hiatus forms I will adhere to the normalized practice outlined above.

6. In addition to the diphthongs, which count as one syllable, in Old Irish so-called *hiatuses* exist. These are sequences of two vowels (mainly *ia, iu* and *ie*) that have to be pronounced as two syllables. They are recognizable in normalized orthography by the fact that unlike the corresponding diphthongs, no *síneadh fada* is written on them. In transcription they are represented by forms with <˙> dieresis or trema[10]: disyllabic *fiach* /f'iǝχ/ 'raven' (but monosyllabic *fíach* /f'iaχ/ 'a legal due'), *nie* /n'ië/ 'nephew,' *friu* /f'r'iü f'r'ihu/ 'towards them.' Sometimes the *dieresis* is also used in text editions to indicate hiatus. Hiatuses fell together with their diphthongic counterparts rather early in the Gaelic language of Ireland, but they have mostly remained until today in spoken Scottish Gaelic.

3.3.11. The marking of palatalization and non-palatalization

As stated in 2.7.4 above, every consonant in Old Irish can appear either palatalized or non-palatalized ('neutral'). In phonological transcriptions palatalization is marked with the apostrophe <'>;[11] but Old Irish orthography uses other means to express this distinction:

1. An *anlauting* consonant is palatalized if followed by one of the front vowels *i, e, í, é*: *síl* /s'īλ/ 'seed, offspring,' *gillae* /g'ile/ 'boy, servant,' *sel* /s'eλ/ 'a while,' *dér* /d'ēρ/ 'tear.'

2. The same is basically true for word interior consonants. In most cases a purely orthographic *i* that has no sound value is added before the consonant in question: *berid* and *beirid* /b'eρ'ǝδ'/ 'he carries,' *céle* and *céile* /k'ēλ'e/ 'client,' *magen* and *maigen* /maγ'ǝv/ 'field.'

3. In *auslaut* palatalization is indicated by a preceding *i*, which is purely orthographic and has no sound value; cf. the minimal pairs:

ben /b'ev/ 'woman'	vs.	*bein* /b'ev'/ 'woman' archaic acc. sg
ór /ōρ/ 'gold'	vs.	*óir* /ōρ'/ 'of the gold' gen. sg
gabál /gaβāλ/ 'the taking'	vs.	*gabáil* /gaβāλ'/ 'the taking' prep., acc. sg.

4. The use of *i* to indicate palatalization of a following consonant creates the non-diphthongic digraphs *ai, ei, oi, ui, ái, éi, ói, úi*, which stand for the monophthongs /a e o u ā ē ō ū/ before a

---

[10] The forms with *dieresis* /ɜ ä ö ü/ in transcription have nothing to do with German *umlaut*! These letters only represent tautosyllabic /ǝ a o u/ in Irish words after another vowel.

[11] Of course the reverse is true as well: if in a phonological transcription no apostrophe <'> is written, the preceding consonant is not palatalized.

palatalized consonant: *gaib* /gaβ'/ 'take!,' *beir* /b'eρ'/ 'carry!,' *óir* /ōρ'/ 'of the gold,' *dúin* /dūv'/ 'of the fort' etc. Real diphthongs are written *aí, áe, oí, óe, uí* (see 3.3.10.5. above). The diphthongs *aí* and *oí* are usually used before palatalized consonants; *áe* and *óe* are consistently used before non-palatalized consonants.

5. If followed by one of the back vowels *a, o, u, á, ó, ú*, any consonant is non-palatalized. A consonant in *auslaut* is non-palatalized if no *i* precedes it.

6. To complicate matters, in unstressed word interior syllables *i may* follow directly a non-palatalized consonant or an *a* can be inserted before it: *berid* and *beraid* can both stand for /b'eρəδ'/ 'he may carry'[12] (see 3.3.10.3 above).

7. In words of one syllable with *i* or *í* as their vowel no distinction between palatalization or non-palatalization of the *auslauting* consonant can be made: *mind* /m'ind/ nom. sg. of 'diadem,' but *mind* /m'in'd'/ gen. sg. of 'diadem.' In later times and in Modern Irish orthography an *o* is written in such cases to indicate non-palatalization: *mionn* /m'in/.

8. In absolute *auslaut* the following conventions are used: *-i* and *-e may* follow directly a non-palatalized consonant, or a purely orthographical *a* can be inserted before them: *dalte, daltae* /dalte/ 'fosterling,' *dalti, daltai* /dalti/ 'fosterlings' (spellings like *dalte* or *dalti* are of course ambiguous, as they could theoretically also indicate a palatalized consonant before the *e/i*). *-iu* stands for a /u/ after a palatalized consonant: *Laigniu, Lagniu* /laγ'v'u/ 'inhabitants of Leinster (acc. pl.);' *-ea* and *-eo* stand for /a/ and /o/ after palatalized consonants: *doirsea, dorsea* /doρ's'a/ 'doors,' *toimseo* /toμ's'o/ 'measure (gen. sg.).'

3.3.12. One final word

You'll find tables displaying the spellings of Old Irish phonemes in Appendix F.1 and F.2. In the previous pages many subtleties of Old Irish orthography had to be silently passed over in order not to extend the length of the lesson. Certain aspects of the orthography changed over the centuries, and the scribes often confused old and modern spelling conventions, so that in the manuscripts you will hardly ever encounter texts that conform 100% to the rules laid out above. In reality Old Irish orthography is much more complicated, and the only way to come to terms with it is to read and read and read...

Illustration 3.3: A sheep after having tried to master Old Irish orthography

---

[12] Note: *berid* can stand for *beirid* /b'eρ'əδ'/ 'he carries' and *beraid* /b'eρəδ'/ 'he may carry'!

3.4. Sample texts with phonological analysis

3.4.1 *Scél lemm dúib*

The following is an Old Irish poem about the coming of winter in Old Irish orthography and a phonological transcription. I followed Gerard MURPHY (*Early Irish Lyrics*, Oxford 1956: 160) in the wording, but I adapted the orthography of the poem a little bit. The translation is rather free.

Scél lemm dúib	phonological transcription	News of Winter
Scél lemm dúib:	s'k'ēλ l'em dūβ'	News for you,
dordaid dam,	dordəð' daμ	hear stags bell,
snigid gaim,	s'n'iγ'əð' gaμ'	winter snows,
ro·fáith sam;	ro·fāθ' saμ	summer's gone;
gáeth ard úar,	ga i̯θ ard uaρ	wind, strong, cold,
ísel grían,	īs'əλ g'r'iav	sun is low,
gair a rith,	gaρ' a r'iθ	short his course,
ruirthech rían;	ruρ'θ'əχ r'iav	heavy sea;
rorúad rath,	roρuaδ raθ	fern rust-red,
ro·cleth cruth,	ro·k'l'eθ kruθ	lost its shape,
ro·gab gnáth	ro·gaβ gnāθ	wild-goose cries
giugrann guth;	g'iṷγρən guθ	usual cry;
ro·gab úacht	ro·gaβ uaχt	cold takes hold
etti én,	et'i h'ēv	of birds' wings,
aigre ré:	aγ'ρ'e r'ē	time of ice:
é mo scél.	ē mo s'k'ēλ	that's my news.

3.4.2 The opening sentences of *Scéla Muicce Meic Dathó*

The following passage is taken (again with some slight adaptations in spelling) from Rudolf THURNEYSEN's edition of *Scéla Mucce Meic Dathó* 'The Tale of Mac Da Thó's Pig' (Dublin Institute for Advanced Studies. Medieval and Modern Irish Series 6, Dublin 1935). The phonological transcription and the translation again are mine.

Text:

Boí rí amrae for Laignib, Mac Dathó a ainm.
Boí cú occo. Im·díched in cú Laigniu uili.
Ailbe ainm in chon, ocus ba lán Ériu dia air-
dircus in chon. Do·eth ó Ailill ocus ó Meidb
do chungid in chon. Immalle dano táncatar
ocus techta Ulad ocus Chonchobair do chungid in chon chétnai. Ro·ferad fáilte friu uili,
ocus ructha cuci-sium isin mbrudin. Is sí-sin
in chóiced bruden ro·boí i nÉrinn isind aim-
sir-sin, ocus bruden Da-Derg i crích Cúa-
lann ocus bruden Forgaill Manaich ocus
bruden Maic Da-Réo i mBréfni ocus bruden
Da-Choca i n-íarthur Midi.

Phonological Transcription:

boị r'ī aμɾe foɾ laɣ'v'əβ', mak daθō a an'm'.
boị kū ogo. im'·d'ɪχ'əð in kū laɣ'v'u huλ'i.
aλ'β'e an'm' in χov, ogus ba lāv ēɾ'u d'iä aɾ'-
ð'ər'k'us in χov. do·eθ ō aλ'əl' ogus ō μ'eð'β'
do χuŋ'g'əð' in χov. iməl'é dəvó tāvgədəɾ
ogus t'eχta uλəð ogus χovχəβəɾ' do χuŋ'g'əð'
in χov χēdvi. ro·f'epəð fāl't'e f'r'ihu huλ'i,
ogus ρugθa kugi-s'uμ is'əv mbruð'əv'. is s'ī-
s'iv' in χōg'əð βρuð'əv ro·βoị i v'ēɾ'ən' is'ənd
am's'əɾ'-s'iv', ogus βρuð'ən da-ð'erg i g'r'ɪχ' kua-
λən ogus βρuð'əv orgəl' μavəχ' ogus βρuð'əv
μak' ða-ρ'ēụ i m'b'r'ēf'v'i ogus βρuð'ən da-
χoga i v'iaɾθuɾ μ'ið'i.

Translation:

There was a famous king over the Laigin (Leinster-men), Mac Da-Thó his name. He had a dog. The dog used to guard all Laigin. Ailbe the name of the dog, and Ireland was full of the dog's renown. There came (men) from Ailill and from Medb to ask for the dog. At the same time then they came and the messengers of the Ulaid (Ulster-men) and of Conchobar came to ask for the same dog. Welcome was given to all of them, and they were brought to him in the hostel. This is the fifth hostel that existed in Ireland at that time, and the hostel of Da-Derg in the district of Cúalu and the hostel of Forgall Manach and the hostel of Mac Da-Réo in Breifne and the hostel of Da-Choca in the West of Mide.

3.5. Exercise

Illustration 3.4: *Pangur Bán*

Now try your own luck in transcribing an Old Irish poem. It is the famous poem about the monk and his cat, found in a manuscript in the monastery of St. Paul im Lavanttal in Austria (*Thes.* ii 293.14–294.4). Don't be afraid of making mistakes. Do it like the monk and his cat Pangur: catch whatever comes into your net. And should nothing come into your net, just enjoy the poem.

Messe ocus Pangur bán

Meisse ocus Pangur Bán,
cechtar nathar fría șaindán;
bíth a menma-sam fri seilgg,
mu menma céin im șaincheirdd.

Caraimm-se fos, ferr cach clú,
oc mu lebrán léir ingnu.
Ní foirmtech frimm Pangur Bán,
caraid cesin a maccdán.

Ó ru·biam (scél cen scís)
innar tegdais ar n-óendís,
táithiunn (díchríchide clius)
ní fris·tarddam ar n-áthius.

Gnáth húaraib ar gressaib gal
glenaid luch inna lín-sam;
os mé, du·fuit im lín chéin
dliged ndoraid cu ndronchéill.

Fúachaid-sem fri frega fál
a rosc anglése comlán.
Fúachaimm chéin fri fégi fis
mu rosc réil, cesu imdis.

Faílid-sem cu ndéine dul,
hi·nglen luch inna gérchrub;
hi·tucu cheist ndoraid ndil,
os mé cheine am faílid.

Cía beimmi ammin nach ré,
ní·derban cách a chéile.
maith la cechtar nár a dán,
subaigthius a óenurán.

Hé feisin as choimsid dáu
in muid du·ngní cach óenláu.
Du thabairt doraid du glé
for mu mud céin am meisse.

The Scholar and his Cat

Myself and Pangur Bán,
each of us at his own art.
His mind is always turned to hunting,
my own mind to my special trade.

I love it quiet, better than fame,
while eagerly studying my book.
Pangur is not envious of me,
he loves his own childish art.

When we two are (no fatigue)
alone in our house,
we have something (unlimited sport)
to point our attention to.

Regularly, after a violent rush,
a mouse clings to his net.
And I, into my own net falls,
a dark, but important statement.

Towards the wall he points
his bright and penetrating glare.
Towards the keenness of knowledge
I point my own clear, but weak glare.

He rejoices in dashing around,
when a mouse clings to his sharp claw;
when I grasp a dark but dear problem,
it is I myself who rejoices.

Though we are like this all time,
no-one disturbs the other.
Each of us loves his art,
and is glad in it alone.

He himself is his master
of the job he does each single day.
But to bring dark to light,
in my own way, that's what I do.

3.6. Exercise

And now go ahead with a longer piece of prose. It tells about the arrival of the greatest hero of the Ulaid (inhabitants of the northern Irish province of Ulster) *Cú Chulainn* as a small boy of five years at the court of the province's king *Conchobar mac Nessa*. The passage is taken from John STRACHAN's *Stories from the Táin* (Dublin 1904), a beginners' reader in Old Irish saga texts. If you want to read the whole story of the Cattle Raid of Cúailnge, the translation of Thomas KINSELLA (*The Tain*, Oxford University Press 1970) can be recommended. Try to analyze each word on its own.

'Altae-som ém,' ol Fergus, 'la máthair 7 la athair ocond Airgdig i mMaig Muirtheimni. Ad·fessa dó airscélae na maccraide i nEmain. Ar bíit trí cóecait macc and,' ol Fergus, 'oca cluichiu. Is samlaid do·meil Conchobar a ḟlaith: trian ind laí oc déicsin na maccraide, a trian n-aill oc imbirt ḟidchille, a trian n-aill oc óul chormae, conid·gaib cotlud de. Cía beimmi-ni for longais riam, ní·fil i nÉire óclaig bas amru,' ol Fergus.

'Guidid Cú Chulainn dia máthair didiu a léiciud dochumm na maccraide. "Ní·regae," ol a máthair, "condit·roib coímthecht di ánrothaib Ulad." "Rochían lemm-sa anad fri sodain," ol Cú Chulainn. "Inchoisc-siu dam-sa ced leth at·tá Emain." "Fathúaid ammne," ol a máthair, "7 is doraid a n-uide," ol sí, "at·tá Slíab Fúait etruib." "Do·bér indass fair," ol Cú Chulainn, "ammin."

Téit ass íarum, 7 a scíath slissen laiss 7 a bunsach 7 a lorg ánae 7 a líathróit. Fo·ceirded a bunsaig riam conda·gaibed ar loss resíu do·rotsad a bun for lár.

Téit cosna maccu íarum cen naidmm a ḟoesma forru. Ar ní·téiged nech cuccu inna cluichemag co·n-arnastae a ḟoesam. Ní·fitir-som a n-í-sin. "Non·sáraigedar in macc," ol Follomon macc Conchobuir, "sech ra·ḟetammar is di Ultaib dó." Arguntais dó. Maidid fóo.

Fo·cerdat a trí cóecta bunsach fair, 7 ar·sissetar isin scíath slissen uili leis-seom. Fo·cerdat dano a líathróiti uili fair-seom. Ocus nos·gaib-seom cach n-oín líathróit inna ucht. Fo·cerdat dano a trí cóecta lorg n-ánae fair. Ara·clich-som connách·ráncatar, 7 gabais airbir diib fria aiss.

Ríastarthae imbi-seom i suidiu. Inda lat ba tindorcun as·n-ort cach foiltne inna chenn lasa coiméirge con·érracht. Inda lat ba oíbell teined boí for cach óenḟinnu. Íadais indala súil connárbo letha indaas cró snáthaite. As·oilgg alaili combo móir béolu fidchoich. Do·rig dia glainíni co·rrici a áu. As·oilg a béolu coa inairdriuch combo ecnae a inchróes. At·recht in lúan láith assa mulluch.

Benaid fona maccu íarum. Do·scara cóecait macc diib resíu rístais dorus nEmna. Fo·rrumai nónbar diib toram-sa 7 Chonchobar; bámmar oc imbirt ḟidchille. Lingid-som dano tarsin fidchill i ndegaid ind nónbuir.

Gaibid Conchobar a rigid. "Ní maith ar·ráilter in maccrad," ol Conchobar. "Deithbir dam-sa, á phopa Conchobuir," ol se. "Dos·roacht do chluichiu óm thaig óm máthair 7 óm athair, 7 ní maith ro·mbátar friumm." "Cía th'ainm-siu?" ol Conchobor. "Sétantae macc Sualtaim atom·chomnaicc-se, 7 macc Dechtire do fethar-su. Níbu dóig mo choinḟére sund." "Ced náro·nass do ḟoesam-so dano forsna maccu?" ol Conchobar. "Ní·fetar-sa a n-í-sin," ol Cú Chulainn. "Gaib it láim mo ḟoesam airriu didiu." "Atmu," ol Conchobar.

La sodain do·ella-som forsin maccraid sechnón in tige. "Cid no·taí dano doib indossa?" ol Conchobar. "Co·ronastar a fóesam-som form-sa dano," ol Cú Chulainn. "Gaib it láim didiu," ol Conchobar. "Atmu," ol Cú Chulainn.

Lotar uili isa cluichemag íarum, 7 ata·rechtatar in maicc-hí ro·ślassa and. Fos·ráthatar a muimmi 7 a n-aitti.'

Lesson 4

4.1. The initial mutations

One of the most striking features of all Insular Celtic languages are the so-called *mutations*, the systematic changes in the *anlaut* of words, governed by the syntactical properties of the preceding word. Mutations seem to be an exclusively Insular Celtic morphonematic phenomenon: there is no certain evidence that Continental Celtic had anything of that kind. In the context of European languages initial mutations take up an 'exotic' position: no other European standard language has them, but, for example, in a number of dialects of Romance languages (Andalusian, Sardian, etc.) comparable phenomena occur.

To give you an impression of how mutations operate and what they can look like (observe only the changes in the *anlaut* of the following words, don't be worried about the changes in the interior and in the end): *ech* means 'horse,' *becc* means 'small.' With the article *in*, the nominative singular 'the small horse' is realized as *int ech becc* /int eχ b'eg/. In the genitive the whole phrase becomes *ind eich bicc* /ind eχ' β'ig'/—nothing has changed in the *anlaut* of *eich*, but the *anlaut* of *becc* /b'eg/ was *lenited* to *bicc* /β'ig'/, due to the influence of the form *eich*. In the accusative the phrase becomes *in n-ech mbecc* /in n'eχ m'b'eg/: an *n* was added to the *anlaut* of *ech*, and in a similar way *becc* was *nasalized* to *mbecc* /m'b'eg/, all these changes triggered by the preceding word.

Mutated forms are those forms that are actually encountered in the texts. If you want to look up a word in the dictionary you always have to look for the unmutated form.

4.2. The mutations of Old Irish

Old Irish has three different types of mutations (British languages can have even more):

1. lenition (Mod. Ir. *séimhiú*)
2. nasalization ('eclipsis') (Mod. Ir. *urú*)
3. aspiration ('h-mutation')

Mutations usually affect words within a phrase (noun phrase, verbal phrase). Phrases are the constituent parts of the sentence, that is subject, object, prepositional phrase, verb, etc. To take an English example: in the sentence *My big brother can see the small, spotted puppy happily playing in the blooming garden with a group of children*, the subject phrase is 'my big brother,' 'the small, spotted puppy' is the object phrase, 'in the blooming garden' and 'with a group of children' are prepositional phrases and 'can see' is the verbal phrase.

Mutations usually, although not absolutely, have no effect across the phrase boundary. That means that, e.g., the last word in a subject phrase would not affect the first word of an object phrase, even though the latter would immediately follow the first. In Early Old Irish mutational effects even across phrase boundaries may be encountered.

4.3. Lenition

Lenition basically means that consonants are pronounced in a more relaxed way than usual. The place of articulation stays the same, but unlike with stops, the tongue or the lips do not completely seal off the stream of air flowing through the mouth. Lenition only affects consonants; *anlauting* vowels do not change. The lenited pronunciation of consonants *per se* is nothing exotic at all; in fact this happens all the time in many languages (think of the way *tt* in words like *matter* is pronounced in American English, or how *b* is pronounced in a word like *lieber* in Austrian German), though in most languages this remains a variant pronunciation, which creates no difference in meaning. This is how lenition started off in Irish and Insular Celtic as a whole, too. But the Insular Celtic languages underwent a series of decisive changes in their prehistory, which in the end resulted in grammatical systems where the lenited articulation of a sound made an important difference in meaning.

The exact way in which this 'relaxation' is realized for each consonant in Old Irish can be seen in illustration 4.2. The entry under the heading 'lenited' shows you how the lenited sounds are

Illustration 4.1: Relaxation

realized in pronunciation. Unfortunately in most cases there is no distinction in orthography between the unlenited sounds and their lenited counterparts (*b, d, g, m, n, r, l, s, f*). Only with *p, c, t* and s_2 is the lenited form always graphically distinct. In the other cases one simply has to know from the context when lenition is present. You will learn this in the course of time. Unlike in Old Irish, in Modern Irish orthography lenition is consistently marked: lenited consonants always have an *h* after them.

Note: In illustrations 4.2 and 4.3 the consonants stand for palatalized and non-palatalized consonants alike.

unmutated	lenited	written		unmutated	lenited	written
m	/μ/	*m*		p	/φ/	*ph*
n	/v/	*n*		c	/χ/	*ch*
r	/ρ/	*r*		t	/θ/	*th*
l	/λ/	*l*		b	/β/	*b*
s_1 (< *s)	/h/	*ṡ, s*		d	/δ/	*d*
s_2 (< *sụ)	/f/	*f, ph*		g	/γ/	*g*
f	/ /	*ḟ, f, -*				

Illustration 4.2: Lenition

Note:

1. There is no difference in pronunciation between s_1 and s_2; the difference is only historical-etymological. s_1 continues PIE *s. s_2, from PIE and Common Celtic *sụ, appears only in a tiny number of words, the most important being *siur* /s'iüρ/ 'sister.' For example, 'my sister' would be *mo fiur, mo phiur* /mo f'iüρ/. The lenition of *s > f* obviously struck the speakers of Irish themselves as very peculiar, as it was soon given up in favor of *s > h*[1] like in the vast majority of cases. *s* is not affected by lenition when followed by *p, t, c, m*.

---

[1] Scottish Gaelic, however, behaved differently from Irish.

2. *f* is actually lenited to / / zero, which may be spelled *ḟ, f* or not at all.

3. In the oldest time both with *s₁* and with *f* lenition was not indicated in spelling, e.g., <f> could both stand for /f/ and for / /: *a fine* /a f'iv'e/ 'her family' and *a fine* /a iv'e/ 'his family.' It was only during the Old Irish period that the *punctum delens* <·>, the dot put over *s* and *f*, came into use to indicate the lenited variants: *a ḟine* /a iv'e/ 'his family.'

4. Lenition is prevented when the final consonant of the leniting word and the consonant to be lenited are 'homorganic,' that is, when they are articulated at the same place in the mouth. This refers to the dental sounds (/d t l n s/), the labial sounds (/b p m/) and the guttural sounds (/g k/).

4.4. Leniting forms

Throughout this book all words and inflectional forms that trigger lenition of the following word will have a superscript *L* after them.

Lenition takes place after the following words and forms:

    1. certain prepositions (e.g., *ar^L* 'in front of,' *imm^L* 'around,' *do^L* 'to, for,' etc.)

    2. certain conjunctions (e.g., *má^L* 'if,' *ocus^L* 'and,' etc.)

    3. certain possessive pronouns and infixed pronouns (e.g., *mo^L* 'my,' *do^L* 'thy,' *a^L* 'his,' *-m^L* 'me,' *-t^L* 'thee,' etc.)

    4. certain case endings within noun phrases (e.g., gen. sg., prep. sg. and nom. pl. of the o-stems, nom. sg. and prep. sg of the ā-stems, etc.)

    5. in certain syntactical constructions (certain relative clauses, etc.)

Don't be worried now; you will learn all the leniting words and forms at the appropriate time. Examples for lenited forms:

peccad /p'ekəδ/ 'sin'	*mo pheccad* /mo φ'ekəδ/ 'my sin'
tech /t'eχ/ 'house'	*imm thech* /im' θ'eχ/ 'around a house'
cíall /k'ial/ 'sense'	*in chíall* /in χ'ial/ 'the sense'
ben /b'ev/ 'woman'	*in ben* /in β'ev/ 'the woman'
dúan /duav/ 'poem'	*di dúain* /d'i δuav'/ 'two poems'
gáir /gāρ'/ 'a shout'	*in gáir* /in γāρ'/ 'the shout'
máthair /māθəρ'/ 'mother'	*do máthair* /do μāθəρ'/ 'thy mother'
nél /n'ēλ/ 'cloud'	*fo néul* /fo v'ēu̯λ/ 'under a cloud'
leth /l'eθ/ 'side'	*do leth* /do λ'eθ/ 'towards'
ríar /r'iaρ/ 'will, wish'	*fo réir* /fo ρ'ēρ'/ 'under the will'
soilse /sol's'e/ 'brightness'	*int ṡoilse, int soilse* /int hol's'e/ 'the brightness'
siur /s'iüρ/ 'sister'	*mo fiur, mo phiur* /mo f'iüρ/ 'my sister'
frecrae /f'r'egρe/ 'answer'	*do ḟrecrae (frecrae, recrae)* /do ρ'egρe/ 'thy answer'
ainm /an'm'/ 'name'	*m'ainm* /man'm'/ 'my name'

4.5. Nasalization

Basically, nasalization means that a nasal sound (/n m ŋ/) is added to the *anlaut* of a word, though this isn't always orthographically and phonetically evident. Both consonants and vowels are affected by nasalization. With nasalization, as in lenition, nasalized sounds in many cases are spelled exactly as their unmutated counterparts (*p, t, c, f, s*). One has to know from the context when a letter represents the nasalized value of a sound. Only with *b, d, g* and words beginning with vowels is nasalization unambiguously expressed in orthography.

unmutated	nasalized	written		unmutated	nasalized	written
p	/b/	*p*		m	/m/	*m(m)*
c	/g/	*c*		n	/n/	*n(n)*
t	/d/	*t*		r	/r/	*r(r)*
b	/mb/	*mb*		l	/l/	*l(l)*
d	/nd/	*nd*		s	/s/	*s*
g	/ŋg/	*ng*		f	/β/	*f*
				vowel	/vV/	*n-V*

Illustration 4.3: Nasalization

Note:

1. The nasalized products of *b* and *d*: *mb* and *nd* probably were pronounced /mb/ and /nd/ in earliest Old Irish, but changed to pronunciation /m/ resp. /n/ before the Middle Irish period.

2. The nasalization of an *anlauting* vowel is indicated in normalized Old Irish orthography by an *n* separated by a hyphen <-> from the word: *inna n-ech* /ina v'eχ/ 'of the horses.' In the manuscripts they are not separated.

3. In addition to the sounds /f/ and / /, the letter *f* can also represent the nasalized variant /β/. So, *a fine* could also stand for /a β'iv'e/ 'their family.'

4. With *m, n, r, l*, nasalization may be indicated by geminate spelling, but need not: *a lles, a les* /a l'es/ 'their benefit.'

Illustration 4.4: Nasalization

4.6. Nasalizing forms

Throughout this book all words and inflectional forms that trigger nasalization of the following word will have a superscript [N] after them.

Nasalization takes place after the following words and forms:

1. certain prepositions (e.g., *íar*[N] 'after,' *i*[N] 'in,' *co*[N] 'with,' etc.)

2. certain conjunctions (e.g., *ara*[N] 'so that,' *dia*[N] 'if,' etc.)

3. certain possessive and infixed pronouns (e.g., *ar*[N] 'our,' *a*[N] 'their,' *-a*[N] 'him,' etc.)

4. certain case endings within noun phrases (e.g., nom. and acc. sg. of neutral o-stems, acc. sg. and gen. pl. of all declensions, etc.)

5. in certain syntactical constructions (certain relative clauses)

Don't be worried now; you will learn all the nasalizing words and forms at the appropriate time. Examples for nasalized forms:

poll /pol/ 'hole'	*i poll* /i bol/ 'into a hole'
túath /tuaθ/ 'tribe'	*far túath* /faρ duaθ/ 'your tribe'
claideb /klaδ'əβ/ 'sword'	*co claidiub* /ko glaδ'uβ/ 'with a sword'
bél /b'ēλ/ 'mouth'	*i mbéul* /i m'b'ēųλ/ 'in a mouth'
dénum /d'ēvuμ/ 'doing'	*íar ndénum* /iaρ n'd'ēvuμ/ 'after doing'
gein /g'ev'/ 'birth'	*íar ngeinimm* /iaρ ŋ'g'ev'əm'/ 'after a birth'
Mide /m'iδ'e/ 'Mide, Meath'	*i Midiu, i mMidiu* /i m'iδ'u/ 'in Mide, in Meath'
nem /n'eμ/ 'heaven'	*i nim, i nnim* /i n'iμ'/ 'in heaven'
leth /l'eθ/ 'half'	*a leth, a lleth* /a l'eθ/ 'the half'
ríched /r'īχ'əδ/ 'heaven'	*i ríchiud, i rríchiud* /i r'īχ'uδ/ 'in heaven'
filid /f'iλ'əδ'/ 'poets'	*ar filid* /aρ β'iλ'əδ'/ 'our poets'
ucht /uχt/ 'bosom, lap'	*i n-ucht* /i vuχt/ 'in a lap'

4.7. Aspiration

Aspiration[2] is rarer than the other two mutations. Aspiration occurs only after certain forms ending in a vowel and affects words beginning with a vowel by adding an /h/ to the *anlaut* of the word. Unfortunately, due to the dubious status of the letter *h* in Old Irish orthography (see 3.3.9), aspiration is rarely orthographically indicated and one has to know from the context where it has to appear: *a ech* /a h'eχ/ 'her horse,' *inna Éirenn* /ina h'ēρ'ən/ 'of Ireland.'

Sometimes *anlauting* consonants are geminated (spelled double) in aspirated position, e.g., *inna mmaccu* /ina maku/ 'the sons (acc. pl.).' This gemination is probably a purely orthographic convention and does not imply a lengthened pronunciation of the sound.

Throughout this book all words and inflectional forms that trigger aspiration of the following word will have a superscript *H* after them.

Aspiration takes place after the following words and forms:

1. certain prepositions (e.g., *fri*[H] 'turned towards,' *co*[H] 'towards,' etc.)

2. the possessive pronoun *a*[H] 'her' and the infixed pronouns of the 3rd singular feminine and 3rd plural (-*a*[H] 'them, her')

3. the negated copula *ní*[H] 'it is not' and *ba*[H] 'was, were'

4. basically, all words that end in a vowel but do not cause lenition or nasalization, e.g., the article of the genitive singular feminine and of the accusative plural of all genders *(in)na*[H], words like *na*[H] 'any' or *úa*[H] 'grandson,' etc.

Don't be worried now; you will learn all the aspirating words and forms at the appropriate time. Examples for aspirated forms:

ed /eδ/ 'it'	*ní ed* /n'ī h'eδ/ 'it is not it'
mod /moδ/ 'manner'	*indala mmod* /indáλa moδ/ 'one of the two ways'

---

[2] In my system *aspiration* is basically the same phenomenon that in GOI 150 is called *gemination*. Do not confuse Irish aspiration with aspiration in Welsh, which is a completely different mutation.

4.8. Exercise

1. *a^H* means 'her' in Old Irish. Try to say of all the following items that they belong to her and try to write the words in Old Irish orthography and in phonological transcription:

> *ainm* /an'm'/ 'name'
> *enech* /ev'əχ/ 'face, honor'
> *indile* /in'd'əλ'e/ 'property'
> *oítiu* /oi̯d'u/ 'youth'
> *uball* /uβəl/ 'apple'

2. *mo^L* means 'my' in Old Irish. Try to say of all the following items that they belong to you, and try to write the words in Old Irish orthography and in phonological transcription:

Illustration 4.5: (Missing) aspiration

> *popul* /pobuλ/ 'people'
> *teine* /t'ev'e/ 'fire'
> *cú* /kū/ 'dog'
> *bó* /bō/ 'cow'
> *dét* /d'ēd/ 'tooth'
> *gním* /g'n'īμ/ 'deed'
> *muin* /muv'/ 'neck'
> *nós* /nōs/ 'custom, tradition'
> *lugbart* /luγβərt/ 'kitchen-garden'
> *ríge* /r'īγ'e/ 'kingdom'
> *serc* /s'erk/ 'love'
> *slúag* /sluaγ/ 'crowd, group'
> *smacht* /smaχt/ 'rule, command'
> *filidecht* /f'iλ'əδ'əχt/ 'poetry'
> *athair* /aθəρ'/ 'father'

3. *ar^N* means 'our' in Old Irish. Now say of the same items as above that they belong to us, and try to write the words in Old Irish orthography and in phonological transcription.

Lesson 5

5.1. The grammatical categories of Old Irish

Like all old Indo-European languages Old Irish is an inflected language. That means that the shapes of words, especially the endings, change according to certain rules in order to indicate grammatical categories: gender, number and case with nouns and adjectives; number, person, mood, voice, tense and dependence with verbs. But unlike most other old Indo-European languages where inflection is expressed in the alternation of transparent and recognizable endings, Old Irish inflection consists to a large amount of alternations of palatalization/non-palatalization in the end of words, of changes in the interior of words and of changes of the mutating effects upon following words.

5.2. Nouns and adjectives: gender

Old Irish, like, for example, Latin, German or Russian, has still fully retained the distinction between the three inherited Indo-European grammatical genders *masculine*, *feminine* and *neuter*. The *neuter* gender, however, disappeared during the Middle Irish period, the greatest part of the old neuter words becoming masculine, some feminine.

Masculine gender is used for naturally male beings and *feminine* gender for naturally female beings. Apart from that, no general rules can be given as to what gender a word has—in the end it has to be learned for each word separately (as in German).

5.3. Nouns and adjectives: number

In the declension of nouns Old Irish has retained the three inherited Indo-European numbers *singular*, *dual* and *plural*.

Illustration 5.1:
cáera (sg.)
'a sheep, one sheep'

5.3.1. Singular

The *singular* is used to refer to individual items or beings (*tech* /t'ex/ 'a house,' *ingen* /iv'γ'əv/ 'a girl') or abstract concepts (*cert* /k'ert/ 'justice').

5.3.2. Dual

Illustration 5.2:
di cháeraig (du.)
'two sheep'

The *dual* expresses duality ('twoness') of things or beings, either accidental pairs ('occasional dual': *di mnaí* /d'i μvaị/ 'two women') or things that naturally come in pairs ('natural dual': *di śúil* /d'i hūλ'/ 'two eyes'). The dual is always used in combination with the numerals *da^L*, *dá^L* (with masculine nouns), *da^N*, *dá^N* (with neuter nouns) and *di^L*, *dí^L* (with feminine nouns) 'two.' The short vowel forms are older than those with long vowels.

Adjectives, pronouns and verbs, however, have lost the category of dual and use the plural instead.

Lesson 5

5.3.3. Plural

The *plural* is used to express more than two elements (*tige* /t'iɣ'e/ 'houses,' *fir* /f'ip'/ 'men,' *súili* /sūλ'i/ 'eyes').

Illustration 5.3: *cáeraig* (pl.) '(many) sheep'

5.4. Nouns and adjectives: case

Old Irish has retained five of the presumably eight Indo-European and Common Celtic cases. These five cases will be called *nominative, genitive, prepositional, accusative* and *vocative* in this course. Every case can appear in any of the three numbers:

	singular (sg.)	dual (du.)	plural (pl.)
nominative (nom.)	*cáera*ᴸ	*di*ᴸ *cháeraig*ᴸ	*cáeraig*
genitive (gen.)	*cáerach*	*da*ᴸ *cháerach*ᴸ	*cáerach*ᴺ
prepositional (prep.)	*co*ᴺ *cáeraig*ᴸ (*cáera?*)	*co*ᴺ *ndib*ᴺ *cáerchaib*	*co*ᴺ *cáerchaib*
accusative (acc.)	*cáeraig*ᴺ	*di*ᴸ *cháeraig*ᴸ	*cáercha*ᴴ
vocative (voc.)	*a*ᴸ *cháera*ᴸ	*a*ᴸ *di*ᴸ *cháeraig*ᴸ	*a*ᴸ *cháercha*ᴴ

Illustration 5.4: all 15 possible cases of *cáera* 'sheep'

5.4.1. Nominative

The main function of the *nominative* is to indicate the subject of the sentence. The subject is that part of the sentence that performs the action of the sentence (with active verbs) or upon which the action of the sentence is performed (with passive verbs). Examples from English: *The impudent boy kisses the shy girl* (active verb) and *The imprudent boy is being slapped by the shy girl* (passive verb).

Furthermore, the nominative is used as predicative nominative, that is, to make a statement about the subject. In the sentence *This little boy is impudent and imprudent*, *this little boy* is the subject, *impudent* and *imprudent* are the predicates—they are the statements that are being made about the boy.

Finally, the nominative in Old Irish is very often used as *nominatiuus pendens*. A *nominatiuus pendens*-construction means that any part of the sentence that is specifically to be stressed is put into the nominative and is 'fronted' to the beginning of the sentence, where it is left without any connection to the rest of the sentence. In most cases a pronoun is used to compensate within the sentence for the fronted phrase. In the English example *This shy girl, I wouldn't want to come across her in a dark alley*, *this shy girl* is the fronted phrase, and *her* is the pronoun that takes its place in the sentence.

5.4.2. Genitive

The main function of the *genitive* is to qualify or to determine another noun. In English the word *house* on its own is undetermined, but in *John's house* the word is qualified by the genitive *John's*—now we are speaking about a specific house. Note that, apart from cases where personal names are involved, in English relations of that type are usually expressed with constructions with *of*. In the above example you could also say *the house of John*; but you cannot use another construction in *house of pain*.

In classical Old Irish prose the genitive is always following the word it defines: *rígthech Cormaic* /r'ï̄γ'θ'eχ[1] gormək'/ 'Cormac's palace,' *Cú Chulainn* /kū χuλən'/ 'hound of Culann, Culann's hound,' *dorus inna boithe* /doρus ina boθ'e/ 'the door of the hut,' *cluichemag inna mac-raide* /kluχ'əμəγ ina makρəδ'e/ 'playing ground of the boy troop.' Sometimes constructions with genitives are more naturally expressed by adjectival constructions in English: *fer saidbre* /f'eρ saδ'β'ρ'e/ 'a man of wealth = a wealthy man.'

Furthermore, genitives can be dependent on a few adjectives (mainly those meaning 'able': *túalaing labartha* /tuaλəŋ'g' laβəρθa/ 'capable of speaking,' cp. German *der Sprache mächtig*), can be used predicatively, e.g., *ammi Dé* /ami d'ē/ 'we are God's = we belong to God' (*Wb.* 6b20), and can have temporal meaning in a few fossilized phrases, e.g., *cecha blíadnae* /k'eχa b'l'iaδve/ 'every year.'

Illustration 5.5:
macc Domnaill 'Donald's son'
macc = nominative singular
Domnaill = genitive singular

Note:

1. In poetry and legal texts ('archaic language') the genitive may precede the word it qualifies.

5.4.3. Prepositional

The *prepositional* case is in Old Irish prose mostly used after certain prepositions like *do^L* /do/ 'to,' *co^N* /ko/ 'with,' *di^L* /d'i/ 'from,' etc. In Old Irish prose this case doesn't seem to have an inherent syntactical meaning, which means it doesn't seem to have a meaning of its own in the sentence, but the relation of the prepositional to the rest of the sentence is dependent upon the preposition preceding it.

There are only a few cases where an 'independent' prepositional (i.e., without a preceding preposition) can be used in classical Old Irish prose: after the comparative to express the compared item, e.g., *ferr gáes gaisciud* /f'er gaịs gas'k'uδ/ 'wisdom is better than weapons' (BFF 6.77), and in a few constructions with pronouns, e.g., *m'óenur* /moịvuρ/ 'I alone,' *ar ndiis* /aρ n'd'iəs'/ 'the two of us.' Independent prepositionals of substantivized neutral adjectives, usually with the article, are used as adverbs, e.g., *in tánisiu* /in tāvəs'u/ 'secondly.'

Note:

1. The prepositional is called *dative* in all traditional grammars. In my view this is an unfortunate designation, since the Old Irish prepositional is a syncretistic case going back functionally and formally to four different Common Celtic and Indo-European cases: dative, instrumental,

---

[1] Don't be confused by seeing a short /e/ here in an unaccented syllable where you would expect /ə/. In the case of compounds, i.e., words that are being made up by two other words (here: *ríg-* 'king' and *tech* 'house'), and especially in the case of transparent compounds, the rules for /ə/ in unaccented syllables can be suspended, and the vocalism of the second compound member may be pronounced as its uncompounded counterpart.

ablative and locative. The datival function (that is, the function as the indirect object of the verb) of this case is nowhere prominent in Old Irish.

2. In poetry and legal texts ('archaic language') independent prepositionals do appear more frequently. They can be used in practically all meanings, which in normal prose are expressed through preposition plus prepositional. But in most of these cases the prepositionals function as instrumentals.

5.4.4. Accusative

The main function of the *accusative* is to designate the object of the verb. The object is that part of the sentence upon which the action is performed in the case of active verbs. Examples in English: *I kiss <u>the girl</u>. Thereupon she slaps <u>me</u>. The girl* and *me* are the respective objects of the two sentences.

Furthermore, the accusative is used to designate periods of time, e.g. *in n-aithchi n-uili* /in naθ'χ'i vuλ'i/ 'the whole night,' or points of time, e.g., *in fecht-so* /in β'eχt-so/ 'at that time.' For this usage compare German: *Diesen Sonntag werde ich nur fernschauen* 'I'll only be watching TV this Sunday,' where the temporal phrase *diesen Sonntag* is also in the accusative.

Furthermore, the accusative is required after certain prepositions like *la^H* /la/ 'with,' *fri^H* /f'r'i/ 'turned towards,' *i^N* /i/ 'into,' etc., and it is used as the case of comparison after *amal* /aμəλ/ 'like' and the equative, e.g., *móir <u>béolu</u> midchuaich* /mōr' b'ēu̯λu m'iδχuə̯χ'/ 'as big as the mouth of a mead-cup' (TBC 431 f.).

5.4.5. Vocative

The *vocative* is the case of addressing. That means that when you speak directly with a person and address him or her with his or her name or title, you have to use the vocative. Example from English: In the sentence *Donald, don't go near that girl!*, *Donald* has the function of a vocative (though it is not a separate case in English!). Of course, this is not only true for proper names but also for all terms that you use on people, as in the following example: *Now that's your own fault, you stupid ass!*

In Old Irish the vocative is always preceded by the leniting particle *a^L, á^L* /a ā/ 'oh': *a Domnaill* /a δομvəl'/ '(oh) Donald,' or *a asain boirb* /a asəv' βor'b'/ '(oh) you stupid ass.'[2]

Note:

1. In the singular only the masculine *o*-declension has a special vocative ending. In all other declensions the vocative is formally identical with the nominative. In the dual the vocative is formally identical with nominative and accusative. In the plural the vocative seems to be formally identical with the accusative, but too few examples are attested to draw secure conclusions.

---

[2] This is an entirely hypothetical and made-up example, as the ass seems not to have been native in early medieval Ireland (Fergus KELLY, *Early Irish Farming*, Dublin 1998, 131 f.).

5.5. Adjectives

Adjectives conform in gender, number and case with the noun they qualify. The only exception occurs when the noun is in the dual: then the plural form is used for the adjective.

Adjectives basically follow their head noun in Old Irish: *Ériu álainn* /ēρ'u āλən'/ 'beautiful Ireland,' *ingen mór* /iv'γ'əv μōρ/ 'big girl.' Only a few adjectives are exceptions to that rule: *uile* /uλ'e/ 'all, whole' and *sain* /sav'/ 'special' may stand before or after the word they qualify. *dag-, deg-* /daγ d'eγ/ 'good,' *droch-* /droχ/ 'bad,' *bith-* /b'iθ/ 'lasting, permanent,' *sith-* /s'iθ/ 'long,' *mí-* /m'ī/ 'ill, wrong,' *so-, su-* /so su/ 'good,' *do-, du-* /do du/ 'bad' and *óen-, oín-* /oịv/ 'one' are prefixed to the nouns they qualify. That means that they appear as the first member of a compound. They do not change according to gender, number and case. Other adjectives like *sen* /s'ev/ 'old,' *il* /iλ/ 'many' or *fír* /f'īρ/ 'true' are mainly used as first members of compounds but may also be used as independent words. Examples: *drochmacc* /droχμak/ 'bad boy,' *senduí* /s'enduị/ 'old fool.'

Illustration 5.6: *óenchaera* 'one sheep, a single sheep'

5.6. The article

Old Irish has no indefinite article. So *ben* /b'ev/ can simply mean 'woman' or 'a woman,' and *fer* /f'eρ/ can mean 'man' or 'a man.'

Old Irish has a definite article. Its basic form is *in* /in/ 'the,' but this form undergoes considerable changes depending on the gender and the case and the *anlaut* of the following word. The article is used to indicate determination: *in fer* /in f'eρ/ means 'the man.' That means we are now speaking about a specific man, not just any man.

It is sometimes used with proper names: *in Cú Chulainn* /in kū χuλən'/ 'the famous Cú Chulainn.' In narrative texts the definite article is sometimes used to introduce new, hitherto unknown characters, where speakers of English and German would put an indefinite article, e.g., *co·n-accai in fer ocond fulucht i mmedón ind feda* /ko·vaki in β'eρ ogənd uλuχt i m'eδōv ind eδa/ 'he saw a man at the cooking-pit in the middle of the forest' (TBC 516).

If a noun is followed by a determined genitive, that is, a genitive which itself has an article or a possessive pronoun or which is a proper name, the first noun as a rule never takes the article: *cluichemag inna macraide* /kluχ'əμəγ ina makρəδ'e/ '*the* playing ground of *the* boy troop,' *prím-apstal Éirenn* /p'r'īμabstəλ ēρ'ən/ '*the* chief apostle of Ireland.'

Remember this rule: within an Old Irish noun phrase there is not more than one article allowed.

Lesson 5

5.7. Word order

Insular Celtic languages stand isolated from the rest of the Indo-European languages in that they exhibit a very peculiar word order. Word order is the order in which the different parts of a sentence are arranged to make up an 'unmarked' sentence, i.e., a sentence in which no part is specifically stressed. Insular Celtic languages have the word order

VSO

V stands for *verb*, *S* for *subject*, *O* for *object*.

That means in an unmarked declarative sentence the verb takes the very first place in the sentence, immediately followed by the subject (nom.), the object (acc.) taking third place. All other parts of the sentence (adverbs, adverbial expression, etc.) follow after that.

So a 'normal' sentence in Old Irish would look like: *caraid in gille in n-ingin* /kapəδ' in gil'e in n'iv'γ'əv'/ 'the lad loves the girl' with *caraid* 'loves' being the verb, the nominative *in gille* 'the lad' the subject and the accusative *in n-ingin* 'the girl' the object.

All other Indo-European languages (including Continental Celtic languages) have either a word order SOV or SVO. An example for SOV is Latin: *puer puellam amat*; English is typical SVO: *the boy loves the girl*. German *der bub liebt das mädchen* would seem to be SVO, too, but things are a bit more complex here.

A basic word order VSO, however, has more and further-reaching consequences: such a word order typologically entails among other things that nouns follow prepositions (Old Irish conforms to this: *i nÉirinn* /i v'ēp'ən'/ 'in Ireland') and that adjectives and attributive genitives follow the noun they qualify (Old Irish conforms to this, too: *Ériu álainn* /ēp'u āλən'/ 'beautiful Ireland,' *inis inna nnóeb* /iv'əs' ina noįβ/ 'the island of the saints').

Lesson 6

6.1. Nouns: declensional classes

Old Irish has retained a large number of the declensional classes of Proto-Indo-European; the nomenclature agrees to a great extent with that of Latin and Greek stem-classes. The names for the different stem-classes used throughout this book (and used by all scholars of Old Irish) are purely historical. If you look at actual Old Irish paradigms you will normally notice that the letter that lends its name to the declensional class appears nowhere in the inflection. For example, there is no *o* to be found anywhere in the paradigms of o-stem words. In Indo-European and in Common Celtic times the eponymous sounds were still there in these declensions and made up the *stems* of the words, that is those parts of the words unto which the inflectional endings were stuck, e.g., Common Celtic o-stem nom. sg. *u̯iros* 'man': the stem vowel in *u̯iro-* is *-o-*, *-s* is the ending of the nominative singular. Due to the radical sound changes, especially the loss of most final syllables, that took place between Common Celtic and Old Irish times, the eponymous sounds largely disappeared from the inflections, so that you won't find any *o* left in the Old Irish continuant of *u̯iros*, namely *fer*.

The stem-classes of Old Irish, together with the genders they can have, are:

> o-stems (masculine and neuter)
> ā-stems (feminine)
> i̯o-stems (masculine and neuter)
> i̯ā-stems (feminine)
> ī-stems (feminine)
> i-stems (masculine, feminine and a few neuters)
> u-stems (masculine and neuter)
> consonantal-stems:
>> k-stems (masculine and feminine)
>> g-stems (masculine and feminine)
>> t/d-stems (masculine and feminine)
>> nt-stems (masculine, feminine and neuter)
>> n-stems with subclasses (masculine, feminine and neuter)
>> r-stems (masculine and feminine)
>> s-stems (neuter)
> some irregular nouns

Don't be afraid; you will learn these one by one in this course.

Lesson 6

6.2. Adjectives: declensional classes

Things are a bit easier with the inflection of adjectives. There are basically four classes:

> o-, ā-stems
> i̯o-, i̯ā-stems
> i-stems
> u-stems

Besides, there are two or three consonantal-stem adjectives.
If an adjective belongs to the o-, ā-declension this means that it uses o-inflection after a masculine or neuter noun and ā-inflection after a feminine noun. The same distribution is true for i̯o-, i̯ā-stem adjectives. The i-stem adjectives use the same inflection for all genders.

6.3. Declension: general remarks

Before we turn to our first declension some preliminary remarks have to be made as regards the presentation of declensional paradigms in this course. Throughout this book I will give you tables that illustrate the inflection of the stem-classes at various stages of Irish, Celtic and Proto-Indo-European (PIE).

In these tables the Old Irish inflection, which is the one important to you, will be given in italics. Declension in Old Irish largely consists of changes in palatalization/non-palatalization of the stem final consonant and in changes of the mutational effects on following words. Always keep an eye on these changes and effects! Superscript *L, N, H* mean that the case form in question causes lenition, nasalization or aspiration respectively on the following word within a phrase.

Keep in mind that not all of the case-forms I present for individual words are actually attested in Old Irish. Especially more marginal cases, e.g., the dual cases of rarely used words, may not be attested at all throughout the whole history of the Irish language. I do not especially mark these purely conjectural case-forms. Whenever I had to make up a form myself I tried to be as consistent with the attested Old Irish system as possible and I used the form that seemed to me the most plausible in a given case.

To the right of the Old Irish forms you will find reconstructions of various earlier stages, usually from the Primitive Irish (the period immediately preceding Old Irish, about which we know mainly from Ogam inscriptions), the Proto-Celtic and the Proto-Indo-European periods. The label 'Pre-Celtic' in some of the reconstructions serves to justify forms, where for the sake of convenience I use Proto-Indo-European sounds and endings, but which as such cannot be reconstructed for Proto-Indo-European for various reasons. The reconstructed forms ultimately reflect my personal opinions about the morphological systems of Celtic and Indo-European, and they will sometimes diverge from the *communis opinio*.

Sometimes you will find forms in pointed brackets < > in the Proto-Celtic or Primitive Irish columns. These are then actually attested forms in their respective spelling. I will use the usual Indo-European diacritic symbols to represent reconstructed phonemes.

An asterisk * means that the form is not attested, but reconstructed.

A double arrow « means that the development from the preceding stage did not go according to sound laws (German: *lautgesetzlich*), but that morphological modifications, usually of analogical nature, took place between the two stages.

One or two question marks *?* mean that I have some or great doubt about the reconstruction of the form in question.

To the left of the italicized Old Irish forms I will give abstract patterns of the inflections in formalistic descriptions. *C* stands for the stem final consonant (or group of consonants) of the word. The symbol *'* means palatalization of the preceding consonant, superscript $^{L, N, H}$ mean lenition, nasalization or aspiration of the following word. *(u)* means that a *u* may appear before the stem final consonant in addition to the root vowel or instead of the /ə/ (the exact rules are a bit complicated). This phenomenon is called u-infection or u-insertion. *{R}* means that raising of the root vowel takes place where applicable, *{L}* means that lowering of the root vowel takes place where applicable.

Illustration 6.1:
cáera ṡamna
'Hallowe'en sheep'

6.4. Nouns: masculine o-stems

Now let's turn our attention to the o-stems. This is probably the stem-class with the largest number of words in Old Irish. o-stems can be both masculine and neuter, but we will first look at masculine o-stems. Our first word will be *ech* /eχ/ 'horse,' stem final consonant /χ/:

case	ending	Old Irish	Prim. Irish	Proto-Celtic	PIE
nom. sg.	{L}C	*ech*	*eχ^uah	*ek^uos	*h₁eḱu̯os
gen.	{R}C'ᴸ	*eich*ᴸ	*eχ^uī	*ek^uī «, *ek^uosi̯o	*h₁eḱu̯os(i̯o)
prep.	{R}(u)Cᴸ	*euch*ᴸ	*eχ^uū	*ek^uūi̯, -ū, -ūδ	*h₁eḱu̯ōi̯, -oh₁, -ōd
acc.	{L}Cᴺ	*ech*ᴺ	*eχ^uav	*ek^uom	*h₁eḱu̯om
voc.	C'ᴸ	*á*ᴸ *eich*ᴸ	*eχ^ue	*ek^ue	*h₁eḱu̯e
nom. pl.	{R}C'ᴸ	*eich*ᴸ	*eχ^uī	*ek^uoi̯ «	*h₁eḱu̯ōs
gen.	{L}Cᴺ	*ech*ᴺ	*eχ^uav	*ek^uom	*h₁eḱu̯ōm
prep.	{L}Cəβ'	*echaib*	*eχ^uaβih	*ek^uobis «	*h₁eḱu̯ōi̯s, -obʰos
acc.	{R}(u)Cuᴴ	*echu*ᴴ, *euchu*ᴴ	*eχ^uūh	*ek^uūs	*h₁eḱu̯ons
voc.	{R}Cuᴴ	*á*ᴸ *echu*ᴴ «	*eχ^uī	*ek^uoi̯ «	*h₁eḱu̯ōs
n.a.v. du.	{L}Cᴸ	*dá*ᴸ *ech*ᴸ	*eχ^ua	*ek^uo «	*h₁eḱu̯oh₁
gen.	{L}Cᴸ	*dá*ᴸ *ech*ᴸ	*eχ^uō	*ek^uou̯ («)	*h₁eḱu̯oh₁s, -oh₁u
prep.	{L}Cəβ'	*dib*ᴺ *n-echaib* «	*eχ^uaβiv	*ek^uobim «	*h₁eḱu̯obʰih₁, -moh₁ ?

Illustration 6.2.: The standard masculine o-stem declension

Note:

1. After the vowel *e*, u-infection may later also be expressed by the vowel *o*. Therefore the prep. sg. may also be spelled *eoch* /eu̯χ/, the accusative plural also *eochu* /eu̯χu/.

6.5. Variants of the o-stem declension

The paradigm of the word *ech* 'horse' gives you the basic pattern of alternations as regards palatalization/non-palatalization of the stem final consonant and the different mutating effects within the o-stem paradigm. Remember that it is this special sequence of alternations that makes up the important part of the declension and distinguishes it from other declensional classes.

What you did not see in the example above, however, are alternations within the root of the word itself. The vowel *e* of *ech* basically remained unchanged throughout the paradigm. Unfortunately the o-stem declension is the one Old Irish declensional class fraught with most variants and irregularities, and therefore it is perhaps the most difficult of all classes. This is largely due to the so-called 'raising' and 'lowering' effects that have to be taken into account in a great number of words. These effects basically mean that the root vowel of monosyllabic (and some disyllabic) words changes in a manner comparable to German *umlaut*. Lowering and raising only affect stressed short syllables (neither long vowels nor diphthongs). They are the effects of historical developments, depending on the type of vowel that originally stood in the following syllable.

'Lowering' means that the stressed short vowels *i* and *u* become *e* and *o* respectively. Whenever in a word stressed short *i* and *u* come to appear in a paradigmatical form where lowering takes place (indicated by *{L}* in my formalistic description), they change into *e* and *o*.

'Raising' is more or less the reverse development, but it is much more restricted in is application and doesn't take place indiscriminately. In the case of raising the stressed short vowels *e* and *o* become *i* and *u*. Some conditions have to be fulfilled, not all details of which have been worked out yet with absolute certainty: no voiceless consonant or no consonant group must follow the vowel. But when a single voiced consonant follows, short stressed *e* or *o* change to *i* and *u* in those paradigmatic forms where raising takes place (indicated by *{R}* in my formalistic description).[1]

A good example for the changes that are brought about by lowering and raising (in addition to the alternations regarding palatalization/non-palatalization of the stem final consonant) is the paradigm of the word *fer* /f'eρ/ 'man' (stem final consonant /ρ/). Note that wherever lowering *{L}* is indicated in the formalistic description, the root vowel is *e* in the following example, and where raising *{R}* is indicated, the root vowel appears as *i*. These effects are *in addition* to the changes in the mutational effects on the following word and in addition to the changes in palatalization/non-palatalization of the root final consonant:

---

[1] Kim MCCONE, *Towards a Relative Chronology of Ancient and Medieval Celtic Sound Change*, Maynooth 1996: 109–115 gives an overview and historical explanation of the two effects.

case	ending	Old Irish	Prim. Irish	Proto-Celtic	Pre-Celtic
nom. sg.	{L}C	*fer*	*u̯iu̯ah	u̯iros <uiros>	*u̯iros
gen.	{R}C'ᴸ	*firᴸ*	*u̯iu̯ī	*u̯irī «, *u̯irosi̯o	*u̯iros(i̯o)
prep.	{R}(u)Cᴸ	*fiurᴸ*	*u̯iu̯ū	*u̯irū i̯, -ū, -ū(δ)	*u̯irōi̯, -oh₁, -ōd
acc.	{L}Cᴺ	*ferᴺ*	*u̯iu̯av	*u̯irom	*u̯irom
voc.	C'ᴸ	*áᴸ fĩrᴸ*	*u̯iu̯e	*u̯ire	*u̯ire
nom. pl.	{R}C'ᴸ	*firᴸ*	*u̯iu̯ī	*u̯iroi̯ «	*u̯irōs
gen.	{L}Cᴺ	*ferᴺ*	*u̯iu̯av	*u̯irom	*u̯irōm
prep.	{L}Cəβ'	*feraib*	*u̯iu̯aβih	*u̯irobis «	*u̯irōi̯s, -obʰos
acc.	{R}Cuᴴ	*firuᴴ*	*u̯iu̯ūh	*u̯irūs	*u̯irons
voc.	{R}Cuᴴ	*áᴸ fĩruᴴ «*	*u̯iu̯ī	*u̯iroi̯ «	*u̯irōs
n.a.v. du.	{L}Cᴸ	*dáᴸ ferᴸ*	*u̯iu̯a	*u̯iro «	*u̯iroh₁
gen.	{L}Cᴸ	*dáᴸ ferᴸ*	*u̯iu̯ō	*u̯irou̯ («)	*u̯iroh₁s, -oh₁u
prep.	{L}Cəβ'	*dibᴺ feraib «*	*u̯iu̯aβiv	*u̯irobim «	*u̯irobʰih₁, -moh₁ ?

Illustration 6.3: o-stem declension and the raising/lowering effects on *e/i* in the root

An example for the same changes in a word with the root vowel *o* is *son* /sov/ 'sound' (stem final consonant /v/). Here you will find *o* in the root where lowering *{L}* takes place and *u* where rasing *{R}* takes place. Since this word is a loan from Latin *sonus* 'id.' and therefore cannot be older than Primitive Irish times I have refrained from reconstructing earlier forms.

case	ending	Old Irish	Prim. Irish
nom. sg.	{L}C	*son*	*sovah
gen.	{R}C'ᴸ	*suinᴸ*	*sovī
prep.	{R}(u)Cᴸ	*sunᴸ*	*sovū
acc.	{L}Cᴺ	*sonᴺ*	*sovav
voc.	C'ᴸ	*áᴸ śoinᴸ*	*sove
nom. pl.	{R}C'ᴸ	*suinᴸ*	*sovī
gen.	{L}Cᴺ	*sonᴺ*	*sovav
prep.	{L}Cəβ'	*sonaib*	*sovaβih
acc.	{R}Cuᴴ	*sunuᴴ*	*sovūh
voc.	{R}Cuᴴ	*áᴸ śunuᴴ «*	*sovī
n.a.v. du.	{L}Cᴸ	*dáᴸ śonᴸ*	*sova
gen.	{L}Cᴸ	*dáᴸ śonᴸ*	*sovō
prep.	{L}Cəβ'	*dibᴺ sonaib «*	*sovaβiv

Illustration 6.4: o-stem declension and the raising/lowering effects on *o/u* in the root

6.6. Nouns: neuter o-stems

The inflection of neuter o-stems is very similar to that of masculine o-stems. There are only a few typical differences: in neuter words the nominative of all numbers is identical with the accusative. That means that, unlike masculine words, neuters always cause nasalization in the nominative singular. The vocative is identical with the nominative/accusative as well.

In the nominative and accusative plural neuter o-stems have two different forms: a so-called 'short' and a so-called 'long' plural. The short plural (which etymologically continues the Celtic and Indo-European preforms) has no further syllable added as ending, looks like the singular form but causes lenition. It is mainly used after numerals and articles, which carry the 'plural-information.' The long plural has a distinct ending -a. For the use of these different forms, cf. the following examples: the short plural *secht scél* /s'eχt s'k'ēλ/ 'seven stories,' *inna scél* /ina s'k'ēλ/ 'the stories' (*inna* = neuter plural of the article), but the long plural *scéla laí brátha* /s'k'ēλa laį βρāθa/ 'tidings of Doomsday.' The following example is *cenn* /k'en/ 'head' (stem final consonant /n/):

case	ending	Old Irish	Prim. Irish	Pre-Celtic
nom. acc. sg.	{L}C^N	*cenn*^{N}	*k^uenav	*k^uennom
gen.	{R}C'^{L}	*cinn*^{L}	*k^uenī «	*k^uennos(įo)
prep.	{R}(u)C^L	*ciunn*^{L}	*k^uenū	*k^uennōį, -oh$_1$, -ōd
voc.	{L}C^N	*á*^{L} *chenn*^{N}	*k^uenav	*k^uennom
nom. acc. pl.	{L}C^L/Ca^H	*cenn*^{L}, *cenna*^{H} («)	*k^uenā	*k^uenneh$_2$
gen.	{L}C^N	*cenn*^{N}	*k^uenav	*k^uennōm
prep.	{L}Caβ'	*cennaib*	*k^uenaβih «	*k^uennōįs, -obʰos
voc.	{L}Ca^H	*á chenna*^{H} «	*k^uenā	*k^uenneh$_2$
nom. acc. du.	{L}C^N	*dá*^{N} *cenn*^{N} «	*k^uena « ??	*k^uennoih$_1$
gen.	{L}C^N	*dá*^{N} *cenn*^{N} «	*k^uenō («)	*k^uennoh$_1$s, -oh$_1$u
prep.	{L}Caβ'	*dib*^{N} *cennaib*	*k^uenaβiv «	*k^uennobʰih$_1$, -moh$_1$?

Illustration 6.5: The neuter o-stem declension

6.7. Exercise

Try to decline some or all of the following o-stem words. To make things a little bit easier, you don't have to form the duals of the words in this and future exercises:

macc /mak/ (m.) 'son, boy'
dún /dūv/ (n.) 'fort, hill-fort'
corp /korp/ (m.) 'body'
ball /bal/ (m.) 'limb, member'
roth /roθ/ (m.) 'wheel, disk'
rosc /rosk/ (n.) 'eye'
sorn /sorn/ (m.) 'furnace, oven'
bech /b'eχ/ (m.) 'bee'
bedg /b'eδg/ (m.) 'leap, start, bound'
leth /l'eθ/ (n.) 'half'

Note:

1. *corp, rosc, sorn* and *bedg* are 'raisable,' resp. 'lowerable.' In *ball* u-infection takes place in the appropriate cases; in *macc* it does not. In all other words the root vowel stays unaltered throughout the paradigm.

6.8. Long vowels, words of more than one syllable and further subtleties

As mentioned above, the o-stem declension is probably the declension with the largest number of variants and apparent irregularities. Below follow some of the most important rules that have to be observed when declining an o-stem word. In the end one really has to know in each individual case which rules apply to a particular word. This is best learned by experience.

6.8.1. Words with long vowels

1. Words of one syllable that have one of the long vowels *á, í, ó, ú* in their root (e.g., *dál* /dāλ/ 'share,' *síl* /s'īλ/ 'seed,' *slóg* /slōγ/ 'host,' *múr* /mūρ/ 'wall') are easily dealt with: this vowel never changes, no u-infection takes place. One only has to be careful as to the change in palatalization/non-palatalization of the final consonant.

2. o-stem words of one syllable that have *é* as their vowel in the nom. sg. (!) are more complicated. The vowel changes depending on the quality of the following consonant. If a palatalized consonant follows, the *é* usually changes to the diphthong /ēu̯/, spelled *éui* or *éoi*; sometimes, however, it changes to /īu̯/, spelled *íui*. Examples: *én* /ēv/ 'bird,' but nom. pl. *éoin, éuin* /ēu̯v'/ 'birds'; *nél* /n'ēλ/ 'cloud,' but gen. sg. *níuil* /n'īu̯λ'/. If a syllable containing *u* follows or in case of u-infection (prep. sg. and acc. pl.), *é* changes to the diphthong /ēu̯/, spelled *éu, éo*; sometimes, however, it changes to /īu̯/, spelled *íu*. Examples: prep. sg. *éun, éon* /ēu̯v/; nom. sg. *trén* /t'r'ēv/ 'strong,' but acc. pl. *tríunu* /t'r'īu̯vu/.

6.8.2. Words with diphthongs

1. Words of one syllable with *úa* as their vowel (e.g., *búar* /buaρ/ 'cattle, herds') are easy: this diphthong never changes.[2] No u-infection takes place; e.g., gen. sg. *búair* /buaρ'/, prep. sg. *búar* /buaρ/.

2. For o-stem words of one syllable with *áe, aí, óe, oí* as their vowel (e.g., *sáer* /sai̯ρ/ 'craftsman,' *nóeb* /noi̯β/ 'saint') this is basically true as well: these diphthongs do not change. But often, especially in normalized spelling, the two possible spellings of these diphthongs (see 3.3.10.5) are utilized to make orthographical distinctions: *áe, óe* are used before non-palatalized consonants, and *aí, oí* frequently occur before palatalized consonants. That way there is an alternation throughout the paradigm (e.g., nom. sg. *sáer* /sai̯ρ/, gen. sg. *saír* /sai̯ρ'/, prep. sg. *sáer* /sai̯ρ/, etc.). I will conform to this use in my course.

3. Words of one syllable with the diphthong *ía* /ia/ in the nominative singular show an alternation with *éi* /ē/ throughout the paradigm: *ía* occurs in those cases where a non-palatalized consonant follows, *éi* where a palatalized consonant follows: nom. sg. *rían* /r'iav/ 'sea, ocean,' gen. sg. *réin* /r'ēv'/, prep. sg. *rían* /r'iav/, etc. No u-infection takes place.

4. The neuter word *céol* /k'ēu̯λ/ 'music' has the diphthong *éo* /ēu̯/ in the nom. and acc. sg. and pl. and in the gen. and prep. pl. In the gen. sg. this changes to *cíuil* /k'ĭu̯λ'/, in the prep. sg. to *cíul* /k'ĭu̯λ/.

So far I have been talking about words of one syllable only. If o-stem words have more than one syllable, though, things get a little bit trickier.

6.8.3. Words with hiatuses

A clear distinction has to be made between words with diphthongs and words with hiatuses (see 3.3.10.6). Hiatuses can only appear in stressed syllables and are distinguished from diphthongs in that no *fadas* (length-marks) are written on them, at least in normalized spelling: compare, e.g., the diphthong *ía* /ia/ (one syllable!) with the hiatus *ia* /iǝ/ (two syllables!). Since a hiatus form like *fiach* /f'iǝχ/ 'raven' actually consists of two syllables /f'i - ǝχ/, the inflectional changes only take place in the second syllable: gen. sg. *fiich* /f'iǝχ'/, prep. sg. with u-infection *fiuch* /f'iu̇χ/. As you can see from this example, a *schwa* in hiatus position /ǝ/ is written *a* before a non-palatalized consonant, but *i* before a palatalized consonant.

Hiatuses can only exist as long as there are no more than the two hiatus-syllables in the word. As soon as another syllable is added, the hiatus is contracted to the corresponding diphthong or long vowel. For example, *ia* becomes the diphthong *ía* /ia/, *ii* becomes long vowel *í* /ī/: prep. pl. *fíachaib* /fiaχǝβ'/ (two syllables) < *fiach* /f'iǝχ/ + *aib* /ǝβ'/. (In the case of certain verb formations, e.g., the future, things are a bit different: *ia* can be contracted to *e* there.)

6.8.4. Behavior of *schwa* /ǝ/

In the case of other words apart from hiatus-words that have *schwa* /ǝ/ in their second syllable it is important to keep in mind that with the change of palatalization/non-palatalization in the final consonant also the orthography of the /ǝ/ before it changes accordingly. That is, you get

---

[2] Note that the diphthong *úa* may always alternate with the long vowel *ó*. This variation, however, has nothing to do with the changes described in this lesson and is completely independent from any phonetic environment.

nom. sg. *claideb* /klaδ'əβ/ 'sword' with non-palatalized final *b*, but gen. sg. *claidib* /klaδ'əβ'/ with palatalized final *b*. In the prepositional where a *u* can be inserted before the final consonant (= 'u-infection') we get *claidiub* /klaδ'uβ/. Or nom. sg. *salann* /saλən/ 'salt,' gen. sg. *salainn* /saλən'/, prep. sg. *salunn* /saλun/.

The difficulties start when an extra syllable is added in the ending. Then a very important rule called *syncope* comes into action.

6.8.5. Syncope

Syncope is a rule by which in pre-Old Irish times after the loss of inherited final syllables the vowel of every second, non-final syllable was deleted. Although this was originally a prehistoric rule it has still enormous repercussions on the way Old Irish words, both nouns and verbs, behave. For example, if we want to put *claideb* into the acc. pl., by adding the ending *-u* we would theoretically get **claidebu*. Now this form would have three syllables—an environment in which syncope applies. Syncope means that every second syllable, unless it is the very last syllable of the word, loses its vowel. In **claidebu* the vowel of the second syllable is *e*, and since it is not the very last syllable of the word, it has to be deleted.

Now another factor has to be observed: if the deleted vowel was historically a 'front vowel,' that is *e*, *ē*, *i*, *ī*, the whole consonant cluster that results from the vowel loss becomes palatalized. In **claidebu* the second vowel was historically one of those four vowels (most probably *i*), therefore in the resultant acc. pl. *claidbiu* /klaδ'β'u/ the cluster *db* /δ'β'/ is palatalized. But it is not always apparent on the surface what the historical vowel was: e.g., in *carpat* /karbəd/ 'chariot' the second vowel was originally *ē*, a front vowel as well. Therefore in the acc. pl. the whole cluster has to be palatalized, too: *cairptiu* /kar'b'd'u/. If, however, the syncopated vowel was historically a 'back vowel,' that is *a*, *ā*, *o*, *ō*, *u* or *ū*, the whole resultant consonant cluster becomes non-palatalized.

Illustration 6.6:
Did you understand it?

Keep in mind that the rules just given do not only apply to the o-stem declension, but to all nouns, adjectives and verbs that have more than two syllables. These rules will be of great importance in advanced lessons, with even higher and more far-reaching consequences in the verbal inflection.

Unfortunately, however, in the prehistory of Old Irish many more counterrules and analogical adjustments took place, so that in many words where syncope would be expected it does not take place or does not seem to take place.

6.8.6. Syncope with long vowels

One of the environments where syncope is often overruled is when a long vowel, especially one resulting from compensatory lengthening, is standing in the second syllable, e.g., the prep. pl. of *cenél* /k'ev'ēλ/ 'race, people, nation' (< Proto-Celtic **kenetlom*) is *cenélaib*, no syncope of *é* takes place.

Lesson 7

7.1. The basic pattern of the masculine article

The basic form of the article is *in* /in/, but this changes considerably depending on the case and the *anlaut* of the following word. I will present the 'normal' paradigm for the masculine article first, which is the one used before words beginning with *b, d, g, p, t, c, m*.

case	transc.	Old Irish	Proto-Celtic
nom. sg.	in	*in*	*(s)indos
gen.	in$^{(')L}$	*in^L*	*(s)indī
prep.	(s'ə)n^L	*-(si)n^L*	*(s)indūi̯, -ū, -ūδ
acc.	in^N	*in^N*	*(s)indom
nom. pl.	in$^{(')L}$	*in^L*	*(s)indī
gen.	(i)na^N	*(in)na^N*	*(s)indoi̯som
prep.	(s)nəβ'	*-(s)naib*	*(s)indobis
acc.	(i)na^H	*(in)na^H*	*(s)indūs
n.a. du.	in	*in dá^L*	*(s)indo
gen.	in	*in dá^L*	*(s)indō
prep.	(s)nəβ'	*-(s)naib dib^N*	*(s)indobim

Illustration 7.1: The basic pattern of the masculine article

Note:

1. The mutational effects of the masculine article are identical to those of the masculine o-stem declension.

2. In the prepositional case the article combines with the preceding preposition, e.g., *do^L* 'to, for,' but *don^L* 'for the (sg.),' *donaib* 'for the (pl.)'; *ar^L* 'in front of,' but *arin^L* 'in front of the (sg.),' *arnaib* 'in front of the (pl.)'; *i^N* 'in,' but *isin^L* 'in the (sg.),' *isnaib* 'in the (pl.)' etc. Independent articles, that means articles without preceding prepositions, are extremely rare in the prepositional case; an example occurs in the poem *Dom·farcai fidbaide fál* (verse 3): *úas mo lebrán ind línech* 'over my little book, the lined one' (*Thes.* ii 290.8). Prepositionless articles in the prepositional case are sometimes encountered in petrified adverbial expressions, e.g., *in chruth-so* 'thus.'

3. Whether the form with *s* or without *s* of the article is used in the prepositional case depends on the preposition. Prepositions that lenite (like *do^L*, *fo^L* etc.) use the s-less forms; all other prepositions (like *la^H*, *i^N* etc.) use the s-forms. Exceptions are *tre^L*, which takes the s-form, *for*, which can take both forms with and without *s*, and *oc*, which is always s-less.

4. In the accusative, too, the article combines with those prepositions that govern an accusative. Again forms with or without *s* are used, following the same rules as in 7.1.3.

5. Only in the oldest texts the article *inna* in the gen. and acc. pl. is disyllabic. The most common variant in Irish is *na*.

6. The article cannot be used in the vocative.

7. It is very difficult to say if there was a change in palatalization of the *n* of *in* throughout the paradigm. It may be suspected that originally palatalization was there in the appropriate cases, but it must have been given up by the rule of depalatalization of proclitics. Therefore I have put the palatalization mark in parentheses in the table above. I will not mark palatalization in the article in further transcriptions in this book.

7.2. Variants in the basic pattern of the masculine article

1. The nominative singular is *int* /int/ with words that begin with a vowel: *int én* /int ēv/.

2. The genitive singular and nominative plural is *ind^L* /in(')d(')/ with words that begin with a vowel, *l, r, n* or *f,* which is lenited to zero: *ind éuin* /ind ēụv'/ 'of the bird, the birds,' *ind loích* /ind λoịχ'/ 'of the warrior, the warriors,' *ind réin* /ind ρ'ēv'/ 'of the sea, the seas,' *ind níuil* /ind v'īụλ'/ 'of the cloud, the clouds,' *ind fir* /ind iρ'/ 'of the man, the men.' The genitive singular and nominative plural is *int^L* /in(')t(')/ with words that begin with *s,* which is lenited to /h/: *int sacairt* /int hagər't'/ 'of the priest, the priests.'

3. The prepositional singular is *-(si)nd^L* /(s'ə)nd/ with words that begin with a vowel, *l, r, n* or *f,* which is lenited to zero: *dond éun, cosind lóech, arind rían, isind níul, fond fiur.* The prepositional singular is *-(si)nt^L* /(s'ə)nt/ with words that begin with *s,* which is lenited to /h/: *dont sacart, cosint sacart.*

7.3. The neuter article

The neuter article is basically identical in form and behavior with its masculine counterpart, except for nominative and accusative singular and nominative and accusative plural:

case	transcript.	Old Irish	Proto-Celtic
nom. acc. sg.	a^N	*a^N*	*(s)osim
gen.	in(')^L	*in^L*	*(s)indī
prep.	(s'ə)n^L	*-(si)n^L*	*(s)indūị, -ū, -ūδ
nom. acc. pl.	(i)na	*(in)na* «	*(s)indā (?)
gen.	(i)na^N	*(in)na^N*	*(s)indoịsom
prep.	(s)nəβ'	*-(s)naib*	*(s)indobis
n.a. du.	in	*in dá^N*	*(s)indo
gen.	in	*in dá^N*	*(s)indō
prep.	(s)nəβ'	*-(s)naib dib^N*	*(s)indobim

Illustration 7.2: The neuter article

Note:

1. The mutational effects of the neuter article are identical to those of the neuter o-stem declension.

2. When combined with a preposition in the accusative, the neuter article a^N, too, appears either with or without *s*, following the same rules as in 7.1.3 above, e.g., *foa*^{N} 'under the' (*fo*^{L} + *a*^{N}), but *isa*^{N} 'into the' (*i*^{N} + *sa*^{N}).

3. Only in the oldest texts the article *inna* in the nom., acc. and gen. pl. is disyllabic. The most common variant in Irish is *na*.

You can find a survey of the article in Appendix F.3. Below are two typical examples of the inflection of masculine and neuter o-stem nouns preceded by the article. Note the mutations indicated in orthography, but also be aware of the mutations (in this case nasalizations) you cannot see in spelling, but which nonetheless have to be pronounced. I will use the preposition *do*^{L} 'to, for' as the default preposition to illustrate the formation of the prepositional case.

case	masculine	transcription	neuter	transcription
nom. sg.	*in fer*	in f'eρ	*a*^{N} *cenn*^{N}	a g'en
gen.	*ind*^{L} *ḟir*^{L}	ind iρ'	*in*^{L} *chinn*^{L}	in χ'in'
prep.	*dond*^{L} *ḟiur*^{L}	dond iụρ	*don*^{L} *chiunn*^{L}	don χ'iụn
acc.	*in*^{N} *fer*^{N}	in β'eρ	*a*^{N} *cenn*^{N}	a g'en
voc.	*á*^{L} *ḟir*^{L}	ā iρ'	*á*^{L} *chenn*	ā χ'en
nom. pl.	*ind*^{L} *ḟir*^{L}	ind iρ'	*inna cenn*^{L}*(-a*^{H}*)*	ina k'en(a)
gen.	*inna*^{N} *fer*^{N}	ina β'eρ	*inna*^{N} *cenn*^{N}	ina g'en
prep.	*donaib feraib*	donəβ' f'eρəβ'	*donaib cennaib*	donəβ' kenəβ'
acc.	*inna*^{H} *firu*^{H}	ina f'iρu	*inna cenn*^{L}*(-a*^{H}*)*	ina k'en(a)
voc.	*á*^{L} *ḟiru*^{H}	ā iρu	*á*^{L} *chenna*^{H}	ā χ'ena
n.a. du.	*in dá*^{L} *fer*^{L}	in dā eρ	*in dá*^{N} *cenn*^{N}	in dā g'en
gen.	*in dá*^{L} *fer*^{L}	in dā eρ	*in dá*^{N} *cenn*^{N}	in dā g'en
prep.	*donaib dib*^{N} *feraib*	donəβ' d'iβ' β'eρəβ'	*donaib dib*^{N} *cennaib*	donəβ' d'iβ' g'enəβ'

Illustration 7.3: Two typical paradigms

Illustration 7.4: *forsin chlaidiub* 'on the sword'

7.4. The o-stem adjectives

The o-stem adjectives are basically identical in inflection with o-stem nouns, with two slight differences: in the neuter nominative and accusative plural the long form with the ending -a is exclusively used, and the masculine accusative plural has a by-form in -a, beside regular -u. After the classical Old Irish period the masculine nominative and accusative plural also take on the ending -a. The two examples below are masculine *in catt bán* 'the white cat' and neuter *a clár ndess* 'the right side (board).'

case	masculine	transcription	neuter	transcription
nom. sg.	*in catt bán*	in kat bāv	*a^N clár^N ndess^N*	a glāp n'd'es
gen.	*in^L chaitt^L báin^L*	in χat' βāv'	*in^L chláir^L deiss^L*	in χλāp' δ'es'
prep.	*don^L chatt^L bán^L*	don χat βāv	*don^L chlár^L dess^L*	don χλāp δ'es
acc.	*in^N catt^N mbán^N*	in gat mbāv	*a^N clár^N ndess^N*	a glāp n'd'es
voc.	*á^L chaitt^L báin^L*	ā χat' βāv'		
nom. pl.	*in^L chaitt^L báin^L*	in χat' βāv'	*inna clár^L(-a^H) dessa^H*	ina klāp(a) d'esa
gen.	*inna^N catt^N mbán^N*	ina gat mbāv	*inna^N clár^N ndess^N*	ina glāp n'd'es
prep.	*donaib cattaib bánaib*	donəβ' katəβ' bāvəβ'	*donaib cláraib dessaib*	donəβ' klāpəβ' d'esəβ'
acc.	*inna^H cattu^H bánu^H(-a^H)*	ina katu bāvu/a	*inna clár^L(-a^H) dessa^H*	ina klāp(a) d'esa
voc.	*á^L chattu^H bánu^H*	ā χatu bāvu		
n.a.v. du.	*in dá^L chatt^L báin^L*	in dā χat βāv'	*in dá^N clár^N ndessa*	in dā glāp n'd'esa
gen.	*in dá^L chatt^L bán*	in dā χat βāv	*in dá^N clár^N ndess^N*	in dā glāp n'd'es
prep.	*donaib dib^N cattaib bánaib*	donəβ' d'iβ' gatəβ' bāvəβ'	*donaib dib^N cláraib dessaib*	donəβ' d'iβ' klāpəβ' d'esəβ'

Illustration 7.5: Inflection of article, noun and adjective

7.5. Exercise

Now try to inflect the following words. Decline them together with the article. Combine them with the adjectives *becc* /b'eg/ 'small' and *mór* /mōp/ 'big.' *Becc* is 'raisable' and/or 'lowerable.' *Dliged*, *sacart* and *cenél* do not exhibit syncope, and *biad* /b'iəδ/ is contracted to *bíad-* /b'iaδ-/ when an extra syllable is added.

in slóg /slōγ/ (m.) 'host, troop'
in tempul /t'empuλ/ (m.) 'temple'
in bél /b'ēλ/ (m.) 'lip, pl.: mouth'
in lóech /loi̯χ/ (m.) 'warrior'
a cenél /k'ev'ēλ/ (n.) 'race, people'
in cúan /kuav/ (m.) 'bay, harbor'
a mbiad /b'iəδ/ (n.) 'food'

a ndliged /d'l'iγ'əδ/ (n.) 'law'
in sacart /sagərt/ (m.) 'priest'
int íasc /iask/ (m.) 'fish'

Illustration 7.6:
in beich déin 'the swift bees'

Lesson 8

8.1. The Old Irish verb

The Old Irish verbal system differs very much from that of other European languages. One of the most striking peculiarities is that in Old Irish every verb has two different inflectional sets, depending on whether the verb is *independent* or *dependent*.

1. A verb is in *dependent* position when a so-called conjunct particle precedes it. Conjunct particles are most of the conjunctions (e.g., *día* 'if,' *co^N* 'so that,' etc.) and sentence particles (e.g., *ní* 'not,' *in^N* '?', etc.).

2. A verb is in *independent* position when no such particle precedes it.

The exact way in which the difference between the two different sets in a given word is realized depends on another feature: whether the verb is *simple* or *compounded*. *Simple* verbs are uncompounded, that is, they consist of the mere verbal root plus the ending. Simple verbs in English would be *to get, to draw* etc., in German *gehen, stehen*. *Compound* verbs have one or more preverbs before the root. In English verbs like *to withdraw, to forget* are compound verbs, in German *ausgehen, verstehen*. In this lesson, we will only look at simple verbs in Old Irish. In simple verbs the independent forms are distinguished from the dependent ones in that the former use the so-called *absolute* endings, the latter the so-called *conjunct* endings.

position	independent	dependent
ending set	*absolute*	*conjunct*

Illustration 8.1: Simple verbs

Only simple verbs that are not preceded by a particle use the absolute endings. In all other cases conjunct endings are used. Remember this basic rule:

> As soon as any element, be it particle or preverb, comes before the verbal root, the verb changes to conjunct inflection.

In this course I will separate the first preverbal element, be it particle or preverb, by a superscript dot <·> from the rest of the verbal form, e.g., *ní·cara* /n'ī·kaρa/ '(s)he does not love' or *do·biur* /do·biuρ/ 'I give.' The accent falls immediately after this dot. In other textbooks instead of the superscript dot <·> a hyphen <-> or colon <:> may be used, e.g., *do-biur, do:biur*, but in a lot of editions no such diacritic sign is used at all, e.g., *ní cara, dobiur*.

8.2. Conjugation: general remarks

In Old Irish grammar books three different classifications of the verbal inflectional classes exist side by side. I will follow Kim MCCONE's classification as set out in *The Early Irish Verb*, 21–25. Other classifications are those of Rudolf THURNEYSEN (GOI 352–357) and of John STRACHAN (OIPG 34). You can find a table comparing the various classifications in Appendix F.6.

Throughout this course I will give you tables to illustrate the inflection of the verbal classes. The Old Irish inflection will be represented in italics. To the right of the Old Irish forms I will give abstract patterns of the inflections in formalistic descriptions. *C* stands for the stem final consonant (or group of consonants) of the verb. The symbol ' means palatalization of the preceding consonant. *{R}* means that raising of the root vowel of the verb takes place where applicable, *{L}* means that lowering of the root vowel of the verb takes place where applicable. I will use *ní·* 'not' as the default conjunct particle to illustrate the inflection in dependent position.

Since Old Irish does not have an infinitive, I will use the form of the independent 3rd sg. present tense as the citation form for all verbs throughout this book. When an independent 3rd sg. present tense verbal form is translated with an English infinitive, e.g., *caraid* 'to love,' this means that I refer to the abstract citational form of the verb. When it is translated with an English 3rd sg. form, however, this means that I specifically refer to the 3rd person, e.g., *caraid* '(s)he loves.'

To distinguish between the 2nd persons singular and plural, which are formally absolutely distinct in Old Irish, I will use the Old English pronouns *thou, thee, thine* for the former, and standard *you, your* only for the latter in all translations, e.g., *carai* 'thou lovest,' but *carthae* 'you (all) love.'

8.3. The verbal inflection

Old Irish has no personal pronouns in the way most other modern Indo-European languages have. Personal pronouns are words like *I, she, him, we, them* in English or *ich, dich, ihr, uns, euch* in German.

In English or German you can form sentences like *I write a book, ich schreibe ein buch*, where the subject is expressed by *I*, resp. *ich*, the 1st person singular pronoun in the nominative case. In Old Irish, however, it is not possible to express the subject through a personal pronoun in a normal sentence. The Old Irish equivalent to the sentence above is *scríbaimm lebor* /s'k'r'iβəm' l'eβəp/. Here the person is solely expressed by the ending of the verb: the inflectional form *scríbaimm* 'I write' already contains the reference to the 1st person singular, so it is not necessary (and indeed impossible) to express it through a pronoun. This is true for all persons in Old Irish. But this also means that a 3rd person singular form like *sóeraid* /soį̃ρəδ/ can stand for 'he saves,' 'she saves' and 'it saves.' One has to infer from the context what or who is meant in a given instance. A similar situation is to be found for example in Latin, where *scribo* means 'I write,' but *scribit* can stand for 'he writes,' 'she writes,' 'it writes.'

We will learn in a later lesson what strategies Old Irish uses to express things like *I save her, ich rette sie, seruo eam*, where in English and German two personal pronouns are involved, and the Latin version at least involves an object pronoun.

8.4. Verbs of the W1-class (ā-verbs)

In Kim MCCONE's classification *W* stands for 'weak verbs.' Weak verbs are characterized by the fact that their root ends in a consonant and that in the 3rd singular active present tense conjunct the verbal form ends in a vowel.

W1 is the first weak class. The characteristic vowel of W1 verbs in the 3rd sg. conjunct is *-a*. Furthermore in W1 verbs the root final consonant remains non-palatalized throughout the whole paradigm. The following example is the present indicative of *caraid* /kaɾəð'/ 'to love,' root *car-* /kaɾ-/ (root final consonant /ɾ/):

W1	absolute (independent)		conjunct (dependent)	
1st sg.	*caraim(m)*	Cəm'	*(ní)·caraim(m)*	Cəm'
2nd sg.	*carai*	Ci	*(ní)·carai*	Ci
3rd sg.	*caraid*	Cəð'	*(ní)·cara*	Ca
1st pl.	*carmai*	Cmi	*(ní)·caram*	Cəμ
2nd pl.	*carthae*	Cθe	*(ní)·caraid*	Cəð'
3rd pl.	*carait*	Cəd'	*(ní)·carat*	Cəd

Illustration 8.2: The conjugation of W1 verbs

Note:

1. The W1-class consists to a large amount of denominative verbs, that is, verbs that are created from already existing nouns or adjectives and mean something like 'to make like the corresponding adjective or noun.' Examples: from *marb* /marβ/ 'dead' the verb *marbaid* /marβəð'/ 'to kill (= to make dead)' is created, from *mór* /mōɾ/ 'big' the verb *móraid* /mōɾəð'/ 'to praise (= to make big)' is created.

2. Many Latin loan words fall into this class as well, like *scríbaid* /s'k'r'īβəð'/ 'to write' from *scribere*, or *légaid* /l'ēɣəð'/ 'to read' from *legere*.

3. The ending of the 1st sg. *-aim(m)* /-əm'/ is always unlenited. But be careful: most often it is only written with a single *-m*: *caraim*.

4. In the 1st pl. absolute the ending *-mai* /-mi/ always has an unlenited *m* /m/. But it is nearly always written with a single *m*. In the 1st pl. conjunct, however, the ending *-am* /-əμ/ has a lenited *-m* /μ/ in Old Irish!

5. If the stem of the verb ends in *n* (like in *glanaid* /glavəð'/ 'to clean,' stem *glan-*), in the 2nd pl. absolute the ending *-thae* /θe/ becomes *-tae* /te/ by the rule of delenition of homorganic sounds (see 4.3.4): *glantae* /glante/ 'you clean.'

Illustration 8.3:
caraid cách a chéile
'they love each other'

8.5. Exercise

Now try to conjugate some of the following verbs in absolute and conjunct inflection:

móraid /mōɾəð'/ 'to praise'
légaid /l'ēɣəð'/ 'to read'
glanaid /glavəð'/ 'to clean'
berraid /b'erəð'/ 'to shear, to shave'

Lesson 9

9.1. Varia

1. In the exercises below you will encounter two of the most important conjunct particles: the negative particle *ní* /n'ī/ 'not,' which turns a positive main clause into a negative one, and the sentence particle *in*ᴺ /iv/, which turns a positive sentence into a positive question. Remember that you have to use dependent verbal forms after these particles.

2. *ocus*ᴸ /ogus/ is the usual Old Irish word for 'and.' It is traditionally abbreviated 7 in manuscripts and editions. Do not confuse this sign with the number '7'!

3. The main disjunctive conjunction in Old Irish is *acht* /aχt/ 'but.'

4. The preposition *ar*ᴸ 'in front of, for the sake of' takes the prepositional.

The preposition *do*ᴸ 'to, for' takes the prepositional.

The preposition *i*ᴺ means 'in' when followed by the prepositional, but 'into' when followed by the accusative.

5. Old Irish has a very odd counter-rule against nasalization: when a word that ends in *n* and that causes nasalization on the following word (especially the accusative singular article and the interrogative particle *in*ᴺ·) comes to stand in front of a word beginning with *d*, the nasalization is not expressed; e.g., the accusative of *in domun* /in doμuv/ 'the world' is also *in domun* /in doμuv/ and not ⁺*in ndomun*, as would be expected.

9.2. Exercise

First translate the Old Irish sentences into your native language. Sentences with one asterisk * are based on authentic Old Irish sentences, but have been modified by me; sentences marked with two asterisks ** are authentic Old Irish; modifications have only been applied to a very slight degree at the best, usually to normalize the orthography.

Then try the reverse: translate from English into Old Irish. The English-Old Irish sentences use the same vocabulary as their Old Irish counterparts. But be careful; the necessary grammatical forms will be slightly different.

Old Irish

1. * Caraimm fos (*Thes.* ii 293.16), carai degscéla, caraid in macc oac echu díanu. 2. Ní·caram libru salm, ní·caraid in catt nderg, ní·carat loích templu sacart. 3. Pridchait int ṡacairt scél nDé donaib lóechaib, acht marbait ind loích inna sacartu cosnaib claidbib. 4. In·mberra in macc cóem folt nderg ind ḟir bicc? 5. Ní·mórai scéla fer n-oac. 6. Carmai fos nóeb i templaib Dé. 7. Á ḟiru, ní·glanaimm in dá chlaideb arin macc ouc. 8. Á lóechu tríunu, sóerthae inna maccu ar drochḟeraib. 9. Techtait fir in domun mór, acht techtaid Día a rríched rrindach. 10. Á maicc léigind, scríbai scél i llibur línech. 11. In·llégaid degscéla i senlebraib? 12. Gerrmai fér nglas donaib echaib díanaib. 13. Marbaimm in n-én mbecc ngorm isin chrunn. 14. In·n-ásat cranna arda isind ḟéur glas? 15. Carthae sunu cíuil, á lóechu. 16. Berrait loích oic in cheníuil inna cenna ⁊ glanait inna curpu. 17. Pridchait in chruimthir dligeda Dé fír. 18. In·techtai ech mór, á maicc bicc? 19. Ní·cara in fer céol inna n-én isnaib crannaib. 20. Á chruimtheru, scríbthae i llibur mór ⁊ légmai a scél.

Transcription

1. kaρəm' fos, kaρi d'eγs'k'ēλa, kaρəδ' in mak oə̈g eχu d'iavu. 2. n'ī·kaρəμ l'iβρu salm, n'ī·kaρəδ' in gat n'd'erg, n'ī·kaρəd loi̯χ' t'empλu sagərt. 3. p'r'iδχəd' int hagər't' s'k'ēλ n'd'ē donəβ' loi̯χəβ', aχt marβəd' ind λoi̯χ' ina sagərtu kosnəβ' klaδ'β'əβ'. 4. iv·m'b'era in mak koi̯μ folt n'd'erg ind iρ' β'ig'? 5. n'ī·mōρi s'k'ēλa f'eρ voə̈g. 6. kaρmi fos noi̯β i d'empλəβ' d'ē. 7. ā iρu, n'ī·glavəm' in dā χλaδ'əβ aρ'ən μak oüg. 8. ā λoi̯χu t'r'īu̯vu, soi̯ρθe ina maku aρ δροχeρəβ'. 9. t'eχtəd' f'iρ' in doμuv mōρ, aχt t'eχtəδ' d'ia a r'īχ'əδ r'indəχ. 10. ā μak' λ'ēγ'ən'd', s'k'r'īβi s'k'ēλ i l'iβuρ λ'īvəχ. 11. in·l'ēγəδ' d'eγs'k'ēλa i s'evλ'eβρəβ'? 12. g'ermi fēρ ŋglas donəβ' eχəβ' d'iavəβ'. 13. marβəm' in n'ēv m'b'eg ŋgorm is'ən χρun. 14. in·nāsəd krana arda is'ənd ēu̯ρ γλas? 15. kaρθe suvu kīu̯λ', ā λoi̯χu. 16. b'erəd' loi̯χ' oə̈g' in χ'evīu̯λ' ina k'ena ogus γλavəd' ina kurpu. 17. p'r'iδχəd' in χρuμ'θ'əρ' d'l'iγ'əδa d'ē īρ'. 18. in·d'eχti eχ mōρ, ā μak' β'ig'? 19. n'ī·kaρa in f'eρ k'ēu̯λ ina v'ēv isnəβ' kranəβ'. 20. ā χρuμ'θ'əρu, s'k'r'īβθe i l'iβuρ μōρ ogus λ'ēγmi a s'k'ēλ.

English

1. I don't love quietness, dost thou love a good story, the young boy does not love a swift horse. 2. We love a book of psalms, you love red cats, warriors love temples of priests. 3. The priest preaches stories of God to the warrior, and the warrior does not kill the priest with a sword. 4. The nice boy shaves the red hair of the small men. 5. We praise the story of the young men. 6. Thou lovest not the holy quietness in a temple of God. 7. Oh man, we do not clean the sword for the young boy. 8. Oh strong warrior, thou savest a boy from a bad man. 9. Men do not possess the big world, but does God possess the starry heaven? 10. Oh sons of study (= students), you write stories in a lined book. 11. We do not read a good story in old books. 12. Do you cut green grass for the swift horse? 13. We do not kill the small blue bird in the tree. 14. A tall tree grows in the green grass. 15. Dost thou love the sound of music, oh warrior? 16. The young warrior does not shave the head, but he cleans the body. 17. Does the priest preach the law of the true God? 18. Thou dost not possess big horses, oh small boy. 19. Do the men love the music of the birds in the tree? 20. Oh priest, dost thou write in a big book? I do not read the story.

Lesson 10

10.1. Nouns: feminine ā-stems

Our first exclusively feminine declension is the ā-stem inflection. It is, fortunately, more homogeneous than the o-stem declension, so that it will suffice to give you two exemplary paradigms. A typical ā-stem is *túath* /tuaθ/ 'people, tribe, petty kingdom' (stem final consonant /θ/):

case	ending	Old Irish	Prim. Irish	Proto-Celtic	PIE
nom. sg.	{L}C^L	*túath*^L	*tōθā	toụtā <-τοουτα>	*teụteh₂
gen.	{R}C'e^H	*túaithe*^H	*tōθiịāh «	toụtās <toutas>	*teụteh₂s
prep.	{R}C'^L	*túaith*^L	*tōθī	*toụtaị «	*teụteh₂eị, -eh₂i
acc.	C'^N	*túaith*^N	*tōθev	*toụtam	*teụteh₂m
voc.	{L}C^L	*á*^L *thúath*^L	*tōθa	*toụta	*teụte(h₂)
nom. pl.	{L}Ca^H	*túatha*^H	*tōθāh	*toụtās	*teụteh₂es
gen.	{L}C^N	*túath*^N	*tōθav	*toụtom (»)	*teụteh₂om
prep.	{L}Caβ'	*túathaib*	*tōθaβih	*toụtābis («)	*teụteh₂bʰis, -eh₂bʰos
acc.	{L}Ca^H	*túatha*^H	*tōθāh	*toụtās	*teụteh₂ns
voc.	{L}Ca^H	*á*^L *thúatha*^H	*tōθāh	*toụtās	*teụteh₂es
n.,a.,v. du.	{R}C'^L	*dí*^L *thúaith*^L	*tōθī	*toụtaị	*teụteh₂ih₁
gen.	{L}C^L	*dá*^L *thúath*^L	*tōθō	*toụtoụ («)	*teụteh₂h₁oh₁s, -(H)oh₁u
prep.	{L}Caβ'^N	*dib*^N *túathaib* «	* tōθaβiv	*toụtābim «	*teụteh₂bʰih₁, -moh₁ ?

Illustration 10.1: The standard ā-stem declension

10.2. Variants of the ā-stem declension

While usually the stem final consonant becomes palatalized in the gen. sg. (cp. *túaithe*), a number of words are exempt from this rule. These are words where the stem ends in a consonant cluster, e.g., *delb* /d'elβ/ 'form' or *deacht* /d'eǝχt/ 'divinity,' the gen. sg. of which are *delbae* /d'elβe/ and *deachtae* /d'eǝχte/ respectively. Words in *-cht* /χt/ never palatalize their *auslauting* cluster in the whole paradigm. Some of the alternations (changes) that we encountered in o-stems have to be taken into consideration with ā-stems as well.

1. The diphthong *ía* of the nom. sg. changes into *é* in cases where the following consonant becomes palatalized: e.g., *cíall* /k'ial/ 'sense,' gen. sg. *céille* /k'ēl'e/, *bríathar* /b'r'iaθǝp/ 'word,' prep. sg. *bréithir* /b'r'ēθ'ǝp'/.

2. In words of more than one syllable the usual syncope rules (see 6.8.5) have to be observed. That means that in forms where an extra syllable is added as an ending (in the gen. sg. and the

nom., acc. and prep. pl.) the vowel of every second, non-final syllable has to be deleted. Again one has to pay attention to whether the deleted vowel was historically a front or back vowel. If the vowel was historically a front vowel (*e, i, ē, ĭ*), the resulting consonant cluster becomes palatalized, irrespective of whether one of the consonants would have been non-palatalized without syncope, e.g., *buiden* /buδ'əv/ 'troop,' acc. pl. *buidnea* /buδ'v'a/. The vowel was historically an **i* here. If it was a back vowel (*a, o, u, ā, ō, ū*), the resulting consonant cluster becomes non-palatalized, irrespective of whether one of the consonants would have been pala-talized without syncope, e.g., *dígal* /d'ɨɣəλ/ 'revenge,' gen. sg. *díglae* /d'ɨɣλe/. The vowel was historically an **a* here.

Many words, however, are exempt from the effects of syncope. In words like *ingen* /iv'ɣ'əv/ 'daughter, girl,' syncope has already taken place historically (< **enigenā*, cf. ENIGENA on the Ogam inscription CIIC 362), so that the gen. sg. *ingine* /iv'ɣ'əv'e/ only on the surface shows no syncope, although historically it did take place regularly (< **enigeniı̯ās*). In other words a long vowel in the unstressed syllable seems to have impeded syncopation: *gabál* /gaβāλ/ 'the taking,' but gen. sg. *gabálae* /gaβāλe/. In yet other words syncope is obviously simply suppressed be-cause the resultant consonant cluster would have been impossible to pronounce. This is true for abstract nouns in *-acht*, like *bendacht* /b'endəχt/ 'blessing,' gen. sg. *bendachtae* /b'endəχte/.

Raising/lowering effects play less a role in this declension than in the o-stems. Raising/lowering can be encountered in monosyllabic words that have *e* and *o*, in most cases followed by a single consonant, as their root vowel in the nom. sg. An example for this behavior is the word *cell* 'church, monastic settlement' (stem final consonant /l/), a loan from Latin *cella*:

case	ending	Old Irish	Primitive Irish
nom. sg.	{L}C^L	*cell*^L	**kelā*
gen.	{R}C'e^H	*cille*^H	**keliı̯āh*
prep.	{R}C'^L	*cill*^L	**kelī*
acc.	C'^N	*ceill*^N	**kelev*
voc.	{L}C^L	*á*^L *chell*^L	**kela*
nom. pl.	{L}Ca^H	*cella*^H	**kelāh*
gen.	{L}C^N	*cell*^N	**kelav*
prep.	{L}Cəβ'	*cellaib*	**kelāβih*
acc.	{L}Ca^H	*cella*^H	**kelāh*
voc.	{L}Ca^H	*á*^L *chella*^H	**kelāh*
n.,a.,v. du.	{R}C'^L	*dí*^L *chill*^L	**kelī*
gen.	{L}C^L	*dá*^L *chell*^L	**kelō*
prep.	{L}Cəβ'^N	*dib*^N *cellaib* «	**kelāβiv*

Illustration 10.2: The ā-stem declension with raising/lowering effects

10.3. *ben* 'woman'

The word for 'woman' *ben* /b'ev/ (stem final consonant /v/) historically belongs to this inflectional class, too, although the synchronic Old Irish paradigm is absolutely anomalous:

case	transcription	Old Irish	Prim. Irish	Proto-Celtic	PIE
nom. sg.	b'ev^L	*ben^L*	*bevā «	bena <-bena>	$*g^u\acute{e}nh_2$
gen.	mnā^H	*mná^H*	*mnāh	*m/bnās	$*g^un\acute{e}h_2s$
prep.	mnai̯^{L}	*mnaí̯^{L}*	*mnai̯	*m/bnāi̯, m/bnai̯	$*g^un\acute{e}h_2ei̯, -\acute{e}h_2i$
acc.	b'ev'^{N}	*mnaí̯^{N} (bein^N)* «	*bevev	*benam <beni>	$*g^u\acute{e}nh_2$
voc.	ā β'ev'^{L}	*á^L ben^L*	*bevā «	*ben	$*g^u\acute{e}n$
nom. pl.	mnā^H	*mná^H*	*mnāh	m/bnās <mnas>	$*g^un\acute{e}h_2es$
gen.	bav^N	*ban^N*	*bavav	*banom <bnanom>	$*g^u\d{n}h_2\acute{o}m$
prep.	mnāə̄β'	*mnáib*	*mnāaβih «	*m/bnābis («)	$*g^u\d{n}h_2b^h\acute{i}s, -b^hos$
acc.	mnā^H	*mná^H*	*mnāh	m/bnās <mnas>	$*g^un\acute{e}h_2ns$
voc.	ā μvā^H	*á^L mná^H*	*mnāh	*m/bnās	$*g^un\acute{e}h_2es$
n.,a.,v. du.	d'ī̆^{L} μvai̯^{L}	*dí̆^{L} mnaí̯^{L}*	*mnai̯	*m/bnai̯	$*g^un\acute{e}h_2ih_1$
gen.	dā^L βav^L	*dá^L ban^L*	*bavō	*banou̯ («)	$*g^u\d{n}h_2h_1\acute{o}h_1s, -(H)\acute{o}h_1u$
prep.	d'ī̆β'^{N} mnāə̄β'	*díb^N mnáib* «	*mnāaβiv «	*m/bnābim «	$*g^u\d{n}h_2b^h\acute{i}h_1, -m\acute{o}h_1$?

Illustration 10.3: The declension of *ben* 'woman'

Note:

1. In the transcription I have mainly taken account of the earliest Old Irish forms. In the prep. pl. and du. the early Old Irish hiatus was later monophthongized to /mnāβ'/. In the acc. sg. the historically correct form *bein^N* was already very early replaced by *mnaí^N*. Very rarely *bein^L* can be used for the prep. sg.

2. Besides *ben^L* in legal texts a neutral form *bé^N* is found, e.g., in the phrase *bé cuitgernsa* /b'ē gud'γ'ərnsa/ 'woman of joint authority' or *bé carna* /b'ē gaρna/ 'whore.'

3. In compounds *ban-* appears, e.g., *banchomairle* /bavχoμəρ'λ'e/ 'advice of a woman' (*comairle* 'advice'). Often this creates feminine variants to otherwise masculine nouns, e.g., *banap* /bavab/ 'abbess' to *ap* 'abbot,' *bantigernae* /bant'iγ'ərne/ 'lady, female ruler' to *tigernae* 'lord, ruler.'

Illustration 10.4: *bancháera* 'she-sheep'

Lesson 11

11.1. The basic feminine article

The basic form of the article is *in* /in/, but again this can change considerably depending on the case and the *anlaut* of the following word. I will present the 'normal' paradigm for the feminine article first, which is the one used before words beginning with *b, d, g, p, t, c, m*.

case	transc.	Old Irish	Proto-Celtic
nom. sg.	in[L]	*in[L]*	*(s)indā
gen.	(i)na[H]	*(in)na[H]*	*(s)indās
prep.	(s'ə)n [(')L]	*-(si)n[L]*	*(s)indai̯
acc.	in [(')N]	*in[N]*	*(s)indam
nom. pl.	(i)na[H]	*(in)na[H]*	*(s)indās
gen.	(i)na[N]	*(in)na[N]*	*(s)indoi̯som
prep.	(s)nəβ'	*-(s)naib*	*(s)indābis
acc.	(i)na[H]	*(in)na[H]*	*(s)indās
n.a. du.	in[(')]	*in dí[L]*	*(s)indai̯
gen.	in	*in dá[L]*	*(s)indō
prep.	(s)nəβ'	*-(s)naib dib[N]*	*(s)indābim

Illustration 11.1: The basic pattern of the feminine article

Note:

1. The mutational effects of the feminine article are identical to those of the ā-declension.

2. As for the way the article is used when combined with prepositions, the same is true as for the masculine article (see 7.1.2–4).

11.2. Variants of the feminine article

1. The nominative singular is *ind[L]* /ind/ with words that begin with a vowel, *l, r, n* or *f*, which is lenited to zero: *ind iress* /ind iṗ'əs/ 'the belief, the faith,' *ind lám* /ind λāµ/ 'the hand,' *ind rún* /ind ρūv/ 'the secret,' *ind náire* /ind vāṗ'e/ 'the shamefulness,' *ind ḟlesc* /ind λ'esk/ 'the rod.' The nominative singular is *int[L]* /int/ with words that begin with *s*, which is lenited to /h/: *int ṡúil* /int hūλ'/ 'the eye.'

2. The prepositional singular is *-(si)nd[L]* /(s'ə)nd/ with words that begin with a vowel, *l, r, n* or *f*, which is lenited to zero: *isind iriss* 'in the belief, in the faith,' *isind láim* 'in the hand,' *arind rúin* 'for the secret,' *dond náiri* 'to the shamefulness,' *cosind ḟleisc* 'with the rod.' The prepositional

singular is -*(si)nt*^L /(s'ə)nt/ with words that begin with *s*, which is lenited to /h/: *isint śúil* 'in the eye.'

3. Only in the oldest texts the article in the gen. sg. and nom., acc. and gen. pl. is disyllabic *inna*. The most common variant, however, is *na*.

11.3. The article after prepositions

In Old Irish the article always has to combine with a preceding preposition. In certain cases something similar happens in German as well: e.g., the preposition *zu* and the article *dem* coalesce to *zum*, *in* and *dem* coalesce to *im*. But whereas in German this is restricted to a few forms, in Old Irish this is always the case, both for prepositions that govern the prepositional, and for prepositions that govern the accusative.

There are two basic variants in which the article can appear in these complexes of preposition and article: one with *s(s)* and one without *s*.

The variant with *s* is used with prepositions that do not lenite (but note *tre*!):

a^H	'out of'
co^H	'towards, against, till'
co^N	'with'
for	'upon, over'
fri^H	'turned towards'
íar^N	'after'
i^N	'in, into'
la^H	'with, by'
ós	'over'
re^N	'before'
tar	'across'
tre^L	'through'

The variant without *s* is mainly used with prepositions that lenite (but note *oc* and *for*!):

ar^L	'in front of, before'
di^L	'of, from'
do^L	'to, for'
etir^L	'between, among'
fíad^L	'in the presence of'
fo^L	'under'
for	'upon, over'
imm^L	'around'
ó^L	'from'
oc	'at'
sech^L	'past, beyond'

Note:

1. In the prep. sg. of all genders the basic form is *-(s)in^L*. Furthermore, *d* or *t* can be appended depending on the *anlaut* of the following word, e.g., *don^L, cos(s)int^L, fond^L*, etc.

2. In the prep. pl. of all genders the basic form is *-(s)naib*, e.g., *asnaib, arnaib,* etc.

3. In the acc. sg. m./f. the form is *-(s)in^N*, e.g., *fris(s)in^N, dín^N*, etc.

4. In the acc. sg. n. the form is *-(s)a^N*, e.g., *foa^N, is(s)a^N*, etc.

5. In the acc. pl. of all genders the form is *-(s)na^H*, e.g., *íarsna^H, óna^H*, etc.

You can find a survey of all variants of the article in Appendix F.3.

11.4. The ā-stem adjectives

The ā-stem adjectives are identical in inflection with the ā-stem nouns. Here follows a complete paradigm with article, ā-stem noun and ā-stem adjective: *ind ingen becc* 'the little girl.'

case	feminine	transcription
nom. sg.	*ind^L ingen^L becc^L*	ind iv'γ'əv β'eg
gen.	*inna^H ingine^H bicce^H*	ina h'iv'γ'əv'e b'ig'e
prep.	*dond^L ingin^L bicc^L*	dond iv'γ'əv' β'ig'
acc.	*in^N n-ingin^N mbicc^N*	in n'iv'γ'əv' m'b'ig'
voc.	*á^L ingen^L becc^L*	ā iv'γ'əv β'eg
nom. pl.	*inna^H ingena^H becca^H*	ina h'iv'γ'əva b'ega
gen.	*inna^N n-ingen^N mbecc^N*	ina v'iv'γ'əv m'b'eg
prep.	*donaib ingenaib beccaib*	donəβ' iv'γ'əvəβ' b'egəβ'
acc.	*inna^H ingena^H becca^H*	ina h'iv'γ'əva b'ega
voc.	*á^L ingena^H becca^H*	ā iv'γ'əva b'ega
n.a.v. du.	*in dí^L ingin^L becca^H*	in d'ī iv'γ'əv' β'ega
gen.	*in dá^L ingen^L becc^N*	in dā iv'γ'əv β'eg
prep.	*donaib dib^N n-ingenaib beccaib*	donəβ' d'iβ' v'iv'γ'əvəβ' b'egəβ'

Illustration 11.2: Inflection of feminine article, noun and adjective

Note:

1. Adjectives belonging to the o-, ā-class are inflected according to the o-stem pattern when following masculine and neuter nouns, and according to the ā-stem pattern when following feminine nouns, irrespective of the declensional class of the preceding noun. The noun need not necessarily belong to the same declensional class. The determining factors for the use of the correct form of the adjective are solely the gender and the case of the preceding noun.

11.5. Exercise

Inflect some of the following words together with the article. Combine them with the adjectives
bán /bāv/ 'white,' *clóen* /kloi̯v/ 'crooked,' *fír* /f'īρ/ 'true' and *gel* /g'eλ/ 'bright.'

in grían /g'r'iav/ (f.) 'sun'
in chorr /kor/ (f.) 'heron'
ind ḟlesc /f'l'esk/ (f.) 'rod, stick'
ind lám /lāμ/ (f.) 'hand'
in ben /b'ev/ (f.) 'woman'
ind ires /iρ'əs/ (f.) 'faith'
int ślat /slat/ (f.) 'twig, branch'
in chloch /kloχ/ (f.) 'stone'

Note:

1. *gel* and *corr* are raisable; the second syllable of *ires* is
not syncopated.

Illustration 11.3: *clocha* 'stones'

Lesson 12

12.1. Verbs of the W2a and W2b-class (ī-verbs)

W2 is the second weak verbal class. The characteristic vowel of W2 verbs in the 3rd sg. conjunct is -*i*. Furthermore, in W2 verbs the stem final consonant basically remains palatalized throughout the whole paradigm.

This class has two subtypes: W2a and W2b. The only difference between the two in the present stem is that W2b verbs have short *o* or *u* as their root vowel (*sluindid* /slun'd'əδ'/ 'to declare, to tell,' *roithid* /roθ'əδ'/ 'to set in motion, to make run'). All other W2 verbs belong to the W2a class. There is no other difference in behavior between these two sub-classes in the present tense, so that the example for the present indicative of W2a, *léicid* 'to leave, to allow,' root *léic*- /l'ēg'/ (root final consonant /g'/), will serve as a model for W2b as well:

W2	absolute (independent)		conjunct (dependent)	
1st sg.	*léiciu, léicim(m)*	C'u, C'əm'	*(ní)·léiciu, ·léicim(m)*	C'u, C'əm'
2nd sg.	*léici*	C'i	*(ní)·léici*	C'i
3rd sg.	*léicid*	C'əδ'	*(ní)·léici*	C'i
1st pl.	*léicmi*	C'm'i	*(ní)·léicem*	C'əμ
2nd pl.	*léicthe*	C'θ'e	*(ní)·léicid*	C'əδ'
3rd pl.	*léicit*	C'əd'	*(ní)·léicet*	C'əd

Illustration 12.1: The conjugation of W2-verbs

Note:

1. The ending -*im(m)* in the 1st sg., which is original only with W1 and S3 verbs (historically speaking, athematic verbs), becomes the only productive ending during the Old Irish period and ousts the original ending -*u* of the thematic verbs. With most verbs only the ending -*imm* is attested in the 1st sg.

2. In W2 verbs the root final consonant is typically palatalized throughout the paradigm. A few verbs with two root final consonants (e.g., *erbaid* /erbəδ'/ 'to entrust') or with *á*, *ó* or *u* in the root (e.g., *rádaid* /rāδəδ'/ 'to speak' and *do·lugai* /do·luγi/ 'to forgive') originally had non-palatalized root final consonants. This 'anomaly' within the W2-class, however, was given up in the Old Irish period and finally these verbs acquired palatalized root final consonants throughout the paradigm as well (e.g., *ráidid* /rāδ'əδ'/ etc.).

3. The W2a-class consists to a large number of denominative verbs from o- and ā-stem nouns, that is, verbs that are created from already existing nouns or adjectives and that mean something like 'to make something with the corresponding adjective or noun.' For example, from *scél* /s'k'ēλ/ 'story' the verb *do·scéulai* /do·s'k'ēṷλi/ 'to make known' is created, from *rím* /rīμ/ 'number' the verb *rímid* /rīμ'əδ'/ 'to calculate' is created.

66

4. The W2b-class consists of old causative and iterative verbs with an historical root vowel *o*, which usually became *u* in Old Irish through raising. Causative verbs mean 'to make somebody do a certain action,' e.g., W2b *do·lugai* 'to forgive (= to make something to lie down)' from S1 *laigid* 'lie,' or W2b *roithid* 'to make run' from S1 *reithid* 'to run.'

12.2. Exercise

Now try to conjugate some of the following verbs in absolute and conjunct inflection:

> *dáilid* /dāλ'əδ'/ 'to distribute'
> *ráidid* /rāδ'əδ'/ 'to speak'
> *guirid* /guρ'əδ'/ 'to make warm, to heat'
> *roithid* /roθ'əδ'/ 'to make run'
> *sluindid* /slun'd'əδ'/ 'to mention, to declare, to name'

12.3. The prehistory of the W1 and W2 ending sets

General remarks: As with the nominal inflections, I will give you tables with reconstructed verbal endings and stem formations throughout this book. I will use basically the same conventions and symbols as laid out in 6.3. There is one symbol we have not met yet: † marks syncopated syllables (syncope took place between the Primitive Irish and Old Irish periods). But be aware of the fact that the tables below can convey only a very rough picture. Reconstructing preforms of verbs is for various reasons much more difficult than reconstructing nominal inflections, and the developments that took place historically are far more complex. This book is not the place to go into any details of this.

W1	OIr.	Prim. Ir.	Insular Celtic	Pre-Celtic
absolute				
1st sg.	*-aimm*	*-āmi «	*-āmi «	*-ah$_2$mi, *-ah$_2$i̯oh$_2$
2nd sg.	*-(a)i*	*-āhi	*-āsi «	*-ah$_2$(i̯e)si
3rd sg.	*-aid*	*-āθi	*-āti «	*-ah$_2$(i̯e)ti
1st pl.	*-†m(a)i*	*-āmohi «	*-āmosi «	*-ah$_2$(i̯o)mosi
2nd pl.	*-†th(a)e*	*-āθē- «	*-ātesi «	*-ah$_2$(i̯e)tesi
3rd pl.	*-ait*	*-ādi «	*-anti «	*-ah$_2$nti, *-ah$_2$i̯onti
conjunct				
1st sg.	*-aimm*	*-āmi «	*-ām	*-ah$_2$mi, *-ah$_2$i̯oh$_2$
2nd sg.	*-(a)i «*	*-āhi «	*-ās	*-ah$_2$(i̯e)si
3rd sg.	*-a*	*-āθ	*-āt	*-ah$_2$(i̯e)ti
1st pl.	*-am*	*-āµah	*-āmos	*-ah$_2$(i̯o)mosi
2nd pl.	*-aid*	*-āθeh	*-ātes	*-ah$_2$(i̯e)tesi
3rd pl.	*-at*	*-ād «	*-ant	*-ah$_2$enti, *-ah$_2$i̯onti

Illustration 12.2: Reconstructed W1 endings

W2	OIr.	Prim. Ir.	Insul. Celtic	Pre-Celtic
absolute				
1st sg.	-(i)u	*-iįū	*-iįū	*-eįoh₂
2nd sg.	-i	*-īhi	*-īsi «	*-i̯esi
3rd sg.	-id	*-īθi	*-īti «	*-i̯eti
1st pl.	-ⁿmi	*-īmohi «	*-īmosi «	*-ei̯omosi
2nd pl.	-ⁿthe	*-īθē- «	*-ītesi «	*-ei̯etesi
3rd pl.	-it	*-īdi	*-īnti «	*-ei̯onti
conjunct				
1st sg.	-(i)u	*-iįū	*-iįū	*-eįoh₂
2nd sg.	-i	*-īh	*-īs	*-i̯esi
3rd sg.	-i	*-īθ	*-īt	*-i̯eti
1st pl.	-em	*-īµah	*-īmos «	*-ei̯omosi
2nd pl.	-id	*-īθeh	*-ītes	*-ei̯etesi
3rd pl.	-et	*-īd	*-īnt «	*-ei̯onti

Illustration 12.3: Reconstructed W2 endings

Note:

1. The *m* of the 1st sg. -(a)im(m) /əm'/ was delenited in analogy to the 1st sg. of the copula am(m), im(m) /am im/ 'I am' (< CC *emmi < PIE *h₁esmi). The ending -(a)imm starts to spread to all verbal classes in Old Irish times and replaces the historically justified -(i)u.

2. The W1 2nd sg. conj. -ai apparently was taken over from the corresponding absolute ending, probably in analogy to the 2nd sg. abs. and conj. of the W2 verbs, where the two forms are regularily identical.

3. The *m* of the 1st pl. abs. -(m)m(a)i /m⁽'⁾i/ was delenited in analogy to the 1st pl. of the copula ammi, immi /ami imi/ 'we are' (< CC *emmosi); the 1st pl. conj. -am, -em /əµ/, however, preserves the historically expected form.

4. In what I represent as one W1 paradigm in fact at least three different PIE stem formations fell together: athematic factitives with the suffix *-ah₂-, thematic denominatives with the suffix *-ah₂i̯e/o-, and primary root presents from roots ending in a vowel like *h₂anh₁ti 'breathes'> CC *anati > OIr. anaid 'to wait' or *skerHti 'separates' > CC *skarati > OIr. scaraid 'to separate, to part.'

5. In what I represent as one W2 paradigm in fact at least two different PIE stem formations fell together: primary verbs with the thematic suffix *-ei̯e/o-, and athematic statives in *-eh₁(i̯e/o-). Furthermore, at least creitid 'to believe' continues a primary verbal collocation PIE *ḱred dʰeh₁- 'to put one's heart.' In the tables above I assume that at some stage in the language history, but in the Insular Celtic period at the latest, *-ī- was generalized as the W2 stem suffix, even where *-ii̯o- would be expected, either in analogy to the verbs with original *-ī- < PIE *-eh₁-, or in analogy to the W1 verbs that had a uniform stem suffix *-ā- throughout the paradigm.

6. The distinction between absolute and conjunct endings in Old Irish has a parallel in the earliest British (Old Welsh) material. It has nothing to do with the distinction between primary and secondary endings in PIE, but is the result of a special Insular Celtic development: early loss of final inherited final short *-i, but retention of the vowel before enclitic particles. Subsequently the forms with and without *-i were redistributed in the whole verbal system. The exact nature of those particles in front of which *-i was retained is a matter of heated disputes.

12.4. Possessive pronouns

In English possessive pronouns are words like *my, your, her*, etc., in German *unser, euer, ihr*, etc. Functionally these pronouns are very similar to the genitive case: they can express possession, e.g., <u>my</u> book = *the book that belongs to me*, but they can also express various other relations, e.g., *tut dies zu <u>meinem</u> Gedächtnis = do this to remember me*, where the possessive pronoun serves as the object of *Gedächtnis* 'rememberance.' This second type of construction is very important in Old Irish, as we shall see in a later lesson.

Illustration 12.4:
mo chuilén 'my puppy'

Fortunately, Old Irish possessive pronouns are not inflected. There is one form for each person that remains unaffected by all inflectional changes of the noun it qualifies. Old Irish possessive pronouns always precede the word they qualify. All possessive pronouns have mutational effects. Which mutation follows which pronoun can be seen in the table below:

person	translation	pronoun
1st sg.	my	*mo*L, *m'*
2nd sg.	thy	*do*L, *t,' th'*
3rd sg.m.	his	*a*L
3rd sg.f.	her	*a*H
3rd sg.n.	its	*a*L
1st pl.	our	*ar*N
2nd pl.	your	*for*N, *far*N, *bar*N
3rd pl.	their	*a*N

Illustration 12.5: Possessive pronouns

Note:

1. The -*o* of *mo*L and *do*L is elided before words beginning with vowels; in the case of *do*L we then get *t'* or lenited *th'* (it is not clear when and why we get the lenited form): *m'athair* 'my father,' *t'ainm, th'ainm* 'thy name.' In early texts *mo*L and *do*L have by-forms with *u*: *mu*L, *du*L.

2. Be careful with *a*! Depending on the mutation it causes it can either mean 'her,' 'his,' 'its' or 'their.' So it is always of highest importance to look at the following word and note the mutational effect exerted on it. In this context it is of greatest importance to be familiar with Old Irish orthography, in order to recognize what mutation could be reflected in the spelling.

3. Just like the article, possessive pronouns combine with preceding prepositions. The possessive pronouns retain their mutational effects.

3.1. In the case of *mo* and *do* we get -*m^L* /m/ and -*t^L* /t/ after prepositions ending in a vowel and after *for*: *dom^L* /dom/ (< *do^L* + *mo^L*) 'to my,' *frim^L* /f'r'im/ (*fri^H* + *mo^L*) 'against my, towards my,' *fort^L* /fort/ (< *for* + *do^L*) 'on thy,' etc. Otherwise *mo^L* and *do^L* remain: *asmo^L* (*a^H* + *mo^L*) 'out of my,' *imdu^L* (*imm^L* + *du^L*) 'around thy,' or *ocdu^L* (*oc* + *do^L*) 'at thy.'

3.2. All *a* behave the same, no matter what mutational effects they cause. In most cases the *a* is simply stuck to the preposition: *fora* (*for* + *a*) 'on his, her, its, their,' *fria* (*fri^H* + *a*) 'against his, her, its, their.' The two prepositions *do^L* 'to, for' and *di^L* 'from' both become *dia* with possessive *a* and one has to decide from the context which of the two is meant in a given case. Nasalizing prepositions display an *n* before the *a*: e.g., *cona* (*co^N* + *a*) 'with his, her, its, their;' in the case of *i^N* this *n* is frequently spelled double: *inna* or *ina* (*i^N* + *a*) 'in(to) his, her, its, their.' *a^H* 'out of' inserts an *s* before the *a*: *asa* 'out of his, her, its, their.'

3.3. *ar^N* 'our' behaves like *a*: *diar^N* (*do^L*/*di^L* + *ar^N*) 'to our; from our,' *íarnar^N* (*íar^N* + *ar^N*) 'after our,' *occar^N* (*oc* + *ar^N*) 'at our,' *asar^N* (*a^H* + *ar^N*) 'out of our.'

3.4. *for^N*, *far^N*, *bar^N* /βoρ βaρ/ 'your' is simply added to the preposition: *dibar^N* (*di^L* + *bar^N*) 'from your,' *ibar^N* or *ifar^N* (*i^N* + *bar^N*) 'in(to) your.'

4. Possessive pronouns are apparently not affected by the mutational effects of preceding particles or prepositions, e.g., *á mmo śruith* /ā mo hρuθ'/ 'oh my wise man' (I2T 10), where *mo* is not lenited after the otherwise leniting vocative particle *á^L*.

Lesson 13

13.1. A poem

The lines below about a scribe form the third stanza of a poem edited by Kuno MEYER in ZCPh 13, 8 (also edited in EIL 70 and GT 159). The poem dates approximately to the 11th century, but it is put into the mouth of Saint Colum Cille, who lived in the 6th century and who was famous for being a tireless scribe. Many miracles in connection with books are ascribed to him. I have normalized the spelling of the stanza.

Sínim mo phenn mbecc mbróenach
tar óenach lebor lígoll
cen scor fri selba ségonn,
dían scíth mo chrob ón scríbonn.

s'īv'əm' mo f'en m'b'eg mbroi̯vəχ
taρ oi̯vəχ l'eβəρ l'ɨɣol
k'ev skoρ f'r'i s'elβa s'ēɣən,
d'iav s'k'ɨθ mo χρoβ ōn s'k'r'ɨβən.

Illustration 13.1: *Cáera Chille oc scríbund* 'the sheep of the church writing'

13.2. Varia

1. In the sentences below we will meet a new conjunct particle: *innád*[N] is the negated interrogative particle 'do … not?,' and as such takes the dependent form of the verb, e.g., *Innad·carai do mnaí, a fir?* 'Dost thou not love thy wife, man?'

2. There are a number of new prepositions:

The preposition *cen*[L] 'without' takes the accusative.

The preposition *co*[N] 'with' takes the prepositional.

The preposition *di*[L] 'from' takes the prepositional.

The preposition *fo*[L] means '(placed) under' when followed by the prepositional, but '(going) under' when followed by the accusative.

The preposition *fri*[H] '(turned) against, towards' takes the accusative.

The preposition *ó*[L] 'from' takes the prepositional.

The preposition *tar* 'across' takes the accusative.

3. Note the use of the verb *creitid* (W2a) 'to believe.' If you want to say 'to believe *in*' you simply have to use an object in the accusative: e.g., *creitiu Día* (*Día* = acc. sg.) means 'I believe *in* God.' There is no need to especially express the 'in' in Old Irish.

4. The phrase *slán co céill*, taken from a poem (in sentence 17) translates as 'safe and sound.' Literally it means 'sound with sense.' This is a so-called *cheville*, or a phrase that is more or less

71

meaningless in the context of the sentence, but which is needed in a poem to achieve rhyme and the necessary number of syllables. Note the special language and the way things are expressed in sentences 16–20, which are all taken from poems.

5. *Colum Cille* 'the Dove of the Church' is the Irish name of Saint Columba, one of the most important of all Irish saints, who amongst other things founded the monastery on the small island of Ioua (*Iona*) off the Scottish coast. He belonged to the royal family of the *Uí Néill* 'descendants of Níall,' who ruled the greatest part of Ireland in the early Middle Ages. Their ancestor was the prehistoric, legendary king *Níall Noígíallach* 'Níall of the Nine Hostages,' the *Níall* alluded to in sentence 17.

13.3. Exercise

Old Irish

1. Ní·léiciu (*or:* ní·léicimm) inna mucca móra forsa fér. 2. Á mo ben lígach, in·sluindi drochscéla do thúaithe dond fiur thríun fo déraib díanaib? 3. Innád·creti Día, á fir bicc? 4. Dáilmi ar mbiad 7 ar ndig forsna ingena 7 maccu. 5. Á thúatha in domuin móir, ní·creitid fírdeacht Críst bíi, acht creitte far ngúdéu. 6. Brisit inna drochingena creitt in charpait cona claidbib. 7. Léiciu (*or:* léicimm) sunu céoil asmo chruitt di ór 7 argut. 8. Sluindi cella línmara do túaithe donaib mnáib, á Emer rúad. 9. Creitid in buiden mór bréithir int šacairt. 10. Ní·léicem claidbiu i llámaib ingen inna fer. 11. In·rráidid rúin ind libuir šalm do dib n-ingenaib cóemaib inna mná gaíthe, á chruim-theru? 12. Guirid in grían gel curpu fer 7 ban 7 delba crann co neurt isin maitin. 13. Brisid in gáeth aicher crann inna luinge. 14. Innád·mmarbat buidnea lóech? 15. Á dí šenmnaí, in·cúraid inna ingena óca co flescaib daingnib tara tóebu? 16. * Crochaid nóeb Colum Cille a chorp forsna tonna glassa. (GT 20) 17. * Colum Cille, caindel Néill, séolaid a luing tarsin sál, slán co céill. (GT 20) 18. * Brisid in nóeb tonna arda ind neimid bled i lluing brisc. (GT 20) 19. * Int én becc, léicid feit din gup glan, in lon din chraíb glais. (EIL 6) 20. ** Dordaid dam, [...] gáeth ard úar, ísel grían. (EIL 160)

Transcription

1. n'ɪ·l'ēg'u (n'ɪ·l'ēg'əm') ina muka mōpa forsa β'ep. 2. ā mo β'ev λ'ɪɣəχ, iv·slun'd'i droχs'k'ēλa do θuaθ'e dond iu̯ρ θ'ρ'ɪu̯v fo δ'eρəβ' d'iavəβ'? 3. ināδ·g'r'ed'i d'ia, ā iρ' β'ig'? 4. dāλ'm'i aρ m'b'iäδ ogus aρ n'd'iɣ' forsna h'iv'ɣ'əva ogus μaku. 5. ā θuaθa in doμuv' μōρ', n'ɪ·k'r'ed'əδ' f'ɪρδ'eä̯χt g'r'ɪs't' β'ïi, aχt k'r'et'e βaρ ŋgūδ'eu̯. 6. b'r'is'əd' ina droχiv'ɣ'əva k'r'et' in χarbəd' kova glaδ'-β'əβ'. 7. l'ēg'u (l'ēg'əm') suvu k'eu̯λ' asmo χput' d'i ōρ ogus argud. 8. slun'd'i k'ela l'ɪvμəρa do θuaθ'e donəβ' mnāäβ', ā eμ'əρ ρuaδ. 9. k'r'ed'əδ' in βuδ'əv μōρ b'r'ēθ'əρ' int hagər't'. 10. n'ɪ·l'ēg'əμ klaδ'β'u i lāμəβ' iv'ɣ'əv ina β'ep. 11. iv·rāδ'əδ' rūv' ind λ'iβuρ' halm do d'iβ' v'iv'ɣ'əvəβ' koi̯μəβ' ina mnā gai̯θ'e, ā χρuμ'θ'əρu? 12. guρ'əd' in ɣ'ρ'iav ɣ'eλ kurpu f'eρ ogus βav ogus δ'elβa kran ko neu̯rt is'ən μad'əv'. 13. b'r'is'əδ' in ɣai̯θ aχ'əρ kran ina luŋ'g'e. 14. ināδ·marβəd buδ'v'a loi̯χ? 15. ā d'ɪ h'evμvai̯, iv·gūρəδ' ina h'iv'ɣ'əva hōga ko β'l'eskəβ' daŋ'g'v'əβ' taρa doi̯βu? 16. kroχəδ' noi̯β koλum k'il'e a χorp forsna tona glasa. 17. koλum k'il'e, kan'd'əλ v'ēl', s'ēu̯λəδ' a λuŋ'g' tars'ən sāλ, slāv ko g'ēl'. 18. b'r'is'əδ' in noi̯β tona harda ind v'eμ'əδ' β'l'eδ i luŋ'g' β'r'is'k'. 19. int ēv b'eg, l'ēg'əδ' f'ed' d'in ɣub ɣλav, in lov d'in χρai̯β' ɣλas'. 20. dordəδ' daμ, gai̯θ ard uaρ, ɪs'əλ g'r'iav.

Illustration 13.2:
caindel isin gaíth
'candle in the wind'

English

1. I allow the big pig (to go) onto the grass. 2. Oh my beautiful women, you relate the bad story of your tribes to the strong men under fierce tears. 3. Don't you believe in God, little men? 4. Do we distribute our food and our drink among the girls and the boys? 5. Oh tribes of the world, you believe in the true divinity of the living Christ, and you do not believe in your false gods. 6. Do the bad girls break the frames of the chariots with their swords? 7. We do not release the sound of music from our harps of gold and silver. 8. You do not enumerate the churches of your tribes to the woman, oh red-haired girls. 9. Doesn't the big troop believe the words of the priest? 10. We leave the sword in the hand of the girl of the man. 11. Thou speakest the secrets of the psalm book to the beautiful daughter of the clever woman, oh priest. 12. Does the sun warm the bodies of men and women and the shapes of the trees with might in the morning? 13. The strong wind does not break the masts of the ships. 14. Does he kill a troop of warriors? 15. Oh old woman, dost thou punish the young girl with a hard rod on her side? 16. Does saint Colum Cille crucify his body on the blue waves? 17. Colum Cille, the candel of Níall, does he not sail his ship over the sea, safe and sound? 18. The saint does not break the high waves of the whales' sanctuary in fragile ships. 19. The little bird, does it release (= give) a whistle from the bright peak, the blackbird from the green branches? 20. The stags bellow.

13.4. Test

Try to recognize the inflectional forms of the following nouns and give as much information about them as possible—gender, stem class, case, number. Where two or more slots follow a form, more than one correct answer is possible:

éoin: _____ or _____   ind lám: _____

gaíth: _____ or _____   in lláim: _____

in n-én: _____   inna rosca: _____ or _____

claidbib: _____   caindil: _____ or _____

inna mban: _____   in macc mbecc: _____

in macc becc: _____   inna macc mbecc: _____

ech: _____ or _____ or _____

inna rosc: _____ or _____ or _____

inna mná: _____ or _____ or _____

á chenn: _____   int én: _____   ceill: _____

láim: _____ or _____   ind leith: _____

in chlaidib: _____ or _____   inna rún: _____

a cenn: _____ or _____   in bech: _____

leth: _____ or _____ or _____

or _____ or _____

Lesson 14

14.1. Nouns: masculine i̯o-stems

Historically speaking i̯o-stems were but a variant of the o-stems in PIE (they simply had a i̯ before the o). But as a result of the drastic sound changes in the prehistory of Irish, the inflection of the i̯o-stems differs radically from that of the o-stems in Old Irish. Unlike the inflectional classes we have learned so far i̯o-stems *do* have something that may be called an ending: there is always a vowel at the end of the word. This vowel may be *e, i* or *u*, depending on the case. As regards the mutational effects on the following word, i̯o-stems go absolutely parallel with the o-stems. As a mnemonic device to remember the endings of the masculine i̯o-stems you can use the word *fer* (to the right of the table below). In nearly all cases the root vowel of *fer* corresponds to the ending of the i̯o-stem.

The root final consonant before the vowel of the ending may either be palatalized (cp. the *l* /λ'/ in *céile* below) or non-palatalized (cp. the *t* /t/ in *daltae* below) throughout the paradigm. In the latter category fall mainly words with consonant clusters before the final vowel. Pay attention to the different spellings of the final vowels in the two inflectional patterns, but be also always aware that the final vowels are identical at the same time. No vowel changes like raising, lowering, etc. take place in the roots of the words. The following examples are *céile* /k'ēλ'e/ 'client, companion' for words with palatalized root final consonants, and *daltae* /dalte/ 'fosterling, foster-son' for words with non-palatalized root final consonants:

case	ending	pal. root final cons.	non-pal. root final cons.	Proto-Celtic	fer
nom. sg.	C⁽ʾ⁾eᴴ	*céile*	*daltae*	*°(i)i̯os	*fer*
gen.	C⁽ʾ⁾iᴸ	*céili*ᴸ	*daltai*ᴸ	*°(i)i̯ī	*fir*ᴸ
prep.	C⁽ʾ⁾uᴸ	*céiliu*ᴸ	*daltu*ᴸ	*°(i)i̯ūi̯, -ū, -ū(δ)	*fiur*ᴸ
acc.	C⁽ʾ⁾eᴺ	*céile*ᴺ	*daltae*ᴺ	*°(i)i̯om	*fer*ᴺ
voc.	C⁽ʾ⁾iᴸ	*á*ᴸ *chéili*ᴸ	*á*ᴸ *daltai*ᴸ	*°(i)i̯e	*á*ᴸ *ḟir*ᴸ
nom. pl.	C⁽ʾ⁾iᴸ	*céili*ᴸ	*daltai*ᴸ	*°(i)i̯oi̯	*fir*ᴸ
gen.	C⁽ʾ⁾eᴺ	*céile*ᴺ	*daltae*ᴺ	*°(i)i̯om	*fer*ᴺ
prep.	C⁽ʾ⁾əβ'	*céilib*	*daltaib*	*°(i)i̯obis	*feraib*
acc.	C⁽ʾ⁾uᴴ	*céiliu*ᴴ	*daltu*ᴴ	*°(i)i̯ūs	*firu*ᴴ
voc.	C⁽ʾ⁾uᴴ	*á*ᴸ *chéiliu*ᴴ	*á*ᴸ *daltu*ᴴ	« *°(i)i̯oi̯	*á*ᴸ *ḟiru*ᴴ
n.-a. du.	C⁽ʾ⁾eᴸ	*dá*ᴸ *chéile*ᴸ	*dá*ᴸ *daltae*ᴸ	*°(i)i̯o	*dá*ᴸ *ḟer*ᴸ
gen.	C⁽ʾ⁾eᴸ	*dá*ᴸ *chéile*ᴸ	*dá*ᴸ *daltae*ᴸ	*°(i)i̯ou̯	*dá*ᴸ *ḟer*ᴸ
prep.	C⁽ʾ⁾əβ'	*dib*ᴺ *céilib*	*dib*ᴺ *ndaltaib*	« *°(i)i̯obim	*dib*ᴺ *feraib*

Illustration 14.1: The masculine i̯o-stem declension

14.2. Nouns: neuter i̯o-stems

Neuter i̯o-stems are just as parallel to masculine i̯o-stems, as neuter o-stems are parallel to masculine o-stems. As a mnemonic device to remember the endings of the neuter i̯o-stems you can use the word *cenn* (to the right of the table below). In nearly all cases the root vowel of *cenn* corresponds to the i̯o-stem endings. Again the root final consonant before the vowel of the ending may either be palatalized or non-palatalized, and stays so throughout the paradigm. No vowel changes like raising, lowering, etc., take place in the roots of the words. The following examples are *cride* /k'riδ'e/ 'heart' for words with palatalized root final consonants, and *cumachtae* /kuμəχte/ 'power, strength, might' for words with non-palatalized root final consonants:

case	ending	pal. root final cons.	non-pal. root final cons.	Proto-Celtic	cenn
nom. acc. sg.	C⁽ʼ⁾eᴺ	*cride*ᴺ	*cumachtae*ᴺ	*°(i)i̯om	cennᴺ
gen.	C⁽ʼ⁾iᴸ	*cridi*ᴸ	*cumachtai*ᴸ	*°(i)i̯ī	cinnᴸ
prep.	C⁽ʼ⁾uᴸ	*cridiu*ᴸ	*cumachtu*ᴸ	*°(i)i̯ūi̯, -ū, -ū(δ)	ciunnᴸ
voc.	C⁽ʼ⁾eᴺ	*á*ᴸ *chride*ᴺ	*á*ᴸ *chumachtae*ᴺ	*°(i)i̯om	*á*ᴸ chennᴺ
nom. acc. pl.	C⁽ʼ⁾eᴸ	*cride*ᴸ	*cumachtae*ᴸ	*°(i)i̯ā	cennᴸ
gen.	C⁽ʼ⁾eᴺ	*cride*ᴺ	*cumachtae*ᴺ	*°(i)i̯om	cennᴺ
prep.	C⁽ʼ⁾əβ'	*cridib*	*cumachtaib*	*°(i)i̯obis	cennaib
voc.	C⁽ʼ⁾eᴸ	*á*ᴸ *chride*ᴸ	*á*ᴸ *chumachtae*ᴸ	*°(i)i̯ā	*á*ᴸ chennaᴴ
nom. acc. du.	C⁽ʼ⁾eᴺ	*dá*ᴺ *cride*ᴺ	*dá*ᴺ *cumachtae*ᴺ	*°(i)i̯o	*dá*ᴺ cennᴺ
gen.	C⁽ʼ⁾eᴺ	*dá*ᴺ *cride*ᴺ	*dá*ᴺ *cumachtae*ᴺ	*°(i)i̯ou̯	*dá*ᴺ cennᴺ
prep.	C⁽ʼ⁾əβ'	*dib*ᴺ *cridib*	*dib*ᴺ *cumachtaib*	« *°(i)i̯obim	*dib*ᴺ cennaib

Illustration 14.2: The neuter i̯o-stem declension

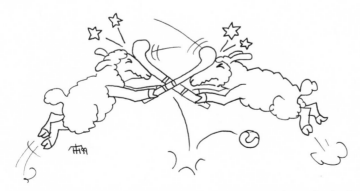

Illustration 14.3: *dá chéile oc cluichiu* 'two companions playing'

14.3. Adjectives: i̯o-stems

In lessons 7 and 11 we learned the o-, ā-adjectives, i.e., adjectives that inflect as o-stems when accompanying masculine and neuter nouns, and as ā-stems when accompanying feminine nouns. There is also a large number of adjectives that inflect as i̯o-stems when qualifying masculine and neuter nouns (and, you guessed correctly, their feminine counterparts are i̯ā-stems. We will look at them in the next lesson).

The root final consonant of i̯o-stem adjectives may either be palatalized or non-palatalized and stays so throughout the paradigm. In the singular i̯o-stem adjectives are identical in inflection with masculine, respectively neuter i̯o-stem nouns. In the plural, however, they show a divergent behavior: they have the ending *-(a)i* in the nominative, accusative and vocative, *-(a)e* in the genitive and *-(a)ib* in the prepositional. The examples below are *buide* /buð'e/ 'yellow' for words with palatalized root final consonants and *rígdae* /r'ɪɣðe/ 'royal, kingly' for words with non-palatalized root final consonants.

case	ending	masc., palat.	masc., non-palat.	ending	neuter, palat.	neuter, non-palat.
nom. sg.	C(ʹ)eᴴ	*buide*	*rígdae*	C(ʹ)eᴺ	*buide*ᴺ	*rígdae*ᴺ
gen.	C(ʹ)iᴸ	*buidi*ᴸ	*rígdai*ᴸ	C(ʹ)iᴸ	*buidi*ᴸ	*rígdai*ᴸ
prep.	C(ʹ)uᴸ	*buidiu*ᴸ	*rígdu*ᴸ	C(ʹ)uᴸ	*buidiu*ᴸ	*rígdu*ᴸ
acc.	C(ʹ)eᴺ	*buide*ᴺ	*rígdae*ᴺ	C(ʹ)eᴺ	*buide*ᴺ	*rígdae*ᴺ
voc.	C(ʹ)iᴸ	*á*ᴸ *buidi*ᴸ	*á*ᴸ *rígdai*ᴸ	C(ʹ)eᴺ	*á*ᴸ *buide*ᴺ	*á*ᴸ *rígdae*ᴺ
nom. pl.	C(ʹ)iᴸ	*buidi*ᴸ	*rígdai*ᴸ	C(ʹ)iᴸ	*buidi*ᴸ	*rígdai*ᴸ
gen.	C(ʹ)eᴺ	*buide*ᴺ	*rígdae*ᴺ	C(ʹ)eᴺ	*buide*ᴺ	*rígdae*ᴺ
prep.	C(ʹ)əβ'	*buidib*	*rígdaib*	C(ʹ)əβ'	*buidib*	*rígdaib*
acc.	C(ʹ)iᴴ	*buidi*ᴴ	*rígdai*ᴴ	C(ʹ)iᴸ	*buidi*ᴸ	*rígdai*ᴸ
voc.	C(ʹ)iᴴ	*á*ᴸ *buidi*ᴴ	*á*ᴸ *rígdai*ᴴ	C(ʹ)iᴸ	*á*ᴸ *buidi*ᴸ	*á*ᴸ *rígdai*ᴸ

Illustration 14.4: i̯o-stem adjectives

14.4. Exercise

Inflect some of the following words. Decline them together with the article. Combine them with the i̯o-stem adjectives *foirbthe* /for'β'θ'e/ 'perfect,' *amrae* /aμρe/ 'wonderful,' *nue* /nuĕ/ 'new,' *dorchae* /ɖorχe/ 'dark.'

> *in céile* /k'ēλ'e/ (m.) 'client, companion'
> *a cluiche* /kluχ'e/ (n.) 'game, sport'
> *in techtaire* /t'eχtəρ'e/ (m.) 'messenger'
> *int ecnae* /egne/ (m.) 'knowledge'
> *a fíadnaise* /f'iaðvəs'e/ (n.) 'witness, testimony'
> *int aitte* /at'e/ (m.) 'foster-father'

Lesson 15

15.1. Verbs: general remarks on compound verbs

Now that you have learned the two weak conjugations W1 and W2 we can turn to a very important chapter of the Old Irish verbal system: the compound verbs. In 8.1 I already pointed out the basic distinction between simple and compound verbs in Old Irish, but I will go into the appropriate details now.

In English compound verbs (like *under-take, over-hear*, etc.) can only consist of a single preverb (*under-, over-*, etc.) and the verbal root (*take, hear*, etc.). They make up only a small part of the verbal system. German has decisively more compound verbs than English. Here, too, in the overwhelming majority they consist of a single preverb followed by the verbal root (*auf-nehmen, bei-legen*, etc.), but sometimes two preverbs are possible as well (*nach-be-arbeiten, vor-unter-suchen*, etc.). In Old Irish on the other hand compound verbs make up the greatest part of the verbal system, and the language loves preverbs: up to four of them can stand before the verbal root. We will only look at compound verbs with one preverb at the beginning.

 One of the greatest differences between simple and compound verbs in Old Irish is that compound verbs only use conjunct endings! I said in 8.1 that as soon as any particle comes before a verb it changes to conjunct inflection. Preverbs count as particles just as well. The first particle in a verbal form always comes before the stress, and this is true for compound verbs, too.

In most cases you will find a basic simple verb in Old Irish from which a compound verb is formed. For example the simple W1 verb *scaraid* 'to part, to separate, to cut off' forms with the preverb *to* the compound W1 verb *do·scara* 'to overthrow, to destroy,' or the simple W2 verb *rímid* 'to count, to estimate' forms with the preverb *ad* the compound W2 verb *ad·rími* 'to count, to compute.' Note that in both cases the whole verb changes to conjunct inflection and that the preverb (as the first particle in the verbal form) comes before the stress and is therefore separated from the rest of the word by the mid high dot <·> in my standardized orthography.

Sometimes the meaning of the basic simple verb is only slightly modified by a preverb (e.g., *rímid* 'to count, to estimate' → *ad·rími* 'to count, to compute,' cf. English *hear* → *overhear* or German *rechnen* → *berechnen*), but more often than not the semantical connection between the simple and the compound verb is weak or hardly visible at all, e.g., W2b *sluindid* 'to relate, to name' → W2b *do·sluindi* 'to deny, to reject, to refuse.' Note that it is usually not possible to find out the meaning of a compound verb by simply adding the meaning of the preverb(s) and the meaning of the verbal root in the translation!

Sometimes no simple verb exists beside a compound verb in Old Irish at all. For example, the compound W1 verb *ad·ella* 'to visit, to approach' consists of the preverb *ad* and a W1 verbal stem *ella-*, but a simple W1 verb **ellaid*, which might be expected, is not found in Old Irish. This verbal root is only attested in composition.

Because of the obscuring effects of assimilation, syncope, vowel affection and other prehistoric sound changes in Irish it is often very difficult to recognize the preverbs and verbal roots involved in a compound. In grammars and dictionaries you will often find a system for the formal representation of compound verbs, to which I will adhere: the *underlying* forms of the preverbs are separated by hyphens from one another and from the *underlying* verbal root (without the stem vowel!). *Do·scara* is thus represented as *to-scar-*, *ad·ella* as *ad-ell-*, *ad·rími* as *ad-rím-*, *do·sluindi* as *di-sluind-*. Or a more complex example: W2 *do·róscai* 'to distinguish oneself' is a compound of *di-ro-od-scoch-*. It is important to be aware of these *underlying* forms: e.g., pretonic[1] *do·* can represent two different preverbs, *to-* and *di-*, which behave completely differently as soon as they leave the pretonic position. In the illustration below you will find all preverbs of Old Irish with their underlying forms and what they look like in pretonic position. The suggested meanings are only an approximation. I will not attempt to give a picture of the preverbs outside of the pretonic position, as this would go far beyond the scope of this book.

underlying form	meaning	pretonic	underlying form	meaning	pretonic
ad	'to, towards'	*ad·*	in	'in, into'	*in·*
are, air	'before, for'	*ar·*	inde	'in, into'	*in·*
aith	'*re-, ex-*'	*ad·*	ne, ni	'down'	n/a
com, cum	'with'	*con·*	oc	'at'	*ocu·, occu·*
de, dī	'from'	*do·*	oss, uss	'up, off'	*as·*
ess	'out of'	*as·*	re, ri, rem-	'before, *prae-*'	*remi·*
eter	'between'	*eter·, etar·*	ro	*grammatical*	*ro·, ru·*
fo	'under'	*fo·*	sech	'past, beyond'	*sechmi·*
for	'on, over'	*for·*	tar, tairm-	'across, over'	*tarmi·, tremi·*
frith, fris	'against'	*fris·*	to	'to, towards'	*do·, du·*
íarm-	'after'	*íarmi·*	tri, tre, trem-	'through'	*tremi·, trimi·*
imbe, imm	'around'	*im·, imm·*			

Illustration 15.1: Underlying and pretonic variants of preverbs

15.2. Verbs: deuterotonic and prototonic verbal forms

So far, so good. But now the difficulties start. You remember that every verbal form in Old Irish has two variants, an independent and a dependent variant. In simple verbs this distinction is made by the use of absolute or conjunct endings. But how is this distinction made in compound verbs where only conjunct endings are possible in the first place?

This distinction is effected by a shift of the stress. Compound verbs in independent position as we saw them above are stressed on the *second* element of the verbal form, the first preverb coming immediately before the stress. Because of this stress pattern these forms are called *deuterotonic* forms (from Greek *deúteros* = 'second,' *tónos* = 'accent, stress'). As soon as any other conjunct particle (like *ní*, *in*[N], etc.) comes before the verbal form, the stress shifts one position to the left, that is onto the first element of the verbal form, which was unstressed so far. These forms are called *prototonic* forms (from Greek *prôtos* = 'first').

---

[1] *Pretonic* = in the position immediately before the stress.

This leads to the following system in Old Irish as regards dependent and independent verbal forms (forms with conjunct endings are underlined):

	independent	dependent
simple verbs (e.g., *scaraid*)	absolute ending *scaraid*	conjunct ending *(ní)·scara*
compound verbs (e.g., *do·scara*)	deuterotonic form *do·scara*	prototonic form *(ní)·tascra*

Illustration 15.2: Dependence and independence

Unfortunately this is not all that has to be said about deutero- and prototonic verbal forms. The shift of the accent one position to the left has heavy consequences. The accent shift means that in the prototonic form the verb usually has one syllable more than it had in the deuterotonic form. Consequently a completely different syncope-pattern applies, and the resulting form can differ vehemently from the form we started from.

Let's look at W1 *ad·ella* /aδ·ela/ 'to visit' first. In the deuterotonic form the accent lies on the *e*. That part of the verb which lies under the stress (·*ella*) has two syllables, therefore no syncope applies. But when we put it into its prototonic form the stress now falls on *ad-*, upon which -*ella* immediately follows. We would get *·adella*. This form, however, has more than two syllables, therefore syncope has to apply. The syncope rule is that the vowel of every second, non-final syllable is deleted. In this case the *e* of *·adella* is affected by deletion. Since *e* is a front vowel and syncopation of a front vowel entails palatalization of all surrounding consonants, the *d* /δ/ and the *ll* /l/ become palatalized, so that we end up with /·aδ'l'a/, which is written ·*aidlea*.

But often even more changes take place. Let's look at the other examples we have had so far.

W2 *ad·rími* /aδ·r'ĩμ'i/ 'to count' becomes *·adrími* first of all. *d* /δ/ is lost before *r*, but before it disappears it lengthens the vowel in front of it (= *compensatory lengthening*), so that we get *·ārīmi*. Now syncope applies: *ī* in the second syllable is a front vowel so that all surrounding consonants are palatalized by its syncopation. The result is /·āρ'μ'i/, written ·*áirmi*.

W1 *do·scara* /do·skaρa/ 'to destroy' is a compound of *to-* (which becomes *do* in the position before the stress, see illustration 15.1.) and *scara-*, so that our starting point for the prototonic variant is *·toscara*. Now a not very clear rule applies that changes *o* of preverbs to *a* especially in cases when the following syllable has an *a* (*scar-*), which gives us *·tascara*. Now we come to syncope. In this case the back vowel *a* has to be deleted, which means that all surrounding consonants become non-palatalized and we finally arrive at /·taskρa/, which is written ·*tascra* 'to destroy.'

But things can get even worse. W2b *do·sluindi* 'to deny' is a compound of *dí-* (which also becomes *do* in the position before the stress, see illustration 15.1.) and *sluindi-*, so that our starting point for the prototonic variant is *·dísluindi*. The first development to take into account here is lenition, which turns *s* into *h*: *·díhluindi*. Now syncope takes place. Since *u* is a back vowel that depalatalizes everything around it we arrive at *·díhlndai* (orthographic *a*!). Now the trouble really starts: as soon as any voiced consonant (here *d*) comes into immediate contact with *h* (< *s*) it gets devoiced, so that in this case *t* results; the *h* disappears. Furthermore, the *n* is assimilated to the *l* so that it itself becomes *l*. The two *l*s then merge into one unlenited *l*. What we get in the end is /·d'īlti/, which is written ·*díltai* 'to deny.' In the case of ·*díltai* it is very important to note that as a result of a secondary development, that is, syncope of a back vowel, the final consonant of the verbal root has become non-palatalized throughout the paradigm, even though ideally W2

verbs always have a palatalized root final consonant! Of course exactly the opposite can be true in the case of W1 verbs, which ideally have a non-palatalized root final consonant throughout the paradigm. For example, W1 *for·cenna* 'to finish' has ·*foircnea* /·for'k'n'a/ (< *·*forkenna*) as its prototonic counterpart, where the consonant cluster before the ending is always palatalized.

Illustration 15.3:
tascarthae 'knocked out'

Be assured that *do·sluindi*, ·*díltai* is not the most extreme alternation found in Old Irish. You can find a short list of representative pairs in GOI 534–536. In the vocabulary I will always give both the 3rd sg. deuterotonic and prototonic forms of any compound verb. Although this will be of some help for you, always be aware that — because of the many and complicated developments within Old Irish — some unexpected form may crop up somewhere that I cannot take into consideration in the vocabulary.

15.3. Exercise

Inflect the following compound verbs both in the independent and dependent form.

> *ad·suidi*, ·*astai* /aδ·suδ'i ·asti/ (W2b) 'to stop, to prevent'
> *con·tibi*, ·*cuitbi* /kon·t'iβ'i ·kud'β'i/ (W2a) 'to laugh at'
> *fo·gella*, ·*foiglea* /fo·g'ela ·foγ'l'a/ (W1) 'to appeal to'
> *con·scara*, ·*coscra* /kov·skaρa ·koskρa/ (W1) 'to destroy'

15.4. Adverbial compounds

In addition to normal composition as discussed in the previous section, it is also possible in Old Irish to use certain adjectives as first members of compounds. The adjectives then have adverbial meaning in such compounds. Usually, though not exclusively, these adjectives stand in pretonic position. Frequently used adjectives are: *caín* 'fine,' *ceta*, *cita* 'first' < *cét-*, *mad* 'well' < *maith*, *mí* 'bad', *mos* 'soon' < *mó*, e.g., *caín·scríbaimm* 'I write well,' *ceta·creti* '(s)he believed first' (preterite of W2a *creitid* 'to believe'), *mad·génair* '(s)he was well born' (preterite of S2 *gainithir* 'to be born'), *mí·airlither* '(s)he gives bad advice' (W2a *airlithir* 'to give advice'), *mos·tairchella* '(s)he takes in soon' (W1 *do·airchella* 'to take in, to absorb').

Lesson 16

16.1. Varia

1. The preposition a^H 'out of' takes the prepositional. When combined with a possessive pronoun this preposition becomes *as-*, e.g., *asmo^L* 'out of my,' *asa* 'out of his, her, its, their,' etc.

The preposition *íar^N* 'after' takes the prepositional. In combination with the possessive pronouns *a* and *ar^N* it becomes *íarn-*: *íarna* 'after his, her, its, their,' *íarnar^N* 'after our.'

The preposition *oc* 'at, by' takes the prepositional.

The preposition *ós* 'over, overhead' takes the prepositional.

2. The masculine i̯o-stem *duine* /duv'e/ 'man, human being' forms its plural from a different stem with i-inflection: nom., acc., voc. *doíni* /doi̯v'i/, gen. *doíne*, prep. *doínib*.

3. *Ulaid* (o, m) are the 'inhabitants of Ulster, the men of Ulster;' at the same time they signify the province Ulster herself. Thus *maccrad Ulad* can be translated 'boygroup of the men of Ulster' and 'boygroup of Ulster.'

4. In the construction *possessive pronoun + óenur* /oi̯vuρ/ (prep. sg. of *óenar*) '... alone' we have one of the few cases in Old Irish prose where a prepositional can be used without preposition: *m'óenur* 'I alone,' *t'óenur* 'thou alone,' *a óenur* '(s)he alone,' etc.

5. Some of the adjectives used show exceptional behavior:

uile /uλ'e/ 'all, whole' may stand before or after the noun it qualifies: *int uile domun* or *in domun uile* 'the whole world.'

The unstressed pronominal *cach, cech* /kaχ, keχ/ 'each' stands before the word it qualifies. Its *anlaut* is never lenited! In the singular they are uninflected, except for the feminine gen. sg. *cacha, cecha*. In the plural, usually (but not necessarily) the ending *-a* appears.

The neuter of *aile* /aλ'e/ 'other, second' is *aill* /al'/ in the nominative and accusative singular. In the phrase *aill... aill...* 'the one... the other..., the ones... the others...' it is also used for masculine and feminine words.

16.2. Exercise

Old Irish

1. Ol Cú Chulainn oac: 'Do·scaraimm inna maccu di maccraid Ulad m'óenur.' 2. Do·sluindi ícc don duiniu athgoítiu. 3. For·cenna gáire mór degscél in techtairi. 4. Innád·tascram cuire llóech trén conar clélámaib? 5. Ní·díltaid bríathra int šoiscélai. 6. In·foircnet in techtairi dáil inna céile co claidbib? 7. Innád·n-áirmiu céiliu mo muintire? 8. In·n-aidli daltu do cheníuil? 9. Ní·astai omun Dé in ngataige ndánae oc gait isin chill. 10. Ad·rímem laithe déidencha aui Chonairi. 11. Ad·ellaid muintir for céili i carput dá roth. 12. Ad·suidet ind notairi dánai inna gataigiu lobru isind luing. 13. In·fursannai in grían inna éunu isnaib crannaib 7 inna íascu isind uisciu? 14. In·díltaid creitim i n-eisséirgiu inna corp asa lligib 7 i nduiniu bíu íarna bás? 15. For·osnai in

grían gel uide in beich buidi a bláth find i mbláth nderg. 16. Á duini nemḟulachtai, ad·suidi mo dá chéile amrai oc cluichiu ḟidchille. 17. Innád·fodlai int echaire arán 7 uisce forsna daltu? 18. Do·fortai Día uisce inna n-uile nnél for domun llethan inna ndoíne n-olc. 19. * Imm·ráidimm popul cáen ind rígi díadai ós nélaib, aill ós laithib lígdaib, aill fo déraib díanaib. (*Fél. Prol.* 21–24) 20. * Máel Rúain, grían mór Midi, íccaid a lige cneit cech cridi. (*Fél. Prol.* 225–228)

Transcription

1. oλ kū χuλən' oȝg: 'do·skapəm' ina maku d'i μakpəð' uλəð moᶖvuꝗ.' 2. do·slun'd'i īk' don duv'u aθγoᶖd'u. 3. foꝗ·k'ena gāp'e mōꝗ d'eγs'k'ēλ in t'eχtəp'i. 4. inād·daskꝗəμ kuꝗ'e loᶖχ d'r'ēv kovəꝗ g'l'ēλāμəβ'? 5. n'ɪ·d'īltəð' b'r'iaθpa int hos'k'ēλi. 6. iv·βoꝗ'k'n'əd in t'eχtəp'i dāλ' ina g'ēλ'e ko glaðβ'əβ'? 7. ināð·vāꝗ'μ'u k'ēλ'u mo μun't'əp'e? 8. in·nað'l'i daltu do χ'ev'īᶙλ'? 9. n'ɪ·asti oᶙuv d'ē in ŋgadəγ'e ndāve og gad' is'ən χ'il'. 10. að·r'īμəμ laθ'e ð'ēð'əvχa haᶙi χovəp'i. 11. að·eləð' mun't'əp' foꝗ g'ēλ'i i garbud dā ꝗoθ. 12. að·suð'əd ind vodəꝗ'i ðāvi ina gadəγ'u loβꝗu is'ənd λuŋ'g'. 13. iv·βuꝗsəni in γ'ꝗ'iav ina h'ēᶙvu isnəβ' kranəβ' ogus ina h'iasku is'ənd us'k'u? 14. in·d'īltəð' k'r'ed'əμ' i v'es'ēꝗ'γ'u ina gorp asa l'iγəβ' ogus i nduv'u β'īᶙ iarna βās? 15. foꝗ·osni in γ'ꝗ'iav γ'eλ uð'e in β'eχ' βuð'i a blāθ ind i mblāθ n'd'erg. 16. ā ðuv'i v'eμuλəχti, að·suð'i mo dā χ'ēλ'e aμꝗi og kluχ'u iðχ'il'e. 17. ināð·βoðλi int eχəꝗ'e aꝗāv ogus us'k'e forsna daltu? 18. do·forti d'ia us'k'e ina vuλ'e n'ēλ foꝗ doᶙuv ina ndoᶖv'e volk. 19. im'·rāð'əm' pobuλ gaᶖv ind ꝗ'ɪγ'i ðiaði ōs n'ēλəβ', al' ōs laθ'əβ' l'īγðəβ', al' fo ð'ēꝗəβ' d'iavəβ'. 20. maᶖλ ꝗuav', g'r'iav μōꝗ μ'ið'i, īkəð' a λ'iγ'e k'n'ed' g'eχ k'r'ið'i.

Illustration 16.1: *do·fortai Día uisce inna nél for domun* 'God pours the water of the clouds upon the world'

English

1. I do not overthrow the boys of the boygroup of the Ulaid alone. 2. Dost thou refuse healing to the severely wounded people? 3. Does not great laughter end the good stories of the messengers? 4. We overthrow the troop of strong warriors with our left hands. 5. You reject the word of the Gospel. 6. The messengers end the meeting of the clients with swords. 7. I recount the clients of thy family. 8. Thou visitest the foster-son of my race. 9. Fear of God prevents the bold thieves from stealing in churches. 10. Do we recount the last day of Conaire's grandson? 11. You do not visit the family of our clients in chariots. 12. Do the bold scribes not stop the weak thief in the ship? 13. The sun lights up the bird in the tree and the fish in the water. 14. Thou rejectest the belief in the resurrection of thy body out of its grave and in the living man after thy (*íar do*) death. 15. Does not the bright sun light up the path of the yellow bees from a red blossom to a white blossom? 16. The unbearable person does not prevent my wonderful companion from playing *fidchell.* 17. The foster-son distributes bread and water among the horse-keepers. 18. Does God pour the water of all the clouds upon the wide world of the bad people? 19. We think of the fine peoples of the divine kingdom over the clouds. 20. Does not his grave heal the sigh of every heart?

Lesson 17

17.1. Nouns: feminine i̯ā-stems

Just as i̯o-stems are historically related to o-stems, so i̯ā-stems are related to ā-stems. Like the ā-stems they are exclusively feminine. The mutational effects are identical to those of the ā-declension. Again, as with i̯o-stems, we have something that could be called endings, i.e., *e* and *i* that alternate in a particular, but different way from the pattern we learned with the i̯o-stems. i̯ā-stems can have palatalized or non-palatalized stem consonants. No raising or lowering effects take place in the root vowel of the word. The two examples below are *guide* /guδ'e/ 'prayer' for words with palatalized root final consonants and *ungae* /uŋge/ 'ounce' for words with non-palatalized root final consonants:

case	ending	pal. root final cons.	non-pal. root final cons.	Prim. Irish	Proto-Celtic
nom. sg.	C⁽ʾ⁾eᴸ	*guide*ᴸ	*ungae*ᴸ	*°ii̯ā	*°(i)i̯ā
gen.	C⁽ʾ⁾eᴴ	*guide*ᴴ	*ungae*ᴴ	*°ii̯āh	*°(i)i̯ās
prep.	C⁽ʾ⁾iᴸ	*guidi*ᴸ	*ungai*ᴸ	*°ii̯ī	*°(i)i̯ai̯
acc.	C⁽ʾ⁾iᴺ	*guidi*ᴺ	*ungai*ᴺ	*°ii̯ev	*°(i)i̯am
voc.	C⁽ʾ⁾eᴸ	*á*ᴸ *guide*ᴸ	*á*ᴸ *ungae*ᴸ	*°ii̯a	*°(i)i̯a
nom. pl.	C⁽ʾ⁾iᴴ	*guidi*ᴴ	*ungai*ᴴ	*°īh «	*°(i)i̯ās
gen.	C⁽ʾ⁾eᴺ	*guide*ᴺ	*ungae*ᴺ	*°ii̯av	*°(i)i̯om
prep.	C⁽ʾ⁾əβʾ	*guidib*	*ungaib*	*°ii̯āβih	*°(i)i̯ābis
acc.	C⁽ʾ⁾iᴴ	*guidi*ᴴ	*ungai*ᴴ	*°īh «	*°(i)i̯ās
voc.	C⁽ʾ⁾iᴴ	*á*ᴸ *guidi*ᴴ	*á*ᴸ *ungai*ᴴ	*°īh «	*°(i)i̯ās
n.-a. du.	C⁽ʾ⁾iᴸ	*dí*ᴸ *guidi*ᴸ	*dí*ᴸ *ungai*ᴸ	*°ii̯ī	*°(i)i̯ai̯
gen.	C⁽ʾ⁾eᴸ	*dá*ᴸ *guide*ᴸ	*dá*ᴸ *ungae*ᴸ	*°ii̯ō	*°(i)i̯ou̯
prep.	C⁽ʾ⁾əβʾᴺ	*dib*ᴺ *nguidib*	*dib*ᴺ *n-ungaib*	*°ii̯āβiv	*°(i)i̯ābim

Illustration 17.1: The i̯ā-stem declension

Note:

1. The immediate preforms of the nominative, vocative and accusative plural must have been taken over from the ī-stems (see 17.3 below) with which the i̯ā-stems are identical to a great extent.

2. The i̯ā-stems frequently form abstract nouns from adjectives, e.g., o-, ā-adjective *slán* 'whole, sound, complete' → i̯ā-stem abstract *sláine* 'soundness, completeness,' or i-stem adjective *énairt* 'weak' → i̯ā-stem abstract *énairte* 'weakness.'

17.2. Adjectives: i̯ā-stems

The i̯ā-stem adjectives are the feminine counterparts to masculine and neuter i̯o-stem adjectives. They inflect exactly like i̯ā-stem nouns. If we again take the two examples from 14.3, *buide* /buδ'e/ 'yellow' for words with palatalized stem final consonant (/δ'/) and *rígdae* /r'ɪ́γδe/ 'royal, kingly' for words with non-palatalized stem final consonant (/γδ/), we get the following inflection:

case	ending	palatalized	non-palatalized
nom. sg.	C⁽'⁾e^L	buide^L	rígdae^L
gen.	C⁽'⁾e^H	buide^H	rígdae^H
prep.	C⁽'⁾i^L	buidi^L	rígdai^L
acc.	C⁽'⁾i^N	buidi^N	rígdai^N
voc.	C⁽'⁾e^L	á^L buide^L	á^L rígdae^L
nom. pl.	C⁽'⁾i^H	buidi^H	rígdai^H
gen.	C⁽'⁾e^N	buide^N	rígdae^N
prep.	C⁽'⁾əβ'	buidib	rígdaib
acc.	C⁽'⁾i^H	buidi^H	rígdai^H
voc.	C⁽'⁾i^H	á^L buidi^H	á^L rígdai^H

Illustration 17.2: i̯ā-stem adjectives

17.3. Nouns: feminine ī-stems

The ī-stems are exclusively feminine. They have a very close connection to the i̯ā-stems. To a large extent the two declensions have identical endings, and it is obvious that in the prehistory and history of the Irish language the two declensions influenced each other. In most cases an extra syllable is added to the root final syllable as 'ending.' Where no such ending is added, the root final consonant is palatalized. Where an extra syllable is added, the root final consonant can either be palatalized or non-palatalized, depending whether a back or front vowel was syncopated before the ending. No raising or lowering effects take place in the root vowel of the word. Unlike the declensions we learned so far, there are no adjectives that inflect as ī-stems.

Two subtypes of the ī-declension can be distinguished: one with 'long' endings and one with 'short' endings. It seems that the 'long' variant must continue the original, inherited inflectional pattern, since many old, frequently used words belong to this variant. The 'short' variant, on the other hand, consists of a number of young loan-words from Latin and of words that may originally have inflected as ā-stems, especially verbal nouns in which the prepositional case has replaced the nominative, e.g., *buith* 'being,' prep./acc. also *buith*, very rarely ā-stem nom. sg. *both*. So the 'short' inflection may in fact be due to influence from the ā- and possibly also the i-declension.

We will look at the 'long' variant first. A number of important words belong to this inflection: *adaig*, gen. sg. *aidche* /aðəɣ' aδ'χ'e/ 'night,' *blíadain*, gen. sg. *blíadnae* /b'l'iaδəv' b'l'iaδve/ 'year,' *Brigit*, gen. sg. *Brigte* /b'r'iɣ'əd' b'r'iɣ'd'e / 'Brigit,' *inis*, gen. sg. *inse* /iv'əs' iv's'e/ 'island,' *séitig*, gen. sg. *séitche* /s'ēd'əɣ' s'ēd'χ'e/ 'wife.' I will use *rígain* /r'īɣəv'/ 'queen' (root final consonant /v/) as the example:

case	ending	Old Irish	Prim. Irish	Proto-Celtic	PIE
nom. voc. sg.	C'ᴸ	*rígain*ᴸ	*rīɣavī	*rīganī	*h₃réĝnih₂
gen.	C(')eᴴ	*rígnae*ᴴ	*rīɣaviiāh	*rīganiās	*h₃réĝnieh₂s
prep.	C'ᴸ, C(')iᴸ	*rígain*ᴸ, *rígnai*ᴸ («)	*rīɣavī	*rīganiai («)	*h₃réĝnieh₂ei, -ieh₂i
acc.	C(')iᴺ	*rígnai*ᴺ	*rīɣaviiev «	*rīganim	*h₃réĝnih₂m
nom. voc. pl.	C(')iᴴ	*rígnai*ᴴ	*rīɣavīh «	*rīganiias	*h₃réĝnih₂es
gen.	C(')eᴺ	*rígnae*ᴺ	*rīɣaviiav	*rīganiom («)	*h₃réĝnieh₂om
prep.	C(')əβ'	*rígnaib*	*rīɣaviiāβih	*rīganiābis («)	*h₃réĝnieh₂bʰis, -ieh₂bʰos
acc.	C(')iᴴ	*rígnai*ᴴ	*rīɣavīh	*rīganīs	*h₃réĝnih₂ns
n.,a.,v. du.	C'ᴸ	*dí*ᴸ *rígain*ᴸ	*rīɣavī	*rīganī	*h₃réĝnih₂ih₁
gen.	C(')eᴸ	*dá*ᴸ *rígnae*ᴸ	*rīɣaviiō	*rīganiou «	*h₃réĝnieh₂h₁oh₁s, -Hoh₁u
prep.	C(')əβ'	*díb*ᴺ *rrígnaib* «	*rīɣaviiāβiv	*rīganiābim «	*h₃réĝnieh₂bʰih₁, -moh₁ ?

Illustration 17.3: The ī-stem declension (long variant)

Illustration 17.4:
guide do Brigti
'a prayer to Brigit'

The 'short' variant is identical in dual and plural with the 'long' variant, but in the prepositional and accusative singular the short variant shows no ending (the form looks just like the nominative singular), whereas the long variant has the ending -*i* there. Since the 'short' declensional pattern probably developed under the influence of the ā- and i-declensions, and thus is secondary to the 'long' variant, I will not give any reconstructed forms. I use *aithis*; gen. sg. *aithise* /aθ'əs' aθ'əs'e/ 'insult, disgrace' (stem consonant /s'/) as an example:

case	ending	Old Irish
nom. voc. sg.	C'L	aithisL
gen.	C(')eH	aithiseH
prep.	C'L	aithisL
acc.	C'N	aithisN
nom. voc. pl.	C(')iH	aithisiH
gen.	C(')eN	aithiseN
prep.	C(')əβ'	aithisib
acc.	C(')iH	aithisiH
n., a., v. du.	C'L	díL aithisL
gen.	C(')eL	dáL aithiseL
prep.	C(')əβ'	díbN n-aithisib

Illustration 17.5: The ī-stem declension (short variant)

Note:

1. The Old Irish ī-stem declension basically continues the so-called PIE *devī*-inflection.

2. The reconstruction of the nominative plural is difficult. We would expect an ending CC *-iįas < PIE *-ih₂es, which is not attested. The Proto-British ending *-iįās (e.g., in Cymric *rhianedd* 'girls' < Proto-British *rīganiįās*) must have been taken over from the ịā-stems. This is not possible for Irish. Several other strategies of explanation are viable for Irish: either the ending was taken over from the i-stems (*-iįas » *-eįes > *-iįes > *-īs), or the isolated nominative plural ending *-as was replaced by the regular nominative plural ending of the consonantal stems *-es (*-iįas » *-iįes > *-īs), or the old nominative plural ending was replaced by the accusative plural ending in analogy to the ā-stems, where nominative and accusative plural were identical (*-iįas » *-īs).

17.4. Exercise

Inflect some of the following words. Decline them together with the article. Combine them with any of the adjectives you learned so far.

in chomairle /koµəρ'λ'e/ (ịā, f) 'advice, counsel'
int śoilse /sol's'e/ (ịā, f) 'light'
ind labrae /laβρe/ (ịā, f) 'speech'
ind inis /iv'əs'/ (long ī, f) 'island'
Brigit /b'r'iγ'əd'/ (long ī, f) 'Brigit' (only singular)
in blíadain /b'l'iaδəv'/ (long ī, f) 'year'
in méit /m'ēd'/ (short ī, f) 'greatness, size, amount' (only singular)
ind luib /luβ'/ (short ī, f) 'herb, plant'
ind epistil /eb'əs't'əλ'/ (short ī, f) 'letter' (gen. sg. epistle)

Lesson 18

18.1. The conjugated prepositions: general remarks

In 8.3, I mentioned that Old Irish basically has no personal pronouns. How then are phrases like German *mit mir, über dich, an ihn* or English *through us, by you, under them* expressed, for which in most languages prepositions are used, followed by personal pronouns? The strategy used in Old Irish is that the preposition in question is 'conjugated,' comparable to the way verbs are inflected. The term 'conjugation' is in fact not absolutely appropriate, as the 'endings' of the conjugated prepositions have nothing in common with the inflectional endings of the verbs. On the other hand, the expression 'conjugated preposition' is widely used in Irish studies, so I will stick to it in this book.

Illustration 18.1:
form 'upon me'

Historically speaking these 'endings' are nothing but the personal pronouns of Proto-Celtic, which formed an accentual unit with the preceding preposition and consequently came into such close contact that the two eventually merged and came to be regarded as a single entity. It is not possible to separate one element from the other. So, for example, *dó* 'to him, for him' (< *do^L* + 3rd sg. masc.) cannot be analyzed and split into two elements, one of which means 'to,' one of which means 'him.' The whole word simply means 'to him.'

In the following lessons I will present you one by one all conjugated prepositions of Old Irish. I will basically follow GOI and OIPG by only presenting those forms that are actually attested in Irish texts. Often there are numerous variant spelings beside the ones I will give in the tables. I will stick to the frequently used ones, but you can find more detailed accounts in GOI and in DIL under the individual prepositions.

Whereas simple prepositions are by nature unstressed in Old Irish, the conjugated forms are fully stressed words. Although this divergent behavior has no import at the moment, it is of consequence for Old Irish metrics.

As you will have noticed in the lessons so far, some of the Old Irish prepositions take the prepositional, some the accusative, and some (*i^N, for, ar^L, fo^L*) can take both, depending on the meaning. In the 1st and 2nd persons of the conjugated prepositions the endings are the same for both cases. In the 3rd persons, however, the endings differ according to the case. This is especially important for the four prepositions that can take both the prepositional and the accusative: e.g., *indib* means 'in them,' but *intiu* means 'into them,' or *fuiri* means 'on her,' *forrae* means 'onto her.' Now and then confusion between the two cases occurs.

Although all conjugated prepositions behave pretty much the same, it is not possible to give one well-defined set of endings that is valid for all prepositions and persons. Instead they all differ slightly from one another and in the end they all have to be learned by heart separately. A basic pattern can be set up, though:

person	ending	transcr.	explanation
1st sg.	*-(u)m,* *-(u)mm*	/(u)μ/ /(u)m/	In the 1st sg. conjugated prepositions end in *-m* (sometimes lenited /μ/ when the preposition lenites, but usually unlenited /m/); often there is u-infection before the *-m*.
2nd sg.	*-(u)t*	/t/ /(u)d/	In the 2nd sg. the ending is *-t* /t d/. Often there is u-infection before the *-t*.
3rd sg. m., n.			No rules can be given for the 3rd sg. masc. and neuter. The forms have to be learned individually.
3rd sg. f.	*-e, -i*	/e/ /i/	In the 3rd sg. f. usually *-e* /e/ with prepositions taking the acc., or *-i* /i/ with prepositions taking the prep., are added to the preposition. Where possible the consonant before the *-e* or *-i* is devoiced.
1st pl.	*-(u)nn,* *-(u)n*	/(u)n/	In the 1st plural the ending is *-n(n)* /n/. Often there is u-infection before the *-n(n)*.
2nd pl.	*-ib*	/β'/	In the 2nd plural the ending is *-ib* /β'/.
3rd pl.	*-u, -ib*	/u/ /əβ'/	In the 3rd plural the ending is *-u* /u/ with prepositions that take the accusative, or *-ib* /əβ'/ (with prepositions that take the prepositional). Where possible the consonant before the *-u* is devoiced.

Illustration 18.2: The endings of the conjugated prepositions

Note:

1. Where both disyllabic and monosyllabic pronunciations are given in the transcription, the disyllabic (= hiatus) variant is the older one, the monosyllabic the younger one.

2. The only preposition that certainly has the lenited ending *-m* /μ/ in the 1st sg. form is *do^L* 'to, for.' One would expect that other leniting prepositions would have had lenited /μ/ originally, too, but the attested forms like *dím* from *de^L* 'from, of' and *trium* from *tre^L* 'through' are too scanty and too ambiguous to allow for a decision. In the later language these forms all clearly have an unlenited *-m* /m/, and I hesitatingly adopted this pronunciation also for the Old Irish period in my tables. The rhymes *dím* : *ríg* /r'īγ/ (EIL 25.1), *úaimm* : *búain* /buav'/ (EIL 17.1), *úaim* : *úair* /uaρ'/ (EIL 46.49), *úaim* : *·lúaid* /·luaδ'/ (*Gosp.* 29) do not prove a lenited quality for *-m*, since after long vowels unlenited liquids may rhyme with lenited voiced consonants.

3. Ideally the *-t* of the 2nd sg. ought to be voiceless /t/ in monosyllabic forms like *frit, lat*, and voiced /d/ in disyllabic forms like *indut, airiut*, etc. I have followed this principle in the phonological transcriptions of the forms, but this probably draws too idealized a picture and a certain amount of variation will actually have existed in the spoken language. In the *Poems of Blath-*

macc lat may rhyme either with *macc*, thus attesting to the expected pronunciation /lat/, or with *fris·accat* (vers 923), which can only mean a pronunciation /lad/.

4. In the 3rd pl. and the 3rd sg. fem. sometimes forms with -*th*- before the ending may be encountered, e.g., *lethu* 'with them' (*Thes.* ii 241.4), *frithiu* 'towards them' (*Gosp.* 17) in old sources, or *fóthu* (LL 8416), *foíthib* (LU 6166) 'under them,' *foithi* 'under her' (*Trip.* 8.10) in younger sources.

18.2. The conjugated prepositions 1

1. Conjugated prepositions with the prepositional:

person	*do*^L 'to, for'	
	ending	transcription
1st sg.	*dom, dam*	/doµ daµ/
2nd sg.	*duit, dait*	/dut' dat'/
3rd sg. m., n.	*dó (dáu)*	/dō/
3rd sg. f.	*dí*	/d'ī/
1st pl.	*dún(n)*	/dūn/
2nd pl.	*dúib*	/dūβ'/
3rd pl.	*do(a)ib, duaib, dóib*	/doəβ' duəβ' dōβ'/

Illustration 18.3: The conjugated prepositions 1: *do*^L

person	*de*^L, *di*^L 'from, of'		*ó*^L, *úa*^L 'from, by'	
	ending	transcription	ending	transcription
1st sg.	*dím*	/d'īm d'īµ (?)/	*úaim(m)*	/uam'/
2nd sg.	*dít*	/d'īt'/	*úait*	/uat'/
3rd sg. m., n.	*de*	/d'e/	*úad*	/uaδ/
3rd sg. f.	*di*	/d'i/	*úadi*	/uaδ'i/
1st pl.	*dín(n)*	/d'īn/	*úain(n)*	/uan'/
2nd pl.	*diib, díb*	/d'iəβ' d'īβ'/	*úaib*	/uaβ'/
3rd pl.	*diib, díib, díb*	/d'iəβ' d'īβ'/	*úadaib, úaidib*	/uaδəβ' uaδ'əβ'/

Illustration 18.4: The conjugated prepositions 1: *di*^L, *ó*^L

Note:

1. *dáu* 'for himself' in *Thes.* ii 294.3 is a hypercorrect spelling for /dō/ that gives evidence that the OIr. diphthong *áu* had already become monophthongized to /ō/ at the time the poem was written.

2. Conjugated prepositions with the accusative:

person	*la*[H] 'with'	
	ending	transcription
1st sg.	*lem(m), lim(m), lium(m)*	/l'em l'im l'iṳm/
2nd sg.	*lat(t)*	/lat/
3rd sg. m., n.	*leis(s), les(s), lais(s)*	/l'es' las'/
3rd sg. f.	*lee*	/l'ehe l'eë/
1st pl.	*linn, leinn, lenn*	/l'in l'en' l'en/
2nd pl.	*lib*	/l'iβ'/
3rd pl.	*leu, léu, leo*	/l'ehu l'eho l'eṳ/

Illustration 18.5: The conjugated prepositions 1: *la*[H]

person	*fri*[H] 'towards, against'		*tre*[L], *tri*[L] 'through'	
	ending	transcription	ending	transcription
1st sg.	*friumm, frim*	/fr'iṳm fr'im/	*trium*	/t'r'iṳm/
2nd sg.	*frit(t), friut(t)*	/fr'it fr'iṳt/	*triut*	/t'r'iṳt/
3rd sg. m., n.	*fris*	/fr'is'/	*triit*	/t'r'iəd'/
3rd sg. f.	*frie*	/fr'ih'e fr'ië/	*tree*	/t'r'ehe t'r'eë/
1st pl.	*frinn*	/fr'in/	*triun, trin*	/t'r'iṳn t'r'in/
2nd pl.	*frib*	/fr'iβ'/	*triib*	/t'r'iəβ'/
3rd pl.	*friu*	/fr'ihu fr'iṳ/	*treu, treo, tréu*	/t'r'ehu t'r'eho t'r'eṳ/

Illustration 18.6: The conjugated prepositions 1: *fri*[H], *tre*[L]

18.3. Verbs of the S1-class

So far we were looking at 'weak' verbal classes only. Now we turn to 'strong' classes. In MCCONE's classification S stands for 'strong verbs.' Strong verbs are characterized by the fact that in the present tense in the 3rd singular conjunct they end in a consonant.

S1 is the first strong class. S1 verbs are characterized by an alternation of palatalization/non-palatalization of the root final consonant throughout the paradigm. That means that in certain persons the root final consonant is palatalized, in certain other persons it is non-palatalized. In the main type of S1 verbs the root final consonant is non-palatalized before the ending of the 1st singular and the 1st and 3rd plural persons, but palatalized before the 2nd and 3rd singular and 2nd plural endings. In the 3rd sg. conjunct S1 verbs end in the plain palatalized root consonant. Be careful; apart from these alternations in palatalization in some cases raising and lowering effects also have to be taken into account in this class. The example below is the present indicative of the very important verb *beirid* /b'ep'əδ'/ 'to carry,' root *ber-* /b'ep/ (root final consonant /p/):

S1	absolute (independent)		conjunct (dependent)	
1st sg.	*biru*	{R}Cu	*(ní)·biur*	{R}(u)C
2nd sg.	*biri*	{R}C'i	*(ní)·bir*	{R}C'
3rd sg.	*beirid*	C'əδ'	*(ní)·beir*	C'
1st pl.	*bermai*	{L}Cmi	*(ní)·beram*	{L}Cəµ
2nd pl.	*beirthe*	C'θ'e	*(ní)·beirid*	C'əδ'
3rd pl.	*berait*	{L}Cəd'	*(ní)·berat*	{L}Cəd

Illustration 18.7: The conjugation of S1 verbs

Note:

1. In MCCONE's classification S1 has many subclasses, all of which are basically characterized by an alternation of palatalization/non-palatalization in the root final consonant:

1.1. S1a is the basic type as outlined above. A few verbs have a root vowel *e* that changes to *a* in front of palatalized *g* or *d*: 3rd sg. *laigid*, ·*laig* /laγ'əδ', ·laγ'/, but 3rd pl. *legait*, ·*legat* /l'eγəd', ·l'eγəd/ 'to lie,' 3rd sg. *saigid*, ·*saig*, but 3rd pl. *segait*, ·*segat* 'to seek, to approach,' and in analogy to that pattern 3rd sg. *saidid*, ·*said*, but 3rd pl. *sedait*, ·*sedat* 'to sit.'

1.2. Verbs with an underlying short *e* as their root vowel and lenited *th* /θ/ and *d* /δ/ as their root final consonants behave like the basic S1a type when the root is stressed, e.g., *reithid*, ·*reith* 'to run.' When the root is unstressed, however, the vowel is reduced in the usual manner, but the final dental becomes a non-palatalized, unlenited *t* /d/, e.g., the compound of *reth-* *fo·timmdiriut* /fo·t'im'δ'əp'ud/ 'I fumigate' (*fo-to-imm-di-reth-*). In some verbs, the non-palatalized, unlenited *t* appears also in the stressed 3rd sg. conjunct, e.g., *ad·fét* /aδ·f'ēd/, but 3rd pl. *ad·fíadat* /aδ·f'iaδəd/ 'to tell, to relate' (root *fēd-* /f'ēδ-/). This type is S1b.

1.3. S1c verbs permanently have *a* or *o* as their root vowel. Their root final consonant is palatalized only in the 2nd and 3rd sg. conjunct, otherwise it is always non-palatalized, e.g., *canaid*, ·*cain* /kavəδ', ·kav'/ 'to sing' or *orgaid*, ·*oirg* /orgəδ', ·or'g'/ 'to slay.'

1.4. A number of verbs have a nasal (*n* or *m*) before their root final consonant, which disappears outside of the present stem. This will be of importance in advanced lessons. This is class S1d; examples are *dingid*, ·*ding* 'to press' or *tongaid*, ·*toing* 'to swear.' Some verbs have *a* or *o* as their root vowel and behave like type S1c in regard to the palatalization of their root final consonant. Otherwise, verbs of this class behave exactly like the basic type.

2. Even in the earliest attestations certain restructurings of the standard conjugation have already taken place: the 1st sg. may also end in -*imm* /əm'/.

3. The S1 class is made up of old e/o-thematic verbs: PIE *bʰereti,*bʰeronti* > CC *bereti, *beronti* > OIr. *beirid, berait*. Where S1a verbs have non-palatalized stem consonants, the thematic vowel was historically *o*; where they have palatalized stem consonants, the thematic vowel was *e*.

18.4. Compound S1 verbs

Compound verbs in this stem class behave exactly analogously to the stem classes we already learned. Let's look, for example, at the important verb *do·beir* /do·b'eρ'/ 'to give, to bring,' prototonic *·tabair* /·taβəρ'/. This is a compound of the preverb *to-* and the verbal root *ber-*:

S1	deuterotonic (independent)		prototonic (dependent)	
1st sg.	*do·biur*	{R}(u)C	*(ní)·tabur*	(u)C
2nd sg.	*do·bir*	{R}C'	*(ní)·tabair*	C'
3rd sg.	*do·beir*	C'	*(ní)·tabair*	C'
1st pl.	*do·beram*	{L}Cəμ	*(ní)·taibrem*	†C(')əμ
2nd pl.	*do·beirid*	C'əð'	*(ní)·taibrid*	†C(')əð'
3rd pl.	*do·berat*	{L}Cəd	*(ní)·taibret*	†C(')əd

Illustration 18.8: The conjugation of compounded S1 verbs

Note:

1. In most cases raising and lowering effects do not apply in unaccented syllables; therefore they can be disregarded for the verbal root in prototonic forms (but note that of course other effects of that sort can again apply to the preverbs when they come under the stress!).

2. Do not forget the effects of syncope! Be aware that in the plural forms of prototonic S1 verbs, due to the effects of syncope, the root final consonant may be secondarily palatalized, like e.g., in 3rd pl. *·taibret* above.

3. Even in the earliest attestations certain restructurings have taken place: in order to disambiguate it from the 3rd sg., in some verbs the 1st sg. may also end in *-u* /u/ and *-(a)imm* /əm'/, the 2nd sg. may end in *-i* /i/, e.g., *ro·iccu, ro·iccimm* 'I reach,' *do·icci, ·ticci* 'thou reachest.'

18.5. Exercise

Now try to conjugate some of the following verbs in absolute and conjunct inflection, or in deuterotonic and prototonic form respectively:

ceilid /k'eλ'əð'/ (S1) 'to hide'
feidid /f'eð'əð'/ (S1) 'to lead'
aigid /aγ'əð'/ (S1) 'to drive'
as·beir, ·eipir /as·b'eρ', ·eb'əρ'/ (S1) 'to say, to speak'
do·icc, ·ticc /do·ig', ·t'ig'/ (S1) 'to come'
for·beir, ·forbair /for·b'eρ', ·forbəρ'/ (S1) 'to increase, to grow'

Note:

1. Lowering has to be applied in *do·icc* in the appropriate persons.

Lesson 19

19.1. From a poem

This is an excerpt from a famous poem called 'St. Patrick's *lorica*' or *breastplate*, in which the poet enumerates the powers with which he girds himself against the adversities of life. I have left out all those lines that contain words in stem-classes we haven't learned so far (source: GT 28–29).

The poet tells that he girds himself today with God's strength to be guided:

cumachtae nDé dom chumgabáil [...]   kuμəχte n'd'ē dom χuμγaβāλ'
clúas Dé dom étsecht   kluas δ'ē dom ēt's'əχt
bríathar Dé dom aurlabrai   b'r'iaθəp δ'ē dom auρλəβρi
lám Dé dom imdegail   lāμ δ'ē dom im'δ'əγəλ'
intech Dé dom remthechtas [...]   in't'eχ d'ē dom ρ'eμ'θ'əχtəs
sochraite Dé dom anaccul   soχρəd'e δ'ē dom avəkuλ
ar intledaib demnae   aρ in't'l'ədəβ' d'eμve
ar aslaigib dúalchae   aρ asləγ'əβ' duaλχe
ar airrechtaib aicnid   aρ ar'əχtəβ' ak'n'əδ'
ar cach nduine [...]   aρ kaχ nduv'e
i n-úathad ocus i sochaidi.   i vuaθəδ ogus i soχəδ'i.

Illustration 19.1:
atom·riug indíu
'I gird myself today'

19.2. Varia

1. There are no separate reflexive pronouns in Old Irish. Reflexive pronouns are pronouns like German *sich* or like English forms ending in -*self*, which refer to the subject of the clause. Instead, any pronominal construction of Old Irish (e.g., conjugated prepositions, infixed pronouns etc.) can refer to the person or thing forming the subject of the clause. Of course this means that sometimes such constructions can be ambiguous: e.g., *as·beir bréithir fris* may mean 'he says a word to him = someone else' (non-reflexive) or 'he says a words to himself = he speaks with himself' (reflexive). One has to judge from the context which is meant in a given instance.

2. The neuter i̯o-stem *lá* 'day' has an older disyllabic inflection: singular nom., acc. *lae^N* /laë/, gen. *laí^L* /lai̯/, prep. *láu^L, lau^L, lao^L* /lau̯/, plural nom., acc. *lae^L* /laë/, gen. *lae^N* /laë/, prep. *laib* /laəβ'/; and a younger monosyllabic inflection: singular nom., acc. *lá^N* /lā/, gen. *laí^L* /lai̯/, prep. *ló^L* /lō/, plural nom., acc. *lá^L* /lā/, gen. *lá^N* /lā/, prep. *láib* /lāβ'/. Moreover there is a longer form *laithe* /laθ'e/ (i̯o, n) 'day' as well.

93

3. The very important S1 verb *téit* 'to go' and its compound *do·tét* 'to come' show many peculiarities. Their present stem is *tíag-* (note that the *ía* turns to *éi* before a palatalized consonant), but in the 3rd sg. they use a stem *tét-* /t'ēd-/. You should learn these forms by heart.

S1	absolute (independent)		conjunct (dependent)	
1st sg.	*tíagu*	t'iaɣu	*(ní)·tíag*	·t'iaɣ
2nd sg.	*téigi*	t'ēɣ'i	*(ní)·téig*	·t'ēɣ'
3rd sg.	*téit*	t'ēd'	*(ní)·tét*	·t'ēd
1st pl.	*tíagmai*	t'iaɣmi	*(ní)·tíagam*	·t'iaɣəμ
2nd pl.	*téit*	t' ēd'	*(ní)·téit, ·téigid*	·t'ēd' ·t'ēɣ'əð'
3rd pl.	*tíagait*	t'iaɣəd'	*(ní)·tíagat*	·t'iaɣəd

Illustration 19.2: The inflection of S1 *téit* 'to go'

S1	deuterotonic (independent)		prototonic (dependent)	
1st sg.	*do·tíag*	do·t'iaɣ	*(ní)·taíg, ·táeg*	·ta i̯ɣ
2nd sg.	*do·téig*	do·t'ēɣ'	*(ní)·taíg*	·ta i̯ɣ'
3rd sg.	*do·tét*	do·t'ēd	*(ní)·taít, ·táet*	·ta i̯d
1st pl.	*do·tíagam*	do·t'iaɣəμ	n/a	
2nd pl.	n/a		n/a	
3rd pl.	*do·tíagat*	do·t'iaɣəd	*(ní)·taígat*	·ta i̯ɣəd

Illustration 19.3: The inflection of S1 *do·tét* 'to come'

4. Sentences containing conjugated prepositions or other prepositional phrases can often be construed without verb in Irish, whereas in translation a verb has to be provided in the target language. See for example the following two lines from Old Irish sagas: *'Carpat dam-sa!'* 'lit.: A chariot to me! = Give me a chariot!' (seven-year-old Cú Chulainn to king Conchobor in TBC 648) and *'In fer úait dam-sa […] nó bás fort béolu!'* 'lit.: The man from thee to me or death upon thy lips! = Leave the man and give him to me, or may death befall thee!' (The jealous future queen of the Laigin to her maiden who had been the first to sleep with the king's son Máel Fothartaig, in FG 71–72).

5. *Bran* is the name of the hero of the tale *Echtrae Brain maicc Febail 7 a Immram* 'The Adventure of Bran mac Febail and his Voyage,' which tells of Bran's sea journey to the 'Other World.'

6. *Inis Fáil* 'the Island of Fál' is a poetical name for Ireland, named after the *Lia Fáil* 'the stone of Fál' in Temair (Tara), which shrieked when the future king stepped on it. Though we would regularily expect lenition after *inis*, the name is usually pronounced without lenition. Only *inis* is inflected in this name; *Fáil* is in the genitive and stays so.

19.3. Exercise

Old Irish

1. As·biur bréithir faílte fritt, acht ní·tabair faílti frimm. 2. * Do thabairt díglae biri in claideb latt. (*Wb.* 6a13) 3. For·osnai soilse inna gréine in n-uile ndomun isind lau, acht do·ceil in grían a agaid isind aidchi. 4. Ní·alam maccu ban mbocht, acht almai daltu do rígnaib. 5. In·n-imbrid fidchill lemm, á šéitchi inna cennaige? 6. Lengait éisc asind fairrgi i soilsi ind laí. 7. Ní·fulang dorchae n-aidche nInse Fáil isin gemriud. 8. Téigi lae 7 dí adaig i do churuch cosin n-insi móir n-aird. 9. Ní·astai airde int šnechtai déini inna n-ech ndonn. 10. Innád·tíagam cosa rríched cona méit noíbe íarnar mbás? 11. Do guidi do Brigti do·iccid ifar ndáil cach n-aidchi. 12. In·forcnat int šacairt gaíth forcetal ind Núfíadnaisi dúnn? 13. ** Bendacht úaimm for Eithni n-ollguirm, ingen Domnaill. (GT 202) 14. * Fo·fúasna in gáeth aicher findfolt inna fairrge innocht. (*Thes.* ii 290) 15. * Á Chríst, sénai mo labrai, á maicc amrai Dé. (*Fél. Prol.* 1) 16. * Fo·ceird Día cen dolmai néim n-óir deirg form labrai. (GT 202) 17. * Lingid in chráeb di láim Brain i lláim inna mná. (IB 31) 18. * Téit in ben úaidib íarum 7 beirid in craíb lee cosin n-insi. (IB 31) 19. * Canaid in fer isin char-put rannu dó 7 donaib comaltaib Brain. (IB 32) 20. * In·foídi Bran fer dia muintir i nInsi Subai? (IB 61)

Transcription

1. as·b'iup b'r'ēθ'əp' βai̯l't'e f'r'it, aχt n'ī·taβəp' fai̯l't'i f'r'im. 2. do θaβər't' d'ī̯γλe b'ip'i in glaδ'əβ lat. 3. for·osni sol's'e ina g'r'ēv'e in nuλ'e ndoμuv is'ənd λau̯, aχt do·k'eλ' in γ'ρ'iav a haγəδ' is'ənd aδ'χ'i. 4. n'ī·aλəμ maku bav mboχt, aχt aλmi daltu do ρ'ī̯γvəβ'. 5. in·n'im'b'r'əδ' f'iδχ'əl' l'em, ā h'ēd'χ'i ina g'enəγ'e? 6. l'engəd' ēs'k' as'ənd ar'g'i i sol's'i ind λai̯. 7. n'ī·fuλəŋg dopχe vaδ'χ'e v'iv's'e fāλ' is'ən γ'eμ'ρ'uδ. 8. t'ēγ'i laë ogus δ'ī aδəγ' i do χupuχ kos'ən niv's'i mōp' var'd'. 9. n'ī·asti ar'd'e int h'v'eχti d'ēv'i ina v'eχ ndon. 10. inād·t'iaγəμ kosa r'ī̯χ'əδ kova μ'ēd' voi̯β'e iapμəp mbās? 11. do γuδ'i do β'ρ'iγ'd'i do·ig'əδ' iβap ndāλ' kaχ vaδ'χ'i. 12. iv·βorknəd int hagər't' γai̯θ' fork'ədəλ ind vūiaδvəs'i dūn? 13. b'endəχt uam' fop eθ'v'i volγur'm', iv'γ'ən doμvəl'. 14. fo·fuasva in γai̯θ aχ'əp f'indolt ina far'g'e inóχt. 15. ā χ'ρ'īs't', s'ēvi mo λaβρi, ā μak' aμpi δ'ē. 16. fo·k'er'd' d'ia k'en doλμi n'ēμ' vōp' δ'er'g' form λaβρi. 17. l'iŋ'g'əδ' in χpai̯β d'i λāμ' βρav' i lāμ' ina mnā. 18. t'ēd' in β'ev uaδ'əβ' iapμμ ogus β'ep'əδ' in grai̯β' l'eh'e kos'ən n'iv's'i. 19. kavəδ' in f'ep is'ən χarbud ranu dō ogus donəβ' koμəltəβ' brav'. 20. iv·βoi̯δi brav f'ep d'iä μun't'əp' i v'iv's'i suβi?

Illustration 19.4: *póc duit, a ingen* 'a kiss for you, girl'

English

1. We do not say a word of welcome to you, but you give welcome to us. 2. Thou dost not carry the sword for the infliction of revenge. 3. Does the light of the sun illuminate the whole world during the day, and does the sun hide his (OIr. *her*!) face in the night? 4. They rear the son of a poor woman, but they do not rear foster-sons for a queen. 5. Thou playest *fidchell* with us, wife of the merchant. 6. A fish jumps out of the sea in the light of the day. 7. We endure the darkness of the nights of Inis Fáil in the winter. 8. Do they go (for) a day and two nights in their *curach* to the big, high island? 9. The height of the snow hampers the swiftness of the brown horse. 10. I go to heaven with its greatness of sanctity after my death. 11. For praying to Brigit they meet (OIr. *they come into their meeting*) every night. 12. The wise priest teaches the teaching of the New Testament to her. 13. Blessing from us on Eithne, the daughter of Domnall. 14. The sharp wind does not disturb the white hair of the sea tonight. 15. Christ, dost thou bless my speech? 16. The gods pour (OIr. *put*) without hesitance the lustre of red gold upon our speech. 17. Do the branches jump from the hand of Bran into (OIr. *i* + acc.!) the hands of the women? 18. The women do not go from him then and they do not carry the branches with them to the island. 19. The man in the chariot does not sing a verse to them. 20. Bran sends men from his retinue into the Island of Joy.

19.4. From the *Táin Bó Cúailnge*

The following sentence is from the *Táin Bó Cúailnge* (TBC 415–416). It tells how Cú Chulainn sets out from his home in Mag Muirthemne to join the boytroop in Emain Macha.

Téit ass íarum 7 a scíath slissen laiss 7 a bunsach 7 a lorg ánae 7 a líathróit.

tʲēdʲ as iaρuμ ogus a sʲkʲiaθ sʲlʲisəv lasʲ ogus a βunsəχ ogus a λorg āve ogus a λiaθρōdʲ.

Note:

1. *ass* is the 3ʳᵈ sg. neuter of the conjugated preposition *a^H* 'out of.' Literally it means 'out of it,' but here it is used for 'away.'

2. Cú Chulainn's *scíath slissen* is a 'shield made of boards,' obviously a toy for young Irish boys.

Illustration 19.5:
Cáera Chulainn cona loirg ánae 7 cona líathróit
'the sheep of Culann with his hurley stick and with his ball'

Lesson 20

20.1. Nouns: masculine and feminine i-stems

All three genders can have i-stems. We will first look at masculine and feminine nouns. Masculine and feminine i-stems basically inflect alike; the only difference lies in the nominative singular: feminine i-stems lenite a following word, while masculine i-stems don't.

In the singular the nominative, prepositional, accusative and vocative end in the palatalized stem final consonant. The genitive singular has an ending attached to the non-palatalized stem final consonant, which in the early Old Irish period is -o, but from the Classical Old Irish period onward is -a. In the genitive singular and dual lowering of short i and u to e and o takes place in the root—otherwise there are no such effects in the i-stem declension. In the plural the stem final consonant in front of the endings -i, -e and -ib is either always palatalized or always non-palatalized (especially after á, ó and consonant clusters).

A typical masculine i-stem is *cnáim* /knāμ'/ 'bone' (stem final consonant /μ/). Note that it is also an example of a word with a non-palatalized stem final consonant in the plural:

case	ending	Old Irish	Prim. Irish	Proto-Celtic	PIE
nom. sg.	C'	cnáim	*knāμih	*knāmis	*knéh₂mis
gen.	{L}Co/aᴴ	cnámoᴴ, cnámaᴴ	*knāμōh «	*knāmēs	*kn̥h₂méi̯s
prep.	C'ᴸ	cnáimᴸ	*knāμē, -μī	*knāmei̯, -mī «	*kn̥h₂méi̯ei̯
acc.	C'ᴺ	cnáimᴺ	*knāμiv	*knāmim	*knéh₂mim
voc.	C'ᴸ	áᴸ chnáimᴸ	*knāμih	*knāmis «	*knéh₂mei̯
nom. pl.	C⁽'⁾iᴴ	cnámaiᴴ	*knāμīh	*knāmii̯es	*kn̥h₂méi̯es
gen.	C⁽'⁾eᴺ	cnámaeᴺ	*knāμii̯av	*knāmii̯om	*kn̥h₂méi̯om
prep.	C⁽'⁾əβ'	cnámaib	*knāμiβih	*knāmibis («)	*kn̥h₂mibʰís, -ibʰós
acc. voc.	C⁽'⁾iᴴ	cnámaiᴴ	*knāμīh	*knāmīs	*kn̥h₂míns
n., a., v. du.	C'ᴸ	dáᴸ chnáimᴸ	*knāμī	*knāmī	*knéh₂mih₁
gen.	{L}Co/aᴸ	dáᴸ chnámoᴸ, -aᴸ «	*knāμii̯ō	*knāmii̯ou̯ («)	*kn̥h₂mih₁óh₁s, -Hóh₁u
prep.	C⁽'⁾əβ'	díbᴺ cnámaib «	*knāμiβiv	*knāmibim «	*kn̥h₂mibʰih₁, -moh₁ ?

Illustration 20.1: Masculine i-stems

An example of a feminine i-stem, and at the same time an example of a word with a palatalized stem final consonant in the plural, is *súil* /sūλ'/ 'eye,' stem final consonant /λ/:

case	singular	plural	dual
nom.	*súil^L*	*súili^H*	*dí^L śúil^L*
gen.	*súlo^H, súla^H*	*súile^N*	*dá^L śúlo^L, śúla^L*
prep.	*súil^L*	*súilib*	*dib^N súilib*
acc.	*súil^N*	*súili^H*	*dí^L śúil^L*
voc.	*á śúil^L*	*á śúili^H*	*á dí^L śúil^L*

Illustration 20.2: Feminine i-stems

Note:

1. Words ending in *g* /γ/ show a special alternation in their root vocalism between *ai* /a/ before palatalized *g* and *e* /e/ before non-palatalized *g*, e.g., nom. sg. *aig* /aγ'/, gen. sg. *ego* /eγo/ 'ice,' or nom. sg. *liaig* /l'iəγ'/, gen. sg. *lego* /l'eγo/, nom. pl. *legai* /l'eγi/ 'doctor, physician.'

20.2. Nouns: neuter i-stems

Neuter i-stems are not very frequent. In the singular they look like masculine or feminine i-stems, with the sole difference that they cause nasalization in the nominative, accusative and vocative. In the plural they have an ending *-e^L* in the nominative, accusative and vocative. A frequent word of this class is *muir* /muρ'/ 'sea,' stem final consonant /ρ/. Note the effect of lowering in the genitive singular:

case	ending	Old Irish	Prim. Irish	Proto-Celtic
nom. acc. sg.	C'^N	*muir^N*	*moρiv* «	*mori*
gen.	{L}Co/a^H	*moro^H, mora^H*	*moρōh* «	*mores*
prep.	C'^L	*muir^L* («)	*moρē, *moρī	*morei̯, *morī
nom. acc. pl.	C(')e^L	*muire^L*	*moρii̯ā	*morii̯ā
gen.	C(')e^N	*muire^N*	*moρii̯av	*morii̯om
prep.	C(')əβ'	*muirib*	*moρiβih	*moribis
nom. acc. du.	C'^N	*dá^N mmuir^N*	*moρī	*morī
gen.	{L}Co/a^N	*dá^N mmoro^N, -a^N* «	*moρii̯ō	*morii̯ou̯
prep.	C(')əβ'	*díb^N mmuirib* «	*moρiβiv	*moribim

Illustration 20.3: Neuter i-stems

Lesson 20

20.3. The i-stem adjectives

Beside o-, ā-adjectives and i̯o-, i̯ā-adjectives, i-stem adjectives form the third and last large group of adjectives. Their inflection differs a little bit from the corresponding i-stem nouns: in the genitive singular they have the endings of o-, ā-adjectives; in the genitive plural they can have either the ending *-e* of the i-stem nouns or an endingless form reminiscent of the o-, ā-adjectives. The two examples below are *maith* /maθ'/ 'good,' stem final consonant /θ/, for words with a palatalized root final consonant throughout the paradigm, and *allaid* /aləδ'/ 'wild,' stem final consonant /δ/, for words with a non-palatalized root final consonant in those cases where a further syllable is attached as ending:

case	ending	masc./neut., pal.	m./n., non-pal.	ending	feminine, pal.	fem., non-pal.
nom. sg.	C'(N)	*maith*(N)	*allaid*(N)	C'L	*maith*L	*allaid*L
gen.	C'L	*maith*L	*allaid*L	C(')eH	*maithe*H	*alltae*H
prep.	C'L	*maith*L	*allaid*L	C'L	*maith*L	*allaid*L
acc.	C'N	*maith*N	*allaid*N	C'N	*maith*N	*allaid*N
voc.	C'L/N	*á*L *maith*L/N	*á*L *allaid*L/N	C'L	*á*L *maith*L	*á*L *allaid*L
nom. pl.	C(')iH	*maithi*H	*alltai*H	C(')i	*maithi*H	*alltai*H
gen.	C(')eN, C'N	*maithe*N, *maith*N	*alltae*N, *allaid*N	C(')eN, C'N	*maithe*N, *maith*N	*alltae*N, *allaid*N
prep.	C(')əβ'	*maithib*	*alltaib*	C(')əβ'	*maithib*	*alltaib*
acc.	C(')iH	*maithi*H	*alltai*H	C(')iH	*maithi*H	*alltai*H
voc.	C(')iH	*á*L *maithi*H	*á*L *alltai*H	C(')iL	*á*L *maithi*H	*á*L *alltai*H

Illustration 20.4: i-stem adjectives

20.4. Exercise

Inflect some of the following words. Decline them together with the article. Combine them with the adjectives *allaid* /aləδ'/ 'wild,' *maith* /maθ'/ 'good,' *sainemail* /sav'əµəλ'/ 'excellent' (fem. gen. sg. *sainemlae*), *sochraid* /soχρəδ'/ 'beautiful, handsome' (fem. gen. sg. *sochraide*).

> *a cuirm* /kur'm'/ (i, n) 'beer, ale'
> *in búachaill* /buaχəl'/ (i, m) 'lad, cowherd, cowboy' (gen. *búachalla*)
> *ind ḟlaith* /flaθ'/ (i, f) 'sovereignty, rule, ruler, prince'
> *a ndruimm* /drum'/ (i, n) 'back'
> *in tailm* /tal'm'/ (i, f) 'sling' (gen. *telmo*)

Illustration 20.5:
Notlaic 'Christmas'

Lesson 21

21.1. The conjugated prepositions 2

Here follow the inflected forms of those four Old Irish prepositions that can take both the prepositional *and* the accusative (the prepositional usually expressing the position or the placement somewhere, and the accusative expressing the direction or the movement somewhere). There is no difference in form in the 1st and 2nd persons between the two cases, but in the 3rd persons there are always two distinct forms, one for the prepositional and one for the accusatival usage.

person		*ar*ᴸ 'for, on account of, in front of'		*fo*ᴸ 'under'	
		ending	transcription	ending	transcription
1st sg.		airium, erum	/aρ'um eρum/	foum	/foǫm foüm?/
2nd sg.		airiut, erut	/aρ'ud eρud/	fout	/foụt foüt?/
3rd sg. m., n.	prep.	airiu	/aρ'u/	fóu, fó	/foụ fō/
	acc.	airi	/aρ'i/	foí	/foị/
3rd sg. f.	prep.	n/a		n/a	
	acc.	airre	/ar'e/	foæ, fóe	/foh'e foë/
1st pl.		erunn, eronn	/eρun/	founn	/foụn/
2nd pl.		airib, eruib	/aρ'əβ' eρuβ'/	fuib	/fuβ'/
3rd pl.	prep.	airib	/aρ'əβ'/	foib	/foəβ' ?/
	acc.	airriu, erru	/ar'u eru/	foo	/foho foö/

Illustration 21.1: The conjugated prepositions 2: *ar*ᴸ, *fo*ᴸ

person		*for* 'on'		*i*ᴺ 'in, into'	
		ending	transcription	ending	transcription
1st sg.		form	/form/	indiumm	/in'd'um/
2nd sg.		fort	/fort/	indiut	/in'd'ud/
3rd sg. m., n.	prep.	for	/foρ/	and	/and/
	acc.	foir, fair	/foρ' faρ'/	ind	/in'd'/
3rd sg. f.	prep.	fuiri, fora	/fuρ'i foρa/	indi	/in'd'i/
	acc.	forrae	/fore/	inte	/in't'e/
1st pl.		fornn	/forn/	indiunn	/in'd'un/
2nd pl.		fuirib, foirib	/fuρ'əβ' foρ'əβ'/	indib	/in'd'əβ'/
3rd pl.	prep.	foraib	/foρəβ'/	indib	/in'd'əβ'/
	acc.	forru	/for'u/	intiu	/in't'u/

Illustration 21.2: The conjugated prepositions 2: *for*, *i*ᴺ

21.2. Secondary or nominal prepositions

We have met a large collection of prepositions so far, e.g., *i^N, co^N, ar^L, fri^H, fo^L*, etc. These are, to put it simply, short, unstressed words, whose syntactical function within a clause is to express certain local, temporal or causal relations of the words they are preposed to. Just the same is true for German (*auf, über, während, wegen*, etc.) or English (*upon, in, for*, etc.) prepositions.

Beside these *primary prepositions*, as they may be called, Old Irish also has so-called *secondary* or *nominal prepositions*. These have basically the same or similar functions and meanings as the primary prepositions, but their syntactic behavior is different. Furthermore, they are not old prepositions inherited from Proto-Celtic or even Proto-Indo-European times, like many of those above, but had only very recently been formed in the prehistory or history of Irish. Usually their most important component is a noun (that is why they are called nominal prepositions).

German and English have secondary prepositions as well: e.g., German *angesichts* is a petrified case form of the noun *Angesicht*, or English *in front of* is a fixed phrase made up of the old preposition *in* and the noun *front*. In the same way the Old Irish secondary preposition *dochum^N* 'towards' is a petrified case form of *tochim* 'the stepping forward,' or *i ndegaid* 'after, behind' is a fixed phrase of the old preposition *i^N* and the prepositional of the noun *degaid* 'the act of seeking, search.'

Secondary prepositions not only differ from old primary prepositions by the fact that they are made up of nouns, but they also behave differently in relation to other elements within the clause. Whereas primary prepositions

Illustration 21.3:
inna degaid
'after her'

in Old Irish either take the prepositional or the accusative of the word that follows, secondary prepositions always take the genitive, e.g., *dochum inna scuile* 'to school' (*inna scuile* is gen. sg. of *in scol* (ā, f) 'the school'), *i ndegaid in charpait* 'after the chariot' (*in charpait* is gen. sg. of *in carpat* (o, m) 'the chariot'). This is true for secondary prepositions in German as well; compare, for example, *angesichts des Weltuntergangs* (gen. sg. of *der Weltuntergang*). Furthermore, in Old Irish the article of the following word does not merge with the secondary preposition.

Secondary prepositions cannot be inflected according to person in the same way as primary Old Irish prepositions are. Instead they are construed with the possessive pronoun of the person intended: *mo dochum* 'towards me,' *a ndochum* 'towards them,' *it degaid* 'after thee' (*it^L* = *i^N* + *do^L*), *innar ndegaid* 'after us' (*innar^N* = *i^N* + *ar^N*), etc. Note that the possessive pronoun always comes immediately before the noun of the nominal preposition, and don't forget about the necessary mutation after the possessive pronoun!

The construction with possessive pronouns again has a parallel in German and English: in German you cannot use normal personal pronouns after secondary prepositions, as you would do with primary prepositions. A construction like *zugunsten mir* or *zugunsten mich* is plainly wrong; instead you have to use a possessive pronoun: *zu meinen Gunsten*. This is also true for English, e.g., *for my sake*, not *for sake me*.

Among the most important of the secondary or nominal prepositions are the following. I will always give one example for the construction with a possessive pronoun in parentheses:

*dochum*ᴺ /doχum/	'to, towards' (*mo dochum* /mo δoχum/ 'to me')
*i*ᴺ *n-arrad*ᴸ /i varəδ/	'near, with, besides' (*it arrad* /id arəδ/ 'near thee, at thy side')
*fo*ᴸ *bíth*ᴸ /fo β'ῑθ/	'because of, on account of, for the sake of' (*foa bíth* /foä β'ῑθ/ 'for his sake')
*i*ᴺ *ndegaid*ᴸ /i n'd'eγəδ'/	'after, behind' (*ina degaid* /iva d'eγəδ'/ 'after her')
*ar*ᴸ *bélaib* /aρ β'ēλəβ'/	'before, in front of' (*ara bélaib* /aρa β'ēλəβ'/ 'in front of it')
*ar*ᴸ *chiunn*ᴸ /aρ χ'iṷn/	'facing, awaiting' (*arar ciunn* /aρəρ g'iṷn/ 'facing us')
*ar*ᴸ *chenn*ᴺ /aρ χ'en/	'towards, against' (*arfar cenn* /aρβaρ g'en/ 'against you')
*tar cenn*ᴺ /taρ k'en/	'for' (*tara cenn* /taρa g'en/ 'for them')
*íar*ᴺ *cúl*ᴸ /iaρ gῡλ/	'behind (position)' (*íarmo chúl* /iaρmo χῡλ/ 'behind me = hinter mir')
*for cúlu*ᴴ /foρ kῡλu/	'behind (direction)' (*fort chúlu* /fort χῡλu/ 'behind thee = hinter dich')
*i*ᴺ *ndead*ᴸ, *i*ᴺ *ndiad*ᴸ /i n'd'eᴂδ, i n'd'iᴂδ/	'after' (*ina dead, ina diad* /iva δ'eᴂδ, iva δ'iᴂδ/ 'after him')
*tar éissi*ᴴ /taρ ēs'i/	'behind, for, instead of' (*tara éissi* /taρa h'ēs'i/ 'behind her, for her')
*i*ᴺ *mmedón* /i m'eδōv/	'in the middle, amidst' (*inna medón* /ina μeδōv/ 'in its midst')

Note:

1. You will find more nominal prepositions, but by no means all, in GOI 536–537. In DIL you will usually find them listed under the noun.

21.3. Demonstrative particles

Demonstrative pronouns are words like *dieser, jener* in German or *this, that, these, those* in English. Old Irish doesn't have words that are directly comparable in form and function to the German or English examples, but instead uses enclitic particles to express the demonstrative meaning. *Enclitic* means that these particles, which are never accented, immediately follow the word they qualify. They always have to be used together with the article. Throughout this course I will separate these particles from the rest of the word by a hyphen.

1. The particle *-so, -sa, -se, -seo, -sea* (always with unlenited *s*) points to something near, present or immediately following and corresponds roughly to English 'this.' *-so, -sa* /so sa/ are used after non-palatalized sounds, *-se, -seo, -sea* /s'e s'o s'a/ after palatalized sounds. *-so* and *-sa* on the one hand, and *-se, -seo, -sea* on the other hand are simply variants of one another; e.g., *in lebor* means 'the book,' *in lebor-sa* means 'this book' (the final *r* of *lebor* is non-palatalized, therefore *-so* or *-sa* have to be used); but *ind libuir* 'the books,' *ind libuir-se* 'these books' (this time the *r* is palatalized, therefore *-se* or *-seo* or *-sea* have to be used).

2. The particle -sin /s'iv'/ (always with unlenited s) is used for 'that.' It points to something more remote or already mentioned before; e.g., in ben means 'the woman,' in ben-sin means 'that woman'; ind ḟir 'the men,' ind ḟir-sin 'those men.'

3. When used alone or only with the article, -so 'this' and -sin 'that' have substantival force, e.g., is deired mbetho in-so 'this is the end of the world' (Wb. 10b3), as·biur sin 'I say that'; the same is true, when -so and -sin are added to prepositions, e.g., amal sin 'like that,' a sin 'from there, therefrom.'

21.4. Verbs of the S2-class

The second strong verbal class, S2, is characterized by palatalization of the stem final consonant throughout the paradigm. It is thus very similar to the W2-class with the one difference that it, like any strong verbal class, ends in the root final consonant in the 3rd sg. conjunct. I will only give an example for a simple verb; the inflection of compound S2 verbs absolutely agrees to the usual rules for compound verbs. The example is gaibid /gaβ'əδ'/ 'to take,' root gaib- /gaβ'/ (root final consonant /β'/):

S2	absolute (independent)		conjunct (dependent)	
1st sg.	gaibiu, gaibimm	C'u, C'əm'	(ní)·gaibiu, ·gaibimm	C'u, C'əm'
2nd sg.	gaibi	C'i	(ní)·gaibi	C'i
3rd sg.	gaibid	C'əδ'	(ní)·gaib	C'
1st pl.	gaibmi	C'm'i	(ní)·gaibem	C'əµ
2nd pl.	gaibthe	C'θ'e	(ní)·gaibid	C'əδ'
3rd pl.	gaibit	C'əd'	(ní)·gaibet	C'əd

Illustration 21.4: The conjugation of S2 verbs

Note:

1. Like in W2, in this class the 1st sg. ending -iu /u/ is being replaced by -imm /əm'/ during the Old Irish period.

2. Though S2 verbs ideally have a palatalized stem final consonant throughout their paradigm, of course in compound verbs the stem consonant can be secondarily depalatalized because of the syncopation of a back vowel: e.g., fo·gaib, ·fagaib /fo·gaβ' ·faɣəβ'/ 'to find, to get,' but 3rd pl. prototonic ·fagbat /·faɣβəd/ 'they find' < *·fagaibet.

3. The S2 class consists of old i̯e/o-thematic verbs: PIE *gʷʰedʰi̯eti, *gʷʰedʰi̯onti > CC *gʷedi̯eti, *gʷedi̯onti (cf. Gaul. uediIumi 'I pray') > OIr. guidid, guidit 'to pray, to request.'

4. Forms like ad·gaur /aδ·gau̯ρ/ 'I sue' (Thes. ii 228.30) or for·congur /foρ·koŋgu̯ρ/ 'I command' (Wb. 19d25) without overt ending, but with u-infection in the 1st sg., or 3rd pl. du·airngerat /du·aρ'ŋ'g'əρəd/ 'they promise' (Ml. 87b15) with non-palatalized instead of palatalized r attest to a certain amount of confusion with the S1-class in the case of some verbs.

Lesson 21

21.5. Verbs of the S3-class

S3 is the third and last strong verbal class. In S1 we had verbs that show an alternation of palatalized and non-palatalized root final consonants in their paradigm, in S2 we had verbs with a palatalized root final consonant throughout, and in S3 we have the third logical possibility: a non-palatalized root final consonant throughout the paradigm. Furthermore, the root final consonant is always n /ν/, which disappears outside the present stem.

In MCCONE's classification there is only a single S3-class. Historically, however, the verbs in this class go back to two slightly different sources and therefore I will distinguish them by calling those that show the vowel e in the present tense S3a (THURNEYSEN's B IV class, see GOI 356), and those with the vowels i or u in the present tense S3b (THURNEYSEN's B V class, see GOI 357). However, apart from the diverging vowels both subclasses behave identically. S3a is by far the better attested subclass in the present indicative: crenaid /k'r'evəð'/ 'to buy,' stem cren- /k'r'ev/, present stem final consonant /ν/:

S3	absolute (independent)		conjunct (dependent)	
1st sg.	crenaim(m)	vəm'	(ní)·crenaim(m)	vəm'
2nd sg.	crenai	vi	(ní)·crenai	vi
3rd sg.	crenaid	vəð'	(ní)·cren	ν
1st pl.	crenmai	vmi	(ní)·crenam	vəμ
2nd pl.	crentae	nte	(ní)·crenaid	vəð'
3rd pl.	crenait	vəd'	(ní)·crenat	vəd

Illustration 21.5: The conjugation of S3a verbs

Note:

1. No simple, active S3b verb seems to be attested, and also of compound verbs only very few present tense forms are actually found in the texts, e.g., 1st sg. as·gninaim 'I know,' do·linaim 'I flow,' ara·chrinim 'I perish,' 3rd sg. do·lin 'flows,' ara·chrin 'perishes,' itar·gnin 'understands,' 3rd pl. do·linat 'they flow,' ara·crinat 'they perish.'

2. The sole exception to the rule that the present stem in S3 verbs ends in a non-palatalized n is at the same time one of the very few S3 deponent verbs (we will learn about them in a later lesson): ro·cluinethar 'to hear.' The stem cluin- /kluv'/ ends in palatalized n.

3. Palatalization of n in the present stem is of course introduced secondarily when the vowel before the n is syncopated, e.g., 1st sg. do·fuibnimm /do·fuβ'v'əm'/ 'I cut, destroy' < *to-fo-benaimm.

4. The S3-class consists of old nasal infix presents of PIE verbal roots ending in a laryngeal: PIE *kʷrinéh₂ti, *kʷrinh₂énti > CC *kʷrinati, *kʷrinanti (cf. Gaul. prinas 'bought,' OW. prinit 'buys') > OIr. crenaid, crenait 'to buy.'

104

21.6. The prehistory of the S1, S2 and S3 ending sets

Below you find my attempts at reconstructing the ending sets of the strong verbs. Whereas the original 'pre-Celtic' (= more or less PIE) input forms are pretty certain, the intermediate stages of the development towards Old Irish have to be viewed with some caution. Especially the forms that I termed 'Insular Celtic' are far from being undisputed. In the case of S3 verbs I refrained from reconstructing further back than the Insular Celtic period (and even these forms are highly simplified), as the PIE input formations are very diverse and show a complicated behavior.

S1	OIr. abs.	Prim. Ir.	Ins. Celtic	Pre-Celtic	OIr. conj.	Prim. Ir.	Ins. Celtic	Pre-Celt.
1st sg.	-u «	*-ū	*-ū	*-oh₂	-ᵘC	*-ū	*-ū	*-oh₂
2nd sg.	-i «	*-ehi	*-esi «	*-esi	{R}-C' «	*-eh	*-es	*-esi
3rd sg.	-id	*-eθi	*-eti «	*-eti	-C'	*-eθ	*-et	*-eti
1st pl.	-†m(a)i	*-omohi «	*-omosi «	*-omosi	-am	*-oµah	*-omos	*-omosi
2nd pl.	-†the	*-eθē- «	*-etesi «	*-etesi	-id	*-eθeh	*-etes	*-etesi
3rd pl.	-ait	*-odi	*-onti «	*-onti	-at	*-od	*-ont	*-onti

Illustration 21.6: Reconstructed S1 endings

S2	OIr. abs.	Prim. Ir.	Ins. Celtic	Pre-Celtic	OIr. conj.	Prim. Ir.	Ins. Celtic	Pre-Celt.
1st sg.	-iu	*-iįū	*-į̥ū	*-įoh₂	-iu	*-iįū	*-į̥ū	*-įoh₂
2nd sg.	-i	*-ihi	*-isi «	*-įesi	-i «	*-ih	*-is	*-įesi
3rd sg.	-id	*-iθi	*-iti «	*-įeti	-C'	*-iθ	*-it	*-įeti
1st pl.	-†mi	*-imohi «	-*įomosi «	*-įomosi	-em	*-iµah «	*-į̥omos	*-į̥omosi
2nd pl.	-†the	*-iθē- «	*-itesi «	*-įetesi	-id	*-iθeh	*-ites	*-įetesi
3rd pl.	-it	*-idi «	*-į̥onti «	*-įonti	-et	*-id «	*-į̥ont	*-įonti

Illustration 21.7: Reconstructed S2 endings

S3	OIr. abs.	Prim. Ir.	Insul. Celtic	OIr. conj.	Prim. Ir.	Insul. Celtic
1st sg.	-naim(m)	*-vami «	*-nami «	-naim(m)	*-vami «	*-nam
2nd sg.	-nai	*-vahi	*-nasi «	-nai «	*-vah	*-nas
3rd sg.	-naid	*-vaθi	*-nati «	-n	*-vaθ	*-nat
1st pl.	-n†mai	*-vamohi «	*-namosi «	-nam	*-vaµah	*-namos
2nd pl.	-n†te	*-vaθē- «	*-natesi «	-naid	*-vaθeh	*-nates
3rd pl.	-nait	*-vadi «	*-nanti «	-nat	*-vad «	*-nant

Illustration 21.8: Reconstructed S3 endings

21.7. Exercise

Now try to conjugate some of the following verbs in absolute and conjunct inflection, or in their deuterotonic and prototonic form respectively. Watch out for depalatalization, resp. secondary palatalization as a consequence of syncope in the plural forms of prototonic verbs (e.g., 3ʳᵈ pl. ·fodmat, ·frecrat, ·freipnet, ·foirbnet):

> airid /aρ'əδ'/ (S2) 'to plough'
> guidid /guδ'əδ'/ (S2) 'to ask, to pray'
> fo·daim, ·fodaim /fo·daμ', ·foδəμ'/ (S2) 'to suffer, to endure'
> fris·gair, ·frecair /f'r'is·gaρ', ·f'r'egəρ'/ (S2) 'to answer'
> ernaid /ernəδ'/ (S3a) 'to bestow'
> renaid /r'evəδ'/ (S3a) 'to sell'
> fris·ben, ·frepen /f'r'is·b'ev, ·f'r'eb'əv/ (S3a) 'to heal'
> for·fen, ·forban /foρ·f'ev, ·forβəv/ (S3a) 'to finish, to complete'

Lesson 22

22.1. From the *Old Irish Triads*

The *Old Irish Triads* are a collection of roughly 250 short and often clever aphorisms, usually comprising three, sometimes more, items typical for certain places, persons or legal aspects. They have been edited by Kuno MEYER in 1906 in volume 13 of the *Todd Lecture Series* of the Royal Irish Academy. Below I give you two examples. Note, that the preposition *fri*ᴴ in *Triad 66* is used in the sense 'for; to attend to,' and that *búaid* (i, n) in *Triad 156* means 'special quality, mark of quality.' I have normalized the spelling.

> *Triad 66*
>
> Trí airgarta ecailse: caillech fri clocc, athláech i n-apdaini, bainne for altóir.
>
> t'r'ī haꞃ'ɣərta egəl's'e: kal'əχ f'r'i klog, aθλaịχ i ʋabδəv'i, ban'e foꞃ altōꞃ'.

> *Triad 156*
>
> Trí búadae étaig: maisse, clithchae, suthaine.
>
> t'r'ī buaδe ēdəɣ': mas'e, k'l'iθχe, suθəv'e.

22.2. From the Old Irish glosses

The following piece is from the Old Irish glosses. The glosses are our most important source for the grammar of Old Irish because they are practically the only texts that have come down to us directly in early medieval manuscripts. The glosses are short commentaries between the lines of books of the bible or grammatical tracts. I have modified and shortened this little piece a bit. Note the unusual word order VOS in the first sentence!

> * [...] Ní·foircnea in fíni ithe neich di anúas. [...] Ad·ellat [in doíni sechmaill] in fíni do thabairt neich doib dia torud. (*Ml.* 102a15)
>
> n'ī·for'k'n'a in β'īv'i iθ'e v'eχ' d'i avúas. aδ·eləd in doịv'i s'eχμəl' in β'īv'i do θaβər't' v'eχ' doə̣β' d'iä toꞃuδ.

Note:

1. *Sechmall* literally means 'the act of passing by'; *doíni sechmaill* therefore are the 'people of passing by,' which means 'passers by.'

2. *Neich* is the genitive of *ní* 'something.'

3. *Anúas* is stressed on the second syllable.

Illustration 22.1:
cáeraig sechmaill oc tabairt neich doib de thorud inna fíne
'sheep passing by taking something from the fruit of the vine for themselves'

22.3. Varia

1. The male personal name *Cormac* (o, m) in sentence 14 below refers to the great and just king *Cormac mac Airt*, one of the legendary prehistoric kings of Ireland. You can find more information about him in Tomás Ó CATHASAIGH's book *The Heroic Biography of Cormac mac Airt* (Dublin Institute for Advanced Studies, 1977).

2. The phrase *gaibid X búaid di Y* 'lit. X takes victory from Y' in sentence 12 means 'X defeats Y, X wins over Y.'

22.4. Exercise

Old Irish

1. ** Guidiu itche asmo chridiu deróil dúr duit, a maicc Dé. 2. In·llenai graig inna n-ech cosin clúain, á búachaill? 3. ** Benaid [*sc.* Cú Chulainn] fona maccu íarum. (TBC 435) 4. Trí búadae glana: rodarc tree, laith indi, fuil asa bruur. 5. * Bentae clocán mbinn inna cille i n-aidchi gaíthe, á sacartu. Ní·tíag ina dáil, co-lléice, acht i ndáil mná baíthe. (GT 113) 6. Fris·gairet ind legai ceisti ind fir thinn. 7. Ní·crenaimm cuirm din chennaigiu dochraid. 8. Fo·daimi mór péine 7 mór ngortae t'óenur isin muir. 9. Ní·air mo dam maith in n-úir-sin arin llóg-so. 10. Ní·sernam ór 7 argat for láma inna mban sochraid. 11. In·mbenaid cenn in chimbedo echtrainn frisin fraig, á lóechu? 12. Agait gataigi mucca inna túaithe ón chlúain. Gaibit búachailli búaid diib íarum. 13. ** Ní·feraimm cuirm maith milis. (GT 49) 14. Gaibid Cormac flaith fer n-Inse Fáil. 15. Brisiu cnáim ndrommo in búachalla co cloich thruimm. 16. Innád·mbeir in techtaire macc inna rígnae lais dochum inna scoile? 17. * Fégthae úaib sair fo-thúaid a muir múad mílach. (GT 205) 18. ** Caíne amrae lasin mBran inna churchán tar muir nglan. (IB 33) 19. ** Úar ind adaig i mMóin Móir, feraid dertan ní deróil. (GT 206 f.) 20. ** Is samlaid do·meil Conchobor a flaith: trian ind laí [...] oc imbirt fidchille, a trian n-aill oc óul chorma. (TBC 402 ff.)

Transcription

1. guδ'u id'χ'e asmo χ'ρ'iδ'u δ'eρōλ' δūρ dut', ā μak' δ'ē. 2. iv·l'evi graγ' ina v'eχ kos'ən gluav', ā βuaχəl? 3. b'evəδ' fona maku iaρuμ. 4. t'r'ī buaδe glava: roδərk t'r'eh'e, laθ' in'd'i, fuλ' asa bruüρ. 5. b'ente klogāv m'b'in' ina k'il'e i vaδ'χ'i γai̯θ'e, ā hagərtu. n'ī·t'iaγ iva δāλ', ko-l'ēg'e, aχt i ndāλ' mnā bai̯θ'e. 6. f'ris·gaρ'əd ind λ'eγi k'es't'i ind iρ' θ'in'. 7. n'ī·k'r'evəm' kur'm' d'in χ'enaγ'u δoχρəδ'. 8. fo·daμ'i mōρ b'ēv'e ogus μōρ ŋgorte toi̯vuρ is'ən μuρ'. 9. n'ī·aρ' mo δaμ maθ' in nūρ'-s'əv' aρ'ən lōγ-so. 10. n'ī·s'ernəμ ōρ ogus argəd foρ lāμa ina mbav soχρəδ'. 11. iv·m'b'evəδ' k'en in χ'im'b'əδo eχtrən' f'r'is'ən βraγ', ā λoi̯χu? 12. aγəd' gadaγ'i muka ina tuaθ'e ōn χλuav'. gaβ'əd'. buaχəl'i buaδ' d'iəβ' iaρuμ. 13. n'ī·f'eρəm' kur'm' maθ' m'iλ'əs'. 14. gaβ'əδ' kormək flaθ' β'eρ v'iv's'e fāλ'. 15. b'r'is'u knāμ' ndromo in βuaχəla ko gloχ' θρum'. 16. ināδ·m'b'eρ' in teχtəρ'e mak ina r'īγve las' doχum ina skoλ'e? 17. f'ēγθe uaβ' saρ' fo-θúaδ' a muρ' muaδ' m'īλəχ. 18. kai̯v'e aμρe las'ən mbrav ina χuρχāv taρ muρ' ŋglav. 19. uaρ ind aδəγ' i mōv' μōρ', f'eρəδ' dertəv nī d'eρōλ'. 20. is saμλəδ' do·m'eλ' kovχəβəρ a λaθ': t'r'iəv ind λai̯ og im'b'ər't' iδχ'əl'e, a d'r'iən nal' og ōṵλ χorma.

English

1. We pray a prayer from our insignificant, hard hearts to thee, Son of God. 2. You follow the stud of the horses to the meadow, lads. 3. Does he make an assault on the boy after that? 4. — 5. Thou ringest a sweet-sounding bell of the church, priest. I go to meet it (in OIr.: *to his [the bell's] meeting*), and I do not go to meet a wanton woman (in OIr.: *to the meeting of a wanton woman*). 6. Does the doctor answer the questions of the sick man? 7. We buy beer from the ugly merchants. 8. She suffers a lot of pain and a lot of hunger alone on the sea. 9. My oxen plough that land for this price. 10. Thou spreadest gold and silver over the hand of the beautiful woman. 11. The soldiers beat the heads of the foreign prisoners against the wall. 12. A thief drives the pigs of the tribe from the meadow. The cowboy takes victory from him after that. 13. We pour good, sweet beer on you (on = *for* + acc.). 14. Does Cormac take the rule of the men of Inis Fáil? 15. Do we break the bones of the back of the lad with a heavy stone? 16. The messengers bring the sons of the queen with them to the school. 17. We see away from us to the North-East the glorious sea full of animals. 18. A wonder of beauty for (OIr.: *la!*) the men in their little *curachs* over the clear sea. 19. Cold the night in the big bog, but no storm does pour. 20. In this way the queens spend their sovereignty: a third of the day playing *fidchell*, another third drinking beer.

Illustration 22.2:
cid ferr? cuirm maith milis no uisce bethad?
'what is better? good sweet beer or water of life?'

22.5. Test

Recognize the following conjugated prepositions. Say which preposition the form belongs to and give person and number, as well as gender and case, where possible.

foir: _____   *lib:* _____   *dít:* _____

úainn: _____   *triit:* _____   *and:* _____

fuiri: _____   *ind:* _____   *foe:* _____

airium: _____   *dúnn:* _____   *inte:* _____

indib: _____   or _____   *fou:* _____

frie: _____   *leis:* _____   *form:* _____

úadi: _____   *friut:* _____   *foo:* _____

22.6. Test

Try to recognize the verbal forms. Give as much information about the words as possible — class, person, number, dependent or independent variant. If the verb is in a dependent form, write the corresponding independent variant into the slot in parentheses, and vice versa:

in·crenaid: _____ (_____)

ní·foircnet: _____ (_____)

biri: _____ (_____)

gairiu: _____ (_____)

ní·eiprem: _____ (_____)

ní·tascraid: _____ (_____)

ní·imbiur: _____ (_____)

ráitte: _____ (_____)

imm·ráidem: _____ (_____)

ní·frecrat: _____ (_____)

guidid: _____ (_____)

for·fenam: _____ (_____)

in·n-airem: _____ (_____)

rentae: _____ (_____)

sernmai: _____ (_____)

in·freipnid: _____ (_____)

ní·fodmam: _____ (_____)

fo·gaibimm: _____ (_____)

gaibit: _____ (_____)

in·díltai: _____ or _____ (_____)

for·cain: _____ or _____ (_____)

22.7. From a poem

Below follows the greatest part of a poem by the poet MUGRÓN (abbot of Í 965–981). It is an invocation of the powers of Christ's cross. Again I have omitted those lines of the poem that have declensional forms we have not learned so far. The complete poem can be found in Gerard MURPHY's *Early Irish Lyrics*, Dublin 1956 (repr. Dublin: Four Courts Press 1998), p. 32 ff.

Cros Chríst tarsin ngnúis-se,   kros χ'ρ'ɪs't' tars'ən ŋgūs'-s'e
tarsin clúais fon cóir-se.   tars'ən gluas' fon gōρ'-s'e
Cros Chríst tarsin súil-se.   kros χ'ρ'ɪs't' tars'ən sūλ'-s'e
Cros Chríst tarsin sróin-se.   kros χ'ρ'ɪs't' tars'ən srōv'-s'e

Cros Chríst tarsin mbél-sa.   kros χ'ρ'ɪs't' tars'ən m'b'ēλ-sa
Cros Chríst tarsin cráes-sa.   kros χ'ρ'ɪs't' tars'ən grais-sa
Cros Chríst tarsin cúl-sa.   kros χ'ρ'ɪs't' tars'ən gūλ-sa
Cros Chríst tarsin táeb-sa.   kros χ'ρ'ɪs't' tars'ən daiβ-sa

[...] Cros Chríst tarsin tairr-se.   kros χ'ρ'ɪs't' tars'ən dar'-s'e
Cros Chríst tarsin druimm-se.   kros χ'ρ'ɪs't' tars'ən drum'-s'e

Cros Chríst tar mo láma [...]   kros χ'ρ'ɪs't' taρ mo λāμa
Cros Chríst tar mo lesa.   kros χ'ρ'ɪs't' taρ mo λ'esa
Cros Chríst tar mo chosa.   kros χ'ρ'ɪs't' taρ mo χosa

Cros Chríst lemm ar m'agaid.   kros χ'ρ'ɪs't' l'em aρ maγəδ'
Cros Chríst lemm im' degaid.   kros χ'ρ'ɪs't' l'em im δ'eγəδ'
Cros Chríst fri cach ndoraid   kros χ'ρ'ɪs't' f'r'i kaχ ndoρəδ'
eitir fán 7 telaig. [...]   ed'əρ' fāv is t'eλəγ'

Cros Chríst tar mo śuide.   kros χ'ρ'ɪs't' taρ mo huδ'e
Cros Chríst tar mo lige.   kros χ'ρ'ɪs't' taρ mo λ'iγ'e
Cros Chríst mo bríg uile [...]   kros χ'ρ'ɪs't' mo β'ρ'ɪγ' uλ'e

Cros Chríst tar mo muintir.   kros χ'ρ'ɪs't' taρ mo μun't'əρ'
Cros Chríst tar mo thempal.   kros χ'ρ'ɪs't' taρ mo θ'empəλ
Cros Chríst isin alltar.   kros χ'ρ'ɪs't' is'ən altəρ
Cros Chríst isin chenntar.   kros χ'ρ'ɪs't' is'ən χ'entəρ

Ó mulluch mo baitse   ō μuluχ mo βat's'e
co ingin mo choise [...]   ko h'iŋ'g'əv' mo χos'e

Co laithe mo báis-se,   ko laθ'e mo βās-s'e
ría ndul isin n-úir-se,[...]   r'ia nduλ is'ən nūρ'-s'e
Cros Chríst tarsin ngnúis-se.   kros χ'ρ'ɪs't' tars'ən ŋgūs'-s'e

Note:

1. The spelling *táeb* for *tóeb*: the orthographical interchangeability of the diphthongs *áe, aí* and *óe, oí* is a feature of later Irish.

2. The word *ingen* /iŋ'əv/ means 'nail (of a finger or a toe),' do not confuse it with *ingen*, pronounced /iv'γ'əv/ 'girl.'

3. Note especially the many demonstrative particles used in the text.

Lesson 23

23.1. Nouns: masculine u-stems

The last 'vocalic' declensional class we will learn are the u-stems. These are mostly masculine; a few are neuter. The feminines that seem to have historically belonged to this class have all gone over to the ā-stems.

Monosyllabic words with root vowel *u* or words with 'infected' *u* before their final consonant in the nominative and accusative singular are at once identifiable as u-stems, e.g., *guth* /guθ/ 'voice,' *giun* /g'iṷv/ 'mouth,' *ammus* /amus/ 'attempt,' etc. Many words, however, do not display a *u* in the nominative and accusative singular, e.g., *bith* /b'iθ/ 'world,' *dán* /dāv/ 'gift,' *cath* /kaθ/ 'battle,' *molad* /moλǝδ/ 'praise,' etc.; these you have to learn by heart as belonging to this class. Some words sometimes show *u* before their final consonant, sometimes not: e.g., the word for 'knowledge' can either appear as *fis* /f'is/ or as *fius* /f'iṷs/. In the prepositional singular, however, these words frequently do show the *u*, e.g., *biuth* 'world.'

The root final consonants of u-stems are basically non-palatalized throughout the paradigm. An exception is of course in those cases, where the root final consonant is secondarily palatalized as a result of syncope: e.g., the genitive singular of *ammus* /amus/ 'attempt,' which goes back to an older *ammessu-, is *aimseo, aimsea* /am's'o am's'a/, because in the second syllable an historical *e* was syncopated < *ammesso.

We will first look at masculine u-stems. A typical word is *guth* /guθ/ 'voice' (root final consonant /θ/):

case	ending	Old Irish	Prim. Irish	Proto-Celtic	Pre-Celtic
nom. voc. sg.	{R}(u)C	*guth*	*guθuh	*gutus «	*ǵʰéṷtus
gen.	{L}Co/aᴴ	*gothoᴴ, gothaᴴ*	*guθōh	*gutoṷs	*ǵʰutéṷs
prep.	{R}(u)Cᴸ	*guth*ᴸ	*guθū (»)	*gutoṷei̯, *gutū «	*ǵʰutéṷei̯, *ǵʰutúh₁
acc.	{R}(u)Cᴺ	*guth*ᴺ	*guθuv	*gutum «	*ǵʰéṷtum
nom. pl.	{L}Ce/i/aᴴ	*gothaeᴴ, -aiᴴ, -aᴴ*	*guθoṷeh	*gutoṷes	*ǵʰutéṷes
gen.	{L}Ceᴺ	*gothaeᴺ «*	*guθoṷav	*gutoṷom	*ǵʰutéṷom
prep.	{L}Cǝβ'	*gothaib*	*guθoβih «	*gutubis	*ǵʰutubʰís, -ubʰos
acc. voc.	{R}(u)Cuᴴ	*guthuᴴ*	*guθūh	*gutūs	*ǵʰutúns
n., a., v. du.	{R}(u)Cᴸ	*dáᴸ guth*ᴸ	*guθū	*gutū «	*ǵʰéṷtuh₁
gen.	{L}Co/aᴸ	*dáᴸ gotho*ᴸ, *-a*ᴸ	*guθoṷō	*gutoṷoṷ (»)	*ǵʰutuh₁óh₁s, -(H)óh₁u
prep.	{L}Cǝβ'	*dibᴺ ngothaib* «	*guθoβiv «	*gutubim «	*ǵʰutubʰih₁, -moh₁ ?

Illustration 23.1: The masculine u-stems

Note:

1. As with the i-stems, the genitive singular of the u-stems can end either in *-o* (oldest form) or *-a* (younger, usual form). In the nominative plural of the masculines three different endings are possible: *-(a)e* /e/, *-(a)i* /i/, *-a* /a/. Of these *-(a)e* is the oldest,[1] *-(a)i* must have been taken over from the i-stems, and *-a* may simply reflect a younger development whereby final vowels lose their independent quality.

23.2. Nouns: neuter u-stems

Just like all neuters, neuter u-stems cause nasalization in the nominative, accusative and vocative singular. In the nominative, accusative and vocative plural they have two forms: a short and a long form. Just like in the neuter o-stems the short form is identical with the singular and causes lenition, whereas the long form adds an extra *-a* to the stem. The addition of the *-a* entails syncope if a form with more than two syllables would result. The example below is *dorus* /doṛus/ 'door' (root final consonant /s/):

case	ending	Old Irish	Prim. Irish	Proto-Celtic
nom. acc. sg.	{R}(u)Cᴺ	*dorus*ᴺ	*doṛesuṿ «	*du̯orestu
gen.	{L}Co/aᴴ	*doirseo*ᴴ, *doirsea*ᴴ	*doṛesōh	*du̯orestou̯s
prep.	{R}(u)Cᴸ	*dorus*ᴸ	*doṛesū («)	*du̯orestou̯ei̯, *du̯orestū
nom. acc. pl.	{R}(u)Cᴸ/{L}Ca	*dorus*ᴸ, *doirsea* «	*doṛesou̯ā	*du̯orestou̯ā
gen.	{L}Ceᴺ	*doirse*ᴺ «	*doṛesou̯av	*du̯orestou̯om
prep.	{L}Cəβ'	*doirsib*	*doṛesoβih «	*du̯orestubis
n., a., v. du.	{R}(u)Cᴺ	*dá*ᴺ *ndorus*ᴺ	*doṛesū	*du̯orestū
gen.	{L}Co/aᴺ	*dá*ᴺ *ndoirseo*ᴺ, *-a*ᴺ	*doṛesou̯ō	*du̯orestou̯ou̯
prep.	{L}Cəβ'	*dib*ᴺ *ndoirsib* «	*doṛesoβiv «	*du̯orestubim

Illustration 23.2: The neuter u-stems

23.3. Adjectives: u-stems

Only a few adjectives belong to this group: a few simple adjectives like *dub* /duβ/ 'black,' *tiug* /t'iu̯γ/ 'thick,' *fliuch* /f'l'iu̯χ/ 'wet,' *accus, ocus* /agus ogus/ 'near,' and some compounded adjectives like *solus* /soλus/ 'bright,' *follus* /folus/ 'clear,' *cumung* /kuμuŋg/ 'narrow,' *díriug, díriuch* /d'īṛ'uγ d'īṛ'uχ/ 'straight,' etc.

Apart from the u-vowel or u-infection, u-stem adjectives inflect like o-, ā-stem adjectives in the singular and like i-stem adjectives in the plural. Only in the genitive plural they behave like o-, ā-stems.

Illustration 23.3: *fliuch* 'wet'

---

[1] For the development CC *-oi̯eC* > OIr. *-ae*, compare ·*robae* 'has been' < *·ro-boi̯e*.

The vocatives probably would have been identical with the nominative forms, but according to GOI 227 no such forms are attested. The two examples below are *dub* /duβ/ 'black' for simple monosyllabic words and *solus* /soλus/ 'bright' for disyllabic compounded words (note the effect of syncope in the latter):

case	ending	masc. and neut.	masc. and neut.	ending	feminine	feminine
nom. sg.	uC	*dub*(N)	*solus*(N)	uCL	*dub*L	*solus*L
gen.	C'L	*duib*L	*solais*L	C(')eH	*dubae*H	*soilse*H
prep.	uCL	*dub*L	*solus*L	C'L	*duib*L	*solais*L
acc.	uCN	*dub*N	*solus*N	C'N	*duib*N	*solais*N
nom. pl.	C(')iL	*dubai*L	*soilsi*L	C(')iH	*dubai*H	*soilsi*H
gen.	uCN	*dub*N	*solus*N	uCN	*dub*N	*solus*N
prep.	C(')əβ'	*dubaib*	*soilsib*	C(')əβ'	*dubaib*	*soilsib*
acc.	C(')iH	*dubai*H	*soilsi*H	C(')iH	*dubai*H	*soilsi*H

Illustration 23.4: u-stem adjectives

23.4. Determining the stem class of adjectives

It is very easy to recognize to which inflectional class a given adjective belongs, as long as you know what its nominative singular looks like. Basically you only have to look at the final portion of the word and you will immediately know its inflectional class.

1. If an adjective ends in -*e*, it belongs to the i̯o-, i̯ā-adjectives.

2. If an adjective ends in a palatalized consonant, it belongs to the i-adjectives.

3. If an adjective has a *u* before the final consonant, it belongs to the u-adjectives.

4. All other adjectives, that is adjectives ending in a non-palatalized consonant, belong to the o-, ā-adjectives.

Illustration 23.5: *dub* 'black'

23.5. Exercise

Inflect some of the following words. Decline them together with the article. Combine them with any of the adjectives you learned so far.

a rrind /r'ind/ (u, n) 'star'

in bith /b'iθ/ (u, m) 'world'

in molad /moλəδ/ (u, m) 'praise, the praising' (gen. sg. with syncope and delenition *molto, -a* /molto molta/, no u-infection in the prep. sg. *molad* /moλəδ/)

a mbir, a mbiur /b'iρ b'iụρ/ (u, n) 'stake, point, spear, spit'

int áes /aịs/ (u, m) 'people, folk'

in fid /f'iδ/ (u, m) 'wood, forest'

a mmind /m'ind/ (u, n) 'diadem, badge, crown' (no lowering of the *i*)

in foilsigiud /fol's'əγ'uδ/ (u, m) 'manifestation, the revealing' (gen. sg. with syncope *foilsigtheo, -a* /fol's'əγ'θ'o fol's'əγ'θ'a/)

Lesson 24

24.1. The cardinal numbers 1–19

Cardinal numbers are the basic numerals *one, two, three*, etc., used to count things. Below are the cardinal numbers from 1 to 10 with their respective mutational effects:

nr.	transcr.	masculine	neuter	feminine	Prim. Irish	Proto-Celtic	PIE
1	oịv-		óen-, oín-		*oịva-	*oịno-	*oịno-
2		daᴸ, dáᴸ	daᴺ, dáᴺ	diᴸ, díᴸ			
3		triᴴ, tríᴴ	(treᴸ)	teoir, téora	see below		
4		cethair		cethéoir, cethéora			
		no distinction of gender					
5	kōg'ᴸ		cóicᴸ		*kʷōgʷe «	*kʷınkʷe «	*penkʷe
6	s'ēᴴ		séᴴ		*sụeh	*sụeχs	*sụek̂s
7	s'eχtᴺ		sechtᴺ		*seχtev	*sextam	*septm̥
8	oχtᴺ		ochtᴺ		*oχtev «	*oχtū («?)	*h₂ok̂toh₁u
9	noịᴺ		noíᴺ		*noụev	*noụan	*h₁neụn̥
10	d'eχ'ᴺ		deichᴺ		*deχev	*dekam «	*dek̂m̥t

Illustration 24.1: The cardinal numbers

Note the following peculiarities in the use of these numbers:

1. Unlike adjectives, cardinal numerals always stand before the word they qualify.

2. The singular of the counted word is used after *óen-, oín-* (which means also after 11, 21, 31, etc.). The dual is used after *dá, dí* (which means also after 12, 22, 32, etc.). The plural is used after the numerals 3–10 and after 13–19, 23–29, 33–39, etc.

3. The numeral *óen-, oín-* '1' is always compounded with the word it counts, causing lenition in this process: *óencháera* 'one sheep,' *óenchíall* 'one sense.'

4. The numbers 2, 3 and 4 are inflected together with the noun they qualify. For the inflection of '2' (OIr. masc. neut. *da, dá* < CC **doụo* < PIE **duụo(h₁)*; OIr. fem. *di, dí* < CC **dụē* < PIE **dụeị?*), compare the dual sections of the respective declensional classes.

5. The inflection of '3' and '4' goes as follows (I do not reconstruct feminine forms as their prehistory is highly problematic):

3	transcr.	Old Irish	Prim. Irish	Com. Celtic	PIE
masc. nom.	t'r'i^H	tri^H	*trīh	*trii̯es	*tréi̯es
neut. nom. acc.	t'r'i^L t'r'e^L	tri^L (tre^L) «	*trii̯ā	*trii̯ā «	*tríh$_2$
gen.	t'r'i^N t'r'e^N	tri^N (tré^N) «	*trii̯av	*trii̯om	*tréi̯om, *trii̯óm
prep.	t'r'iβ'	trib	*triβih	*tribis «	*tribʰí, tribʰ(i)ós
masc. acc.	t'r'i^H	tri^H	*trīh	*trīs	*tríns
fem. nom.	t'eu̯p' t'eu̯pa^H	teoir, teuir, téora^H			*tisrés
gen.	t'eu̯pa^N	téora^N			*tisróm
prep.	t'eu̯pəβ'	téoraib			*tisr̥bʰí, -bʰ(i)ós
acc.	t'eu̯pa^H	téora^H			*tisr̥ńs

Illustration 24.2: The inflection of the cardinal '3'

4	transcription	Old Irish	Prim. Irish	Com. Celtic	PIE
masc. nom.	k'eθəp'	cethair	*kʷeθu̯opeh	*kʷetu̯ores	*kʷetu̯óres
n. nom. acc.	k'eθəp'^{L}	cethair^L «	*kʷeθupā	*kʷeturā «	*kʷetu̯ōr
gen.	k'eθ'p'e^N	ceithre^N	*kʷeθupii̯av «	*kʷeturom	*kʷeturóm
prep.	k'eθ'p'əβ'	ceithrib	*kʷeθupiβih «	*kʷetrubis «	*kʷetrubʰí, -ubʰ(i)ós
acc.	k'eθ'p'i^H	cethri^H	*kʷeθupīh «	*kʷeturās	*kʷeturńs
fem. nom.	k'eθ'eu̯p' k'eθ'eu̯pa^H	cethéoir, cethéora^H			*kʷétesres
gen.	k'eθ'eu̯pa^N	cethéora^N			*kʷétesrom
prep.	k'eθ'eu̯pəβ'	cethéoraib			kʷétesr̥bʰi, -bʰ(i)os
acc.	k'eθ'eu̯pa^H	cethéora^H			*kʷétesrńs

Illustration 24.3: The inflection of the cardinal '4'

6. The numbers 5–10 are not inflected. Note, however, the mutational effects of the numbers. *cóic* '5' and *sé* '6' nasalize the following word when used in genitival position.

7. The 'teens' (the numbers 11–19) are formed by adding the word *deac, deec* /d'eəg/, later *déc* /d'ēg/ '-teen' (< Prim. Ir. *dehegav < *deχēgav < *dekenkom < CC *dekam-kom 'with ten') after the counted word: e.g., *dá lae deac* 'twelve days,' *téoir aidchi deac* 'thirteen nights,' *a ocht deac* /a hoχt d'eəg/ 'eighteen,' etc.

8. When the cardinal numbers are used on their own as substantives (that is without counting an object), the particle *a^H* precedes them. In this case *óen* can be used on its own without being compounded to another word; instead of *dá, dí* the form *dáu, dó* is used: *a óen* /a hoi̯v/ 'one,' *a dáu, a dó* /a dau̯ a dō/ 'two,' *a trí, a cethair, a cóic, a sé, a secht, a ocht* /a hoχt/, *a noí, a deich*.

9. The cardinal numbers cannot be used to count people. For this purpose a separate numeral series exists, which we will learn in a later lesson.

24.2. The ordinal numbers 1–19

Ordinal numbers are those forms of the numerals that are used to specify the order of elements, e.g., in English *first, second, third* etc.

Ordinal numbers basically behave like adjectives, in that they conform in case, number and gender with the words they qualify. *Cétnae, aile* and *tánaise* inflect as i̯o-, i̯ā-adjectives, all others as o-, ā-adjectives. But unlike normal adjectives, ordinal numbers *precede* the word they qualify, e.g., *in chethramad rann* 'the fourth part,' *in seissed lebor* 'the sixth book.' The only exceptions are *cét-*, which is compounded with the word it qualifies (e.g., *cétadaig* 'first night,' *cétmuinter* /kʼēdµunʼtʼəp/ 'first wife'; cp. Gaulish *Cintugnatos* 'first born'), and *tánaise* and occasionally *aile*, which follow the words they qualify. As you can see in the reconstructions below, a large amount of restructuring has taken place in these words.

nr.		Old Irish	Prim. Irish	Proto-Celtic	PIE
1	kʼēd- kʼēdve	*cét-, cétnae*	kēdu-, kēdavii̯ah	kɪntu-, kɪntanii̯os	-
2	tāvəsʼe aλʼe	*tánaise, aile*	taδvihessii̯ah, aλii̯ah	tʼadnisetsii̯os, alii̯os	*h₂élii̯os
3	tʼrʼis tʼrʼes	*tris(s), tres(s)*	trisah («)	tristos, trit(ii̯)os «	*trih₂ós
4	kʼeθpəµəδ	*cethramad*	kᵘeθupaµeθah «	kᵘetu̯arii̯os «	*kᵘturih₂ós
5	kōgʼəδ	*cóiced*	kᵘōgᵘeθah «	kᵘɪnkᵘetos «	*pn̥kᵘtós
6	sʼesʼəδ	*seissed*	su̯eseθah «	su̯eχsos «	*suk̂sh₂ós
7	sʼeχtµəδ	*sechtmad*	seχtaµeθah «	seχtametos «	*septm̥h₂ós
8	oχtµəδ	*ochtmad*	oχtaµeθah «	oχtūmetos «	*h₂ok̂th₁uh₂ós
9	nōµəδ	*nómad*	nou̯aµeθah «	nou̯ametos «	*h₁nun̥h₂ós
10	dʼeχµəδ	*dechmad*	deχaµeθah «	dekametos «	*dek̂m̥h₂ós
11	oi̯vµəδ … dʼeäg	*óenmad … deac*	oi̯vaµeθah	oi̯nometos	-

Illustration 24.4: The ordinal numbers

The ordinal numbers 12–19 are formed by adding *deac* /dʼeäg/ after the word qualified: e.g., *ind aile ingen deac* 'the twelfth girl,' *in tress lóech deac* 'the thirteenth warrior.'

Illustration 24.5:
cétnae etir chomthromma
'primus inter pares'

24.3. The copula

We have dealt with two weak verbal classes and three strong verbal classes so far. There are still three further classes to look at. We will learn them in the next lesson. Completely outside of the system of verbal classes stands one very important, but in many languages notoriously irregular, word: the *copula*, that is, the verb 'to be.' Now, first of all, you cannot talk about the verb 'to be' simply like that in Old Irish. A statement like *ich bin* in German or *I am* in English can be rendered by three different verbs in Old Irish, depending on exactly what I mean. Do I want to speak about some characteristic trait of mine that is part of my very individuality and existence, or do I want to speak about a momentary condition, or do I want to speak about a regular condition? In the first case in Old Irish I would have to use the copula, in the second case the *substantive verb*, and in the third case the *habitual* variant of the substantive verb.[1] We will look at the copula first. I will talk about the substantive verb in the next lesson.

The copula is used to form a connection between a subject and its predicate, that is, it is used to make an equation between the subject and another word, noun or adjective. Examples for this use would be: *am Duid-se* 'I am David' (that is true for me for all of my life, and there is no other David like me; or as a response to someone calling me 'Daniel'), *is mór in trúaige* 'the sorrow is great' (it is a characteristic of this particular sorrow that it is great and unbearable), *at ben dánae* 'thou art a bold woman' (a characteristic trait of your nature), *it insi Ériu 7 Albu* 'Ireland and Britain are islands' (won't change for a couple of more years).

However, in cases where existence, presence, a condition or a state is meant, the copula cannot be used: statements like 'I think, therefore I am,' 'you are here,' 'she is with child' or 'we are in rage' call for the use of the substantive verb. But the substantive verb may apparently also always be employed instead of the copula, especially when the predicate does—for whatever reason—not immediately follow the verb (see paragraph 2 below), e.g., *biid duine slán 7 fírián* 'man is sound and righteous' for normal **is slán 7 fírián duine* (*Wb.* 4d33).

> The following hints may serve as a rough guideline: wherever a connection with a noun or adjective is made, usually the copula is used; wherever a connection between a noun and a prepositional phrase is made, the substantive verb is used.
> Or: wherever you can put an equal sign '=' between words or between two statements, the copula has to be used.

There are some peculiarities in the use of the copula:

1. No form of the copula, either absolute or conjunct, is ever accented. The copula is enclitic, that is, it merges with preceding sentence particles or conjunctions where possible.

2. The word order in normal predicative sentences of the type *X is Y* diverges from German or English. Whereas in the latter the word order is SCP (subject S – copula C – predicate P), e.g., *Hans* (S) *ist* (C) *ein Mann* (P) or *Mary* (S) *is* (C) *a woman* (P), the word order in Old Irish is CPS. That means that the predicate immediately follows the copula and the subject is placed at the very end of the statement: *is* (V) *fer* (P) *Éoin* (S) 'John is a man,' *is* (V) *ben* (P) *Maire* (S) 'Mary is a woman.'

---

[1] The distinction between the copula and the substantive verb is not peculiar to Old Irish. A very similar distinction exists in Spanish with its two verbs *ser* = copula and *estar* = substantive verb. The copula and the *uerbum substantiuum* in Old Irish and Spanish match perfectly from an etymological point of view: both *ser* in Spanish and *is* in Old Irish go back to the PIE root √*h₁es* 'to be,' and both *estar* and *at·tá* go back to the root √*steh₂* 'to stand.' But this is only a coincidence and does not go back to a common Indo-European distinction between the two functions of 'to be.'

3. A very frequent use of the copula is to stress a certain part of the sentence by placing it at the beginning of the sentence and introducing it with the copula, with the rest of the sentence following in a relative construction. For example, a normal, unmarked sentence would be: *benaid in manach in clocc i n-aidchi* 'the monk rings the bell in the night.' Now I can front any of the constituent elements of the sentence:

Is i n-aidchi benaid in manach in clocc 'it is in the night, that the monk rings the bell' or: 'the monk rings the bell *in the night.*'

Is in manach benas² in clocc i n-aidchi 'it is the monk who rings the bell in the night' or: '*the monk* rings the bell in the night.'

Is in clocc benas in manach i n-aidchi 'it is the bell that the monk rings in the night' or 'the monk rings *the bell* in the night.'

Is béimm in chluicc do·gní in manach i n-aidchi 'it is ringing the bell that the monk makes in the night' or 'the monk *rings* the bell in the night.'

Illustration 24.6:
is dall in cháera-so
'this sheep is blind'

4. Pronouncing the stressed part of the sentence louder and with more emphasis, as is usual in German and English and expressed by the use of *italics* in writing, is not possible in Old Irish! If you want to stress a word or phrase, it has to be fronted to the beginning of the sentence. The copula may also be left away in these cases: *I n-aidchi benaid in manach in clocc* 'in the night the monk rings the bell' or: 'the monk rings the bell *in the night.*'

24.3.1. Independent forms of the copula

Independent and dependent forms of the copula look very different from each other, so we will have to go through them one by one:

person	Old Irish	Prim. Ir.	Proto-Celtic	PIE
		absolute	(independent)	
1st sg.	*am*	*emi	*emmi	*h₁ésmi
2nd sg.	*it, at* «	*ihi	*esi	*h₁ési
3rd sg.	*is*	*isi	*esti	*h₁ésti
1st pl.	*ammi(n)* «	*emohi	*emmosi «	*h₁smés
2nd pl.	*adi(b)* «	*eðihi «	*etesi «	*h₁sté
3rd pl.	*it*	*idi	*(s)ınti («)	*h₁sénti

Illustration 24.7: The absolute inflection of the copula

Note:

1. The reconstructions, morphological and phonetical changes and explanations offered above and in the tables below are highly conjectural. I do not claim any reliability for them.

2. In the 2nd sg. absolute *it, at* the *t* has been added to the expected form **i* in analogy to the conjugated prepositions and/or the infixed pronouns, according to the proportion

pronominal 1st sg. *-m* : 2nd sg. *-t* = copula 1st sg. *am* : X (X = *at, it*).

---

² *Benas* is a relative form of the verb *benaid*. Don't worry about it now; you will learn it soon enough.

The same explanation is true for the -n of 1st pl. *ammin* and the -b of 2nd pl. *adib*.

24.3.2. Dependent forms of the copula

The dependent forms of the copula go as follows:

person	Old Irish	Prim. Ir.	Insular Celtic	Proto-Celtic
		conjunct (dependent)		
1st sg.	-da^L «	*-d/δem	*-d/δ'em	*-de emmi
2nd sg.	-da^L «	*-d/δeh	*-d/δ'eh	*-de esi
3rd sg.	-t, -id, -did	*-d/δih	*-d/δ'iss	*-de esti
1st pl.	-dan^L «	*-d/δemah	*-d/δ'emoh	*-de emmosi
2nd pl.	-dad^L «	*-d/δeδih «	*-d/δ'eθih	*-de etesi
3rd pl.	-dat^L «	*-d/δid	*-d/δ'ɪnt	*-de ɪnti

Illustration 24.8: The conjunct inflection of the copula

Note:

1. I have no explanation why the conjunct forms (except for the 3rd sg. forms) lenite.

2. The conjunct forms are added directly to a preceding particle or conjunction. For example, together with the interrogative particle *in*^N this gives forms like 1st sg. *inda*^L 'am I?,' 2nd sg. *inda*^L 'art thou?,' 3rd pl. *indan*^L 'are we?', etc. The interrogative of the 3rd sg. of the copula is simply *in*^N 'is he, is she, is it?' The negated forms of the copula, 'I am not,' 'she is not,' etc., are special:

person	Old Irish	Prim. Ir.	Insular Celtic	Proto-Celtic
		negated		
1st sg.	*níta*^L, -da^L «	*nīδ(i)δem «	*nītiδ'em	*ne eti de emmi
2nd sg.	*níta*^L, -da^L «	*nīδ(i)δeh «	*nītiδ'eh	*ne eti de esi
3rd sg.	*ní*^H	*nīh	*nīss	*ne esti
1st pl.	*nítan*^L, -dan^L «	*nīδ(i)δemah «	*nītiδ'emoh	*ne eti de emmosi
2nd pl.	*nítad*^L, -dad^L «	*nīδ(i)δeδih «	*nītiδ'eθih	*ne eti de etesi
3rd pl.	*nítat*^L, -dat^L «	*nīδ(i)δid «	*nītiδ'ɪnt	*ne eti de (s)ɪnti

Illustration 24.9: The negative inflection of the copula

3. After the conjunctions *cía* 'although' and *má* 'if,' special forms of the 3rd persons are used: 3rd sg. *cíasu*^L, *cíaso*^L, *ceso*^L, *cesu*^L, neg. *cenid*, 3rd pl. *ceto*^L, *cetu*^L; 3rd sg. *maso*^L, *masu*^L, neg. *manid*, 3rd pl. *matu*^L.

You can find all forms of the copula in Appendix F.12.

Lesson 25

25.1. Infixed pronouns class A

I already mentioned earlier that Old Irish basically has no independent personal pronouns. In 18.1. we learned what strategy the language uses to express a sequence of preposition and personal pronoun: the prepositions are actually 'inflected' or 'conjugated' like verbs. Now we will look at the way Old Irish expresses things like German *ich liebe dich* or English *she/he loves me not*, i.e., cases where object pronouns (most often in the accusative case, but sometimes also with datival meaning) are dependent on verbs. The strategy used is to *infix* (= to put into) the pronominal forms right into the middle of the verbs they are dependent on. Therefore they are called *infixed pronouns*.

Let's take the S2 verb *fo·gaib* 'to find,' for example. Imagine a game of hide-and-seek. Things like the following could be said during the game (note that the ending = the subject of the verb, and the infixed pronoun = the object of the verb, are totally independent from an-  other): *fom·gaib* /fom·ɣaβ'/ 'he finds me,' *fos·ngaibiu* /fos·ŋgaβ'u/ 'I find her,' *fob·gaibem* /foβ·gaβ'əµ/ 'we find you,' *fot·gaibet* /fod·ɣaβ'əd/ 'they find thee.' Other participants of the game could be more successfully hiding, and things like the following could be said (note the regular use of the prototonic variant of the verb after the negative particle and the infixation of the pronoun immediately after the negative particle): *ním·fagbai* /n'ĩm·aɣβi/ 'thou dost not find me,' *ní·fagaib* /n'ɪ·βaɣaβ'/ 'she does not find him,' *nínn·fagbaid* /n'ɪn·faɣβəδ'/ 'you do not find us,' *nís·fagaib* /n'ɪs·faɣaβ/ 'he does not find them.'

The basic idea should be clear. But of course Old Irish wouldn't be Old Irish if matters weren't a little bit more complicated altogether.

1. There are different sets of infixed pronouns in Old Irish, their use depending on phonetical and syntactical factors. What we are talking about in this lesson are the so-called class A pronouns. These are used after preverbs and particles that historically ended in vowels. These comprise the preverbs *ro·*, *do·* (< *to*), *do·* (< *dí*), *fo·*, *ar·* (< *are*) and *imm·* (< *imbi*), and the particles *no·* and *ní·*.

Illustration 25.1:
Fob·géb, fob·géb!
'I'll find you, I'll find you!'

2. The pronouns are always infixed after the first particle in a verbal form. That means that in deuterotonic forms of compound verbs the pronoun is infixed after the first preverb (cf. *fom·gaib* above). In prototonic forms of compound verbs and in conjunct forms of simple verbs the pronoun is infixed immediately after the conjunct particle (cf. *ním·fagbai* above, or *ním·gaib* 'he doesn't take me').

3. If a pronoun is to be infixed into an independent simple verb, which *per se*, of course, has no particle in front of it, the meaningless and 'empty' particle *no·* has to be put before the verb. The pronoun is infixed after this particle, but of course the inflection of the simple verb has to

122

change from absolute to conjunct. For example, W1 3rd sg. absolute *caraid* means 'he loves.' If I want to say 'he loves her' I have to use the empty particle *no·*, unto which I then stick the infixed 3rd sg. feminine pronoun *-s^N*. At the same time I change the verb to conjunct inflection (because now a particle stands in front of it): *nos·cara* /nos·gapa/ 'he loves her.' If, however, a conjunct particle (like negative *ní·*) already stands before the verb, the pronoun simply has to be infixed according to the normal rules: *ní·cara* /n'ī·kapa/ 'she does not love,' but *nít·chara* /n'īd·χapa/ 'she does not love thee.'

4. The infixed pronouns class A are usually simply added to the final vowel of the preverb or particle: *do·* + 2nd pl. *-b* > *dob·*, *fo·* + 2nd sg. *-t^L* > *fot^L·*, *ní·* + 3rd sg. fem. *-s^N* > *nís^N·*, etc. Those two preverbs, however, which do not show a vowel in their standard form (*ar·* and *imm·*), add a vowel between preverb and pronoun: 1st sg. *arum·, arom·, aram·*, 2nd sg. *arat·*, 1st pl. *arun·, arin·*, 2nd pl. *arub·, arob·*; 1st sg. *immum·, immim·*, 1st pl. *immun(n)·, imman(n)·*, 3rd pl. *immus·*.

The 3rd sg. pronouns masc. *-a^N* and neuter *-a^L* behave differently. In preverbs and particles that end in *-o* they replace (elide) the *-o*: *do·* + *-a^{N/L}* > *da^{N/L}·*, *no·* + *-a^{N/L}* > *na^{N/L}·*, etc. With *ar·* and *imm·* we get *ara^{N/L}·* and *imma^{N/L}·* (and older *are^{N/L}·* and *imme^{N/L}·*). After *ní·*, however, *-a^{N/L}* disappears, only the mutational effects remain: *ní·* + *-a^{N/L}* > *ní^{N/L}·*!

5. The infixed pronouns have various mutational effects. 1st sg. *-m* and 2nd sg. *-t* lenite. 3rd sg. feminine and 3rd pl. *-s* may or may not nasalize. Historically the 3rd sg. feminine nasalized, the 3rd pl. aspirated. At the time of classical Old Irish the original distribution had become completely obscured and both options are viable for both persons. 1st pl. *-nn* and 2nd pl. *-b* have no effect. The 3rd sg. masculine *-a* nasalizes, the 3rd sg. neuter *-a* lenites. In the case of the 3rd persons do not mix up the mutational effects of the infixed pronouns with the different mutational effects of the possessive pronouns!

6. Because of the lack in Old Irish of special reflexive pronouns (e.g., German *sich*, the English forms in *-self*, Latin *sui, sibi, se*, etc.), the infixed pronouns cannot only be used to refer to an object, but also to the subject of the sentence. This can lead to ambiguous sentences like *na·mmarba* 'he kills him,' but also 'he kills himself.'

Infixed pronouns are nothing exotic at all. They are just a variant of the enclitic use of pronouns, which is very widespread among many languages like French *je t'aime* 'I love you' (*je aime* 'I love' + enclitic *t'* 'thee'), or Spanish *dígamelo* 'tell it to me' (*diga* 'tell' + enclitic *-me* 'to me' + enclitic *-lo* 'it') or Austrian German *wannstn gsiagst* 'when you see him' (conjugated conjunction[1] *wannst* 'when thou' + enclitic *-n* 'him').

---

[1] The conjugated conjunctions of Austrian German are even more outlandish than the conjugated prepositions of Old Irish!

person	translation	pronoun	
		class A	
1st sg.	me	-m^L, -mm^L	/m^L/
2nd sg.	thee	-t^L	/d^L/
3rd sg. masc.	him	-a^N	/a^N/
3rd sg. fem.	her	-s^(N)	/s^(N)/
3rd sg. neutr.	it	-a^L	/a^L/
1st pl.	us	-n, -nn	/n/
2nd pl.	you	-b	/β/
3rd pl.	them	-s^(N)	/s^(N)/

Illustration 25.2: The infixed pronouns class A

You'll find a survey of all infixed pronouns in Appendix F.4. Below follow two model paradigms for the use of infixed pronouns: one for the compound S2 verb *fo·gaib, ·fagaib* 'to find,' the other for the simple W1 verb *caraid, ·cara* 'to love.' For variation's sake I will use different persons in the verbal endings (1st sg., 3rd sg., 1st pl., 3rd pl.). Note the various ambiguous cases, where the infixed pronouns can also be understood with reflexive meaning.

pronoun	Old Irish	transcription	translation
	independent (deuterotonic)		
1st sg.	*fom·gaibiu*	/fom·γaβ'u/	I find me (myself)
2nd sg.	*fot·gaibiu*	/fod·γaβ'u/	I find thee
3rd sg. m.	*fa·ngaibiu*	/fa·ŋgaβ'u/	I find him
3rd sg. f.	*fos·(n)gaibiu*	/fos·ŋgaβ'u, fos·gaβ'u/	I find her
3rd sg. n.	*fa·gaibiu*	/fa·γaβ'u/	I find it
1st pl.	*fonn·gaibiu*	/fon·gaβ'u/	I find us
2nd pl.	*fob·gaibiu*	/foβ·gaβ'u/	I find you
3rd pl.	*fos·(n)gaibiu*	/fos·gaβ'u, fos·ŋgaβ'u/	I find them

Illustration 25.3: Paradigm of infixed pronouns class A with *fo·gaib*

Illustration 25.4: *Not·charaimm!* 'I love you'

pronoun	Old Irish	transcription	translation
dependent (prototonic)			
1st sg.	ním·fagaib	/n'ɪm·aɣəβ'/	he does not find me
2nd sg.	nít·fagaib	/n'ɪd·aɣəβ'/	he does not find thee
3rd sg. m.	ní·fagaib	/n'ɪ·βaɣəβ'/	he does not find him (himself)
3rd sg. f.	nís·fagaib	/n'ɪs·βaɣəβ', n'ɪs·faɣəβ'/	he does not find her
3rd sg. n.	ní·fagaib	/n'ɪ·aɣəβ'/	he does not find it
1st pl.	nínn·fagaib	/n'ɪn·faɣəβ'/	he does not find us
2nd pl.	níb·fagaib	/n'ɪβ·faɣəβ'/	he does not find you
3rd pl.	nís·fagaib	/n'ɪs·faɣəβ', n'ɪs·βaɣəβ'/	he does not find them

Illustration 25.5: Paradigm of infixed pronouns class A with fo·gaib

pronoun	Old Irish	transcription	translation
independent (particle no·, conjunct)			
1st sg.	nom·charam	/nom·χaρəμ/	we love me
2nd sg.	not·charam	/nod·χaρəμ/	we love thee
3rd sg. m.	na·caram	/na·gaρəμ/	we love him
3rd sg. f.	nos·caram	/nos·gaρəμ nos·kaρəμ/	we love her
3rd sg. n.	na·charam	/na·χaρəμ/	we love it
1st pl.	nonn·caram	/non·kaρəμ/	we love us (ourselves)
2nd pl.	nob·caram	/noβ·kaρəμ/	we love you
3rd pl.	nos·caram	/nos·kaρəμ nos·gaρəμ/	we love them

Illustration 25.6: Paradigm of infixed pronouns class A with caraid

pronoun	Old Irish	transcription	translation
dependent (conjunct)			
1st sg.	ním·charat	/n'ɪm·χaρəd/	they do not love me
2nd sg.	nít·charat	/n'ɪd·χaρəd/	they do not love thee
3rd sg. m.	ní·carat	/n'ɪ·gaρəd/	they do not love him
3rd sg. f.	nís·carat	/n'ɪs·gaρəd n'ɪs·kaρəd/	they do not love her
3rd sg. n.	ní·charat	/n'ɪ·χaρəd/	they do not love it
1st pl.	nínn·carat	/n'ɪn·kaρəd/	they do not love us
2nd pl.	níb·carat	/n'ɪβ·kaρəd/	they do not love you
3rd pl.	nís·carat	/n'ɪs·kaρəd n'ɪs·gaρəd/	they do not love them (themselves)

Illustration 25.7: Paradigm of infixed pronouns class A with caraid

25.2. Exercise

Use all possible pronouns of class A with the following verbal forms:

do·cil /do·kʼiƛ'/ (S1) 'thou hidest'
ní·léicet /n'ī·l'ēg'əd/ (W2) 'they do not let'
do·scara /do·skaρa/ (W1) '(s)he overthrows'
ní·taibrem /n'ī·taβ'ρ'əμ/ (S1) 'we do not bring'
renaimm /r'evəm'/ (S3) 'I sell'
gairthe /gaρ'θ'e/ (S2) 'you call'

25.3. Conjugated prepositions 3

In this lesson you will learn six new conjugated pronouns: two that take the prepositional and four that take the accusative. Often certain persons are not attested at all; in these cases their slots are left free. Certain forms are only attested relatively late. I will not, however, specially mark these younger forms.

In the accusatival pronominal forms the 3rd sg. feminine and 3rd pl. forms show a divergent behavior from the other persons. The former two have voiceless consonants before their ending (e.g., *cuicce* /kukʼe/, *impu* /imρu/ etc.); the latter have voiced consonants (e.g., *cuccum* /kugum/, *imbi* /imʼbʼi/ etc.). We had the same difference already in 21.1, e.g., between 3rd sg. fem. *inte* /inʼťe/ and 3rd sg. masc. neut. *ind* /inʼd'/. The same difference exists between lenited *r* (e.g., 1st sg. *airium* /aρ'um/) and unlenited *rr* (e.g., 3rd pl. *airriu* /ar'u/).

1. Conjugated prepositions with the prepositional:

| person | *aᴴ* 'out of' | | *fíadᴸ* 'in the presence of' | |
	ending	transcription	ending	transcription
1st sg.	asum	/asum/	fíadam, fíadum	/fʼiaδəm fʼiaδum/
2nd sg.	essiut	/esʼud/	fíadut	/fʼiaδud/
3rd sg. m., n.	ass, as	/as/	fíado, fíada	/fʼiaδo fʼiaδa/
3rd sg. f.	eissi, eisti	/esʼi esʼťi/	n/a	
1st pl.	n/a		n/a	
2nd pl.	n/a		fíadib	/fʼiaδəβ'/
3rd pl.	eissib, eistib	/esʼəβ' esʼťəβ'/	fíadib, fíadaib	/fʼiaδəβ'/

Illustration 25.8: The conjugated prepositions 3: *aᴴ*, *fíadᴸ*

2. Conjugated prepositions with the accusative:

person	co^H 'to'		eter^L 'between'	
	ending	transcription	ending	transcription
1st sg.	cuccum	/kuɡum/	etrom, etrum	/edρəm edρum/
2nd sg.	cuc(c)ut	/kuɡud/	etrut	/edρud/
3rd sg. m., n.	cuc(c)i, cuccai	/kuɡi/	etir, itir	/ed'əρ' id'əρ'/
3rd sg. f.	cuicce, cuccae	/kuk'e kuke/	n/a	
1st pl.	cucunn	/kuɡun/	etronn, etrunn	/edρən edρun/
2nd pl.	cuc(c)uib	/kuɡuβ'/	etruib	/edρəβ'/
3rd pl.	cuccu	/kuku/	etarru, etarro	/etəru etəro/

Illustration 25.9: The conjugated prepositions 3: co^H, eter

person	imm^L 'around about'		tar 'over, across, beyond'	
	ending	transcription	ending	transcription
1st sg.	immum	/imum/	torom, torum	/toρəm toρum/
2nd sg.	immut	/imud/	torut	/toρud/
3rd sg. m., n.	imbi, immi	/im'b'i im'i/	tarais	/taρəs'/
3rd sg. f.	impe	/im'p'e/	tairsi, tairse	/taρ's'i taρ's'e/
1st pl.	immunn	/imun/	torunn	/toρun/
2nd pl.	immib	/im'əβ'/	toraib	/toρəβ'/
3rd pl.	impu, impo	/impu impo/	tairsiu	/taρ's'u/

Illustration 25.10: The conjugated prepositions 3: imm^L, tar

25.4. Emphasizing particles

If you want to stress pronominal forms in English or German, you can do this by uttering the pronoun in question with more emphasis, that is, louder and stronger. In writing this emphatic pronunciation is often rendered by *italics*, e.g., 'I love you (and not this guy with the Ferrari—he just wants your sex)' or 'I love *you* (and not this long-legged blonde)' or 'Das ist *mein* Sitzplatz (und nicht Ihrer, Sie haben sich vorgedrängt).'[2]

This option, however, does not exist in Old Irish. In Old Irish all pronominal forms are un-stressed (with one exception, which we will learn in a later lesson), and therefore it is of course not possible to pronounce them with more emphasis. Instead, enclitic particles, so-called *empha-sizing particles*, have to be added, very much like the enclitic particles we met in 21.3 about demonstrative particles.

---

2 Excuse my use of drastic language, but this often helps to make things clearer in grammatical explanations.

Where in the table below more than one form is given, the variants before the semicolon are used after words ending in a non-palatalized consonant or in the vowels *a, o,* or *u;* those after the semicolon are used after words ending in a palatalized consonant or in the vowels *e* or *i.* Throughout this course I will separate the particles from the word they are attached to by a hyphen <->.

person	emphasizing particle	
1st sg.	*-sa; -se, -sea*	/sa/ /s'e s'a/
2nd sg.	*-so, -su; -siu*	/so su/ /s'u/
3rd sg. masc.	*-som, -sam; -sem, -sium, -seom*	/soμ saμ/ /s'eμ s'uμ s'oμ/
3rd sg. fem.	*-si*	/s'i/
3rd sg. neutr.	*-som, -sam; -sem, -sium, -seom*	/soμ saμ/ /s'eμ s'uμ s'oμ/
1st pl.	*-ni*	/n'i/
2nd pl.	*-si*	/s'i/
3rd pl.	*-som, -sam; -sem, -sium, -seom*	/soμ saμ/ /s'eμ s'uμ s'oμ/

Illustration 25.11: The emphasizing particles

The enclitic emphasizing particles have to follow another accented word. Since the pronouns that have to be emphasized themselves are unaccented this practically means that emphasizing particles immediately follow the next accented word after the pronoun. Although both the pronominal form and the emphasizing particle remain unstressed, the whole construction is equivalent to a strongly stressed form in English or German.

Emphasizing particles can emphasize any pronominal form.

   1. They can emphasize subjects (= inflectional endings) and objects (= infixed pronouns) of verbal forms: *not·charaimm-se* 'I love thee,' *not·charaimm-siu* 'I love *thee,*' *nom·charai-siu* '*thou* lovest me,' *nom·charai-se* 'thou lovest *me.*'

   2. They can emphasize possessive pronouns: *a lám-som* '*his* hand,' *inna láim-sem* 'in *his* hand' (*innaL* = *iN* + *aL*), *a catt-si* '*her* cat,' *dia cattaib-si* 'for *her* cats' (*diaH* = *doL* + *aH*).

   3. They can emphasize conjugated prepositions: *leis-sem* 'with *it,*' *dún-ni* 'for *us,*' *díb-si* 'from *you,*' *forru-som* 'upon *them.*' Sometimes a form changes a bit when emphasized, e.g., 3rd sg. masc. *dó* 'for him' becomes *do-som* 'for *him*' with short *o.*

Emphasizing particles are important to distinguish between forms that otherwise would be ambiguous: e.g., *a ech* could either mean 'his horse' /a eχ/ or 'her horse' /a h'eχ/, *a ech-som* makes it clear that it is 'his horse'; 3rd sg. *ásaid* could either mean 'he grows,' 'she grows' or 'it grows,' *ásaid-si* makes it clear that we are talking about a feminine subject; *nos·caraimm* could either mean 'I love her' or 'I love them,' *nos·caraimm-seom* 'I love *them*' makes it clear that I am in a moral dilemma.

Emphasizing pronouns are frequently used to contrast two persons: *nom·charai-siu, acht nít·charaimm-se* '*thou* lovest me, but *I* do not love thee,' or *is mór ar slúag-ni, acht is lobur for slúag-si* '*our* army is big, but *your* army is weak.'

Lesson 26

26.1. Test

Emphasize the pronominal forms in the following words:

immum:	_____	*cuicce:*	_____	*etarru:*	_____
friss:	_____	*torunn:*	_____	*dúib:*	_____
latt:	_____	*fair:*	_____	*imbi:*	_____
leis:	_____	*mo chos:*	_____	*do maicc:*	_____
ar n-echu:	_____	*a argat:*	_____	or	_____
for ngáire:	_____	*a túath:*	_____	or	_____
a fir:	_____ or	_____	or	_____
nos·crenaimm:	_____ or	_____	or	_____
nínn·feid:	_____ or	_____	or	_____
nít·glanat:	_____ or	_____		
na·mbenai:	_____ or	_____		
immum·agaid:	_____ or	_____		
níb·taibrem:	_____ or	_____		
da·beirid:	_____ or	_____		
fot·daimet:	_____ or	_____		

Illustration 26.1: *nonn·celam-ni* 'we hide ourselves'

26.2. Varia

1. The demonstrative particles *-so* and *-sin* (see 21.3) can be used with the article alone. They are stressed on the second syllable and are used like substantives: *in-so* 'this' (referring to present place and time), *in-sin* 'that' (anaphorically referring to something already mentioned); e.g., *as·beir-si in-so* 'she says this,' or *(is) airde serce móire in-sin* 'that (= what I was talking about) is a sign of great love' (*Wb.* 24c2). Together with the adverb *sís* /s'īs/ 'down below' *in-so* is sometimes used in the title of stories, e.g., *Immram Brain 7 a Echtrae in-so sís* 'The Voyage of Bran and his Adventure (follow) down here.'

2. Neuter adjectives can be used as substantives. They can then either have the meaning of a neuter abstract noun, e.g., *mór* (o, n) 'something big = a great amount, a lot,' *becc* (o, n) 'something little = little amount' (sentence 11 of the exercise), or sometimes they come to signify a concrete object, e.g., *dub* (u, n) 'something black = ink' (sentence 20 of the exercise).

3. We will meet our first Old Irish conjunctions in this exercise. Conjunctions are words that connect a dependent clause with a main clause. These are words like *while, after, because, that,* etc. in English or *weil, nachdem, damit, dass,* etc. in German. Conjunctions can be very tricky in their construction in Old Irish, but the two examples in this lesson are simple in their use: after the causal conjunction *ar^L, air^L* 'because, since, for' and after connective *sech* 'and moreover' a normal independent form of the verb is used.

26.3. Exercise

Old Irish

1. Fo·gaibi-siu ubla isind fid 7 nos·biur-sa [*or* nos·mbiur-sa] cosin rrígnai. Is i mmedón ind feda fos·gaibi (*or* fos·ngaibi). 2. * Benaid-seom [= Cú Chulainn] a cethair cenn diib 7 fos· ceird for ceithéora benna inna gablae. (TBC 334 f.) 3. Níb·caram-si, á áes catha, 7 is úath dún-ni cumachtae for claideb. 4. Crenaid in cennaige glicc fid ndarae ar théoraib cumalaib, acht na·rren frisna rrígnai ar cheithéoraib cumalaib. 5. It móra aslacha in betha 7 ammi cimbithi-ni doaib-sem. 6. ** Ní ar formut frib-si as·biur-sa in-so. (*Wb.* 12c29) 7. ** Níta chummae-se friu-som. (*Wb.* 20c25) 8. * It fáilti inna ingena oc techt Beltaini. (GT 49) 9. * Is deithbir dom-sa brón, sech am tróg, am sentuinne. (GT 49) 10. ** Is becc, is líath mo thrilis, ní líach drochcaille tarais. (GT 49) 11. ** Techt do Róim, mór sáetho, becc torbai. (*Thes.* ii 296.3-4) 12. Do·linat tri srothae folo a tóeb ind loích 7 asa láim 7 asa chiunn íarna guin. 13. Is dorchae int uile bith 7 is lán de rúnaib isind aidchi. 14. Ním·gaib format frit-su, á fir saidbir, ar is aire tromm duit indeb mór. 15. * Fúachaid-sem a rosc fri fál inna frega, fúachaimm-se mo rosc réil fri féigi ind fessa. (*Thes.* ii 293.22 ff.) 16. Cóic lae 7 sé aidchi tíagait-sem tar druimm in mora, 7 do·tíagat co insi solais láin di énlaith isint sechtmad láu. 17. ** Fo·cerdat a llíathróiti uili fair-seom 7 nos·gaib-seom cach n-óenlíathróit inna ucht. (TBC 424 f.) 18. * Fo·cerdat dano a llorga ánae uili fair, acht arus·clich-seom 7 gaibid airbir diib fria aiss. (TBC 425 ff.) 19. ** 'Nída sáithech dim chluichiu beos, á phopa Chonchobuir,' ol in gillae. (TBC 565 f.) 20. * Is scíth mo lám ón scríbund; sceithid mo phenn sruth di dub glégorm. (GT 159)

Transcription

1. fo·gaβ'i-s'u uβla is'ənd iδ ogus vos·b'iṵp-sa (nos·m'b'iṵp-sa) kos'ən r'īɣvi. is i m'eδōv ind eδa fos·gaβ'i (fos·ŋgaβ'i). 2. b'evəδ-s'oṃ a g'eθəp' k'en d'iäβ' ogus os·k'er'd' fop k'eθ'eṵpa b'ena ina gaβλe. 3. n'īβ·kapəṃ-s'i, ā ai̯s kaθa, ogus is uaθ dūn-n'i kuṃəχte βop glaδ'əβ. 4. k'r'evəδ' in k'enəɣ'e g'l'ik' f'iδ ndape ap θ'eṵpəβ' kuṃəλəβ', aχt na·r'ev f'r'isna r'īɣvi ap χ'eθ'eṵpəβ' kuṃəλəβ'. 5. id mōpa asləχa in β'eθa ogus ami k'im'b'əθ'i-n'i doäβ'-s'eṃ. 6. n'ī ap ormud f'r'iβ'-s'i as·b'iṵp-sa in-so. 7. n'īda χume-s'e f'r'ihu-soṃ. 8. id fai̯l't'i ina h'iv'ɣ'əva og t'eχt β'eltəv'i. 9. is d'eθ'β'əp' doṃ-sa brōv, s'eχ am trōɣ, am s'entun'e. 10. is b'eg, is l'iaθ mo θ'p'iλ'əs', n'ī l'iaχ droχkal'e tapəs'. 11. t'eχt do pōṃ', mōp sai̯θo, b'eg dorβi. 12. do·l'ivəd t'r'i sroθe foλo a toi̯β ind λoi̯χ' ogus asa λāṃ' ogus asa χ'iṵn iapva ɣuv'. 13. is dopχe int uλ'e b'iθ ogus is lāv de pūvəβ' is'ənd aδ'χ'i. 14. n'īm·ɣaβ' forməd f'r'it-su, ā ip' haδ'β'əp', ap is ap'e trom dut' in'd'əβ mōp. 15. fuaχəδ'-s'eṃ a posk f'r'i fāλ ina f'r'eɣa, fuaχəm'-s'e mo posk r'ēλ' f'r'i f'ēɣ'i ind esa. 16. kōg' λaë ogus h'ē haδ'χ'i t'iaɣəd'-s'eṃ tap drum' in ṃopa, ogus δo·t'iaɣəd ko h'iv's'i soλəs' lāv' d'i ēvλəθ' is'ənt h'eχtṃəδ λau̯. 17. fo·k'erdəd a l'iaθpōd'i huλ'i fap'-s'oṃ ogus vos·gaβ'-s'oṃ kaχ voi̯vλ'iaθpōd' ina uχt. 18. fo·k'erdəd davo a lorga hāve huλ'i fap', aχt apus·k'l'iχ'-s'oṃ ogus ɣaβ'əδ' ar'β'əp' d'iäβ' f'r'iha as'. 19. 'n'īda hāθ'əχ d'im χluχ'u b'eṵs, ā φoba χovχəβup',' oλ in g'ile. 20. Is s'k'īθ mo λāṃ ōn s'k'r'īβund; s'k'eθ'əδ' mo φ'en sruθ d'i δuβ ɣ'λ'ēɣorm.

English

1. I find an apple in the wood and thou carriest it to the queens. It is in the middle of the wood that we find it. 2. They strike their three heads off them and they put them on three points of the fork. 3. I love you, oh people of the war, and the power of your swords is no horror for me. 4. The clever merchants do not buy oak-wood for four *cumals*, and they do not sell it to the queens for three *cumals*. 5. Are not the temptations of the world great, and am I a captive to them? 6. It is not out of envy for thee that we say that. 7. I am like her. 8. Is the girl joyful at the coming of *Beltaine*? 9. Sorrow is not fitting for us, because (*ar*) we are not miserable and we are not old women. 10. My hair is not short, it is not grey, a bad veil over it is a pity. 11. Is a pilgrimage to Rome a lot of trouble and little profit? 12. One stream of blood flows from the side of the warrior after his wounding. 13. The whole world is not dark. But is it full of secrets in the night? 14. Envy for you does not seize us, rich men, because great wealth is a heavy burden for you. 15. Do they not point their eyes towards the enclosing wall (*OIr*.: enclosure of the wall), and do we not point our clear eyes towards penetration of knowledge? 16. Six days and seven nights he goes over the back of the sea, and he comes to a bright island full of birds on the eighth day. 17. He throws all his balls at them, and they catch them, every single ball, in their lap. 18. Then he throws all his driving sticks at them, but they do not ward them off and do not take a bundle of them on their back. 19. 'We have enough of our game, father Conchobar,' said the lads. 20. My hands are tired of writing, my pen does not pour fourth a stream of bright dark blue ink.

26.4. From the *Old Irish Triads*

Triad 233 enumerates three of the highest spirits:

Scolóc íar llégud a ṡalm 7 gillae íar lléiciud a airi úad 7 ingen íar ndénum mná dí.

skoλōg iaρ l'ēγuδ a halm ogus γ'ile iaρ l'ēg'uδ a aρ'i uaδ ogus iv'γ'əv iaρ n'd'ēvuμ μvā d'ī.

Lesson 27

27.1. Hiatus verbs

All H-verbs, that is hiatus verbs, basically behave very much alike in the present stem, so the three different classes can be dealt with in one lesson. The word 'hiatus' signifies the slight pause in pronunciation that occurs in a sequence of two vowels. This indicates the main characteristic of verbs of the H-classes: their stem ends in a vowel, and the vowel of the inflectional endings (e.g., 3rd pl. abs. -*(a)it* /əd'/, 1st pl. conj. -*am* /əμ'/, 2nd pl. conj. -*(a)id* /əð'/) is added directly onto the stem vowel: e.g., stem *rā*-, 3rd sg. abs. *ráid, raid* /raᵊð'/ 'he rows,' 3rd pl. abs. *ráit, rait* /raᵊd'/ 'they row'; or stem *bī*-, 1st pl. conj. ·*bíam*, ·*biam* /·b'iᵊμ/ 'we are usually,' 3rd pl. conj. ·*bíat*, ·*biat* /·b'iᵊd/ 'they are usually'; or stem *so*-, 3rd sg. abs. *so(a)id* /soᵊð/ 'he turns,' 3rd pl. conj. ·*soat* /·soᵊd/ 'they turn.'

In the 3rd sg. conjunct hiatus verbs end in their stem vowel. But unlike W1 and W2 verbs, which end in a vowel in the 3rd sg. conjunct, too, in H-verbs this vowel is not a personal ending, but the pure stem: ·*rá* /·rā/, ·*bí* /·b'ī/, ·*soí* /·soi̯/.

When the verbal root loses its accentuation in deuterotonic forms or when the verb has more than one preverb, the stem vowel with the inflectional ending becomes reduced. H1 and H2 verbs look very much like W1 and W2 verbs respectively in these positions, so be careful not to mix up the different inflectional classes. In other words, 3rd sg. H1 *ad·cota* 'to get' looks like a W1 verb with its final -*a*, but in fact it is a compound of the substantive verb *tā*- with two preverbs (*ad-con-tā*-); 3rd sg. H2 *fris·accai* 'to expect' looks like a W2 verb with its final -*i*, but it is a compound of *ci*- 'to see' with two preverbs (*fris-ad-ci*-). To illustrate the reduced stem vowels in unstressed position, I will give a separate third column for the variants with unstressed roots besides the usual absolute and conjunct column in the following sections.

 Illustration 27.1: *ciid* 'she weeps'

Many hiatus verbs are not very well attested. Some of the persons never occur. Therefore, for H1 and H3 verbs no complete paradigms can be given.

27.2. Verbs of the H1-class

The stem vowel of H1 verbs is *a, ā*. Of the absolute inflection only the third persons are attested (present indicative of *ráid* /raȝð'/ 'to row,' stem *rā-* /rā-/). The conjunct inflection is extremely well attested, because the substantive verb *at·tá* 'to be,' stem *tā-* /tā-/, belongs to this class. For the unaccented column I will use the forms of *ad·cota, ·éta* /aδ·koda ·ēda/ 'to get, to obtain,' a compound of *tā-*:

H1	absolute		conjunct		unaccented	
1st sg.	n/a		(at)·táu, (at)·tó	aṵ, ō	ad·cotaim	Cəm'
2nd sg.	n/a		(at)·taí	aị	ad·cotai	Ci
3rd sg.	ráid	aȝð'	(at)·tá	ā	ad·cota	Ca
1st pl.	n/a		(at)·taam	aȝµ	·étam	Cəµ
2nd pl.	n/a		(at)·taid	aȝð'	*ad·cotaid	*Cəð'
3rd pl.	rait	aȝd'	(at)·taat	aȝd	ad·cotat	Cəd

Illustration 27.2: The verbs of the H1 class

27.3. Verbs of the H2-class

Of all hiatus classes H2 is best attested. This is due to the fact that a group of important verbs belongs to this class, namely *ad·cí* 'to see,' *biid* 'to be usually,' *do·slí* 'to earn,' *gniid* 'to do, to make,' and many compounds thereof. The stem vowel of H2 verbs is *i, ī*. For the absolute inflection I will use *biid* /b'iȝð'/ 'to be usually,' stem *bī-* /b'ī-/. For the conjunct and unaccented column I will use the compound verb *do·gní, ·dénai* /do·g'n'ī ·d'ēvi/ 'to do, to make' (with normalized spelling) and *do·écai, ·décai* /do·ēgi ·d'ēgi/ 'to see':

H2	absolute		conjunct		unaccented	
1st sg.	bíuu	iü	do·gníu	iṵ	·dénaim, ·déccu	C⁽ʼ⁾əm', C⁽ʼ⁾u
2nd sg.	bii	ïï	do·gní	ī	·dénai	C⁽ʼ⁾i
3rd sg.	biid	iȝð'	do·gní	ī	·dénai	C⁽ʼ⁾i
1st pl.	bímmi	īm'i	do·gniam	iȝµ	·dénam	C⁽ʼ⁾əµ
2nd pl.	n/a		do·gniid	iȝð'	·dénaid	C⁽ʼ⁾əð'
3rd pl.	biit	iȝd'	do·gniat	iȝd	·dénat	C⁽ʼ⁾əd

Illustration 27.3: The verbs of the H2 class

27.4. Verbs of the H3-class

The attestation is worst in the case of the H3 verbs. For the absolute endings only the third persons can be given, for the conjunct endings little more. The H3 class covers verbs whose stem ends in one of the other vowels, that is, in *e*, *o*, or *u*. In the case of the stem vowel *e* the 3rd sg. conjunct ends in -*é*. In the case of the stems vowels *o* and *u* the 3rd sg. ends in the diphthongs -*oí* and -*uí*, but in -*ai* in unaccented position.

I will illustrate the attested personal forms of H3 verbs with examples of the simple verbs *foid*, ·*foí* /foəδ' ·foį̃/ 'to spend the night' (for words with vowel *o*) and *sceid*, ·*scé* /s'k'eəδ' ·s'k'ē/ 'to vomit' (for vowel *e*), and with the compound verbs *ad·noí*, *·*aithni* /aδ·noį̃ ·aθ'v'i/ 'to entrust,' *con·oí*, ·*comai* /kov·oį̃ ·koµi/ 'to protect,' *for·comai*, ·*forcmai* (foɼ·koµi ·foɼkµi/ 'to keep,' *do·intai*, ·*tintai* /do·inti ·t'inti/ 'to return' (all vowel *o*), *as·luí*, ·*élai* /as·luį̃ ·ēλi/ 'to escape' (vowel *u*).

H3	absolute		conjunct		unaccented	
1st sg.	n/a		at·noim (?)	oəm' (?)	n/a	
2nd sg.	n/a		n/a		n/a	
3rd sg.	fo(a)id, sceid	oəδ', eəδ'	·foí, ·scé, as·luí	oį̃, ē, uį̃	·comai, ·élai	Ci
1st pl.	n/a		n/a		do·intam	Cəµ
2nd pl.	n/a		cot·dóith	oəδ'	n/a	
3rd pl.	fo(a)it	oəd'	·foat, ·sceet, as·luat	oəd, eəd, uəd	for·comat, ·élat	Cəd

Illustration 27.4: The verbs of the H3 class

You can find a table with all verbal classes in Appendix F.7.

27.5. Exercise

Conjugate the following verbs:

> *ad·cí*, ·*accai* /aδ·k'ī ·aki/ (H2) 'to see'
> *im·soí*, ·*impai* /im'·soį̃ ·impi/ (H3) 'to turn around'
> *liid*, ·*lí* /l'iəδ' ·l'ī/ (H2) 'to accuse'

Illustration 27.5: *líu-sa!*
'j'accuse!'

27.6. The prehistory of the hiatus verbs

There is neither a uniform etymological origin for H3 verbs nor a correspondence between subclasses and historical preforms.

1. PIE roots of the structure $Ceu̯$: intervocalic ('lenited') $u̯$ disappeared around the early Old Irish period, e.g., H3 *con·oí* 'to protect' < *$au̯eθi$ from PIE √$h_2eu̯$ 'to help.'

2. PIE roots of the structure Ces: intervocalic s was lenited to h, which eventually disappeared in the interior of words, e.g., H2 *ad·cí* 'to see' < *$k^u̯iheθi$ from PIE √$k^u̯ei̯s$ 'to notice.'

3. *i̯e/i̯o*-verbs from PIE roots of the structure CeH: intervocalic $i̯$ disappeared before the Old Irish period, e.g., H2 *gniid* 'to do' < *$gnīi̯eθi$ < *$ĝneh_1i̯eti$ from PIE √$ĝenh_1$ 'to create.' Peter SCHRIJVER (*Studies in British Celtic Historical Phonology*, Amsterdam 1995, 406) extends the explanation as *i̯e-/i̯o*-verbs also to those H2 verbs that continue PIE laryngeal-final roots (e.g., H1 *baid* 'to die' < $g^u̯(e)h_2$-i̯e-); Kim MCCONE (*From Indo-European to Old Irish*, Oxford 1986, 228) explains these (*baid*, also *·tá*) as secondarily thematized athematic verbs.

27.7. The complete dependent forms at a glance

As a broad rule it may be stated that dependent forms of verbs (conjunct endings, prototonic forms) are used after conjunct particles. But by closer inspection a more complex picture emerges. Many conjunct particles do not entail dependent verbal forms. The following list contains all those conjunct particles that do have dependent forms after them:

1. After the negative particles *nĭ·*, *nĭcon·*, *nă·*, *năd·*, *nach-*, *nacon·*, and after compounds thereof like *cani·* 'nonne?,' *mani·* 'if not,' *ceni·* 'although not,' *coni·*, *conná·*, *cona·* '(so) that not,' *arná·* 'in order not to.'

2. After the interrogative particle *in^N·*, *innád^N·*; *co^H·* 'how?'; *cecha·*, *cacha·* 'whoever, whatever'; sometimes also after the interrogative pronoun *cía (ce·, ci·)*.

3. After the prepositional relative particle *(s)a^N·* as in *ara^N·*, *dia^N·*, *fua^N·*, *occa^N·*, *fora^N·*, *forsa^N·*, *cosa^N·*, *frisa^N·*, *lasa^N·*, *trisa^N·*; and after relative *i^N·* 'in(to) which.'

4. After the conjunctions *ara^N·* 'in order that,' *dia^N·* 'if,' *co^N·*, *con^N·* '(so) that.'

In all the above forms conjunct endings of verbs are used. Furthermore, conjunct endings are used:

1. in compound verbs

2. and in simple verbs after the verbal particles *ro* and *no*.

Lesson 28

28.1. The substantive verb

This lesson immediately continues 24.3 about the copula, one way of expressing the verb 'to be' in Old Irish. The so-called *substantive verb* covers another aspect of the verb 'to be' and differs very much from the copula in its syntactical use. The substantive verb is especially used to denote:

1. Existence: *at·tá in Coimmdiu* 'there is the Lord, the Lord is/exists.' (German *es gibt*)

2. Physical presence: *at·taam i Finnbain indossa* 'we are now in Vienna.'

3. Being in a certain condition: *at·tó i mo ṡuidiu ar bélaib rímairi* 'I am sitting (lit.: in my seat/sitting) in front of the computer,' *at·tó i ngalur* 'I am in illness = I am ill.' Note the difference in construction with the adjective *galrach* 'ill, sick,' where the copula has to be used: *am galrach-sa* 'I am ill.'

Sometimes, however, the substantive verb can also replace the copula, especially when the predicate does not immediately follow, that is, in certain relative constructions, about which we will learn later, and in those cases where the subject stands between verb and predicate, e.g., *at·taat mesai Dé nephchomtetarrachti amal abis* 'the judgements of God are incomprehensible like an abyss' (*Ml.* 55d11); the normal word order here would be **it nephchomtetarrachti mesai Dé*; or *ro·bátar ind liss dúntai* 'the ramparts were closed' (IB 1), where **robtar dúntai ind liss* would normally be expected.

The basic present stem of the substantive verb is *at·tá* /at·tā/ and belongs to the H1 class. This compound is used in positive main clauses. You can find the paradigm in 27.2. After conjunct particles the preverb *at·* is dropped and only the stem *·tá* is used, but only when a datival pronoun is infixed after the particle, e.g., *nín·tá* 'there is not to us = we have not' (more about that construction in a later lesson), or when the conjunct particle consists of preposition plus relative element *-(s)a^N*, e.g., *lasa·tá* 'with whom is,' etc.

Apart from the cases just mentioned, however, the conjunct forms of *at·tá* are supplied by a completely different construction with the defective verb *·fil* (literally an imperative meaning 'see!'). The 'subject' of this construction is expressed by the accusative or by an infixed pronoun; e.g., with the interrogative particle: *in·fil in mnaí* (acc.!) *sund?* 'is the woman here?' or *in·fil inna echu* (acc.!) *arind achud?* 'are the horses on the pasture?,' and the answer would be: *nís·fil* 'she is not,' resp. 'they are not' (infixed pronoun 3rd sg. feminine and 3rd pl. *-s^(N)*). Accordingly, the whole paradigm for the personal pronouns 'I am not,' etc., is:

person	Old Irish	Ogam Ir.	translation
1st sg.	*ním·fil*	/n'ɪm·iλ'/	I am not
2nd sg.	*nít·fil*	/n'ɪd·iλ'/	thou art not
3rd sg. m.	*ní·fil*	/n'ɪ·β'iλ'/	he is not
3rd sg. f.	*nís·fil*	/n'ɪs·fiλ' n'ɪs·β'iλ'/	she is not
3rd sg. n.	*ní·fil*	/n'ɪ·iλ'/	it is not
1st pl.	*nínn·fil*	/n'ɪn·f'iλ'/	we are not
2nd pl.	*níb·fil*	/n'ɪβ·f'iλ'/	you are not
3rd pl.	*nís·fil*	/n'ɪs·f'iλ' n'ɪs·β'iλ'/	they are not

Illustration 28.1: The negative inflection of the substantive verb

Note:

1. In the earliest literature, *fil* without conjunct particle is used just like *at·tá* in the meaning 'there is, there are,' e.g., *fil and bile* 'there is a sacred tree there' (IB 7).

You can find all forms of the substantive verb in Appendix F.11.

28.2. The verbal noun

One feature that distinguishes Old Irish, together with the British languages, from 'normal' European languages is that it has no infinitive. Instead, a lot of the functions typical of infinitives in languages like English or German is fulfilled by so-called verbal nouns in Old Irish. Verbal nouns are abstract nouns, carrying the meaning of the corresponding verb, but otherwise behaving completely like nouns. In grammatical jargon nouns of this type are also called action nouns (*nomina actionis*). Something similar can be achieved by using the *-ing*-forms of English verbs together with the article, e.g., *the going, the leaping, the loving*, or by using the neuter article together with the infinitive in German, e.g., *das Gehen, das Springen, das Lieben*. But note that you will never be able to form verbal nouns in Old Irish in any comparably regular way. Therefore it is better to compare them to German abstract nouns like *der Gang, der Sprung, die Liebe* in relation to the verbs they belong to.

Notwithstanding the fact that verbal noun constructions are often similar to infinitival constructions in other languages, verbal nouns and infinitives are not equivalent, and there are major differences between the two categories, syntactically and morphologically:

1. Infinitives are formed by predictable rules (in English: *to* + present stem, e.g., *to go*; in German: present stem + *-en*, e.g., *geh-en*; Latin: present stem + *-re*, e.g., *i-re*). Verbal nouns are not formed by any predictable rules. This means that one has to learn by heart which verbal noun belongs to each single verb, e.g., *techt* to *téit* 'to go,' *gabál* to *gaibid* 'to take,' or *serc* to *caraid* 'to love.'

2. Infinitives, like verbs, govern accusatives to express their object (e.g., in German *ich will meinen Mann lieben und ehren*, the inifinitives *lieben* und *ehren* require the accusative *meinen Mann*, just like they do in the finite construction *ich liebe und ehre meinen Mann*). Verbal nouns, however, like all other substantives, govern genitives to express their object: *gaibid ind ingen áin inna líathróite* (gen.!) 'the girl begins to drive the ball.' This sentence could be translated literally into English as 'the girl begins the driving *of the ball*,' or into German 'das Mädchen beginnt das Treiben *des Balls.*'

3. In many languages infinitives express tense and voice. For example, in Latin, in the ending of the infinitive the three tenses present (*laudare*), future (*laudaturum esse*) and past (*laudauisse*) can be expressed, and a distinction between active (*laudare*) and passive (*laudari*) can be achieved. In German, too, you can make the fourfold distinction between *zu loben* (present active), *gelobt zu werden* (present passive), *gelobt zu haben* (past active) and *gelobt worden zu sein* (past passive). Verbal nouns are absolutely indifferent to these distinctions, and one has to know from the context what is meant: OIr. *molad* just means neutrally 'praise, praising.'

4. Infinitives are often restricted to certain constructions, usually being dependent from other words. Verbal nouns are inflected like any other noun and can be used in any position where nouns are admissible.

But now let's look at the Old Irish verbal noun in detail:

1. First, there is no rule in Old Irish as to how to form a verbal noun from a given verb:

1.1. Sometimes the verbal noun looks like the root of the verb, e.g., *ás* (o, n) 'the growing, growth' to W1 *ásaid* 'to grow,' or *rád* (o, m) 'the speaking, speech' to W2a *ráidid* 'to speak.'

1.2. Sometimes special suffixes are added to the verbal root. A very frequent suffix for example is *-ad*, *-iud*, which inflects as a masculine u-stem and is usually employed with weak verbs, e.g., *léiciud* (u, m) 'the letting, the leaving' to W2a *léicid* 'to let, to leave.' But actually many other suffixes exist, e.g., *-ál* in *gabál* (ā, f) 'the taking, the seizing' to S2 *gaibid* 'to take, to seize,' or the i̯o-stem ending in *suide* (i̯o, n) 'the sitting, seat' to S1a *saidid* 'to sit,' and many, many more.

1.3. Sometimes the verbal noun is built on a totally different root, e.g., *serc* (ā, f) 'the loving, love' to W1 *caraid* 'to love,' or *dígal* (ā, f) 'revenge' to S1 *do·fich* 'to revenge.'

In the wordlist verbal nouns will be marked with the abbreviation *v.n.*, and the verb they belong to will be cited.

2. As with all nouns, only genitives and possessive pronouns can be dependent on verbal nouns. The genitives/possessive pronouns usually denote the object (!) of the verbal noun, e.g., *gat ind óir* 'the theft of the gold' (the gold is being stolen), *ícc dóenachta* 'the salvation of mankind' (mankind is being saved), *serc inna mná* 'the love of the woman' (the woman is being loved), *m'adall* 'my visit' (I am being visited), *a ithe* 'his/its eating' (he/it is being eaten). You have to be very careful here because from English or German usage you are trained to understand things like *mein Besuch* or *John's visit* to mean that it is you/John who visits someone else. The superficially 'identical' construction in Old Irish *m'adall, adall Éoin*, however, can only mean that you are/John is being visited. Only with intransitive verbs a dependent genitive denotes the subject: *mo thecht* 'my going' (I am going), *techt Chonairi* 'Conaire's going' (Conaire is going).

The agent of verbal noun constructions is expressed by the prepositions *do^L* and *la^H*: e.g., *marbad inna maccraide la Hiruath* 'the killing of the infants by Herod,' or *mo śerc do Día* 'God's love for me.' Be especially careful with this last example! The translation 'my love for God' is wrong!

3. Verbal nouns in Old Irish are used in a variety of constructions with prepositions in place of participle constructions in other languages. Most important of these is the use of verbal nouns preceded by the preposition *oc* 'at,' usually together with the substantive verb. This corresponds to the English continuous constructions *I am doing, I was going*, etc., and denotes an action that is/was extending over a long period of time or denotes an action that is/was going on while another action happens/happened, e.g., *at·tó oc scríbund* 'I am writing,' *bámmar oc imbirt fidchille* 'we were playing *fidchell* (when Cú Chulainn jumped across the board)' (TBC 437). Since in this construction the verbal noun stands in the prepositional case, the *anlaut* of the following genitive is of course lenited: *oc mórad Chonchobuir* 'praising Conchobar,' *oc tabairt libuir don scolóic* /og taβər't' λ'iβuρ'/ 'giving a book to the scholar.'

28.3. Infixed pronouns class B

In contrast to infixed pronouns class A, class B pronouns are used after preverbs that originally ended in a consonant. This comprises the preverbs *for, etar, fris, con, ad* (< *ad*), *ad* (< *aith*), *as* (< *ess*), *as* (< *oss*) and *in*. Class B pronouns are characterized by a /d/ before the proper pronominal part. This is spelled *t* or *d* after *for* and *etar* (e.g., *etardom^L·, forta^H·*), but *t* only with all other preverbs. *fris* becomes *frit°·* and *con* combines with *t* to *cot°·* (e.g., *fritamm^L·, coton·*). For the last three preverbs (*ad, as, in*) a single form *at°·* appears (e.g., *atot^L·, at^L·, ata^H·, atab·*), so that it is not possible to distinguish between the three preverbs when a pronoun is infixed.

The 1st and 2nd persons look very much like the corresponding forms of class A pronouns (except for the additional *d* or *t*, of course) and they have the same mutational effects. But note that the 3rd persons differ essentially in their appearance: the 3rd sg. masculine and neuter simply end in *t*, followed by nasalization and lenition respectively. The 3rd sg. feminine and 3rd pl. end in *-da*, *-ta*, which aspirates.

person	translation	pronoun	
		class B	
1st sg.	me	*-dom^L, -dum^L, -tom^L, -tum^L, -dam(m)^L, -tam(m)^L*	/dəm^L/
2nd sg.	thee	*-tot^L, -tat^L, -t^L*	/dəd^L d^L/
3rd sg. m.	him	*-t^N*	/d^N/
3rd sg. f.	her	*-da^H, -ta^H*	/da^H/
3rd sg. n.	it	*-t^L*	/d^L/
1st pl.	us	*-don, -ton, -tan(n)*	/dən/
2nd pl.	you	*-dob, -dub, -tob, -tab*	/dəβ/
3rd pl.	them	*-da^H, -ta^H*	/da^H/

Illustration 28.2: The infixed pronouns class B

Next follow two model paradigms for the use of infixed pronouns, one for the S1b compound verb *for·cain* 'to teach,' the other for the H2 compound verb *ad·cí*, *·accai* 'to see.' For variation's sake I will use different persons in the verbal endings (3rd pl., 1st sg.).

pronoun	Old Irish	transcription	translation
1st sg.	fordom·chanat	/fordom·χavəd/	they teach me
2nd sg.	fordot·chanat	/fordod·χavəd/	they teach thee
3rd sg. m.	fort·canat	/ford·gavəd/	they teach him
3rd sg. f.	forda·canat	/forda·kavəd/	they teach her
3rd sg. n.	fort·chanat	/ford·χavəd/	they teach it
1st pl.	fordonn·canat	/fordon·kavəd/	they teach us
2nd pl.	fordob·canat	/fordoβ·kavəd/	they teach you
3rd pl.	forda·canat	/forda·kavəd/	they teach them (themselves)

Illustration 28.3: Paradigm of infixed pronouns class B with *for·cain*

pronoun	Old Irish	transcription	translation
1st sg.	atom·chíu	/adom·χ'iu̯/	I see me (myself)
2nd sg.	atot·chíu	/adod·χ'iu̯/	I see thee
3rd sg. m.	at·cíu	/ad·g'iu̯/	I see him
3rd sg. f.	ata·cíu	/ada·k'iu̯/	I see her
3rd sg. n.	at·chíu	/ad·χ'iu̯/	I see it
1st pl.	atonn·cíu	/adon·k'iu̯/	I see us (ourselves)
2nd pl.	atob·cíu	/adoβ·k'iu̯/	I see you
3rd pl.	ata·cíu	/ada·k'iu̯/	I see them

Illustration 28.4: Paradigm of infixed pronouns class B with *ad·cí*

Note that in negative statements, of course, class A pronouns have to be used, e.g., *ata·ciam* 'we see them,' but *nís·accam* (*nís·n·accam*) 'we do not see them.' You'll find a survey of all infixed pronouns in Appendix F.4.

28.4. Exercise

Use all possible pronouns of class B with the following verbal forms:

con·gairi /kovˑgaᵖʼi/ (S2) 'thou summonest, thou invitest'
in·fét /ivˑfʼēd/ (S1) '(s)he relates, tells'
fris·benaimm /fʼrʼisˑbevəmʼ/ (S3a) 'I heal'
ad·ciat /aδˑkʼiəd/ (H3) 'they see'
as·renam /asˑrʼevəμ/ (S3) 'we sell'
for·osnai /foᵖˑosni/ (W2b) 'it illuminates'

Illustration 28.5: *oc oul chorma maith* 'drinking good beer'

28.5. The conjugated prepositions 4

These are the last six conjugated prepositions that take the prepositional. Many of these forms are only attested in late Old Irish or Middle Irish texts, but I refrain from specifically indicating the younger forms.

person	íar^N 'after'		oc 'at, with'	
	ending	transcription	ending	transcription
1st sg.	n/a	`	ocum, ocom	/ogum ogəm/
2nd sg.	íarmut	/iaᵖμud/	ocut	/ogud/
3rd sg. m., n.	íarum, íarma	/iaᵖuμ iaᵖμa/	occo, occa	/ogo oga/
3rd sg. f.	n/a		occai, occae	/oki oke/
1st pl.	n/a		ocunn	/ogun/
2nd pl.	n/a		occaib	/ogəβʼ/
3rd pl.	íarmaib	/iaᵖμəβʼ/	occaib, occo	/ogəβʼ oko/

Illustration 28.6: The conjugated prepositions 4: *íar^N, oc*

| person | ós, úas 'over, above' | | reN, riN 'before' | |
	ending	transcription	ending	transcription
1st sg.	úasum	/uasum/	rium, remum	/r'iu̯m r'eμum/
2nd sg.	úasut	/uasud/	remut	/r'eμud/
3rd sg. m., n.	úaso, úasa	/uaso uasa/	riam, ríam	/r'iə̯μ r'iau̯μ/
3rd sg. f.	úaise, úaisti	/uas'e uas't'i/	remi	/r'eμ'i/
1st pl.	úasunn	/uasun/	reunn, riun	/r'eu̯n r'iu̯n/
2nd pl.	n/a		reuib	/r'eu̯β'/ (?)
3rd pl.	úasaib, úaistib	/uasəβ' uas't'əβ'/	remib	/r'eμəβ'/

Illustration 28.7: The conjugated prepositions 4: úas, reN

| person | ís 'under' | | coN 'with' (archaic) | |
	ending	transcription	ending	transcription
1st sg.	ísum, íssum	/īsum/	n/a	
2nd sg.	n/a		n/a	
3rd sg. m., n.	íssa	/īsa/	cono, conu	/kovo kovu/
3rd sg. f.	n/a		n/a	
1st pl.	ísund ísaind	/īsun isən'/	n/a	
2nd pl.	n/a		n/a	
3rd pl.	íssaib	/īsəβ'/	condaib	/kondəβ' ?/

Illustration 28.8: The conjugated prepositions 4: ís, coN

Lesson 29

29.1. Test

Try to recognize the inflectional forms. Give as much information about the words as possible—gender, stem class, case, number:

a cride: _____ or _____

inna umae: _____ or _____

ingin n-allaid: _____   *srothae nglas:* _____

inna céile: _____   *cnámai báin:* _____

súili: _____ or _____

inna rrígnae maith: _____   *búaid amru:* _____

in soilsi follais: _____   *in chathai:* _____

mindaib órdaib: _____   *liaig becc:* _____

méit móir: _____ or _____

inna comairli: _____ or _____

búachaill rrígdae: _____   *muire n-ard:* _____

áth chían: _____   *ingin allaid:* _____

legai amrai: _____ or _____

int áesa oic: _____ or _____

ungae: _____ or _____ or _____

aidchi dorchai: _____ or _____ or _____

29.2. Varia

1. Combined with the article the ordinal number/pronominal *aile* 'second, other,' also 'the one... the other,' becomes *indala, indara* /indáλa indápa/ 'the second, the other' for all genders and cases, always standing in front of the word it qualifies. In Old Irish it has the same mutating effect on the following word as the article.

2. In Old Irish circumstantial conditions affecting a person are often rendered by a construction with the preposition *do^L* for the person affected. This can be translated in various ways, depending on the context. Examples would be *a chlaideb briste dó* 'his sword broken to him = his sword was broken,' or *at·tá dom* 'there is to me = I have = I am.'

29.3. Exercise

Old Irish

1. ** Ní·dénaimm gnímu maccthai. (*Wb*. 12c9) 2. Atonn·ciid-si oc gait inna n-ech, 7 at·ḟéidid donaib echairib. 3. Ata·agam-ni ón chlúain tarsin n-áth. 4. Cotot·chil-siu etir cranna 7 dusu i mmedón ind ḟeda for slóg inna mberg, acht atot·chiat-som 7 ḟot·gaibet. 5. * Atom·riug indíu co niurt tríun. (GT 27) 6. Ata·gairiu (*or:* ata·ngairiu) cuccum do thabairt chomairle maithe dom-sa, ar at·tá mór fessa doaib-seom. 7. * In·n-accaid Áed isin chath? Ní·n-accam-som, acht ad·ciam a scíath occa imdegail. (GT 109) 8. Is dó da·gniat: is maith leo ithe ḟeola 7 ól fína. 9. ** Is oc precept ṡoiscélai at·tó. (*Wb*. 21c19) 10. Nít·ḟil sund isind áth, acht at·taí i mmedón inna caille oc dénum chlúana indi. 11. At·tá Día. 12. * Imma·raat (*sc.* in n-insi) immacúairt 7 at·tá slóg mór oc ginig 7 oc gáirechtaig. (IB 61) 13. At·taam-ni for longais riam 7 ní dóich ar techt ar ais dúnn. 14. Níb·ḟil oc tabairt uball dind abaill. Innád·ḟil ubla isnaib crannaib? 15. * Ní·fil nert i lláim Brain do gabáil inna croíbe. (IB 31) 16. * Fil dúnn o thossuch inna ndúile cen áes, [...] nín·taidlea int immarmus. (IB 44) 17. ** Is i persain Chríst da·gniu-sa sin. (*Wb*. 14d26) 18. * Ad·cí [*sc.* Cú Chulainn] in fer ara chiunn 7 leth a chinn fair 7 leth fir aili fora muin. (TBC 492 f.) 19. ** Fa·n-éirig Cú Chulainn 7 benaid a chenn de cosind luirg ánae 7 gaibid immáin líathróite riam [...]. (TBC 501 f.) 20. * Ad·cí [*sc.* Cú Chulainn] in fer ocond ḟulucht i mmedón ind ḟeda, indala lám dó cona gaisciud indi, ind lám aile oc fuini in tuirc. Is mór a úathmaire ind ḟir. Fa·n-ópair-seom ar apu 7 do·beir a chenn 7 a muicc lais. (TBC 516 ff.)

Illustration 29.1: *oc seinm 7 oc léimm* 'making music and dancing'

Lesson 29

Transcription

1. n'ɪ·d'ēvəm' g'n'ɪ̯μu makθi. 2. adon·k'iǝð'-s'i og gad' ina v'eχ, ogus ad·ēð'əð' donəβ' eχəp'əβ'. 3. ada·haγəμ-n'i ōn χλuav' tars'ən nāθ. 4. kodod·χ'iλ'-s'u ed'əp' krana ogus δusu i m'eðōv ind eða foρ slōγ ina m'b'erg. aχt adod·χ'iǝd-soμ ogus od·γaβ'əd. 5. adom·ρ'iμ̯γ in'd'ɪ̯μ ko n'iμrt t'r'iμv. 6. ada·gaρ'u (ada·ŋgaρ'u) kugum do θaβər't' χoμəp'λ'e maθ'e doμ-sa, aρ at·tā mōρ β'esa doǝβ'-s'oμ. 7. in·nakəð' aǐ̯ð is'ən χaθ? n'ɪ·vakəμ-soμ, aχt að·k'iǝμ a s'k'iaθ oga im'ð'əγaλ'. 8. is dō da·γ'v'iǝd: is maθ' leho iθ'e eμλa ogus ōλ f'ɪva. 9. is og ρ'r'ek'əρt hos'k'ēλi at·tō. 10. n'ɪd·iλ' sund is'ənd āθ, aχt at·ta̯i i m'eðōv ina kal'e og d'ēvuμ χλuava in'd'i. 11. at·tā d'ia. 12. ima·raǝd imakúar't' ogus at·tā slōγ mōρ og g'iv'əγ' ogus og gāρ'əχtəγ'. 13. at·taǝμ-n'i foρ loŋgəs' r'iǝμ ogus v'ɪ dōχ' aρ d'eχt aρ as' dūn. 14. n'ɪβ·f'iλ' og taβər't' uβəl d'ind aβal'. ināð·β'iλ' uβla isvəβ' kranəβ'? 15. n'ɪ·f'iλ' n'ert i lāμ' βρav' do γaβāλ' ina kroi̯β'e. 16. f'iλ' dūn ō θosuχ δūλ'e k'ev ai̯s, [...] n'ɪn·tað'l'a int iməρμus. 17. is i b'ersəv' χ'ρ'ɪs't' da·γ'v'iμ-sa s'iv'. 18. að·k'ɪ in β'eρ apa χ'iμn ogus λ'eθ a χ'in' faρ' ogus λ'eθ β'iρ' aλ'i fopa μuv'. 19. fa·v'ēρ'əγ' kū χuλən' ogus β'evəð' a χ'en d'e kos'ənd λur'g' āve ogus γaβ'əð' imāv' l'iaθρōd'e r'iǝμ. 20. að·k'ɪ in β'eρ ogənd uλuχt i m'eðōv ind eða, indáλa λāμ' dō kova γas'k'uð in'd'i, ind λāμ aλ'e og fuv'i in tur'k'. is mōρ a uaθμəρ'e ind iρ'. fa·vōbəρ'-s'oμ aρ abu ogus δo·b'eρ' a χ'en ogus a μuk' las'.

English

1. I do a childish deed. 2. We see you stealing (*OIr.*: at the theft of) a horse, and we tell it to the horse-keeper. 3. You drive it (*OIr.*: him = the horse) from the meadow across the ford. 4. I hide myself from the troop of bandits between the trees and the bushes in the middle of the forest, but they see me and they find me. 5. We gird ourselves today with great strength. 6. He calls thee to him to give good advice to him, because thou hast a lot of knowledge. 7. Dost thou see the men in the battle? No (*OIr.*: I do not see them), but I see their shields protecting them (*OIr.* at their protecting). 8. It is therefore that she does it: she does not like (*OIr.*: it is not good with her) to eat meat (*OIr.*: the eating of meat) and to drink wine (*OIr.*: the drinking of wine). 9. We are not preaching the Gospel (use the construction from above). 10. We are here in the ford, and we are not in the middle of the forest making a glade in it. 11. Does God exist? 12. We row around it, but there is no large group gaping and laughing. 13. Are you in exile from her, and is your return likely for you (do you have hope of returning)? 14. Thou art taking an apple from the apple tree. There are apples in the tree. 15. There is strength in Bran's hand to grab the branch. 16. We are not without age from the beginning of creation (*OIr.*: there is not to us without age...), sin touches us. 17. It is in the person of Christ that we do that. 18. He sees her with half her head on her. 19. Cú Chulainn attacks her and strikes her head from her with the driving stick. 20. He sees her at the cooking-pit, her other hand roasting the boars. He attacks her nevertheless and takes her head and her pig with him.

Lesson 30

30.1. Nouns: the consonant stems

The last large group of declensional classes includes the so-called consonant stems. Historically (still in Proto-Celtic) they formed one declensional pattern, but due to the radical sound changes that took place in the prehistory of Irish they branched off into a wide range of sub-classes in Irish, behaving differently in the details, but still adhering to a certain common pattern. The name 'consonant stems' results from the fact that originally, in the Proto-Celtic and Proto-Goidelic period, their stems ended in consonants, onto which the endings were immediately added. The different consonant classes of Old Irish are:

> guttural stems:
> > g-stems (masculine and feminine)
> > k-stems (masculine and feminine)
> dental stems:
> > t/d-stems (masculine and feminine)
> > nt-stems (masculine, feminine and neuter)
> nasal stems:
> > on-stems (masculine, feminine)
> > men-stems (neuter)
> r-stems (masculine and feminine)
> s-stems (neuter, one masculine)
> some irregular nouns

The following general points have to be observed:

1. With the exception of the r- and the s-stems, the common pattern of Old Irish consonant stems is that the eponymous (= stem final) consonant is lost in the nominative and vocative singular but can be seen in all other cases.

2. The nominative singular may end in a vowel or in a consonant, depending on whether the vowel before the stem final consonant was originally long or short: in the first case the word ends in a vowel in Irish (e.g., nom. *cáera*, gen. *cáerach* 'sheep' < **kaịrāk-*, k-stem = stem final consonant *ch* /χ/ after an originally long *ā*), while in the latter case it ends in a consonant (e.g., nom. *sail*, gen. *sailech* 'willow' < **salik-*, k-stem = stem final consonant *ch* /χ/ after an originally short *i*).

3. In the prepositional singular most consonantal declensions have, at least in the earlier period, two variants, a short and a long one. The short form is usually, but not always, identical with the nominative singular (which means that the eponymous consonant is not to be seen), the long form, however, is identical with the accusative singular—apart from the different mutational effects. The short form, usually called 'short dative' in standard grammars, appears mainly in archaic texts, whereas the long form ('long dative') is the standard Old Irish form.

4. In the prepositional plural and dual and in the accusative plural, where extra syllables are added to the words, syncope regularly applies, with the odd exceptions, of course.

146

What follows below is the basic pattern of the consonant stems. Keep in mind, however, that certain classes behave somewhat differently in detail. You will note the actual differences when we will look at the individual classes.

case	Old Ir.	Prim. Irish	Proto-Celtic	Pre-Celtic
nom. voc. sg.	Ø	*-h	-Cs	*-Cs
gen.	{L}C	-Cah	-Cos «	*-Cos, *-Ces
prep.	C'ᴸ, Øᴸ	*-Cē (?), *-C	-Cei̯, -Ci	*-Cei̯, -Ci
acc.	C'ᴺ	*-Cev	-Cam	*-Cm̥
nom.pl.	C'	*-Ceh	-Ces	*-Ces
gen.	{L}Cᴺ	*-Caν	-Com	*-Com
prep.	{L}Cəβ'	*-Caβih «	-Cbis («)	*-Cbʰis, -bʰos
acc. voc.	{L}Caᴴ	*-Cāh	-Cās	*-Cn̥s
n. a. v. dual	C'ᴸ	*-Ce	*-Ce	*-Ch₁e
gen.	{L}Cᴸ	*-Cō	*-Cou̯ «	*-Ch₁oh₁s, -C(H)oh₁u
prep.	{L}Cəβ'ᴺ	*-Caβiv «	*-Cbim «	*-Cbʰih₁, -moh₁ ?

Illustration 30.1: The basic pattern of the consonantal declension

Note:

1. The above table applies only to masculine and feminine nouns. The neuters behave a little bit differently, e.g., their nominatives and accusatives are always identical. The neuters will be dealt with in greater detail in later lessons.

Illustration 30.2:
Fech in rríg! Behold the king!

30.2. Guttural stems: consonantal declension in g

Consonant-stem words whose stems end in guttural sounds (spelled *g, ch, c*) are called 'guttural stems.' These can be further grouped into three sub-types: g-stems, k-stems and a single instance of an nk-stem.

There are only a few words attested with a stem ending in *g* /γ/. These can be masculine or feminine. A frequent example is the word for 'king' *rí* m., stem *ríg-* /r'īγ/:

case	ending	Old Irish	Prim. Irish	Proto-Celtic	Pre-Celtic
nom. sg.	Ø	*rí*ᴴ	*rīh	rīχs <-ρειξ, -ριγς, -rix>	*h₃rēĝs
gen.	{L}γ	*ríg*	*rīγah	*rīgos	*h₃rēĝos
prep.	γ'ᴸ, Øᴸ	*rígᴸ, (ríᴸ)* «	*rīγ («)	*rīgei̯, rīgi <-ριγι,-ρειγι>	*h₃rēĝei̯, *h₃rēĝi
acc.	γ'ᴺ	*rígᴺ*	*rīγev	*rīgam	*h₃rēĝm̥
voc.	Ø	*áᴸ rí*ᴴ	*rīh	*rīχs	*h₃rēĝs
nom.pl.	γ'	*ríg*	*rīγeh	rīges <-ριγες, -riges>	*h₃rēĝes
gen.	{L}γᴺ	*rígᴺ*	*rīγav	*rīgom	*h₃rēĝom
prep.	{L}γəβ'	*rígaib*	*rīγaβih «	*rīgbis («)	*h₃rēĝbʰis, -bʰos
acc.	{L}γaᴴ	*ríga*ᴴ	*rīγāh	rīgās <-rigas>	*h₃rēĝn̥s
voc.	{L}γaᴴ	*áᴸ ríga*ᴴ «	*rīγeh	*rīges	*h₃rēĝes
n. a. v. du.	γ'ᴸ	*dáᴸ rígᴸ*	*rīγe	*rīge	*h₃rēĝh₁e
gen.	{L}γᴸ	*dáᴸ rígᴸ*	*rīγō	*rīgou̯ («)	*h₃rēĝh₁oh₁s, -(H)oh₁u
prep.	{L}γəβ'	*dibᴺ rrígaib* «	*rīγaβiv «	*rīgbim «	*h₃rēĝbʰih₁, -moh₁ ?

Illustration 30.3: The g-stems

Note:

1. The words of this class continue old root nouns.

30.3. Guttural stems: consonantal declension in k

Illustration 30.4:
oc scribund ar lieic
'writing on a stone'

More frequent than the words in *g* are those that for historical reasons are called k-stems. In some books they are called ch-stems. They can be masculine and feminine. The stem of these words basically ends in *ch* /χ/, but there is an important rule whereby palatalized *ch* /χ'/ becomes *g* /γ'/, but only when the final syllable is unstressed and stands in absolute *auslaut*. Thus there is actually an alternation between *auslauting* non-palatalized *ch* and palatalized *g* throughout the paradigm in most words of this declension. A typical example for a k-stem is *sail* f. 'willow-tree,' stem *sailech-* /saλ'əχ/:

case	ending	Old Irish	Prim. Irish	Proto-Celtic	Pre-Celtic
nom. sg.	Ø	sail	*saλih	*saliχs	*saliks
gen.	{L}χ	sailech	*saλiχah	*salikos	*salikos
prep.	γ'ᴸ, Øᴸ	sailigᴸ, sailᴸ «	*saλiχ («)	*salikei̯, *saliki	*salikei̯, *saliki
acc.	γ'ᴺ	sailigᴺ	*saλiχev	*salikam	*salikm̥
voc.	Ø	áᴸ ṡail	*saλih	*saliχs	*saliks
nom.pl.	γ'	sailig	*saλiχeh	*salikes	*salikes
gen.	{L}χᴺ	sailechᴺ	*saλiχav	*salikom	*salikom
prep.	{L}χ⁽'⁾əβ'	sailchib	*saλiχaβih «	*saligbis («)	*salikbʰis, -bʰos
acc.	{L}χ⁽'⁾aᴴ	sailcheaᴴ	*saλiχāh	*salikās	*salikn̥s
voc.	{L}χ⁽'⁾aᴴ	áᴸ ṡailcheaᴴ «	*saλiχeh	*salikes	*salikes
n. a. v. du.	γ'ᴸ	díᴸ ṡailigᴸ	*saλiχe	*salike	*salikh₁e
gen.	{L}χᴸ	dáᴸ ṡailechᴸ	*saλiχō	*salikou̯ («)	*salikh₁oh₁s, -(H)oh₁u
prep.	{L}χ⁽'⁾əβ'	dibᴺ sailchib «	*saλiχaβiv «	*saligbim «	*salikbʰih₁, -moh₁ ?

Illustration 30.5: The k-stems

There is one guttural stem that does not end in lenited g or ch, but in c(c) /g/: lie, lia m. 'stone.' For historical reasons this is called an nk-stem:

case	singular	transcr.	dual	transcr.	plural	transcr.
nom.	lie, lia	/lieᴴ liäᴴ/	dáᴸ liicᴸ	/λiäg'ᴸ/	lieic, liaic, liic	/liëg' liäg'/
gen.	liac(c)	/liäg/	n/a		liac(c)ᴺ	/liägᴺ/
prep.	lieicᴸ, liaicᴸ, liicᴸ	/liëg'ᴸ liäg'ᴸ/	n/a		*lecaib	/legəβ'/
acc.	lieicᴺ, liaicᴺ, liicᴺ	/liëg'ᴺ liäg'ᴺ/	n/a		lec(c)aᴴ	/legaᴴ/

Illustration 30.6: The paradigm of lie, lia 'stone'

30.4. Exercise

Try to inflect some of the following words. I have given the genitive singular in each case and the prepositional plural in those cases where no syncope applies. Decline them together with the article. Combine them with any of the adjectives you have learned so far.

cáera /kai̯ra/, gen. cáerach /kai̯rəχ/ (k, f) 'sheep'
cathair /kaθər'/, gen. cathrach /kaθrəχ/ (k, f) 'town'
brí /b'r'ī/, gen. breg (g, f) /b'r'eγ/ 'hill'
Lugaid /luγəδ'/, gen. Luigdech /luγ'δ'əχ/ (k, m) 'Lugaid (man's name)'
coí /koi̯/, gen. cuach /kuäχ/, prep. cuich /kuäχ'/ (k, f) 'cuckoo'
aire /ar'e/, gen. airech /ar'əχ/, prep. pl. airechaib /ar'əχəβ'/ (k, m) 'noble man'
nathair /naθər'/, gen. nathrach /naθrəχ/ (k, f) 'snake'

30.5. The conjugated prepositions 5

These are the last conjugated prepositions that take the accusative. Now you have learned all conjugated prepositions of Old Irish. Try to get a feeling for them when you come across them in texts.

| person | amal^L 'like, as' | | cen^L 'without' | |
	ending	transcription	ending	transcription
1st sg.	samlum	/sau̯λum/	n/a	
2nd sg.	samlut	/sau̯λud/	cenut	/k'evud/
3rd sg. m., n.	saml(a)id, samlith	/sau̯λəδ'/	cene, cenae	/k'eve/
3rd sg. f.	n/a		n/a	
1st pl.	n/a		n/a	
2nd pl.	n/a		cenuib	/k'evuβ'/
3rd pl.	samlaib	/sau̯λəβ'/	cenaib	/k'evəβ'/

Illustration 30.7: The conjugated prepositions 5: *amal^L, cen^L*

| person | sech 'over, beyond' | |
	ending	transcription
1st sg.	sechum	/s'eχum/
2nd sg.	sechut	/s'eχud/
3rd sg. m., n.	sechæ	/s'eχe/
3rd sg. f.	secce	/s'ek'e/
1st pl.	sechunn	/s'eχun/
2nd pl.	sechaib	/s'eχəβ'/
3rd pl.	seccu	/s'eku/

Illustration 30.8: The conjugated prepositions 5: *sech*

Lesson 31

31.1. Deponent verbs

The forms of the verbal classes that we have learned so far are all so-called active verbal forms. Apart from these there exists a special group of verbs with an inflection of its own, basically distinguished by an *r* in the ending. These verbs are called *deponent verbs*. Students with a knowledge of Latin will already know deponent verbs with their typical *r*-endings from there. In Old Irish these verbs behave just like the verbs that we have learned so far, except for their different endings. 'The difference between active and deponent inflection is purely lexical and has no semantic significance whatsoever.' (EIV 74)

The deponent endings are basically the same for all verbal classes. One can roughly say that deponent endings are distinguished by an additional *r* /ρ/ from their corresponding active endings. Only in the 2nd plural are active and deponent endings identical. The 3rd singular ending can have *th* /θ/ (e.g., *-thir*) or *d* /δ/ (e.g., *-dir*), and this varies even within the same word from attestation to attestation.

Illustration 31.1:
oc suidigiud chlaidib i curp
'placing a sword in a body'

Deponent verbs are numerous only in the W2 class. Apart from these there are some deponent verbs in the W1, a few in the S2 and even fewer in the S3 classes. No deponent verbs belong to the S1 class and nearly none, with a few exceptional forms (see GOI 376), to the H-verbs. Only W2 deponent verbs are well attested in absolute and conjunct inflection. Of the other classes mostly conjunct forms can be found, so that a complete absolute paradigm can only be given for W2 verbs.

31.2. W2 deponent verbs

The present indicative of *suidigidir* /suδ'əγ'əδ'əρ/ 'to place' serves as the model for W2 deponent verbs. The synchronic root is *suidig-* /suδ'əγ'-/ (root final consonant /γ/):

W2	absolute		conjunct	
1st sg.	*suidigiur*	C'uρ	*(ní)·suidigiur*	C'uρ
2nd sg.	*suidigther*	C'(ə)θ'əρ	*(ní)·suidigther*	C'(ə)θ'əρ
3rd sg.	*suidigidir*	C'əθ'əρ', C'əδ'əρ'	*(ní)·suidigedar*	C'əθəρ, C'əδəρ
1st pl.	*suidig(m)mir*	C'(ə)m'əρ'	*(ní)·suidig(m)mer*	C'(ə)m'əρ
2nd pl.	*suidigthe*	C'(ə)θ'e	*(ní)·suidigid*	C'əδ'
3rd pl.	*suidigitir*	C'əd'əρ'	*(ní)·suidigetar*	C'ədəρ

Illustration 31.2: The conjugation of W2 deponent verbs

Note:

1. In the 3rd persons the syllable before the proper ending is *never* syncopated, even though the normal rules would demand it.

2. The overwhelming majority of W2 deponent verbs belong to the very productive group of denominative verbs formed with the suffix *-(a)ig-*, which is the main suffix used in Old Irish to form new verbs from nouns, e.g., *cruth* 'shape, form' → *cruthaigidir* 'to shape,' *fírián* 'just' → *fíriánaigidir* 'to justify,' or *follus* 'clear, bright' → *foilsigidir* 'to clarify, to publish' etc. These verbs inflect exactly like *suidigidir* 'to place' (←*suide* 'place, seat').

3. In addition, there are also some 'original' W2 deponents like *seichithir* 'to follow' (cp. the etymologically identical Latin *sequitur* 'to follow'), which are not derived from other words. Be careful: In these cases the syncope pattern may deviate from that of *suidigidir* in that those syllables which I put into parentheses in the pattern above have to be syncopated.

31.3. W1 deponent verbs

Except for the 2nd singular *labraither* 'thou speakest' I could find no other attested absolute active, non-relative form in Old Irish sources. A typical W1 deponent verb is *molaithir* /moλəθ'əρ'/ 'to praise,' root *mol-* /moλ-/ (root final consonant /λ/):

W1	absolute		conjunct	
1st sg.	n/a		*(ní)·molor, (ní)·molur*	Coρ, Cuρ
2nd sg.	*labraither*	Cəθ'əρ	*(ní)·molaither*	Cəθ'əρ
3rd sg.	n/a		*(ní)·molathar*	Cəθəρ
1st pl.	n/a		*(ní)·molammar*	Cəməρ
2nd pl.	n/a		*(ní)·molaid*	Cəδ'
3rd pl.	n/a		*(ní)·molatar*	Cədəρ

Illustration 31.3: The conjugation of W1 deponent verbs

31.4. S2 deponent verbs

As with W1 verbs, only a few absolute S2 forms are attested. The following example is *midithir* /mˈiδˈəθˈəρ/ 'to judge,' root *mid-* /mˈiδ-/, root final consonant /δ/:

S2	absolute		conjunct	
1st sg.	*midiur*	C'uρ	*(ní)·midiur*	C'uρ
2nd sg.	n/a		*(ní)·mitter*	C'θ'əρ, C't'əρ
3rd sg.	*midithir*	C'əθ'əρ'	*(ní)·midethar*	C'əθəρ
1st pl.	n/a		*(ní)·midemmar*	C'əməρ
2nd pl.	n/a		*(ní)·midid*	C'əδ'
3rd pl.	n/a		*(ní)·midetar*	C'əδəρ

Illustration 31.4: The conjugation of S2 deponent verbs

Note that in the 2nd singular the /θ/ of the ending is delenited to /t/ when it comes into contact with a *d, t* or *n* of the stem.

31.5. S3 deponent verbs

There are only two S3 deponent verbs, *ro·cluinethar* /ro·kluvˈəθəρ/ 'to hear' and *ro·finnadar* /ro·fˈinəδəρ/ 'to find out.' Both have the peculiarity of losing their preverb *ro·* in dependent position, so that, e.g., 'I hear' would be *ro·cluiniur*, but 'I hear not' would be *ní·cluiniur*.

S3	*ro·cluinethar*	*ro·finnadar*
1st sg.	*(ro)·cluiniur*	n/a
2nd sg.	*(ro)·cluinter*	n/a
3rd sg.	*(ro)·cluinethar*	*(ro)·finnadar*
1st pl.	*(ro)·cluinemmar*	*(ro)·finnammar*
2nd pl.	*(ro)·cluinid*	n/a
3rd pl.	*(ro)·cluinetar*	*(ro)·finnatar*

Illustration 31.5: The conjugation of the S3 deponent verbs

Illustration 31.6: *ro·cluiniur fogur* 'I hear noise'

31.6. Exercise

Try to conjugate the following deponent verbs.

foilsigidir /fol's'əγ'əð'əρ'/ (W2) 'to clarify, to publish'
béoaigidir /b'eu̯əγ'əð'əρ'/ (W2) 'to make alive, to animate'
samlaithir /saµλəθ'əρ'/ (W1) 'to compare, to liken'
airlithir /aρ'λ'əθ'əρ'/ (W2) 'to advise'
labraithir /laβρəθ'əρ'/ (W1) 'to speak'
ad·muinethar /að·muv'əθəρ/ (S2) 'to remember' (only independent!)

31.7. The 3rd person passive forms

Until now we have only met verbs with active meaning, that is, verbs where the subject of the sentence is performing an action aimed at an object in the accusative case (= transitive verbs, as in English *I love you*, German *ich liebe dich*), or an action without an object (= intransitive verbs, as in English *I weep*, German *ich weine*). Now we will turn to the Old Irish passive voice, that is, constructions where the action is being performed upon the subject by somebody or something else, as in English *they are being driven from their homes* or German *ich werde geliebt*. The formation of the passive voice is a bit more complicated in Old Irish than it is in English, German or Latin, as there is no uniform formation of the passive for all persons.

Special passive endings exist in Old Irish only for the 3rd persons. They are the same for non-deponent and deponent verbs. Be careful: They must not be mistaken for the corresponding deponent endings, although they look very similar:

| | 3rd sg. | | 3rd pl. | |
	absolute	conjunct	absolute	conjunct
W1	carthair	·carthar	cartair, caraitir	·cartar, ·caratar
W2	léicthir	·léicther	léictir, léicitir	·léicter, ·léicetar
S1	berair	·berar	bertair	·bertar
S2	gaibthir	·gaibther	gaibtir	·gaibter, ·gaibetar
S3	crenair	·crenar	crentair	·crentar
H1	rāithir	·rāthar	n/a	·rātar
H2	gníthir	·gníther	gnītir	·gníter
H3	nuithir	·soíther	?[1]	?

Illustration 31.7: The passive forms

---

[1] I could find no examples for 3rd pl. forms, although it is not unlikely that such forms exist.

31.7.1. 3rd singular

1. The basic passive ending in the 3rd sg. is *-thair, -thir* /θ(ʹ)əρʹ/ in the absolute and *-thar, -ther* /θ(ʹ)əρ/ in the conjunct forms. The /θ/ is non-palatalized in the W1 class and palatalized everywhere else. If after the application of syncope the /θ/ comes to stand immediately after a *d, t* or *n*, it is delenited to /t/, e.g., **midithir > mittir* 'he is being judged.'

2. Historically there was a vowel before the /θ/ of the ending, but this is nearly always syncopated, even where according to the normal rules syncope shouldn't apply. This is especially important for deponent verbs for which thus a distinction between the 3rd sg. deponent ending *-C-ithir (-C-ither), -C-athair (-C-athar)* and the 3rd sg. passive ending *-C-thir (-C-ther), -C-thair (-C-thar)* is created: before the deponent ending there is a vowel (even against the rules of syncope); in the passive there is no vowel (even against the rules of syncope), e.g., *foilsigidir* '(s)he explains,' *foilsigthir* 'it is being explained.' In rare cases, however, the rules of syncope are applied nevertheless, and then there is no way to formally distinguish between deponent and passive forms: the distinction can then only be made from the context.

3. In the S1 and S3 classes the ending is *-air* /əρʹ/ in the absolute and *-ar* /əρ/ in the conjunct, without /θ/. If the root of the verb in question ends in *r*, and the ending *-ar* is in no immediate proximity to the accent of the word, the vowel of the ending is lost. That means that, e.g., prototonic **·tabarar*, the deuterotonic form of *do·berar* 'is being brought,' becomes *·tabarr*, with loss of the *a* between the two *r*'s. The 3rd sg. ending *-ar* is sometimes also found in S2 verbs, e.g., in the compound verb *fo·ácabar (fo-ad-gab-)* 'is being left behind.' The corresponding simple verb *gaibid*, however, has the 3rd sg. passive *gaibthir* with /θ/.

4. In Old Irish the 3rd sg. passive is also used to express impersonality, that is, an action where no subject is specified. In German impersonality is expressed by the pronoun *man*: *man sagt, man tut, man geht*, and this can be directly expressed in Old Irish by 3rd sg. passive forms: *ráittir, do·gnither, tíagair*. In English impersonal forms are expressed by 'one,' e.g., 'one speaks,' or by 'there is,' e.g., 'there is speaking.'

31.7.2. 3rd plural

1. The ending of the 3rd plural is *-tair, -tir* /d(ʹ)əρʹ/ in the absolute and *-tar, -ter* /d(ʹ)əρ/ in the conjunct. The historical vowel in front of the ending may or may not be syncopated, even if the rules of syncope would demand it, e.g., *marbtair* and *marbaitir*, *·gaibter* and *·gaibetar*.

2. Among S1 and S3 verbs only forms without a vowel before the ending are found, e.g., *bentair* and *bertair*. In the deponent verbs the 'syncopated' forms are preponderant, even though there are also forms without syncope, e.g., passive *miditir* 'they are being judged,' which cannot be distinguished formally from deponential *miditir* 'they judge.'

31.8. The 1st and 2nd person passive forms

In Old Irish separate passive endings exist only for the 3rd persons. In order to express the passive voice in other persons, it is necessary to infix the respective personal pronoun into the 3rd person singular passive form, e.g., 3rd sg. *gairthir* '(s)he/it is being called,' but 1st sg. *nom·gairther* 'I am being called.' For the 1st and 2nd plural the 3rd sg. passive form is used, too, e.g., 3rd pl. *do·bertar* 'they are being brought,' but 2nd pl. *dob·berar* 'you are being brought.'

Complete paradigms for the passive of the verbs W1 *caraid* 'to love' and S2 *ad·gair, ·acair* 'to sue' follow here:

pronoun	Old Irish	transcription	translation
		independent	
1st sg.	nom·charthar	/nom·χαρθəρ/	I am being loved
2nd sg.	not·charthar	/nod·χαρθəρ/	thou art being loved
3rd sg.	carthair	/kaρθəρ'/	he/she/it is being loved
1st pl.	nonn·carthar	/non·kaρθəρ/	we are being loved
2nd pl.	nob·carthar	/noβ·kaρθəρ/	you are being loved
3rd pl.	cartair, caraitir	/kaρdəρ' kaρəd'əρ'/	they are being loved
		dependent	
1st sg.	ním·charthar	/n'ɪm·χαρθəρ/	I am not being loved
2nd sg.	nít·charthar	/n'ɪd·χαρθəρ/	thou art not being loved
3rd sg.	ní·carthar	/n'ɪ·kaρθəρ/	(s)he/it is not being loved
1st pl.	nínn·carthar	/n'ɪn·kaρθəρ/	we are not being loved
2nd pl.	níb·carthar	/n'ɪβ·kaρθəρ/	you are not being loved
3rd pl.	ní·cartar	/n'ɪ·kaρdəρ/	they are not being loved

Illustration 31.8: Passive paradigm of *caraid*

Illustration 31.9:
fonn·ácabar inar cotlud
'we are left sleeping'

pronoun	Old Irish	transcription	translation
		independent (deuterotonic)	
1st sg.	*atom·gairther*	/adom·γaρ'θ'əρ/	I am being sued
2nd sg.	*atot·gairther*	/adod·γaρ'θ'əρ/	thou art being sued
3rd sg.	*ad·gairther*	/aδ·gaρ'θ'əρ/	(s)he/it is being sued
1st pl.	*atonn·gairther*	/adon·gaρ'θ'əρ/	we are being sued
2nd pl.	*atob·gairther*	/adoβ·gaρ'θ'əρ/	you are being sued
3rd pl.	*ad·gairter, ad·gairetar*	/aδ·gaρ'd'əρ ·gaρ'ədəρ /	they are being sued
		dependent (prototonic)	
1st sg.	*ním·acarthar*	/n'ɪm·agəρθəρ/	I am not being sued
2nd sg.	*nít·acarthar*	/n'ɪd·agəρθəρ/	thou art not being sued
3rd sg.	*ní·acarthar*	/n'ɪ·agəρθəρ/	(s)he/it is not being sued
1st pl.	*nínn·acarthar*	/n'ɪn·agəρθəρ/	we are not being sued
2nd pl.	*níb·acarthar*	/n'ɪβ·agəρθəρ/	you are not being sued
3rd pl.	*ní·acartar*	/n'ɪ·agəρdəρ/	they are not being sued

Illustration 31.10: Passive paradigm of *ad·gair*

31.9. Exercise

Try to inflect all persons of the passive of the following verbs (be careful—they are cited in the 3rd sg. active/deponent):

> *ad·rími* /aδ·r'ɪμ'i/ (W2a) 'to count'
> *do·scara* /do·skaρa/ (W1) 'to destroy, to overthrow'
> *ní·cuirethar* /n'ɪ·kuρ'əθəρ/ (W2b dep.) 'to put (negative)'
> *aigid* /aγ'əδ'/ (S1) 'to drive, to impel'
> *molaithir* /moλəθ'əρ'/ (W1 dep.) 'to praise'
> *ní·crena* /n'ɪ·k'r'eva/ (S3) 'to buy (negative)'
> *ní·gaib* /n'ɪ·gaβ'/ (S2) 'to take (negative)'

Illustration 31.11: *guirthir in tón* 'the hind side is being warmed'

Lesson 32

32.1. Varia

1. Outside of standardized orthography one repeatedly encounters the variation between *nn* and *nd* in Old Irish texts. Although originally these spellings were used for two different sounds, /n/ and /nd/ respectively, they had fallen together in /n/ already in the Old Irish period and eventually became freely interchangeable orthographical variants. So whenever you encounter *nn* or *nd* in an unknown word, keep in mind the possibility of looking it up both under *nd* or *nn* in the dictionary. In the exercises below, for example, *binn* stands for older *bind*.

2. Note the stem variation in *coí* /koị/, gen. *cuach* /kuəχ/ 'cuckoo' and *céo* /k'eụ/, gen. *ciach* /k'iəχ/ 'fog.' In the oblique cases they are disyllabic with a hiatus between the two syllables.

3. A number of compound verbs lose their first preverb in dependent position. I pointed out this peculiarity already in 31.4 with regard to *ro·cluinethar* and *ro·finnadar*, which become *·cluinethar* and *·finnadar* outside of independent position. Other verbs share this peculiarity as well, e.g., *ad·ágathar* (W2!) 'to fear, to be afraid of' becomes *·ágathar*.

4. The verb *fo·ceird* (S1) 'to put' has the peculiarity that its dependent form is supplied by a completely different stem: *·cuirethar*, which belongs to the W2b class and is a deponent verb. So 'we put' would be *fo·cerdam*, but 'we do not put;' *ní·cuiremmar*.

5. You will notice that in sentence 18 *fo·ácabar*, the passive of *fo·ácaib*, *·fácaib* (S2) 'to leave,' shows no syncope (we would expect **fo·ácbar*). This sometimes happens in other words as well and is probably due to the influence of the 3rd sg. active form.

6. The prototonic passive of *ad·cí*, *·accai* (H2) is irregular: an *s* appears before the ending, so that we get *·accastar*. The deuterotonic passive is the regular *ad·cíther*.

7. One of the ways to express possession in Old Irish is the construction *at·tá X la Y* 'Y has X,' literally 'there is X with Y,' e.g., *at·tá a rígain la cach ríg* 'every king has his queen.' A more emphatic construction, where the owner is especially stressed, is provided by the copulaic construction *is la Y X* 'X is Y's', e.g., *is lim-sa in cauradmír* 'the hero's portion is mine.'

32.2. Exercise

Old Irish

1. Ra·chluiniur: benair clocán binn i n-aidchi gaíthe. 2. Ní·ágatar ind airig saidbri cumachtae ríg túaithe. 3. In·llabraither bríathra faílte frisin rríg ⁊ fria rígnai n-oïc oca techt don chathraig? 4. ** Béoigidir in spirut in corp. (*Wb.* 13d7) 5. Is for fertaib ar carpait suidigmir cenna cróderga inna n-airech marb. 6. Innád·cluinid feit inna gaíthe isnaib sailchib ardaib ar brú inna Bóinne? 7. In·samlatar in scolairi baíth cáercha fri echu? Ní·samaltar-som friu. 8. Cruthaigtir doíni i cosmailius Dé. 9. Ní·fil nathracha isind insi glais, ar ata·aig nóeb Pátraic inna uili eissi. 10. Ní·trebtar rátha ⁊ šenchathraig inna ngeinte. 11. Foilsigthir deacht i Críst, acht foilsigithir Críst fírinni nDé do doínib domuin. 12. **Ad·fíadar dom-sa at·tá macc maith lat-su. (FR 17 f.) 13. Is tre fír flatha miditir túatha móra ⁊ chathraig inna n-úasal. 14. Canair trírech ind luin ⁊ loíd

Lesson 32

inna cuach immum-sa i mmedón ind ḟedo. 15. Á aiti, innád·cluinter-su ríg inna fern oc labrad frimm-sa? 16. Á maicc, ní rí in-so, acht is nél ciach 7 in gáeth oc glúasacht inna nduille. 17. Scríbthair ogom i tóeb liacc aird 7 ṡuidigthir in lie-sin ar mulluch thulchae. 18. Ním·gairther cosin cath, fom·ácabar imo chotlud. 19. Atot·chíther oc áin inna cáerach ón chlúain, nít·accastar oca n-airi. 20. Tíagair ó ríg inna n-Ulad co Temair do dénum chairdessa etarro.

Transcription

1. ra·χλuv'uρ: b'evəρ' klogāv b'in' i vaδ'χ'i γai̯θ'e. 2. n'ï·āγədəρ ind aρ'əγ' saδ'β'ρ'i ku̯μəχte r'ïγ tuaθ'e. 3. iv·laβρəθ'əρ b'r'iaθpa fai̯l't'e f'r'is'ən r'ïγ' ogus f'r'iha ρ'ïγvi voȯg' oga d'eχt don χaθρəγ'? 4. b'eu̯əγ'əδ'əρ' in s'p'iρud in gorρ. 5. is foρ f'ertəβ' aρ garbəd' suδ'əγ'm'əρ' k'ena krōδ'erga ina vaρ'əχ marβ. 6. ināδ·gluv'əδ' fed' ina gai̯θ'e isnəβ' saλ'χ'əβ' ardəβ' aρ βρū ina bōn'e? 7. iv·saμλədəρ in skoλəρ'i βai̯θ' kai̯ρχa f'r'i h'eχu? n'ï·saμəλdəρ-so̯μ f'r'ihu. 8. kruθəγ'd'əρ' doi̯v'i i gosμəλ'us δ'ē. 9. n'ï·f'iλ' naθρəχa is'ənd iv's'i γλas', aρ ada·haγ' noi̯β pādρəg' ina huλ'i es'i. 10. n'ï·t'r'eβdəρ rāθa ogus h'evχaθρəγ' ina ŋ'g'en't'e. 11. fol's'əγ'θ'əρ' d'ēəχt i g'r'ïst, aχt fol's'əγ'əθ'əρ' k'r'ïst f'ïρ'ən'i n'd'ē do δoi̯v'əβ' doμuv'. 12. aδ·f'iaδəρ doμ-sa at·tā mak maθ' lat-su. 13. is t'r'e ïρ βlaθa m'iδ'əd'əρ' tuaθa mōρa ogus χaθρəγ' ina vuasəλ. 14. kavəρ' t'r'iρ'əχ ind λuv' ogus λoi̯δ' ina kuȯχ imum-sa i m'eδōv ind eδo. 15. ā at'i, ināδ·glun't'əρ-su r'ïγ ina β'ern og laβρəδ f'r'im-sa? 16. ā μak', n'ï rï in-so, aχt is n'ēl k'iȯχ ogus in γai̯θ og gluasəχt ina ndul'e. 17. s'k'r'ïβθəρ' oγəm i doi̯β λ'iȯg ar'd' ogus huδ'əγ'θ'əρ' in l'ië-s'iv aρ μuluχ θuλχe. 18. n'ïm·γaρ'θ'əρ kos'ən gaθ, fom·āgəβəρ imo χodλuδ. 19. adod·χ'ïθ'əρ og āv' ina gai̯ρəχ ōn χλuav', n'ïd·akəstəρ oga vaρ'i. 20. t'iaγəρ' ō ρ'ïγ' ina vuλəδ ko t'eμəρ' do δ'ēvu̯μ χaρ'd'əsa etəro.

English

1. We hear it: sweet-sounding bells are struck in a windy night. 2. The rich nobleman fears the power of the tribal kings. 3. You (*OIr.*: pl.) do not say words of welcome to the kings and to their young queens at their coming to the town. 4. Does not the spirit vivify the bodies? 5. It is on the rear shaft of my chariot that I place the blood-red head of the dead nobleman. 6. I hear the whistling of the wind in the high willow at the bank of the Boyne. 7. The scholar does not compare a sheep to a horse. It (= the sheep, feminine in Old Irish) is not being compared to it (= the horse, masculine in Old Irish). 8. Is a human shaped in the likeness of God? 9. There are snakes in the green island, Saint Patrick does not drive out all of them from it (*OIr.*: does not drive them out all). 10. The *rath*s and old cities of the pagans are inhabited. 11. Is not divinity revealed in Christ, and does not Christ reveal God's truth to the people of the world? 12. We are told (*OIr.*: it is being told to us) you (*OIr.*: pl.) have good sons. 13. It is through the ruler's righteousness that the small tribe and its city are judged. 14. The trilling of the blackbirds and the lay of the cuckoos is sung around thee in the middle of the wood. 15. Dad, thou hearest the kings of the aldertree speaking to me. 16. Son, are these kings? 17. Ogam inscriptions (= ogams) are being written on the side of high stones and the stones are being placed at the tops of hills. 18. We are being called to the battle, we are not being left sleeping (*OIr.*: in our sleep). 19. Are you (*OIr.*: pl.) being seen driving the sheep from the meadow? You are being seen herding them (*OIr.*: at their watching). 20. Messengers are coming (*OIr.*: there is a going) from the kings of the Ulaid to Tara to make a covenant between them.

Lesson 33

33.1. Dental stems: consonantal declension in t

The majority of words of this class go back to formations with suffixal *t* in Proto-Celtic and PIE. In Old Irish this sound appears as lenited *d* /ð/ or *th* /θ/. When the dental is at the absolute end of the word it is usually written *d* /ð/, although, especially in old texts, it can appear as *th* /θ/ as well. When an extra syllable is added, e.g., in the prepositional and accusative plural, and the dental comes to stand in the interior of the word, it usually appears as *th* /θ/, seldom as *d* /ð/. This variation is partly due to regular sound changes, but obviously a lot of levelling and simple 'confusion' must have taken place as well. Other words of this stem class go back to forms with etymological *d*. These show the *d* /ð/ more regularly throughout the paradigm, but even here *th* /θ/ may occasionally appear in analogy to words with etymologically justified *th* /θ/. As in guttural stems, in dental stems, too, the nominative singular may end in a vowel or in a consonant, depending on whether the etymological vowel before the dental was long or short. This can apply to words with both etymological *th* or *d* alike. Nouns of this class can be masculine and feminine. Below follows the inflection of *cing* m. 'warrior,' stem *cingeth-* /k'iŋ'g'əθ/:

case	ending	Old Irish	Prim. Irish	Proto-Celtic	Pre-Celtic
nom. sg.	Ø	*cing*	*kıŋgeh	*kıŋgets	*keŋgĕts
gen.	{L}ð/θ	*cinged/th*	*kıŋgeθah	*kıŋgetos	*kengetos
prep.	ð/θ'ᴸ, Øᴸ	*cingid/thᴸ, cingᴸ* «	*kıŋgeθ (»)	*kıŋgeteı̯, -ti	*kengeteı̯, *kengeti
acc.	ð/θ'ᴺ	*cingid/thᴺ*	*kıŋgeθev	*kıŋgetam	*kengetm̥
voc.	Ø	*áᴸ ching*	*kıŋgeh	*kıŋgets	*keŋgĕts
nom. pl.	ð/θ'	*cingid/th*	*kıŋgeθeh	*kıŋgetes	*kengetes
gen.	{L}ð/θ ᴺ	*cinged/thᴺ*	*kıŋgeθav	*kıŋgetom	*kengetom
prep.	{L}θ(')əβ'	*cingthib* (?)	*kıŋgeθaβih «	*kıŋgedbis (»)	*kengetbʰis, -bʰos
acc.	{L}θ(')aᴴ	*cingtheaᴴ* (?)	*kıŋgeθāh	*kıŋgetās	*kengetn̥s
voc.	{L}θ(')aᴴ	*áᴸ chingtheaᴴ* (?) «	*kıŋgeθeh	*kıŋgetes	*kengetes
n. a. v. du.	ð/θ'ᴸ	*dáᴸ chingid/thᴸ*	*kıŋgeθe	*kıŋgete	*kengeth₁e
gen.	{L}ð/θ ᴸ	*dáᴸ chinged/thᴸ*	*kıŋgeθō	*kıŋgetoṷ (»)	*kengeth₁oh₁s, -(H)oh₁u
prep.	{L}θ(')əβ'	*dibᴺ cingthib* (?) «	*kıŋgeθaβiv «	*kıŋgedbim «	*kengetbʰih₁, -moh₁ ?

Illustration 33.1: The t-stems (etymological *t*)

Note:

1. The prepositional plural and dual, and the accusative and vocative plural of this word, that is, those cases where due to an added extra syllable syncope has to apply, are not actually attested. I have hesitatingly set up the paradigm above with syncopated forms, on the grounds that other words like prep. pl. *traigthib* 'feet' from *traig* (f, t) or acc. pl. *lochtha* (t, f) 'mice' from *luch* do

display syncope here. But it seems that actually dental and guttural stems that denote certain classes of persons like *fili* (t, m) 'poet,' *míl* (t, m) 'soldier,' *ruiri* (g, m) 'king,' *aire* (k, m) 'freeman' for whatever reasons avoided syncope.

The next paradigm, which has a vowel in the nominative singular, is probably from a word with etymological *d*. It is the word for the 'driver of a chariot' *arae* m., stem *arad-* /aρəδ/. Note also that in this word there is no syncope in those cases where an extra syllable is added (the omission of syncope is etymologically justified here).

case	ending	Old Irish	Prim. Irish	Proto-Celtic	Pre-Celtic
nom. sg.	Ø	*arae*^{H}	*aρeheh	*aresets	*pr̥h₂iseds
gen.	{L}δ/θ	*arad*	*aρeheδah	*aresedos	*pr̥h₂isedos
prep.	δ/θ'^{L}, Ø^L	*araid*^{L}, (*arae*^{L}) «	*aρeheδ («)	*aresedei̯, -di	*pr̥h₂isedei̯, *pr̥h₂isedi
acc.	δ/θ'^{N}	*araid*^{N}	*aρeheδev	*aresedam	*pr̥h₂isedm̥
voc.	Ø	*á*^{L} *arae*^{H}	*aρeheh	*aresets	*pr̥h₂iseds
nom. pl.	δ/θ'	*araid*	*aρeheδeh	*aresedes	*pr̥h₂isedes
gen.	{L}δ/θ ^{N}	*arad*^{N}	*aρeheδav	*aresedom	*pr̥h₂isedom
prep.	{L}θ(')əβ'	*aradaib*	*aρeheδaβih «	*aresedbis (»)	*pr̥h₂isedbʰis, -bʰos
acc.	{L}θ(')a^H	*aradu*^{H}, *arada*^{H}	*aρeheδāh	*aresedās	*pr̥h₂isedn̥s
voc.	{L}θ(')a^H	*á*^{L} *arada*^{H} (?) «	*aρeheδeh	*aresedes	*pr̥h₂isedes
n. a. v. du.	δ/θ'^{L}	*dá*^{L} *araid*^{L}	*aρeheδe	*aresede	*pr̥h₂isedh₁e
gen.	{L}δ/θ ^{L}	*dá*^{L} *arad*^{L}	*aρeheδō	*aresedou̯ («)	*pr̥h₂isedh₁oh₁s, -(H)oh₁u
prep.	{L}θ(')əβ'	*dib*^{N} *n-aradaib* «	*aρeheδaβiv «	*aresedbim «	*pr̥h₂isedbʰih₁, -moh₁ ?

Illustration 33.2: The t-stems (etymological *d*)

Note:

1. The accusative plural ought to be *arada*. The attested form *aradu* owes its *-u* to the influence of the o-stems.

Illustration 33.3: *arae 7 eirr* 'chariot-driver and chariot-fighter'

33.2. Dental stems: consonantal declension in nt

A second large group of dental stems has its stem ending in unlenited *t* /d/, which ultimately goes back to PIE and CC *nt*. Words of this class can belong to any of the three genders of Old Irish. The inflection of neuters, however, differs somewhat from that of masculines and feminines. We will start with the latter, with the word *carae* m. 'friend,' stem *carat-* /kaɸəd/. Note that the /d/ can be written *t* or *d* in word interior position after a consonant.

case	ending	Old Irish	Prim. Irish	Common Celt.	Pre-Celtic
nom. sg.	V^H	*carae*^{H}	*kaɸēh	*karants «	*kh₂rénts
gen.	əd	*carat*	*kaɸēdah	*karantos	*kh₂r̥ntós
prep.	əd'^{L}	*carait*^{L} «	*kaɸēd («)	*karantei̯, -nti	*kh₂r̥ntéi̯, *kh₂r̥ntí
acc.	əd'^{N}	*carait*^{N}	*kaɸēdev	*karantam «	*kh₂réntm̥
voc.	V^H	*á*^{L} *charae*^{H}	*kaɸēh	*karants «	*kh₂rénts
nom. pl.	əd'	*carait*	*kaɸēdeh	*karantes «	*kh₂réntes
gen.	əd^N	*carat*^{N}	*kaɸēdav	*karantom «	*kh₂r̥ntóm
prep.	(ə)d⁽'⁾əβ'	*cairtib*	*kaɸēdaβih «	*karandbis («)	*kh₂r̥ntbʰís, -bʰós
acc.	(ə)d⁽'⁾a^H	*cairt/dea*^{H}	*kaɸēdāh	*karantās	*kh₂r̥ntń̥s
voc.	(ə)d⁽'⁾a^H	*á*^{L} *chairt/dea*^{H} «	*kaɸēdeh	*karantes «	*kh₂réntes
n. a. v. du.	əd'^{L}	*dá*^{L} *charait*^{L}	*kaɸēde	*karante	*kh₂rénth₁e
gen.	əd^L	*dá*^{L} *charat*^{L}	*kaɸēdō	*karantou̯ («)	*kh₂r̥nth₁óh₁s, -(H)óh₁u
prep.	(ə)d⁽'⁾əβ'	*dib*^{N} *cairt/dib* «	*kaɸēdaβiv «	*karandbim «	*kh₂r̥ntbʰih₁, -moh₁ ?

Illustration 33.4: The nt-stems

There are only a few neuters, the most important being the word for 'tooth' *dét* /d'ēd/:

case	ending	Old Irish	Prim. Irish	Common Celt.	Pre-Celtic
nom. acc sg.	d^N	*dét*^{N} «	*dēd	*dant «	*h₁dónt
gen.	d	*dét*	*dēdah	*dantos «	*h₁dn̥tós
prep.	d'^{L}	*déit*^{L}	*dēdē	*dantei̯	*h₁dn̥téi̯
voc.	d^N	*á*^{L} *dét*^{N} «	*dēd	*dant «	-
nom. acc. pl.	d^L	*dét*^{L}	*dēdā	*dantā «	-
gen.	d^N	*dét*^{N}	*dēdav	*dantom «	-
prep.	dəβ'	*détaib*	*dēdaβih «	*dandbis «	-
n. a. v. du.	d^N	*dá*^{N} *ndét*^{N}	?	?	-
gen.		n/a	?	?	-
prep.		n/a	?	?	-

Illustration 33.5: The neuter nt-stems

33.3. Exercise

Inflect some of the following words. I have given the genitive singular in each case and I have noted those words where no syncope applies. Decline them together with the article. Combine them with any of the adjectives you have learned so far.

> *druí* /druį̄/, gen. *druad* /druəδ/ (t, m) 'druid' (original *d*)
>
> *námae* /nāμe/, gen. *námat* /nāμəd/ (nt, m) 'enemy'
>
> *fili* /f'iλ'i/, gen. *filed* /f'iλ'əδ/ (t, m) 'poet' (no syncope!)
>
> *teine* /t'ev'e/, gen. *teined* /t'ev'əδ/ (t, m) 'fire' (original *th*)
>
> *fíado* /f'iaδo/, gen. *fíadat* /f'iaδəd/ (nt, m) 'lord, the Lord'
>
> *luch* /luχ/, gen. *lochad* /loχəδ/ (t, f) 'mouse' (original *th*)
>
> *traig* /traγ'/, gen. *traiged* /traγ'əδ/ (t, f) 'foot' (original *th*)

33.4. The cardinal numbers 20–1000

1. The decades 20–90 inflect like masculine nt-stems, e.g., nom. *fiche*, gen. *fichet*, prep. *fichit*, or nom. *trícho*, gen. *tríchat*, prep. *tríchait*. They can also be used in the dual and in the plural, e.g., in the frequent expressions *dá fichit* 'two twenties = forty' or *trí fichit* 'three twenties = sixty.' The final vowel of the decades 30–90 in the nominative singular is *-o* in the earliest period of Old Irish, *-a* in later Irish. The earlier variant in *-o* is not always attested.

2. *cét* is a neuter o-stem.

3. *míle* is a feminine į̄ā-stem.

4. The multiples of 10, 100 and 1000 are nouns. That means that syntactically they behave differently from the numbers 1–10 which are basically adjectives. After them the counted elements stand in the genitive plural, e.g., *trícha cáerach* 'lit. thirty of sheep = thirty sheep.' The multiples of 10, 100 and 1000 are used for people and things alike.

5. In combination of digits and decades the digits come first and the latter follow in the genitive singular, e.g., *a ocht fichet* /a hoχt β'iχ'əd/ '28 (lit.: eight of twenty).' Note that the elements counted immediately follow the digit, e.g., *cóic ṡailm sechtmogat* '75 psalms (lit.: five psalms of seventy)' (*Ml.* 2c2). Digits and decades are combined with hundreds by means of the preposition *ar^L* + prep., e.g., *a dáu cóicat ar chét* '152,' *cóic míli ochtmugat ar chét* '185.000 (lit.: five thousand of eighty upon hundred' (*Ml.* 34b17).

Illustration 33.6:
...a cethair sechtmagat, a cóic ṡechtmagat...
'...seventy-four, seventy-five...'

The Proto-Celtic reconstructions in the table below are tentative proposals only.

nr.	transcr.	Old Irish	Prim. Irish	Common Celt.	PIE
20	fʲiχʲe	fiche	*u̯iχēh «	*u̯ikantī «	*du̯idḱm̥tih₁
30	tʲrʲɪχo	trícho	*trīχōh	*trikonts	*tridḱomts
40	kʲeθərχo	cethorcho	*kʷeθrūχōh	*kʷetrūkonts	*kʷetrudḱomts
50	koi̯ga	cóeca	*kʷoi̯gʷōh < *kʷōgʷīχōh «	*kʷɪnkʷīkonts	*penkʷedḱomts
60	sʲeska	sesca	*su̯eskōh	*su̯eχskonts	*su̯eḱsdḱomts
70	sʲeχtµəγo	sechtmogo	*seχtaµāχōh	*seχtamākonts «	*septm̥dḱomts
80	oχtµəγa	ochtmoga	*oχtaµāχōh «	*oχtākonts	*h₂oḱtoh₃dḱomts
90	nōχa	nócha	*nou̯āχōh ? «	*nou̯ankonts ?	*h₁neu̯n̥dḱomts
100	kʲēd	cét	*kēdav	*kantom	*dḱm̥tom
1000	mʲīʎʲe	míle	-	-	-

Illustration 33.7: The cardinal numbers 20–1000

33.5. The ordinal numbers 20–1000

1. The ordinal numbers 20–1000 are formed by adding the suffix -mad /µəδ/, which we already met in 24.2, to the stem of the corresponding cardinals.

2. In combinations of digits with tens and hundreds the digit alone has the ordinal form, the tens are expressed by the genitive of the cardinal, the hundreds are attached by means of arᴸ, e.g., *ind óenmad rann fichet* 'the 21st part' (LU 2455), *isin fichetmad blíadain ar chét* 'in the 120th year' (*Trip.* 258, 13).

number	Old Irish	transcription
20th	fichetmad	fʲiχʲədµəδ
30th	tríchatmad	tʲrʲīχədµəδ
40th	cethrachatmad	kʲeθrəχədµəδ
50th	cóecatmad	koi̯gədµəδ
60th	sescatmad	sʲeskədµəδ
70th	n/a	
80th	n/a	
90th	n/a	
100th	cétmad	kʲēdµəδ
1000th	mílmad	mʲīʎµəδ

Illustration 33.8: The ordinal numbers 20–1000

Lesson 34

34.1. Relative clauses

We will now start with a new complex of Old Irish syntax and morphology: relative constructions. This is a large and complicated area of Old Irish grammar, and we will approach it cautiously, progressing step by step over the next lessons.

Relative clauses are subordinate clauses that define parts of a superordinate clause and that are introduced by relative pronouns, for example, in English or German. Relative pronouns are inflected pronouns like *der, die, das, welcher, welche, welches* in German, or *qui, quae, quod* in Latin. English uses the only partially inflectable words *who (whose, whom), which, that.* In other languages like Spanish or Italian uninflected particles like *que, che* mark the relativity of a clause. Examples for relative clauses are English *is this all __that__ you know* or German *grüss mir die Frau, __die__ ich liebe.*

In Old Irish things are completely different. Old Irish does not have inflectable relative pronouns, and although there is something like a relative particle, it is only used in very limited contexts. This may not seem unusual to speakers of English, where sometimes relative clauses can be construed without any overt relative marking, e.g., *this one goes out to the one I love*, where *I love* is a relative clause dependent on *the one*, without being especially marked as such by a pronoun. But this is only an option in English, whereas it is the rule in Old Irish. This lack of a relative pronoun does not mean, however, that relativity remains unexpressed. In fact a highly complex system is involved to express relativity in specifically relative verbal forms. So you always have to turn your attention first to the verb of the clause to determine if you are dealing with a relative clause, and which type of relative clause it is. To make things more complicated there are a number of completely different strategies to mark relativity, depending on the person, the dependence/independence of the verb, the infixed pronoun, the relation of the subordinate to the superordinate clause, and the syntactical category of the relativized phrase.

Strictly speaking, relative clauses are only those clauses that qualify a part of the superordinate clause and that, in 'normal' European languages, are introduced by a relative pronoun or particle. In Old Irish grammar, however, when speaking of relative clauses, usually all possible kinds of subordinate clauses are subsumed, like causal, temporal or concessive clauses, etc. This is due to the fact that the constructions of these types of dependent clauses are very much like and follow rules similar to 'real' relative clauses. It would perhaps be more appropriate to speak of subordinate constructions and subordinate verbal forms in Old Irish, but 'relative' is the traditional term to which I will adhere, too.

34.2. Absolute relative verbal endings

Many different strategies exist to express relativity, depending on the type of relation between subordinate and superordinate clause and on the shape of the verb. Let's turn to the latter question first. For simple verbs separate inflectional endings exist to express relativity, but only for the 3rd person singular and the 1st and 3rd persons plural, and only in the absolute inflection.

For the 1st and 2nd persons singular and the 2nd person plural and for dependent forms a different strategy has to be used, which I will discuss in the next section.

1. In the active inflection the ending of the 3rd sg. is /əs/, spelled -as after non-palatalized consonants and vowels and -es after palatalized consonants.

2. The 1st pl. ending is /m⁽ʲ⁾e/, spelled -mae /me/ after non-palatalized consonants and -me /m'e/ after palatalized consonants and i. When the rules of syncope demand it, a vowel appears before the ending, which then always has a palatalized m.

3. The 3rd pl. ending is /d⁽ʲ⁾e/, spelled -tae /de/ after non-palatalized consonants and -te /d'e/ after palatalized consonants and i. This /d/ can be written with a d if it immediately follows a consonant. When the rules of syncope demand it, but sometimes also without any apparent reason, a vowel appears before the ending, which then always has a palatalized t.

The active relative endings of Old Irish are as follows:

class	person	Old Irish	transcription
	3rd sg.	*caras*	Cəs
W1	1st pl.	*carmae, pridchimme*	C(ə)m⁽ʲ⁾e
	3rd pl.	*cartae, caraite, pridchite*	Cde, Cəd'e
	3rd sg.	*léices*	C'əs
W2	1st pl.	*léicme*	C'm'e
	3rd pl.	*léicte, léicite*	C'd'e, C'əd'e
	3rd sg.	*beires*	C'əs
S1	1st pl.	*bermae*	Cme
	3rd pl.	*bertae*	Cde
	3rd sg.	*gaibes*	C'əs
S2	1st pl.	*gaibme*	C'm'e
	3rd pl.	*gaibte*	C'd'e
	3rd sg.	*crenas*	vəs
S3	1st pl.	*crenmae*	vme
	3rd pl.	*crentae*	nde

Illustration 34.1a: The active absolute relative endings

class	person	Old Irish	transcription
	3rd sg.	*taas, snás*	aə̌s, ās
H1	1st pl.	n/a	
	3rd pl.	**rátae*	āde
	3rd sg.	*bíis, gnís*[1]	iə̌s, īs
H2	1st pl.	*bímme*	īm'e
	3rd pl.	*bíte, gníte*	ĭd'e
	3rd sg.	*foas*	Və̌s
H3	1st pl.	n/a	
	3rd pl.	*foite*	Vd'e

Illustration 34.1b: The active absolute relative endings

Not only active, but also deponent and passive verbs have special relative endings in the absolute inflection. These are easy to remember, however, since their final consonants are non-palatalized, which means that they are formally identical with the corresponding conjunct endings (with the one difference, of course, that they occur without a particle before them). The deponent relative forms are as follows:

class	person	Old Irish	transcription
	3rd sg.	*labrathar*	Cəθəρ, Cəδəρ
W1	1st pl.	*labrammar*	C(ə)məρ
	3rd pl.	*labratar*	Cədəρ
	3rd sg.	*suidigedar*	C'əθəρ, C'əδəρ
W2	1st pl.	*suidigmer*	C'm'əρ, C'əməρ
	3rd pl.	*suidigetar*	C'ədəρ
	3rd sg.	*midethar*	C'əθəρ, C'əδəρ
S2	1st pl.	*midemmar*	C'm'əρ, C'əməρ
	3rd pl.	*midetar*	C'ədəρ

Illustration 34.2: The deponent absolute relative endings

---

[1] Further attested forms of the 3rd sg. relative of the H2 class are *cías, liess* and *sníes*; beside *foas*, in H3 there are *sceas, sceis, soas, luas, lues* and *cloas.*

The passive relative forms are as follows:

class	person	Old Irish	transcription
W1	3rd sg.	carthar	Cθəρ
	3rd pl.	cartar, caratar	Cdəρ, Cədəρ
W2	3rd sg.	léicther	C'θ'əρ
	3rd pl.	léicter, léicetar	C'd'əρ, C'ədəρ
S1	3rd sg.	berar	Cəρ
	3rd pl.	bertar	Cdəρ
S2	3rd sg.	gaibther	C'θ'əρ
	3rd pl.	gaibter	C'd'əρ
S3	3rd sg.	crenar	vəρ
	3rd pl.	crentar	ndəρ
H1	3rd sg.	n/a	
	3rd pl.	látar	
H2	3rd sg.	bither, líther, gnither	iθ'əρ, īθ'əρ
	3rd pl.	líter, gniter	id'əρ, īd'əρ
H3	3rd sg.	clóither	Vθ'əρ
	3rd pl.	n/a	

Illustration 34.3: The passive absolute relative endings

Relative constructions that use the above listed relative verbal forms without any further particle express the following relations:

1. Subjectival relation (subject antecedent):

The relativized phrase, that is, the word on which the relative clause is dependent, is the subject of the relative clause, e.g., *ad·cíu in n-ingin caras libru maithi* 'I see the girl who loves good books.' The relativized phrase in the superordinate clause is *in n-ingin* 'the girl (acc.),' whose role in the relative clause is that of the subject (she is the one who loves good books).

2. Objectival relation (object antecedent):

The relativized phrase, that is, the word on which the relative clause is dependent, is the object of the relative clause, e.g., *ad·cíu in n-ingin caras in rí* 'I see the girl whom the king loves.' The relativized phrase in the superordinate clause again is *in n-ingin* 'the girl (acc.),' but in this case her role in the relative clause is that of the object (she is the one who is the object of the king's love).

This, of course, means that sometimes we can get ambiguous constructions, e.g., *in fer móras in macc* may either mean 'the man who praises the boy' or 'the man whom the boy praises.' A sentence like *in macc móras in fer* is superficially—at least orthographically—ambiguous, too, but there is a difference in pronunciation: 'the boy whom the man praises' would be pronounced /in mak mōβəs in f'eρ/ (*in fer* being the subject of the relative clause, therefore in the nominative case); 'the boy who praises the man' would be pronounced /in mak mōβəs in β'eρ/ (*in fer* being the object of the relative clause, therefore in the accusative case). But in most cases it is clear from the context and/or especially from the inflectional endings who is the subject of the relative clause.

Examples for all possible uses of the different relative forms are:

> *in lebor caras ind ingen* 'the book which the girl loves' (object antecedent)
> *ind ingen caras in llebor* 'the girl who loves the book' (subject antecedent)
> *in lebor carmae* 'the book which we love' (object antecedent)
> *in lebor cartae (inna ingena)* 'the book which they (the girls) love' (object antecedent)
> *inna ingena cartae in llebor* 'the girls who love the book' (subject antecedent)
> *in lebor carthar* 'the book which is being loved' (subject antecedent)
> *ind libuir cartar* 'the books which are being loved' (subject antecedent)

34.3. Leniting relative clauses

In the last section I talked about the constructions used for simple verbs in the 3rd singular or 1st or 3rd persons plural. If, however, the verb of the relative clause is in the 1st or 2nd person singular or 2nd plural, or if it is compounded, a completely different strategy has to be used. Then what is called a *leniting relative clause* construction has to be used. Syntactically this construction does not correspond absolutely to the relative clauses in the last section, in that it is only used where the relativized phrase is the subject of the relative clause, or where a neuter pronoun is the object of the relative clause.

How is the lenition in a leniting relative clause expressed? In compound verbs the *anlauting* consonant of the stressed part of the verb is lenited, e.g., *ad·chíu* /aδ·χ'iṷ/ 'which I see,' *ad·fíadar*, *ad·fíadar* /aδ·iaδəρ/ 'which is being told,' *do·thíagat* /do·θ'iaγəd/ 'who come.' This lenition is, of course, often not to be seen in the orthography, but has to be pronounced nevertheless, e.g., *do·gniam* /do·γ'v'iəμ/ 'which we make,' *do·beirid* /do·β'eρ'əδ'/ 'which you bring.' If, however, the stressed part of a verbal form starts with a vowel, the lenition is neither to be seen nor to be pro-nounced, e.g., *ad·ellat* /aδ·eləd/ 'who visit,' *fo·ácabar* /fo·āgə-βəρ/ 'who is being left behind.' In these cases you simply have to know that syntactically a leniting relative clause is deman-ded in the construction.

In those cases where a simple verb in the 1st or 2nd person sin-gular or 2nd plural appears in a relative construction the empty particle *no·*, which you already know from the infixed pro-nouns, has to be used to create a 'forced' compound. Then the same rules as for original compounds are applied, e.g., *no·char-aimm* /no·χaρəm'/ 'which I love,' *no·gaibi* /no·γaβ'i/ 'which thou takest,' *no·aigid* /no·aγ'əδ'/ 'which you drive.'

Illustration 34.4:
oclach berthaigethar a chlaideb
'a warrior who brandishes his sword'

34.4. Negative leniting relative clauses

For the negation of subordinate clauses a special negative particle *nád·*, *nă·* is used. As with all particles, verbs must take their dependent forms after it, that is conjunct inflection in the case of simple verbs, the prototonic form in compound verbs. Of course no special relative endings can be applied in dependent forms.

In constructions that demand leniting relative clauses *nád·* also lenites the *anlaut* of the following verb, e.g., *ind ingen nád·chara in fer* 'the girl who does not love the man,' *in lebor nád·berar* /nāδ·β'epəρ/ 'the book which is not carried,' *nád·fácabar* /nāδ·āgəβəρ/ 'who is not left behind,' *nád·accam* /nāδ·akəμ/ 'which we do not see,' etc.

34.5. Special relative forms

1. Deuterotonic compound verbs with *imm·* and *ar·* as their first preverb add *-a* (earlier *-e*) to *imm·*, *ar·* in relative position, e.g., non-relative *imm·tét* '(s)he goes around,' but relative *imme·thét* 'who goes around, which (s)he goes around,' or non-relative *ar·fognat* (H2!) 'they serve,' but relative *ara·fognat* 'who serve.'

2. The 3rd sg. relative of S1 *téit* '(s)he goes' is *téite* 'who goes.'

3. The relative forms of the copula *is* and of the substantive verb *at·tá* will be discussed in the next lesson.

34.6. The prehistory of the relative endings

1. The relative forms of the 1st pl. *-m(a)e* /me/ and 3rd pl. *-t(a)e* /de/ go back to forms where the relative particle **i̯o* was added to the absolute endings, i.e. **-mohii̯o* and **-ntii̯o*.

2. In compound verbs the relative particle **i̯o* was added to the first preverb. This explains the lenition in leniting relative forms, and it is also responsible for the relative variants *imme·* and *are·* < **ambii̯o-* and **arei̯o-*.

3. The 3rd sg. relative ending *-as/-es* /əs/ has been analogically transferred from the relative form *as* of the copula which itself perhaps continues a weakly accentuated form with relative *-i̯o*, i.e. **estii̯o* > **etsii̯o* > **essi̯o* > **esso* > *as* (cp. MW *yssyd* < **estii̯o*).

34.7. Independent personal pronouns

There is one exception to my earlier claim (see 25.1) that Old Irish has no independent personal pronouns: In fact in one construction personal pronouns like *I, thou, he, she*, etc. are used, namely when they form the topic of the sentence and are therefore moved to its stressed beginning, usually being introduced by the copula, e.g., *is é mo druí, Ísu Críst*, 'he is my druid, namely Jesus Christ,' or *in tú rí inna n-Iudaide?* 'art *thou* the king of the Jews?' (lit.: 'is it thou the king of the Jews?'). Often the independent pronoun is followed by a relative clause, e.g., *is mé for·chain in Sengoídelc* 'it is I who teaches Old Irish.' These are the independent personal pronouns, with their emphatic variants on the right:

person	translation	pronoun		emphatic pronoun	
1st sg.	I	*mé*	/m'ē/	*me(s)se, meisse*	/m'es'e/
2nd sg.	thou	*tú*	/tū/	*tussu, tusu*	/tusu/
3rd sg. masc.	he	*é, hé*	/ē/	*é-som, hé-som*	/ē-soμ/
3rd sg. fem.	she	*sí*	/s'ī/	*sisi, sissi*	/s'is'i/
3rd sg. neutr.	it	*ed, hed*	/eδ/	n/a	
1st pl.	we	*sní*	/s'n'ī/	*snisni, sinni*	/s'n'is'n'i s'in'i/
2nd pl.	you	*sí, sib*	/s'ī s'iβ'/	*sisi, sissi, sib-si*	/s'is'i s'iβ'-s'i/
3rd pl.	they	*é, hé*	/ē/	*é-som, hé-som*	/ē-soμ/

Illustration 34.5: The independent personal pronouns

Note:

1. The emphatic forms are used to confront different persons: *messe ocus Pangur Bán, cechtar náthar fria śaindán* 'I (on the one hand) and Pangur the White (on the other hand), each of us two is at his own task' (*Thes.* ii 293.14).

2. All independent personal pronouns except for the 3rd pl. can be construed with the 3rd sg. of the copula: *is mé* 'it is I,' *is tú* 'it is thou,' *is é* 'it is he,' *is sí* 'it is she,' *is ed* 'it is it,' *is sní* 'it is we,' *is sib* 'it is you.' Only the 3rd pl. always takes the 3rd pl. form of the copula: *it é* 'it is they' (the same, of course, is true for all other manifestations of the copula, e.g., negated *ní^H*, interrogative *in^N*, etc.). The same is true for relative clauses that have a relativized personal pronoun as their subject: all except for the 3rd pl. pronoun are construed with a 3rd sg. verbal form, e.g., *is snisni as·beir in mbréithir-seo* /is s'n'is'n'i as·β'eρ' iv m'b'r'ēθ'əρ'-s'o/ 'it is we who say (lit. who says) this word.'

3. Stressed pronouns can only be used as nominatives. Where a stressed personal pronoun in the genitive is asked for special forms exist. These are very rare, however. In predicative constructions (that is constructions of the type *X is mine, hers, yours*, etc.) they are usually replaced by constructions with *la*, and they are more frequently used as partitive genitives (that is, in constructions like *two of us, some of them*, etc.). They are 1st sg. *muí* /muị/ 'mine,' emphasized *muisse* /mus'e/ 2nd sg. *taí* /taị/ 'thine' (e.g., *is and nad·bí muí na taí* 'it is there that there is neither mine nor thine,' LU 10848), 1st pl. *náthar* or *nár* /nāθəρ nāρ/ 'of us (two),' 2nd pl. *sethar* or *sár* /s'eθəρ sāρ/ 'of you (two),' and *aí, áe* /aị/ for all 3rd persons 'his, hers, its, theirs, of them,' e.g., *cía náthar* 'who of us two,' *a n-aí* 'his, their (things),' etc.

Lesson 35

35.1. Varia

1. In Irish texts you will constantly encounter the sign *.i.* This is originally a Latin abbreviation for *id est* 'that is,' but in Irish texts it is usually read as *ed ón* /eð ōv/ 'that is; that means; namely,' introducing an explanation or illustration of something said before.

2. *ol* is a causal conjunction, and like *ar* and *sech*, which we met in 26.2, it is followed by the independent form of the verb. Only the 3ʳᵈ sg. of the copula appears in its relative form after *ol*.

3. Adjectives without a noun beside them can be used substantivally to refer to persons or things, e.g., *oac* 'someone young = a young person,' *lobur* 'someone weak = a weak, sick person,' *dorchae* 'something dark = darkness, dark place,' *ard* 'something high = height.' When refering to a person the adjective is masculine or feminine (depending on the gender of the person); when refering to a thing, the adjective is neuter.

4. The preposition *la*ᴴ is used to express the agent (that is the one, by whom the action is done) in a passive construction, e.g., *nít·áigther-su linn* 'thou art not being feared by us.'

35.2. Exercise

Old Irish

1. ** Is ed in-so no·guidimm. (*Wb.* 21a8) 2. ** Do rígrad no·molur, ol is tú mo ruiri. (*Fél. Prol.* 13 f.) 3. Tongu do Día toinges mo thúath, is sib-si in druid bertae brichtu forar nnáimtea-ni. 4. ** Rethait uili 7 is óenḟer gaibes búaid diib inna chomalnad. (*Wb.* 11a4) 5. * Is é [*sc.* Día] fo·cheird cen dolmai néim n-óir deirg form labrai. (GT 202) 6. Bendacht úaimm forsin n-oígid ndil beires scéla diar cairtib leis. 7. ** A mbás tíagmae-ni do·áirci bethaid dúib-si, .i. is ar bethaid dúib-si tíagmai-ni bás. (*Wb.* 15b28) 8. Is sinni téite isin fid 7 ro·chluinethar inna éunu oc cétul. 9. Innád·n-accaid inna cáercha dubai aiges int augaire a medón inna cáerach find? 10. Is sí ind ingen dáiles biad 7 do·fortai fín donaib oígedaib, 7 nos·ngairiu cuccum. 11. At·taat ind araid inna suidiu ar bélaib inna n-eirred, nís·fil inna suidiu fora clíu. 12. It é filid prímgráid ind ḟir cantae cóecait ndúan ar thríb cétaib, .i. secht cóecait ndúan. 13. ** Ní·caraimm in n-uisce ndúabais imma·thét sech tóeb m'árais. (AU 845) 14. ** It moíni cartar lib, nídat doíni. (GT 48) 15. ** Á gelgrían for·osnai ríched co mméit noíbe, á Rí con·ic aingliu, á Choimmdiu inna ndoíne! (*Fél. Prol.* 5-8) 16. ** Trí buirb in betha: óc con·tibi sen, slán con·tibi galrach, gáeth con·tibi báeth. (*Triad* 82) 17. ** Trí dorchae nád·dlegat mná do imthecht: dorchae ciach, dorchae n-aidche, dorchae feda. (*Triad* 100) 18. ** Trí fuili nád·dlegat frecor: fuil chatha, 7 eóit, 7 etargairi. (*Triad* 154) 19. ** Trí soír do·gniat dóeru díb féin: tigernae renas a déiss, rígain téite co aithech, mac filed léices a cheird. (*Triad* 167) 20. ** Trí orbai rannatar fíad chomarbaib: orbae drúith 7 orbae dásachtaig 7 orbae sin. (*Triad* 205)

Transcription

1. is eδ in-so no·γuδ'əm'. 2. do ρ'ɪγρəδ no-μoλuρ, oλ is tū mo ρuρ'i. 3. toŋgu do δ'ia toŋ'g'əs mo θuaθ, is s'iβ'-s'i in druϧδ' b'eρde b'r'iχtu foρəρ nāμ'd'a-n'i. 4. r'eθəd' uλ'i ogus is oḭv'eρ gaβ'əs buaδ' d'iϧβ' ina χoμəλvəδ. 5. is ē fo·χ'er'd' k'en doλμi n'ēμ vōρ' δ'er'g' form λaβρi. 6. b'endəχt uam' fors'ən noḭγ'əδ' n'd'iλ' b'eρ'əs s'k'ēλa d'iϧρ gaρ'd'əβ' les'. 7. a mbās t'iaγme-n'i do·ǎρ'k'i b'eθəδ' dūβ'-s'i, eδ ōv is aρ β'eθəδ' dūβ'-s'i t'iaγmi-n'i bās. 8. is s'in'i t'ēd'e is'ən β'iδ ogus ρo·χλuv'əθəρ ina h'eṷvu og k'ēduλ. 9. ināδ·vakəδ' ina kaḭρχa duβi aγ'əs int aṷγəρ'e a meδōv ina gaḭρəχ β'ind? 10. is s'ɪ ind iv'γ'əv dāλ'əs b'iϧδ ogus δo·orti f'ɪv donəβ' oḭγ'əδəβ', ogus vos·ŋgaρ'u kugum. 11. at·taϧd ind aρəδ' ina suδ'u aρ β'eλəβ' ina ver'əδ, n'ɪs·f'iλ' ina suδ'u foρa g'l'iṷ. 12. id ē f'iλ'əδ' ρ'r'ɪμγρāδ' ind iρ' kande koḭgəd' nduav aρ θ'ρ'ɪβ' k'ēdəβ', eδ ōv s'eχt goḭgəd' nduav. 13. n'ɪ·kaρəm' in nus'k'e nduaβəs' ima·θ'ēd s'eχ toḭβ māρəs'. 14. id moḭv'i kaρdəρ l'iβ', n'ɪδəd doḭv'i. 15. ā γ'eλγ'ρ'iav foρ·osni r'ɪχ'əδ ko m'ēd' voḭβ'e, ā ρ'ɪ kov·ig aŋ'g'λ'u, ā χom'δ'u ina ndoḭv'e. 16. t'r'ɪ bur'b' in β'eθa: ōg kon·t'iβ'i s'ev, slāv kon·t'iβ'i gaλρəχ, gaḭθ kon·t'iβ'i baḭθ. 17. t'r'ɪ doρχe nād·d'l'eγəd mnā do im'θ'əχt: doρχe g'iϧχ, doρχe vaδ'χ'e, doρχe β'eδa. 18. t'r'ɪ fuλ'i nād·d'l'eγəd f'r'egəρ: fuλ' χaθa, ogus eṷd', ogus edəργəρ'e. 19. t'r'ɪ soḭρ' do·γ'v'iϧd doḭρu d'ɪβ' f'ēv': t'iγ'ərne r'evəs a δ'ēs', r'ɪγəv' t'ēd'e ko haθ'əχ, mak f'iλ'əδ l'ēg'əs a χ'er'd'. 20. t'r'ɪ horbi ranədəρ f'iaδ χoμərbəβ': orbe drūθ' ogus orbe dāsəχtəγ' ogus orbe s'iv'.

English

1. This is it what we pray for. 2. (It is) thy royal household that we praise, because thou art our king. 3. We swear by the god by which our tribes swear, thou art the druid who says (*OIr.*: gives, brings) charms on our enemy. 4. Do all run and is it one man of them who wins (*OIr.*: who takes the victory) at completing it? 5. It is they who put without delay the lustre of red gold upon our speech. 6. A blessing from us upon the dear guests who bring news from our friend with them. 7. The death that I go to causes life to thee, that means, it is for life to thee I go to death. 8. It is they who go into the wood and hear the birds singing. 9. We see the (one) black sheep which the shepherds drive out of the middle of the white sheep. 10. She is the girl, who does not distribute food and who does not pour wine to the guest, and thou dost not call her to thee. 11. The charioteer is sitting in front (*OIr.*: before the lips) of the chariot-fighter, he is not sitting at his left. 12. Are not they poets of the first grade who sing 350 poems? 13. Does she love the ill-omened water, which goes around past her habitation? 14. It is not riches, which are being loved by us, it is (*OIr.*: they are) people. 15. O bright sun, which does not lighten up the heaven, o king, who does not have power over the angels. 16. Three wise people (*gáeth*) of the world: a young person who does not laugh about an old person, a healthy person, who does not laugh about a sick person, a wise person, who does not laugh about a stupid person. 17. Three dark places (where) a woman is entitled to go. 18. Three (types of) blood(-shed) that entitle attendance. 19. Three free persons who do not make unfree persons of themselves: a lord who does not sell his prerogatives, a queen who does not go to a peasant, a son of a poet who does not leave his art. 20. Three inheritances that are not divided in front of heirs.

35.3. A poem: *The dead princes in the mill*

In men meiles in muilenn,   in μ'ev m'eλ'əs in muλ'ən,
ní coirce acht dergthuirenn;   n'ī kor'k'e aχt d'ergθuρ'ən;
is do ḟorglu in chruinn máir   is do orglu in χρun' μāρ'
fothae muilinn Máelodráin.   foθe muλ'ən' μai̯λoδρāv'.

Source: AU 650.

35.4. A poem: *A kiss*

Cride é,   k'r'iδ'e ē,
daire cnó,   daρ'e knō,
ócán é,   ōgāv ē,
pócán dó.   pōgāv dō.

Source: GT 112

Illustration 35.1:
Is é mo lóech, mo gille mer
'He is my hero, my nimble lad'

Lesson 36

36.1. Nouns: consonantal declension in r

The few Old Irish words whose stem ends in *r* /ρ/ denote family relations. They are *athair* m. /aθəρ/ 'father,' *bráthair* m. /brāθəρ/ 'brother,' *máthair* f. /māθəρ/ 'mother,' *siur* f. /s'iüρ/ 'sister' and the very rare *amnair* /aμvəρ/ 'maternal uncle.' The *r* is visible throughout the whole paradigm. In the plural the *th* and *r* of the stem can be palatalized or non-palatalized. r-stems can be masculine or feminine, e.g., *máthair* f. /māθəρ/ 'mother':

case	endg.	Old Irish	Prim. Irish	Proto-Celtic	PIE
nom.	ρ'	*máthair*	*māθīρ	mātīr <matir>	*meh$_2$tér
gen.	ρ	*máthar*	*māθρah	*mātros «	*meh$_2$trés
prep.	ρ'L	*máthair*L	*māθeρē «	*mātreị̯	*meh$_2$tréị̯
acc.	ρ'N	*máthair*N	*māθeρev	māteram <materem>	*meh$_2$térm̥
voc.	ρ'	*á*L *máthair*	*māθīρ	*mātir «	*méh$_2$ter
nom.pl.	ρ'	*máithir*	*māθρeh «	*māteres	*meh$_2$téres
gen.	ρ$^{(')}$eN	*máithre*N, *máthrae*N («)	*māθρiị̯av «	mātrom <ματρον>	*meh$_2$tróm
prep.	ρ$^{(')}$əβ'	*máithrib, máthraib*	*māθρiβih	mātribis <ματρεβο> («)	*meh$_2$tr̥bʰís, -bʰós
acc.	ρ$^{(')}$aH	*máithrea*H «	*māθρāh	*mātrās	*meh$_2$tr̥ŋ́s
voc.	ρ$^{(')}$aH	*á*L *máithrea*H «	*māθρeh «	*māteres	*méh$_2$teres
n. a. v. du.	ρ'L	**dí*L *máthair*L (?)	*māθρe « (?)	*mātere	*meh$_2$térh$_1$e
gen.	ρ'L	**dá*L *máthar*L	*māθρō	*mātroṵ («)	*meh$_2$tr̥h$_1$óh$_1$s, -(H)óh$_1$u
prep.	ρ$^{(')}$əβ'	**dib*N *máithrib* (?)	*māθρiβiv	*mātribim «	*meh$_2$tr̥bʰih$_1$, -moh$_1$?

Illustration 36.1: The r-stems

Note:
1. In later Irish these words inflect as k-stems, e.g., gen. sg. *sethrach*. The inflection is similar to that of *nathair, nathrach* 'snake' and *cathair, cathrach* 'city.'

The inflection of *siur* f. /s'iüρ/ 'sister' is irregular:

case	transcr.	Old Irish	Prim. Irish	Proto-Celtic	PIE
nom.	s'iüρ	*siur*	*su̯ihūρ	*su̯esūr	*su̯ésōr
gen.	s'eθəρ	*sethar*	*su̯eθρah «	*su̯erros «	*su̯esrés
prep.	s'iəρ'ᴸ	*sieir*ᴸ, *siair*ᴸ	*su̯ihepē «	*su̯errei̯	*su̯esréi̯
acc.	s'iəρ'ᴺ	*sieir*ᴺ, *siair*ᴺ	*su̯ihoρev	su̯esoram	*su̯ésorm̥
voc.	f'iəρ	*á*ᴸ *fiur*, *á*ᴸ *phiur*	*su̯ihūρ	*su̯esūr «	*su̯ésor
nom.pl.	s'eθ'əρ'	*seithir*	*su̯eθρeh «	*su̯esores	*su̯ésores
gen.	s'eθəρᴺ	*sethar*ᴺ (?) «	*su̯eθρii̯av «	*su̯errom	*su̯esróm
prep.	s'eθρəβ'	*sethraib*	*su̯eθρiβih «	*su̯erribis («	*su̯esr̥bʰís, -bʰós
acc.	s'eθρaᴴ	*sethra*ᴴ	*su̯eθρāh «	*su̯esorās	*su̯ésorn̥s
voc.		n/a	*su̯eθρeh «	*su̯esores	*su̯ésores
n. a. v. du.	f'iəρ'ᴸ	*dí*ᴸ *fieir*ᴸ	*su̯ihoρe	*su̯esore	*su̯ésorh₁e
gen.		n/a	*su̯eθρō «	*su̯errou̯ («	*su̯esr̥h₁óh₁s, -(H)óh₁u
prep.		n/a	*su̯eθρiβiv «	*su̯erribim «	*su̯esr̥bʰih₁, -moh₁ ?

Illustration 36.2: The paradigm of *siur* 'sister'

Note:

1. In early Old Irish the *anlauting s* of *siur* becomes /f/ when lenited, so, e.g., 'my sister' would be *mo fiur* or *mo phiur*! In later Irish this is 'normalized' to *síur* /s'iu̯ρ/, lenited *śíur* /h'iu̯ρ/. In Sc. Gaelic the 'normalization' went the other way, so that there 'sister' now is *piuthar*, lenited *phiuthar*.

36.2. Nouns: consonantal declension in s

With one exception all s-stems are neuter. And, with the same exception, in none of the s-stems can the eponymous *s* ever be seen because, as is so often the case with Old Irish, the name for this inflectional class is purely historical. The example below is *nem* /n'eμ/ 'sky, heaven,' stem final consonant /μ/:

Illustration 36.3:
di mulluch int ṡléibe (Ml. 58c4)
'from the top of the mountain'

case	ending	Old Irish	Prim. Irish	Proto-Celtic	Pre-Celtic
nom. acc. sg.	{L}C^N	*nem^N* «	*neμah	*nemos «	*néb^{h}os
gen.	{R}C'e^H	*nime^H*	*neμihah	*nemisos «	*neb^{h}ése/os
prep.	{R}C'^{L}	*nim^L*	*neμih («)	*nemiseị, *nemisi «	*neb^{h}éseị, neb^{h}ési
nom. acc. pl.	{R}C'e^L	*nime^L*	*neμiha	*nemisa	
gen.	{R}C'e^N	*nime^N*	*neμihav	*nemisom	
prep.	{R}C'əβ'	*nimib*	*neμihaβih «	*nemizbis	
n.a. du.	{L}C^N	*dá^N nnem^N*	?	?	
gen.	{R}C'e^N	*dá^N nnime^N*	*neμihō (?)	*nemisoụ (?)	
prep.	{R}C'əβ'	*díb^N nnimib*	*neμihaβiv (?) «	*nemizbim (?)	

Illustration 36.4: The s-stem declension

Note:

1. The word *tech* /t'ex/ 'house' exhibits some variation in its stem: the nom. sg. is in the oldest period *teg* /t'eγ/, later *tech*; in those cases where raising takes place the stem can be *tig-* /t'iγ'/ and *taig-* /taγ'/, e.g., gen. sg. *taige*, prep. sg. *taig* and *tig*, nom. pl. *tige* and *taige*.

2. Note the variation in the root vowel in *slíab* /s'l'iaβ/ 'mountain,' gen. sg. *sléibe* /s'l'ēβ'e/, which you know already from many other examples.

The only masculine word of this class is *mí* /m'ī/ 'month,' where you can actually see an *s* in the inflection. Note the change in the quality between palatalization and non-palatalization of the stem-final *s* in the paradigm, which is not expressed orthographically:

case	singular	transcr.	dual	transcr.	plural	transcr.
nom.	*mí^H*	/m'ī^H/	*dá^L mí^L*	/μ'ī^L/	*mís*	/m'īs'/
gen.	*mís*	/m'īs/	*dá^L mí^L*	/μ'ī^L/	*mís^N*	/m'īs^N/
prep.	*mís^L, mí^L*	/m'īs'^{L} m'ī^L/	n/a		*mísaib*	/m'īsəβ'/
acc.	*mís^N*	/m'īs'^{N}/	*dá^L mí^L*	/μ'ī^L/	*mísa^H*	/m'īsa^H/

Illustration 36.5: The paradigm of *mí* 'month'

Illustration 36.6: *i mmís Enáir* (SR 234)
'in the month of January'

36.3. Exercise

Inflect some of the following words. Decline them together with the article. Combine them with any of the adjectives you have learned so far.

athair /aθəρ'/ (r, m) 'father'
bráthair /brāθəρ'/ (r, m) 'brother'
glenn /g'l'en/ (s, n) 'valley'
mag /maγ/ (s, n) 'plane, open field'
og /oγ/ (s, n) 'egg'
leth /l'eθ/ (s, n) 'side' (no raising in this word!)

Lesson 37

37.1. The habitual present of the substantive verb

The H2 verb *biid* supplies the habitual or consuetudinal present of the substantive verb *at·tá*. 'Habitual' means that *biid* expresses a usual condition, or activities that are done regularly or on a 'habitual' basis. In English *biid* is usually translated as 'is wont to be, is continually, is regularly,' in German 'ist gewöhnlich, pflegt zu sein.' Syntactically *biid* is used like *at·tá* (see 28.1). The difference in meaning between the two verbs can be seen in sentences like *bíuu-sa oc irbáig darfar cenn-si* 'I am always boasting about you' (*Wb.* 16d8) versus *at·tó oc irbáig darfar cenn-si* 'I am boasting about you (right now).'

person		absolute	transcr.	conjunct	transcr.	unstressed after *ro*	
1st sg.		*bíuu*	b'iü	·*bíu*	·b'ı̄u̯	n/a	
2nd sg.		*bí*	b'ı̄	·*bí*	·b'ı̄	n/a	
3rd sg.		*bíid*	b'iəð'	·*bí*	·b'ı̄	·*rubai*	·ruβi
	rel.	*bíis, bís*	b'iəs b'ı̄s	-		-	
	impers.	*bíthir*	b'ı̄θ'əp'	·*bíther*	·b'ı̄θ'əρ	·*rubthar*	·ruβθəρ
	impers. rel.	*bíther*	b'ı̄θ'əρ	-		-	
1st pl.		*bímmi*	b'ı̄m'i	·*biam*	·b'iə̯µ	n/a	
	rel.	*bímme*	b'ı̄m'e	-		-	
2nd pl.		n/a		n/a		n/a	
3rd pl.		*bíit*	b'iəd'	·*biat*	·b'iə̯d	·*rubat*	·ruβəd
	rel.	*bíte*	b'ı̄d'e	-		-	

Illustration 37.1: The habitual present of the substantive verb

Note:

1. The column on the right shows the form of *bí-* in unstressed position after the verbal particle *ro* (which is here raised to *ru-*). This is not of importance for you at the moment but will become relevant in a later lesson.

2. The copula has a relic habitual form in the 3rd sg., which only appears in enclitic position as *-bi, -pi* /b'i/, e.g., *nipi cían a maisse in choirp* 'the beauty of the body is not long-lasting' (*Wb.* 28c25).

37.2. Relative forms of the substantive verb and the copula

1. The relative form of the substantive verb in leniting relative clauses is *fil* /f'iλ'/, negated *nád·fil* /nāδ·iλ'/, e.g., *in fer nád·fil oc labrad* 'the man who is not speaking.' Sometimes *file* with the additional relative ending *-e* is found, e.g., *in fochraicc file dó i nnim* 'the reward which he has (*lit.* which is to him) in heaven' (*Wb.* 26b29). The 3rd plural relative *filet* is a younger form.

2. The relative form of the 3rd sg. of the copula is *as* /as/, the 3rd pl. *ata* /ada/, in negated leniting relative clauses 3rd sg. *nád^L* /nāδ/ and 3rd pl. *natat^L* /nadəd/. In leniting relative clauses *as* and *ata* 'pass on' the lenition, which should be expressed on the verb, to the following word, e.g., *it sib ata chomarbai Abracham* 'it is you who are the heirs of Abraham' (*Wb.* 19c20). Be careful not to confuse *ata* /ada/, the 3rd pl. relative of the copula, with *at·tá* /a(d)·tā/, the 3rd sg. non-relative form of the substantive verb, which in the manuscripts and in editions of texts is usually written *atá* or even *ata* with omission of the length mark.

37.3. The imperative

The imperative is that mood of the verb which is used to give orders, e.g., English *Love me or leave me!* or German *Nimm! Lies! Schaut nicht so blöd!* In English imperatives are restricted to the 2nd persons; orders can only be given to someone directly addressed. For other persons constructions with *let* are used, e.g., 1st pl. *Let us go to the pub!*, 3rd pl. *Let them not spill our pints!* In German orders to all plural persons are possible, e.g., 1st pl. *Trinken wir!,* 2nd pl. *Trinkt mit!,* 3rd pl. (only when formally addressing a person) *Nehmen Sie sich doch auch ein Glas!* A 3rd sg. imperative did in fact exist in German, but this came out of use more than a century ago, e.g., *Fülle Er mir das Glas nach!* (you wouldn't have a lot of success today if you said this to a waiter). In Latin, orders to 3rd persons can regularly be made, e.g., *sumito* 'let him/her take,' *legunto* 'let them read.' Old Irish takes the system of imperatives even a step further than Latin in that orders can be given also to all 1st persons, plural and singular, e.g., *biur* 'let me carry,' *cluinem* 'let us hear.'

Illustration 37.2:
ben nach n-echraig! 'hit any key!'

Old Irish does not distinguish between absolute and conjunct endings in the imperative. Compound verbs appear in their prototonic variant in the imperative unless a pronoun is infixed (see 38.1). Separate imperative endings exist only for the 2nd and 3rd singular:

1. The 2nd sg. active imperative consists simply of the bare stem of the verb, e.g., *car!* 'love!,' *léic!* 'leave!,' *beir!* 'carry!,' *fagaib!* 'find!' (from *fo·gaib*), *éiren!* 'pay!' (from *as·ren*), etc. The 2nd sg. deponent imperative ending is *-the/-de* /θ'e δ'e/, e.g., *labraithe! labraide!* 'speak!,' *suidigthe!* 'place!,' *cluinte!* 'listen!,' *frecuirthe !* 'worship!' (from *fris·cuirethar*).

2. The 3rd sg. imperative ending is /əδ/ for active and deponent verbs alike, i.e., *-ad* after non-palatalized stems, *-ed* after palatalized stems, e.g., *crenad!* 'let him/her buy!,' *gaibed!* 'let him/her take!,' *cluined!* 'let him/her listen!,' *tascrad!* 'let him/her overthrow!' (from *do·scara*), *díltad!* 'let him/her deny!' (from *do·sluindi*). Instead of /δ/ in the ending *th* /θ/ may also appear, e.g., *éirneth!* 'let him/her pay!,' *frecuireth!* 'let him/her worship!,' *intam-lath!* 'let him/her imitate!' (from *in·samlathar*).

In all other persons the imperative is identical with the corresponding dependent form of the present indicative. That means that the 2nd pl. imperative of a simple verb has the form of the 2nd pl. conjunct, e.g., *guidid!* 'pray!,' *comalnaid!* 'fulfil!'; a compound verb, of course, appears in its prototonic variant, e.g., 1st pl. *taibrem!* 'let us bring! let us give!' (from *do·beir*), 3rd pl. *acrat!* 'let them sue!' (from *ad·gair*).

Still, imperative and dependent present indicative forms cannot be confused: dependent forms always need a particle before them, whereas the positive imperative goes without particle. When negated, the imperative uses a special negative particle *ná·* /nā/. This negative particle goes into pretonic position before the imperative form, without any further change in the ending, e.g., *car!* 'love!,' but *ná·car!* 'do not love!,' *guidid!* 'pray! (pl.),' but *ná·guidid!* 'do not pray! (pl.),' or passive *tabarr!* 'let it be given!,' but *ná·tabarr!* 'let it not be given!'

The following table gives you the active imperative forms of simple and compound verbs. The compound verbs are W1 *ad·ella* 'to visit,' W2 *fo·dáili* 'to distribute,' *fo·ric* 'to find,' S1 *do·beir* 'to bring, to give,' S2 *ad·gair* 'to sue,' S3 *fris·ben* 'to heal,' H2 *do·gní* 'to make,' *con·sní* 'to contend, to contest,' H3 *ad·noí* 'to entrust,' *con·oí* 'to protect.' Note for the compound verbs that the underlying palatalization/non-palatalization of the stem-final consonant can be obscured by the effects of syncope:

class	person	singular	ending	plural	ending
W1	1st	n/a		caram, aidlem	Cəμ
	2nd	car, adall	C	caraid, aidlid	Cəδ'
	3rd	carad, aidled	Cəδ	carat, aidlet	Cəd
W2	1st	fuircim	C'əm'	léicem, fodlam	C'əμ
	2nd	léic, fodail	C'	léicid, fodlaid	C'əδ'
	3rd	léiced, fodlad	C'əδ	léicet, fodlat	C'əd
S1	1st	biur, tabur	uC	beram, taibrem	Cəμ
	2nd	beir, tabair	C'	beirid, taibrid	C'əδ'
	3rd	beired, taibred	C'əδ	berat, taibret	Cəd
S2	1st	n/a		gaibem, acram	C'əμ
	2nd	gaib, acair	C'	gaibid, acraid	C'əδ'
	3rd	gaibed, acrad	C'əδ	gaibet, acrat	C'əd
S3	1st	n/a		crenam, freipnem	vəμ
	2nd	cren, freipen	v	crenaid, freipnid	vəδ'
	3rd	crenad, freipned	vəδ	crenat, freipnet	vəd
	1st	n/a		n/a	

Illustration 37.3a: The active imperative endings

class	person	singular	ending	plural	ending
H1	2nd	n/a		n/a	
	3rd	n/a		n/a	
	1st	n/a		dénam, cosnam	*C'iəμ, Cəμ
H2	2nd	bí	ī	bíid, biid, bíth	C'iəδ', C'īδ', Cəδ'
	3rd	bíid, biid, bíth	iəδ	bíat, biat	C'iəd, Cəd
	1st	n/a		n/a	
H3	2nd	suí, comae	V	aithnid, comaid	Cəδ'
	3rd	at·noad, comad	Vəδ, Cəδ	n/a	

Illustration 37.3b: The active imperative endings

Note:

1. The 2nd sg. imperative continues forms ending in the plain stem vowel of the respective verbal class, e.g., S1 *beir* < **bere* < PIE **bʰere*, W2b *guir* < **gʷorī* < PIE **gʷʰorei̯e*, etc. In the 2nd pl. the PIE ending **-te* was added to the stem, which eventually resulted in Old Irish *-(a)id*. The 3rd person endings continue PIE forms in **-tu* and **-ntu*, which were somehow reformed to **-tō* and **-ntō* in the prehistory of Irish.

2. A number of verbs have a rather irregular 2nd sg. imperative, which actually continues a subjunctive formation. The other imperative persons of these verbs are formed regularly:

class	verb	imperative	meaning
S1	at·reig	at·ré	'rise!'
	con·éirig	coméir	'arise!'
	fo·reith	*foir	'help!'
	aingid	ain	'protect!'
	do·icc, do·tét	tair	'come!'
	teit	eirg	'go!'
S2	ad·guid	aicc	'invoke!'
H2	do·gní	déne	'make!'
	con·gní	cungne	'help!'
	do·écci	décce	'look!'
H3	do·goa	tog	'choose!'

Illustration 37.4: Irregular imperatives

The substantive verb *at·tá* does not form its imperative from the stem *tā-*. Instead the stem *bī-* of the habitual forms is used for the imperative:

person	imperative	transcr.
1st sg.	n/a	
2nd sg.	*bí*	b'ī
3rd sg.	*bíid, biid, bíth*	b'iəð' b'īθ'
1st pl.	n/a	
2nd pl.	*bíid, biid, bíth*	b'iəð' b'īθ'
3rd pl.	*bíat, biat*	b'iəd

Illustration 37.5: The imperative of the substantive verb

The imperative of the copula 'be!' is:

person	absolute	after particles
1st sg.	n/a	n/a
2nd sg.	*ba^L*	*-ba^L, -pa^L*
3rd sg.	*bed^L, bad^L*	*-bad^L*
1st pl.	*baan^L, ban^L*	n/a
2nd pl.	*bed^L, bad^L*	*-bad^L*
3rd pl.	*bat^L*	*-bat^L*

Illustration 37.6: The imperative of the copula

An example for the use of the imperative of the copula is maxim §2.7 of *Bríathra Flainn Fína maic Ossu* 'The Sayings of Flann Fína mac Ossu':[1] *Ba umal corba úasal* 'Be humble so that you may be exalted.'

---

[1] *Flann Fína mac Ossu* was the Irish name for king *Aldfrith of Northumbria* (ca. 685–705), to whom a number of Old Irish texts are ascribed.

37.4. The deponent and passive imperative forms

The following table gives you the deponent imperative forms. Note that the 1st pl. sometimes shows active endings. Note also that although S3 verbs generally have a non-palatalized stem, the one frequent verb *ro·cluinethar* exceptionally has a palatalized stem final consonant:

class	person	singular	ending	plural	ending
W1	1st	n/a		n/a	
	2nd	*labraithe, labraide*	C(ə)θ'e, C(ə)δ'e	*labraid*	Cəδ'
	3rd	*labrad*	Cəδ	*labratar*	Cədəp
W2	1st	*águr, *suidigiur*	C'uρ	*suidigem, *suidigmer*	C'əμ, C'm'əρ
	2nd	*suidigthe*	C'θ'e	*suidigid*	C'əδ'
	3rd	*suidiged*	C'əδ	**suidigetar*	C'ədəp
S2	1st	n/a		n/a	
	2nd	*mitte*	C'θ'e	*midid*	C'əδ'
	3rd	*mided*	C'əδ	n/a	
S3	1st	n/a		*cluinem, finnamar*	Cəμ, Cəməp
	2nd	*cluinte*	nte	*cluinid*	Cəδ'
	3rd	*cluined*	vəδ	*cluinetar*	Cədəp

Illustration 37.7: The deponent imperative endings

The passive imperative forms look like the corresponding relative forms, yet the two are easily distinguishable: imperatives basically stand at the beginning of sentences, whereas relative forms always have to appear in the interior of sentences after relativized nouns or pronouns:

class	person	Old Irish	ending
W1	3rd sg.	*carthar*	Cθəρ
	3rd pl.	*cartar*	Cdəρ
W2	3rd sg.	*léicther*	C'θ'əρ
	3rd pl.	*léicter*	C'd'əρ
S1	3rd sg.	*berar*	Cəρ
	3rd pl.	*bertar*	Cdəρ
S2	3rd sg.	*gaibther*	C'θ'əρ
	3rd pl.	*gaibter*	C'd'əρ

Illustration 37.8a: The passive imperative endings

class	person	Old Irish	ending
S3	3rd sg.	*crenar*	vəρ
	3rd pl.	*crentar*	ndəρ
H1	3rd sg.	n/a	
	3rd pl.	n/a	
H2	3rd sg.	*déntar*	θəρ
	3rd pl.	n/a	
H3	3rd sg.	n/a	
	3rd pl.	n/a	

Illustration 37.8b: The passive imperative endings

37.5. Exercise

Try to form the imperative forms of all possible persons, positive and negative, of some of the following verbs:

as·ren, ·éiren /as·r'ev ·eρ'əv/ (S3) 'to pay, to expend' (no syncope in the passive!)
glanaid /glavəδ'/ (W1) 'to clean'
ceilid /k'eλ'əδ'/ (S1) 'to hide'
ro·finnadar, ·finnadar /ro·f'inəδəρ, ·f'inəδəρ/ (S3) 'to find out'
fris·gair, ·frecair /f'r'is·gaρ' ·f'r'egəρ'/ (S2) 'to answer'
midithir /m'iδ'əθ'əρ'/ (S2) 'to judge'
foilsigidir /fol's'əγ'əδ'əρ'/ (W2) 'to reveal, to publish'

Illustration 37.9:
naba thoirsech! (*Wb.* 29d19)
'don't be grieved!'

Lesson 38

38.1. Infixed pronouns in imperatives

When pronouns have to be infixed into imperatives, e.g., in expressions like *push it!, call me!* etc., the 'normal' strategy is used: the pronoun is infixed after the first preverb in deuterotonic compound verbs, or after the empty particle *no·* in the case of simple verbs. This means, however, that no longer a formal distinction can be made between present indicative and imperative forms, except for the 2nd and 3rd persons singular with their special endings.

For example, simple verb forms like *nom·charaid!* 'love (pl.) me!,' *nom·charat!* 'let them love me!' and *nom·charthar!* 'let me be loved!' look exactly like the corresponding present indicative forms 'you love me,' 'they love me,' 'I am being loved.' The same is true for compound verbs like *atom·ágaid!* 'fear (pl.) me!,' *atom·ágatar!* 'let them fear me!,' *atom·áigther!* 'let me be feared!,' which could just as well mean 'you fear me,' 'they fear me,' 'I am being feared.' It has to be inferred from the context whether the imperative or present indicative is meant.

Note also that a 2nd sg. imperative with infixed pronoun looks like a 3rd sg. present indicative: *da·beir!* 'bring it! give it!' could also be read '(s)he brings it, gives it.' Again, special attention has to be given to the context. On the other hand, a form like 3rd sg. imperative *ata·gaired!* 'let him/ her call them' is unambiguous because of the ending.

Negated imperatives with infixed pronouns, however, are always unambiguous, because a special negative particle and a special class of infixed pronouns is used for the imperative (see 38.3).

38.2. Infixed pronouns class C

Class C infixed pronouns look very much like class B pronouns, with the difference that they always start with a *d*, and that the masculine and neuter 3rd singular have a number of variant forms depending on the particle they are attached to. The initial *d* is basically lenited /ð/, but after relative *n* (which we will learn in a later lesson) and after the nasalization of certain particles it is delenited to /d/.

The use of infixed pronouns classes A and B depends on phonological factors. That means that whether class A or B is used depends on the form of the preverb to which the pronoun is attached: class A comes after preverbs that originally ended in a vowel (see 25.1), class B after preverbs that originally ended in a consonant (see 28.3).

In contrast to this the use of class C infixed pronouns is syntactically conditioned: they have to be used after relative prepositions (we will learn about them in a later lesson), after certain conjunctions (*dia^N* 'if, when,' *ara^N* 'in order that,' *co^N* 'so that') and after the interrogative particle *in^N*; finally, they replace pronouns of the other two classes when the verb stands in relative position. But note that class A 1st and 2nd person infixed pronouns can always be used instead of class C pronouns in relative position.

An example for the use after the interrogative particle is: *indam·charai?* 'dost thou love me?'

Examples for the use of class C pronouns in leniting relative position are: *nodam·chrocha* 'which crucifies me' (*Ml.* 32d28), *adid·n-opair* 'who offers himself' (*Ml.* 66b4), *fod·dáili* 'who distributes it' (*Wb.* 12a8), *doda·aidlea* 'who visits her' (*Wb.* 9d5), *nodon·nerta-ni* 'who strengthens us' (*Wb.* 6d11).

person	translation	pronoun	
		class C	
1st sg.	me	*-dom^L, -dum^L, -dam(m)^L*	/ðəm^L/
2nd sg.	thee	*-dat^L, -dit^L*	/ðəd^L/
3rd sg. m.	him	*-id^N, -did^N, -d^N*, rarely *-da^N*	/ið$^{(')N}$ ðið$^{(')N}$ ð^N (ða^N)/
3rd sg. f.	her	*-da^H*	/ða^H/
3rd sg. n.	it	*-id^L, -did^L, -d^L*	/ið$^{(')L}$ ðið$^{(')L}$ ð^L/
1st pl.	us	*-don, -dun, din, -dan(n)*	/ðən/
2nd pl.	you	*-dob, -dub, -dib, -dab*	/ðəβ/
3rd pl.	them	*-da^H*	/ða^H/

Illustration 38.1: The infixed pronouns class C

Note:

The usage of the 3rd singular masculine and neuter forms is as follows:

1. *-d* is used after preverbs that end in vowels: *fod·, nod·, rod·,* etc.

2. *-did* is used after relative *i^N·* 'in(to) which' and after the conjunction *co^N·* 'so that': *indid·, condid·* (later *conid·*).

3. *-id* is used after preverbs ending in a consonant: *conid·, forid·, adid·, frissid·,* etc.

38.3. Infixed pronouns after negative *ná, nád*

If pronouns are infixed after the negative particles *ná* (imperative) and *nád* (interrogative and relative), a special stem *nach-* is used with endings similar to class C pronouns:

person	translation	pronoun	
1st sg.	not me	*nacham·^{L}, nachim·^{L}*	/naχəm^L/
2nd sg.	not thee	*nachat·^{L}, nachit·^{L}*	/naχəd^L/
3rd sg. m.	not him	*nach·^{N}*	/naχ^N/
3rd sg. f.	not her	*nacha·^{H}*	/naχa^H/
3rd sg. n.	not it	*nach·^{L}, nachid·^{L} (nadid·^{L})*	/naχ^L naχəð$^{(')L}$ naðəð$^{(')L}$/
1st pl.	not us	*nachan·*	/naχən/
2nd pl.	not you	*nachab·, nachib·*	/naχəβ/
3rd pl.	not them	*nacha·^{H}*	/naχa^H/

Illustration 38.2: The infixed pronouns after *ná, nád*

Examples for the use in relative position are: *nachid·chúalatar* '(they) who have not heard it' (*Wb.* 25d14), *húare nachan·soírai-ni* 'because thou dost not deliver us' (*Ml.* 93d10).

An example for the interrogative use is: *innachan·caraid* 'don't you love us?'

Examples for the imperative use are: *nacham·dermainte!* 'forget me not!' (*Ml.* 32d5), *nachib·eirpid-si!* 'entrust not yourselves!' (*Wb.* 22d6).

You'll find a survey of all infixed pronouns in Appendix F.4.

38.4. Exercise

Try to infix all possible pronouns into the 2nd singular imperative, positive and negative, of the verbs in the exercise in 37.5.

Illustration 38.3: *Atom·ágaid! Am olc-sa!* 'Fear me! I am evil!'

38.5. The deictic particle *í*

Any form of the article can be combined with the so-called deictic particle *í* /ī/ (also spelled *hí*), which is always stressed. The article can thus function as a substantive. As a rule, a determiner has to follow after the deictic particle. The determiner can be:

1. The demonstrative particles *-sin, -siu,* e.g., masc. nom. sg. *int í-sin* 'that one; *der (Mann dort*),' masc. nom. pl. *ind í-siu* 'these ones; *die (Männer da*),' fem. gen. sg. *inna hí-siu* 'of this one; *dieser (Frau da*),' neuter nom. acc. sg. *a n-í-siu* 'this one; *das (Ding da*),' gen. pl. *inna n-í-sin* 'of those; *dieser (Leute, Dinge dort*),' etc., e.g., *as·beir a n-í-siu* 'he says this' (*Wb.* 12d21) or *adib mogae ind í-sin* 'you are slaves of that one' (*Wb.* 3b15).

2. A relative clause, e.g., *donaib hí gníte* 'to those who do,' *forsna hí comalnatar toil Dé* 'upon those, who fulfil God's will' (*Wb.* 20d1); cf. German *der-, die-, dasjenige,* etc.).

3. A personal name, which is thus emphasized, e.g., *int í Cú Chulainn* 'he, the famous Cú Chulainn,' *forsin n-í Dauid* 'on him, David ' (*Ml.* 52).

The deictic particle *í* may also stand after a noun, which then must also be followed by a determinator either of type 1 or 2, e.g., *in gním-í-sin* 'that deed,' or *in gním-í do·rigénus* 'that deed I have done.'

38.6. Indefinite pronouns

The substantival indefinite pronoun *nech, ní* in Old Irish has the meaning 'someone, something; anyone, anything,' in negative sentences 'noone, nothing.' It bears the stress. The plural is supplied by *alaili, araili* 'some people; some things.'

case	masc., fem.	neuter
nom. sg.	*nech* /n'eχ/	*ní* /n'ī/
gen.	*neich*^{L} /n'eχ'^{L}/	
prep.	*neuch*^{L}, *neoch*^{L} /n'eu̯χ^L/	
acc.	*nech*^{N} /n'eχ^N/	*ní* /n'ī/

Illustration 38.4: The substantival indefinite pronoun

When used adjectivally, the indefinite pronoun has the meaning 'some, any' and is unstressed, standing in proclitic position before the word it qualifies. The plural occurs only in negative sentences.

case	masc., fem.	neuter
nom. sg.	*nach* /naχ/	*na*^{H} /na^H/
gen.	*nach* /naχ/, fem. *nacha*^{H} /naχa^H/	
prep.	*nach*^{L} /naχ^L/	
acc.	*nach*^{N} /naχ^N/	*na*^{H} /na^H/
nom. pl.	n/a	*nacha*^{H} /naχa^H/
gen.	n/a	
prep.	*nach, nacha* /naχ naχa/	
acc.	*nacha*^{H} /naχa^H/	

Illustration 38.5: The adjectival indefinite pronoun

Note:

1. Be careful not to confuse the stressed neuter indefinite pronoun *ní* with the negative particle *ní·* 'not' and the negated copula *ní*^{H} 'is not.'

2. The adjectival and the substantival forms of the indefinite pronoun are often combined, especially in the neuter *na nní, na ní* /na n'ī/ 'anything whatsoever,' followed by a partitive *de*^{L}, e.g., *slogait na nní de uisciu doda·icc* 'they swallow all of the water which comes to them' (*Ml.* 123d3).

38.7. The anaphoric pronoun *suide*

You have already learned that the article can be used substantivally together with the particles *-so, -se, -sin*: e.g., *in-so* 'this (thing),' *in-sin* 'that (thing)' (see 8.9) and together with the deictic particle *í* (see 38.5). There is one more word to be mentioned in this context. The form *suide* has an anaphoric function. That means it points to something already mentioned before. For example, it often appears in the phrase *ol suide* '(s)he (= that is the one mentioned just before) said.'

1. The stressed form *suide* /suð'e/ inflects like a i̯o-, i̯ā-stem, except for the nom. acc. sg. neuter *sodain, sodin* /soðəv'/. It occurs practically only after prepositions, e.g., *do śuidiu* 'to that,' *itir suidiu* 'between those,' *amal śodain* 'like that,' and together with the particle *ol* 'says, said.'

2. The unstressed form *side* /s'ið'e/, *ade* /að'e/, nom. acc. sg. neuter *són* /sōv/ and *ón* /ōv/ is enclitic and emphasizes pronominal elements: *is é-side as éola* 'it is he (the afore-mentioned) who is knowledgeable' (*Wb.* 4b1), *de-side* 'from this' (*de* = 3rd sg. neuter of *di*L), *a banchéile-side* 'his (the aforementioned's) wife,' *as·beir-side* 'he says.' You have already met the neuter enclitic form *ón* in the abbreviation *.i.*, which expands as *ed ón* /eð ōv/ 'that means; lit.: it the aforementioned.'

38.8. Interrogative pronouns

There are two forms of the interrogative pronoun, an unstressed form (indifferent to gender and number) *ce*H, *ci*H, *cia*H /k'e k'i k'ia/, and a stressed form *cía*H /k'ia/ 'who is it?,' neuter *cid, ced* /k'ið k'eð/ 'what is it?,' plural *citné* /k'idv'ē/ (sometimes *cisné* /k'isv'ē/) 'who, what are they?' The copula is never used after these interrogatives, because they already contain the copulaic meaning in themselves.

1. The unstressed form functions as a conjunct particle before verbs, taking the place both of subject and object of the verb, e.g., *cia·beir* 'who carries?,' *cia·accai* 'whom dost thou see?,' *ce·ricc* 'to what does it come?'

2. The stressed form of the interrogative pronoun is not incorporated into the verbal complex but is instead followed by a relative construction, e.g., *cía nodom·chara* 'who (is it who) loves me?,' *cid as maith nó as olc do dénum* 'what (is it that) is good or is bad to do?'

Both forms, stressed and unstressed, can refer to a following substantive in the nominative case; the unstressed form, however, chiefly appears in a few stereotyped phrases. Stressed *cía*H is in this case used as a masculine interrogative pronoun, the feminine being supplied by *cesí*L, *cessi*L *cisí*L /k'es'ī k'is'ī/, the neuter by *cid*L, *ced*L, e.g., *cía tussu* 'who art thou?,' *cid chenél* 'what is the gender?' (*Sg.* 197b3), *cisí chonar do·llod-su* 'what is the way along which thou camest?' (LL 24529). Examples for the unstressed variant are *ce méit* 'what is the amount? how much?,' *ce chruth* 'what is the manner? how?,' *ce hé* 'who is he?' etc. This latter construction, *ce* or *cía* followed by a substantive, is often used to furnish interrogative pronouns of manner, place, time, etc., e.g., *cía airm, c'airm* 'what is the place? = where?,' followed by a relative clause.

Other interrogative pronouns are

1. *cote, caite* /kod'e kad'e/, pl. *coteet, coteat, cateet, cateat* /kod'eəd kad'eəd/ 'what is? what are?'

2. Genitival *coich* /koχ'/ 'whose is?,' e.g., *is inderb coich in mug* 'it is uncertain whose is the slave' (*Sg.* 209b30).

3. *can* /kaʋ/ 'from where is? whence is?'

4. *cis lir* /k'is l'iρ'/ 'how many are there?,' e.g., *cis lir gráda filed?* 'how many grades of poets are there?' (UR §1), or *cis lir ata chórai do ríg do giull?* 'How many (things) are there, which are appropriate for a king as a pledge?' (CG 505 f.).

5. The interrogative pronoun *co*[H]. /ko·/ 'how' is a conjunct particle, e.g., *co·accai in slúag* 'how dost thou see the host?' (LU 4530).

Illustration 38.6:
cissi chonar luide-sem?
'which way did he go?'

Lesson 39

39.1. Varia

1. The sentence particle *trá* /trā/ has a modifying force 'then, therefore, so, however, etc.' and is often used to give the sentence a slightly different coloring, very much like German '*also.*' Similar Old Irish words are *dano* /davo/, *didiu* /d'ið'u/, *immorro* /imóro/.

2. The adverb *tall, thall* expresses distance of place and time. *tall* 'yonder, over there' is the third degree of remoteness beside *-so, -sa, -se* 'this (here),' *-sin* 'that (there),' e.g., *isint ṡalm tall* 'in that psalm,' *ó chéin thall* 'from (that time) long ago.'

3. We will encounter two new conjunctions in this lesson: *má*^{L} means 'if' and is followed by the independent form of the verb, the first consonant of which it lenites. However, as *má*^{L} introduces a dependent clause; infixed pronouns inserted into the verb following it have to be of class C.

4. The conjunction *co*^{N} 'so that' is followed by the dependent form of the verb which it nasalizes, e.g., *co·mbeir* 'so that he carries,' *co·tabair* /ko·daβəp'/ 'so that he gives.' Together with the copula it forms an accentual unit: *conid* 'so that it is;' together with the habitual form of the copula we get *combi* 'so that it usually is.' Take special notice of *conid*, because it is an extremely frequent form in Irish texts. I will return in much more detail to the conjunctions in later lessons.

39.2. Exercise

Old Irish

1. ** Dom·eim-se! (*Ml.* 72d11) ** Ná·dénae ainmnit! (*Ml.* 55a1) 2. ** 'Congnae lem, á Chú Chulainn! […] Beir síst lim!' (TBC 494 f.) 3. ** Indaig brot forsin n-echraid trá! (TBC 663) 4. ** 'Eirg-siu trá, á Chonaill, don dún 7 nom·léic-se oc forairi sund co-lléic!' (TBC 672 f.) 5. ** Nachit·tróethad do mescae! (IB 30) 6. ** Nachib·mided, .i. nachib·berar i smachtu rechta fetarlaicce! (*Wb.* 27a24) 7. ** 'Tíagam diar tig!' ol Conchobar. (TBC 520) 8. ** Hóre ammi maicc laí 7 soilse, ná·seichem inna hí-siu! (*Wb.* 25c6) 9. ** Bed athramlai .i. gaibid comarbus for n-athar 7 intamlaid a béssu! (*Wb.* 9a14) 10. ** Ná·aimdetar! (*Ml.* 56a23) 11. ** Léicther [*sc.* int árchú] dia ṡlabradaib, dáig ar n-indile 7 ar cethrae, 7 dúntar in less! (TBC 573 f.) 12. ** Trí seithir oíted: tol, áilde, féile. (*Triad* 206) 13. ** Fo chen duit, a maccáin, fo déig cridi do máthar! (TBC 592) 14. ** Fossad air-sin imrad Bran, ní cían co tír inna mban. (IB 60) 15. ** 'Ced ṡlíab in-so thall?' ol Cú Chulainn, […] 'Cia carn ngel in-so thall i n-úachtur int ṡléibe? […] Ced mag a n-í thall? […] Cissí ṡlabrae, in díscir-se thall?' (TBC 691 ff.) 16. ** Ní tú nod·n-ail acht is é not·ail. (*Wb.* 5b28) 17. ** Is mór in deithiden file dom-sa diib-si. (*Wb.* 26d19) 18. ** Má nodub·fil i n-ellug coirp Chríst, adib cland *Abrache* [= Latin genitive!] amal ṡodin, 7 it sib ata chomarbai *Abracham.* (*Wb.* 19c20) 19. ** Is bés trá dosom a n-í-siu, cosc inna mban i tossug 7 a tabairt fo chumachtae a fer […] combi íarum coiscitir ind fir 7 do·airbertar fo réir Dé. (*Wb.* 22c10) 20. * 'Is é a bés,' ol Ísu, 'nach indeúin benar for·cain in cách noda·ben; ocus ní sí for·chanar.' (*Gosp.* 26)

Lesson 39

Transcription

1. dom·eɥ'-s'e! nā·d'ēve an'm'n'əd'! 2. ˈkoŋgne l'em, ā χū χuλən'! b'ep' s'ɪs't' l'im!' 3. indəγ' brod fors'ən n'eχpəδ' trā! 4. ˈer'g'-s'u trā, ā χovəl', don dūv ogus nom·λ'ēg'-s'e og fopəp'i sund ko-l'ēg'!' 5. naχəd·troi̯θəδ do μ'eske! 6. naχəβ·m'iδ'əδ, eδ ōv naχəb·b'epəp i smaχtu r'eχta f'edəpλək'e! 7. ˈt'iaγəɥ d'iəp d'iγ'!' oλ kovχəβəp. 8. hōp'e ami mak' λai̯ ogus soλ's'e, nā·s'eχ'əɥ ina h'ɪ-s'u! 9. b'eδ aθpəμλi, eδ ōv gaβ'əδ' koμərbus βop vaθəp ogus intəμλəδ' a β'ēsu! 10. nā·am'δ'ədəp! 11. l'ēg'θ'əp d'iä hλaβpəδəβ', dāγ' ap v'in'd'əλ'e ogus ap g'eθpe, ogus dūntəp in l'es! 12. t'r'ɪ s'eθ'əp' oi̯d'əδ: toλ, āl'd'e, f'ēλ'e. 13. fo χ'ev dut', ā μakāv', fo δ'ēγ' k'r'iδ'i do μāθəp! 14. fosəδ ap'-s'iv' im'·raäδ brav, n'ɪ k'iav ko t'ɪp ina mbav. 15. ˈk'eδ h'λ'iaβ in-so θal?' oλ kū χuλən'. ˈk'ia karn ŋ'g'eλ in-so θal i vuaχtup int h'λ'ēβ'e? k'eδ μaγ a v'ɪ θal? k'is'ɪ hλaβpe, in d'ɪs'k'əp'-s'e θal?' 16. n'ɪ tū noδ·vaλ' aχt is' ē nod·aλ'. 17. is mōp in deθ'əδ'əv f'iλ'e doμ-sa d'iəβ'-s'i. 18. mā voδuβ·f'iλ' i v'elug kor'p' χ'p'ɪs't', aδ'əβ' kland *Abrache* aμəλ hoδ'əv', ogus id' s'iβ' ada χoμərbi *Abracham*. 19. is b'ēs trā do-soμ a v'ɪ-s'u, kosk ina mbav i dosuγ ogus a daβər't' fo χuμəχte a β'ep komb'i iapuμ kos'k'əd'əp' ind ip' ogus do·ap'β'əpdəp fo p'ēp' δ'ē. 20. ˈis ē a β'ēs,' oλ ɪsu, ˈnaχ in'd'eɥv' b'evəp fop·kav' in gāχ noδa·b'ev; ogus n'ɪ s'ɪ fop·χavəp.'

English

1. Protect (pl.) us! Be (pl.) patient (*OIr.*: make patience!)! 2. Help (pl.) us! Carry (pl.) a while with us! 3. Do not (pl.) apply the goad on the horses! 4. Don't go, oh Conall, to the fort, and don't leave us here at the guard! 5. Don't let your (pl.) drunkenness overcome you! 6. Don't let them judge thee, that means don't let thyself be brought under the sway of the Old Law! 7. 'Let's not go to my house!' said Conchobar. 8. Let us follow these (things)! 9. Let us be fatherlike, that means let us take the heritage of our fathers and let us imitate their customs. 10. Do not (sg.) attempt (it)! 11. Let them be released from their chains, for the sake of my wealth and my cattle, but don't let the court be closed. 12. One sister, two sisters, three sisters. 13. Welcome to you, little boys, for the sake of the hearts of your mothers! 14. Steadily therefore let the men row, it is not long to the lands of the women. 15. 'What are the mountains over there?' said Cú Chulainn, 'What are the bright mounds over there on top of the mountains? What are the plains there? What are the herds, the wild ones there?' 16. It is not you who nourish them, but it is they who nourish you. 17. The concern is not great which we have for thee. 18. If thou art in communion with the body of Christ, thou art a son/a daughter of Abraham like that, and it is thou who is an heir of Abraham. 19. This then is a custom for them, reproval of a woman in the beginning and then giving her under the power of her man... so that it is afterwards that the man is reprimanded and is bent under the will of God. 20. 'This is its custom,' said Jesus, 'the anvils which are being struck do not teach everyone, who strikes them; and it is they who are being taught.'

39.3. Test

Try to recognize the verbal forms (give as much information about the words as possible—class, person, number, mood, relative or not, infixed pronoun):

eipred: _____	comalnaithe: _____	áirim: _____
crochaid: _____	ná·crochaid: _____	biur: _____
immráidet: _____	nach·ngairem: _____	eiperr: _____
foilsigid: _____	rom·chluinter: _____	sóertar: _____
crochthar: _____	ná·crochthar: _____	finntae: _____
áirmem: _____	cotob·ceilid: _____	ná·déne: _____
da·gniad: _____	nach·chluined: _____	eirg: _____
dos·mbeir: _____	ná·comalnatar: _____	tair: _____
dáiles: _____	pridchimme: _____	rímte: _____
téite: _____	do·thíagat: _____	gattae: _____
crentar: _____	fíriánaigemmar: _____	nád·fil: _____
for·chaun: _____	nád·fodmat: _____	sernas: _____
nod·carat: _____	indat·chluinter: _____	adid·chí: _____

39.4. Test

Try to recognize the inflectional forms (give as much information about the words as possible—gender, stem class, case, number):

inna traiged: _____	or	_____	ind fíadat:	_____
Temraig: _____	or	_____	aithir:	_____
cethrachat: _____	or	_____	tengthaib:	_____
ciach: _____	or	_____	ind uige:	_____
sieir: _____	or	_____	cathracha:	_____
cáera: _____	or	_____	míledaib:	_____
slíab: _____	or	_____	airecha:	_____
dét: _____	or	_____	or	_____
or _____	or	_____	or	_____
int ṡenduid: _____	á ríga: _____		ríga:	_____

Lesson 40

40.1. Nasal stems: neuter n-stems

The neuter n-declension, also called men-declension, mainly consists of verbal nouns of strong verbs. The eponymous *n* appears only in the plural and the dual. It is unlenited and it is therefore written *nn* or *n*. In most of the words the *m* /m/ of the stem is palatalized throughout the paradigm. An example is *céimm* /k'ēm'/ 'step, the stepping,' stem *céimmenn-* /k'ēm'ən/, the verbal noun of *cingid* (S1) 'to step':

case	ending	Old Irish	Prim. Irish	Proto-Celtic	Pre-Celtic
n. a. sg.	m'ᴺ	*céimm*ᴺ	*kēmev	*kanχsman «	*kéngsmņ
gen.	m'eᴴ	*céimme*ᴴ	*kēmēh	*kanχsmēs	*kņgsméns
prep.	m'əm'ᴸ, m'ᴸ	*céimmimm*ᴸ, *céimm*ᴸ «	*kēmevē, -mev	*kanχsmenei̯, -meni	*kņgsménei̯, -méni
n. a. pl.	m'ənᴸ	*céimmenn*ᴸ	*kēmevā «	*kanχsmanā	
gen.	m'ənᴺ	*céimmenn*ᴺ	*kēmevav «	*kanχsmanom	
prep.	m'ənəβ'	*céimmennaib* «	*kēmevaβih «	*kanχsmambis	
n. a. du.	m'ᴺ	*dá*ᴺ *céimm*ᴺ	?	?	
gen.		n/a	?	?	
prep.	m'ənəβ'	*díb*ᴺ *céimmennaib*	?	?	

Illustration 40.1: The neutral n-stem declension

In some words the *m* of the stem becomes non-palatalized as soon as an extra syllable is added, the most important example being the word for 'name' *ainm* /an'm'/, stem *anmann-* /anmən/:

case	ending	Old Irish	Prim. Irish	Proto-Celtic	PIE
n. a. sg.	m'ᴺ	*ainm*ᴺ	*anmev	*anman «	*h₁né(h₃)mņ
gen.	meᴴ	*anmae*ᴴ	*anmēh	*anmēs	*h₁ņ(h₃)méns
prep.	məm'ᴸ, m'ᴸ	*anmaimm*ᴸ, *ainm*ᴸ «	*anmevē, -mev	*anmenei̯, -meni	*h₁ņ(h₃)ménei̯, -méni
n. a. pl.	mənᴸ	*anmann*ᴸ	*anmevā «	anmanā (anuana)	
gen.	mənᴺ	*anmann*ᴺ	*anmevav «	*anmanom	
prep.	mənəβ'	*anmannaib*	*anmevaβih «	anmambis (anmanbe)	
n.a. du.	m'ᴺ	*dá*ᴺ *n-ainm*ᴺ	?	?	
gen.		n/a	?	?	
prep.	mənəβ'	*díb*ᴺ *n-anmannaib*	?	?	

Illustration 40.2: The declension of *ainm* 'name'

Note:

1. In nearly all words in this class the nom. sg. ends in /m/, which is spelled *m* or *mm*. Exceptions are *imb* /im'b'/, gen. *imbe* /im'b'e/ 'butter,' *mír* /m'ɪɸ'/, gen. *míre* /m'ɪɸ'e/ 'bit, morsel' and *gein* /g'ev'/, gen. *geine* /g'ev'e/ 'birth.'

2. A few words behave irregularly. Neuter *arbor* /arβuɸ/ 'grain, corn' inflects like an n-stem in the oblique cases: gen. *arbae* /arβe/, prep. *arbaimm* /arβəm'/ etc.; *neim* /n'eμ'/ 'poison' is an n-stem in the singular, but an i-stem in the plural, e.g., nom. pl. *neimi* /n'eμ'i/.

3. In the later language the ending -a was added to the nom. and acc. pl., e.g., *céimmenna* 'steps' or *imbenna* 'butters.'

4. The prehistory of the long ending -*imm*ᴸ in the prep. sg. is unclear.

Illustration 40.3: *mír curad* 'the hero's portion'

40.2. Exercise

Inflect some of the following words. Decline them together with the article. Combine them with any of the adjectives you learned so far.

> *béimm* /b'ēm'/ (n, n) 'the striking, stroke, blow' (v.n. of S3 *benaid*)
> *imb* /im'b'/ (n, n) 'butter'
> *léimm* /l'ēm'/ (n, n) 'the leaping, a jump' (v.n. of S1 *lingid*)
> *seinm* /s'en'm'/, gen. *senmae* /s'enme/ (n, n) 'the sounding, the playing of an instrument' (v.n. of S1 *seinnid*)
> *ingrimm* /iv'ɣ'ɸ'əm'/, gen. *ingrimme* /iv'ɣ'ɸ'əm'e/ (n, n) 'persecution' (no syncope!, v.n. of S1 *in·greinn*)
> *togairm* /toɣər'm'/, gen. *togarmae* /toɣərme/ (n, n) 'the calling, the shouting' (no syncope!, v.n. of S2 *do·gair*)

40.3. Comparison of adjectives

Comparison means the formation of different degrees of adjectives, which means the formation of forms like *big, bigger, biggest* in English or *gross, grösser, am grössten* in German. German and English have three different degrees of adjectives: the positive (the basic form of the adjective, e.g., *gross, big*), the comparative (the grade used for comparing two or more nouns with regard to a certain quality, e.g., *grösser, bigger*) and the superlative (which expresses the highest degree possible in a quality, e.g., *am grössten, biggest*). The different degrees are expressed by special suffixes attached to the basic form of the adjective: -*er* in the comparative both in English and in German, -*est* in the superlative in English, -*(e)ster* in German.

As you may have guessed things are a bit different in Old Irish. In addition to the three degrees mentioned above Old Irish has a fourth degree called equative.[1] The equative is used when a

---

[1] You will find the four degrees positive, equative, comparative and superlative in the standard handbooks. Actually, more degrees can be added. I will talk about them in a later lesson.

noun possesses a certain quality in the same degree as another one. In English or German such an equation has to be expressed analytically, e.g., *he is as tall as a tree* or *ihre Lippen sind so rot wie Kirschen*. In Old Irish these forms are expressed by a single word with a special ending, e.g., *deirgithir* 'as red as' and *móir* 'as tall as.'

A number of syntactical and morphological peculiarities have to be observed in all degrees of comparison apart from the positive, that is in the equative, comparative and superlative:

1. Equative, comparative and superlative are uninflected. Only a single form exists for each of them, which does not change according to gender and number.

2. All three forms of comparison can only be used predicatively. That means they only appear as predicates in copulaic sentences of the type *X is as big as/bigger than/the biggest*. It is not possible to use them attributively, like in English *the greatest love of all* or in German *mit längeren Wartezeiten ist zu rechnen*. Instead these sentences would have to be reformulated as *mit Wartezeiten, die länger sind, ist zu rechnen*, and *the love, which is greatest of all*. In Old Irish the forms of comparison have to follow the word they qualify in a relative clause.

3. Neither of the three can be substantivized. If you do want to use them as substantives, they have to follow the deictic particle *í* in a relative clause, e.g., *ind í as áildem* 'she who is most beautiful = the most beautiful, *die Schönste*' or *inna hí ata nessa* 'they who are nearer = the nearer (things), *die Näheren*.'

In the lessons so far you have only encountered the positive degree of Old Irish adjectives. In the following lessons the other degrees of comparison will be discussed one after the other, starting with the equative in the following section.

40.4. Comparison: the equative

The equative suffix, which is attached to the positive stem of the adjective, is *-ithir* /ˈəθʼəρʼ/ (usually after monosyllabic adjectives) and *-idir* /ˈəðʼəρʼ/ (usually after polysyllables). This suffix causes raising where possible, but it never undergoes syncope, e.g.:

gel /gʼeλ/ 'bright' → *gilithir* /gʼiλʼəθʼəρʼ/ 'as bright as'
tromm /trom/ 'heavy' → *truimmithir* /trumʼəθʼəρʼ/ 'as heavy as'

Other examples:

dían /dʼiaν/ 'swift' → *déinithir* /dʼēνʼəθʼəρʼ/ 'as swift as' (the change from *ía* to *éi* is not raising, but the regular development of *ía* before a palatalized consonant!)
tiug /tʼiṵγ/ 'thick' → *tigithir* /tʼiγʼəθʼəρʼ/ 'as thick as'
cas /kas/ 'curly' → *caissithir* /kasʼəθʼəρʼ/ 'as curly as'

Syncope, of course, takes place in adjectives of more than one syllable when the suffix *-ithir* is added:

solus /soλus/ 'clear' → *soilsidir* /soλʼsʼəðʼəρʼ/ 'as clear as'
deimin /dʼeμʼəν/ 'certain' → *deimnithir* /dʼeμʼνʼəθʼəρʼ/ 'as certain as'

Note also cases where syncope causes non-palatalization of the adjective's stem final consonant:

amrae /aμρe/ 'wonderful' → *amraidir* /aμρəðʼəρʼ/ 'as wonderful as' (< *amar-ithir*) or where syncope has already taken place somewhere else in the word:

erlam /ɛρλəμ/ 'ready' → *erlamaidir* / ɛρλəμəδ'əρ'/ 'as ready as' (< *are-lām-ithir*, syncope has taken place between *r* and *l*!).

There are a few irregular formations of the equative:

positive	equative
il /iλ/ 'many'	*lir* /l'iρ'/
lethan /l'eθəv/ 'broad'	*leithir, lethithir* /l'eθ'əρ' l'eθ'əθ'əρ'/
már, mór /māρ mōρ/ 'great, much, big'	*móir* /mōρ'/
remor /r'eμəρ/ 'thick'	*reimithir, reimir* /r'eμ'əθ'əρ' r'eμ'əρ'/
sír /s'īρ/ 'long'	*sithir, sithithir* /s'iθ'əρ' s'iθ'əθ'əρ'/
trén /t'r'ēv/ 'strong'	*treisithir* /t'r'es'əθ'əρ'/

Illustration 40.4: Irregular equative forms

Note:

1. The person or thing to which the subject is compared immediately follows the equative in the accusative case, e.g., *[is] leithir damseichi ind óensúil* 'the single eye is as broad as an ox-hide (*damseiche*)' (after TBDD 44.4), *is mór sléibe fírinne Dé* 'God's truth is as great as the mountains' (*Ml.* 55d11), or it is expressed by a conjunctionless clause, e.g., *soilsidir bid i llugburt* 'as bright (as if) it were in a garden' (*Thes.* II 294.16).

2. In the later language the compared person or thing may be expressed by a prepositional phrase with *fri^H* (later: *ri^H*, *re^H*), e.g., *duibidir ri bran a bráe, géirithir a gáe ri ailt, gilidir a chness ri áel... airdithir a scíath ri scál, sithithir a lám ri láe* 'his brow is as black as a raven (*bran*), his spear is as sharp as a blade (*ailt*), his skin is as bright as lime (*áel*)... his shield is as high as a phantom (*scál*), his hand is as long as a foot (*láe*)' (LL 6390–6395).

3. Another method of equating things and persons is to prefix *com-* to the positive form of an adjective and by introducing the compared element with *fri^H*, e.g., *is comdub fri éc a drech* 'his face is as black as death' (*Corm.* 36), *bid comard a slíab fri fán* 'the mountain will be as high as the valley' (*Blathm.* 949).

You'll find a table with irregular comparison in Appendix F.5.

Illustration: 40.5: *dían, déiniu, déinem, déinithir* 'fast, faster, fastest, as fast as'

Lesson 41

41.1. The preterite

So far we were dealing with the different stem formations of the present tense of the Old Irish verb. The imperative (see 37.3) is formed from the present stem. But some moods and tenses are formed from separate stems in Old Irish. First we will look at that of the preterite. The simple preterite (as opposed to the 'augmented preterite' or 'perfect,' which we will learn in a later lesson) denotes a single, unrepeated action that was completed in the past and has no immediate relevance to the present. Thus it is roughly equivalent to the English past tense; in German it is most appropriately rendered by the *Präteritum*, for example:

> *Im·luid Bran laa n-and a óenur…, co·cúala a céol íarna chúl… Con·tuil asendath frissa céol ara bindi. A ndo·fúsig asa chotlud, co·n-acca in cróíb n-argait… ina farrud.* (IB 2)

'One day Bran was walking[1] there by his own…, he *heard* music in his back… Instantly he *fell* asleep at the music because of its sweetness. When he *woke* from his sleep, he *saw* a silver branch beside him.'

'Eines Tages *wanderte* Bran allein dort…, er *hörte* Musik hinter sich… Sofort *fiel* er bei der Musik in Schlaf aufgrund ihrer Süsse. Als er aus dem Schlaf *erwachte*, *sah* er einen silbernen Zweig neben sich.'

The distinction between the different present stem classes is only marginally relevant to the formation of the various types of Old Irish preterite stems. Other factors like the opposition between weak and strong verbs or the root structure of the strong verbs are more important: whereas all weak verbs and most hiatus verbs in some way or the other form a so-called s-preterite, in the case of the strong verbs the preterite stem formation depends largely on the shape of the root.

These are the different preterite formations. We will learn all of them in the next two lessons:

> s-preterite:
> > simple s-preterite
> > reduplicated s-preterite
> t-preterite
> suffixless preterite:
> > reduplicated preterite
> > é-, í-, ó-preterite
> > á-preterite
> irregular and suppletive formations

---

[1] The Old Irish preterite cannot be rendered by an English past tense in this case.

199

41.2. The s-preterite

The simple, unreduplicated s-preterite is formed by all weak verbs, by H3 verbs (except for ·*foí* 'to sleep' and *do·goa* 'to choose') and by the S1 verb *ibid* 'to drink' and the S2 verb *gaibid* 'to take.' The s-preterite is characterized by an *s* that is added to the stem vowel in all persons except for the 3ʳᵈ sg. conjunct. The vowel before the *s* is syncopated appropriately where an extra syllable is added. In *gabais* /gaβəs'/, the preterite of *gaibid* 'to take,' the stem final consonant /β/ is non-palatalized throughout; in *ibis* /iβ'əs'/, the preterite of *ibid* 'to drink,' it is palatalized throughout /β'/.

The ending set of the s-preterite is reminiscent of that of S1 verbs. In the passive no *s* appears, instead a dental suffix in various forms is added to the root.

41.2.1. The s-preterite of W1 verbs

In W1 verbs the consonant before the *s* is non-palatalized throughout. In the 3ʳᵈ sg. conjunct the bare root appears, e.g., ·*car*:

person		absolute		conjunct	
1ˢᵗ sg.		*carsu*	Csu	(ní)·*carus*	Cus
2ⁿᵈ sg.		*carsai*	Csi	(ní)·*carais*	Cəs'
3ʳᵈ sg.		*carais*	Cəs'	(ní)·*car*	C
	rel.	*caras*	Cəs	-	
	pass.	*carthae*	Cθe	(ní)·*carad*	Cəδ
	pass. rel.	*carthae*	Cθe	-	
1ˢᵗ pl.		*carsaimmi*	Csəm'i	(ní)·*carsam*	Csəμ
	rel.	*carsaimme*	Csəm'e	-	
2ⁿᵈ pl.		n/a		(ní)·*carsaid*	Csəδ'
3ʳᵈ pl.		*carsait*	Csəd'	(ní)·*carsat*	Csəd
	rel.	*carsaite*	Csəd'e	-	
	pass.	*carthai*	Cθi	(ní)·*cartha*	Cθa
	pass. rel.	*carthai*	Cθi	-	

Illustration 41.1: The conjugation of W1 s-preterites

41.2.2. The s-preterite of W2 verbs

In W2 verbs the consonant before the *s* is basically palatalized throughout the whole paradigm. Verbs where the vowel of the root is *á, o,* or *u* form an exception, though. In the 3ʳᵈ sg. conjunct the oldest ending was *i*, e.g., ·*léici*. Since this was indistinguishable from the 3ʳᵈ sg. conjunct present tense, which in the example above is also ·*léici*, later the *i* was dropped and the bare root remained, e.g., ·*léic*:

person	absolute		conjunct	
1st sg.	*léicsiu*	C's'u	*(ní)·léicius*	C'us
2nd sg.	*léicsi*	C's'i	*(ní)·léicis*	C'əs'
3rd sg.	*léicis*	C'əs'	*(ní)·léici, ·léic*	C'i, C'
rel.	*léices*	C'əs	-	
pass.	*léicthe*	C'θ'e	*(ní)·léiced*	C'əð
pass. rel.	*léicthe*	C'θ'e	-	
1st pl.	*léicsimmi*	C's'əm'i	*(ní)·léicsem*	C's'əµ
rel.	*léicsimme*	C's'əm'e	-	
2nd pl.	n/a		*(ní)·léicsid*	C's'əð'
3rd pl.	*léicsit*	C's'əd'	*(ní)·léicset*	C's'əd
rel.	*léicsite*	C's'əd'e	-	
pass.	*léicthi*	C'θ'i	*(ní)·léicthea*	C'θ'a
pass. rel.	*léicthi*	C'θ'i	-	

Illustration 41.2: The conjugation of W2 s-preterites

41.2.3. Deponent s-preterite forms

Only a few absolute deponent s-preterite forms are attested:

1. 3rd sg.: *cíchnaigistir* (W2b) 'creaked,' *eissistir* (W2a) 'besought,' *ráthaigestair* (W2b) 'perceived'
2. 1st pl. rel.: *célsammar* 'which we foreboded' (W1)
3. 3rd pl.: *tuilsitir* (W2) 'they slept'

The absolute passive forms are a bit better attested, in fact their formation is not different from that of the active inflection: 3rd sg. *suidigthe* (W2b) 'was placed,' 3rd pl. *suidigthi* 'were placed.'

The conjunct inflection, on the other hand, is well attested:

	W1		W2	
1st sg.	*(ní)·labrasur*	Cəsuµ	*(ní)·suidigsiur*	C's'uµ
2nd sg.	*(ní)·labraiser*	Cəs'əp	*(ní)·suidigser*	C's'əp
3rd sg.	*(ní)·labrastar*	Cəstəp	*(ní)·suidigestar*	C'əstəp
pass.	*(ní)·labrad*	Cəð	*(ní)·suidiged*	C'əð
1st pl.	*(ní)·labrasammar*	Cəsəməp	*(ní)·suidigsemmar*	C's'əməp
2nd pl.	*(ní)·labraisid*	Cəs'əð	*(ní)·suidigsid*	C's'əð'
3rd pl.	*(ní)·labrasatar*	Cəsədəp	*(ní)·suidigsetar*	C's'ədəp
pass.	*(ní)·labartha*	Cθa	*(ní)·suidigthea*	C'θ'a

Illustration 41.3: The conjugation of the W1 and W2 deponent s-preterite

41.3. Special formations of the s-preterite

Illustration 41.4:
do·génus-sa dermat
'I made a mistake'

1. In W2b verbs (except for deponent verbs in *-(a)igithir*) the root vowel *u* of the present stem becomes *o* in the preterite and the root final consonant becomes non-palatalized except for the endingless 3rd sg. conjunct, e.g., 1st sg. *con·tolus* 'I slept' (*con·tuili*), 3rd sg. deponent *do·corastar* '(s)he put' (*do·cuirethar*), 3rd sg. *slocais* '(s)he swallowed' (*sluicid*), but *do·loig* '(s)he forgave' (*do·luigi*).

2. All H1 and some H2 verbs form their preterite stem by 'reduplicating' their *anlauting* consonant. That means that the root initial consonant is 'doubled,' with an *e* appearing between the two consonants, e.g., *bebais* /b'eβəs/ '(s)he died' from *báid* /baᵹ̃/ 'to die.' Unfortunately the reduplication can often be blurred by further sound changes. For example, the reduplicated s-prèterite:

2.1. of *gníid* /g'n'iᵹ̃/ is *génais, ·génai* /g'ēvəs' ·g'ēvi/ < *ge-gnī-s-* (the *g* was lost in front of the *n*, but caused the lengthening of the *e* = 'compensatory lengthening').

2.2. of *do·gní* it is *do·génai, ·digni* /do·g'ēvi ·d'iɣ'v'i/; but the syncope is analogically avoided in some forms, e.g., 3rd pl. *·digénsat* /·d'iɣ'ēvsəd/.

2.3. of *con·sní, ·cosnai* /kov·s'n'ī ·kosni/ 'to strive for' it is *con·senai, ·coissenai* /kov·sevi ·kos'əvi/ < *se-snī-s-*.

2.4. In the preterite of *ad·cota, ·éta* /aδ·koda ·ēda/ 'to get' (a compound of *tā-*) the reduplication is between *t* and *d* and the reduplicating *e* has become /ə/, spelled *a*, in unstressed position: 3rd sg. *ad·cotadae, ·étadae* /aδ·kodəδe ·ēdəδe/ '(s)he got,' 3rd pl. *ad·cotatsat, ·étatsat* /aδ·kodətsəd ·ēdətsəd/.

3. The 3rd sg. conjunct usually has a final vowel *-(a)e* in H1 verbs, e.g., *·bebae* /·b'eβe/ from *báid*, *imm·rerae* /im'·r'epe/ '(s)he rowed around' from *imm·rá* 'to row around,' and *-(a)i* in H2 verbs, e.g., *do·génai* /do·g'ēvi/ '(s)he did' from *do·gní* 'to do.' But in all other persons the *s* is visible, e.g., 3rd pl. *do·génsat* /do·g'ēvsəd/.

41.4. The t-preterite

The t-preterite is characterized by the suffix *t*, which is added to the root and which is followed by the ending. The *t* basically stands for /t/, except in the preterite of the two roots **em-* and **sem-*, where it stands for /d/. Conjunct forms are very well attested, but absolute forms are rather rare. The t-preterite is formed by all strong verbs—irrespective of their present stem class—whose roots end in *r* or *l*, and also by a few strong verbs ending in *g* and by the two strong roots S1 *em-* and S2 *sem-* (of these two roots no simple verbs exist, only compounds like *ar·foím* 'to accept' < **are-fo-em-* or *do·essim* 'to pour out' < **to-ess-sem-*; therefore I cite them as abstract roots). Of course compounds of these verbs form t-preterites as well, e.g., *as·bert* 'he said' from *as·beir*, compound of *beirid*. This is a list of all verbs that form a t-preterite:

	present	preterite stem
r	*beirid* 'to carry'	*bert-*
	fo·geir 'to heat'	*fo·gert-*
	marnaid 'to betray'	*mert-*
	sernaid 'to strew'	*sert-*
	dairid 'to bull'	*dart-*
	gairid 'to call'	*gart-*
l	*at·baill* 'to die'	*(*belt-) -balt-*
	ceilid 'to hide'	*celt-*
	geilid 'to graze'	*gelt-*
	meilid 'to grind'	*melt-*
	ailid 'to rear'	*alt-*
m	**em-* 'to take/protect'	*ét-* /ed/
	*sem- 'to pour'	*(*sét-) -set-, -sat- /-s⁽ʲ⁾əd-/*[2]
g	*aigid* 'to drive'	*acht-*
	aingid 'to protect'	*anacht-*
	dligid 'is due'	*dlecht-*
	do·formaig 'to increase'	*do·formacht-, tormacht-*
	at·reg (ess-reg-) 'to rise'	*recht-, -racht-*[3]
	orgaid 'to slay'	*ort-*
	saigid 'to seek'	*siacht- /sʲiəχt-/*
	ro·saig 'to reach'	*ro·siacht, ·roacht /roəχt/*

Illustration 41.5: Verbs forming t-preterites

A few more verbs ending in nasals and gutturals analogically acquired a t-preterite in the history of Old Irish; see GOI 422 for details.

The ending set of the t-preterite is reminiscent of the present of strong verbs in the singular, but similar to the preterite of deponent verbs in the plural. Because outside of the s-preterite the formation of the passive preterite is much more complicated, I will talk about the preterite passive of strong verbs in a later lesson and do not give them in the following tables. The following example is the most frequent of all t-preterites, the preterite of *beirid* 'to carry':

---

[2] Only unstressed forms are attested.
[3] t-preterite only in compounds of the root *reg-*; the simple verb *regid, rigid* forms a reduplicated preterite.

person	absolute		conjunct	
1st sg.	n/a		(ní)·biurt	{R}(u)Ct
2nd sg.	n/a		(ní)·birt	{R}C't'
3rd sg.	birt	{R}Ct	(ní)·bert	Ct
rel.	berte	Cte	-	
1st pl.	n/a		(ní)·bertammar	Ctəməρ
2nd pl.	n/a		(ní)·bertaid	Ctəδ'
3rd pl.	bertatar	Ctədəρ	(ní)·bertat, ·bertatar	Ctəd, Ctədəρ
rel.	bertar, bertatar	Ctəρ, Ctədəρ	-	

Illustration 41.6: The conjugation of the t-preterite

Note:

1. When the *t* is added to a root ending in *g* /γ/, the *g* becomes *ch* /χ/, e.g., *aigid* 'to drive' → preterite stem *acht-*.

2. When added to a root ending in *m* /μ/, the two sounds merge to give a new sound /d/, spelled *t*.

3. Sometimes the root can be very hard to identify in the actual attested verbal forms, especially when it is pushed out of the stressed position by additional preverbs. For example, the verb S1 *do·fuissim* 'to beget, to create, to bear' (a compound of the root **sem-* with the preverbs **to-uss-*) has the t-preterite *do·fosat* /do·fosəd/, or the prototonic form of the t-preterite of *do·meil* 'to spend, to consume' is *·tomalt* /·toμəlt/, deuterotonic *do·melt* /do·m'elt/. Some of the preterite forms below are never attested in stressed position, therefore I cite them with a hyphen before them, e.g., *-balt-*.

41.5. The prehistory of the s- and t-preterites

Necessarily I can only offer you a very simplified survey of the prehistory of the various preterite formations of Old Irish. The Old Irish s-preterite continues Proto-Indo-European s-aorists: the suffix s was added to the root and so-called athematic endings were immediately added. This formation underwent heavy reshapings in the prehistory of Irish. The most important step was the reinterpretation of the 3rd sg. form as a new basic stem form, unto which in all other persons the usual thematic endings (those of, e.g., the S1 class) were stuck. True weak, i.e., secondary, verbal classes originally had no preterite. The s-preterite formation was taken over from some historically strong verbs that became reinterpreted as weak verbs within Irish or Celtic, like the verb W1 *scaraid* (preterite stem *scaras-*) in the table below. I will give you only a reconstruction of the W1 s-preterite. The prehistory of W2a and W2b s-preterites is very much similar, with only the suffix **-ī- < *-eie-* and **-e-* respectively before the *s*, instead of the **-a-* in W1 s-preterites. The absolute forms of the s- and t-preterites were probably created at the Insular Celtic stage in analogy to the absolute/conjunct-opposition in the present tense by adding **-i* at the end of the forms.

conj.	OIr.	Prim. Ir.	Insular Celtic	Proto-Celtic	PIE
1st sg.	·scarus	*skaρasū	*skaraʦū «	*skerasam «	*skérHsm̥
2nd sg.	·scarais	*skaρaseh	*skaraʦes «	*skeras «	*skérHss
3rd sg.	·scar	*skaρah	*skaraʦ	*skerast «	*skérHst
1st pl.	·scar†sam	*skaρasoμah	*skaraʦomos «	*skerasmo/me	*skérHsmo/me
2nd pl.	·scar†said	*skaρaseθeh	*skaraʦetes «	*skeraste	*skérHste
3rd pl.	·scar†sat	*skaρasod	*skaraʦont «	*skerasant	*skérHsn̥t

Illustration 41.7: The prehistory of the s-preterite

The Old Irish t-preterite developed out of the same PIE s-aorist formation as the s-preterite, but due to a different sound environment the *s* was lost at some stage in Celtic. Again the 3rd sg. form was reinterpreted as the new basic stem form unto which the thematic endings were added in all other persons. Furthermore the ending of the suffixless preterite was taken over in the plural in Old Irish.

conj.	OIr.	Prim. Irish	Insular Celtic	Proto-Celtic	PIE
1st sg.	·biurt	*birtū	*birtū «	*bīrsam	*bʰérsm̥
2nd sg.	·birt	*birteh	*birtes «	*bīrs	*bʰérss
3rd sg.	·birt	*birt	*birt	*bīrst	*bʰérst
1st pl.	·bertammar «	*birtoμah	*birtomos «	*bersmo/me	*bʰérsmo/me
2nd pl.	·bertaid «	*birteθeh	*birtetes «	*berste	*bʰérste
3rd pl.	·bertatar «	*birtod	*birtont «	*bersant	*bʰérsn̥t

Illustration 41.8: The prehistory of the t-preterite

41.6. Exercise

Try to inflect the following verbs in the appropriate preterite formation:

anaid /avəð'/ (W1) 'to stay'
do·sluindi, ·díltai /do·slun'd'i ·d'īlti/ (W2b) 'to deny'
soid, ·soí /soäð' ·soi̯/ (H3) 'to turn' (s-pret. soais, ·soí /soäs' ·soi̯/)
ad·ella, ·aidlea /að·ela ·að'l'a/ (W1) 'to visit'
cruthaigidir /kruθəɣ'əð'əρ'/ (W2b) 'to shape'
do·gní, ·dénai /do·g'n'ī ·d'ēvi/ (H2) 'to do, to make'
fo·ácaib, ·fácaib /fo·āgəβ' ·fāgəβ'/ (S2) 'to leave' (no syncope in the middle
                    syllable in the plural forms; cp. 32.1.5)
imm·beir, ·imbir /im'·b'eρ' ·im'b'əρ'/ (S1) 'to play'
do·eim, ·dim /do·eμ' ·d'iμ'/ (S1) 'to cover, to protect'

Lesson 42

42.1. An indecent poem

At·tá ben is' tír	ad·tā b'eʋ is t'īρ'
—ní·eiprimm a ainm—	—n'ī·eb'r'əm' a han'm'—
maidid eissi a deilm	maδ'əδ' es'i a d'el'm'
amal chloich a tailm.	aμəλ χλοχ' a tal'm'

Note:

1. *is' tír* stands for classical Old Irish *isin tír*

2. *·eiprimm* is a younger variant for what in classical Old Irish would be *·epur*.

Source: Kuno MEYER, *Bruchstücke der älteren Lyrik Irlands*, Berlin 1919, 34

42.2. Varia

1. The abbreviation *⁊rl* stands for *ocus araile* /ogus aρáλ'e/ 'and the other (things)' and is the Irish equivalent of Latin *etc.*

2. In compound verbs that have the preverbs *do·* (< **to-*), *fo·* and *ro·* as their first preverbs and in which the stressed part of the verb in the deuterotonic form starts with a vowel, very frequently the *o* of the preverb is elided, that means dropped, so that eventually the deuterotonic form of the verb looks like the prototonic form. For example, independent, deuterotonic *fo·ácaib* /fo·āgəβ'/ 'to leave' → *fθ·ácaib* → *fácaib* /fāgəβ'/, which looks exactly like prototonic, dependent *·fácaib*, or *ro·icc, ·ricc* /ro·ig' ·r'ig'/ 'to reach' → *ricc, ·ricc*. Note that in the case of the preverb *do·* (< **to-*) the elided variant starts with a *t-*, e.g., *do·aisféna* /do·as'f'ēva/ 'to show, to demonstrate' → *taisféna* /tas'f'ēva/. Basically both forms can stand side by side in independent position, although in some words the elided variants are preponderant.

3. I said in 3.2 that mutational effects (lenition and nasalization) usually do not extend across phrases. This is no absolute rule, though, and in the example below *fácab Pátraicc a daltae n-and* 'Patrick left his foster-son there' as a result of the nasalizing effect of the accusative *daltae* 'foster-ling' an *n* appears before *and* 'there,' although this is a different part of the sentence.

42.3. Exercise

Old Irish

1. * Cladair a ḟertae íarum. Sáitir a lia. Scríbthair a ainm n-ogaim. Agair a gubae. (TBC 1385 f.)
2. * It gilithir snechtae n-óenaidche in dí dóit 7 it dergithir sian sléibe in dá ngrúad nglanáilli. (TBDD 19-21) 3. * It duibithir druimne ndoíl in dí malaig. (TBDD 22) 4. * It glaisithir bugae in dí ṡúil. (TBDD 24) 5. * At·tá cosmailius aile leis-seom [*sc.* St. Paul] in-so .i. cosmailius gotho fri tob, ar at·taat ilṡenmann do ṡuidiu 7 is sain cach n-áe .i. is sain seinm fri cath, sain fri súan 7rl. (*Wb.* 12c46). 6. Is trí garmann gartae in cailech isin maitin. 7. ** Cisi in máthair con·bert a ngein-se? (*Gosp.* 32) 8. * Delbais Ísu dá énán deac, passir a n-anmann; dia Sabbait dos·géni de chrí cen madmann. (*Gosp.* 2) 9. * Gabais éulchaire in n-í Connlae immon mnaí adid·ngládastar 7 do·chorastar ubull dó. (EC 7) 10. * Ní·tomult-sa far mbiad nó far n-étach, acht is sisi doda·melt. (*Wb.* 18a10) 11. * Con·gab Pátraicc íar n-aidbairt i nDruimm Daro [...] Fácab Pátraicc a daltae n-and, *Benignus* a ainm. (*Thes.* ii 238.14-15). 12. ** Is ed ainm inna inse-so Inis Subai. Fa·n-ácabsat and íarum. (IB 61) 13. * Con·gartat ind fir *Iudas* cuccu; ar·foet argat úadib ar mrath in choimded. (*Blathm.* 177-180) 14. * Ar·gabsat ind Iudaidi Ísu 7 na·sroigliset 7 at·n-ortat tara grúaide. (*Blathm.* 181-184) 15. ** Gabthae tí chorcrae immun ríg. (*Blathm.* 205) 16. ** Látharsat dó dig séto ar lainni a mochéco; con·mescsat [...] domblas dó ar ḟínacet. (*Blathm.* 233-236) 17. ** Do·celt grían a sollsi sain, [...] búiristir rían trethanbras. (*Blathm.* 241-244) 18. * Is Ísu in fer as·éracht i nIsraél; is inna anmaimm fris·accat uili cenél. (*Blathm.* 921-924) 19. * I Cétaín chrúaid scarsu-sa fri Máel Rúanaid. Dia Dardaín gabsu-sa céill for ingnais maicc m'athar. (*Bruchst.* 116) 20. Con·garad prímḟili ind ríg cosa rrígtech do ṡenmaimm inna cruitte. Indat·chongrad-su leis-seom?

Transcription

1. klaðəp' a erte iapuµ. sāt'əp' a λ'iä. s'k'r'ïβθəp' a an'm' voɣəm'. aɣəp' a ɣuβe. 2. id g'iλ'əθ'əp' s'n'eɣte voịṷað'χ'e in d'ï ðōd' ogus id d'er'g'əθ'əp' s'iäṽ s'l'ēβ'e in dā ŋgruað ŋglavāl'i. 3. id duβ'əθ'əp' drum'v'e ndoịλ' in dī µaləɣ'. 4. id glas'əθ'əp' buɣe in d'ï hūλ'. 5. at·tā kosµəλ'us aλ'e l'es'-s'oµ iv-so, eð ōv kosµəλ'us goθo f'r'i toβ, ap ad·taəd iλh'enmən do huð'u ogus is sav' kaχ vaị, eð ōv is sav' s'en'm' f'r'i kaθ, sav' f'r'i suav ogus apáλ'e. 6. is t'r'ï garmən garte in kal'əχ is'ən µad'əv'. 7. k'is'i in µāθəp' kov·β'ert a ŋ'g'ev'-s'e? 8. delβəs' ïsu dā ēvāv d'eäg, pasəp' a vanmən; d'iä sabəd' dos·g'ēvi d'e χ'ṗ'ï k'ev µaðmən. 9. gaßəs' eṷλχəp'e in n'ï gonλe imən mnaị að'əð·ŋglāðəstəp ogus do·χopəstəp ußul dō. 10. n'ï·toµult-sa βap m'b'iäð nō βap v'ēdəχ, aχt is s'is'i doða·m'elt. 11. kov·gaß Pādpəg' iap vað'bər't' i ndrum' ðapo. fāgəß Pādpəg' a ðalte vand, *Benignus* a an'm'. 12. is eð an'm' ina h'iv's'e-so iv'əs' sußi. fa·vāgəßsəd and iapuµ. 13. kov·gartəd ind ip' *Iudas* kuku; ap·foäd argəd uaðəß' ap µpaθ in χoµ'ð'əð. 14. ap·gaßsəd ind ịuðəð'i ïsu ogus va·sroɣ'l'əs'əd ogus að·vortəd tapa ɣpuað'e. 15. gaße t'ï χorkpe imən r'ïɣ'. 16. lāθəpsəd dō d'iɣ' s'ēdo ap λan'i a µoχēgo; kov·m'esksəd domblas dō ap ïvak'əd. 17. do·k'elt g'r'iav a soλ's'i sav', buß'əs't'əp' r'iav t'r'eθəvßras. 18. is ïsu in f'ep as·ēpaχt i v'israēλ; is ina anməm' f'r'is·akəd uλ'i k'ev'ēλ. 19. i g'ēdaịṽ' χpuað' skapsu-sa f'r'i maịλ ruavəð'. d'iä dardaịṽ' gaßsu-sa k'ēl' fop iŋgnəs' mak' maθəp'. 20. kov·gapəð p'r'ïµ'iλ'i ind ṗ'ïɣ kosa r'ïɣθ'eχ do h'enməm' ina krut'e. indəd·χoŋgpəð-su l'es'-s'oµ?

English

1. Then their mounds are dug. Their (grave-)stones are set up. Their names are written in Ogam (*OIr.*: their ogam-names are written). They are mourned (their mourning is done). 2. Her arm is as white as snow and her cheek is as red as blood (*fuil*). 3. Her brow is as black as the night (*adaig*). 4. Her eye is as blue as the sea (*muir*). 5. Are there many sounds to the trumpet? Is the sound for war special? Is the sound for sleep special? 6. It is a single (*óen-*) cry that the cocks made (*OIr.*: shouted) in the morning. 7. She is the mother who conceived this birth. 8. Jesus formed a single bird, 'sparrow' its name. Did he make it (*OIr.*: him) on Saturday? 9. Did longing seize the men for the women who spoke to them and who threw apples to them? 10. We consumed thy food and thy clothes. It is not thou who consumed them. 11. Did Patrick settle in Druimm Daro after its offering (*i.e.* after it had been offered to him)? Did Patrick leave his fostersons there? 12. These are the names of these islands. He left her there then. 13. The man called Judas to him; he received money from him for betraying his lord. 14. Did the Jew take hold of Jesus and did he flog him and did he beat him across his cheeks? 15. Was a purple cloak put around the kings? 16. He gave her a 'parting drink' for her swift death's sake; he mixed for her gall with vinegar. 17. The sun did not hide its (*OIr.*: her) light, the sea did not roar. 18. They are the men who arose again; is it in their names that the whole people puts its hope? 19. On a Wednesday we parted from Máel Rúanaid. On Thursday we realized the loss of our father's son. 20. Were the chief poets of the king called to the palace to play their harps? We were not called together with them.

Lesson 43

43.1. Nasal stems: masculine and feminine n-stems

There is some morphological variation among masculine and feminine n-stems. Some words end in a consonant in the nominative singular, some in a vowel. Many words have a lenited *n* /v/ in their stem, but others show an unlenited *nn* /n/.

43.1.1. Stems in -n

I start with the group of words with lenited *n*; the example is *talam* m. 'earth,' stem *talman-* /taλµəv/:

case	ending	Old Irish	Prim. Irish	Proto-Celtic	PIE
nom.	µ	*talam*	*taλαµū	*telamū	*télh₂mō(n)
gen.	µəv	*talman*	*taλαµovah	*telamonos «	*tl̥h₂mnés
prep.	µəv'ᴸ, µᴸ	*talmain*ᴸ, *talam*ᴸ «	*taλαµov («)	*telamonei̯, -oni «	*tl̥h₂mnéi̯, *tl̥h₂méni
acc.	µəv'ᴺ	*talmain*ᴺ	*taλαµovev	*telamonam	*télh₂monm̥
voc.	µ	*á*ᴸ *thalam*	*taλαµū	*telamū «	*télh₂mon
nom.pl.	µəv'	*talmain*	*taλαµoveh	*telamones	*télh₂mones
gen.	µəvᴺ	*talman*ᴺ	*taλαµovav «	*telamonom «	*tl̥h₂mnóm
prep.	µ(ə)vəβ'	*talmanaib*	*taλαµovaβih «	*telamombis («)	*tl̥h₂mn̥bʰís, -bʰós
acc.	µ(ə)vaᴴ	*talmana*ᴴ	*taλαµovāh «	*telamonās «	*tl̥h₂mnń̥s
voc.	µ(ə)vaᴴ	*á*ᴸ *thalmana*ᴴ «	*taλαµoveh	*telamones	*télh₂mones
n. a. v. du.	µəv'ᴸ	*dá*ᴸ *thalmain*ᴸ	*taλαµove	*telamone	*télh₂monh₁e
gen.	µəvᴸ	*dá*ᴸ *thalman*ᴸ	*taλαµovō	*telamonou̯ «	*tl̥h₂mn̥h₁óh₁s, -(H)óh₁u
prep.	µ(ə)vəβ'	*díb*ᴺ *talmanaib*	*taλαµovaβiv «	*telamombim «	*tl̥h₂mn̥bʰih₁, -moh₁ ?

Illustration 43.1: The n-stems

Note:

1. Like *talam* inflects the semantic class of Old Irish agent nouns in *-am/-em* like *ollam*, gen. *ollamon* 'chief poet,' *brithem*, gen. *brithemon* 'judge,' *flaithem*, gen. *flaithemon* 'ruler,' etc. The *a/e* in these words is never syncopated.

2. A large group of masculine and feminine n-stems end in a vowel in the nominative singular, e.g., *noídiu* /noi̯δ'u/ 'child.' Outside of the nominative singular these words replace the vowel by *-en/-an* /əv/: gen. *noíden* /noi̯δ'əv/, nom. sg. *toimtiu* f. /toµ'd'u/, gen. *toimten* /toµ'd'əv/ 'opinion' or nom. sg. *ordu* /ordu/, acc. *ordain* /ordəv'/ 'thumb.' In the prepositional singular these words have three possible forms:

2.1. one with an ending *e*, e.g., *toimte* /tou̯'d'e/ which is the oldest form,

2.2. one that looks like the nominative, e.g., *toimtiu*,

2.3. and one that looks like the accusative, e.g., *toimtin*.

3. *animm* /avəm'/ 'soul' has an irregular inflection: it is an n-stem in the plural, e.g., nom. *anmain*, acc. *anmana*, but in the singular it can behave both like a short ī-stem, e.g., prep., acc. *animm*, and like an n-stem, gen. *anme*, prep., acc. *anmain*.

43.1.2. Stems in -nn

Another large group of n-stems has a stem ending in an unlenited *nn*. To a large extent the words belonging to this class have a syllable beginning with lenited *r* /ρ/, *l* /λ/or unlenited *m(m)* /m/[1] before the *nn*, like *Ériu*, gen. *Éirenn* f. 'Ireland.' The example below, *gobae* m. 'smith,' stem *gobann-* /goβən/, is actually an exception to this, as here the syllable before the *nn* starts with *b* /β/:

case	ending	Old Irish	Prim. Irish	Proto-Celtic
nom.	C(')V^H	*gobae*^H	*goβēh	*gobanns
gen.	C(')ən	*gobann*	*goβenah	*gobannos
prep.	C(')ən'^L, C(')V ^L	*gobainn*^L, *gobae*^L «	*goβen* («)	*gobannei̯, -nni
acc.	C(')ən'^N	*gobainn*^N	*goβenev	*gobannam
voc.	C(')V	*á*^L *gobae*	*goβēh «	*gobann
nom. pl.	C(')ən'	*gobainn*	*goβeneh	*gobannes
gen.	C(')ən^N	*gobann*^N	*goβenav	*gobannom
prep.	C(')(ə)nəβ'	*goibnib*	*goβenaβih «	*gobannbis
acc.	C(') (ə)na^H	*goibnea*^H	*goβenāh	*gobannās
voc.	C(') (ə)na^H	*á*^L *goibnea*^H «	*goβeneh	*gobannes
n. a. v. du.	C(')ən'^L	*dá*^L *gobainn*^L	*goβene	*gobanne
gen.	C(')ən^L	*dá*^L *gobann*^L	*goβenō	*gobannou̯
prep.	C(') (ə)nəβ'	*díb*^N *ngoibnib*	*goβenaβiv «	*gobannbim

Illustration 43.2: The unlenited n-stems

Note:

1. *aub* f. /au̯β/ 'river' has an irregular inflection: gen. *abae* /aβe/, prep. *abainn* /aβən'/, prep. pl. *aibnib* /aβ'n'əβ'/.

---

[1] This phenomenon is called *NacNeill's Law*. For a discussion see Karin Stüber, *The Historical Morphology of n-Stems in Celtic*, Maynooth 1998, 39–44.

43.2. Exercise

Inflect some of the following words. Decline them together with the article. Combine them with any of the adjectives you learned so far.

> *ollam* /oləμ/, gen. *ollamon* /oləμəv/ (n, m) 'professor, poet of the highest grade'
> *Ériu* /ēρ'u/, gen. *Éirenn* /ēρ'ən/ (n, f) 'Ireland'
> *cú* /kū/, gen. *con* /kov/ (n, m) 'hound'
> *rétglu* /r'ēdγλu/, gen. *rétglann* /r'ēdγλən/ (n, f) 'star'
> *menmae* /m'enme/, gen. *menman* /m'enməv/ (n, m) 'mind'
> *derucc* /d'eρuk/, gen. *dercon* /d'eρkəv/ (n, f) 'acorn'
> *brú* /brū/, gen. *bronn* /bron/ (n, f) 'belly, womb'
> *aisndís* /as'n'd'īs'/, *aisndísen* /as'n'd'īs'əv/ (n, f) 'act of telling, relating; narration' (v.n. of *as·indet* 'to tell, to relate')

43.3. Comparison: the superlative

The superlative suffix, which is attached to the positive stem of the adjective, usually is *-em* /'əμ/, but *-am* /əμ/ after consonants that resist palatalization. It causes raising where possible, e.g.:

> *sen* /s'ev/ 'old' → *sinem* /s'iv'əμ/ 'oldest'

Other examples:

> *cóem* /koįμ/ 'lovely → *coímem* /koįμ'əμ/ 'loveliest'
> *ard* /ard/ 'high' → *ardam* /ardəμ/ 'highest'
> *ansae* /anse/ 'difficult' → *ansam* /ansəμ/ 'most difficult'

Syncope, of course, takes place in adjectives of more than one syllable when the suffix *-em/-am* is added:

> *follus* /folus/ 'clear' → *foilsem* /fol's'əμ/ 'clearest'
> *úasal* /uasəλ/ 'high, noble' → *úaislem* /uas'λ'əμ/ 'highest, noblest'

Note also cases where syncope has already taken place somewhere else in the word:

> *toísech* /toįs'əχ/ 'leading' → *toísigem* /toįs'əγ'əμ/ 'most leading, foremost' (< **touesaχ°*, the syncope has taken place between *u* and *s*, before the *u* vanished!).

There are a few irregular formations, and some adjectives form their superlative from different roots altogether:

positive	superlative
accus, ocus /agus ogus/ 'near'	nessam /nesəμ/
becc /b'eg/ 'small, few'	lugam (lugimem) /luγəμ luγ'əμ'əμ/
maith, dag- /maθ' daγ-/ 'good'	dech, deg /d'eχ d'eγ/
már, mór /māρ mōρ/ 'great, much, big'	máam, moam /maə̆μ moə̆μ/
oac, óc /oə̆g ōg/ 'young'	óam /oə̆μ/
olc, droch- /olk droχ-/ 'bad'	messam /m'esəμ/
sír /s'īρ/ 'long'	síam /s'iə̆μ/
trén /t'r'ēv/ 'strong'	tressam /t'r'esəμ/

Illustration 43.3: Irregular superlative forms

Examples of the use of the superlative are: *is sí ind ingen as áildem i nÉirinn* 'she is the most beautiful girl in Ireland' (from *álaind* 'beauiful'), *it é ata húaislem and* 'they are the noblest there' (*Ml.* 116a11), or *téit i telaig as nessam* 'he goes to the nearest hill.'

You'll find a table with irregular comparison in Appendix F.5.

Lesson 44

44.1. The suffixless preterite

Unlike the s- and the t-preterite, where recognizable suffixes (-s- and -t- respectively) are added to form the preterite stem, no separate preterite suffix is added to the root in the various suffixless preterite formations. Instead the appearance of the root itself is changed in various ways, without any overt marking being added. The suffixless preterite has a separate set of endings, which is basically identical both for absolute and conjunct. The main difference between absolute and conjunct forms are the passive forms and the fact that the absolute inflection has special relatives forms for the 3rd sg. and the 1st and 3rd pl., whereas the conjunct inflection has not. Of course, you still have to make the distinction between deuterotonic and prototonic verbal forms in the case of compound verbs.

In the active inflection all persons are endingless in the singular, with the 1st and 2nd singular being absolutely identical and showing a non-palatalized root final consonant, the 3rd sg. showing a palatalized root final consonant. In the 3rd sg. absolute relative form the ending -e /e/ is added. Deponent verbs have the ending -ar /əp/ in the 1st and 2nd sg., -air /əp'/ in the 3rd sg. In the plural active and deponent verbs have identical endings, the same endings that we met already in the plural of the t-preterite, 1st pl. -(a)mmar /(ə)məp/, 2nd pl. -aid /əð'/, 3rd pl. -(a)tar /(ə)dəp/. Sometimes a special 3rd pl. absolute ending -(a)tir /(ə)dəp'/ can be met.

Roughly the following formations can be distinguished within the suffixless preterite class (note that slight differences may exist between the classification presented here and those of GOI and EIV):

> reduplicated preterite:
> > e-reduplication
> > o-reduplication
> > a-reduplication
> > i-reduplication
> long vowel preterite:
> > various formations (ē, úa, ía)
> > ī-preterite
> > ā-preterite
> irregular preterites

Except for a few irregular verbs all suffixless preterite formations ultimately can be explained as historically going back to reduplicated formations. As already seen in 41.3.2, reduplication basically means that the verbal root's initial consonant is doubled and a so-called reduplication vowel comes to stand between the 'twin' consonants. Furthermore, in Irish the second of these consonants is regularly lenited and the original vowel of the root is usually reduced to *schwa* /ə/. Reduplication can be represented structurally as follows:

Illustration 44.1:
Reduplication

213

$$\text{root:} \qquad\qquad \text{preterite:}$$
$$C_1(R)V_xC_2\text{-} \quad\rightarrow\quad C_1V_y\text{-}C_{1[+\text{len}]}(R)\text{\textschwa}C_2\text{-}$$

Yet in Old Irish in a whole range of formations for diverse reasons the vowel of the reduplication syllable has been lengthened and the second consonant has been lost, so that synchronically no reduplication can be seen at all. The list of suffixless preterites above represents the perspicuity of reduplication in descending order.

In compound verbs where the reduplicated root would come to stand in unstressed position, i.e., in compounds with two or more preverbs, or in prototonic verbal forms, the reduplication is often lost as a result of syncope, e.g., *con·boing* 'to break,' reduplicated preterite *con·bobaig* /kov·boβəγ'/ 'broke,' but prototonic *·combaig* /·kombəγ'/ < **·kombᵻbaig* < **·kom-bobaig*.

You can find a table with all preterite formations in Appendix F.8.

44.2. The reduplicated preterite

Most of the strong verbs whose roots begin and end in a consonant form their preterite stem by overt reduplication. The reduplication vowel is usually *e*, e.g., the preterite stem of *maidid* 'to break (intrans.)' is *memad-* /m'eµəδ/. Note that the second of the two originally identical consonants must be lenited in Irish, as it comes to stand between two vowels, e.g., *cingid* 'to step' has the preterite stem *cechang-* /k'eχəŋg/ < Proto-Celtic **kekong-*. Furthermore, it is always non-palatalized, even if in the present stem a palatalizing vowel follows, as in, e.g., S1 *ligid* /l'iγ'əδ'/ 'to lick,' but preterite stem *lelag-* /l'eλəγ/ (note that only the 3ʳᵈ sg. conj. and the 3ʳᵈ pl. abs. are actually attested in this verb; all other forms are constructed by me in the form in which they ought to appear, if they were attested):

		absolute		conjunct	
1st sg.		*lelag*	{L}C	*(ní)·lelag*	{L}C
2nd sg.		*lelag*	{L}C	*(ní)·lelag*	{L}C
3rd sg.		*lelaig*	C'	*(ní)·lelaig*	C'
	rel.	*lelgae*	Ce	-	
1st pl.		*lelgammar*	{L}Cəməp	*(ní)·lelgammar*	{L}Cəməp
	rel.	*lelgammar*	{L}Cəməp	-	
2nd pl.		n/a		*(ní)·lelgaid*	Cəδ'
3rd pl.		*lelgatar*	{L}Cədəp	*(ní)·lelgatar*	{L}Cədəp
	rel.	*lelgatar*	{L}Cədəp	-	

Illustration 44.2: The conjugation of the reduplicated preterite

Note:

1. S1 *lingid* 'to leap' has *leblang-* as its preterite stem (the earliest form was **eblang-*, but this is attested only indirectly in compounds!). By analogy with it S1 *dringid* 'to climb' has acquired the 3ʳᵈ sg. preterite *drebraing*.

2. S1 *seinnid* 'to play an instrument' and *do·seinn, ·tophainn* 'to hunt' (root **su̯en-*) have *sephann-* /s'efən/ < **su̯esu̯on-* as their preterite stem.

3. Verbs of the S1d-class lose their *n* (resp. *m*) of the present stem, e.g., *dingid* 'to press, to crush,' preterite stem *dedag-* /deδəγ/.

4. Roots beginning with *sl-* and *sn-* usually lose the *s* in reduplication, e.g., S2 *sligid* 'to fell' → preterite stem *selag-*; S2 *snigid* 'to drip' → *senag-*.

44.3. Reduplication with vowels other than *e*

Some verbs use other reduplication vowels:

1. One verb with root vowel *a* reduplicates with *a*: S1 *canaid* 'to sing,' preterite stem *cachan-* /kaχəv/. Forms with reduplication vowel *e* also exist, e.g., the 1st sg. preterite *for·cechan* /foɾ·k'eχəv/ 'I taught' of the compound *for·cain*.

Illustration 44.3:
leblaing-si 'she leapt'

2. S1d verbs with an apparent *o* (< **u*) in their root have *o* (< **u*) as reduplication vowel, e.g., *bongaid* 'to break,' preterite stem *bobag-* /boβəγ/, or *in·loing* 'to occupy,' preterite stem *in·lolag-* /iv·loλəγ/.

3. Verbs that are synchronically felt to have *i* as their root vowel form their preterite stem by reduplicating their *anlauting* consonant with *i* and 'dropping' the rest of the root. This applies to most S3 and some H2 verbs. Remember that S3 verbs lose their *n* outside the present stem so that in fact the root of an S3 verb like *renaid* 'to sell' is *rī-*. The rules of lowering the vowel before the final consonant, which I gave in illustration 44.2, are valid for these and other formations, too. Therefore you will find, e.g., 1st sg. or 3rd pl. forms with vowel *e* that has been lowered from underlying *i*. The following forms are found in GOI 427 f.:

1. S3 *denaid* 'to suck' has 3rd sg. preterite *did* /d'iδ'/, rel. *dide*.

2. S3 *lenaid* 'to follow': 3rd sg. *·lil*, 3rd pl. *·leldar* /l'eλdəɾ/.

3. S3 *renaid* 'to sell': 1st sg. *·rer*, unstressed *as·comrar* (from *as·ren* 'to pay, expend' with augment *cum-*) 3rd sg. *·rir*, rel. *rire*.

4. H2 *ciid* 'to weep': 3rd sg. *cich*.

44.4. Long vowel preterites

1. The following verbs actually belong to the same type of formation as the one described in 44.3.3, but further sound changes have obscured the reduplication and resulted in long vowels and diphthongs respectively where the reduplication syllable would be expected. The important development here is the loss of the lenited fricatives **γ, *χ, *δ,* and **θ* with compensatory lengthening of the preceding vowel before *l, n, r* in the prehistory of Irish:

1. *crenaid* 'to buy': 1st sg. *·cér*, 3rd sg. *·cíuir* /k'iu̯ρ'/ (< **kiχρ-*)

2. *ara·chrin* 'to decay': 3rd sg. *ara·ruichíuir*,[1] *ar·rochíuir*, 3rd pl. *ar·rochíuirtar*, *·arrchéoratar*.

3. *glenaid* 'to stick': 3rd sg. *·gíuil* (< **giγλ-*), abs. rel. *gíulae*.

4. *·gnin* 'to know': 1st and 2nd sg. *·gén*, 3rd sg. *·géuin*, 1st pl. *·génammar*, 3rd pl. *·génatar*.

5. *tlenaid* 'to take away': 3rd sg. *·rothíuil*.

2. The preterite of *benaid* 'to strike' is 1st sg. *beo*, 2nd sg. unstressed *·ruba*, 3rd sg. *bii*, *bí*, *·bí*, unstressed *·rubai*, rel. *bie*, 2nd pl. unstressed *fo·rubid*, 3rd pl. *·béotar* (< **biu̯-* < **biβ-*).

3. A few strong verbs, whose roots originally contained an *i*, form an ī-preterite. On the surface it looks as if they simply replaced the vowel of the present stem by /ī/ to form the preterite stem:

1. S1a *fichid* 'to fight': 3rd sg. preterite *fích* /f'īχ'/ (< **u̯iu̯iχ-*), rel. *fíche*, 1st pl. *fíchimmar*. Unstressed 3rd sg. *da·ruïch* (from the compound *do·fich* 'to avenge, to punish').

2. S1b *in·fét* 'to relate, to tell': 3rd sg. *in·fíd* (< **u̯iu̯iδ-*); similar to its compounds: *as·indet* 'to declare, to tell' has 3rd sg. *as·rindid*, and *do·adbat/tadbat* 'to show' has a 3rd sg. *do·árbith*, *do·árbuid*, *do·árbaid*.

3. S3 *ernaid* 'to grant': 3rd sg. *·ír*.

4. Compounds of S3 **fenaid* (root *fī-*; not attested as a simple verb): *ar·fí* 'he fenced.'

Two more verbs without an etymological *i* in the root have been secondarily drawn into this group:

5. S2 deponent *midithir* 'to judge': deponent 1st sg. *·mídar*, 3rd sg. *·mídair*, 3rd pl. *·mídatar*. When the root falls out of the stressed position reductions take place: 1st sg. *·ammadar*, 3rd sg. *do·rumadir*, 3rd pl. *·irmadatar*, *·imruimdetar*.

6. Maybe S1 *sichid*, *seichid* 'to declare': 3rd sg. *sich* (*Gosp.* §13, 22, 29; read: *sích* /s'īχ'/?).

4. The H3 verb *foaid* 'to sleep' has the 3rd sg. preterite *·fíu*, 1st pl. *femmir*, 3rd pl. *·féotar* (< **u̯iu̯-*; PIE √*h₂u̯es*). The unstressed 2nd sg. after *ro-* is *·roa* /roä/.

5. In some words the reduplication with vowel *e* has been obscured by the loss of fricatives (see 1. above).

1. The 3rd sg. preterite of deponent *gainithir* 'to come to life, to be born' is deponent *génair* /g'ēvəρ'/ (< **geγv°*).

2. By analogy *·moinethar* 'to think' has *·ménair*.

3. The preterite of active *saidid* 'to sit' is deponent (!) 3rd sg. *siasair* /s'iəsəρ'/, 3rd pl. rel. *siassatar* (ultimately < Common Celtic **sesod-*).

6. The preterite of deponent S3 *ro·cluinethar* 'to hear' (root **klu-*) is active (!) 1st and 2nd sg. *·cúala*, 3rd sg. *·cúalae*, 1st pl. *·cúalammar*, 2nd pl. *·cúalaid*, 3rd pl. *·cúalatar* (< **koχλou̯°* < Common Celtic **kukluu̯°*).

---

[1] In the following sections you will sometimes encounter forms where an *ro-* (*ru-*) or *r-* is added. You need not take notice of them at the moment. *ro* is a verbal particle that we will learn in full detail in a later lesson.

44.5. The ā-preterite

In this last type of regularly formed suffixless preterites, the ā-preterite, the underlying reduplication has been most thoroughly obscured in the course of time. The ā-preterite is formed by strong verbs whose roots basically conform to the structure CeT: Their roots start with a consonant and usually end in a dental or guttural stop. The vowel of the root is basically *e* but sometimes appears as *a*. In the preterite these verbs replace the *e* (or *a*) of the root by an *á* /ā/ to form the preterite stem. So the 3rd sg. preterite of S1 *teichid* 'to flee' (root: *tech-*) is *táich* '(s)he fled,' S1 *reithid* 'to run' (root: *reth-*): *ráith* '(s)he ran,' S1 *feidid, feithid* 'to go' (root: *fed/feth-*): *fáid, fáith* 'he went.' In some verbs the vowel *e* is not apparent as such in the present stem: S2 *figid* 'to weave' (root: *fig-*): *fáig* 'she wove,' or in the example below S2 *guidid* 'to pray' (root: *ged-*!):

		absolute		conjunct	
1st sg.		*gád*	āC	*(ní)·gád*	āC
2nd sg.		*gád*	āC	*(ní)·gád*	āC
3rd sg.		*gáid*	āC'	*(ní)·gáid*	āC'
	rel.	*gáde*	āCe	-	
1st pl.		*gádammar*	āCəməp	*(ní)·gádammar*	āCəməp
	rel.	*gádammar*	āCəməp	-	
2nd pl.		n/a		*(ní)·gádaid*	āCəδ'
3rd pl.		*gádatar*	āCədəp	*(ní)·gádatar*	āCədəp
	rel.	*gádatar*	āCədəp	-	

Illustration 44.4: The inflection of the ā-preterite

The following verbs and their compounds form ā-preterites:

verb	preterite stem
damaid (S2) 'to suffer, to grant'	*·dámair* (dep.!)
feidid, feithid (S1) 'to go'	*fád-, fáth-*
figid (S2) 'to weave'	*fág-*
guidid (S2) 'to pray'	*gád-*
ro·laimethar (S2) 'to dare'	*·lámair* (dep.!)
reithid (S1) 'to run'	*ráth-*
scoichid, scuichid (S1) 'to depart'	*scách-*
teichid (S1) 'to flee'	*tách-*

Illustration 44.5: Verbs forming ā-preterites

Note:

1. A few verbs have short a-preterites: S1 *fo·ceird* 'to throw, to put' has a preterite 3rd sg. *fo·caird*, 3rd pl. *fo·cartar*, S1 *sceirdid* 'to strip, to scrape off' has a 3rd sg. preterite *·scaird*. The short *a* in these verbs is probably due to shortening of original long *á* before two consonants.

Illustration 44.6:
gádammar do Brigti
'we prayed to Brigit'

44.6. The preterite of the copula and the substantive verb

The preterite of the substantive verb goes as follows (note the vowel reduction when the root comes into unstressed position):

		absolute		conjunct		unstressed	
1st sg.		*bá*	bā	(*ní*)·*bá*	·bā	·*roba*, ·*raba*	·ro/aβa
2nd sg.		*bá*	bā	(*ní*)·*bá*	·bā	·*raba*	·raβa
3rd sg.		*boí*, *baí*	boi̯, bai̯	(*ní*)·*boí*, ·*baí*	·boi̯, ·bai̯	·*robae*, ·*rabae*	·ro/aβe
	rel.	*boíe*	boi̯e	–		–	
	impers.	*bothae*	boθe	(*ní*)·*both*	·boθ	·*rabad*	·raβəδ
1st pl.		*bámmar*	bāməp	(*ní*)·*bámmar*	·bāməp	·*robammar*	·roβəməp
	rel.	**bámmar*	bāməp	–		–	
2nd pl.		n/a		(*ní*)·*baid*	·baə̯δ'	·*robaid*	·roβə̯δ'
3rd pl.		*bátar*, *bátir*	bādəp, bādəp'	(*ní*)·*bátar*	·bādəp	·*robatar*, ·*rabatar*	·ro/aβədəp
	rel.	*bátar*	bādəp	–		–	

Illustration 44.7: The preterite of the substantive verb

In the case of the copula one doesn't speak of a preterite, but of a past tense. The copula is always unstressed and attaches itself to any particle that comes before it, thereby becoming further reduced. Examples of the conjunct use would be *níbo*, *nípu* 'he/she/it was not,' *níbtar*, *níptar* 'they were not.' Note that the *b* of the copula can sometimes be assimilated to a preceding nasal and disappear completely, e.g., *comtar* < *combtar* < **co^N batar* 'so that they were.'

	absolute		conjunct	
1st sg.	*basa*	basa	*-psa, -bsa*	-bsa
2nd sg.	*basa*	basa	*-psa, -bsa*	-bsa
3rd sg.	*ba^H*	ba^H	*-po^L, -bo^L, -pu^L, -bu^L*	-bo^L, -bu^L
rel.	*ba^L*	ba^L	-	
1st pl.	n/a		*-bummar*	-buməp
rel.	n/a		-	
2nd pl.	n/a		n/a	
3rd pl.	*batir, batar*	badəp, badəp'	*-ptar, -btar*	-bdəp
rel.	*batar*	badəp	-	

Illustration 44.8: The past tense of the copula

44.7. Irregular preterite formations

As if this were not bad enough, some verbs form irregular preterites or use suppletive stems:

1. The preterite of S1 *téit* 'to go' is 1st and 2nd sg. *lod* /loð/, 3rd sg. *luid* /luð'/, rel. *luide* /luð'e/, 1st pl. *lodmar* /loðməp/, 3rd pl. *lotar* /lodəp/.

2. The reduplicated preterite of S1 *·icc* (as in *do·icc* 'to come,' *ro·icc* 'to reach') is *ánacc-* /āvəg/: 1st and 2nd sg. *·ánacc*, 3rd sg. *·ánaicc*, 1st pl. *· áncammar* /·āvgəməp/, 2nd pl. *·áncaid*, 3rd pl. *·áncatar* /·āvgədəp/.

3. The preterite of H2 *ad·cí* 'to see' is formed without apparent reduplication: 1st and 2nd sg. *·acca* /·aka/, 3rd sg. *·accae*, 1st pl. *·accamar*, 3rd pl. *·accatar*. If it is used independently, a meaningless conjunction *co^N* is prefixed, e.g., *co·n-acca* 'I saw,' but *ní·acca* 'I did not see.' Other compounds of the root *cī-* 'to see' do show reduplication, e.g., 1st sg. *fris·acacha* /f'r'is·akəχa/ 'I expected' from *fris·accai* 'to expect.'

4. The preterite of S3 *(ro)·finnadar* 'to find out' has the present meaning 'to know': 1st and 2nd sg. *(ro)·fetar* /·f'edəp/, 3rd sg. *·fitir* /f'id'əp'/, 1st pl. *·fitemmar*, *·fetammar*, 2nd pl. *·fitid*, 3rd pl. *·fitetar* (seldom *·fetatar*, *·fetar*). An old variant of the 2nd pl. is *·fitis*.

5. The suppletive preterite of S2 *fo·gaib* 'to find' is 1st sg. *·fúar*, 3rd sg. *·fúair* /·fuap'/, 1st pl. *·fúarammar*, 3rd pl. *·fúaratar*. If it is used independently the preverb *fo·* is added, e.g., *fo·fúar-sa* 'I found,' but *ní·fúar* 'I did not find.'

6. The suppletive preterite of S1 *do·tuit* 'to fall' is *do·cer*, *·tochair* /do·k'ep ·toχər'/. Attested forms are: 1st sg. *·torchar* /·topχəp/, 2nd sg. *·torchair*, 3rd sg. *do·cer*, unstressed *do·rochair*, 3rd pl. *do·certar*, unstressed *do·rochratar*, *·torchartar*, *·torchratar*. Originally it did not inflect like a suffixless preterite, but in the course of Old Irish time it adopted the behavior of the suffixless preterite.

7. 3rd sg. *at·bath* /ad·βaθ/, *·apad* /·abəð/ 'he died,' 3rd pl. *at·bathatar* /ad·βaθədəp/ is without a corresponding present.

44.8. Exercise

Try to inflect the preterite of some of the following verbs:

Illustration 44.9: *fíu* 'he slept'

> *teichid* (S1), pret. *tách-* /tāχ/ 'to flee'
> *rigid* (S1), pret. *rerag-* /reρəγ/ ' to stretch'
> *lenaid* (S3), pret. *lil-* /l'iλ'/ 'to follow, to adhere'
> *gainithir* (S2), deponent (!) pret. *gén-* /g'ēv/ 'to be born'
> *ro·icc* (S1), pret. *ro·ánac-* /·āvəg/ 'to reach'
> *crenaid* (S3), pret. *cíur-* /k'iụρ/ 'to buy'
> *for·cain* (S1), pret. *for·cachan-* /·kaχəv/ 'to teach'

44.9. The prehistory of the suffixless preterite

The suffixless preterites go back to PIE reduplicated perfects. The prehistory of the various suffixless preterite stem formations of Old Irish is very complex and ought to be discussed for every one of them separately. In this introductory course I can only give you a brief glimpse at the development of the basic ending set of the suffixless preterite, exemplified by the reduplicated preterite of *ligid*, i.e., *lelag-*:

conj.	OIr. transcr.	Prim. Irish	Insular Celtic	Proto-Celtic	PIE
1st sg.	·*lelag*	*liloi̯ga «	*leloi̯ga	*leloi̯ga	*lelói̯ĝʰh₂e
2nd sg.	·*lelag*	*liloi̯gah «	*leloi̯gas « ?	*leloi̯χta	*lelói̯ĝʰth₂e
3rd sg.	·*lelaig*	*liloi̯ge «	*leloi̯ge	*leloi̯ge	*lelói̯ĝʰe
1st pl.	·*lel†gammar* «	*liloi̯gaμe «	*leloi̯game «	*leligme	*leliĝʰmé
2nd pl.	·*lel†gaid*	*liloi̯gaθeh «	*leloi̯gate «	*lelige	*leliĝʰé
3rd pl.	·*lel†gatar*	*liloi̯gontaρ «	*leloi̯gar «	*leligar	*leliĝʰr̥

Illustration 44.10: The prehistory of the suffixless preterite endings

Note:

1. Whereas in PIE the reduplication vowel was *e*, in Irish it depended on the vowel of the root: where the root contained an *i/i̯*, the reduplication vowel was *i*, whereas in roots containing *u/u̯*, the reduplication vowel was *u*.

2. The prehistory of the 2nd sg. ending is unclear. The above presented explanation is just a possibility.

3. In the prehistory of Irish the inherited 3rd pl. ending *-ar* was conflated with the 3rd pl. ending *-(o)nt* of the other tenses and moods. Since the resulting ending *-ontar > Old Irish -atar looked like the deponent ending, the 1st pl. took on the deponent ending *-ammar* as well.

Lesson 45

45.1. From *Uraicecht na Ríar*

The *Uraicecht na Ríar* 'The Primer of the Stipulations' is an Old Irish law text from the later eighth century, which concerns itself with the requirements and privileges of the seven grades of *filid* 'poets.' It consists of 24 paragraphs with lots of notes, of which I give four excerpts. It has been edited by Liam BREATNACH, *Uraicecht na Ríar. The Poetic Grades in Early Irish Law*, Early Irish Law Series Vol. II, Dublin 1987.

§1 Cis lir gráda filed? Ní ansae: a secht: ollam, ánruth, clí, cano, dos, macḟuirmid, fochloc. Trí ḟográd leo, .i. taman, drisiuc, oblaire.

§2 Ceist, caite dán 7 grád 7 lóg n-enech cach aí ó biuc co mór? Ní ansae: dán olloman cétomus: secht cóecait dréct lais, .i. cóec cach gráid; is éola i cach coimgniu, 7 is éola i mbrithemnacht ḟénechais. Cethorcha sét a díre.

§6 Ceist, cía cruth do·berar grád for filid? Ní ansae, taisbénad a dréchtae do ollamain — 7 biit inna secht ngráda fis occa — 7 na·gaib in rí inna lángrád…

§9 Ocus ḟer de chlaind ḟiled do·gní frithgnum íar scarad frie dia athair 7 dia ṡen-athair, cid grád do·berar dó? Ní ansae, grád foa dán fodeisin, air is sí óenoíbell in-sin ad·annai bréo.

Transcription

§1 k'is l'iρ grāδa f'iλ'əδ? n'ī hanse: a s'eχt: oləμ, āνρuθ, k'l'ī, kavo, dos, makuρ'μ'əδ', foχλəg. t'r'ī oγρāδ l'eụ, eδ ōν taμəν, d'r'is'ug, oβλəρ'e.

§2 k'es't', kad'e dāv ogus γρāδ ogus λōγ v'ev'əχ kaχ aị ō β'iụg ko mōρ? n'ī hanse: dāv oləμəv k'ēdəμus: s'eχt goịgəd' d'r'ēχt las', eδ ōν koịg kaχ grāδ'; is eụλa i kaχ koμ'γ'v'u, ogus is eụλa i m'b'r'iθ'əμvəχt ēv'əχəs'. k'eθəρχa s'ēd a δ'īρ'e.

§6 k'es't', k'ia kruθ do·β'eρəρ grāδ foρ f'iλ'əδ'? n'ī hanse, tas'β'ēvəδ a δ'ρ'ēχte do oləμəv — ogus β'iǝd' ina s'eχt ŋgrāδa f'is' oga — ogus va·γaβ' in r'ī ina λāνγρāδ…

§9 ogus eρ d'e χλan'd' iλ'əδ do·γ'v'ī f'r'iθγvuμ iaρ skaρəδ f'r'ih'e d'iä aθəρ' ogus diä h'evaθəρ, k'iδ grāρ do·β'eρəρ dō? n'ī hanse, grāδ foä δāv foδ'és'əv', aρ' is s'ī oịvoịβ'əl in-s'iv' aδ·ani b'r'eụ.

Illustration 45.1:
fili 'a poet'

45.2. From the *Old Irish Triads*

Triad 35: Trí óenaig hÉrenn: óenach Tailten, óenach Crúachan, óenach Colmáin Ela.

t'r'ī hoịvəγ' ēρ'ən: oịvəχ tal't'əv, oịvəχ kruaχəv, oịvəχ koλmāv' eλa.

Lesson 45

45.3. Test

Try to recognize the verbal forms (give as much information about the words as possible — class, person, number, mood, relative or not, infixed pronoun). Give also the quotation form of the verb and say to which present class it belongs:

nád·eipert: _____   fo·lolgaid: _____   ro·cúalae: _____

rersait: _____   ná·dignius: _____   sirt: _____

co·n-accae: _____   do·logsam: _____   molaiser: _____

fo·caird: _____   do·gádatar: _____   sóerthai: _____

ní·éracht: _____   do·fíchatar: _____   cachnae: _____

do·lod: _____   or _____   sephainn: _____

at·gén: _____   do·génais: _____   génair: _____

in·n-ibis: _____   fort·ndedgatar: _____   boíe: _____

fo·cíuir: _____   ní·phridchus: _____   ráncatar: _____

cich: _____   fúarammar: _____   na·mbí: _____

ro·lámar: _____   or _____   ní·ded: _____

síasar-su: _____   innád·fetar: _____   or _____

·roacht: _____   or _____   or _____

45.4. Test

Try to recognize the inflectional forms (give as much information about the words as possible — gender, stem class, case, number):

céimm: _____ or _____   arbaimm: _____

inna anmann: _____ or _____   ollomnaib: _____

toimtin: _____ or _____   or _____

seinmimm: _____   abae: _____   in chon: _____

goibnea: _____   Ére: _____   bronna: _____

Albain: _____ or _____   aisndís: _____

airmitin: _____ or _____   or _____

talman: _____ or _____   airecha: _____

noídin: _____ or _____   or _____

suthainidir: _____   ansam: _____   toísigem: _____

foilsithir: _____   lir: _____   messam: _____

222

45.5. Varia

1. The two letters *ae*, e.g., in *daltae*, can be written with the ligature *æ*. Accordingly, *oe* is sometimes written *œ*.

2. A word designating a period of time in the accusative followed by *and* 'there' (3rd sg. neuter prepositional of *i*N 'in'), means 'one X' (X = the specified period of time). Frequently, the nasalizing effect of the accusative can be seen on *and*, e.g., *lae n-and* /laë vand/ 'one day,' or *fecht n-and* /fʲeχt vand/ 'one time.'

3. The conjunction *co*N· followed by a dependent verbal form in the indicative can mean 'that, so that' and also 'until.'

4. The conjunction *dia*N·, followed by a dependent verbal form in the preterite, means 'when.'

5. *Nád·*, *nach*°· 'that not' introduces dependent clauses, even if there is no overt sentence from which it depends, e.g., in sentence 14.

45.6. Exercise

Old Irish

1. * At féchem dom, níta ḟéchem-sa duit. (*Wb.* 32a21) 2. ** Tánaicc aimser mo aidbairte-se. (*Wb.* 30d11) 3. * Do·cer in biáil dia ṡamthaig issa mmuir 7 fo·caird *Eliseus* a ṡamthig inna diaid 7 do·luid in biáil arithissi ar chenn inna samthaige, co·mboí impe. (*Tur.* 131) 4. * Dia·luid Dauid for longais tri glenn […], da·mbidcset a námait di chlochaib oca thecht 7 do·bertatar maldachta foir dano di mulluch int ṡléibe. (*Ml.* 58c4) 5. ** Im·luid Bran lae n-and a óenur i comocus dia dún. Co·cúalae a céol íarna chúl. (IB 2) 6. ** Leblaing in chróeb di láim inna mná co·mboí for láim Brain, 7 ní·boí nert i lláim Brain do gabáil inna croíbe. (IB 31) 7. ** Níbu cían íar-sin co·ráncatar tír inna mban. (IB 62) 8. ** Ní·lámair Bran techt isa tír. (IB 62) 9. * Fo·caird Bran a láim forsin ceirtli. Lil in cheirtle dia dernainn. (IB 62) 10. * Boí in snáithe inna ceirtle i lláim inna mná. Con·sreng in curach dochum poirt. (IB 62) 11. * Lotar íarum i tech mór. Ar·áncatar imdai cecha lánamnae and .i. trí noí n-imdæ. (IB 62) 12. * Co·n-accatar ní, éill ngéisse ara ciunn […] Láthrais Cú Chulainn cloich mbicc forsna éonu co·mbí ocht n-éonu díb. (TBC 785 ff.) 13. * Batar foidirci ind uisci, bátar hi fudumnaib talman, tri indlach inna talman í-sin. (*Ml.* 40d16) 14. * Nád·tochair nem inna cenn, nacha·loisc in teine, nacha·báid rían […], nacha·sloic in talam! (*Blathm.* 269–273) 15. ** Do·cer mac […] fo aill, bebais i n-óenúair; táchatar uili acht Ísu, anais ar chiunn ṡlúaig. (*Gosp.* 41) 16. * Trí ata dech do ḟlaithemuin: fír, síd, slóg. (*Triad* 242). 17. * Ba é lóech ba áildem boíe di ḟeraib Érenn 7 Alban, acht níbo ṡuthain. (TBF 2–3) 18. * […] is ed as moam serc linn-ni ad·chotadsam triar sáethar saindíles […]. (*Ml.* 92c5) 19. * Is ed tréide in-sin as toísigem do duiniu .i. bairgen 7 ḟín 7 olae. (*Ml.* 20d2) 20. * Trí luchra ata messam: luchair tuinne, luchair mná baíthe, luchair con fo léimmimm. (*Triad* 238)

Lesson 45

Transcription

1. ad f'ēχ'əµ doµ, n'ɪda ēχ'əµ-sa dut'. 2. tāvəg' am's'əp mo aδ'βər't'e-s'e. 3. do·k'eρ in b'iäλ' d'iä haµθəγ' isa muρ' ogus fo·kar'd' *Eliseus* a haµθəγ' ina δ'iəδ' ogus δo·luδ' in b'iäλ' aρ'íθ'əs'i aρ χen ina saµθəγ'e, ko·mboį im'p'e. 4. d'iä·luδ' dau̯əδ' foρ longəs' t'r'i γ'λ'en, da·m'b'iδ'γ's'əd a vāµəd' d'i χλoχəβ' oga θ'eχt ogus δo·b'ertədəp maldəχta foρ' davo d'i µuluχ int h'λ'ēβ'e. 5. im·luδ' brav laë vand a oi̯vuρ i goµogus d'iä δū̯v. ko·guaλe a geu̯λ iapva χūλ. 6. l'eβλəŋ'g' in χρoįβ d'i λāµ' ina mnā ko·mboį foρ lāµ' βρav', ogus v'ɪ·boį n'ert i lāµ' βρav' do γaβāλ' ina kroįβ'e. 7. n'ɪbu k'iav iap-s'iv ko·rāvgədəp t'ɪρ' ina mbav. 8. n'ɪ·lāµəρ' brav t'eχt isa d'ɪρ'. 9. fo·kar'd' brav a λāµ' fors'ən g'er't'l'i. l'iλ' in χ'er't'l'e d'iä δ'ernən'. 10. boį snāθ'e ina k'er't'l'e i lāµ' ina mnā. kov·s'r'eŋg in guρəχ doχum bor't'. 11. lodəp iapuµ i d'eχ mōρ. aρ·āvgədəp imδi k'eχa lāvəµve and, eδ ōv t'r'ɪ noį v'imδe. 12. ko·vakədəp n'ɪ, ēl' ŋ'g'ēs'e aρa g'iu̯n. lāθρəs' kū χuλən' kloχ' m'b'ig' forsna heu̯vu ko·m'b'ɪ oχt v'eu̯vu d'ɪβ'. 13. badəp foδ'ər'k'i ind us'k'i, bādəp i βuδəµvəβ' taλµəv, t'r'i indλəχ ina taλµəv ɪ-s'iv'. 14. naδ·toχəρ' n'eµ ina g'en, naχa·los'k' in t'ev'e, naχa·bāδ' r'iav, naχa·slog' in taλəµ! 15. do·k'eρ mak fo al', b'eβəs' i voį̯vuaρ'; tāχədəp uλ'i aχt ɪsu, avəs' aρ χ'iu̯n hλuaγ'. 16. t'r'ɪ hada d'eχ do λaθ'əµəv': f'ɪρ, s'ɪδ, slōγ. 17. Ba h'ē in loį̯χ ba āl'd'əµ boį̯e d'i eρəβ' ēρ'ən ogus albəv, aχt n'ɪbo huθəv'. 18. is eδ as moäµ s'erk l'in-n'i aδ·χodəδsəµ t'r'iäρ saį̯θəp san'd'ɪλ'əs. 19. is eδ t'r'ēδ'e in-s'iv as toį̯s'əγ'əµ do δuv'u, eδ ōv bar'g'əv ogus ɪv ogus oλe. 20. t'r'ɪ luχρa ada m'esəµ: luχəρ' dun'e, luχəρ' mnā baį̯θ'e, luχəρ' gov fo λ'em'əm'.

English

1. We are debtors to you (pl.), you (pl.) are not debtors to us. 2. Did the time of our offering come? 3. The axes (*bélai*) fell off their handles into the sea and *Eliseus* threw his handles after them and the axes came back again onto the heads of the handles, so that they were around them. 4. When the judges (*brithem*) went into exile through glenns, their enemies pelted them with stones while they were going (*OIr.*: at their going) and they cursed them (*OIr.*: gave curses upon them) from the tops of the mountains. 5. One day we walked alone near (*OIr.*: in the proximity of) our fort. Did we hear music behind our back? 6. Did the branch jump from the hand of the woman, so that it was in Bran's hand? Was there no power in Bran's hand to take the branch? 7. It was long afterwards until he reached the land of the woman. 8. They dared to go into the land. 9. They did not put their hands on the clew. The clew did not stick to their palms. 10. The clew's thread was not in the hand of the woman. Did she pull the boats towards the port? 11. He went into a large house. He found a bed for himself. 12. She saw something, a flock of swans before her. They placed (= shot) a small stone at the birds, so that they slew fifteen birds of them. 13. The water, which was in the depths of the earth, was not visible through the cleavings of the earth. 14. Heaven did not fall upon her head, the fire did not burn her, the sea did not drown her, the earth did not swallow her. 15. Boys fell down a cliff, they died at once. Did all flee? Did nobody wait for the host? 16. Three that are best for rulers: truth, peace, armies. 17. Were they the most beautiful warriors who were in Ireland and Scotland? But they did not live long. 18. Is this the greatest love that I have, (for that) which I obtained though my own labor? 19. Are these the three foremost things for people? 20. Were these the three worst splendors: the splendor of waves, the splendor of wanton women, the splendor of dogs at the jump?

Lesson 46

46.1. Irregular nouns

Only a few nouns inflect really irregularly in Old Irish (disregarding the fact that one can't avoid the impression that nearly all nouns of Old Irish show some sort of irregular behavior). These are the words *bó* /bō/ (f.) 'ox, cow,' *nó, nau* /nō nau̯/ (f.) 'boat' and *día, dia, die* /d'ia d'iä d'ië/ 'day.' Forms marked with + are not Old Irish, but belong to a later period.

46.1.1. *bó* 'cow'

case	transcr.	Old Irish	Prim. Irish	Proto-Celtic	PIE
nom.	bōᴸ	*bóᴸ*	*bōh	*bou̯s	*gʷóu̯s
gen.	bōᴴ, bou̯ᴴ	*bóᴴ* (arch. *bou*ᴴ)	*bou̯ah	*bou̯os «	*gʷéu̯s
prep.	bov'ᴸ	*boin*ᴸ «	*bou̯ («)	*bou̯ei̯, *bou̯i	*gʷéu̯ei̯, *gʷéu̯i
acc.	bov'ᴺ	*boin*ᴺ	*bovev «	*bom	*gʷṓm < *gʷóu̯m
voc.	āᴸ βōᴸ	*áᴸ bó*ᴸ	*bōh	*bou̯s «	*gʷóu̯
nom.pl.	bai̯ᴴ, baᴴ	+*baí*ᴴ, +*ba*ᴴ (< *boí*ᴴ)	*bou̯eh	*bou̯es	*gʷóu̯es
gen.	bōᴺ, bau̯ᴺ	*bó*ᴺ (arch. *bao*ᴺ)	*bou̯av	*bou̯om	*gʷéu̯om
prep.	buaβ'	*búaib*	*bou̯βih	*bou̯bis («)	*gʷéu̯bʰis, -bʰos
acc.	būᴴ	*bú*ᴴ	*būh	*būs	*gʷṓs < gʷóu̯n̥s
voc.	āᴸ βoi̯ᴴ	*áᴸ boí*ᴴ	*bou̯eh	*bou̯es	*gʷóu̯es
n. a. v. du.	βai̯ᴸ, βov'ᴸ	*díᴸ baí*ᴸ, +*dáᴸ boin*ᴸ	*bou̯e	*bou̯e	*gʷóu̯h₁e
gen.	βōᴸ	*dáᴸ bó*ᴸ	*bou̯ō	*bou̯ou̯ («)	*gʷéu̯h₁oh₁s, -(H)oh₁u
prep.	mbuaβ'	*dib*ᴺ *mbuaib*	*bou̯βiv	*bou̯bim «	*gʷéu̯bʰih₁, -moh₁ ?

Illustration 46.1: The inflection of *bó* 'cow'

Illustration 46.2:
isind noí 'in the boat'

46.1.2. *nó* 'boat'

nó, nau 'boat' is actually a feminine ā-stem, but because of its vocalic stem /nō- nau̯-/ this does not become apparent at first glance.

ending	transcr.		Old Irish	Prim. Irish	Proto-Celtic	PIE
nom.	nōᴸ, nau̯ᴸ	*nóᴸ* (arch. *nau̯ᴸ*)	*nāu̯ā «	*nau̯s ?	*néh₂us
gen.	noëᴴ, nau̯eᴴ	*noeᴴ* (arch. *naueᴴ*)	*nāu̯ijah «	*nāu̯os ? «	*n̥h₂u̯és
prep.	noi̯ᴸ	*+noíᴸ* «	*nāu̯ («)	*nāu̯ei̯ ?, *nāu̯i ?	*n̥h₂u̯éi̯, *néh₂ui
acc.	noi̯ᴺ	*+noíᴺ*	*nāu̯ev «	*nāu̯m ?	*néh₂um
nom.pl.	noäᴴ	*noaᴴ*	*nāu̯āh «	*nāu̯es ?	*néh₂u̯es
gen.	nōᴺ	*nóᴺ*	*nāu̯av	*nāu̯om	*n̥h₂u̯óm
prep.	noäβ'	*nōib*	*nāu̯āβih «	*nāu̯bis ? («)	*n̥h₂ubʰís, -bʰós
acc.	noöᴴ	*nooᴴ*	*nāu̯āh	*nāu̯ās	*néh₂u̯n̥s

Illustration 46.3: The inflection of *nó, nau* 'boat'

Note:

1. Like *nó, náu* inflects *gó, gáu* 'falseness, falsehood.'

46.1.3. *dia* 'day'

An old word for 'day' is nom. sg. *dieᴴ, diaᴴ* /d'ië d'iä/ (this form may also appear as an adverbially used genitive), later *díaᴴ* /d'ia/, prep. *díuᴸ* /d'iu̯/, acc. *déᴺ, deiᴺ* /d'ē/. It is only used in stereotyped phrases like the days of the week, e.g., *dia Aíne* /d'iä hai̯v'e/ '(on) Friday,' *dia Sathairn* '(on) Saturday,' *dia Samna* 'at Samain-tide,' *co dé mbrátha* 'till Judgement Day, forever,' *fri dé* 'by day, in daytime,' *indíu* /in'd'íu̯/ 'today.'

46.2. Indeclinable words

1. Many personal names from foreign languages like Hebrew, Latin and Greek remain uninflected, e.g., Hebrew (via Latin) *Ísu* 'Jesus,' *Dauid, Duid* 'David,' Greek (via Latin) *Agatha* or Latin *Pátricc* /pādɾəg'/ 'Patricius.' This, however, does not imply that all foreign names are uninflected: many are adapted to Old Irish inflectional classes, e.g., the Latin n-stem *Nero* is an n-stem in Old Irish as well: nom. *Neir*, gen. *Neran*.

2. Certain obsolete Irish names in the sagas also remain uninflected, like the rather obscure name element *Daᴸ* (perhaps 'god'?) in names like *Da Derga, Da Thó, Da Réo*, etc.

3. A group of Latin loan words ending in palatalized consonants are not inflected in the singular, but behave like i-stems in the plural, e.g., *apgitir* f. /ab'g'əd'əɾ'/ 'alphabet,' *sapait* f. /sabəd'/ 'Sabbat,' *testimin* m. /t'es't'ə-μ'əv'/ 'text, testimony,' etc.

Illustration 46.4: *Pátraicc* 'Patricius'

4. The native words *togu, rogu, uccu* n. 'choice, wish' are indeclinable. In the later language, however, these words start to inflect as i̯o-stems.

46.3. Consonantal stem adjectives

In addition to the four large classes of adjectives (see 23.4) there are a few isolated adjectives that inflect as consonant stems. These are

> 1. *éula, éola* /eu̯λa/ 'knowing, knowledgeable,' negative *anéola,* which has nom. pl. *éulaig, éolaig* /eu̯λəɣ'/, prep. pl. *éulachaib* /eu̯λəχəβ'/ (k-stem). Early on, however, a by-form *éulach* develops, which is an o-, ā-stem.

> 2. *tee, té* /t'eë t'ē/ 'hot' has a nom. pl. *téit* /t'eə̈d'/ (nt-stem).

> 3. *ainb* /an'β'/ 'ignorant' is regularly inflected as an i-stem, but is once found in archaic language with the expected t-stem gen. sg. *ainbed* /an'β'əδ/ < *ṇu̯id-.

Other adjectives where etymologically consonantal inflection would be expected, have either given it up and, like *ainb* above, adopted another inflection or are only attested in the nominative singular (e.g., *sothnge* /soθ'ŋ'g'e/, *dothge* /doθ'ŋ'g'e/, *étnge* /ēd'ŋ'g'e/, 'having a good, bad, no tongue') so that no statement about the stem class of these words can be made.

46.4. Comparison: the comparative

The comparative suffix, which is attached to the positive stem of the adjective, basically is *-iu* /'u/, but *-u* /u/ after consonants or consonant clusters that resist palatalization. It causes raising where possible, e.g.:

> *sen* /s'ev/ 'old' → *siniu* /s'iv'u/ 'older'
> *oll* /ol/ 'great, ample' → *uilliu* /ul'u/ 'greater, more ample'

Other examples:

> *tiug* /t'iu̯ɣ/ 'thick' → *tigiu* /t'iɣ'u/ 'thicker'
> *ard* /ard/ 'high' → *ardu* /ardu/ 'higher'
> *assae* /ase/ 'easy' → *assu* /asu/ 'easier'

Syncope, of course, takes place in adjectives of more than one syllable when the suffix *-iu/-u* is added:

> *álaind* /āλən'd'/ 'beautiful' → *áildiu* /al'd'u/ 'more beautiful'
> *lobur* /loβup/ 'weak' → *lobru* /loβρu/ 'weaker'

Note also cases where syncope has already taken place somewhere else in the word:

> *toísech* /tois̩'əχ/ 'leading, first' → *toísigiu, toísegu* /tois̩'əɣ'u tois̩'əɣu/ 'more leading' (< *to-u̯esaχ-*, syncope has taken place between *u̯ and *s, before *u̯ was lost!).

There are a few irregular formations, and some adjectives form their comparative from completely different stems altogether:

positive	comparative
accus, ocus /agus ogus/ 'near'	*nessa* /nesa/
becc /b'eg/ 'small, few'	*laugu, lugu, laigiu* /lau̯γu luγu laγ'u/
il /iλ/ 'many'	*lia* /l'ia/
lethan /l'eθəv/ 'broad'	*letha* /l'eθa/
maith, dag- /maθ' daγ-/ 'good'	*ferr* /f'er/
már, mór /māρ mōρ/ 'great, much, big'	*mó, móu, moo* /mō mōu̯ moö/
oac, óc /oäg ōg/ 'young'	*óa* /oä/
olc, droch- /olk droχ-/ 'bad'	*messa* /m'esa/
remor /r'eμəρ/ 'thick'	*reime* /r'eμ'e/
sír /s'īρ/ 'long'	*sia, sía* /s'ia/
trén /t'r'ēv/ 'strong'	*tressa* /t'r'esa/

Illustration 46.5: Irregular comparative forms

Note:

1. Beside the above listed forms the comparative of *mór, már* 'great, much, big' has a great number of orthographical by-forms, such as *máo, máa, móa, má* /māu̯ maä moä mā/.

2. The person or thing with which the subject is compared

2.1. immediately follows the comparative in the plain prepositional case, e.g., *ní ardu ní nim* 'nothing is higher than the sky (lit.: not is higher anything (subject = *ní*) than the sky)' (*Thes.* ii 248.3), or *(is) áildiu cach dath alailiu* 'every color is more beautiful than the other' (TBDD 999).

2.2. or it is expressed by a dependent clause, which is introduced by *ol-daas* /ol-dáäs/ (singular subject) or *ol-dáte* /ol-dáde/ (plural subject), later also *in-daas, in-dáte*, e.g., *is ansu lim-sa mo thech ol-daas mo threbad uile* 'my house is dearer (= *ansu*) to me (= *lim-sa*) than all my husbandry' (FB 26), or *[it] lia ar mmairb ol-dáte ar mbíi* 'our dead are more than our living' (FB 5), or *is laigiu deacht Maicc in-daas deacht Athar* 'the godliness of the Son is less than the godliness of the Father' (*Ml.* 17c7), or contracted *at coímiu-siu in-dás lá samraid* 'thou art more lovely than a summer's day.'

ol-daas etc. is a combination of the nasalizing conjunction *ol^N* 'than' and a relative form of the substantive verb 'who/which is.' The *d* /d/ of *ol-daas* is simply the nasalized *anlaut* of the 3rd sg. relative **taas* of the substantive verb. It can be fully conjugated in all persons and tenses, e.g., 1st sg. present tense »*is sochraidiu lám ol-dó-sa*« *ol coss* '»Hand is more handsome than I am« says Foot' (*Wb.* 12a21), or 3rd pl. preterite *nibo mailliu (ind fir) do·lotar ol-mbátar in charpait* '(the men) who came were not slower than were the chariots' (TBC 3537).

In the later language the comparative also takes over the function of the superlative and ousts the latter completely, e.g., *ind rand as trummu 7 as reime* 'the part which is strongest and which is stoutest' (ITS xiv 42.11), or *in chuit as saidbriu den phopul* 'the richest part of the people (lit.: the part which is richest of the people)' (*Ps.* 45.12).

You'll find a table with irregular comparison in Appendix F.5.

46.5. Special formations of the comparative

1. To express a gradual increase *assa*[H] is inserted between two identical comparatives, e.g., *ferr assa ferr* 'better and better; immer besser,' *nesso assa nesso* 'nearer and nearer; immer näher.' The first vowel of *assa* may be elided: *lia 'sa lia* 'more and more; immer mehr.'

2. Adverbial 'the; *German*: umso, desto' with the comparative is expressed in Old Irish by the comparative followed by *de*, e.g., *(is) mou de a adúath tri sodain* 'the greater is the fear of him through this; *German*: dadurch ist die Furcht vor ihm umso grösser' (*Ml.* 40c11). In Middle Irish this enclitic *de* merged orthographically with the comparative and was spelled *-te* or *-ti*; at the same time these forms more or less took on the meaning of the plain comparative, e.g., *is gnáth mirr do thabairt im chorpaib [...] conid maillite (= mailliu de) thinaid* 'it is usual to give myrrh around the corpses [...] so that it may waste away (the) slower' (PH 7023).

46.6. Exercise

Form the three degrees of comparison of the following adjectives:

> *cóir* /kōρ'/ (i) 'right, proper, correct' (depalatalized when a suffix is added!)
> *cosmail* /kosμəλ'/ (i) 'similar' (no syncope of the second syllable)
> *deithbir* /d'eθ'β'əρ'/ (i) 'fitting, suitable' (no syncope of the second syllable)
> *fírián* /f'īρ'āv/ (o, ā) 'just' (no syncope of the second syllable)
> *léir* /l'ēρ'/ (i) 'eager, diligent'
> *sen* /s'ev/ (o, ā) 'old'
> *sollus* /solus/ (u) 'clear, bright' (syncope of the second syllable and palatalization of the surrounding consonants when a suffix is added!)
> *úasal* /uasəλ/ (o, ā) 'high, noble' (syncope of the second syllable and palatalization of the surrounding consonants when a suffix is added!)

Illustration 46.6:
lúaithiu assa lúaithiu
'faster and faster'

46.7. Additional degrees of comparison

1. The *elative* or *absolute superlative* expresses a very high degree or intensity of a quality. English or German do not have a special morphological category for the elative, but use periphrastic constructions instead, e.g., the sentence *Old Irish grammar is extremely difficult* contains the elatival expression *extremely difficult*. Other ways of expressing the elative in English or German are, e.g., the use of the adverbs *very, most, highly*, resp. *sehr, äusserst*, or in colloquial speech the prefix *ur-*: *die altirische Grammatik ist urschwierig*. In Old Irish the elative can be expressed artificially by the superlative in literal translations of Latin, e.g., *doíni saibem* (*Ml.* 3a5) for Latin *peruersissimi homines* 'very pervert people.'[1] Outside of translated literature various prefixes are used: *ér-, der-, rug-*, as in *deramrae* 'very famous,' *érḟot* 'very long,' *rugil* 'quite many,' or *rucloín* (= *rug-clóen*) 'very unfair.' Modern Irish has the prefix *an(a)-* as in *an-bhréa* 'very fine.'

2. The *excessive degree* expresses the presence of 'too much' of a quality without an implied contrast. This corresponds to constructions with *too* in English and with *zu* in German. Old Irish uses the prefix *ro-/ru-* for the excessive degree, e.g., *roólach* 'too bibulous' or *rubecc* /ruß'eg/ 'too small.' It can also be added to nouns to give them an excessive meaning, e.g., *rochor* is an 'excessive contract (*cor*),' meaning a contract that is disadvantageous for one of the involved parties. But note that *ro-/ru-* added to an adjective can also be used for the mere elative degree.

Illustration 46.7: *derchrúaid* 'very urgent'

---

[1] Note also the artificial attributive use of the superlative *saíbem* in this case, which would be impossible in authentic Old Irish.

Lesson 47

47.1. Personal numerals and other numeral substantives

In order to count persons, unspecified things or particular periods of time, in Old Irish specific numeral words have to be used, i.e., personal numerals, numeral substantives and temporal substantives.

47.1.1. Personal numerals

When counting persons in Old Irish special personal numbers have to be used.

nr.	transcription	Old Irish	Prim. Irish	Proto-Celtic
1	oi̯vəρ^N	óenar^N	*oi̯vau̯iρav	*oi̯nou̯irom
2	d'iəs^L	dias^L	*du̯ihasā	*du̯isatsā < °ad-tā (?)
3	t'r'iəρ^N	triar^N	*triu̯iρav	*triu̯irom
4	k'eθρəρ^N	cethrar^N	*kʷeθρu̯u̯iρav	*kʷetru̯irom
5	kōg'əρ^N	cóicer^N	*kʷōgʷeu̯iρav	*kʷinkʷeu̯irom
6	s'es'əρ^N	seisser^N	*su̯esu̯iρav	*su̯eχsu̯irom
7	mōpf'es'əρ^N	mórfesser^N	*māρahu̯esu̯iρav	*mārosu̯eχsu̯irom
8	oχtəρ^N	ochtar^N	*oχtau̯iρav «	*oχtūu̯irom
9	nōnβəρ^N	nónbor^N	*nou̯anβiρav	*nou̯anu̯irom
10	d'eχ'ənβəρ^N	deichenbor^N «	*deχanβiρav	*dekamu̯irom

Illustration 47.1: The personal numerals

Note:

1. The numbers *óenar* and from *triar* to *deichenbor* are compounds of the cardinal numbers and a neuter o-stem abstract probably derived from the word *fer* 'man.' Attested forms apart from the nominative singular are: gen. sg. *oínair*, prep. sg. *oínur*; gen sg. *triir* /t'r'iəρ'/, prep. pl. *trírib* /t'r'ĭρ'əβ'/ 'in groups of three' (*Fél. Prol.* 210); *cethrairib* 'in groups of four' (*Thes.* I 497, 16); prep. sg. *cóiciur* /kōg'uρ/.

2. *dias* 'two men, a pair' is a feminine ā-stem: gen. sg. *deisse* /d'es'e/, prep. and acc. sg. *diis*, *díis* /d'iəs'/, prep. pl. *deissib* /d'es'əβ'/ 'in pairs' (*Fél. Prol.* 210).

3. Numbers above 10 are expressed in the same way that we already learned in 33.4, i.e., only the digit is expressed by the personal numeral: *dias ar fichit* '22 persons,' *deichenbor ar dib fichtib ar trib cétaib* '350 persons (*lit.*: ten persons on twice twenty on three hundred).'

4. It seems that, unlike in Modern Irish, in Old Irish the personal numerals were solely used to signify 'a group of persons,' specifically 'men.' If any other type of person was meant, ordinary numbers were used, e.g., *trí maicc* 'three sons,' *trí* (!) *seithir* 'three sisters,' *trí soír* 'three free persons,' etc., in the Old Irish *Triads*. A younger construction is to use the personal numeral

followed either by the counted word in the genitive plural, e.g., *cethrur airech* 'four noble-men' (LL 480), *tánaicc Calcus 7 a thriar ban* 'Calcus and his three wives came' (*St. Ercuil* 1952), or in a partitive construction with the preposition *de^L* 'of, from,' e.g., *dechinbor ar dib fichtib ar tríb cétaib de epscopaib* '350 bishops.' This construction is not restricted to persons only, but can be used for animals and things also.

5. A very frequent use of the personal numerals is in the plain singular prepositional case immediately after a possessive pronoun, e.g., *tusu t'óenur* 'thou alone,' *at·taam ar ndiis i cuimriug* 'we two are in bonds' (*Wb.* 32a28), *a cethrur* /a g'eθρυρ/ 'the four of them.'

6. The plain prepositional case of a personal numeral without a preposition or possessive pronoun before it signifies accompaniment, e.g., *at·tá mí nád·n-imthet rí acht cethrur* 'there is a month when a king journeys only with four (companions)' (CG 535–536).

47.1.2. Numeral substantives

Something comparable to personal numerals exists for things as well: if things are to be enumerated (without specific mention of the things in question) numeral substantives are used:

1. *úathad* 'single thing, single number, singular'
2. *déde* 'two things'
3. *tréide* 'three things'
4. *cethardae* 'four things'
5. *cóicde* 'five things'
6. *séde* 'six things'
7. *sechtae* 'seven things'
8. *ochtae* 'eight things'
9. *noíde* 'nine things'
10. *deichde* 'ten things'

With the exception of *úathad*, which is a neuter o-stem, all these numerals are neuter i̯o-stems. Examples for their use are *tréde neimthigedar gobainn* 'three things that qualify a blacksmith' (*Triad* 120) or *cethardae forná·bí cosc nó ríagail* 'four things on which there is neither restraint nor rule' (*Triad* 234).

47.1.3. Temporal substantives

Finally, sometimes a special suffix *-aige* (i̯ā-stem) for periods of time can be found, e.g., *fichtige* 'period of 20 days,' *noíchtige* 'period of 29 days,' *trichtaige* 'period of 30 days.' These are abstracts from adjectives in *-ach*, e.g., *fichtech* 'having 20 (days, years),' *cétach* 'having 100 (years).'

Illustration 47.2: *a mmórfeisser nníamgorm* 'The Magnificent Seven'

Lesson 47

47.2. Possession in Irish

There is no verb in Irish that corresponds to English *to have*. Instead possession in Irish is expressed by various other means.

47.2.1. The substantive verb and infixed pronouns

One possibility is to infix a pronoun with datival force into the 3rd sg. of the substantive verb *tá·* 'there is' or into one of its suppletive stems, e.g., *nom·thá* 'there is to me; *mir ist* = I have; *ich habe*,' or *nob·tá* 'there is to you; *euch ist* = you have; *ihr habt*.' Before forms of the substantive verb beginning with *b-* the particle *ro·* has to be used to infix pronouns: *rot·bí* 'there is usually to thee; *dir ist gewöhnlich* = thou hast usually; *du hast gewöhnlich*,' or *ronn·boí* 'there was to us; *uns war* = we had; *wir hatten*.' Be careful that the negated form *ním·thá* means 'there is not to me = I have not,' but *ním·fil* means 'I am not;' *indat·tá* means 'is there to thee? = dost thou have?', whereas *indat·fil* means 'art thou?' (see 28.1).

47.2.2. The substantive verb and suffixed pronouns

More common than constructions with infixed pronouns are forms where the pronoun is suffixed to the verb, meaning attached at its end. The relevant forms of the substantive verb[1] are:

person		present tense	preterite
1st sg.	I have, I had, etc.	*táthum*	*baíthum, baíthium*
2nd sg.	thou hast, etc.	*táthut*	*baíthut*
3rd sg. m. n.	he/it has, etc.	*táithi, táthai*	*baíthi*
3rd sg. f.	she has, etc.	*táthus*	*boíthus*
1st pl.	we have, etc.	*táthunn, táithiunn*	n/a
2nd pl.	you have, etc.	*táthuib*	n/a
3rd pl.	they have, etc.	**táthus*	**boíthus*

Illustration 47.3: The 'inflection' of *táthum*

Further attested forms are: present habitual *bíthi* 'there is usually to him = he usually has,' imperative *bithom!* 'let there be to me! = let me have!,' present subjunctive *bethum-sa* 'may there be to me = may I have,' future *bethiumm* 'there will be to me = I will have' and *bethib* 'there will be to you = you will have.'

The negative *I don't have*, etc., for both the infixed and the suffixed variant is simply constructed with *ní*: *ním·thá* 'there is not to me = I don't have,' *nít·tá* 'thou hast not,' *ní·tá* 'he does not have,' *níb·boí* 'you did not have,' etc. Be careful to distinguish between *ním·fil* 'I am not,' the negative of *at·tá*, and *ním·thá* 'I don't have,' the negative of the possessive construction!

---

[1] A more detailed account of suffixed pronouns will follow in a later lesson.

233

Lesson 47

47.2.3. Prepositional constructions

Another way of expressing possession is to use prepositional constructions.

1. *la*^H 'with' expresses possession in various constructions. With the substantive verb it means 'to have': *at·tá X la Y* 'there is X with Y = Y has X,' e.g., *in·fil scéla lib?* 'do you have stories?'; the substantive verb can also be left off, e.g., *scél lemm dúib* 'I have news for you' (GT 98), or *rosc nglan lais* 'he has a clear eye.' With the copula the possessor is more strongly emphasized: *is la Y X* 'Y possesses X,' e.g., *is lim-sa in cauradmír* 'the hero's portion is mine' (FB 73).

2. The construction with the preposition *oc* emphasizes the fact of possession: *at·tá X oc Y* 'Y has X, Y is in possession of X,' e.g., *boí cú occo* 'he had a dog' (SMMD 1), *is occa at·tá cach maith, … oc macc mo Dé* 'he has all good, the son of my God (lit.: it is with him that all good is, with the son of my God)' (BColm. 100.16). *oc*, too, can be used in a verbless construction, e.g., *bél occai i·tallfad cú* 'she had a mouth (lit.: mouth with her) in which a hound would fit' (*Echtra Mac Echdach Mugmedóin* 35).

3. For affections and afflictions, meaning emotions, physical and mental states or conditions like joy, pain, hunger, sickness etc., which are often expressed by *to have* in English or by *haben* in German, the preposition *for* is used in Old Irish, followed by the person affected, e.g., *biith galar fort-su* 'illness is on thee = thou hast an illness, thou art ill' (*Wb.* 29a26), *ní·bí nach deithiden foir* 'there is no care on him = he doesn't care at all; er hat keine Sorgen' (*Wb.* 10b9).

47.2.4. Stressed possessive pronouns

Sometimes the stressed variants of the possessive pronouns (see 34.6) are used to express possession, e.g., *is aí talam ocus muir* 'His is the earth and the sea' (IB 27).

Illustration 47.4: *is limm-sa a mbúaid* 'victory is mine'

234

47.3. The preterite passive stem

I already presented the forms of the preterite passive of weak verbs without going into any detail in 41.2, but refrained from doing so in the case of all other preterite formations. The reason for this is that apart from the weak verbs the preterite passive forms are built on separate stems, which are totally unconnected with the active preterite formations.

Unlike the passive in all other tenses and moods where simply a special ending is added to the respective stem (e.g., *-thair, -thar* in the 3rd sg. present), the formation of the preterite passive is rather difficult and depends on the verbal class and the root shape. The ending of the preterite passive basically consists of an underlying *t* (in some forms followed by a vowel), but depending on the verbal class and the root structure this *t* can appear in various forms:

1. as a lenited *th* /θ/ with a voiced variant *d* /ð/,

2. as a voiced *t* /d/,

3. as an *s* or *ss* /s/, and finally

4. as a *t* /t/.

In addition to this, two verbs build their preterite passive forms on suppletive stems. When citing attested forms in the following paragraphs I will use the 3rd sg. absolute or conjunct unless otherwise stated. From the 3rd sg. all other forms can easily be derived (see 47.4).

47.3.1. Ending *th* /θ/

When the basic formant *t* is added to a vocalic stem or a root ending in a vowel, the dental is lenited to *th* /θ/, which in absolute *auslaut* is usually voiced to *d* /ð/ in forms of two or more syllables. Vocalic stems, resp. roots ending in a vowel are typical of the weak verbs, all hiatus verbs, nearly all S3 verbs, the two strong verbs with roots in *-b* and S2 *gairid*.

1. We already saw in 41.2 that the preterite passive of W1 and W2 verbs is apparently built on the root, not on the s-preterite stem: the active s-preterite stem of W1 *caraid* 'to love' is *caras-*, but the absolute 3rd sg. passive '(s)he was loved' is *carthae*, the ending *-the* (< *-te*) is directly added to what seems to be the root *car-*.[2] In most cases the preterite passive stem is identical to the present stem of weak verbs. But in W2b verbs the root vowel *u* of the present stem, e.g., *for·cuirethar* 'to overpower,' becomes *o* in the preterite passive, *for·corad* '(s)he was overpowered.'

2. The two strong verbs with a root ending in *-b* are S2 *gaibid* 'to take' (root *gab-*) → *gabthae*, *·gabad* 'was taken' (non-palatalized root!), and S1 *ibid* 'to drink' (root *ib-*) → *·ibed* 'was drunk.'

3. The strong root *gar-* 'to call' forms its preterite passive in the same way, e.g., S2 *ar·gair* 'to forbid' → *ar·garad* 'it was forbidden,' *do·airngir* 'to promise' → *do·airngerad* 'it was promised.'

Things get much more complicated outside of the above cases. Now the shape of the roots starts to change (be careful to note that in the examples below absolute and conjunct and singular and plural forms are wildly mixed, due to the chances of attestation).

---

[2] Actually, the ending *-te* is added to the root + a stem vowel (*a* in case of W1 verbs, *e* in case of W2 verbs).

4. H1 and H3 verbs add *-ad/-th-* to the root, e.g., H3 *soaid* 'to turn' (root *so-, soí-*) → *·soad* 'it was turned,' 3rd pl. conj. *·soíthea* 'they were turned,' H1 *ro·lā-* (perfect stem of *fo·ceird*): *ro·laad* 'it has been put,' 3rd pl. *·látha* 'they have been put.'

5. Roots with final *i* (that is all H2 verbs and many S3 verbs) add the *-th-* directly to the root whereby the *i* is lengthened, e.g., H2 *gniid* 'to do' (root *gni-*) → *·gníth* 'it was done,' S3 *benaid* 'to strike' (root *bi-*) → *·bíth* '(s)he was struck,' S3 *renaid* 'to sell' (root *ri-*) → *ríthae* 'it was sold.' When the root is moved out of the accented position, the vowel is reduced to /ə/: e.g., S3 *imm·diben* 'to circumcise' (root *bī-*) → *·immdibed* /·imʼδʼəβʼəδ/ 'he was circumcised,' or H2 *ad·slí* 'to earn' (root *sli-*) → *ad·roilled* /aδ·rolʼəδ/ 'it has been earned' (the root is represented by *-lled*).

6. Roots ending in *-er* and *-el* usually 'metathesize' this sequence and add the *th* to the vowel, e.g., S1 *beirid* 'to carry' (root *ber-*) → *brethae* 'it was carried,' S1 *do·beir* 'to give, to bring' → *do·breth, ·tabrad* 'it was given, it was brought,' S1 *ceilid* 'to hide' (root *kel-*) → *·cleth* 'it was hidden,' S3 *sernaid* 'to arrange' (root *ser-*) → *·sreth* 'it was arranged.' S3 *ernaid* 'to grant' (root *er-*) behaves differently, in that it has a preterite passive *·rath* 'it was granted.'

47.3.2. Ending *t* /d/

In strong verbs with root final *m* or *n* the *t* is added directly to the nasal. In consequence the *t* is voiced to /d/ and the nasal disappears with compensatory lengthening of the preceding vowel:

1. °*em/nt* and °*am/nt* > °*ét* /ēd/, e.g., S2 *daimid* 'to suffer' (root *dam-*) → *·dét* /·dʼēd/ 'it was suffered,' S1 *canaid* 'to sing' (root *kan-*) → *·cét* /·kʼēd/ 'it was sung.' When the root vowel is not stressed, it is shortened, e.g., *do·eissim* /do·esʼəμʼ/ 'to pour out' (root *sem-!*) → *do·esset* /do·esʼəd/ 'it was poured out.'

2. The preterite passive of *gonaid* 'to wound' (root *gon-*) is irregular in that it becomes *góetae, ·gáet* /goi̯de ·gai̯d/ '(s)he was wounded.'

47.3.3. Ending *s* and *ss* /s/

In strong verbs with roots ending in a dental (*d, t, th*) or *nn* these combine with the basic **t* of the preterite passive to give *s* or *ss*:

1. S2 *guidid* 'to ask, to pray' (root *ged-*) → *gessae* 'he/she/it was asked,' S2 *midithir* 'to judge' (root *med-*) → *·mess* 'he/she/it was judged,' S1a *do·seinn* 'to hunt' (root *senn-*) → *do·sessa* 'they were hunted,' *ro·fitir* 'to know' (root *finn-*) → *·fess* 'it is known, it was known.' Note that the root of S1c *naiscid* 'to bind' ends in a dental, too (*nad-*), so the preterite passive is *·nass* 'he/she/it was bound.'

2. The important H2 verb *ad·cí* 'to see' forms its preterite passive this way, too: *ad·cess, ·accass/·aiccess* 'he/she/it was seen.' In analogy to this in the other important verb of sensorial perception S3 *(ro)·cluinethar* 'to hear' already in classical Old Irish the analogical formation *(ro)·clos* 'he/she/it was heard' replaced the Early Old Irish preterite passive *(ro)·cloth*.

47.3.4. Ending *t* /t/

Strong verbs with a root ending in a guttural (*g* /γ g/) add the dental directly onto the guttural. The guttural is then realized as *ch* /χ/ after a vowel, or is dropped after an *r*; the *t* stays /t/:

1. S1 *aigid* 'to drive' → ·*acht* 'was driven,' S1 *aingid, ·anaich* 'to protect' (root *aneg-*) → ·*anacht* 'he/she/it was protected,' S1d *boingid* 'to break' (root *bog-*) → ·*bocht* 'it was broken,' S1 *orgaid* 'to slay' (root *org-*) → ·*ort* '(s)he was slain.'

2. The S1 verb *ailid* 'to rear' (root *al-*) also has a preterite passive in /t/: *altae* 'he was reared.'

47.3.5. Suppletive stems

Two verbs have a suppletive preterite passive stem: S2 *fo·gaib* 'to find' has *(fo)·fríth* 'he/she/ it was found,' and the preterite passive (only in impersonal use) of the compounds of S1 *téit* 'to go' is ·*eth* 'one went = a messenger was sent; man ging = ein Bote kam.' Both suppletive forms behave like normal preterite passives in *th.*

47.4. The preterite passive inflection

Like all passive forms of Old Irish the preterite passive has separate endings only for the 3rd persons. All other persons have to be formed by infixing the appropriate pronoun into the 3rd sg. form. The 3rd person forms are:

person		under-lying	1. th /θ/		2. t /d/	3. ss /s/	4. t /t/
3rd sg.	abs. + rel.	*-te	carthae	gníthe	cétae	gessae	altae
	conj.	*-t	·carad	·gníth	·cét	·gess	·alt
3rd pl.	abs.	*-ti	carthai	gníthi	cétai	gessai	altai
	conj.	*-ta	·cartha	·gnítha	·céta	·gessa	·alta

Illustration 47.5: *The inflection of the preterite passive*

Note:

1. The absolute 3rd sg. form is used both in non-relative and relative constructions.

2. The 3rd pl. absolute forms are only weakly attested.

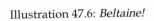

Illustration 47.6: *Beltaine!*

47.5. The past passive participle (P.P.P.)

Formally closely connected to the preterite passives are the past passive participles. They are formed by adding the suffix *-th(a)e* (or the variants *-t(a)e, -sse* according to the rules set out in 47.3) in the same way as in the case of the preterite passive forms. Past passive participles are adjectives; the suffix *-th(a)e* inflects like a i̯o-/i̯ā-adjective. Examples are:

W1 *caraid* 'to love' → *carthae* 'loved'
W2a *léicid* 'to leave' → *léicthe* 'left'
W2b dep. *suidigidir* 'to place, to set' → *suidigthe* 'placed, set'
S1 *canaid* 'to sing' → *céte* 'sung'
S1 *gonaid* 'to wound' → *goíte* 'wounded'

Participles of compound verbs are always stressed on their first syllable. That means they appear in their prototonic shape:

S3 *im·diben* 'to circumcise' → *imdibthe* 'circumcised'
S1 *do·formaig* 'to increase' → *tórmachtae* 'increased'
S1 *con·rig* 'to bind' → *cuimrechtae* 'bound'
S1 *for·cain* 'to teach' → *foircthe* 'taught'
S1 *im·said* 'to besiege' → *impesse* 'besieged' (< *imbi-śed-te*)
S3 *ro·cluinethar* 'to hear' → *clothe* 'heard'

Note that a few strong verbs with roots ending in *-er* and *-el* have their root raised in the past passive participle, unlike the preterite passive:

S1 *beirid* 'to carry' → *brithe* 'carried,' but preterite passive *brethae* '(s)he was carried'
S1 *ceilid* 'to hide' → *clithe* 'hidden,' but preterite passive *clethae* '(s)he was hidden'

A few verbs behave irregularly:

H2 *gniid* 'to do' → pl. *gnethi* 'done' (*Ml.* 115b2)
H2 *fris·accai* 'to hope' → *frescastae* 'hoped, expected'

47.6. Exercise

Form the preterite passive and the past passive participle of the following verbs.

bendachaid /b'endəχəð'/ (W1) 'to bless'
fíriánaigidir /f'ïɼ'āvəɣ'əð'əɼ'/ (W2) 'to justify'
crenaid /k'r'evəð'/ (S3), root *crī-* 'to buy'
fo·cren, ·fochren /fo·k'r'ev ·foχ'ɼ'ev/ (S3), root *crī-* 'to hire'
as·beir, ·eipir /as·b'eɼ' ·eb'əɼ'/ (S1), root *ber-* 'to say'
ar·naisc, ·arnaisc /aɼ·nas'k' ·aɼvəs'k'/ (S1), root *nad-* 'to bind, to guarantee'
fo·cain, ·fochain /fo·kav' ·foχəv'/ (S1), root *kan-* 'to sing to'
fris·oirg, ·frithoirg /f'r'is·oɼ'g' ·f'r'iθoɼ'g'/ (S1), root *org-* 'to offend'

Lesson 48

48.1. Exercise

This is a stanza from a longer poem describing a hermitage out in nature:

Ceithri triir, trí cethrair,
cuibdi fri cach les;
dá ṡeiser i n-eclais
eter túaid is tes.

Source: EIL 30.12

k'eθ'ρ'i t'r'iȧρ', t'r'ī k'eθρəρ'
kuβ'δ'i f'r'i kaχ l'es;
dā h'es'əρ i v'egləs'
ed'əρ tuaδ' is t'es.

Note:

1. *is* in line 4 is a short variant of *ocus* 'and.'

48.2. Exercise

The following stanza is part of a long religious poem on Jesus Christ by the poet *Blathmacc macc Con Brettan*. The language of Blathmacc's poems belongs to the early period of Old Irish. In the passage below this is reflected by the fact that adjectival 'each, every' still appears as *cech*, not as reduced *cach* as in the later language.

Sainemlu cech dóen a chruth,
brestu cech sáer a balcbruth,
gaíthiu cech bruinniu fo nim,
fíriánu cech breithemain.

Source: *Blathm*. 29–33

sav'əμλu k'eχ doi̯v a χρuθ,
b'r'estu k'eχ sai̯ρ a βalkβρuθ,
gai̯θ'u k'eχ brun'u fo v'iμ',
f'īρ'āvu k'eχ b'r'eθ'əμəv'.

Note:

1. *cech dóen* and *cech sáer* in lines 1 and 2 are, like their counterparts *cech bruinniu* and *cech breithemain* in lines 3 and 4, independent prepositionals.

48.3. Varia

1. a^N followed by a leniting relative clause is a relative particle with the meaning 'that, which.' Don't confuse it with a^N followed by a nasalizing relative clause, which is the conjunction 'when.'

2. Indirect speech after words of saying is expressed by a nasalizing relative clause. But like most nasalizing relative clauses, it may also be replaced by a main clause construction.

48.4. Exercise

Old Irish

1. ** Íadais Cú Chulainn indara súil dó connábo letha in-daas cró snáthaite. As·oilgg alaile combo móir béolu midchúaich. (TBC 430 ff.) 2. ** Is demniu linn a n-ad·chiam húa śúilib ol-daas a rro·chluinemmar húa chlúasaib. (*Ml.* 112b13) 3. ** Is ed as·berat ind heretic as laigiu deacht Maicc in-daas deacht Athar. (*Ml.* 17c7). 4. * 'Fír,' ol é-seom, 'is moo serc inna deisse-ucut la Tigernae in-dáu-sa!' (LL 36647f.) 5. ** At·tá árchú lem-sa. […] Téora slabrada fair ⁊ triar cacha slabraide. (TBC 572 f.) 6. ** Rom·boí denus la ríga oc ól meda ⁊ ḟína; indíu ibim medguisce […]. (GT 51) 7. * In maccrad móeth maith, táthus subae i mbithḟlaith; acht Heroaid, táthai bithbrón ⁊ bithifernn. (*Blathm.* 81 ff.) 8. ** Is lais cach alam ad·chí, it aí alltai ⁊ chethrai. (*Blathm.* 774 f.) 9. ** Luid Bran […] for muir. Trí nonbuir a lín. Óenḟer forsnaib tríb nonburaib dia chomaltaib ocus chomáesaib. (IB 32) 10. * At·tá cethrar ar ḟichit do ollamain for túathaib, dá ḟer deac oc acru, dechenbor dó for fledaib féile, ochtar for coí la ríg. (UR §5). 11. ** Ní·fessa a imthechta ónd úair-sin. (IB 66) 12. ** Céol caille fom·chanad la Cuirithir, la fogur fairrge flainne. (GT 73) 13. * Do·breth míl úathmar la Saxanu do bás Áedáin isin chath. (CM 5 f.) 14. ** Is hed in-so sís ro·chlos ⁊ ad·chess inna bésaib ⁊ a gnímaib. (*Wb.* 23c11) 15. * Do·breth corann […] delgae timchell a chinn. Bíthi cloi tria chossa, alaili tria bossa. (*Blathm.* 201 ff.) 16. * Ro·classa garmann inna n-én for luamain. (*Gosp.* 7) 17. * 'Día lat, á Maire […]' ol Gabrial. 'At bendachtae ó chiunn co fonn ⁊ torad do bronn.' (*Blathm.* 605 ff.) 18. * Altae-som [*sc.* Cú Chulainn] la máthair ⁊ la athair i mMaig Muirthemni. Ad·fessa dó airscéla inna maccraide i nEmain. (TBC 399 ff.) 19. ** Trí aithgine in domuin: brú mná, uth bó, ness gobann. (*Triad* 148) 20. * Ad·cessa noí fichit én, rond argait eter cach dá én. […] Do·scartha trí éuin díb. (CCC 2)

Transcription

1. iaδəs' kū χυλən' indápa sūλ' dō konāβo λ'eθa in-dáẹs krō snāθəd'e. as·ol'g' aλáλ'e kombo μōp' beụλu m'iδχuaχ'. 2. is d'eμ'v'u l'in a vaδ·χ'iẹμ ua hūλ'əβ' ol-dáẹs a ro·χλuv'əməp ua χλuasəβ'. 3. is eδ as·β'epəd ind ep'əd'əg' as λaγ'u d'eẹχt μak' in-dáẹs d'eẹχt aθəp. 4. 'f'īp,' ολ ē-s'oμ, 'is moö s'erk ina d'es'e-ugud la t'iγ'ərne in-dáụ-sa!' 5. ad·tā āpχū l'em-sa. t'eụpa slaβpəδa fap' ogus t'r'iẹp kaχa slaβpəd'e. 6. rom·boị d'evus la r'īγa og ōλ μ'eδa ogus īva; in'd'íụ iβ'əm' m'eδgus'k'e. 7. in μakpəδ μoịθ μaθ', tāθus suβe i m'b'iθλaθ'; aχt epoaδ', tāθi b'iθβρōv ogus β'iθ'if'ərn. 8. is las' kaχ aλəμ aδ·χ'ī, id aị alti ogus χ'eθρi. 9. luδ' brav fop μup'. t'r'ī novβup' a l'īv. oịv'ep forsnəβ' t'r'īβ' novβupəβ' d'iä χoμəltəβ' ogus χoμaịsəβ'. 10. ad·tā k'eθpəp ap iχ'əd' do oləμəv' for tuaθəβ', dā ep d'eẹg og agru, d'eχ'əvβəp dō fop f'l'eδəβ' f'ēλ'e, oχtəp fop koị la r'īγ'. 11. n'ī·f'esa a im'θ'əχta ōnd uap'-s'iv. 12. k'eụλ gal'e fom·χavəδ la kup'əθ'əp', la foγup βar'g'e flan'e. 13. do·b'r'eθ m'īλ' uaθμəp la saχsəvu do βās aịδāv' is'ən χaθ. 14. is eδ in-so s'īs ro·χλos ogus aδ·χ'es ina β'esəβ' ogus a γ'v'íμəβ'.

15. do·b'r'eθ koρən d'elge t'im'χ'əl a χ'in'. b'īθ'i kloï t'r'iä χosa, aλáλ'i t'r'ia βosa. 16. ro·klosa garmən ina v'ēv foρ luaμəv'. 17. 'd'ia lat, ā μa're' oλ gaβ'ρ'iäλ. 'ad b'endəχte ō χ'iụn ko fon ogus toρəδ do βρon.' 18. alte-soμ la māθəρ' ogus la haθəρ' i maγ' μuρ'θ'əμvi. aδ·f'esa dō aρ's'k'ēλa ina makρəδ'e i v'eμəv'. 19. t'r'ī aθ'γ'əv'e in doμuv': brū mnā, uθ bō, n'es goβən. 20. aδ·k'esa noị β'iχ'əd' ēv, rond argəd' ed'əρ kaχ dā ēv. do·skaρθa t'r'ī h'eụv' d'ïβ'.

English

1. Did Cú Chulainn close his two eyes so that they were no wider than eyes (*cruí*) of needles? 2. It is not more certain for thee what thou seest through the eyes than what thou hearest through the ears. 3. This is what the heretic does not say, that the godliness of the Son is greater than the godliness of the Father. 4. Love by the Lord for those three men is greater than it is for thee (*OIr.* than thou art). 5. She has four watch-dogs. Four chains upon them and four men for each. 6. We had a while with a king, drinking mead and wine; today we drink whey-water. 7. The tender, good boy, he has eternal joy in heaven (*nem*). 8. Is hers every herd that we see, are hers the wild animals and the cattle? 9. The men went to sea. Nine (times) three men their number. 10. Are there ten men to ollams? 11. Their wandering from that hour on is known. 12. The music of the woods used to play around you with him. 13. Terrible warriors were brought by the Saxons for his death in the battle. 14. These below are (the things) that were heard and seen in their manners and in their deeds. 15. Was a crown of thorns given around his head? Were nails beaten through his feet, others through his palms? 16. Was a cry of the bird on his flight heard? 17. You (pl.) are blessed from your heads to your soles and the fruits of your wombs. 18. They were reared with their mothers and fathers. A tale of the boygroup in Emain was told to them. 19. Bellies of women, udders of cows, furnaces of smiths. 20. Were seventeen birds seen? Was one bird of them brought down?

Lesson 49

49.1. The imperfect

Like the Latin imperfect, the Old Irish imperfect expresses repeated or customary action in the past. An example for repeated action is TBC 416 *fo·cerded a bunsaig riam conda·gaibed ar loss* 'he kept throwing his javelin ahead of himself, and he kept catching it at its rear end.' Customary action can be seen in TBC 418 f. *ní·téiged nech cuccu inna cluichemag co n-arnastae a ŧoesam forru* 'nobody used to come to them onto their playing ground, until his protection had been bound upon them (= until his security had been entrusted to them).'

The imperfect is formed by adding a special set of endings, sometimes called 'secondary endings,' to the present stem. These endings are also utilized by two other secondary moods, the past subjunctive and the conditional, which we will learn in later lessons.

No distinction is made between absolute and conjunct forms in tenses/moods with secondary endings: practically speaking only conjunct forms exist. Simple verbs in independent position are *per force* prefixed with the 'meaningless' particle *no·* to create a compound verb. We already saw something similar happening to simple verbs when pronouns have to be infixed (see 25.1.3) and in certain relative constructions (see 34.3). All other verbs (compound verbs, verbs in dependent position) use the same stem form for the imperfect as in the corresponding present form. Furthermore, there is no distinction between active and deponent forms with secondary endings. The same endings are used for active and deponent verbs alike.

Some examples for imperfects (and their corresponding presents):

3rd pl. *no·cantais* 'they used to sing' (S1 *canait*, stem *can-*)
3rd sg. pass. *no·léicthe* 'he/she/it used to be let go' (W2 *léicthir*, stem *lēc-*)
1st pl. *no·téigmis* 'we used to go' (S1 *tíagmai*, stem *tēg-*)
3rd sg. *as·beired, ·eipred* '(s)he used to say' (S1 *as·beir*, stem *as·ber-*)
1st sg. *imm·téiginn, ·imtheginn* 'I used to go around' (S1 *imm·tíag*, stem *imm·tēg-*)
1st sg. *do·gnínn, ·dénainn* 'I used to do' (H2 *do·gníu*, stem *do·gnī-*)
3rd pl. *imm·réiditis* 'they used to ride around' (S1 *imm·ríadat*, stem *imm·rēd-*)
3rd sg. *imm·raad* 'he used to row around' (H1 *imm·rá*, stem *imm·rā-*)
3rd pl. pass. *con·gairtis, ·congairtis* 'they used to be called' (S2 *con·gairtir*, stem *con·gar-*)

Examples for deponent verbs:

3rd sg. *ro·cluined* '(s)he used to hear' (S3 dep. *ro·cluinethar*, stem *ro·clun-*)
3rd pl. *no·seichitis* 'they used to follow' (W2 *seichitir*, stem *sech-*)
3rd pl. *no·ainmnigtis* 'they used to be named' (W2 *ainmnigtir*, stem *ainmnig-*)

The formation and inflection of the imperfect follows a simple and uniform pattern. It will suffice to use a few sample verbs in the table below to demonstrate its formation for all verbs, irrespective of their stem class: W1 *caraid* 'to love' for simple active verbs, W2 *suidigidir* 'to place' for simple deponent verbs, S1 *do·beir, ·tabair* 'to give, to bring' for compounded verbs in prototonic and deuterotonic position; the imperfect of the substantive verb *at·tá* is built on the suppletive H2 stem *bī-*:

person		W1	W2	S1	H2	ending
1st sg.		·carainn	·suidiginn	do·beirinn, ·taibrinn	·biinn, ·bíinn	ən'
2nd sg.		·cartha	·suidigthea	do·berthea, ·taibrithea	n/a	(ə)θ⁽'⁾a
3rd sg.		·carad, -ath	·suidiged, -eth	do·beired, ·taibred	·biid, ·bíth	əð əθ
	pass.	·carthae	·suidigthe	do·beirthe, ·taibrithe	·bíthe	(ə)θ⁽'⁾e
1st pl.		·carmais	·suidigmis	do·beirmis, ·taibrimis	·bímmis	(ə)m⁽'⁾əs'
2nd pl.		·carthae	·suidigthe	do·beirthe, ·taibrithe	n/a	(ə)θ⁽'⁾e
3rd pl.		·cartais	·suidigtis	do·beirtis, ·taibritis	·bítis	(ə)d⁽'⁾əs'
	pass.	·cartais	·suidigtis	do·beirtis, ·taibritis	-	(ə)d⁽'⁾əs'

Illustration 49.1: The conjugation of the imperfect

Note:

1. Depending on the syncope pattern a vowel can appear before the ending.

2. In the case of the hiatus-verbs, the forms of the 1st and 3rd sg. are disyllabic in classical Old Irish, e.g., 1st sg. ·biinn /b'iən'/, later ·bínn /b'īn'/ 'I used to be,' 3rd sg. im·soad /im·soəδ/ '(s)he turned around and around and around.'

3. The ending of the 1st pl. -mais/-mis /m⁽'⁾əs'/ always has an unlenited /m/, although it is usually written with a single m.

4. Be careful with the 3rd pl. forms: the ending -tais/-tis /d⁽'⁾əs'/ is used for both the active and the passive voice! The correct meaning can solely be determined by the context!

5. The copula has no imperfect; instead for both the imperfect and the preterite a combined past form is used (see 44.6).

6. Because the prehistory of the Old Irish secondary endings is largely unclear, I will not discuss it in this course.

Illustration 49.2: no·scothad 'he peeled and peeled and peeled'

49.2. Exercise

Try to inflect the following verbs in the imperfect. In the case of compound verbs inflect them in both the deuterotonic and the prototonic form:

ad·ella, ·aidlea /aδ·ela ·aδ'l'a/ (W1) 'to visit'
cingid /k'iŋ'g'əδ'/ (S1) 'to step'
ad·cí, ·accai /aδ·k'i ·aki/ (H2) 'to see'
renaid /revəδ'/ (S3) 'to sell'
midithir /m'iδ'əθ'əρ'/ (S2) 'to judge'
fo·gaib, ·fagaib /fo·gaβ' ·faγəβ'/ (S2) 'to find'
do·ceil, ·dichil /do·k'eλ', ·d'iχ'əλ'/ (S1) 'to hide'

49.3. Nasalizing relative clauses

In 34.3 we learned about leniting relative clauses. We saw which syntactic relations they express and how they are constructed. Nasalizing relative clauses are basically identical in formation with leniting relative clauses, except for the crucial difference that instead of lenition of the accented portion of the verb the nasal mutation appears. The syntactic environments, however, where nasalizing relative clauses are used, are completely different:

1. When the antecedent, that is the relativized phrase, expresses the time at which the action of the relative clause takes place: *a llaithe nundam·ṡoíra* 'the day when he delivers me' (*Ml.* 62c6b). Therefore nasalizing relative clauses are also used after the temporal conjunctions *in tain, in tan* 'when,' *céin, céne* 'as long as,' *a^N* 'while, when,'[1] *lase, lasse* 'while,' e.g., *in tan do·lluid in cú cuccai-seom* 'when the dog came towards him' (TBC 581 f.), *céin bas mbéo in fer* 'as long as the man is alive' (*Wb.* 10b23), *a ndo·n·écad tar a éissi* 'whenever he turned to his back' (IB 2), *lasse nad·n-adraim-se* 'when I do not adore' (*Ml.* 132c1).

Optionally a nasalizing relative construction can be used after *(h)óre, (h)úare* 'because,' which originally was a temporal conjunction, e.g., *hóre nandat filii promissionis* 'because they are not *filii promissionis*' (*Wb.* 4c8) (*nandat* = nasalized negative 3rd pl. relative of the copula); independent, non-relative constructions are very frequent after *(h)óre, (h)úare*, however.

After the temporal conjunction *resíu* 'before' no relative construction is used, but an independent, non-relative construction follows.

2. When the antecedent specifies the manner or extent of the action of the relative clause: *méit ata n-echtrainn* 'to the extent that they are foreigners' (*Ml.* 72d15), *in chruth fo·ndáilter* 'how (= the manner) it is divided' (*Wb.* 33b19). Therefore, nasalizing relative constructions are also used after conjunctions like *amal, amail* 'as,' *feib, fib* 'as,' e.g., *amal nguides athair a macc* 'as a father asks his son' (*Wb.* 24d19), *Buchet ní·bia feib ro·mboí riam* 'Buchet will not be as he has been before' (ETB 493).

Into this category fall also those cases where a neuter adjective is moved forward to the front of the sentence, where it is used as an adverbial expression of the following relative clause: *ní maith ar·ráilter in macrad* 'the boy-group is not being treated well (*lit.*: it is not good how the boy-group is being treated)' (TBC 439).

3. When the antecedent is the verbal noun of the verb of the relative clause, that is in the so-called *figura etymologica* 'etymological construction' (see 49.5).

4. When the antecedent expresses the predicative nominative of the relative clause: *plebs dei asndan·berthe-ni* '*plebs dei* (is) what we used to be called' (*Ml.* 114a7).

5. When the antecedent is the object of the relative clause, a nasalizing relative construction can be used instead of a leniting one; a clear exception to this option are neuter pronouns, which are practically always followed by leniting relative clauses.

6. Causal conjunctions like *fo bíth, dáig, dég* and *ol* 'because, since' may be followed by nasalizing relative clauses, but more often than not non-relative, independent sentence constructions are used, e.g., *ol as rann* 'because it is a part' (*Sg.* 25b8) with a relative verbal

---

[1] Don't confuse *a^N* 'when, while', followed by a nasalizing relative clause, with *a^N* 'that, which', followed by a leniting relative clause!

form, but *ol is tú mo ruiri* 'because Thou art my great king' (*Fél. Prol.* 14) with a non-relative construction.

7. In Old Irish nasalized relative constructions are dependent on verbs of saying and thinking, without any conjunction intervening; furthermore, they appear after expressions like 'it is clear, possible, necessary, important,' 'it happens' and the like. In this use the nasalizing construction is similar to constructions with 'that' in English or with '*dass*' in German. Examples are *is derb linn non·soírfea* 'it is certain for us that he will deliver us; *es ist gewiss, dass er uns erlösen wird*' (*Wb.* 24c18), *ba doig bed n-ingcert in testimin-so* 'probably this text is corrupt (*lit.*: it would be likely that this text would be incorrect; *es wäre wahrscheinlich, dass dieser Text unrichtig ist*)' (*Ml.* 61b15).

However, dependent clauses of this type are frequently introduced by conjunctions like *ara^N, co^N, cía* 'that,' and the use of the conjunction *co^N* becomes the normal way of expressing these constructions later on.

Nasalizing relative constructions can in many cases be replaced by formally independent constructions, meaning by constructions with non-relative verbal forms.

49.4. The marking of nasalization in nasalizing relative clauses

The nasal mutation in nasalizing relative clauses is marked in the following ways:

1. Special relative forms of simple verbs (see 34.2) show the nasalization in their *anlaut*, e.g., *amal nguides* 'as he prays' (*Wb.* 24d19), or *fo bíth n-óenaigedar* 'because he unites' (*Sg.* 172a4). Especially in texts from the oldest time, however, nasalization can be omitted in such cases, e.g., *in tain bíis* 'when he is' (*Wb.* 28b28) or *lasse gabas imbi* 'when he takes (it) around himself' (*Wb.* 13d22).

2. In compound verbs, in simple verbs compounded with the empty particle *no·*, in forms with *ro·* (which we will learn later) and after the negative relative particles *nád·* and *ná·*, the *anlaut* of the accented part of the verb after the mid-high dot <·> in the normalized orthography is nasalized, e.g., *do·n-imchella* 'whom it encompasses' (EC 14), *hóre do·rrigeni* 'because he has made' (*Wb.* 15d13), *a n-as·mbert*[2] 'when she said' (EC 9), *in tan no·mbiinn* 'when I was' (*Ml.* 91c1), *in tan nád·n-acastar 7 nád·forchluinter* 'when he is not seen and is not heard' (*Wb.* 25b28).

3. When a pronoun of class C is infixed into a relative verbal form, nasalization appears immediately before the *-d-* of the infixed pronoun, which consequently becomes *-nd-* and later even *-nn-*, e.g., *íarsint śóerad-sin rond·sóer* 'after that deliverance by which he has delivered him' (*Ml.* 52) (infixed pronoun 3rd sg. masc. *-d^N* 'him'), *amal dundat·mecetar-su* 'as they despise thee' (*Ml.* 106c11) (*do·meiccethar* 'to despise,' infixed pronoun 2nd sg. *-dat^L* 'thee').

4. Absolute relative forms of the copula pass on the nasalization to the following word, e.g., *in tan ba n-imdírech do·gnítis* 'when it was mutual stripping which they made' (TBC 558 f.), *céin bas mbéo* 'as long as he is alive' (*Wb.* 10b23).

---

[2] Be careful: the first *n* of *n-as·mbert* has nothing to do with nasalizing clauses; it is the result of the plain nasalizing effect of the conjunction *a^N* 'when.'

49.5. The *figura etymologica*

The so-called *figura etymologica* is a stylistic device where the relativized antecedent is the verbal noun of the verb in the nasalizing relative clause. This kind of wordplay is a frequent and popular feature of Irish texts, e.g.,

a forcital forndob·canar 'the teaching that (= how) you are taught' (*Wb.* 3b23) (*forcetal* 'teaching' v.n. of S1 *for·cain* 'to teach;' the nasalizing relative clause is indicated by the *n* in front of the infixed pronoun *-dob·*),

ba léimm ro·leblaing-seom tarsin cathraig ammuich 'it was a leap that he had leaped over the fort' (*FB* 82) (*léimm* 'leap' v.n. of S1 *lingid* 'to leap;' the initial *l* of *ro·leblaing* is unlenited, thus indicating the nasalized relative clause).

A nice example is

luigim luige luiges mo thúath 'I swear the oath that my people swear' (*TBC* 2749 f.).

This construction also applies to cases where the verb and the verbal noun are not actually etymologically related, e.g.,

frisin seirc ro·car Críst in n-eclais 'to the love wherewith Christ loved the church' (*Ml.* 65d5) (*serc* 'love' v.n. of W1 *caraid* 'to love;' read /ro·gaρ/ with nasalization of the *c*).

Of course, the verbal noun can also simply be the object of the verb, although this doesn't properly belong to a chapter on relative construction:

ro·gád-sa mo guidi 'I have prayed my prayer' (*Fél. Ep.* 412).

This construction was so popular that it was imitated in Hiberno-Latin, that is, in Latin texts written by Irish writers. A few examples from the *Nauigatio Sancti Brendani* shall suffice: *exsultabant exsultatione* 'they rejoiced in rejoicing' (NSB 1), *opus operatus est* 'he did a work' (NSB 5), *de habitatione in qua habitaui* 'from the dwelling in which I dwelled' (NSB 7). Another nice example of this love of etymological charades, though strictly speaking no *figura etymologica*, is *quomodo potest in corporali creatura lumen incorporale corporaliter ardere* 'how can a non-physical light burn physically in a physical thing?' (NSB 12).

Illustration 49.3:
ba léimm ro·leblaing 'it was a leap he leaped'

49.6. Conjunctions and dependent clauses

The following is a list of Old Irish conjunctions, mainly compiled from GOI 546–564. Note these conventions:

1. Superscript ^{L} and ^{N} mean, as usual, that the conjunction lenites/nasalizes the *anlaut* of the immediately following element, irrespective of the type of clause.

2. Superscript ^{RN} means that a nasalizing relative clause follows the conjunction. But keep in mind that instead of a nasalizing relative clause often an independent non-relative construction can be used.

3. In case a conjunction is not especially marked by a superscript ^{RN}, an independent non-relative main clause construction follows it.

4. 'Independent' means that independent verbal forms (i.e., absolute, resp. deuterotonic forms) follow the conjunction.

5. 'Dependent' means that dependent verbal forms (i.e., conjunct, resp. prototonic forms) follow the conjunction.

6. The arrow → highlights frequently used conjunctions.

49.6.1. Copulative and disjunctive conjunctions

Independent:

→   1.1. *ocus^L, ocuis^L, acus^L; os* 'and' (the usual connector of coordinated phrases and clauses)

     1.2. *scéo^L, scéu^L* 'and' (only in early poetry and 'rhetorics')

     1.3. *-ch* 'and' (in early texts only, usually suffixed to proclitics)

     1.4. *noch* 'and; however' (sometimes used at the head of a main clause as an emphatic form of 'and;' more often used in adversative or causal meaning, may be accompanied by *ém, ám* 'indeed', *immurgu* 'however' or *colléic* 'yet')

     1.5. *sech$^{(L?)}$* 'and' (combines two parallel clauses)

     1.6. *eter (etir, itir)... ocus^L... (ocus^L...)* 'and' (links parallel elements into a larger unit)

→   1.7. *sech* 'however, that means' (usually followed by the copula)

     1.8. *emid* $^{(RN\,?)}$*... emid*$^{(RN\,?)}$ 'as well... as' (on its own *emid* means 'nearly; as it were')

→   1.9. *no^L, nó^L, nu^L, nú^L* 'or'

     1.10. *rodbo^L, rodbu^L, robo^L, robu^L* 'either... or' (in coordinated disjunctive phrases; *rodbo* appears either before the first element, with the other elements introduced by *no*, or before all elements, or before later elements only)

     1.11. *airc, airg(g)* 'or'

     1.12. *cenmithá*$^{RN\ or\ independent\ clause}$ 'besides that'

49.6.2. Temporal conjunctions

Independent:

→   2.1. *in tain*^{RN}, *in tan*^{RN}, *tan*^{RN} 'when'
→   2.2. *a*^{N + RN}, neg. *an(n)a* ^{RN}, with *ro: arru-*^{RN}, *anru-*^{RN} 'when, while'
→   2.3. *lase*^{RN}, *lasse*^{RN} 'while, when; *rarely*: whereas'
→   2.4. *céin*^{RN}, *cé(i)ne*^{RN} 'as long'
→   2.5. *ó*^L 'since; after; because'
      2.6. *íarsindí* 'after'
→   2.7. *resíu, risíu* 'before' (followed by a perfective subjunctive; later followed by ^{RN})

Dependent:

→   2.8. *dia*^N 'when' (this meaning only with the narrative preterite)

49.6.3. Consecutive and final conjunctions

Independent:

→   3.1. *co*^L, *coni* 'so that, in order that' (in the glosses in translation of Latin constructions)
      3.2. *afameinn*^{RN}, *abamin*^{RN} '*utinam*, if only'
→   3.3. *dano (dana, daniu, daneu)* 'then; so, also' (never at the beginning of clauses)
→   3.4. *didiu* 'then; now'
→   3.5. *tra* 'now, therefore, then'

Dependent:

→   3.6. *co*^N, *con*^N, *con(n)a*, *con(n)ac(h)on* 'until; so that; in order that, that (explicative)'
→   3.7. *ara*^N, neg. *arna, arná, arnac(h)on* '(so) that; in order that; that (explicative)'

49.6.4. Conditional conjunctions

Independent:

→   4.1. *ma*^L, *má*^L, neg. *mani* 'if'
→   4.2. *acht* 'provided that; if only' (followed by a perfective subjunctive)

Dependent:

→   4.3. *dia*^N 'if' (only in positive conditional clauses with the subjunctive)

49.6.5. Causal conjunctions

Independent:

→   5.1. *(h)óre*^{RN}, *húare*^{RN} 'because, since'
      5.2. *fo bíth*^{RN} 'because'
      5.3. *dég*^{RN} 'because'
      5.4. *ol*^{RN}, neg. *ol ni* 'because'
→   5.5. *air*^(L), *ar*^(L) 'since, for'

49.6.6. Adversative conjunctions

Independent:

     6.1. *cammaib, cammaif, camaiph* 'however, nevertheless'

→   6.2. *immurgu* 'however'

→   6.3. *acht* 'but, except' (in the context of negative clauses also 'only')

→   6.4. *cía*^{L}, *cé*^{L}, neg. *cení, ceni, cini* 'although, even if; also: that (explicative)'

Dependent:

     6.5. *in*^{N}... *in*^{N}... 'be it… or be it…'

→   6.6. *in*^{N}... *fa*^{L}... 'be it… or be it…'

49.6.7. Comparative conjunctions

Independent:

→   7.1. *amal*^{RN} 'as; as if'

     7.2. *feib*^{RN} 'as; as if'

     7.3. *in chruth*^{RN} 'so, as'

     7.4. *is cumme*^{RN} 'it is the same as if' (the compared clauses are linked by *ocus*)

Lesson 50

50.1. The augment (the particle *ro*, etc.)

We will now turn to a very important, but at the same time highly complex lesson of Old Irish grammar. Certain particles, i.e., grammatical elements, can be added to nearly all verbal forms to modify aspects of their meaning, i.e., to convey perfectivity (e.g., non-perfective *as·bert* '(s)he said' vs. perfective *as·rubart* '(s)he has said') or potentiality (e.g., *as·beir* '(s)he says' vs. potential *as·robair* '(s)he can say'). MᶜCONE (EIV 91) calls the elements responsible for the semantic shift the *augment*, because they are *augmented* (= added) to an already existing verbal form. I will follow his suggestion. In dictionaries and grammars you will frequently find the term *perfect(ive) forms*, what I call *augmented forms* in this book. Since by far the most frequent of these elements is *ro*, these forms are sometimes called *ro*-forms, but this is imprecise as other particles are used as well.

With the exception of the imperative, the augment may fundamentally be added to all tenses and moods of Old Irish (including the subjunctive and the future, which we have not learned so far). Most frequently, however, it appears in the preterite, thereby transforming it into a perfect. Less frequently, in descending order, it appears in the present and imperfect subjunctive and in the present indicative. In other tenses and moods it is very rare indeed.

The augment characterizes a verbal action either from a *resultative* point of view, or characterizes it as *potential*. *Resultative* means that the verbal action happened at a previous time but has a significance within the contextual frame of reference. *Potential* means that the verbal action, which does not necessarily take place at the present, is characterized as possible or probable in various degrees. Below I will give a brief account of what this actually means. But you can best read about these questions in all necessary detail in EIV 93–11.

50.1.1. The resultative augment

In its resultative meaning the augment is most frequently used with Old Irish preterites. Augmented preterites have a certain similarity with English 'have'-perfects and are very often called *perfects* even in Irish. Unaugmented preterites ('true preterites') are used in purely narrative contexts in Old Irish and can practically always be rendered by English past tense verbs; on the other hand, where in English a perfect would naturally be used the verbal action is usually expressed by an augmented preterite in Old Irish, too, e.g., compare the unaugmented preterite *carsu in fer-so* 'I loved this man' (but that was a folly of my past and I no longer have any feelings for him) vs. the augmented preterite *ro·carus Connle Rúad* 'I have fallen in love with red-haired Connle' (and I desire him now) (EC 3).

But between these two relatively well-defined poles a large grey zone exists, where Old Irish uses augmented preterites, which cannot be translated by English perfects. Compare the following example: *ad·opart Crimthann in port-sin du Pátricc, ar ba Pátric du·bert baithis du Chrimthunn 7 i Slébti ad·ranact Crimthann* 'Crimthann offered that place to Patrick, for it was Patrick who conferred baptism upon Crimthann, and (it is) in Slébte that Crimthann was/is buried' (*Thes.* ii 242.9–10). The first three verbal forms (*ad·opart, ba, du·bert*) are unaugmented preterites and correspond to English verbs in the past tense. The fourth verbal form, however, *ad·ranac[h]t*, is the preterite passive *ad·anacht* 'was buried,' augmented by the particle *ro-*. By using the augmented preterite and thus giving the verb a resultative meaning, the author of the story wanted to emphasize the significance which the fact that Crimthann had been buried in Slébte had for his own present time and, last but not least, for the narration. It looks as if augmented forms can always be used where a present significance of a past action is understood.

Where one of two or more verbal actions is characterized by a resultative augment, the action of the augmented verb has to be understood as having been completed before that of the other verbs. 'The use of the resultative to express such anteriority appears to be confined to the subordinate clause.' (EIV 99) Compare the example: *ó ro·boí dá laa 7 dí aidchi forsin muir, co·n-accae a dochum in fer isin charput íarsin muir* 'when he had been two days and two nights on the sea, he saw a man in a chariot coming towards him along the sea' (IB 32). The action of the subordinate clause *ro·boí* 'had been' has taken place earlier than that of the main clause *co·n-accae* 'saw' and is therefore characterized by a resultative augment.

Apart from referring to a true present action the Old Irish present tense can also be used for habitual or general statements. Clauses dependent on such presents usually contain present indicatives or subjunctives themselves. To stress the chronological precedence of the dependent clause's action, the augmented tense or mood demanded by context and syntax is used. Compare the following example: *is in núall do·ngniat hó ru·maid fora naimtea remib* 'it is the cry that they make when their enemies are/have been routed before them' (*Ml.* 51c9). The statement of the main clause ('it is the cry that they make') is of a general nature and therefore in the present tense. Old Irish syntax demands that the dependent clause be also in the present tense in this case. In order to express the logical precedence of the action in the dependent clause (first the enemies have to be routed, then the winners can make a cry of victory) the resultative augment *ro* is added to the present tense form *maidid → ro·maid*. While in English such a combination of present tense and anteriority is impossible, this is easy to achieve in Old Irish by augmentation.

Basically the same rules apply in the case of habitual or general statements in the past. Instead of the present indicative and subjunctive, in this case the imperfect indicative and past subjunctive are used. Both can be augmented to indicate anteriority: *Baí carpat ríg hi Temair. No·gabtais dá ech óendatha nad·ragbatais ríam for carpat.* 'There was a king's chariot in Tara. Two horses of the same color that had never been yoked before used to be put under the chariot' (*Ériu* 6, 134.5–6). *ragbatais* is the 3rd pl. passive imperfect *·gaibtis* 'used to be taken' with the augment *ro*, with assimilation of its vowel to the *a* of the root *gab-*.

50.1.2. The potential augment

The augment with potential force is formally identical to the resultative augment, but it can be used in any tense and mood (with the exception of the imperative) and it is not restricted to dependent clauses. It is, however, mainly used with the present and past subjunctive, less so with the present indicative, and rarely outside of these. An example for the augmented present indicative is: *at·robair cach cenél* 'every [sc. grammatical] gender can say [= express] it' (*Sg.* 190b4). An augmented present subjunctive and present indicative is found in *cia ru·bé cen ní diib, ní·rubai cenaib huli* 'though it may be able to be without one of them, it cannot be without them all' (*Ml.* 20d4). The following example contains an augmented preterite with resultative force and an augmented past subjunctive with potential meaning: *connacon·rabae ní ro·scrútais* 'so that there was nothing that they could examine' (*Ml.* 80b9).

Direct orders are given in the imperative in Old Irish, e.g., 2nd pl. *dílgid* 'forgive!' (*Wb.* 18a11) (from W2b *do·luigi*); more general requests can be made in the jussive subjunctive, e.g., *du·logaid do chách* '(you are to) forgive everyone' (*Ml.* 65a10). Jussives can be augmented to express a less determined wish, e.g., *da·rolgid dom tra in frithorcuin-sin* 'may you forgive me, then, that offence' (*Wb.* 18a12).

Final clauses that are introduced by the conjunctions *ara^N* 'in order that,' *co^{L/N}* 'so that,' *arna* 'in order that not,' *cona, conna, coni* 'so that not' contain augmented and unaugmented subjunctives in free distribution.

50.2. The choice of the correct augment

Most verbs use *ro* as their augment. This particle was originally an ordinary preverb and is indeed still used as such in a handful of verbs, e.g., *ro·icc* 'to reach,' *ro·cluinethar* 'to hear,' etc., but eventually it acquired mainly grammatical functions within Old Irish. *ro* has the by-form *ru*, e.g.,

as·rubartammar 'we have said.' When *ro* comes to stand in stressed position immediately before a reduplicated verbal form, it is changed to *róe-* and the first syllable of the reduplication is lost on the surface, e.g., unaugmented reduplicated preterite *ní·memaid* 'it did not break,' but augmented *ní·róemaid* 'it has not broken' (see also 55.3.2 note 8). As a consequence of *ro*'s 'preverbal prehistory' it still largely appears in the appropriate position in compound verbs demanded by the rules of positional hierarchy (see 50.3 below). But a number of verbs either use other particles/preverbs as their augment or take recourse to different means of augmentation altogether:

Illustration 50.1:
dom·roilge, a muimme!
'may you forgive me, mum!'

50.2.1. Simple verbs

1. Most simple verbs use *ro* as their augment. As to the position of *ro* see 50.3 below.

2. A few verbs are augmented by preverbs other than *ro*. I will give a few actually attested forms for every case, citing the underlying forms in formal representation (see 15.2):

   1. *ib-* (S1a) 'to drink': *ess-ib-* (3rd sg. pret. deut. *as·ib* '(s)he has drunken,' 3rd sg. pres. subj. prot. *·esbe* '(s)he may drink')

   2. *lu-* (H3) 'to drink': *ess-lu-* (3rd sg. pres. subj. deut. *as·lú* '(s)he may drink')

   3. *ith-/ed-* (S1a) 'to eat': *dī-uss/fo(?)-ith-/-ed-* (3rd sg. pret. prot. *·duaid* '(s)he has eaten')

   4. *sed-* (S1a) 'to sit': *dī-in-sed-* (3rd pl. pres. subj. prot. *·deset* 'they may sit,' 3rd sg. pret. deut. *do·esid* '(s)he has sat')

   5. *leg-* (S1a) 'to lie': *dī-in-leg-* (3rd pl. pres. subj. prot. *·deilset* 'they may lie,' 3rd sg. pret. prot. *·dellig* '(s)he has lain')

   6. *mlig-* (S1a) 'to milk': *to-uss-mlig-* (1st sg. pret. deut. *do·ommalg* 'I have milked')

   7. *to(n)g-* (S1c) 'to swear': *to-cum-to(n)g-* (3rd sg. pret. deut. *du·cuitig* '(s)he has sworn')

3. Two, possibly three verbs use suppletion to create their augmented forms. That means these are built on completely different roots altogether. The first two verbs are extremely important; augmented verbal forms of these occur frequently:

   1. *ber-* (S1a) 'to carry': *ro-uc-* inflects as a W2b verb: 1st sg. pres. prot. *·rucaim-se* 'I can carry,' 3rd sg. pres. subj. prot. *·ruca* '(s)he may carry,' 2nd sg. pret. deut. *ro·ucais* 'thou hast carried,' etc.

2. *tēg-* (S1a) 'to go': *dī-cum-feth-* inflects as a S1b verb: 3rd sg. pres. s-subj. deut. *do·coí*, prot. *·dich* '(s)he may go,' 3rd pl. *do·coíset*, *·dichset*, *·dechsat* 'they may go,' 1st sg. suffixless pret. deut. *do·coad*, prot. *·dechud* 'I have gone,' 3rd sg. *do·cuaid*, *·dechuid* '(s)he has gone,' 3rd pl. *do·cotar*, *·dechutar* 'they have gone,' etc.

3. *gat-* (W1) 'to steal': *to-ell-* (W1) (3rd sg. pret. deut. *du·ell* '(s)he has stolen')

50.2.2. Compound verbs

1. Most compound verbs use *ro* as their augment. As to the position of *ro* see 50.3 below.

2. Augment *ad*: With only a few exceptions, all compound verbs that have the preverb *cum/con* as their first element and whose second element (a further preverb or the root) begins with a consonant other than *f* use the particle *ad* as their augment. Used as augment, *ad* always comes after *cum/con*. Because of the effects of syncope the augment *ad* may disappear completely as a visible element in certain prototonic forms, but it can be securely inferred from its effects on the syncope pattern of the following syllables, e.g., unaugmented 3rd sg. impf. subj. *·cosctrad* '(s)he would destroy' (< **cum-scarad*) vs. augmented *·comtscarad* '(s)he might destroy' (< **cum-ad-scarad*) from *con·scara* (W1) 'to destroy,' or unaugmented 3rd pl. pret. *·cottlaiset* 'they slept' (< **cum-tolaiset*) vs. augmented *·comttaltsat* 'they have slept' (< **cum-ad-tolaiset*) from *con·tuili* (W2b) 'to sleep.'

3. Augment *cum/con*: No simple rule can be set up for the use of *cum/con* as augment. It seems to be restricted to a few compound S1 and S3-verbs. It is attested for the following roots: S1 *aneg-*, *bo(n)g-*, *fed-*, *féd-*, *lo(n)g-*, *nig-*, *org-*, *rig-*, *to(n)g-*, S3 *be(n)-*, *fe(n)-*, *re(n)-*. In the case of compounds of *org-* 'to slay' *cum/con* is the only possible augment; in the case of compounds of the other roots *cum/con* is restricted to certain preverbs, e.g., S1 *do·indnaig* 'to bestow' → unaugmented 3rd sg. t-pret. *do·indnacht* '(s)he bestowed,' augmented *do·écomnacht* '(s)he has bestowed' (< **to-in-cum-anacht*); S3 *do·ben* 'to cut off' → unaugmented 3rd sg. redupl. pret. *do·bí* '(s)he cut off,' augmented *do·combai* '(s)he has cut off;' note especially S1 *in·fét* 'to tell, to relate' → unaugmented 3rd sg. pret. *in·fíd*, augmented *in·cuaid*; similarly S1 *ad·fét* 'to tell' → augmented 3rd sg. pret. *ad·cuaid*.

4. A few verbs create their augmented stems by suppletion:

1. *do·beir* 'to bring, to give' is unique in having two different augmented stems, depending on the meaning: *to-r(o)-at-*, which inflects as a W2a verb, is used for the meaning 'to give,' *to-uc-*, which inflects as a W2b verb, for the meaning 'to bring': e.g., 3rd sg. s-pret. *do·rat*, *·tarat* '(s)he has given,' 3rd pl. *do·ratsat*, *·tartsat* 'they have given' 3rd sg. a-subj. *do·rata*, *·tarta* '(s)he may give,' 3rd pl. *do·ratat*, *·tartat* 'they may give;' and 3rd sg. s-pret. *do·ucc/do·uicc/do·uccai*, *·tucc/·tuicc* '(s)has brought,' 3rd pl. *do·uccsat*, *·tuccsat* 'they have brought,' 3rd sg. a-subj. *do·ucca*, *·tucca* '(s)he may bring,' 3rd pl. *do·uccat*, *·tuccat* 'they may bring.'

2. Some compounds of *téit* 'to go' replace *tēg-* with *de-cum-feth-*, which inflects as a S1b verb (see 50.3.1.2.3): *do·tét* 'to come,' *fris·táet* 'to come against, to oppose,' *for·tét* 'to help,' *remi·tét* 'to go before, to precede.'

3. *fo·ceird* (S1a), *·cuirethar* (W2b) 'to put' and its compounds combine the augment *ro* with a change to the root H1 *la-*: *ro-la-*, e.g., 3rd sg. unaugm. pret. *fo·caird* '(s)he put,' but augmented s-pret. *ro·lá*, *·rala* '(s)he has put,' 3rd pl. *ro·láiset*, *·rolsat* 'they have put,' 1st sg. a-subj. prot. *·rol* 'I may put,' 3rd pl. prot. *·rolat* 'they may put.'

4. The augmented deuterotonic (!) preterite of *ad·cí* 'to see' is *ad·condairc* 'has seen' (inflecting like a suffixless preterite). There is no prototonic form, after conjunct particles the dependent form of the unaugmented preterite *·accae* is used (see 44.7.3.). Apart from the preterite, *ad·cí* has no augmented forms.

5. A few verbs do not distinguish between unaugmented and augmented forms at all:

1. Compounds of *·ic* (S1a) and *·gni(n)* (S3) are never augmented, even where the syntax would demand it.
2. Compounds with the lexical preverb *ro* like *ad·roilli, ·áirilli* (H2) 'to deserve' (< *ad-ro-slī-) cannot be augmented.
3. The compounds *ro·finnadar* (S3) 'to find out,' its preterito-present *ro·fitir* 'to have found out, to know,' *ro·cluinethar* (S3) 'to hear' and *ro·laimethar* (S2) 'to dare' have *ro* in independent position, but lose it in dependent position, irrespective of whether the syntax would demand an augment or not.
4. The root *tā-* (H1) in the substantive verb *at·tá* and in *do·esta* 'to be absent, to be wanting' cannot be augmented, but its suppletive stem *bī-* (H2; see Appendix F.11) can be augmented in the normal way. The compound *in-tā-/ad-cum-tā-* 'to get' retains the root *tā-* throughout the paradigm. Its dependent form is *·éta*, its independent form *ad·cota*. Neither can be augmented.
5. *fo·gaib* (S2) (with its suppletive preterite *fo·fúair*) 'to find' cannot be augmented. *ad·cí* (H2) 'to see' can only be augmented in the independent preterite.

50.3. The position of the augment

McCONE (EIV 90) established for Old Irish the following positional hierarchy of preverbs in compounds:

1	2	3	4	5
to	for	ad	cum	uss
	fris	ath(e)	ro	ne
	eter	ar(e)		
	imb(e)	de/dī		
	ess			
	fo			
	in(de)			

Illustration 50.2: The positional hierarchy of Old Irish preverbs

Positional hierarchy means that in compounds containing more than one preverb like *do·imthiret* 'to serve' (< *to-imbe-athe-reth- = three preverbs) there is a tendency for a preverb belonging to column 2 (like *imb(e)*) to come before a preverb of column 3 (like *ath(e)*); *to* will always be the first preverb in a compound. The hierarchy within a column cannot be determined with absolute certainty. This hierarchy seems to have been observed fairly rigidly in so-called 'primary' composition, meaning in old, genuinely Irish formations (see EIV 89 for examples). In 'secondary' composition, meaning in calques on Latin compounds on the one hand and in new formations that build on existing, already lexicalized compounds on the other hand, this positional hierarchy need no longer be adhered to.

Regarding the position of the augment, the following complex development is observable within the history of early Irish:

1. In the oldest system of augmentation grammatical *ro* is placed at that position within a compound where it belongs according to the positional hierarchy of preverbs, i.e., before *uss*, *ne* and *cum/con*, but after any other preverb, with the one provision that it never comes to stand before the first lexical preverb. In the later period this rule is weakened. McCone calls this system of placement the *preverbal ro*. Due to the added syllable of the augment, the syncope pattern of augmented verbal forms can differ decisively from that of unaugmented forms. In the case of compound verbs, this adds yet another dimension to the already existing opposition between deuterotonic and prototonic verbal forms. Look at the following example, the 3rd pl. s-preterite of *do·sluindi* 'to deny':

	deuterotonic	prototonic
unaugmented	*do·sluind†set*	*·díl†tiset*
augmented	*do·ríl†tiset*	*·der†lind†set*

Illustration 50.3: The result of augmentation on the deuterotonic/prototonic-opposition

This high degree of alternations led to a propensity towards levelling within the paradigm, for example in the form of 'wrong' syncope patterns or other consequences of mutual influence, e.g., in the example above *do·ríltiset* instead of historically expected **do·roltaiset*.

In the case of simple verbs *ro* was treated as a normal preverb. In independent position it came to stand in unstressed position, e.g., *rom·gabsat* 'they have taken me,' *ro·memdatar* 'they have broken,' in dependent position, however, it was promoted into stressed position with all concomitant shifts of the syncope pattern, e.g., *condom·ragbaiset* 'so that they have taken me,' *ní·róemdatar* 'they have not broken.'

2. This state of synchronic 'unpredictability' of augmented forms with *preverbal ro* compared to the underlying unaugmented forms put pressure on the system towards its simplification as a whole. The first step was the introduction of *prevocalic ro* in compound verbs: this is prefixed as elided *r'* immediately before a vocalically *anlauting* preverb in the stressed part of the verb, even if *ro* ought to follow this preverb according to the positional hierarchy, e.g., original augmented *do·argart* (to-ad-<u>ro</u>-gar-) '(s)he has pleaded' → *do·racart* (to-<u>ro</u>-ad-gar-). This new augmented preterite *do·racart* is very easily recognizable beside the unaugmented preterite *do·acart*. *Prevocalic ro* may also stand before the first lexical preverb of a compound, e.g., original augmented prototonic present passive *·immforlangar* (imbi-fo-<u>ro</u>-long-) 'it can be caused' → *·rimmfolngar*, which is easily recognizable beside unaugmented *·immfolngar*. The great advantage of *prevocalic ro* is that because of the elision of its *o* the syllable count of the word as a whole is not disrupted and the syncope pattern doesn't change. This leads to a higher degree of paradigmatic homogeneity.

3. To avoid the complications caused by the shifting syncope pattern, in simple verbs *ro* developed into a plain conjunct particle during the Old Irish period. That means it always came to stand in pretonic position; if another conjunct particle was added, it coalesced with *ro*. To use the examples from above, instead of classical Old Irish *condom·ragbaiset*, now *corom·gabsat* would be used, or *níro·memdatar* instead of *ní·róemdatar*. This state of affairs can be termed *proclitic ro*.

4. In the case of compound verbs, *prevocalic ro* could of course not be used where the stressed part of the verb began with a consonant. In order to avoid the complex system of *preverbal ro* even in these cases, the *proclitic ro*-solution of simple verbs was utilized, which always appeared in pretonic position. This means that in dependent position *ro* was added directly to a conjunct particle, in independent position it was added to the first pretonic preverb, e.g., original augmented preterite *do·ríltisset* (*di-ro-slond-*) 'they have denied' → *doro·sluindset*, which is easily recognizable beside unaugmented *do·sluindset*. Thus the syncope pattern of the verb was not disrupted. *Proclitic ro* has a leniting effect on the stressed part of the verb.

5. In a further step of simplification the use of *ro* as augment was extended to verbs that originally had no augment or used a different one.

6. In a final step *ro* was treated as a true conjunct particle: after it the regular dependent form of the verb was used.

If the above has left you totally confused, don't let that discourage you. The position of the augment actually is a highly complex question. I have only given a very rough description of all the problems involved. For a thorough and truly comprehensive discussion you should read the relevant chapters in Kim MCCONE's *Early Irish Verb* (127–161).

Lesson 51

51.1. From the *Táin Bó Cúailnge*

The following short episode is from the *Macgnímrada Con Culainn* (TBC 552–560), the 'boyhood deeds of Cú Chulainn.' It tells us how one day on his way to a banquet King Conchobar visits the playground of the boys of the Ulaid to receive their blessings for the journey. He watches the boys at their usual games, but there is one boy standing out among all the others. They are playing *áin phuill* 'driving of the hole,' a mixture of golf and hockey.

Co·n-accae [*sc.* Conchobar] íarum Coin Culaind oc áin líathróite frisna trí cóecta mac, 7 birt a rróenu forru. In tan ba [n-]áin phuill do·gnítis, no·línad-som in poll dia líathróitib 7 ní·cumcaitis in maic a ersclaigi. In tan batar [n-]é-seom uili do·bidctis in poll, ara·cliched-som a óenur conná·téiged cid óenlíathróit ind. In tan ba n-imthrascrad do·gnítis, do·scarad-som inna trí cóecta mac a óenur 7 ní·comricced imbi-seom lín a thrascartha. In tan dano ba n-imdírech do·gnítis, dos·riged-som uili co·mbítis tornochta, 7 nocon·ructais-seom immorro cid a delg asa brot-som nammá.

Transcription

ko·vake koνχǝβǝp iapuµ kov' guλǝn' og āv' λ'iaθōōd'e f'r'is-na t'r'ī koigda mak, ogus b'ir't' a roivu foru. in dav ba vāv' φul' do·γ'v'īd'ǝs', no·l'īvǝd-soµ in bol d'iä λ'iaθōōd'ǝβ' ogus v'ī·kuµgǝd'ǝs' in µak' a erskǝy'i. in dav badǝp vē-s'oµ uλ'i do·β'iδ'g'd'ǝs' in bol, apa·k'l'iχ'ǝδ-soµ a oivup konā·d'ēγ'ǝδ k'iδ' oivλ'iaθōōd' in'd. in dav ba v'im'θǝǝskpǝδ do·γ'v'ī-d'ǝs', do·skapǝδ-soµ ina t'r'ī koigda mak a oivup ogus v'ī·koµ'p'ǝg'ǝδ im'b'i-s'oµ l'īv a θǝaskǝpθa. in dav davo ba v'im'δ'īp'ǝχ do·γ'v'īd'ǝs', dos·r'iγǝδ-soµ uλ'i ko·m'b'īd'ǝs' tornoχta, ogus vokǝv·rugdǝs'-s'oµ k'iδ' a δ'elg asa βpot-soµ namā.

Illustration 51.1:
isin chluichemaig 'on the playground'

257

Lesson 51

51.2. Varia

1. The phrase *is marb, ba marb*, literally 'is dead, was dead,' actually means 'dies, died'.

2. Apart from being the augmented suppletive stem of *do·beir* in the meaning 'to bring,' *do·uccai, ·tuccai* (W2b) can also be used as an independent verb in its own right with the meaning 'to understand.'

3. The interrogative pronoun *cid/ced* 'what is it,' followed by a nasalizing relative clause, means 'why.'

4. The particles *olse, olsi, olseat* /oλs'e oλs'i oλs'ead/ mean 'he, she, they said' respectively. In the later language they were reinterpreted as containing the independent pronouns: *ol sé, ol sí, ol síat.*

5. The *Donn Cúailnge*, the Brown Bull of Cúailnge, is the object of contention in the *Táin Bó Cúailnge.*

6. The particle *os*, followed by an independent pronoun (see 34.6.), is translated 'and (at the same time)' and introduces a side remark on the main statement, e.g., in UR §3: *fili ón at óga fíriána folad*, [enumerating a large number of qualifications here], *os é mac filed 7 aue araili* 'that is a poet whose qualifications are complete and genuine, […], and he is the son of a poet and the grandson of another,' i.e., while at the same time he is the son and grandson of a poet. The particle takes the form *ot* before the 3rd pl. pronoun, e.g., in the following statement apparently on zombies: *delb anmandae foraib, ot hé marbdai ca-lléic* 'a living form on them, and they dead at the same time nevertheless' (*Ml.* 130a3) (actually this gloss speaks of worldly treasures, which, although beautiful and desirable, are spiritually dead).

7. The nom. pl. *beóa*, instead of classical *bíi*, in sentence 20 shows the spread of the ending *-a* also to masculine adjectives.

51.3. Exercise

Old Irish

1. ** Tarḃfeis ḟer nÉrenn: no·marbthae tarb leo 7 no·ithed óenḟer a ṡáith de 7 no·ibed a enbruithe 7 no·cantae ór fírinne fair inna ligiu. (TBDD 123 ff.) 2. ** Do·bert goiste imma brágait fadesin, conid marb, húare nád·ndigni Abisolón a chomairli. (*Ml.* 23b10) 3. * Cach tan do·rrigénsaid maith arnaib bochtaib im' anmaim-se, is form-sa do·rigénsaid. (LU 2335) 4. * Cach tan ná·ndergénsaid maith arnaib bochtaib im' anmaim-se is form-sa ní·dergénsaid. (LU 2353) 5. ** Ro·lil dím m'ernaigde 7 ní·dechaid úaimm. (*Ml.* 54d7) 6. ** hÚare is hi foscud menman ro·rádus-sa inna bríathra as·ruburt, is airi in-sin ro·cúala-su guth m'ernaigde-se. (*Ml.* 50d7) 7. ** No·scrútainn-se, in tan no·mbiinn isnaib fochaidib, dús in·retarscar cairde nDé 7 a remcaissiu, 7 ní·tucus-sa in-sin, inru·etarscar fa naic. (*Ml.* 91c1) 8. * Ro·légsat canóin fetarlaici 7 nuḟíadnaissi amal ronda·légsam-ni, acht ronda·saíbset-som nammá. (*Ml.* 24d24) 9. ** Is hé forcenn du·rat-som forsna mmórchol du·rigensat a námait fris, díltud remdéicsen Dé de-som, húare nád·tarat dígail forsna hí du·rigénsat inna hí-sin fris-sium. (*Ml.* 91a21) 10. ** Ced ná·ronass do ḟóesam-su […] forsna maccu? (TBC 446) 11. * Nípu chían íarsin gním, ad·chuaid Fergus indossa, co·ndergéni-som [*sc.* Cú Chulainn] bét n-aile. (TBC 543 f.) 12. ** Con·aggab enech 7 anmain dam-sa, […] in fer muintire ruccad úaimm .i. mo chú. (TBC 594 ff.) 13. ** 'Indat é-side [*sc.* trí bráithir bat námait-som do

Ultaib] as·berat,' ol Cú Chulainn, 'nach móo fil do Ultaib i mbethaid ol-dás ro·mbeótar-som díb?' (TBC 704 f.) 14. ** [...] is do chuingid chomraic fri fer do·dechaid in mac fil and. (TBC 729 f.) 15. * 'Rot·ánacc-sa, á Cheltchair,' ol Cet mac Mágach, 'co dorus do thige. Ro·éiged immum. Tánaicc cách. Tánacc-su dano.' (SMMD 13.4-6) 16. * 'Do·reilcis gáe form-sa. Ro·léicius-sa gáe n-aile cucut-su co·ndechaid tret šlíasait ocus tre úachtar do macraille.' (SMMD 13.7–9) 17. ** 'Do·uccus-sa in mboin-se éim,' olsi, 'a síd Chrúachan conda·rodart in Donn Cúailnge lem.' (TBR 64-65) 18. ** In moltai, do·ngniinn-se tri bindius 7 chlais, ara·ruichíuir mo guth occaib. (*Ml.* 136a8) 19. * Ind fir, ind oic, ind eich, no·bítis im Maíl Fothertaig, do·gnítis cen chosc i-mmaig, fo·fertais graffaind [...]. (FR 221-224) 20. ** Cless maicc Con Culainn: Do·beired cloich inna chranntabaill 7 dos·léiced táthbéimm forsna éonu, co·ngaibed inna airberta díb, ot é béoa, conda·léiced úad isin n-áer do·ridissi. (AOA 2)

Transcription

1. tarβes' eᵖ v'ēp'ən: no·marβθe tarβ l'ehu ogus no·iθ'əδ oi̯v'eᵖ a hāθ' d'e ogus no·iβ'əδ a evβɾuθ'e ogus no·kante ōᵖ f'ı̆p'ən'e fap' ina λ'iɣ'u. 2. do·b'ert gos't'e ima βɾāɣəd' fəδ'és'əv', kov'iδ marβ, uap'e nāδ·n'd'iɣ'v'i *Abisolon* a χoμəp'λ'i. 3. kaχ dav do·r'iɣ'ēvsəδ' maθ' apnəβ' boχtəβ' im anməm'-s'e is form-sa do·r'iɣ'ēvsəδ'. 4. kaχ dav nā·n'd'ep'ɣ'ēvsəδ' maθ' apnəβ' boχtəβ' im anməm'-s'e is form-sa n'ı̆·d'ep'ɣ'ēvsəδ'. 5. ro·l'iλ' d'ı̆m m'epvəɣ'δ'e ogus n'ı̆·d'eχəδ' uam'. 6. uap'e is i βoskuδ μ'enməv ro·rāδus-sa ina b'r'iaθpa as·ruβurt, is ap'i in-s'iv ro·kuaλa-su guθ m'epvəɣ'δ'e-se. 7. no·skrūdən'-s'e, in dav no·m'b'iän' isnəβ' foχəδ'əβ', dūs in·r'edərskəp kap'd'e n'd'ē ogus a ρ'eμkəs'u, ogus n'ı̆·tugus-sa in-s'iv, inru·edərskəp fa nak'. 8. ro·l'ēɣsəδ kavōv' β'edəpλək'i ogus nuïaδvəs'i aμəλ ronda·l'ēɣsəμ-n'i, aχt ronda·saiβ's'əd-soμ nəmá. 9. is ē fork'en du·rad-soμ forsna mōpχoλ du·r'iɣ'ēvsəd a vāμəd' f'r'is', d'ıltuδ r'eμ'δ'ēg's'əv d'ē d'e-soμ, uap'e nāδ·dapəd d'ıɣəλ' forsna h'ı̆ du·ρ'iɣ'ēvsəd ina hı̆-s'iv f'r'is'-s'uμ. 10. k'eδ nā·rovəs do oi̯səμ-su forsna maku? 11. n'ı̆bu χ'iav iars'in ɣ'v'ı̆μ, aδ·χuäδ' f'epɣus indósa, ko·n'd'ep'ɣ'ēv'i-soμ b'ēd vaλ'e. 12. kov·agəβ ev'əχ ogus avμəv' daμ-sa, in f'ep mun't'əp'e rugəδ uam', eδ ōv mo χū. 13. 'indəd ē-s'iδ'e as·β'epəd,' oλ kū χuλən', 'naχ moö f'iλ' do ultəβ' i m'b'eθəδ' ol-dās ro·m'b'eu̯dəp-soμ d'ıβ?' 14. is do χuŋ'g'əδ' χoμpəg' f'r'i f'ep do·d'eχəδ' in mak f'iλ' and. 15. rod·āvəg-sa, ā χ'eltχəp',' oλ k'ed mak māɣəχ, 'ko dopus do θ'iɣ'e. ro·ēɣ'əδ imum. tāvəg' kāχ. tāvəg-su davo.' 16. 'do·r'eλ'g'əs' gai̯ form-sa. ro·l'ēg'us-sa gai̯ vaλ'e kugud-su ko·n'd'eχəδ' t'r'ed h'λ'iasəd' ogus t'r'e uaχtəp do μagpəl'e.' 17. 'do·ugus-sa in mbov'-s'e ēμ',' oλs'i, 'a s'ı̆δ' χɾuaχav konda·roδərt in don kual'ŋ'g'e l'em.' 18. in μolti, do·ŋ'g'iän'-s'e t'r'i β'in'd'us ogus χlas', apa·ρuχ'ı̆μp' mo ɣuθ ogəβ'. 19. ind iρ', ind oög', ind eχ', no·β'ı̆d'əs' im' mai̯λ' βoθ'ərtəɣ', do·g'n'ı̆d'əs' k'ev χosk i-máɣ', fo·f'epdəs' grafən'd'. 20. do·b'ep'əδ kloχ' ina χpantəβəl' ogus δos·l'ēg'əδ tāθβ'ēm' forsna hēu̯vu, ko·ŋgaβ'əδ ina hap'β'ərta d'ıβ', od ē bēu̯a, konda·l'ēg'əδ uaδ is'ən nai̯p do·ρ'ı̆δ'əs'i.

English

1. Bulls used to be killed by them, and they used to eat their fill of them, and they used to drink their broths and a song of truthfulness used to be sung upon them lying. 2. They gave nooses around their necks so that they died because their friends did not carry out (*OIr.*: make) their piece of advice. 3. Every time thou hast done a good thing for a poor (person) in our names, it is on us thou hast done it. 4. Every time thou hast not done a good thing for a poor (person) in our names, it is on us thou hast not done it. 5. Our prayers have not clung to us, but they have gone from us. 6. Since it is in darkness of mind they have spoken the words that they have spoken, it is therefore you have heard the voices of their prayers. 7. She did not use to investigate, when she was in tribulations, whether God's friendship had departed. It is therefore (*airi*) she has not understood it. 8. Thou hast read the canon as I have read it, but thou hast not perverted it (*OIr.*: her). 9. This is the end which they have put (*OIr.*: given) to the sins which my enemy had done against me because I had not given revenge on him who had done those things against me.

10. Your protection has been bound on the boy. 11. It was long after the deeds, which we have related now, that they have made another deed. 12. They have preserved (our) honor for us, the men of (our) household who have been taken from us. 13. It is he who used to say that there are more of the men who are alive than he has slain of them. 14. It is not to seek encounter against men that the boys who are here have come. 15. We did not reach you by the doors of your houses. Alarm was not sounded around us. Everybody did not come. You did not come. 16. You have not thrown spears at us. We have not cast other spears at you so that they have gone through your thighs. 17. They have brought these cows, so that the bulls (*tarb*) of the Laigin have bulled them for them. 18. The praise which we used to make in melody and choir, our voices have failed at it. 19. The man, who used to be around Máel Fothertaig, was he wont to act without reproof outside, was he wont to prepare a horse-race (= horse-races)? 20. I would (*OIr.:* imperfect) put (*OIr.:* give) stones into my sling and I would cast (them) a stunning blow on a bird, so that it would take the conscience from it (*OIr.:* him), and it (*os é*) still alive, so that I would release it from me into the air again.

51.4. Test

Explain which unaugmented verbal form underlies the following augmented forms.

·torchar:	_____	ro·carus:	_____	as·robair:	_____
·érbart:	_____	do·rónad:	_____	·dergénsaid:	_____
do·róet:	_____	as·ib:	_____	ro·suidigser:	_____
con·acab:	_____	do·raidled:	_____	ad·ráigsetar:	_____
ro·laus:	_____	con·acairt:	_____	for·róechan:	_____
do·cuaid:	_____	do·ratais:	_____	do·ruménair:	_____
·tuidchid:	_____	do·uccai:	_____	con·ascrasat:	_____
·tartsam:	_____	tucsat:	_____	·fargabsat:	_____
do·dechad:	_____	or	_____	ad·cuadatar:	_____
·robae:	_____	ro·nass:	_____	ro·bátar:	_____

Lesson 52

52.1. Prepositional relative constructions

Illustration 52.1:
fer snige dia·ruilil-si
'the snowman
to which she has clung'

Old Irish relative clauses can be introduced by prepositions, and such constructions are consequently called prepositional relative clauses. Compare German, English or Latin examples like *the man of whom I dream*, or *die Frau, für die mein Herz schlägt*, or *uir de quo nil nisi bonum narretur*. In Old Irish these are the only relative constructions where something like a separate relative particle is actually visible. This particle has the form *-a^N* after leniting prepositions, *etir*, *oc* and sometimes *for*, and *-sa^N* after all other prepositions. It is added directly to the preposition that stands at the head of the relative clause. The verb immediately follows in the dependent form. These are the possible combinations of Old Irish prepositions and the relative particle:

preposition	prepos. relative
a^H 'out of'	*asa^N·*
ar^L 'in front of, for'	*ara^N·*
co^H 'up to, until'	*cosa^N·*
co^N 'with'	
di^L 'from'	*dia^N·*
do^L 'to, for'	
etir, itir 'between'	*etera^N·, etira^N·*
fo^L 'under'	*foa^N·, fua^N·, fo^N·*
for 'upon'	*forsa^N·, fora^N·*
fri^H 'against'	*frisa^N·, frissa^N·*
i^N 'in, into'	see below
imm^L 'around'	*imma^N·, immo^N·*
la^H 'with, by'	*lasa^N·*
ó^L 'from'	*óa^N·, ua^N·, ó^N·*
oc 'at, by'	*occa^N·, oca^N·*
tri^L 'through'	*tresa^N·*

Illustration 52.2: The prepositional relatives

261

Examples for the use of these forms are:

intí fora·tuit-som 'the one upon whom it falls' (*Wb.* 4d15): *for* 'upon' + rel. *-a^N* + *do·tuit,
·tuit* 'to fall' = /fopa·dut'/

fil inis [...] imma·taitnet gabra réin 'there is an island [...] around which sea-horses glitter'
(IB 4): *imm^L* 'around' + rel. *-a^N* + *do·aitni, ·taitni* 'to shine' = /ima·dat'n'əd/

cid dia·tá Cophur in dá Muccida? 'What is it from which (the title) *Cophur in dá Muccida*
is?' (LL 32931): *di^L* 'from' + rel. *-a^N* + substantive verb *at·tá, ·tá* = /d'iä·dā/

cid ara·n-eperr Críth Gablach? 'Why (= what is it for which) is it called *Críth Gablach*?' (CG
1): *ar^L* + rel. *-a^N* + *as·beir, ·epir* 'to say' = apa·v'eb'ər/

cid asa·fordailtea grád túaithe? 'What is it out of which the grades of a *túath* have been
divided?' (CG 6): *as* 'out of' + rel. *-sa^N* + augmented *fo·dáli, ·fodlai* 'to divide' =
/asa·βordəl't'a/

Note:

1. The prepositional relative for both *di^L* 'from' and *do^L* 'to' is *dia^N·*.

2. The same formation underlies the conjunctions (!) *ara^N·* 'in order that' and *dia^N·* 'if, when.'

3. The only exception to the addition of the relative particle *-(s)a^N* is the preposition *i^N* 'in,' for
which no special relative form exists. Instead, plain *i^N·* is used, followed by a dependent verbal
form, e.g., *intí i·mbíi in spirut* 'the one in whom the spirit is' (*Wb.* 8b10), or *síd már i·taam* '(it is)
great peace in which we are (= live)' (EC 3).

4. In poetry in general and in prose before the substantive verb *bíid*, the vowel *a* of the particle
-sa^N may be dropped, but the remaining *-s^N* still retains its nasalizing effect, e.g., *mag find
fris'·mben muir* /f'r'is·m'b'ev/ 'a fair plain against which the sea beats' (IB 16), *las'·luid* /las·luð'/
'with whom he went' (*Fél.* June 15), or *táithiunn ní fris'·tarddam ar n-áthius* /f'r'is· dapdəµ/ 'we
have something against which we can put up our keenness' (*Thes.* ii, 203, 18 f.).

5. Before the *d* of infixed pronouns class C and before 3rd sg. forms of the copula in *-d* and *-b/-p*
the relative particle appears in the variant *-(s)in-, -(s)im-*, e.g., *arind·epur* 'for which I say it.' If the
added form of the copula contains one or more syllables, the vowel of the relative particle is
syncopated, e.g., *airmtis* 'so that they might be' < **ar-im-b(i)tis*. Exceptions to this rule are *dian-*
/d'iän-/, *foan* /foän-/ and *oan-* /oän-/.

6. In negative constructions instead of the particle *-(s)a^N* the negative relative *-na (-nach-)* or
-nacon- is used, e.g., *ocna·bíat* 'with which there are not,' *asnacha·tucad* 'out of which he would
not have brought them' (*Ml.* 125b7), or *(tíre) inna·bí bás na peccad na immarmus* 'lands in which
there are neither death nor sin nor transgression' (EC 3).

52.2. Word order

As stated already at the beginning of this book (see 5.7), in a 'normal' Old Irish sentence the
verbal form always comes first. It may only be preceded by a few conjunctions and particles like
ní·, in^N·, co^N·, etc. The verb is followed by the subject, the object and then by all other parts of the
sentence (VSO-order). Thus a typical Old Irish sentence would go, e.g., *benaid Cú Chulainn
omnai ara ciunn i suidiu* 'Cú Chulainn cuts down a tree before them there' (TBC 827 f.). But
building sentences exclusively that way would result in a rather dull and tedious narrative style
without syntactical variation, and in fact Old Irish word order is much more flexible, as you will

already have noticed a couple of times yourself while translating sentences from the exercises. I pointed out a few things in paragraph 3 of 24.3, but I will now explain other possible sentence constructions in more detail.

1. First of all, any part of the sentence may be promoted to the first position to award it special attention. This is called *fronting*. The fronted phrase is usually introduced by a form of the copula.

1.1. If the fronted phrase is the subject of the sentence (= *subject antecedent*), or if it is a neuter object pronoun, the rest of the sentence follows in a leniting relative construction (see 34.2 and 34.3).

1.2. If it is the object (= *object antecedent*), the rest of the sentence follows in a nasalizing or leniting relative construction (see 49.3).

1.3. If the relativized word stands in a prepositional construction within the relative clause, but does not do so in the superordinate clause, a prepositional relative construction (see 52.1) is used.

1.4. If, however, the fronted phrase itself is a prepositional phrase (= *prepositional antecedent*), the relativity of the rest of the sentence finds no formal expression, but a straightforward main clause construction is used, e.g., *is do thabairt díglae beirid in claideb-sin* 'it is to inflict (*lit.* give) vengeance (that) he carries that sword' (*Wb.* 6a13), i.e., here the fronted phrase *do thabairt díglae* 'for the inflicting of vengeance' is a prepositional expression containing the preposition *do^L*.

But in addition to nominal phrases, even subordinate clauses may be thus fronted, e.g., *is combat maithi coisctir* 'it is in order that they may be good they are reproved' (*Wb.* 31b25). In this case the subordinate clause *combat maithi* 'in order that they may be good' is fronted, and then followed by the rest of the sentence in a normal main clause construction.

2. Structurally different are constructions where some part of the sentence is brought to the front without copulaic introduction, and the rest of the sentence follows without any relative marking, but the fronted part is resumed by a pronoun, e.g., *barr buide fordut·tá ós gnúis chorcordai, bid ordan do rígdelbae* 'the blond hair, which is upon thee above a purple face, it will be a noble sign of thy kingly appearance' (EC 5), or *cluiche n-aímin inmeldach, agtait [...] fir 7 mná* 'a pleasant and delightful game, men and women play it' (IB 41). Sentences of this type are called 'cleft sentences.'

3. The VSO-order can be overridden if the subject of the sentence is further determined by a relative clause or a genitival or prepositional phrase. Thus in effect a word order VOS is arrived at, e.g., *imm·folngi inducbáil dó in molad ro·mmolastar Día* 'it causes glory to himself, the praise by which he has praised God' (*Ml.* 126b16). The subject *in molad* has the nasalizing relative clause *ro·mmolastar Día* dependent from it and is therefore moved to a position after the object *inducbáil*; or *ní·foircnea in fíni ithe neich di anúas* 'eating something of it from above does not put an end to a vine' (*Ml.* 102a15), where the genitive *neich* 'of something' and the prepostional phrase *di* 'from it (= her)' and the adverb *anúas* 'from above' are all part of the subject *ithe* 'eating.' Apparently, the sentence would sound rather clumsy if the whole subject phrase stood in its appropriate place immediately after the verb. Overlong phrases of this kind may also be moved to the very beginning of the sentence.

4. Other closely connected parts of the sentence, too, can be separated for the same reason. In the following example *(ní)·gáid do Día dígail for Saul inna n-olc do·rigéni-side fris* 'he did not pray to God for vengence on Saul for the bad things he had done to him' (*Ml.* 55d4), the genitive *inna n-olc* 'of the bad things' is directly dependent on *dígal* 'revenge,' nevertheless they are separated by a prepositional phrase to allow *inna n-olc* to be moved to the final position of the clause in order to be relativized.

5. A special case of suspension of the VSO-order is the omission of the verb, usually the copula or the substantive verb. This omission occurs frequently in descriptive passages, e.g., *súil glas bannach ina chind* 'a grey, lively eye in his head' (LU 9265), where a form of the substantive verb,

Illustration 52.3:
do fuil dom-sa! 'your blood for me!'

at·tá or *fil*, has been suppressed, or *maic-ni do-som* 'we are sons to him' (*Wb.* 19d8), with omission of *ammi*, 1st pl. of the copula. In fronted constructions of the type described in paragraph 1 above the copula may also always be left out. Depending on the context, sometimes other verbs have to be understood, e.g., in commands like *carpat dam-sa* 'a chariot to me!' (TBC 648), where Cú Chulainn certainly omitted the imperative *tabair!* 'give!' because of his impetuous character (not to mention the fact that he forgot the magic word *not·guidiu* 'please').

6. In poetry and in archaizing style, that means in certain stylized, rhetorical passages in Old Irish literature, which are called *retoiric* or *roscada* in Irish, it is possible to separate the stressed part of the verb from a preverbal particle or from its first preverb. The particle or first preverb remains at the very beginning of the sentence, but the rest of the verb is moved to the end. This feature is called *tmesis*, e.g., *nom- Choimmdiu -coíma* 'may God be kind to me' (*Thes.* ii 290.11). You will note that the lenition of the infixed pronoun *-mᴸ*, which in normal order *nom·choíma Coimmdiu* would be on the stressed part of the verb, in this case affects the subject, i.e., the first element immediately following the infixed pronoun.

7. In archaizing style, the complete verb may stand at the end of the sentence if there is no conjunct particle or infixed element involved. It then appears in the prototonic form, if it is a compound, or has conjunct endings, if it is a simple verb, even in independent position, e.g., *ar mind nAxal n-acallad* 'our diadem of apostles was spoken to' (ACC 82), which in normal prose would be *ad·gládad ar mind nAxal.*

Lesson 53

53.1. The subjunctive

The subjunctive mood (German *Konjunktiv*) has its name from the fact that it is frequently employed in subordinate clauses. That means it often appears in contexts which are 'subjugated' to other clauses. But this etymological explanation falls short of covering all of its aspects. The use of the subjunctive in Old Irish is rather similar to that in Latin. It usually conveys a certain measure of indefiniteness, indetermination or uncertainty of a verbal action. Try to keep this 'uncertainty' in mind when you encounter a subjunctive form in an Old Irish text—and you will encounter subjunctives very often indeed, as they are far more common in Old Irish than in English or German. The basic connotations of the subjunctive can be classified thus:

1. The subjunctive mood denotes that a verbal action is willed, wished or commanded. In main clauses it may thus serve as a kind of less determined imperative, e.g., *sén Dé don·fé* 'may God's blessing lead us' (*Thes.* ii 299.29) (*do·fé* = pres. subj. of S1 *do·feid* 'to lead'), or *druídecht nís·grádaigther* 'druidry, thou (rather) not love it' (EC 11), or *ní·comris fri báeth* 'thou (rather) not meet with a stupid person' (*Tecosca Cormaic*, LL 46159) (*·comris* = prototonic 2nd sg. pres. subj. of S1 *con·ricc* 'to meet, to encounter').

2. Related to this use in main clauses is the use of the subjunctive in subordinate final or consecutive clauses, especially after the final and consecutive conjunctions *araN·* and *coN·* '(so) that, in order that,' e.g., *as·bert Conchobor fria muintir ara·scortais a cairptiu* 'Conchobor told his people that they should unyoke their chariots' (CCC 2), or *conna·dechsam i n-adradu idal* 'that we may not go to adore idols' (*Ml.* 62d1).

3. Because the imperative is excluded from subordinate clauses, in its stead the subjunctive renders orders in indirect speech, e.g., *apair fris ad·mestar dúili dúilemon* 'tell him that he estimates the creations of the creator' (AM 32) (*ad·mestar* = 3rd sg. pres. subj. of *ad·midethar* 'to evaluate, to estimate;' the direct order to the 2nd person in the imperative would be: *aimmdithe dúili dúilemon!* 'estimate the creations of the creator!')

4. Because the subjunctive implies uncertainty, it has to be used whenever a statement is not completely real, but rather possible, probable, doubted or assumed. Therefore it is used after *bés* /b'ēs/ 'perhaps,' in indirect questions after *duus, dús* /duüs, dūs/ 'to see if,' in conditional ('if,' see 49.6.4) and concessive ('although,' see 49.6.6) clauses, when the conditioning or conceded action lies in the future or at an indefinite time, or whenever reference is made to an indefinite action. Not in all of these cases would an equivalent subjunctive construction be used in English or German. Examples are: *bés as·bera-su* 'perhaps thou mayest say' (*Thes.* ii 7.29); *dúus ind·aithirset* 'to see if they repent it' (*Wb.* 30b30) (*·aithirset* is prot. 3rd pl. pres. subj. of *ad·eirrig* 'to repent'); *má gabthair do neoch, is dam-sa ceta·gébthar* 'if it be taken by anyone, it will be taken by me first' (SergCC 4 f.); *cía bróenae·su do brattán, ní hé mo maccán chaíne* 'although thou wettest thy cloak (although thou shouldst wet thy cloak) it is not my son whom thou lamentest' (FR 191 f.); an example for the use of the subjunctive for a general, indefinite action is *cach anál do·ngneid* 'every breath you (should) take.'

5. After *acht* 'provided that; if only' and *resíu* 'before' augmented subjunctives (also called: perfective subjunctives) have to be used, e.g., *for·bia ardléigend nÉrenn co bráth acht nad·rogba for forcetal ná for scríbend* 'he will have supreme status of learning in Ireland forever, provided he would not take to teaching and writing' (TBDM); *do·scara cóecait macc diib resíu rístais dorus nEmna* 'he overthrows fifty of the boys, before they could reach the door of Emain Macha' (TBC 435 f.).

The negative of the subjunctive is formed with the negative particle *ní·* in non-relative contexts, and with *ná·, nád·* in relative constructions. In Old Irish the subjunctive mood is built on a separate subjunctive stem of the verb. Three different types of stem formation can be distinguished, depending on the inflectional class of the verb and/or its root shape. We will look at them in detail in the following lessons:

a-subjunctive
e-subjunctive
s-subjunctive

Illustration 53.1:
indat·ber-su lem-sa?
'may I take you with me?'

53.2. The a-subjunctive

The a-subjunctive is formed by all weak verbs, by H1 and H3 verbs, by strong verbs whose roots end in *-b, -r, -l, -m* or single *-n* (all S3 and some S1 and S2 verbs) and by *agaid* 'to drive' and its compounds. With the exception of W2a verbs the root final consonant is always non-palatalized before the ending of the a-subjunctive. In W2a verbs the root final consonant is always palatalized.

53.2.1. The standard a-subjunctive

The present of the a-subjunctive (and some future formations that we will learn in the next lesson) uses a separate set of endings, which may be termed 'a-ending set.' The a-ending set looks very much like the endings of W1 verbs, with the one great difference that the endings of the 1st and 2nd persons singular, both absolute and conjunct, have forms of their own. In the example below I use the S1 verb *beirid* 'to carry.' Note how the root final *r* /ρ/ is always non-palatalized throughout the paradigm:

person	absolute (independent)		conjunct (dependent)	
1st sg.	*bera*	Ca	*·ber*	C
2nd sg.	*berae*	Ce	*·berae*	Ce
3rd sg.	*beraid*	Cəδ'	*·bera*	Ca
rel.	*beras*	Cəs	-	
pass.	*berthair*	Cθəρ'	*·berthar*	Cθəρ
pass. rel.	*berthar*	Cθəρ	-	
1st pl.	*bermai*	Cmi	*·beram*	Cəμ
rel.	*bermae*	Cme	-	
2nd pl.	*berthae*	Cθe	*·beraid*	Cəδ'
3rd pl.	*berait*	Cəd'	*·berat*	Cəd
rel.	*bertae, beraite*	Cde, Cəd'e	-	
pass.	*bertair, beraitir*	Cdəρ', Cəd'əρ'	*·bertar*	Cdəρ
pass. rel.	*bertar, beratar*	Cdəρ, Cədəρ	-	

Illustration 53.2: The a-subjunctive of S1 *beirid*

Note:

1. Apart from the 1st and 2nd sg. the present subjunctive of W1 verbs is formally identical with the respective present indicative forms. This is also true of H1 verbs.

2. Apart from the 1st and 2nd sg. and the 3rd sg. conjunct the present subjunctive of W2a verbs is formally identical with the respective present indicative forms. The 1st sg. has the ending -*ea* /-a/ in the absolute, e.g., *léicea*, and zero / / in the conjunct, e.g., *·léic*; the 2nd sg. has the ending -*e*, e.g., *(·)léice*; the 3rd sg. conjunct has the ending -*ea* /-a/, e.g., *·léicea*. In early texts the 3rd sg. conjunct seems to have had the ending -*e*, e.g., *Día nime, ním·reilge* 'God in heaven, may he not leave me' (ACC 0).

3. In non-deponent W2b verbs and in deponent W2b verbs without the suffix -*aig*- the subjunctive is completely distinct from the present stem. Whereas in the present stem these verbs have the root vowel *u*, sometimes *o*, and usually a palatalized root final consonant, in the subjunctive stem the root vowel is *o* and the root final consonant is non-palatalized, e.g., pres. *ad·suidi* 'to hold fast,' but 2nd sg. pres. subj. *ad·sode* /aδ·soδe/, pres. *·cuirethar* 'to put,' but pres. subj. *·corathar* /·koρəθəρ/. When, however, the syllable after the root is syncopated, the root final consonant does become palatalized even here, e.g., 2nd sg. *·coirther* /·koρ'θ'əρ/. This is also true of most H3 verbs.

4. Among those verbs of the S1 and S3 classes that form an a-subjunctive, the present subjunctive is formally largely distinct from the present indicative, but the odd formal identity may occur here, too; compare, e.g., the 3rd pl. of *beirid*, which is *berait* /b'eρəd'/ both in the present indicative and in the subjunctive.

53.2.2. The a-subjunctive of S3 verbs

The subjunctive of S3 verbs deserves a more detailed treatment. In S3 verbs with roots ending in a vowel (usually *i*), the subjunctive forms are highly dissimilar to the present forms. For example, in *crenaid* 'to buy,' the subjunctive endings are added directly to the root *cri-*. Where an extra syllable is added after the subjunctive *a*, the *i* of the root and the *a* of the subjunctive stem coalesce into a short *e*, e.g., 3rd pl. relative *crete* < *cri-a-te*:

person		absolute (independent)		conjunct (dependent)	
1st sg.		n/a		·*créu*	eu̯
2nd sg.		*criae, crie*	ië	·*criae,* ·*crie*	ië
3rd sg.		*criaid, crieid*	iᴅ̇ꞌ	·*cria*	iä
	rel.	n/a		-	
	pass.	*crethir*	eθꞌəρꞌ	·*crethar*	eθəρ
	pass. rel.	n/a		-	
1st pl.		n/a		·*criam*	iᴅ̇µ
	rel.	n/a		-	
2nd pl.		n/a		n/a	
3rd pl.		n/a		·*criat*	iᴅ̇d
	rel.	*crete*	edꞌe	-	
	pass.	*cretir*	edꞌəρꞌ	n/a	
	pass. rel.	n/a		-	

Illustration 53.3: The a-subjunctive of S3 *crenaid*

Note:

1. Only a few persons are actually attested for the subjunctive of this class.

2. When the root vowel is moved out of stressed position, it first coalesces with the subjunctive *a*, the resulting vowel then being further reduced to /ə/ *schwa*. This can make certain forms very hard to identify, e.g., *co etir·dibet* /ko h'ed'əp·d'iβ'əd/ 'so that they may destroy' (*Ml.* 114c8) is the 3rd pl. present subjunctive of *etir·diben*, a compound of *benaid* 'to cut.'

3. In those S3 verbs where the root ends in a consonant the subjunctive stem shows a short *e* in the root, irrespective of what the root vowel in the present stem is. The S3 verbs *ernaid* 'to bestow,' *sernaid* 'to strew,' *marnaid,* ·*mairn* 'to betray' and *at·baill* 'to die' have the subjunctive stems *era-, sera-, mera-* and *at·bela-* respectively.

53.2.3. The a-subjunctive of deponent verbs

Apart from the 1st sg., deponent a-subjunctive forms, too, are largely identical with their respective present indicative forms in the W1 and W2-inflections. I will give a complete paradigm only for the largest group of deponent verbs, which is W2. The example below is again *suidigidir* 'to place,' the subjunctive stem is *suidig-* /suδ'əɣ'-/, which is identical with the present stem:

person		absolute (independent)		conjunct (dependent)	
1st sg.		*suidiger*	C'əρ	*·suidiger*	C'əρ
2nd sg.		*suidigther*	C'θ'əρ	*·suidigther*	C'θ'əρ
3rd sg.		*suidigidir*	C'əδ'əρ'	*·suidigedar*	C'əδəρ
	rel.	*suidigedar*	C'əδ'əρ		
	pass.	*suidigthir*	C'θ'əρ'	*·suidigther*	C'θ'əρ
	pass. rel.	*suidigther*	C'θ'əρ		
1st pl.		*suidigmir*	C'm'əρ'	*·suidigmer*	C'm'əρ
	rel.	*suidigmer*	C'm'əρ		
2nd pl.		*suidigthe*	C'θ'e	*·suidigid*	C'əδ'
3rd pl.		*suidigitir*	C'əd'əρ'	*·suidigetar*	C'ədəρ
	rel.	*suidigetar*	C'əd'əρ		
	pass.	*suidigtir*	C'd'əρ'	*·suidigter*	C'd'əρ
	pass. rel.	*suidigter*	C'd'əρ		

Illustration 53.4: The a-subjunctive of W2 *suidigidir*

Note:

1. The 1st sg. of W1 deponent subjunctives ends in *-ar*, e.g., *·comalnar* 'I may fulfil.' Apart from this all persons are formally identical with the respective present indicative forms.

2. The a-subjunctive stem of deponent S2 *·mainethar* 'to think' is *men-* /m'ev-/, i.e., 1st sg. *·menar*, 2nd sg. *·mentar*, 3rd sg. *·menathar*, 1st pl. *·menammar*, 2nd pl. *·menaid*, 3rd pl. *·menatar*.

3. The slightly irregular a-subjunctive of S3 *(ro)·cluinethar* 'to hear' shows the two stems *(ro)·cloa-* and *(ro)·cloí-* /ro·kloə̈- ro·kloi̯-/:

person	conjunct (dependent)	
1st sg.	*(ro)·cloor*	oöρ
2nd sg.	*(ro)·cloíther*	oi̯θ'əρ
3rd sg.	*(ro)·cloathar*	oə̈θəρ
	pass. *(ro)·cloíther*	oi̯θ'əρ
1st pl.	*(ro)·cloammar*	oə̈məρ
2nd pl.	n/a	
3rd pl.	*(ro)·cloatar*	oə̈dəρ
	pass. n/a	

Illustration 53.5: The a-subjunctive of *ro·cluinethar*

Illustration 53.6:
bid maith mo menme-se acht ro·cloor for caínscél-si (*Wb.* 23d2)
'my mind will be glad, provided I hear good news of you'

53.3. The e-subjunctive

The e-subjunctive is a very small class among subjunctive formations. It is formed by most H2 verbs, whereby the *i* of the H2 stem is exchanged for a short *e*, which becomes *é* in stressed absolute final position. If the root comes to stand in unstressed position, the forms are identical with the corresponding a-subjunctive forms. This means that H2 compounds verbs with two or more preverbs like *ad·roilli, ·áirilli* 'to deserve' (< **ad-ro-slī-*), where the root is always in unstressed position, only have a-subjunctive forms attested. Best attested are forms of the substantive verb. As an example for the use of the a-subjunctive when the root is unstressed, I supply prototonic forms of *do·gní* 'to do.'

person		absolute (independent)		conjunct (dependent)		unstressed
1st sg.		béo, béu	eu̯	·béo	eu̯	·dén
2nd sg.		bee, bé	ē	·bé	ē	·déne
3rd sg.		beith, beid	eθ' eð'	·bé	ē	·roib, ·déna
	rel.	bess	es	-		-
	pass.	bethir	eθ'əρ'	·bether	eθ'əρ	·déntar
	pass. rel.	bether	eθ'əρ	-		-
1st pl.		bemmi	em'i	·bem	eμ	·robam, ·dénam
	rel.	*bemme	em'e	-		-
2nd pl.		bethe	eθ'e	·beid	eð'	·robith, ·dénaid
3rd pl.		beit	ed'	·bet	ed	·robat, ·dénat
	rel.	bete	ed'e	-		-
	pass.	n/a		do·gneter	ed'əρ	·dénatar
	pass. rel.	-		-		-

Illustration 53.7: The e-subjunctive

Note:

1. Compounds of *-cí* 'to see' show deponent inflection in the present subjunctive, e.g., 1st sg. *ad·cear, ·accar*, 3rd sg. *·accathar* or 3rd pl. *ad·ceter, ·accatar*. In the 3rd sg. passive compounds of *-cí* exhibit traces of an s-subjunctive: *·accastar*.

2. The augmented subjunctive stem of *do·gní* looks somewhat irregular: e.g., augmented subjunctive 1st sg. *do·rón, ·dern*, 3rd sg. *do·róna, ·derna*, 3rd sg. pass. *do·róntar, ·derntar*, compared to unaugmented subjunctive 1st sg. *do·gnéo, ·dén*, 3rd sg. *do·gné, ·déna*, 3rd sg. pass. *do·gnether, ·déntar*.

53.4. The s-subjunctive

The s-subjunctive is one of the most demanding formations of Old Irish, but perhaps not so much the formation itself as its transparency and recognizability for the reader who comes across such a form. Not infrequently the stressed part of a verb may be reduced to a single letter, in rare cases even less. The s-subjunctive is formed by strong verbs with roots ending in dental or guttural consonants or double *n*, that is, *th* /θ/, *d* /δ/, *t* /d/, *nn* /n/, *ch* /χ/, *g* /γ/, *c* /g/. The only exception is S1 *agaid* 'to drive,' which forms an a-subjunctive. Furthermore, the three hiatus verbs H3 *luid* 'to drink,' H3 *do·goa* 'to choose' and compounds of H2 *cī-* 'to see' sometimes show s-forms alongside more regular a-subjunctives.

The s-subjunctive is formed by adding the suffix *-s-* immediately to the root final consonant. The two coalasce into a mere /s/ whereby the root final consonant completely disappears. The /s/ is usually written double *ss* after short vowels and single *s* after long vowels, e.g., *reithid* 'to run': root *reth-* + *-s-* → subjunctive stem *res(s)-*, or *téit* 'to go': root *tēg-* + *-s-* → subjunctive stem *tēs(s)-*. The quantity and quality of the root vowel depends on the underlying root shape; note that verbs of the S1c class lose the *n* of the root outside of the present stem:

1. Roots with underlying short Proto-Indo-European *a* have long *ā* in the s-subjunctive, e.g., S2 *fo·saig* 'to tempt' → 3rd pl. pres. subj. *fo·sāsat*; other verbs that behave like this are *claidid* (*clās-*) 'to dig,' *maidid* (*mās-*) 'to break,' *nascid* (*nās-*) 'to bind,' *saigid* (*sās-*) 'to seek,' *slaidid* (*slās-*) 'to slay,' *snaidid* (*snās-*) 'to carve.'

2. Roots with underlying Proto-Indo-European *i/į*, usually have long *ē* (= *é/ía*) in the s-subjunctive, e.g., S1 *téit* 'to go' < PIE *(s)teigʰ-* → 2nd sg. *téisi*, 1st pl. *tíasmai*; other verbs that behave like this are S1c *·ding* (*dēs-*) 'to press, to shape,' *rigid* (*rēs-*) 'to bind,' *snigid* (*snēs-*) 'to drip;' in roots with initial *f* < PIE *u̯* the quantity may vary: *ro·fitir* 'to know' has, e.g., 3rd sg. *·festar* /f'estəp/ and *·fiastar* /f'iastəp/. Other verbs show only short *e*, e.g., *ad·fét, in·fét* 'to tell,' root *fēd-* < PIE *u̯ei̯d-* has the subjunctive stem *fess-*, perhaps to distinguish it from the future stem *fíass-*; also *do·fich* < PIE *u̯ik-* has the subjunctive stem *fess-*.

3. Roots with underlying vowel *o/u* usually have long *ō* in the s-subjunctive, e.g., S1c *fo·loing* 'to endure' < PIE *leu̯g-* → 1st sg. *fo·lós*; other verbs with this behavior are *as·boind* (*·bōs-*) 'to refuse,' *bongid* (*bōs-*) 'to break,' *·oid* (*·ōs-*) 'to lend,' *tongid* (*tōs-*) 'to swear.' In the case of *do·tuit, ·tuit* 'to fall,' the s-subjunctive seems to have a short *o*: *tos-*.

Illustration 53.8:
fa·lós-sa co neurt
'may I endure it with strength!'

4. Roots with *n* that do not disappear outside of the present stem (although the *n* becomes invisible before the *s* of the s-subjunctive!) have a long vowel in the s-subjunctive, usually *ē* (= *é/ía*), e.g., *do·seinn* 'to hunt' → 1st sg. *du·sés*; other verbs that behave like this are *·bruinn* (*brēs-*) 'to spring forth,' *cingid* (*cēs-*) 'to step.' *·gleinn* (*glēs-*) 'basically: to collect,' *·greinn* (*grēs-*) 'basically: to collect,' *lingid* (*lēs-*) 'to jump;' *·icc* 'to reach' < PIE *h₂enḱ* has the s-subjunctive *·ís-*.

5. Where an *l* or *r* precedes the final consonant of the root, it coalesces with the *s* of the s-subjunctive to give *ll* and *rr* respectively. No *s* is actually to be seen in the s-subjunctive of these verbs, e.g., S1 *fo·ceird* 'to put' → 2nd sg. *fo·ceirr*; other verbs that behave like this are *mligid* (*mell-*) 'to milk' and *orgid* (*orr-*) 'to slay.'

6. All other verbs show a short *e* in the s-subjunctive, even if in the present stem they exhibit a different vowel, e.g., S1 *feidid* 'to lead' → *fess-*, S1 *laigid* 'to lie' → *less-*, S2 *guidid* 'to pray, to ask' → *gess-*; other verbs that behave like this are *aingid* < root *aneg-* (*aness-*) 'to protect,' root *arc-* in *·dúthraiccair* 'to wish,' *·comairc* 'to ask' → *-ress-*, *ar·clich* (*cless-*) 'to ward off,' *at·reig* (*at·ress-*) 'to rise,' *dligid* (*dless-*) 'to be due,' *midithir* (*mess-*) 'to judge,' *reithid* (*ress-*) 'to run,' *saidid* (*sess-*) 'to sit,' *scuchid* (*scess-*) 'to move,' *teichid* (*tess-*) 'to flee.'

Illustration 53.9:
acht ro·clá mo ślúasat
'if only my shovel
would dig!'

7. Into the latter group also belongs the augmented stem of *téit* which is formed from a different root, i.e., S1 *do·cuaid, ·dichuid* 'can go, etc.' < *di-cum-feth-* (see 50.2.2.4.2). Its s-subjunctive stem is *do·coas-, ·diches-*, and it can become rather difficult to identify at times, e.g., 1st sg. *do·cous, ·dichius*, 3rd sg. *do·coí, ·dich/·dig*, 3rd pl. *do·coíset, ·dichset/ ·dechsat*. Some compounds of *téit* use this augmented stem, too, e.g., *do·tét* 'to come' → 3rd sg. augmented s-subj. *do·dig, ·tuidig*, 3rd pl. *do·dechsat, ·tuidchiset*.

Of many roots no subjunctive forms are attested in old texts, so that nothing can be said with certainty about their subjunctive stem formation.

53.4.1. The active s-subjunctive

The endings of the s-subjunctive are those of the S1 inflection, with the exception of the 3rd sg., which—not unlike the s-preterite—is endingless in the absolute and even 'suffixless' in the conjunct, ending in the plain root vowel. Apart from the 3rd sg. conjunct, the *s* of the s-subjunctive can be seen in all persons.

person		absolute (independent)		conjunct (dependent)		unstressed	
1st sg.		*gessu*	su	*·gess*	s	*-gus*	us
2nd sg.		*gessi*	s'i	*·geiss*	s'	*-gais*	əs'
3rd sg.		*geiss*	s'	*·gé*	∇	*-g*	C
	rel.	*gess*	s	-			
	pass.	*gessair*	səp'	*·gessar*	səp		
	pass. rel.	*gessar*	səp	-			
1st pl.		*gesmai*	smi	*·gessam*	səµ		
	rel.	*gesmae*	sme	-			
2nd pl.		*geiste*	s't'e	*·geissid*	s'əð'		
3rd pl.		*gessait*	səd'	*·gessat*	səd		
	rel.	*gestae*	sde	-			
	pass.	n/a		*·gessatar*	sədəp		
	pass. rel.	n/a		-			

Illustration 53.10: The s-subjunctive

272

Note:

1. When the root vowel is stressed, the 3rd sg. conjunct of the s-subjunctive always has a long vowel, irrespective of whether the vowel of the subjunctive stem is long or short, e.g., *ní·má* 'may it not break' ← *maidid* (*mās-*), *fo·ló* 'may (s)he endure' ← *fo·loing* (*lōs-*), *at·ré* 'let him get up' ← *at·reig* (*ress-*), *slán·sé* 'may (s)he sit safely' ← *saidid* (*sess-*).

2. But when the root is unstressed, strange things happen. It would be expected that subjunctive stems with inherent short vowels like *ress-* ← *reithid* lose everything except for the initial consonant, e.g., the compound *fo·reith* 'to help' → *arndom·foir* 'that (s)he may help me': only the *r* of the root 'survives' as a visible element, the *e* of the subjunctive stem is reflected by the palatalization of the *r*; or *do·infet* 'to inspire' (root *feth-*) → *mani·tinib* 'if he do not inspire': the palatalized *b* reflects unstressed *f* in absolute *auslaut*, with an *e* lost after it. Subjunctive stems with inherent long vowels ought to be reflected by the root's initial consonant and the shortened root vowel in absolute *auslaut*, e.g., *in·greinn* 'to persecute' → *·ingre* '(s)he may persecute,' *con·dieig* 'to seek' (< **cum-di-sag-*) → *·cuintea* 'he may seek,' or *ar·icc* 'to come' → *·airi* '(s)he may come,' which actually has no initial consonant in the root.

3. This predictable state of affairs is indeed sometimes encountered, but more often than not even in those cases with an inherent long vowel in the subjunctive stem, where the 3rd sg. conjunct would be expected to end in a short vowel in unstressed position, the vowel may be lost, with only the initial consonant remaining of the root, e.g., *do·etet* 'to track down' (< **to-in-tēg-*, a compound of *téit*, subjunctive stem *tēss-*) → *do·eit* '(s)he may track down,' *fo·loing* 'to suffer' (subjunctive stem *lōss-*) → *·ful* '(s)he may suffer,' or *do·airic* 'to come' (subjunctive stem *tīss-*) → *tair* '(s)he may come.' Note that in the last example no trace remains of the root except for a mark of palatalization on the *r*.

> Although this is a highly difficult formation, I will not quote more forms here. You will find a lot of these collected in GOI 391–395 and other handbooks. Don't be disheartened: even the greatest among Old Irish scholars admit to having difficulties in recognizing 3rd sg. conjunct forms of s-subjunctives at times.

53.4.2. The deponent s-subjunctive

A few verbs inflect as deponents: S2 *midithir* (*mess-*) 'to judge,' S1 *ithid* (*ess-*) 'to eat,' *do·futhraccair*, *·dúthraccair* (*·dúthairs-*, *·dúthras*) 'to wish.' The most important of these is *ro·fitir*, subjunctive stem *fess-*, sometimes *fēs-* (2nd sg. *·fésser*, 3rd sg. *·fíastar*). Only very few absolute deponent forms are attested: 2nd sg. *meser* and 3rd sg. relative *mestar*, 3rd sg. *estir*. I will only give the conjunct paradigm of *fess-* in the following table:

person		conjunct (dependent)	
1st sg.		·fessur	sur
2nd sg.		·feisser	s'əρ
3rd sg.		·festar	stəρ
	pass.	·fessar	səρ
1st pl.		·fessamar	səməρ
2nd pl.		·fessid	s'əδ'
3rd pl.		·fessatar	sədəρ
	pass.	·fessatar	sədəρ

Illustration 53.11: The conjunct deponent s-subjunctive

53.5. Exercise

Form the subjunctive stem of some of the following verbs and inflect them in the present subjunctive:

> scríbaid /s'k'r'ïβəδ'/ (W1) 'to write'
> millid /m'il'əδ'/ (W2a) 'to ruin'
> reithid /r'eθ'əδ'/ (S1) 'to run'
> lenaid /l'evəδ'/ (S3) 'to follow'
> do·cuirethar, ·tochraither /do·kuρ'əθəρ ·toχρəθ'əρ/ (W2b) 'to put, to throw'
> ar·midethar, ·airmidethar /aρ·m'iδ'əθəρ ·aρ'μ'əδ'əθəρ/ (S2) 'to aim at'

53.6. The past subjunctive

The past subjunctive or imperfect subjunctive has the following uses:

1. It has the same connotations as described in 53.1 for the subjunctive in general when the action of the sentence is set in the past, e.g., *as·bert Conchobor fria muintir ara·scortais a cairptiu* 'Conchobor told his men that they should unyoke their chariots; C. sagte seinen Männern, sie sollten ihre Wagen ausspannen' (CCC 2). Since the action of the sentence lies in the past (*as·bert* 'said') the past subjunctive *·scortais* 'they should unyoke' has to be used in the final clause. If the action were present, the present subjunctive *·scorat* had to be used, e.g., **as·beir Conchobor fria muintir ara·scorat a cairptiu* 'Conchobor tells his men that they should unyoke their chariots; C. sagt seinen Männern, sie sollen ihre Wagen ausspannen.'

2. Without any temporal connotation it is used in various types of subordinate clauses to characterize a verbal action as hypothetical, doubtful, improbable or unreal. In this sense it is especially common in conditional ('if') and concessive ('although, even if') clauses. Examples are: *no·meilinn léini mbithnuí; indíu táthumm dom śéimi ná·melainn cid aithléini* 'I used to wear an evernew shirt; but today I have become so thin that I could not even wear a worn-out shirt' (GT 48); *ba lóithred fo chétóir amal bid i talam no·beth tresna ilchéta*

blíadnae 'instantly he turned to dust, as if he had been in earth for many hundred years (*lit.*: as if it had been in earth that he had been for many hundred years)' (IB 65); *is fochen lim-sa ém* […], *má cot·ísinn; ní·cumgaimm ní duit* 'it is (= would be) right with me, if I could do it; but I can't do anything for thee' (TBF 128); Cú Chulainn says: *maith limm, cenco·beinn acht óenlá for domun* 'I want it (= fame), even if I should be (= live) but a single day in this world' (TBC 640 f.).

3. Sometimes the past subjunctive is used where a present subjunctive would be expected syntactically.

The past subjunctive is simply formed by adding the 'secondary endings,' which we have learned in 49.1, to the subjunctive stem. As in the case of the imperfect, no distinction between absolute and conjunct forms exists; simple verbs without a preceding particle are compounded with the empty particle *no·*. Active and deponent verbs inflect alike. The sample verbs below are the same as in 49.1:

person		W1	W2	S1	H2	ending
1st sg.		·carainn	·suidiginn	do·berainn, ·taibrinn	·beinn	ən'
2nd sg.		·cartha	·suidigthea	do·bertha, ·taibrithea	·betha	(ə)θ⁽'⁾a
3rd sg.		·carad, -ath	·suidiged, -eth	do·berad, ·taibred	·beth, ·bed	əδ əθ
	pass.	·carthae	·suidigthe	do·berthae, ·taibrithe	·bethe	(ə)θ⁽'⁾e
1st pl.		·carmais	·suidigmis	do·bermais, ·taibrimis	·bemmis	(ə)m⁽'⁾əs'
2nd pl.		·carthae	·suidigthe	do·berthae, ·taibrithe	·bethe	(ə)θ⁽'⁾e
3rd pl.		·cartais	·suidigtis	do·bertais, ·taibritis	·betis	(ə)d⁽'⁾əs'
	pass.	·cartais	·suidigtis	do·bertais, ·taibritis	–	(ə)d⁽'⁾əs'

Illustration 53.12: The inflection of the past subjunctive 1

The two examples below for the past of the s-subjunctive are S2 *guidid* 'to ask, to pray,' subjunctive stem *ges-* /g'es-/, and S1 *do·tét* 'to come,' subjunctive stem *do·tēs-*, ·*taís-* or ·*táes-* /do·t'ēs-, ·taĩs-/. Note the difference between deutero- and prototonic forms in the case of the latter:

person		S2	S1	ending
1st sg.		·gessinn	do·téisinn, ·taísinn	ən'
2nd sg.		·gesta	do·tíasta, ·táesta	(ə)θ⁽'⁾a
3rd sg.		·gessed	do·téised, ·taísed	əδ əθ
	pass.	·gestae	do·tíastae, ·táestae	(ə)θ⁽'⁾e
1st pl.		·gesmais	do·tíasmais, ·táesmais	(ə)m⁽'⁾əs'
2nd pl.		·geste	do·téiste, ·taíste	(ə)θ⁽'⁾e
3rd pl.		·gestais	do·tíastais, ·táestais	(ə)d⁽'⁾əs'
	pass.	·gestais	do·tíastais, ·táestais	(ə)d⁽'⁾əs'

Illustration 53.13: The inflection of the past subjunctive 2

53.7. Exercise

Form the subjunctive stem of the following verbs and inflect them in the past subjunctive:

> *do·meil, ·tomail* /do·m'eλ' ·toμəλ'/ (S1) 'to consume'
> *fo·reith, ·foiret* /fo·reθ' ·foρ'əd/ (S1) 'to help'
> *ad·cí, ·accai* /aδ·k'i ·aki/ (H2) 'to see'
> *ro·icc, ·ricc* /ro·ig' ·r'ig'/ (S1) 'to reach'
> *do·cuirethar, ·tochraither* /do·kuρ'əθəρ ·toχρəθ'əρ/ (W2b) 'to put, to throw'

53.8. The subjunctive of the copula

I already discussed the subjunctive of the substantive verb in the preceding sections. The copula has special forms of the present and past subjunctive. Note that the copula has separate absolute forms in the past subjunctive, whereas otherwise no distinction between absolute and conjunct exists in this mood.

	present subjunctive		past subjunctive	
	absolute	conjunct	absolute	conjunct
1st sg.	*ba*	-*ba*^{L}	n/a	-*bin*, -*benn*
2nd sg.	*ba, be*	-*ba*	n/a	-*ptha*
3rd sg.	*ba*	-*b, -p, -dib, -dip,* -*bo, -po, -bu*	*bid, bith*	-*bad, -pad, -bed*
rel.	*bes, bas*	-	*bed*^{L}, *bad*^{L}	-
1st pl.	n/a	-*ban*^{L}	*bemmis, bimmis*	-*bemmis, -bimmis*
2nd pl.	*bede*	-*bad*	n/a	n/a
3rd pl.	n/a	-*bet*^{L}, -*bat*^{L}, -*pat*^{L}	*betis, bitis*	-*bdis, -ptis, -dis, -tis*
rel.	*bete, beta, bata*	-	n/a	-

Illustration 53.14: The subjunctive of the copula

Note:

1. After nasalizing particles and conjunctions the nasalization appears as -*m*-, e.g., *arimp* 'in order that it may be.' Sometimes the -*b*- of the copula may be assimilated completely to a preceding -*m*-, e.g., *comman* 'so that we may be' for *comban*, or *airmtis* beside *airmbtis*.

2. The variant -*dib, -dip* can appear instead of -*b, -p*, e.g., *airndib* 'in order that it may be' beside *arimp*, or *condib, condip* 'that it may be.'

3. After the conjunctions *cía* 'although' and *má* 'if' special forms of the 3rd persons are used. The present subjunctive has 3rd sg. *cid, cith, ced, ceith*, neg. *cinip, cenip, cenib*, 3rd pl. *cit*; 3rd sg. *mad*, neg. *manip*, 3rd pl. *mat*. The past subjunctive has 3rd sg. *cid, mad*, 3rd pl. *cetis, matis*.

4. When *cía* 'although' and *má* 'if' are used with the indicative of verbs that have no infixed pronoun, the subjunctive -*d* is added to the two conjunctions.

You can find a table with the subjunctive classes in Appendix F.9.

53.9. The prehistory of the subjunctive

The Old Irish a-, e- and s-subjunctives all go back to the same PIE formation, the thematic s-aorist subjunctive. The split into a- and s-subjunctives was triggered by different phonetic environments and probably took place within Insular Celtic, the split between a- and e-subjunctives took place only within Irish. The reshaping of the original 3rd sg. s-subjunctive *-set(i) > *-s(i) happened in analogy to the 3rd sg. of the s-preterite.

abs.	OIr.	Prim. Irish	Insular Celtic	Proto-Celtic	Pre-Celtic
1st sg.	*mela* «	*meλāhū	*melāsū «	*melasū	*melh$_2$soh$_2$
2nd sg.	*melae*	*meλāhehi	*melāsesi «	*melasesi	*melh$_2$sesi
3rd sg.	*melaid*	*meλāheθi	*melāseti «	*melaseti	*melh$_2$seti
1st pl.	*mel†mai*	*meλāhomohi «	*melāsomosi «	*melasomosi	*melh$_2$somosi
2nd pl.	*mel†tae*	*meλāheθē «	*melāsetesi «	*melasetesi	*melh$_2$setesi
3rd pl.	*melait*	*meλāhodi	*melāsonti «	*melasonti	*melh$_2$sonti

Illustration 53.15: The prehistory of the absolute a-subjunctive

conj.	OIr.	Prim. Irish	Insular Celtic	Proto-Celtic	Pre-Celtic
1st sg.	·*mel* «	*meλāhū	*melāsū «	*melasū	*melh$_2$soh$_2$
2nd sg.	·*melae* «	*meλāheh	*melāses «	*melasesi	*melh$_2$sesi
3rd sg.	·*mela*	*meλāheθ	*melāset «	*melaseti	*melh$_2$seti
1st pl.	·*melam*	*meλāhoμohi	*melāsomos «	*melasomosi	*melh$_2$somosi
2nd pl.	·*melaid*	*meλāheθeh	*melāsetes «	*melasetesi	*melh$_2$setesi
3rd pl.	·*melat*	*meλāhodi	*melāsont «	*melasonti	*melh$_2$sonti

Illustration 53.16: The prehistory of the conjunct a-subjunctive

abs.	OIr.	Prim. Irish	Insular Celtic	Proto-Celtic	Pre-Celtic
1st sg.	*tíasu* «	*tēsū	*tēχsū	*teiχsū	*(s)teig̑soh$_2$
2nd sg.	*téisi* «	*tēsehi	*tēχsesi «	*teiχsesi	*(s)teig̑sesi
3rd sg.	*téis*	*tēsi	*tēχsi «	*teiχseti	*(s)teig̑seti
1st pl.	*tías†mai*	*tēsomohi «	*tēχsomosi «	*teiχsomosi	*(s)teig̑somosi
2nd pl.	*téis†te*	*tēseθē-	*tēχsetesi «	*teiχsetesi	*(s)teig̑setesi
3rd pl.	*tíasait*	*tēsodi	*tēχsonti «	*teiχsonti	*(s)teig̑sonti

Illustration 53.17: The prehistory of the absolute s-subjunctive

conj.	OIr.	Prim. Irish	Insular Celtic	Proto-Celtic	Pre-Celtic
1st sg.	·tías	*tēsū	*tēχsū	*teiχsū	*(s)tei̯ĝsoh₂
2nd sg.	·téis	*tēseh	*tēχses	*teiχsesi	*(s)tei̯ĝsesi
3rd sg.	·té	*tēh	*tēχs «	*teiχseti	*(s)tei̯ĝseti
1st pl.	·tíasam	*tēsoμah	*tēχsomos	*teiχsomosi	*(s)tei̯ĝsomosi
2nd pl.	·téisid	*tēseθeh	*tēχsetes	*teiχsetesi	*(s)tei̯ĝsetesi
3rd pl.	·tíasat	*tēsod	*tēχsont	*teiχsonti	*(s)tei̯ĝsonti

Illustration 53.18: The prehistory of the conjunct s-subjunctive

Lesson 54

54.1. A poem

'In·n-esser dom to á?'	'in·n'es'əp doμ to ā?'
'Tó, mani·má mo á!	'tō, mav'i·mā mo ā!
Ara·tair mo á mó!'	aρa·daρ' mo ā mō!'
'Mani·má to á, tó.'	'mav'i·mā to ā, tō.'

Note:

1. *to*ᴸ is an early form of *do*ᴸ 'thy.'

2: Source: Calvert WATKINS, 'Varia III. 2. »In essar dam do á?«,' *Ériu* 29 (1978), 161–165

54.2. Varia

1. *acht* followed by an augmented subjunctive means 'provided that, if only.'

2. *nícon·* is a variant of the negative particle *ní·*; the two are freely interchangeable.

3. *·ribuilsed* in sentence 16 is the augmented 3ʳᵈ sg. conditional 'could jump' of S1 *lingid* 'to jump' < *ro-iblḗs-eth < *φi-φlang-se-ti-.

54.3. Exercise

Old Irish

1. ** Cid fáilte ad·cot-sa 7 do·ngnéu, is tussu immid·folngai dam, a Dé. (*Ml.* 92a17) 2. ** Ní imned limm, acht rop Críst pridches 7 imme·ráda cách. (*Wb.* 23b24) 3. ** Cía beith ara·n-accathar nech inna rétu inducbaidi in betha-so, arnach·corathar i mmoth 7 machthad dia seirc 7 dia n-accobur. (*Ml.* 68b9) 4. * Cía beith a ndéide-sin im labrad-sa, .i. gáu 7 fír, combad sain a n-as·berainn ó bélaib 7 a n-í imme·rádainn ó chridiu. (*Wb.* 14c23) 5. ** Is dó do·gniinn-se a n-í-sin, combin cosmail fri encu. (*Ml.* 91b7) 6. ** Ba torad saíthir dúnn […] ce do·melmais cech túarai 7 ce do·gnemmis a ndo·gniat ar céili. (*Wb.* 10c21) 7. * Níbu machthad do·rróntae día dind lieicc la geinti ainchreitmechu. (*Sg.* 65a1) 8. ** Is toísigiu ad·ciam teilciud in béla resíu ro·cloammar a guth-side. (*Ml.* 112b12) 9. ** Cía théis [*sc.* Día] i loc bes ardu, ní ardu de. Ní samlaid són dún-ni, air immi ardu-ni de tri dul isna lucu arda. (*Ml.* 23d23) 10. ** Cech nóeb boíe, fil, bias (= will be) co bráth, […] ro·bet ocom chobair! (*Fél. Ep.* 289-292) 11. * Rom·ṡóerae, á Ísu, lat nóebu tan tíastae, amal sóersai Ísac de lámaib a athar. (*Fél. Ep.* 467-470) 12. ** 'Cía bemmi-ni for longais riam [*sc.* Conchobar], ní·fil i nÉire óclaig bas amru,' ol Fergus. 13. ** Ba ingnad la Conn nícon·taibred Connlae taithesc do neoch acht tísed in ben. (*EC* 12) 14. * Na·mbert lais dochum a scuile ara·ngabad léigend lais amal cach nduine. (*Gosp.* 23) 15. ** Ní·fetar ní arndot·áigthe do neoch. (*TBC* 1325 f.) 16. * Is é int ogam ro·scríbad i toíb inna omnae, arná·dechsad nech secce co·rribuil-sed eirr óencharpait tairse. (*TBC* 827 ff.) 17. ** Íarmi·foacht araile di ḟelmaccaib do ṡuidiu cid

279

diambad maith a llae-sa. (TBC 612 f.) 18. ** As·bert Pátraic: Toisc limm fer oínṡéitche doná·rruc-thae acht óentuistiu. (*Thes.* ii 241.9) 19. ** Nícon·robae rann di rannaib in domuin inná·ructais i ndoíri 7 asnacha·tucad Día. (*Ml.* 125b7) 20. * Ad·taat trí glantae do cach róut, téora aimsera i·nglanatar, téora tucaiti ara·nglanatar. (*Corm.* 1082)

Transcription

1. k'iδ' fāl't'e aδ·god-sa ogus δο·ŋgnēy̨, is tusu im'iδ·oλŋgi day̨, a δ'ē. 2. n'ī h'im'n'əδ l'im, aχt rob k'r'īst p'r'iδ'χ'əs ogus im'e·rāδa kāχ. 3. k'ia β'eθ' apa·vakəθəp n'eχ ina r'ēdu h'indugβəδ'i in β'eθa-so, apvāχ·gopəθəp i moθ ogus µaχθəδ d'iä s'er'k' ogus δ'iä vakəβup. 4. k'ia β'eθ' a n'd'ēd'e-s'iv' im λaβpəδ-sa, eδ ōv gāy̨ ogus ịp, kombəδ sav' a vas·β'epən' ō b'ēλəβ' ogus a v'ī im'e·pāδən' ō χ'p'iδ'u. 5. is dō do·g'n'iǒn'-s'e a v'ī-s'iv', komb'in kosµəλ' f'r'i h'engu. 6. ba topəδ saịθ'əp' dūn k'e do·m'eλmes' k'eχ duapi ogus k'e do·g'n'em'es' a ndo·γ'v'iäd ap g'ēλ'i. 7. n'ību µaχθəδ do·rōnte d'ia d'ind λ'iǒg' la g'en't'i hav'χ'p'ed'µ'əχu. 8. is toịs'əγ'u ad·k'iǒy̨ t'el'g'uδ in β'ēλa r'es'īy̨ ro·kloǒməp a γuθ-s'iδ'e. 9. k'ia θ'ēs' i log b'es ardu, n'ī hardu d'e. n'ī saµλəδ' sōv dun-n'i, ap' imi ardu-n'i de t'r'i δuλ isna lugu harda. 10. k'eχ noịβ boịe, f'iλ', b'iäs ko brāθ, ro·b'et ogəm χoβəp'! 11. rom·hoịpe, ā ịsu, lat voịβu tan d'iasde, aµəλ soịpsi īsag d'e λāµəβ' a aθəp. 12. ‘k'ia β'em'i-n'i fop loŋges' r'iǒµ, n'ī·f'iλ' i v'ēp'e ōgλəγ' bas aµpu,' oλ f'epγus. 13. ba h'iŋgnəδ la kon n'īkon·taβ'p'əδ konλe taθ'əsk do vey̨χ aχt t'īs'əδ in βev. 14. na·m'b'ert las' doχum a skuλ'e apa·ŋgaβəδ l'ēγ'ənd las' aµəλ kaχ nduv'e. 15. n'ī·f'edəp n'ī arndəd·āγ'θ'e do v'ey̨χ. 16. Is ē int oγəm ro·s'k'rīβəδ i doịβ' inna hoµve, arnā·d'eχsəδ n'eχ s'ek'e ko·r'iβuλ's'əδ er' oịvχarbəd' tap's'e. 17. iapµi·foǒχt apáλ'e di eλµəkəβ' do huδ'u k'iδ d'iǒmbəδ µaθ' a laë-sa. 18. tos'k' l'im f'ep oịv'h'eδ'χ'e dovā·rugθe aχt oịntus'd'u. 19. n'īkov·roβe ran di panəβ' in doµuv' inā·rugdəs' i ndoịp'i ogus asnəχa·tugəδ d'ia. 20. ad·taǒd t'r'ī glante do kaχ pōy̨d, t'ēy̨pa ham's'əpa i·ŋglavəδəp, t'ēy̨pa tugəd'i apa·ŋglavəδəp.

English

1. Though it be happiness which we should attain and which we should make, it is they who cause it to us. 2. It is no grievance for us, provided it be God whom all people preach and think of. 3. Though it be that thou should see a glorious thing of this world, that it may not put thee into amazement out of love of it and desire for it. 4. So that it may be different what they should say from their lips and what they should think in their hearts. 5. It is therefore she used to do this, so that she might be similar to the innocent. 6. It were a fruit of labor for me if I consumed every food and if I did what my companion does. 7. It were a wonder that gods should not be made from (the) stones. 8. Isn't it first (*OIr.*: comparative) they see the throwing of the axes before they should hear their sounds? 9. Even though thou should go into a higher place, thou art not higher from it. 10. All (*uile*) saints that were, that are, shouldn't they be helping us? 11. May you deliver us, ye saints when you should come, as you have delivered (use *ro*!) the sons from the hands of their fathers. 12. Though I be in exile before you, there are no warriors in Ireland who would be more wonderful than you. 13. It was not strange for Conn that Connlae would give answers provided that the women would not come. 14. We took you with us to our school in order that you might take up reading with us like all people. 15. Have you found anything why (*OIr.*: on account of which) I should be feared by anybody? 16. These are the ogam inscriptions that had been written on the sides of the trees, that they should not go past them until warriors (*eirr*) of chariots should have jumped across them. 17. Some of the students asked him (*do*) for what these days would be good. 18. She desires men of many (*il-*) wives to whom many children should have been born. 19. There were parts of the world into which I should have been carried into captivity and out of which God should not have brought me. 20. Is there one cleaning for a road, one time at which it is cleaned, one reason for which it is cleaned?

54.4. Test

Try to recognize the verbal forms (give as much information about the words as possible—class, person, number, mood, dependent or independent, relative). Give also the quotation form of the verb and say to which present class it belongs:

cara: _____	·mille: _____	·goram: _____
rethir: _____	do·gnetis: _____	or _____
con·melae: _____	·messatar: _____	sláiss: _____
do·tías: _____	·folus: _____	·seiss: _____
for·chana: _____	ro·cloítis: _____	ad·fé: _____
imm·soa: _____	·tuidchissem: _____	·lie: _____
·coratar: _____	·máissed: _____	bad: _____
·tísmais: _____	do·rónmais: _____	do·dig: _____
ar·menar: _____	fris·n-orratar: _____	nád·rí: _____
as·roibre: _____	·accastar: _____	·criat: _____
·dernatar: _____	do·rotsad: _____	fo·lóis: _____
ad·cetha: _____	do·roilcea: _____	ro·sásam: _____
·ré: _____	or _____	·foir: _____

Lesson 55

55.1. The future tense

The future tense is used for verbal actions that will take place in the future, e.g., *I will always love you* or *ein Schiff wird kommen*. In contrast to German, where you can always also use the present tense to denote future actions (e.g., *und das bringt mir den einen*), in Old Irish the future tense has to be applied with the same rigor for future actions as in English. Among all the intricate treasures of Old Irish grammar, the formation of the future is perhaps the most complicated chapter because of the many different classes and the even more numerous exceptions. Old Irish has the following different future formations, which we will learn in this lesson:

f-future
s-future:
    unreduplicated s-future
    reduplicated s-future
i-future:
    reduplicated i-future
    íu-future
a-future:
    reduplicated a-future
    é-future
irregular and suppletive formations

Illustration 55.1: *tarmi·regam!*
Pasaremos! 'We will get through!'

55.2. The f-future

The f-future is formed by nearly all weak verbs (except W1 *caraid* 'to love,' W1 *gataid* 'to steal,' compounds of W1 *scaraid* and W2 *ad·gládathar* 'to talk to'), by H3 verbs, by compounds of S1 *·icc*, by compounds of S2 *·moinethar* and by H2 *ad·roilli* 'to earn.' The underlying suffix of the f-future is *-if-*, which is added directly to the present stem. Originally, that meant in early Old Irish, the suffix caused palatalization of the root final consonant in all verbal classes. During the course of the Old Irish period, however, in the W1 class and in some W2b verbs the root final consonant and the *f* of the suffix become analogically depalatalized under influence from the present stem, e.g., old 3rd pl. abs. *soírfid* /soiɾ'f'əð'/ '(s)he will deliver,' but later *sóerfaid* /soiɾ-fəð'/, in: *ní·fetar indam·ṡoírfad Día fa nacc* 'I do not know whether God will deliver me or not' (*Ml.* 90c19). The *i*, that is to say the vowel of the suffix, is usually absent on the surface due to syncope; it only becomes visible when it comes to stand in an unsyncopated syllable. The *f* /f/ of the suffix may appear as voiced *b* /β/ in absolute *auslaut* or intervocalically, e.g., syncopated 1st sg. abs. *léicfea* /l'ēg'f'a/, but unsyncopated 1st sg. conj. *·léiciub* /·l'ēg'uβ/ 'I will let.' The endings of the f-future are those of the a-ending set (see 53.2), with the one difference that the 1st sg. conjunct is endingless and shows u-infection before the *f/b*.

55.2.1. The active f-future

The paradigm of W2 *léicid* 'to let,' future stem *léicf-* /l'ēg'f'-/, shall suffice to demonstrate the inflection of the f-future:

person		absolute (independent)		conjunct (dependent)	
1st sg.		*léicfea*	C'f'a	*·léiciub*	C'uβ
2nd sg.		*léicfe*	C'f'e	*·léicfe*	C'f'e
3rd sg.		*léicfid*	C'f'əδ'	*·léicfea*	C'f'a
	rel.	*léicfes*	C'f'əs	-	
	pass.	*léicfithir*	C'f'əθ'əρ'	*·léicfither*	C'f'əθ'əρ
	pass. rel.	*léicfither*	C'f'əθ'əρ	-	
1st pl.		*léicfimmi*	C'f'əm'i	*·léicfem*	C'f'əμ
	rel.	*léicfimme*	C'f'əm'e	-	
2nd pl.		*léicfithe*	C'f'əθ'e	*·léicfid*	C'f'əδ'
3rd pl.		*léicfit*	C'f'əd'	*·léicfet*	C'f'əd
	rel.	*léicfite*	C'f'əd'e	-	
	pass.	*léicfitir*	C'f'əd'əρ'	*·léicfiter*	C'f'əd'əρ
	pass. rel.	*léicfiter*	C'f'əd'əρ	-	

Illustration 55.2: The f-future

Note:

1. Instead of *th* /θ/ in the forms above voiced *d* /δ/ may also appear, e.g., *léicfidir*.

2. When the rules of syncope demand it, a vowel is retained before the *f*, which then usually appears as voiced *b* /β/. Furthermore, vowels after *f/b* may then be syncopated, e.g., 3rd sg. abs. *pridchibid* '(s)he will preach' from W1 (!) *pridchid*, 1st pl. *do·aidlibem* 'we will visit' from W1 *do·aidlea* or 3rd sg. pass. *do·díuscibther* '(s)he will be awakened' from W2 *do·díuschi*.

3. If the root final consonant is a *b*, it and the *f* of the future-suffix usually merge in *f* or *b*, e.g., *ad·trefea* and *ad·trebea* /ad·t'r'ef'a ad·t'r'eβ'a/ '(s)he will dwell' < *ad·treb-fea* from W1 *ad·treba*.

4. In the later language the f-future spreads to other verbal classes and ultimately replaces most other future formations in Irish.

55.2.2. The deponent f-future

The inflection of deponent f-futures is absolutely parallel to that of the a-subjunctive. The handbooks cite no forms of the f-future passive of deponent verbs; apparently there are no attestations in early texts. But judging by texts like the prophetic passages in *Immacallam in dá Thúarad*, the passive forms seem to have been formally identical with the deponent forms: e.g., *dichrechnaigfither, digradaigfider* (I2T 224):

person		absolute (independent)		conjunct (dependent)	
1st sg.		suidigfer	C'f'əp	·suidigfer	C'f'əp
2nd sg.		suidigfider	C'f'əδ'əp	·suidigfider	C'f'əδ'əp
3rd sg.		suidigfidir	C'f'əδ'əp'	·suidigfedar	C'f'əδəp
	rel.	suidigfedar	C'f'əδəp	-	
	pass.	suidigfidir	C'f'əδ'əp'	·suidigfedar	C'f'əδəp
	pass. rel.	suidigfedar	C'f'əδəp	-	
1st pl.		suidigfimmir	C'f'əm'əp'	·suidigfemmar	C'f'əməp
	rel.	suidigfemmar	C'f'əməp	-	
2nd pl.		suidigfide	C'f'əδ'e	·suidigfid	C'f'əδ'
3rd pl.		suidigfitir	C'f'əd'əp'	·suidigfetar	C'f'ədəp
	rel.	suidigfetar	C'f'ədəp	-	
	pass.	suidigfitir	C'f'əd'əp'	·suidigfetar	C'f'ədəp
	pass. rel.	suidigfetar	C'f'ədəp	-	

Illustration 55.3: The deponent f-future

55.3. The s-future

All strong verbs that form an s-subjunctive also form an s-future. The only exceptions are compounds of ·icc, which have an f-future, and téit and its compounds, which use a suppletive stem. In the s-future the suffix s is added to the verbal root in exactly the same way as described for the s-subjunctive (see 53.4). The endings of the s-future are basically those of the s-subjunctive, with influence from the a-ending set in the 1st sg. absolute. Two subtypes can be distinguished, a reduplicated and an unreduplicated type:

55.3.1. The unreduplicated type

As far as can be judged from the meagerly attested forms, in S1 verbs with a basic short e in the present and subjunctive stems, the futures look exactly the same as the subjunctives; the correct translation will have to be inferred from the context. The verbs and compounds in question are:

verb	future stem
aingid 'to protect'	aness-
at·reig 'to rise'	ress-
feidid 'to lead'	fess-
laigid 'to lie'	less-
reithid 'to run'	ress-
saidid 'to sit'	sess-
teichid 'to flee'	tess-

Illustration 55.4: The unreduplicated s-future

55.3.2. The reduplicated type

All other verbs form their s-future by basically reduplicating their s-subjunctive stem, using *i* as the reduplicating vowel. Reduplication in the s-future can basically be represented structurally as follows:

root:		s-future:
$C_1(R)VC_2$-	$\rightarrow$	C_1i-$C_{1[+len, +pal]}(R)$əs-

Due to reduplication the verbal root is always unstressed in this formation and the root vowel is reduced to *schwa* /ə/. In the 3rd sg. conjunct, just as in the majority of s-subjunctives, the *s* of the s-future and the preceding vowel are completely lost, leaving the bare *anlauting* consonant of the root after the reduplication syllable. The example below is the future of S2 *guidid* 'to ask, to pray,' subjunctive stem *gess-*, future stem *giges-* /g'iɣ'əs-/. Note that C in this table refers to the lenited root initial consonant, not to the root final consonant as usual:

person		absolute (independent)		conjunct (dependent)	
1st sg.		*gigsea*	C's'a	·*gigius*	C'us
2nd sg.		*gigsi*	C's'i	·*gigis*	C'əs'
3rd sg.		*gigis*	C'əs'	·*gig*	C'
	rel.	*giges*	C'əs	-	
	pass.	*gigestir*	C'əs't'əp'	·*gigestar*	C'əstəp
	pass. rel.	*gigestar*	C'əstəp	-	
1st pl.		*gigsimmi*	C's'əm'i	·*gigsem*	C's'əµ
	rel.	*gigsimme*	C's'əm'e	-	
2nd pl.		*gigeste*	C'əste	·*gigsid*	C's'əδ'
3rd pl.		*gigsit*	C's'əd'	·*gigset*	C's'əd
	rel.	*gigsite*	C's'əd'e	-	
	pass.	*gigsitir*	C's'əd'əp'	·*gigsetar*	C's'ədəp
	pass. rel.	*gigsetar*	C's'ədəp	-	

Illustration 55.5: The reduplicated s-future

Note:

1. Again, you may have already guessed: the vocalization of the endings may vary depending on diverging syncope patterns.

2. The *anlauting* sound of roots beginning with *f-* is regularly lenited away when reduplicated, i.e., **fife- > fie-*; furthermore, the resulting hiatus sequence *ie/ia* /iɜ/ is in many positions contracted into a single short *e*, thus rendering the reduplicated s-future virtually indistinguishable from the corresponding s-subjunctive, e.g., the s-future of S3 *ro·fitir* 'to know' is 1st sg. ·*fessur*, 3rd sg. with hiatus ·*fiastar*, 2nd pl. ·*fessid*, 3rd pl. ·*fessatar;* or from S1 *fichid* 'to fight': 3rd sg. ·*fí*, 3rd sg. pass. ·*fiastar*, but 1st sg. *fessa*, 3rd pl. pass. *fessaitir*. Analogically, S2 *midithir* behaves the same way.

3. Vocalically *anlauting* verbs reduplicate with *i* alone, e.g., S1 *orgaid* 'to slay,' subjunctive stem *orr-* → future stem *iorr-*, *iurr-* /iör- iür-/; S1 *ithid* 'to eat,' subjunctive stem *ess-* → *iëss-*, further contracted to future stem *íss-* /īs-/.

4. Roots beginning with *sl-* and *sn-* lose the *s* in reduplication, e.g., S2 *sligid* 'to fell' → future stem *siles-*; S2 *slaidid* 'to strike' → *selas-*; S2 *snigid* 'to drip' → *sines-*.

5. S1 *seinnid* 'to play an instrument; to strike' and *do·seinn* 'to hunt' have the future stem *sifes-* /sibes-/.

6. S1 *lingid* 'to jump' has the future stem *iblis-*, but this is only found in usually obscured form in compounds.

7. In roots containing etymological *u* or *a* the root initial consonant remains unpalatalized, e.g., 2nd sg. abs. *memais* /m'eµəs'/ 'thou wilt break' from S2 *maidid* or 1st sg. conj. *fo·lilus* /fo·l'iλus/ 'I will suffer' from S1 *fo·loing*. Likewise; the *s* in these cases is depalatalized if the vowel in front of it is syncopated, e.g., 1st sg. abs. *bibsa* /b'iβsa/ 'I will break' from S1 *bongaid* or 3rd pl. conj. *·memsat* /m'eµsəd/ 'they will break' from S2 *maidid*.

8. Where the verbal root has an underlying *a* (see 53.4.1. for examples), the *i* of the reduplicating syllable is lowered to *e*, e.g., *maidid* 'to break' → future stem *memas-* /m'eµəs-/. Note that these verbs retain the *a* of the root in the 3rd sg. conjunct, e.g., *·mema* '(s)he will break.' The reduplicated s-future of *saigid* 'to seek' is disyllabic *sias-* /s'iəs-/.

9. When the preverbs *fo-* and *to-* come to stand in accented position immediately before the reduplicating syllable, they change to *fóe-/foí-*, resp. *tóe-/toí-* and the reduplication is lost (see also 50.2), e.g., 1st sg. deuterotonic *fo·cichiurr* /fo·k'iχ'ur/ 'I will put,' but prototonic *·foíchiurr* /·foiχ'ur/, future of S1 *fo·ceird*.

10. Reduplication is regularly lost when the verbal root is preceded by two or more preverbs.

I cannot go into every irregular detail here. For many more divergent or otherwise special formations see GOI 411–413.

55.4. The i-future

Verbs with a root final *i*, i.e., H2 verbs (except for *·gní* and *·sní*) and most S3 verbs (except for compounds of *·gnin* and *·cluinethar*, *·fitir* and other verbs without a root final *i*.), form an i-future. The endings of the i-future are similar to those of W2 and H2 presents except for the 2nd sg., which ends in *-e*. As in the case of the s-future, two subtypes can be distinguished: a reduplicated type and the so-called íu-type:

55.4.1. The reduplicated type

Roots with a single initial consonant reduplicate this consonant using *i* as reduplication vowel. The endings are added immediately to the root initial consonant. Reduplication can be represented structurally like this:

root: i-future:

Cĭ-   →   Ci-C[+len, +pal]-E

Not too many forms of this formation are attested; a full paradigm of S3 *renaid* 'to sell,' future stem *rir-* /r'iρ'-/, would probably look like this:

person		absolute (independent)		conjunct (dependent)	
1st sg.		*ririu*	C'u	*·ririu*	C'u
2nd sg.		*rire*	C'e	*·rire*	C'e
3rd sg.		*ririd*	C'əδ'	*·riri*	C'i
	rel.	*rires*	C'əs	-	
	pass.	*rirthir*	C'θ'əρ'	*·rirther*	C'θ'əρ
	pass. rel.	*rirther*	C'θ'əρ	-	
1st pl.		*rirmi*	C'm'i	*·rirem*	C'əμ
	rel.	*rirme*	C'm'e	-	
2nd pl.		*rirthe*	C'θ'e	*·ririd*	C'əρ'
3rd pl.		*ririt*	C'əd'	*·riret*	C'əd
	rel.	*ririte* (?)	C'əd'e	-	
	pass.	*rirtir*	C'd'əρ'	*·rirter*	C'd'əρ
	pass. rel.	*rirter*	C'd'əρ	-	

Illustration 55.6: The reduplicated i-future

Note:

1. The future stem of H2 *ad·cí* 'to see' and other compounds of *·cí* is a mixture of s- and i-future. The i-future type includes 3rd sg. *·accigi*, *du·écigi*, 3rd pl. *·aiccichet*; the reduplicated s-future type includes 1st sg. *do·écuchus*, 3rd sg. pass. *ad·cigestar*, 3rd pl. *ad·cichset*.

2. S3 *benaid* has an i-future stem *bī-* < *biβ-*: 1st sg. *bíu*, *·bíu*, 3rd sg. *bíthus* '(s)he will beat them,' *·bí*, rel. *bias*. The attested 3rd sg. pass. is *bethir*; likewise, the 3rd sg. pass. i-future of S3 *ad·fen* 'to requite' is *ad·fether*.

55.4.2. The íu-type

Instead of showing overt reduplication, S3 verbs with roots beginning with consonant and *r/l* insert *íu* /iṷ/ in front of the latter. The endings are the same as in the reduplicated type, but the 'stem' before the ending is always unpalatalized. This formation can be represented structurally like this:

root: íu-future:

CRĬ-   →   CíuR$_{[+len, -pal]}$-E

Examples are 3rd pl. *gíulait* 'they will stick' from *glenaid*, *ara·chíurat* 'they will perish' and 3rd sg. *ara·chíuri* 'it will perish' from *ara·chrin*.

55.5. The a-future

There is no easy rule as to which verbs have an a-future. The a-future is formed by strong verbs with roots ending in *b, r, l, m, n*, by S3 *·gnin* and compounds and by *ro·cluinethar*, by W1 *caraid* 'to love' and *gataid* 'to steal,' W2 *ad·gládathar* 'to talk to,' by H1 verbs, by H2 *·gní* and *·sní* and by H3 *do·goa* 'to choose.' The a-future is so called because it uses the same a-ending set for its inflection as the a-subjunctive (see 53.2). Again two subtypes can be distinguished: a reduplicated type and the so-called é-future:

55.5.1. The reduplicated type

It is not easy to give simple rules about the formation of reduplicated a-futures. It may be best to just list the various formations together with the relevant verbs. Note that, when the reduplication syllable is moved out of the stressed position, reduplication is lost!

1. A few verbs reduplicate with *i*; the vowel of the root is regularly syncopated. The stem final consonant basically becomes palatalized, but analogically loses palatalization again in a few verbs:

    1. S2 *gainithir* 'is born' → future stem *gigne-* /g'iɣ'v'ə-/, e.g., 3rd sg. *gignithir*, *·gignethar*, 3rd pl. *gignitir*

    2. S1 *gonaid* 'to slay' → *gigne-* /g'iɣ'v'ə-/, 3rd sg. pass. *·gignether* 'will be slain'

    3. S2 *ro·laimethar* 'to dare' → *lilme-* /l'iλ'µ'ə-/, 3rd pl. *·lilmatar*

    4. S2 *daimid* 'to suffer' → *didme-* /d'iδ'µ'ə-/, 1st sg. *·didem*, *·didam*, 2nd sg. *·didmae*, 3rd sg. *·didma*, 3rd pl. *·didmat*; 3rd sg. conditional *·didmed*

    5. S1 *ibid* 'to drink' → **iïba-* which is further contracted to *íba-* /ıβə-/, 1st sg. *íba*, *·íb*, 3rd sg. *·íba*, 3rd pl. *íbait*

2. The following verbs reduplicate with *e*. The stem final consonant is not palatalized.

    1. W1 *caraid* 'to love' → future stem *cechra-* /k'eχρə-/, e.g., 3rd sg. *·cechra*, 3rd pl. *cechrait*

    2. W2 *ad·gládathar* 'to talk to' → *ad·gegallda-*, *·acellda-* /aδ·g'eɣəldə- ·ag'əldə-/, sometimes with further assimilation of *-lld-* to *-ll-*, 1st sg. *ad·gegallar*, 3rd sg. *ad·gegalldathar*

    3. S1 *canaid* 'to sing' → *cechna-* /k'eχvə-/, 3rd sg. rel. *cechnas*, 1st sg. *for·cechan* 'I will teach,' 3rd sg. *for·cechna*

    4. H1 *baid* 'to die' → *beba-* /b'eβə-/, 3rd sg. *bebaid*, 2nd pl. *bebthe*

    5. H1 *raid* 'to row' → *rera-* /r'epə-/, 3rd sg. *do·rera*

    6. H1 *ad·cota*, *·éta* 'to obtain' → *·étatha-*/*·étada-* /·ēdəθə- ·ēdəδə-/, 3rd sg. *·étada*, 1st pl. *·étatham*; but pass. *·étastar* and 2nd sg. conditional *·étaste* with influence from the s-future

    7. H3 *do·goa* 'to choose' → *·gega-* /·g'eɣə-/, 3rd sg. *do·gega*, 3rd pl. *do·gegat*

    8. S3 *ro·cluinethar* 'to hear' → *·cechla-* /k'eχλə-/, 3rd sg. *·cechladar*; the passive has s-forms under influence from the corresponding forms of the other word for sensorial perception *ad·cí*, e.g., 3rd sg. *·cechlastar*

3. Strong verbs whose roots begin with a vowel and end with *r* or *l* substitute *eb-* for the initial vowel in the future stem:

1. S3 *ernaid* 'to bestow,' root *er-* → future stem *ebra-* /eβρə-/, e.g., 3rd sg. with suffixed pronoun *ebarthi* < **ebraid-i* '(s)he will bestow it,' 3rd sg. pass. *ebarthir*

2. S1 *ailid* 'to rear,' root *al-* → *ebla-* /eβλə-/, 3rd sg. *·ebla*, 3rd sg. pass. *ebaltair*

3. S2 *airid* 'to plough,' root *ar-* → *ebra-* /eβρə-/, 3rd sg. *·ebrat*

55.5.2. The é-future

Verbs with roots beginning with a consonant and ending in *r*, *l* or *b*, H2 and S3 verbs that begin with *Cn-* and the S1 verbs *do·eim* 'to protect' and *do·fuissim* 'to create' have an é-future. This is basically formed by substituting the root vowel of the corresponding a-subjunctive stem with *ē*. You will note that quite a number of verbs have identical, homophonous future stems. The verbs in question are:

1. S1 *beirid* 'to carry' → future stem *béra-* /b'ēρə-/, e.g., 2nd sg. *·bérae*, 3rd sg. *béraid*, etc. The future stem of *do·beir*, *·tabair* 'to bring, to give' is *do·béra-*, *·tibéra-* /do·b'ēρə- t'iβ'ēρə-/; note that the *é* is not syncopated in the oldest time. Similarly: *ceilid* 'to hide' → *céla-* /k'ēλə-/, *meilid* 'to grind' → *méla-* /m'ēλə-/, *fo·geir* 'to heat' → *·géra-* /·g'ēρə-/.

2. S1 *do·fuissim* 'to create' has the future stem *do·fusséma-* /do·fus'ēμə-/, *do·eim* 'to protect' → *do·éma-* /do·ēμə-/.

3. S1 *marnaid* 'to betray' → *méra-* /m'ēρə-/, *at·baill* 'to die' → *·béla-* /·β'ēλə-/.

4. S2 *gaibid* 'to take' → *géba-* /g'ēβə-/, *gairid* 'to call' → *géra-* /g'ēρə-/, S1 *maraid* 'to remain' → *méra-* /m'ēρə-/

5. W1 *gataid* 'to steal' → *géta-* /g'ēdə-/, compounds of W1 *scaraid* 'to separate' → *·scéra-* /s'k'ēρə-/.

6. S1 *gonaid* 'to slay,' beside showing reduplicated forms (see 55.5.1.1.2 above), also has a é-future stem → *géna-* /g'ēvə-/, 3rd sg. *·géna*.

In the case of the H2 and S3 verbs in question, the *ē* is inserted between the initial consonant and the following *n*:

1. H2 *gniid* 'to do' → future stem *géna-* /g'ēvə-/, e.g., 1st sg. *do·gén*, 2nd sg. *·génae*, 3rd sg. *·géna*, 1st pl. *·génam*, 2nd pl. *·génaid*, 3rd pl. *·génat*. Originally the *é* seems not to have been syncopated, e.g., 1st pl. *·digénam* 'we will make,' but later it could be syncopated as well, e.g., *·dignem*.

2. Likewise, H2 *con·sní* 'to contend' → *·séna-* /s'ēvə-/, 3rd sg. *·coisséna*, and S3 *·gnin* 'to know' → *·géna* /g'ēvə-/, 3rd pl. *·génat*, 3rd sg. pass. *·géntar*.

55.6. Suppletive futures

1. S1 *téit* 'to go' and its compounds with a single preverb use the suppletive future stem *riga-* or *rega-* /r'iɣə- r'eɣə-/. *riga-/rega-* uses the a-ending set for inflection, e.g., 3rd sg. abs. *regaid* '(s)he will go,' rel. *rigas*, 3rd sg. *do·rega, ·terga* '(s)he will come,' 2nd sg. conj. *for·regae* 'thou wilt help.'

2. S1 *agaid* 'to drive' and its compounds use the stem *ebla-* /eβλə-/ in the future. *ebla-* uses the a-ending set for inflection, e.g., 3rd sg. conj. *ad·ebla* '(s)he will drive.'

3. The substantive verb H1 *at·tá* has the hiatus future stem *bia-* /b'iə̃-/, which uses the a-ending set; for the forms see 56.2.1. But compounds of *·tá* have a regular reduplicated a-future.

You can find tables with the future formations in Appendix F.10.

Illustration 55.7:
fa·géba he will find it'

55.7. Exercise

Form the future stem of some of the following verbs and inflect them in the future:

> *rannaid* /ranəð'/ (W1) 'to divide'
> *gairid* /gaρ'əð'/ (S2) 'to hide'
> *slaidid* /slaδ'əð'/ (S2) 'to strike'
> *grádaigidir* /grāδəɣ'əð'əρ'/ (W2b) 'to love'
> *do·seinn, ·tophainn* /do·s'en' ·tofən'/ (S1) 'to pursue, to hunt' (You don't have to attempt to form the prototonic future forms of this verb. This would get too absurd!)

55.8. The prehistory of the future formations

As with the synchronic formation of the future in Old Irish itself, so its diachronic explanation is a difficult field, and I can only give a very general impression of what happened. In the f-future, in Primitive Irish the suffix *-if- was added to the root, followed by the a-ending set. The further prehistory of this suffix is unclear and will therefore not be dealt with here. All other future formations basically go back to reduplicated formations with *i* as reduplication vowel and the suffix *-se/o- added to the root.

An example for the 'normal' reduplicated s-future is *gigis-* /g'iɣ'əs'/, the future stem of S2 *guidid*. Note that in the 1st sg. absolute the ending of the a-future was taken over:

abs.	OIr.	Prim. Irish	Insular Celtic	Proto-Celtic	Pre-Celtic
1st sg.	gig†sea «	*gʷiɣʷesū	*gʷigʷetsū	*gʷigʷetsū	*gʷʰigʷʰedsoh₂
2nd sg.	gig†si «	*gʷiɣʷesehi	*gʷigʷetsesi «	*gʷigʷetsesi	*gʷʰigʷʰedsesi
3rd sg.	gigis	*gʷiɣʷesi	*gʷigʷetsi «	*gʷigʷetseti	*gʷʰigʷʰedseti
1st pl.	gig†simmi	*gʷiɣʷesomohi «	*gʷigʷetsomosi «	*gʷigʷetsomosi	*gʷʰigʷʰedsomosi
2nd pl.	giges†te «	*gʷiɣʷeseθē-	*gʷigʷetsetesi «	*gʷigʷetsetesi	*gʷʰigʷʰedsetesi
3rd pl.	gig†sit	*gʷiɣʷesodi	*gʷigʷetsonti «	*gʷigʷetsonti	*gʷʰigʷʰedsonti

Illustration 55.8: The prehistory of the absolute reduplicated s-future

conj.	OIr.	Prim. Irish	Insular Celtic	Proto-Celtic	Pre-Celtic
1st sg.	·gigius	*gʷiɣʷesū	*gʷigʷetsū	*gʷigʷetsū	*gʷʰigʷʰedsoh₂
2nd sg.	·gigis	*gʷiɣʷeseh	*gʷigʷetses	*gʷigʷetsesi	*gʷʰigʷʰedsesi
3rd sg.	·gig	*gʷiɣʷes	*gʷigʷets «	*gʷigʷetseti	*gʷʰigʷʰedseti
1st pl.	·gig†sem	*gʷiɣʷesoμah	*gʷigʷetsomos	*gʷigʷetsomosi	*gʷʰigʷʰedsomosi
2nd pl.	·gig†sid	*gʷiɣʷeseθeh	*gʷigʷetsetes	*gʷigʷetsetesi	*gʷʰigʷʰedsetesi
3rd pl.	·gig†set	*gʷiɣʷesod	*gʷigʷetsont	*gʷigʷetsonti	*gʷʰigʷʰedsonti

Illustration 55.9: The prehistory of the conjunct reduplicated s-future

Although being synchronically a completely irregular formation in Old Irish, on the historical level the future stem *ebra-* /eβρa/ of S3 *ernaid* (root *perh₃*) is a perfectly regular example for the development of the reduplicated a-future: originally a *p* was reduplicated at the beginning of the word. Eventually the first *p* was lost altogether and the second *p* developed into /β/. é-futures arose exactly in the same way, only the reduplicated consonant was lost in the interior of the word and caused lengthening of the preceding vowel, e.g., *kiχλāheθi > *ke(χ)λāheθi > célaid, future of S1 *ceilid*:

abs.	OIr.	Prim. Irish	Insular Celtic	Proto-Celtic	Pre-Celtic
1st sg.	ebra «	*iβρāhū	*φiβρāsū	*φiφρāsū	*pipr̥h₃soh₂
2nd sg.	ebrae	*iβρāhehi	*φiβρāsesi «	*φiφρāsesi	*pipr̥h₃sesi
3rd sg.	ebraid	*iβρāheθi	*φiβρāseti «	*φiφρāseti	*pipr̥h₃seti
1st pl.	ebraimmi	*iβρāhomohi «	*φiβρāsomosi «	*φiφρāsomosi	*pipr̥h₃somosi
2nd pl.	ebar†the	*iβρāheθē-	*φiβρāsetesi «	*φiφρāsetesi	*pipr̥h₃setesi
3rd pl.	ebrait	*iβρāhodi	*φiβρāsonti «	*φiφρāsonti	*pipr̥h₃sonti

Illustration 55.10: The prehistory of the absolute reduplicated and é a-future

conj.	OIr.	Prim. Irish	Insular Celtic	Proto-Celtic	Pre-Celtic
1ˢᵗ sg.	·ebar «?	*iβρāhū	*φiβrāsū	*φiφrāsū	*pipr̥h₃soh₂
2ⁿᵈ sg.	·ebrae «	*iβρāheh	*φiβrāses	*φiφrāsesi	*pipr̥h₃sesi
3ʳᵈ sg.	·ebra	*iβρāheθ	*φiβrāset	*φiφrāseti	*pipr̥h₃seti
1ˢᵗ pl.	·ebram	*iβρāhoμah	*φiβrāsomos	*φiφrāsomosi	*pipr̥h₃somosi
2ⁿᵈ pl.	·ebraid	*iβρāheθeh	*φiβrāsetes	*φiφrāsetesi	*pipr̥h₃setesi
3ʳᵈ pl.	·ebrat	*iβρāhod	*φiβrāsont	*φiφrāsonti	*pipr̥h₃sonti

Illustration 55.11: The prehistory of the conjunct reduplicated and é a-future

And finally an example for the reduplicated i-future, the future stem *lili-* of S3 *lenaid*:

abs.	OIr.	Prim. Irish	Insular Celtic	Proto-Celtic	Pre-Celtic
1ˢᵗ sg.	liliu	*liλīhū	*lilīsū	*lilīsū	*h₂lih₂liHsoh₂
2ⁿᵈ sg.	lile	*liλīhehi	*lilīsesi «	*lilīsesi	*h₂lih₂liHsesi
3ʳᵈ sg.	lilid	*liλīheθi	*lilīseti «	*lilīseti	*h₂lih₂liHseti
1ˢᵗ pl.	lil†mi	*liλīhomohi «	*lilīsomosi «	*lilīsomosi	*h₂lih₂liHsomosi
2ⁿᵈ pl.	lil†the	*liλīheθē-	*lilīsetesi «	*lilīsetesi	*h₂lih₂liHsetesi
3ʳᵈ pl.	lilit	*liλīhodi	*lilīsonti «	*lilīsonti	*h₂lih₂liHsonti

Illustration 55.12: The prehistory of the absolute reduplicated i-future

conj.	OIr.	Prim. Irish	Insular Celtic	Proto-Celtic	Pre-Celtic
1ˢᵗ sg.	·liliu	*liλīhū	*lilīsū	*lilīsū	*h₂lih₂liHsoh₂
2ⁿᵈ sg.	·lile	*liλīheh	*lilīses	*lilīsesi	*h₂lih₂liHsesi
3ʳᵈ sg.	·lili	*liλīheθ	*lilīset	*lilīseti	*h₂lih₂liHseti
1ˢᵗ pl.	·lilem	*liλīhoμah	*lilīsomos	*lilīsomosi	*h₂lih₂liHsomosi
2ⁿᵈ pl.	·lilid	*liλīheθeh	*lilīsetes	*lilīsetesi	*h₂lih₂liHsetesi
3ʳᵈ pl.	·lilet	*liλīhod	*lilīsont	*lilīsonti	*h₂lih₂liHsonti

Illustration 55.13.: The prehistory of the conjunct reduplicated i-future

Lesson 56

56.1. The conditional

The conditional (also called *secondary* or *past future*) has three principal functions:

1. It characterizes a verbal action as possible under certain conditions (X *could happen*) or, more often, as hypothetical or unreal (X *would, should, could happen* or *have happened*, but the necessary conditions are not met or were not met), e.g., *fo·lilsainn-se matis mo námait doda·gnetis* 'I would have endured (them) if it had been my enemies that would have done them' (*Ml.* 73d1) (the 1st sg. conditional *fo·lilsainn* 'I would have endured' refers to a hypothetical verbal action, whereas the two past subjunctives *matis* 'if they had been' and *doda·gnetis* 'who would have done them' characterize the conditions as unreal).

2. It refers to future actions from a past point of view, e.g., *as·bert Cathbad, óclách no·gébad gaisced and, for·biad a ainm hÉrinn co bráth* […] *7 no·mértis a airscélae co bráth* 'Cathbad said that a warrior who would take arms then, his name would be upon Ireland forever and stories about him would remain forever' (TBC 613 ff.); transferred into a present frame of reference, the future tense would be used where the conditional appears in the sentence above, namely **as·beir Cathbad, óclách gébas gaisced indíu, for·bia a ainm hÉirinn co bráth 7 méraid a airscélae co bráth* 'Cathbad says that a warrior who will take arms today, his name will be upon Ireland forever and stories about him will remain forever.'

3. It is used in negative and interrogative clauses to characterize assumed verbal actions as false, e.g., *ní·digned Dauid* 'David would not have done' (*Ml.* 14b4), *cía no·regad acht mad messe* 'who would go, if not I' (LU 7052 f.).

The conditional is formed by adding the 'secondary endings,' which we have learned in 49.1, to the future stem. As in the case of the imperfect or the past subjunctive, no distinction between absolute and conjunct forms is made; simple verbs without a preceding particle are compounded with the empty particle *no·*. Active and deponent verbs inflect alike. The sample verbs below are the same as in 49.1, except that for W1 *caraid* 'to love' W1 *móraid* 'to praise' has been substituted. Note that, although originally the root final consonant and the suffix *f* in *·móirfinn* /mōρ'f'ən'/, etc., would have been palatalized, it was analogically depalatalized to *·mórfainn* /mōρfən'/, etc., in the later language:

Illustration 56.1:
óclách gébas gaisced indíu, méraid a airscélae co bráth
'a warrior who will take arms today, stories about him will remain forever'

293

person		W1	W2	S1	ending
1st sg.		·móirfinn	·suidigfinn	do·bérainn, ·tibérainn	ən'
2nd sg.		·móirfithea	·suidigfithea	do·bértha, ·tibértha	(ə)θ(')a
3rd sg.		·móirfid, -ith	·suidigfed, -feth	do·bérad, ·tibérad	əδ əθ
	pass.	·móirfithe	·suidigfithe	do·bérthae, ·tibérthae	(ə)θ(')e
1st pl.		·móirfimmis	·suidigfimmis	do·bérmais, ·tibérmais	(ə)m(')əs'
2nd pl.		·móirfide	·suidigfithe	do·bérthae, ·tibérthae	(ə)θ(')e
3rd pl.		·móirfitis	·suidigfitis	do·bértais, ·tibértais	(ə)d(')əs'
	pass.	·móirfitis	·suidigfitis	do·bértais, ·tibértais	(ə)d(')əs'

Illustration 56.2: The inflection of the conditional

56.2. Exercise

Try to form the future stem of some of the following verbs and inflect them in the conditional:

> do·gni, ·dénai /do·g'n'ī ·d'ēvi/ (H2) 'to do, to make'
> do·scara, ·tascra /do·skaρa, ·taskρa/ (W1) 'to overthrow'
> fo·loing, ·fulaing /fo·loŋ'g' ·fuλəŋ'g'/ (S1) 'to suffer, to endure'
> do·icc, ·ticc /do·ig' ·t'ig'/ (S1) 'to come'

56.3. The future of the substantive verb and the copula

		future		conditional
		absolute	conjunct	
1st sg.		bia	*·bia	·beinn
2nd sg.		bie	*·bie	·betha
3rd sg.		bieid, bied	·bia	·biad
	rel.	bias	-	-
	impers.	bethir	·bether	·bethe
1st pl.		bemmi	·biam	·bemmis
2nd pl.		bethe	·bieid, ·bied	n/a
3rd pl.		bieit	·biat	·betis
	rel.	bete	-	-

Illustration 56.3: The future of the substantive verb

As in the case of the subjunctive, the forms of the copula are special in the future and conditional. Note again that unlike any other verb the copula has absolute forms in the conditional.

	future		conditional	
	absolute	conjunct	absolute	conjunct
1st sg.	*be*	n/a	n/a	n/a
2nd sg.	*be, ba*	*-be, -ba, -pa*	n/a	n/a
3rd sg.	*bid, bith*	*-be, -pe, -ba, -pa*	*bed^L*	*-bad^L, -pat^L*
rel.	*bes^L, bas^L*	-	*bed^L*	-
1st pl.	*bemmi, bimmi*	n/a	n/a	n/a
2nd pl.	n/a	*-beth*	n/a	n/a
3rd pl.	*bit*	*-bat^L, -pat^L*	*beitis*	*-ptis*
rel.	*beta^L, bat*	-	n/a	-

Illustration 56.4: The future of the copula

Note:

1. The absolute forms of the conditional are very rare; usually *ro-* is prefixed to the conjunct form of the conditional when no other particle precedes it.

2. For most of those persons that are designated as 'not attested' in the table, in the later language analogical, unclassical formations can be found. I did not take them into account.

You can find all forms of the copula and the substantive verb in Appendixes F.11 and F.12.

56.4. Suffixed pronouns

Apart from the normal type of Old Irish pronouns (classes A–C), which are inserted into verbal forms, in the classical Old Irish period another way of expressing pronominal forms existed: They could also be suffixed to simple verbs, meaning they could be added after the ending of simple verbs.[1] We already met the most frequent use of suffixed pronouns in 47.2.2, i.e., after the 3rd sg. of the substantive verb to denote possession. But ideally suffixed pronouns can be added to all verbs. Practically, however, suffixed pronouns are nearly exclusively added to verbs in the 3rd sg. When the pronoun that always consists of an extra syllable is added, the vowel in the syllable before it is syncopated. The *-d* /ð/ of the 3rd sg. ending is automatically changed to *-th-* /θ/ in this process, e.g., *móraid* '(s)he praises' + suffixed pronoun *-us* 'her' → *mórthus* '(s)he praises her,' or *geguin* '(s)he slew' + suffixed pronoun *-i* 'him' → *gegni* '(s)he slew him.' Apart from instances of the substantive verb **táith* in the meaning 'to have' (see 47.2.2 and Appendix F.11), in Old Irish prose only 3rd person pronouns are used, and practically only after verbs in the 3rd sg. absolute. In poetry 1st and 2nd person pronouns appear as well. The suffixed pronouns are:

---

[1] Historically speaking, the conjugated prepositions of Old Irish are also combinations of prepositions with suffixed pronouns that eventually merged into a single unsegmentable form.

person	ending	transcription	example
1st sg.	-um	/-uμ -um (?)/	sástum 'satisfies me' < sásaid
2nd sg.	-ut	/-ud/	nóíthiut 'celebrates thee' < noïd
3rd sg. m., n.	-i	/-i/	foídsi 'sent him' < pret. foídis
3rd sg. f.	-us	/-us/	itius 'eats her' < ithid
1st pl.	-unn	/-un/	snáidsiunn 'may he protect us' < snáidid
2nd pl.	-uib	/-uβ'/	táthuib 'you have' < tā-
3rd pl.	-us	/-us/	sexus 'followed them' < pret. sechsidir

Illustration 56.5: The suffixed pronouns

Note:

1. Apart from the 3rd sg. absolute, the only other verbal forms to which suffixed pronouns may be attached are 3rd plurals in -it, 1st plurals in -mi and the 1st sg. future in -a. The only pronoun that may be suffixed to these endings is the 3rd sg. masc./neuter, which, however, appears in the form -it /-əd'/ in these cases, e.g., promfit 'I will try it' < 1st sg. future proimfea, guidmit 'we ask it' < 1st pl. guidmi, gébtit 'they will take him' < 3rd pl. future gébait.

56.5. A 'consecutio temporum' in Old Irish

In Latin grammar the rules of *consecutio temporum* 'sequence of tenses' define the correct use of tenses and moods in dependent clauses to express the possible levels of time (German: *Zeitstufen*), i.e., *contemporaneity* = present time, *anteriority* = past time and *posteriority* = future time, in relation to the time of the main clause. These rules have to be strictly observed in Latin in order to achieve a logical construction of the sentences.

Something along these lines can also be set up for Old Irish, though not with the same consequence as in Latin. The table below gives you the possible combination for contemporaneous and posterior actions and for the various applications of the subjunctive (see 53.1). A separate column for anterior actions has not been included, since these may be variously expressed by past tenses or by the use of the augment with other tenses. Note that the present time in the main clause is expressed by the present tense; the past time in the main clause can be expressed by the past tense and by the imperfect, or by augmented forms thereof.

main clause	dependent clause		
	contemporaneous	future	subjunctive
present time	present tense	future tense	present subjunctive
past time	var. past tenses	conditional	past subjunctive

Illustration 56.6: The Old Irish 'consecutio temporum'

Lesson 57

57.1. A legal episode[1]

The following short Old Irish text with legal content is found in two manuscripts from the modern period, printed in CIH iii 1859.6–15 and v 907.36–908.6. I have normalized the spelling.

Ninne mac Magach d'ḟéinib, luid fo thúaid i crích nUlad triur marcach do ṡaigid charat and, 7 scoirsit a n-echu i tír ba cheníuil doib riam; nibu do chuingid chota ind.

Co·n-eipert int í ba thír friu: 'Beirid far n-echu asin tír!'

As·bert didiu in dias boíe la Ninne: 'Ní mó dán dún-ni ci ad·cotam scor ar n-ech sund; nibu ar chuingid chota and.'

'Ní airassa són, robo lib-si riam. Ní·biat and ém airi!'

Ní·fetatar-som co-sin armba leo riam a tír. Ní·léicset a n-echu as. Cartaid didiu int í ba thír a n-echu as ar éicin. Fo·gellsat íarum imbi Conchobor mac Nessa 7 bert-side fíach n-ecair étechtai forsin n-í cartas a n-echu asin tír 7 chomlóg ind í cartas as, 7 do·combaig selba doib a chummai-sin di thelluch.

Transcription

n'in'e mak maɣəχ d'ēv'əβ, luδ' fo θuaδ' i g'r'ɪχ vuləδ t'r'iür μarkəχ do haɣ'əδ' χapəd and, ogus skoρ's'əd' a v'eχu i d'ɪρ' ba χ'ev'ɪμλ' doəβ' r'iəμ; n'ibu do χuŋ'g'əδ' χoda in'd'. ko·v'eb'ərt int-ɪ ba θ'ɪρ f'r'ihu: 'b'eρ'əδ' βaρ v'eχu as'ən t'ɪρ'!' as·b'ert d'iδ'u in d'iəs boi̯e la n'in'e: 'n'ɪ mō dāv dun-n'i k'i aδ·kodəμ skoρ aρ v'eχ sund; n'ibu aρ χuŋ'g'əδ' χoda and.' 'n'ɪ haρ'asa sōv, robo l'iβ'-s'i r'iəμ. n'ɪ·b'iəd and ēμ aρ'i!' n'ɪ·f'edədəρ-soμ ko-s'iv aρmba leμ r'iəμ a d'ɪρ. n'ɪ·l'ēg'səd a v'eχu as. kartəδ' d'iδ'u int-ɪ ba θ'ɪρ a v'eχu as aρ ēg'əv'. fo·g'elsəd iaρuμ im'b'i koνχəβəρ mak n'esa ogus β'ert-s'iδ'e f'iaχ v'egəρ' ēd'əχti fors'ən n'ɪ kartəs a v'eχu as'ən t'ɪρ' ogus χoμλōɣ ind-ɪ kartəs as, ogus δo·kombəɣ' s'elβa doəβ' a χumi-s'əv d'i θ'eluχ.

Note:

1. The purpose of this story is that of a legal example: Ninne unwittingly performed the necessary actions for a legal procedure called *tellach* 'legal entry,' by which claim is laid upon a piece of land. The author of the episode demonstrates that even though Ninne did not intend the *tellach* and did not even know of his right to a claim on the land, the accidentally performed action is valid and he has to be paid compensation.

2. *triur marcach* in the first line does not mean 'with three riders,' but must mean, as becomes evident from the following, 'three riders including him.' Another instance of such an inclusive use of the independent prepositional of personal numerals can be found in the story *Tucait Buile Mongáin*: *at·recht Mongán mórfessiur* 'Mongán arose, seven men altogether' (IB 56.14). That Ninne is accompanied by two men is not accidental: To perform a legally correct *tellach* one has to be accompanied by a witness and a surety.

3. *dán* is here used in the meaning 'payment,' which is not noted in DIL.

4. *ba thír* is a genitival relative clause: 'whose the land was.'

---

[1] The legal and grammatical commentaries to this piece were kindly supplied by Neil MCLEOD and Dennis KING.

5. *fíach ecair étechta* is a legal term for a 'penalty for improper observance of [the law of] entry': By driving off the horses of Ninne and his men and by not submitting the case to a judge, the owner of the land on his part is guilty of breaking the proper procedure of *tellach*.

57.2. Varia

1. Sometimes pronouns can be infixed into Irish verbs where no pronoun would be used in English, e.g., the neuter pronoun in sentence 2 below *adid·trefea* 'lit.: who will dwell it = who will dwell.' Often infixed and suffixed pronouns are used proleptically to refer to objects that themselves are expressed in the sentence, e.g., as in *foilsigthi in spirut and-som a rrath* 'the Spirit manifests (it) in him the grace' (*Wb.* 12a7), where the neuter suffixed pronoun *-i* 'it' refers to *a rrath* 'the grace.' The pronoun should not be translated in such cases.

2. The impersonal phrase *maidid re X for Y* 'lit.: it breaks before X upon Y' is a fixed expression that means 'X defeats Y.' Either of the two prepositonal complements may be left off, i.e., *maidid re X* 'it breaks before X = X wins, X is victor,' and *maidid for Y* 'it breaks upon Y = Y is defeated, Y loses,' as in sentence 10 below.

3. *Níallmag* 'lit.: Níall's (= Níall Noígíallach's) plain' is a *kenning* for Ireland.

57.3. Exercise

Old Irish

1. * Is suaichnid, mani·creitid eisséirge Críst 7 inna mmarb, níb·noíbfea far n-ires in chruth-sin 7 níb·scairfea fribar pecthu. (*Wb.* 13b19) 2. ** Bid sochaide ad·trefea indiut-su 7 bid fáilid nach óen adid·trefea. (*Ml.* 107a15) 3. ** Nonn·samlafammar frinn fesine. (*Wb.* 17b12) 4. ** A lliles dind ainchreitmiuch bid ainchreitmech. (*Wb.* 10a5) 5. ** A n-í as·beirinn co-sse, is ed as·bér beus. (*Ml.* 91b10) 6. ** [...] sech is airde són do·mbéra Día do neuch nod·n-eirbfea ind 7 génas triit. (*Ml.* 51b10) 7. ** Co·n-eipred: 'Do·gén a nnóeb-sa 7 ní·digén a n-airgairthe-se, cid accobar lium,' ní·eiper in-sin. (*Ml.* 69a21) 8. * Níba madae dam m'fóisitiu, air na nní no·gigius, na·ebra Día. (*Ml.* 46b12) 9. ** Gigeste-si Día linn ara·fulsam ar fochaidi. (*Wb.* 14c2) 10. ** Mani·roma fora cenn, ní·mema forsna baullu. (*Ml.* 89c11) 11. * Do·géntar aidchumtach tempuil leis, 7 pridchibid smachtu rechto fetarlaicce, 7 na·ngébat Iudaidi i n-apaid, 7 chon·scéra recht nufiadnaissi. (*Wb.* 26a8) 12. * 'Acht ro·feissinn bed tú níbad samlaid no·scarfammais,' ol Cú Chulainn. (TBR 60) 13. * Bid comard a slíab fri fán, [...] bid cosmail do chlár in domun conid·reissed uball. (*Blathm.* 949-952) 14. * Is lat macc bethir [...] sochaide isin mórtheinid resíu ro·mestar ruiri for gnímu cach óenduini. (*Blathm.* 956-959) 15. ** 'As·rubart,' ol Cú Chulainn, 'ní·regad co·rruccad mo chenn-sa nó co·farcbad-som dano a chenn lem-sa.' (TBC 1373 f.) 16. * Ar·dáilfea fuil cach duini fil isind lius, mani·foichlither 7 mani·dichset mná airnochta friss. (TBC 84 f.) 17. ** 'Ní·regae,' ol a máthair [sc. fri Coin Culainn], 'condit·roib coimthecht di ánrothaib Ulad.' (TBC 408 f.) 18. * Ebeltair culén [...] lem-sa duit 7 be cú-sa do imdegail duit [...] co-lléice, co·rrása in cú í-sin 7 chorop ingnímae. 7 im·dius-sa Mag Muirthemne n-uile. (TBC 598 ff.) 19. * Tabraid biad, tabraid dig do choin Maíle Fothertaig, cú fir do·bérad biad do neoch, cid ar lúaig na·chriad. (FR 205-208) 20. ** Con·mélat námait Níallmaige, [...] fessaitir im chella cathaisi, [...] regaid cach óen asa richt [...], do·bebat flathai ré n-anflathaib, [...] soífithir ecnae i sóebbretha. (I2T 182, 184, 187, 191, 214)

Lesson 57

Transcription

1. is suəχ'v'əδ, mav'i·k'r'ed'əδ es'ēp'γ'e g'r'ïs't' ogus ina marß, n'ïß·noi̯f'a fap v'ip'əs in χpuθ-s'iv' ogus v'ïß·skap'f'a f'r'ißap b'ekθu. 2. b'ïδ soχəδ'e ad·t'r'ef'a in'd'ud-su ogus β'ïδ fāλ'əδ' naχ oi̯v aδ·əd·t'r'ef'a. 3. non·saμλəfəməp f'r'in f'es'əv'e. 4. a l'iλ'əs d'ind av'χ'p'ed'μ'uχ b'ïδ av'χ'p'ed'μ'əχ. 5. a v'ï as·β'ep'ən' ko-s'e, is eδ as·β'ēp b'eu̯s. 6. s'eχ is ap'δ'e sōv do·m'b'ēpa d'ia do v'eu̯χ noδ·v'er'b'f'a in'd' ogus γ'ēvəs t'r'iäd'. 7. ko·v'eb'r'əδ: 'do·g'ēv a noi̯ß-sa ogus v'ï·d'iγ'ēv a vap'γəp'θ'e-s'e, k'iδ akəßəp l'iu̯m,' n'i·eb'əp in-s'iv'. 8. n'ïba maδe daμ moi̯s'əd'u, ap' na n'ï no·γ'iγ'us, na·eβpa d'ia. 9. g'iγ'əs't'e-s'i d'ia l'in apa·βuλsəμ ap βoχəδ'i. 10. mav'i·roμa fopa g'en, n'ï·m'eμa forsna bau̯lu. 11. do·g'ēntəp aδ·χuμdəχ d'empuλ' l'es', ogus p'r'iδ'χ'əß'əδ' smaχtu r'eχto f'edəpλək'e, ogus va·ŋ'g'eßəd i̯uδəδ'i i vabəδ', ogus χov·s'k'ēpa r'eχt nuïaδvəs'i. 12. aχt ro·f'es'ən' b'eδ tū n'ïbəδ haμλəδ' no·skapf'əməs',' oλ kū χuλən'. 13. b'ïδ koμard a s'l'iaß f'r'i fāv, b'ïδ kosμəλ' do χλāp in doμuv kov'iδ·r'es'əδ ußəl. 14. Is lat μak b'eθ'əp' soχəδ'e is'ən mopθ'ev'əδ' r'es'íu̯ ro·m'estəp rup'i fop g'n'īμu kaχ oi̯nduv'i. 15. 'as·rußərt,' oλ kū χuλən', 'n'ï·r'eγəδ ko·rugəδ mo χ'en-sa nō ko·βapgßəδ-soμ davo a χ'en l'em-sa.' 16. ap·daλ'f'a fuλ' kaχ δuv'i f'iλ' is'ənd λ'iu̯s, mav'i·foχ'λ'əθ'əp ogus μav'i·d'iχ's'əd mnā hap'voχta f'r'is'. 17. 'n'ï·r'eγe,' oλ a μāθəp', 'kond'id·poß' koμ'θ'əχt di āvpəθəß' uλəδ.' 18. eß'əltəp' kuλ'ēv l'em-sa dut' ogus β'e kū-sa do im'δ'əγəλ' dut' ko-l'ēg'e, ko·rāsa in kū ï-s'iv' ogus χopob iŋ'g'n'īμe. ogus im'·d'iüssa maγ mup'θ'əμ'v'e vuλ'e. 19. taßpəδ' b'ïδδ, taßpəδ' d'iγ' do χov' μai̯λ'e foθ'ərtaγ', kū f'ip' do·β'ēpəδ b'ïδδ do veu̯χ, k'iδ ap λuaγ' na·χ'p'iäδ. 20. kov·m'ēλəd nāμəd' n'ialμaγ'e, f'esəd'ər' im' χ'ela kaθəs'i, r'eγəδ' kaχ oi̯v asa p'iχt, do·b'eßəd flaθi r'ē vavλaθəß', soi̯f'əθ'əp' egne i soi̯ßß'p'eθa.

English

1. If I should not believe in the resurrection of the dead, my faith will not sanctify me and will not separate me from my sins. 2. Will it be a multitude that will dwell in it? Will all people who dwell in it (*OIr.:* it) be happy? 3. Will he compare himself with himself (*OIr.:* *féin*)? 4. They (*use i*) who will follow the unbelieving, will be unbelieving. 5. That what we used to say so far, we will say it still. 6. This is the sign which the gods will give to those (*use i*) who will entrust themselves to them (*OIr.:* *i*), and who will work through them. 7. We will do this holy thing and we will not do this prohibited thing, although we should wish it. 8. Will thy confession be in vain to thee? Whatever thou wilt ask, will God give it? 9. I will pray (to) God for him in order that he may endure his tribulations. 10. If his head is defeated, his members will be defeated. (*OIr.:* If it breaks upon his head, it will break upon his members.) 11. No rebuilding of the temple will be undertaken by them, and they will not preach the commands of the law of the Old Testament, and the Jews will not receive them as lords (*OIr.:* abbots), and they will not overthrow the law of the New Testament. 12. If he had known it was (*OIr.:* would have been) them, it wouldn't have been thus that they (would have) parted. 13. The mountains will be as high as valleys. Will the world be like a board, so that apples might run (across) it? 14. It is by their sons that a multitude will be struck down into the fire, before the great kings pass judgement on the deeds of all people. 15. They have said they wouldn't go until they had taken our heads or until they had left their heads with us. 16. They will shed the blood of all people who are in the enclosure, unless they be taken care of and a stark naked woman go against them. 17. We will not go, unless we have accompaniment from a great warrior. 18. He will raise a puppy for us and he will be a dog to guard for us. And he will guard all Ireland. 19. Give (sg.) food, give (sg.) a drink to the dogs of men who would have given food to everyone, though they had to buy it at a price. 20. Enemies will not destroy Ireland, sentries will not be fought around churches, no-one will go out of his proper state, rulers will not perish before usurpers, knowledge will not be turned into perverted judgements.

57.4. Test

Try to recognize the verbal forms (give as much information about the words as possible — class, person, number, mood, dependent or independent, relative). Give also the quotation form of the verb and say to which present class it belongs:

glanfaid: _____   ·glainfed: _____   ·ebrainn: _____

rires: _____   ·digéntais: _____   or _____

fo·géram: _____   ·moilfithe: _____   do·lugub: _____

cechnaite: _____   do·gigius: _____   seiss: _____

fo·didma: _____   ro·chechlar: _____   at·ré: _____

regthae: _____   ·regtha: _____   gérmae: _____

do·fí: _____   ·memsad: _____   lilid: _____

·íssainn: _____   lesstae: _____   bieid: _____

fris·iurr: _____   ·sáidfimmis: _____   ro·iccfe: _____

·tibértha: _____   fo·gébmais: _____   fo·lilais: _____

gigner: _____   for·fether: _____   ·tergad: _____

ad·cichset: _____   selsammai: _____   ro·sia: _____

·fessed: _____   or _____   or _____

57.5. Test

Try to recognize the suffixed pronouns and the underlying verbs. Give as much information about the verbs as possible — class, person, number, tense.

mórsus: _____   comallaidi: _____

táthut: _____   bethum: _____

gegni: _____   beirthi: _____

filus: _____   boíthunn: _____

Lesson 58

58.1. Old Irish metrics

Classical Old Irish poetry, or *dán dírech*, can be characterized in a few words as *syllabic, stanzaic, rhyming, non-rhythmic* and *non-quantitative*.[1]

1. *Syllabic* means that the number of syllables per line is fixed, unlike, e.g., the Greek or Latin hexameter or the Germanic long-line, where the number of syllables varies from line to line.

2. *Stanzaic* means that a certain number of lines, in the overwhelming majority four lines, are grouped together in stanzas, again unlike the hexameter, where you can freely add one line after the other without any restriction.

3. *Rhyming* means that certain words rhyme with each other across the lines, unlike Greek or Latin poetry where rhyme is not used.

4. *Non-rhythmic* means that stressed and unstressed syllables are not arranged according to fixed rhythmical patterns as in classical modern German poetry.

5. *Non-quantitative* means that long and short syllables are not arranged in fixed patterns as in Greek or Latin poetry.

58.2. The features of classical Irish poetry

Ten basic features can be defined that must be taken into account when analyzing classical Irish verse (and of course when writing classical Irish verse!). These are: syllabic count, cadence, stanza, rhyme, *aicill*, internal rhyme, consonance, alliteration, *fidrad freccomail*, closing. I will discuss these now in some detail:

58.2.1. Syllabic count

In classical Irish poetry the number of syllables in a line is fixed for each type of metre. The numbers can range from one to thirteen syllables, both of which, however, are very rare extreme poles. The vast number of Irish metres uses lines of seven syllables or thereabouts. In Irish philology, the syllabic count of an Irish metre is indicated by writing the number of syllables of each line of a stanza in arabic numerals one after the other. If you look at the two poems in 3.4 and 3.5 you will see that the first one, *Scél lemm dúib*, has three syllables in each line (schematically: 3 3 3 3), the second one, *Messe ocus Pangur Bán*, seven (7 7 7 7). The poem in 42.1, *At·tá ben is tír*, shows slightly more variation: it has a syllabic count of 5 7 7 7. A comprehensive list of all attested combinations in Irish metrics can be found in MURPHY 1961: 74 ff.

Determining the number of syllables of a line is very easy: you just have to count them! There are only two things that have to be observed: *elision* and *hiatus*. Elision means that an un-

---

[1] I use the term 'classical Irish poetry' to distinguish the main corpus of Irish poetry from the so-called 'archaic style,' which is basically *non-syllabic, rhymeless, non-stanzaic, non-quantitative*, but probably *rhythmic*. A good introduction into the archaic style can be found in CORTHALS 1999.

stressed vowel has to be dropped when another unstressed vowel immediately precedes it.[2] For example, the following line from the poems of BLATHMACC should have seven syllables:

nípu ar onóir ná adrad

To arrive at the required number the vowel of the unstressed preposition *ar* has to be elided after the unstressed *u* of *nípu*. The line has actually to be read *nípu 'r onóir ná adrad*. You could ask yourself why the first *a* of *adrad* is not elided, too. *adrad* is a normal noun that bears the stress on the first syllable. So the *a* is stressed and consequently cannot be dropped.

Another factor important in the calculation of the syllabic count is how hiatus words are pronounced. In poems from the early and classical Old Irish period hiatuses as in *biad* /b'iəð/ 'food' or *ree* /r'eë/, gen. sg. of *ré* 'time,' are pronounced as two syllables. Later these forms are reduced to monosyllabic, i.e., diphthongic pronunciation like in *bíad* /b'iað/, or to long vowels like in *ré* /r'ē/. Sometimes the poets play with the two possibilities, and readings with hiatus stand side by side with monosyllabic readings. This is the case, for example, in the *Poems of Blathmacc*.

58.2.2. Cadence

In poetry generally the end of a line is called *cadence*. In Irish metrics cadence specifically refers to the final word of a line. The native Irish terms for it are *rinn* /r'in/ and *tarmḟorcenn* /tarmork'ən/. Just like the syllabic count of a line, the number of syllables in the cadence is fixed for each metre. It ranges from one to three, rarely four syllables. It is important to bear in mind that for the cadence the syllabic count of a word starts with the stress! That means that in terms of cadence irregularly stressed words like *indíu* /in'd'íu̯/ 'today' (stress on *íu*) or *inuraid* /ivúṛəð'/ 'last year' (stress on *u*) count as one and two syllables respectively. A large group of words where this rule applies are dependent and compound verbal forms: the part taken into account for the cadence starts immediately after the superscript dot <·>; e.g., in *imme·ḟolngi* 'which does produce' only the two syllables *·folngi* can be considered the cadence. From this rule it also follows that unstressed words cannot stand at the end of a line.

In schematic representation the cadence is indicated by a superscript arabic numeral, which immediately follows the number of syllables in a line. *Scél lemm dúib* is thus schematically represented as $3^1 3^1 3^1 3^1$, *Messe ocus Pangur Bán* as $7^1 7^2 7^1 7^2$.

58.2.3. Rhyme

The native Irish term for *rhyme* is *comardad* /koμərdəð/. Irish rhyme is markedly different from what speakers of English or German would perceive as rhyming words. Whereas in those languages the rhyming portions of words must be absolutely identical, there is much more freedom in Irish poetry. To modern ears this sometimes gives the impression that no rhyme is involved at all in classical Irish poems, but then Old Irish *filid* would probably find our modern compositions extremely boring!

Rhyme starts with the stressed vowel. The stressed vowels of two rhyming words must be identical in quantity and quality. Identical quantity means that the two vowels must both be either short or long; a short vowel does not rhyme with a long one. Identity in quality means that the 'color' (the simple vowels /a e i o u/ or the diphthongs /ai̯ oi̯ au̯ eu̯/) must be the same. When

---

[2] Elision of the Latin type, where every time a vowel meets another vowel one of them has to be dropped, does not occur in classical Irish poetry.

the rhyming words consist of more than one syllable, a *schwa* /ə/ of course rhymes with another *schwa*, but vowels in absolute final position again must be identical.[3]

In certain types of metres a stressed syllable may rhyme with an unstressed syllable, e.g., in the poem about *Pangur Bán*: *bán : maccdán, scís : óendís, clius : áithius, dáu : óenláu, dul : gérchrub*. In this type of rhyme, which is called *rinn-airdrinn* rhyme, a stressed long vowel in final position may rhyme with a final unstressed vowel of the same quality, e.g., *ré : céile*.

Things get more complicated when we turn to the consonants of rhyming words. In respect to rhyme Irish consonants fall into six classes:

Class I (voiced stops): /b d g/ (spelled *p, bb; t, dd; c, gg, cc*)

Class II (voiceless stops): /p t k/ (spelled *p, pp; t, tt; c, cc*)

Class III (voiceless spirants): /f θ χ/ (spelled *f, ph; th; ch*)

Class IV (voiced spirants and lenited liquids): /β δ γ λ ρ ν μ/ (spelled *b; d; g; l; r; n; m*)

Class V (unlenited liquids): /l r n ŋg m/ (spelled *ll; rr; nn, nd; ng; m, mm*)

Class VI: /s/ (spelled *s, ss*)

In perfect rhyme a consonant of one class may correspond to any other consonant of the same class. The only exception is that, especially after long vowels, consonants of class IV and V may correspond to each other.

Rhyming consonants must not only belong to the same class, but they must also have the same quality. That means they must either be palatalized or non-palatalized. A palatalized consonant does not rhyme with a non-palatalized one.

Where consonant clusters are involved in rhyme, things get more complicated, but I can't go into the details here. This question is treated in Ó CUÍV 1966.

58.2.4. Stanza

The Irish word for *stanza* is *rann* /ran/. The vast majority of Irish stanzas consist of four lines, called lines *a, b, c* and *d*. Only in a few cases eight or another number of lines is involved. The type of stanza, that is the metre, is typically characterized by fixed syllable counts and cadences in the individual lines. For example, in the metre called *dían airṡeng impóid* the stanza always looks like this: 4^3 8^1 4^3 8^1; or in the metre called *deibide smitach* like this: 3^2 7^3 7^2 3^2. Gerard MURPHY lists 84 different metres in *Early Irish Metrics*, but this hardly includes all variants found in Irish literature.

You don't have to know all the different metres by heart, of course! But of the 84 metres listed by MURPHY nearly all belong to one of two basic types, which are called *rannaigecht* /ranəɣˈəχt/ and *deibide* /dˈeβˈəδˈe/ respectively, and you should be able to recognize to which of the two a given poem belongs. This is indeed very easy and has to do with rhyme.

---

[3] In Middle Irish, after unstressed final vowels had become /ə/, all final vowels, whatever their origin, rhyme with each other.

1. In *rannaigecht*-types of metres there is end-rhyme between lines *b* and *d*, as in the following example (MURPHY 1961: 55; GT 113):

> Clocán binn,
> benar i n-aidchi g*aíthe*.
> Ba ḟerr lim dul ina dáil
> indás i ndáil mná b*aíthe*.

Sometimes lines *a* and *c* may join in the rhyme as well, but important for determining if a poem is *rannaigecht* are lines *b* and *d*.

2. In *deibide*-types of metres there is end-rhyme between lines *a* and *b* and between lines *c* and *d*. Furthermore in *deibide* very often *rinn-airdrinn*-rhymes are utilized, as in the following example (MURPHY 1961: 66; GT 111):

> Ní·ḟ*etar*
> cía lassa·ḟífea *Etan*.
> Acht ro·fetar Etan b*án*
> nícon·ḟífea a hóenur*án*.

58.2.5. *aiccill*

There is no English word for the feature *aiccill* /akʼəlʼ/. *Aiccill* means the rhyme between the end of one line and the beginning or interior of the following line. This feature is especially frequent in *rannaigecht*, where it regularly connects the end of line *c* with the interior of line *d*, but of course it may be employed in *deibide* and in other lines as well. An example for *aiccill* in lines *a/b* and *c/d* (MURPHY 1961: 58):

> Óengus *oll*
> f*onn* fri nath,
> febda f*íal*,
> r*ían* fri rath.

58.2.6. Internal rhyme

In the case of *internal rhyme*, for which no special Irish word exists, there is rhyme between a word in the interior of one line and a word in the interior of the following line. In the following example there is even double internal rhyme in lines *a* and *b* (n*óemrí* : c*óemchlí*, n*ime* : b*ine*) and one internal rhyme between lines *c* and *d* (b*orggaig* : n-*ordaig*)

> N*óemrí* n*ime*, nert cech slúaig,
> c*óemchlí* cen b*ine* bithbúaid,
> rí betha b*orggaig* cen bráth
> ros·n-*ordaig* feib ro·bátar.
>
> (*Saltair na Rann* 3785–3788)

58.2.7. Consonance

For the feature *consonance* various alternative names can be found in the literature, namely *assonance* or *half-rhyme*. In Irish it is called *úaithne* /uaθʼvʼe/. This is in fact just rhyme with relaxed rules: stressed vowels do not have to have the same quality, they must only correspond in quantity; diphthongs correspond to long vowels. Unstressed final vowels, however, must correspond in quantity and quality, just as in normal rhyme. Furthermore, in consonance interior consonants need not correspond in quality; thus a palatalized consonant may half-rhyme with a non-palatalized one. Final consonants, however, must rhyme in a proper fashion. In the following example lines *a* and *c* make consonance with lines *b* and *d*, which rhyme in a normal *rannaigecht* way:

Ro·sonnta fíad sl*ó*gaib,
ot é cona mbr*í*gaib;
ro·bruithea i nd*á*laib,
ro·orta fíad r*í*gaib.

(*Fél. Prol.* 33–36)

58.2.8. Alliteration

The native word for *alliteration* is *úaimm* /uam'/ or *comúaimm* /koµuam'/. Words beginning with the same radical consonant alliterate, and words beginning with any vowel alliterate. Only stressed words can alliterate, which means that articles, prepositions, conjunctions and preverbal particles are ignored for alliterative purposes. Alliteration does not apply if a stressed word with a different initial sound stands between two words with identical radical sounds; but an unstressed word does not prevent alliteration. That means that, for example, in the poem about *Pangur Bán* in the line

fúachimm chéin fri fégi fis

fúachimm does not alliterate with *fégi* and *fis* because the stressed word *chéin* stands between them. Neither does *fri* count for alliteration, as it is an unstressed preposition. *fégi* and *fis* of course do make alliteration as they are both stressed and immediately follow one another. On the other hand, in the line

ó ru·biam — scél cen scís —

scél and *scís* do alliterate, since they are only separated by the unstressed preposition *cen*.

Basically the radical initial, that is, the underlying initial sound irrespective of any mutation, counts for alliteration: thus the unmutated sound *t* /t/, lenited *th* /θ/ and nasalized *t* /d/ all alliterate with each other, but unmutated *m* /m/ and nasalized *mb* /mb/ (< radical *b*) do not count as alliteration. There are only a few exceptions to this rule. Lenited *ḟ* / /, which is silent, is ignored for the purpose of alliteration, thus *ḟlann* alliterates with *lám*, and *ḟerr* with *óc*; lenited *p* = *ph* /f/ alliterates only with another *ph* or with *f*; lenited *s* = *ṡ* /h/ alliterates only with another lenited *ṡ*; the double consonant *sc* only alliterates with itself; the same is true for *sp*, *st* and *sm*; *sl*, *sr* and *sn* alliterate with each other and with *s* followed by any vowel; a lenited *s* after the article = *int ṡ°* can only alliterate with another *s* thus affected.

Rhyme, *aicill*, internal rhyme, consonance and alliteration put together can lead to highly intricate compositions like the following poem, where practically every stressed word is linked with at least two other words. The sense of the poem, however, suffers under the extreme artificiality (MURPHY 1961: 30):

Úa Bricc Bregain ónd Licc lebair
tic i Temair toraib,
mair dar Mumain, daig ná·dubaig,
traig dar Tulaig Tomair.

58.2.9. *fidrad freccomail*

The feature *fidrad freccomail* /f'iðρəð f'r'ekəμəλ'/ (*lit.* 'letter of correspondence') means that the last line of one stanza has to be linked with the first line of the next stanza. This can either be achieved by completely repeating or rephrasing the last line, by repeating the last word, or by somehow alliterating the last word of the first stanza with the first word of the second. Many irregularities to the normal rules of alliteration can occur in *fidrad freccomail*: unstressed words may alliterate here, too, as may the nasalizing *n-* in front of a vowel; *s* and *ṡ*, *f* and *ḟ* alliterate, mutated forms of *p* and *b*, *t* and *d* and *c* and *g* are joined in alliteration; sometimes the initial sound of one word is linked with the interior sound of another word (as in *uil̯i* : *ro·l̯énad* or *tróge* : *c̯o mmárbuidin*) or with the initial of the second member of a compound.

58.2.10. Conclusion

Conclusion is the translation of the Irish term *dúnad* /dūvəð/. It is prescribed in Irish poetry that a poem be closed, meaning that at the very end the very first word or the very first line of the poem is repeated. Sometimes *dúnad* consists of simply repeating the first syllable or first morphem of the initial word. This feature is only employed when the poem consists of more than one stanza.

Illustration 58.1: *dúnad* 'conclusion'

58.3. An exemplary poem

The following Middle Irish poem by the poet CELLACH ÚA RÚANADA († 1079) is a didactic poem, in which every stanza belongs to a different metre. Furthermore, the name of the metre is mentioned in each stanza. The poem has been edited by Rudolf THURNEYSEN in *Zu irischen Handschriften und Litteraturdenkmälern*, Berlin 1912, 73–77 (repr. in: *Gesammelte Schriften. Band II. Keltische Sprachen und Literaturen*, ed. by Patrizia DE BERNARDO STEMPEL and Rolf KÖDDERITZSCH, Tübingen: Niemeyer Verlag 1991, 658–662). Try to identify all metrical features that I have discussed in this lesson. If you attempt a translation but can't find any sense in it, don't be discouraged. The qualities of this poem lie in its formal perfection, not in its meaning:

1. Sluindfet dúib dagaisti in dána
bid díglaim rátha do ráith,
etir ísil ocus úasail
co·rrabat i clúasaib cáich.

2. *Sétrad fata* ferr a ḟégad,
aiste drumchla dána déin,
rind airchetail robuicc ríagla
gabait na clíara do chéin.

3. *Sétrad ngairit* gres sáer sorcha,
suairc a dath;
ní·fil co n-anmain nach·molfa,
romtha a rath.

4. In *rannaigecht* menmach *mór*
assin topor engach úar,
fégaid mar at·tá a áeb,
is cáem do dénaim na ndúan.

5. In *rannaigecht bec* builid,
cen mangairecht, cen mebail,
ní·gláma sund 'ca saigid
i ndairib dána dremain.

6. *Dechnad mór*, at millsi a laíde
úas insi gil gréine
gaiste re dán seng na síde,
aiste as ḟerr i nÉire.

7. *Lethdechnad* lugbairt cráeb chumra
ní sáeb selba;
and-sain ní laiste mo labra,
aiste ergna.

8. Is aiste rathmar co rrind,
is éicse athlam indlim;
bágaim conid bairdne bind
deibide álaind *imrind*.

9. *Deibide scaílte* na scél,
ní hí-side nád·aithgén;
is hí-seo ind aiste bláith brass
i·ngnáthaigther in senchas.

10. Aiste úallach aile ocum,
ní hord aicnid imníabthaig;
maith maisse cech raind réil rigim
a *déin midṡing* milbríathraig.

11. *Snám sebaicc* so sluindébthair,
ro·sía firu fungaire;
déntar lim-sa dúas, ní gó,
do chnúas na cnó cumraide.

12. *Cassbairdne* chas chumaide,
is brass má ros·binnige;
nocho chóir a cammḟige
dar cenn n-oír is indile.

13. *Anamain* irdairc,
úasal in slonnad;
nís·dénand duine
uile acht ollam.

14. Is íat-sain ardaiste in dána
fognas na llaíde mar loing;
do Día beram buide ar mbérla,
cía duine ségda nach·sloind?

Note:

1. The language of the poem is Middle Irish and therefore contains a number of grammatical forms that you have not learned in this course, e.g., the future stem *sluindéf-* of W2b *sluindid* 'to enumerate, to mention,' the verbal ending *-and* /ən/ of the 3rd sg. conjunct present tense, the 3rd pl. independent pronoun *íat* instead of *é* 'they,' the word *mar* 'as, like' and many, many more.

APPENDIXES

INDEX

Appendix A—Abbreviations

Cited literature:

ACC   *Amra Choluim Chille*: Whitley STOKES, 'The Bodleian Amra Choluimb Chille,' *RC* 20 (1899), 31–55, 132–183, 248–289, 400–437

AM   *Audacht Morainn*, ed. Fergus KELLY, Dublin 1976

AOA   *Aided Óenḟir Aífe*: in: *Compert Con Culainn and other Stories*, ed. A. G. VAN HAMEL, Dublin 1978, 1–15

AU   *The Annals of Ulster (to A.D. 1131)*, ed. Seán MAC AIRT and Gearóid MAC NIOCAILL, Dublin 1983

BColm   *Betha Coluim Cille*: in *Lives of Saints from the Book of Lismore*, ed. Whitley STOKES, Oxford 1890

BFF   *Bríathra Flainn Ḟína maic Ossu: Old Irish Wisdom Attributed to Aldfrith of Northumbria. An Edition of Bríathra Flainn Fhína maic Ossu*, ed. Colin A. IRELAND, Tempe, Arizona 1999

Blathm.   *The Poems of Blathmacc*: in: *The Poems of Blathmac Son of Cú Brettan together with the Irish Gospel of Thomas and A Poem on the Virgin Mary*, ed. James CARNEY, Dublin 1964, 1–88

Bruchst.   Kuno Meyer, *Bruchstücke der älteren Lyrik Irlands*, Berlin 1919

CCC   *Compert Chon Culainn*: in: *Compert Con Culainn and Other Stories*, ed. A. G. VAN HAMEL, Dublin 1978, 1–8

CCCG   Henry LEWIS and Holger PEDERSEN, *A Concise Comparative Celtic Grammar*, Göttingen 1937

CG   *Críth Gablach*, ed. D. A. BINCHY, Dublin 1979

CIH   *Corpus Iuris Hibernici*, ed. D. A. BINCHY, Dublin 1978

CM   *Compert Mongáin*: in: *The Voyage of Bran Son of Febal to the Land of Living*, ed. Kuno MEYER, London 1895, 58–84 (repr. Felinfach 1994)

Corm.   *Sanas Cormaic. An Old-Irish Glossary compiled by Cormac Úa Cuilennáin*, ed. Kuno MEYER, Halle—Dublin 1905 (repr. Felinfach 1994)

EC   *Echtrae Chonnlai*: in: Kim MCCONE, *Echtrae Chonnlai and the Beginnings of Vernacular Narrative Writing in Ireland: A Critical Edition with Introduction, Notes, Bibliography and Vocabulary*, Maynooth 2000, 121–123

EIL   Gerard MURPHY, *Early Irish Lyrics*, Oxford 1956 (repr. Dublin 1998)

EIV   Kim MCCONE, *The Early Irish Verb. 2nd Edition Revised with Index*, Maynooth 1997

ETB   *Esnada Tige Buchet*: in: *Fingal Rónáin and other Stories*, ed. David GREENE, Dublin 1955, 27–44

FB   *Fled Bricrenn: The Feast of Bricriu*, ed. George HENDERSON, London 1899

Fél.	*Félire Óengusso Céli Dé. The Martyrology of Oengus the Culdee*, ed. Whitley STOKES, Dublin 1984
FG	*Fingal Rónáin*: in: *Fingal Rónáin and other Stories*, ed. David GREENE, Dublin 1955, 1–15
GOI	Rudolf THURNEYSEN, *A Grammar of Old Irish*, Dublin 1946
Gosp.	*The Irish Gospel of Thomas*: in: *The Poems of Blathmac Son of Cú Brettan together with the Irish Gospel of Thomas and A Poem on the Virgin Mary*, ed. James CARNEY, Dublin 1964, 89–105
GT	David GREENE and Frank O'CONNOR, *A Golden Treasury of Irish Poetry* AD *600–1200*, 1967 (repr.: Dingle 1990)
I2T	*Immacallam in dá Thúarad*: Whitley STOKES, 'The Colloquy of the Two Sages,' *RC* 26 (1905), 4–64
IB	*Immram Brain*: in: *The Voyage of Bran Son of Febal to the Land of Living*, ed. Kuno MEYER, London 1895, 1–41 (repr. Felinfach 1994)
ITS	Irish Texts Society
KP	Stefan SCHUMACHER, *Die keltischen Primärverben. Ein vergleichendes, etymologisches und morphologisches Lexikon*, Innsbruck 2004
LL	*The Book of Leinster*, ed. Osborn BERGIN, Richard BEST, M. O'BRIEN, Anne SULLIVAN, Dublin 1954–1983
LU	*Lebor na hUidre. Book of the Dun Cow*, ed. Richard BEST, Osborn BERGIN, Dublin 1929
Ml.	*Milan Glosses*: in: *Thes.* i , 7–483
NSB	*Nauigatio Sancti Brendani Abbatis from Early Latin Manuscripts*, ed. Carl SELMER, University of Notre Dame 1959 (repr. Dublin 1989)
NWÄI	Patrizia DE BERNARDO STEMPEL, *Nominale Wortbildung des älteren Irischen. Stammbildung und Derivation*, Tübingen 1999
PH	*The Passions and Homilies of the Leabhar Breac*, ed. Robert ATKINSON, Dublin 1887
SergCC	*Serglige Con Culainn*, ed. Myles DILLON, Dublin 1975
Sg.	*St. Gall Glosses*: in: *Thes.* ii, 49–224
SMMD	*Scéla Mucce Meic Dathó*, ed. Rudolf THURNEYSEN, Dublin 1935
SnaG	*Stair na Gaeilge in Ómós do P(h)ádraig Ó Fiannachta*, ed. K. MCCONE, D. MCMANUS, C. Ó HÁINLE, N. WILLIAMS agus L. BREATNACH, Maigh Nuad 1994
TBC	*Táin Bó Cúailnge*: Cecile O'RAHILLY, *Táin Bó Cúailnge. Recension I*, Dublin 1976
TBDD	*Togail Bruidne Da Derga*, ed. Eleanor KNOTT, Dublin 1936
TBF	*Die Romanze von Froech und Findabair. Táin Bó Froích*, ed. Wolfgang MEID, Innsbruck 1970

TBR *Táin Bó Regamna*: Johan CORTHALS, *Táin Bó Regamna. Eine Vorerzählung zur Táin Bó Cúailnge*, Wien 1987

Thes. *Thesaurus Palaeohibernicus. A Collection of Old-Irish Glosses Scholia Prose and Verse, I + II*, ed. W. STOKES and J. STRACHAN, Cambridge 1901 and 1903; repr.: Dublin 1987

Triad Kuno MEYER, *The Old Irish Triads*, Dublin 1906

Trip. *The Tripartite Life of St. Patrick*, ed. Whitley STOKES, London 1887

Tur. *Turin Glosses*: in: *Thes.* i, 484–494

UR *Uraicecht na Ríar. Uraicecht na Ríar. The Poetic Grades in Early Irish Law*, ed. Liam BREATNACH, Dublin 1987

Wb. *Würzburg Glosses*: in: *Thes.* i, 499–714

Abbreviations of grammatical terms:

ā	ā-stem	m	masculine
abs.	absolute verbal form	n	n-stem
acc.	accusative	n	neuter
adj.	adjective	ᴺ	causes nasalization
adv.	adverb	nas. rel.	nasalizing relative clause
augm.	augmented	nk	guttural stem in nk
C	consonant	nom.	nominative
compar.	comparative	n.sg.	nominative singular
cond.	conditional	nt	dental stem in t
conj.	conjunct verbal form	o	o-stem
dep.	dependent verbal form	pal.	palatalization, palatalized
depon.	deponential	pl.	plural
deut.	deuterotonic	poss.pron.	possessive pronoun
du.	dual	prep.	prepositional
f	feminine	pret.	preterite
fut.	future tense	prot.	prototonic
g	guttural stem in g	r	r-stem
gen.	genitive	rel.	relative verbal form
g.sg.	genitive singular	s	s-stem
H b	hiatus verb	S	strong verb
ᴴ	causes aspiration	sg.	singular
i	i-stem	subj.	subjunctive
ī	ī-stem	superl.	superlative
i̯ā	i̯ā-stem	t	dental stem in t
i̯o	i̯o-stem	u	u-stem
ind.	indicative	v.n.	verbal noun
indep.	independent verbal form	V	vowel
k	guttural stem in k	W	weak verb
ᴸ	causes lenition		

Appendix B — Selected Bibliography

Introductions:

Ernest Gordon QUIN, *Old-Irish Workbook*, Dublin 1975
Ruth P.M. and Winfried P. LEHMANN, *An Introduction to Old Irish*, New York 1975
Pádraig Ó FIANNACHTA, *SeanGhaeilge gan Dua*, Maigh Nuad 1981
Kim MCCONE, *A First Old Irish Grammar and Reader. Including an Introduction to Middle Irish*, Maynooth 2005

Grammars:

[VGK] Holger PEDERSEN, *Vergleichende Grammatik der keltischen Sprachen, I + II*, Göttingen 1909 and 1913; repr.: Göttingen 1978
[CCCG] Henry LEWIS and Holger PEDERSEN, *A Concise Comparative Celtic Grammar*, Göttingen 1937
[GOI] Rudolf THURNEYSEN, *A Grammar of Old Irish*, Dublin 1946
[KP] Stefan SCHUMACHER, *Die keltischen Primärverben. Ein vergleichendes, etymologisches und morphologisches Lexikon*, Innsbruck 2004
[OIPG] John STRACHAN, *Old-Irish Paradigms and Selections from the Old-Irish Glosses*, Dublin 1949
[EIV] Kim MCCONE, *The Early Irish Verb. 2nd Edition Revised with Index*, Maynooth 1997
[SnaG] *Stair na Gaeilge in Ómós do P(h)ádraig Ó Fiannachta*, ed. K. MCCONE, D. MCMANUS, C. Ó HÁINLE, N. WILLIAMS agus L. BREATNACH, Maigh Nuad 1994
[NWÄI] Patrizia DE BERNARDO STEMPEL, *Nominale Wortbildung des älteren Irischen. Stamm-bildung und Derivation*, Tübingen 1999

Dictionaries:

[DIL] *Dictionary of the Irish Language. Based Mainly on Old and Middle Irish Materials*, Dublin 1983
[LEIA] Joseph VENDRYES, *Lexique étymologique de l'irlandais ancien*, Paris — Dublin 1959– (appeared: A, B, C, D, M N O P, R S, T U)
Antony GREEN, *Old Irish Verbs and Vocabulary*, Somerville 1995
[PACDIL] *Published Additions and Corrections to the Dictionary of the Irish Language*: http://www.pacdil.org
Dennis KING and Caoimhín Ó DONNAÍLE, *Cuardach ins an Dúil Bélrai*: http://www.smo.uhi.ac.uk/gaeilge/foclora/duil-belrai/lorg.php

Related matters:

[Thes.] *Thesaurus Palaeohibernicus. A Collection of Old-Irish Glosses Scholia Prose and Verse, I + II*, ed. W. STOKES and J. STRACHAN, Cambridge 1901 and 1903; repr.: Dublin 1987
Richard I. BEST, *Bibliography of Irish Philology and of Printed Irish Literature. To 1912*, Dublin 1970
Richard I. BEST, *Bibliography of Irish Philology and Manuscript Literature. Publications 1913–1941*, Dublin 1969
Rolf BAUMGARTEN, *Bibliography of Irish Linguistics and Literature 1942–71*, Dublin 1986

Kim MCCONE and Katharine SIMMS (ed.), *Progress in Medieval Irish Studies*, Maynooth 1996
Martin J. BALL, *The Celtic Languages*, with James FIFE, London—New York 1993, 64–98
Paul RUSSEL, *An Introduction to the Celtic Languages*, London—New York 1995, 15–20
James MACKILLOP, *Dictionary of Celtic Mythology*, Oxford 1998

Journals:

[BBCS]	*The Bulletin of the Board of Celtic Studies*, Caerdydd
[Celtica]	*Celtica*, Dublin
[CMCS]	*Cambrian* (formerly *Cambridge*) *Medieval Celtic Studies*, Cambridge, now Aberystwyth
[ÉC]	*Études Celtiques*, Paris (continues RC since 1936)
[Éigse]	*Éigse. A Journal of Irish Studies*, Dublin
[Emania]	*Emania. Bulletin of the Navan Research Group*, Belfast
[Ériu]	*Ériu. Founded as the Journal of the School of Irish Learning*, Dublin
[KF]	*Keltische Forschungen*, Vienna
[Ogam]	*Ogam. Tradition celtique*, Rennes
[Ollodagos]	*Ollodagos. Actes de la societe belge d'etudes celtiques*, Bruxelles
[Peritia]	*Peritia. Journal of the Medieval Academy of Ireland*, Cork
[RC]	*Revue Celtique*, Paris
[SC]	*Studia Celtica*, Caerdydd
[SCJ]	*Studia Celtica Japonica*
[ZCPh]	*Zeitschrift für celtische Philologie*, Bonn

Web sites of interest:

Lisa SPANGENBERG, *What do I need to learn Old Irish*: http://www.digitalmedievalist.com/faqs/oldirish.html
Celtic Studies Bibliography of the Celtic Studies Association of North America (CSANA): http://www.humnet.ucla.edu/humnet/celtic/csanabib.html
Books for Scholars: http://www.booksforscholars.com/
Old Irish and Early Christian Ireland: A Basic Bibliography: http://www.smo.uhi.ac.uk/gaeilge/sean_ghaeilge.html
Sabhal Mór Ostaig, *Gaeilge ar an Ghréasán*:http://www.smo.uhi.ac.uk/gaeilge/gaeilge.html
CELT (Corpus of Electronic Texts): http://www.ucc.ie/celt/
ISOS (Irish Script on Screen): http://www.isos.dcu.ie/
TITUS (Thesaurus Indogermanischer Text- und Sprachmaterialien): http://titus.uni-frankfurt.de/
Dennis KING, *Sengoídelc—Quotations from Early Irish Literature*: http://www.sengoidelc.com/

E-mail discussion lists:

Old-Irish-L: http://listserv.heanet.ie/lists/old-irish-l.html
Early Medieval Ireland: http://groups.yahoo.com/group/Early-Medieval-Ireland
Iron Age Ireland: http://groups.yahoo.com/group/Iron-Age-Ireland
Kelten: http://www.univie.ac.at/keltologie/Kelten/start.htm

Appendix C — Further Reading

1.2. The classification of the Celtic languages: SnaG 64–65; Kim MCCONE, *Towards a Relative Chronology of Ancient and Medieval Celtic Sound Change*, Maynooth 1996, pp. 67–104; Karl Horst SCHMIDT, 'Insular Celtic: P and Q Celtic', in: Martin J. BALL, *The Celtic Languages*, with James FIFE, London — New York 1993, 64–98; Paul RUSSELL, *An Introduction to the Celtic Languages*, London — New York 1995, 15–20; KP Einleitung §7

1.3. The Continental Celtic languages and their attestation: Wolfgang MEID, 'Forschungsbericht: Altkeltische Sprachen', *Kratylos* 43–47 (1998–2002); Joseph F. ESKA, 'Continental Celtic,' in: *The Cambridge Encyclopedia of the World's Ancient Languages*, ed. Roger D. WOODARD, Cambridge 2004, 857–880; Kim MCCONE, *Towards a Relative Chronology of Ancient and Medieval Celtic Sound Change*, Maynooth 1996, pp. 3–17; Pierre-Yves LAMBERT, *La langue gauloise. Description linguistique, commentaire d'inscriptions choisies*, Paris 1994; Wolfgang MEID, *Gaulish Inscriptions. Their interpretation in the light of archaeological evidence and their value as a source of linguistic and sociological information*, Budapest 1992; Michel LEJEUNE, *Lepontica*, Paris 1971 (= ÉC 12 [1968–1971], 337–500); Filippo MOTTA, 'La documentazione epigrafica e linguistica', in: *I Leponti tra mito e realtà*, ed. Raffaele DE MARINIS, Simonetta BIAGGIO SIMONA, Locarno 2000, 181–222; Jürgen UHLICH, 'Zur sprachlichen Einordnung des Lepontischen', in: *Akten des zweiten deutschen Keltologen-Symposiums. Bonn 2.–4. April 1997*, ed. Stefan ZIMMER, Rolf KÖDDERITZSCH, Arndt WIGGER, Tübingen 1999, 277–304; Carlos JORDÁN CÓLERA, *Celtibérico*, Zaragoza 2004; Wolfgang MEID, *Celtiberian Inscriptions*, Budapest 1994

1.4. The Insular Celtic languages and their attestation: SnaG; Martin J. BALL, *The Celtic Languages*, with James FIFE, London — New York 1993, 64–664; Paul RUSSEL, *An Introduction to the Celtic Languages*, London — New York 1995, 25–196; Kim MCCONE, *Towards a Relative Chronology of Ancient and Medieval Celtic Sound Change*, Maynooth 1996, pp. 17–35; KP Einleitung §7.1 and §11.4–7

1.5. What is Old Irish?: GOI 4–9; SnaG 61–63; David GREENE, 'Archaic Irish', in: *Indogermanisch und Keltisch. Kolloquium der Indogermanischen Gesellschaft am 16. und 17. Februar 1976 in Bonn*, ed. Karl Horst SCHMIDT, Rolf KÖDDERITZSCH, Wiesbaden 1977, 11–33; Kim MCCONE, 'Prehistoric, Old and Middle Irish', in: *Progress in Medieval Irish Studies*, ed. Kim MCCONE, Katharine SIMMS, Maynooth 1996, 7–53

2.2. Ogam: Damian MCMANUS, *A Guide to Ogam*, Maynooth 1991; Sabine ZIEGLER, *Die Sprache der altirischen Ogam-Inschriften*, Göttingen 1994; Richard Alexander Stewart MACALISTER, *Corpus Inscriptionum Insularum Celticarum. Volume I*, Dublin 1945 (repr. Dublin 1996); MAC-ALISTER's book is the standard edition of Ogam stones; a more modern edition is Jost GIPPERT's *Ogam Project*: http://titus.uni-frankfurt.de/ogam/; another Internet resource is *Gach uile rud faoi Ogham ar an Líon/Every Ogham thing on the Web*: http://www.evertype.com/standards/og/ogmharc.html

2.3. Cló Gaelach: In Irish manuscripts many more special signs (abbreviations and contractions: Latin *notae*, Modern Irish *noda*) are used to abbreviate the written text. You can find examples of these *noda* and their use at: Vincent MORLEY's Web site *Comhad na Nod*: http://www.fainne.org/noda/; Gary INGLE's *noda*: http://www.quidnunc.net/~garyi/noda/notae.html; Timothy O'NEILL, *The Irish Hand*, introduction by Francis John BYRNE, Portlaoise 1984; Vincent MORLEY's Web site *An Cló Gaelach* offers many examples for the past and present use of the

Cló Gaelach: http://www.connect.ie/users/morley/cloanna/; he also offers a range of fonts based on the *Cló Gaelach* for free download at: http://www.fainne. org/gaelchlo/

3.1. The phonological system of Old Irish in comparison: the numbers of phonemes for Scots Gaelic, North Welsh, Russian and English are from the following handbooks respectively: William GILLIES, 'Scottish Gaelic', in: *The Celtic Languages*, ed. Martin J. BALL, London—New York 1993, 151 ff.; David A. THORNE, *A Comprehensive Welsh Grammar. Gramadeg Cymraeg Cynhwysfawr*, Oxford 1993, 1 ff.; Bernard COMRIE and Greville G. CORBETT, *The Slavonic Languages*, London—New York 1993, 829 ff.; Ekkehard KÖNIG and Johan VAN DER AUWERA, *The Germanic Languages*, London—New York 1994, 534 ff.; the numbers for German are my personal count. In Routledge's *The Germanic Languages* (ed. Ekkehard KÖNIG and Johan VAN DER AUWERA, London—New York 1994, 350 ff.) the count is 21 consonants and 14 vowels; diphthongs are not counted.

3.2. The phonological system of Old Irish: GOI 27–111; SnaG 90–92; Ruth P.M. and Winfried P. LEHMANN, *An Introduction to Old Irish*, New York 1975, 8–10

3.3. Pronunciation rules: GOI 18–26; SnaG 26–33; EIV 243–248; Ernest Gordon QUIN, *Old-Irish Workbook*, Dublin 1975, 1–5; Fergus KELLY, *A Guide to Early Irish Law*, Dublin 1988, 296–300; Paul RUSSELL, *An Introduction to the Celtic Languages*, London—New York 1995, 223–227; Dennis KING's page: http://www.smo.uhi.ac.uk/old-irish/labhairt.html

4.2. The mutations of Old Irish: GOI 140–141; James FIFE, 'Introduction', in: Martin J. BALL, *The Celtic Languages*, with James FIFE, London—New York 1993, 8–13; Paul RUSSELL, *An Introduction to the Celtic Languages*, London—New York 1995, 231–257; Elmar TERNES, 'Konsonantische Anlautveränderungen in den keltischen und romanischen Sprachen', *Romanistisches Jahrbuch* 28 (1977), 19–53; Henning ANDERSEN (ed.), *Sandhi Phenomena in the Languages of Europe*, Berlin—New York—Amsterdam 1986

4.3. Lenition: Kim MCCONE, *Towards a Relative Chronology of Ancient and Medieval Celtic Sound Change*, Maynooth 1995, 81–98

4.4. Leniting forms: GOI 141–146; CCCG 127–147

4.6. Nasalizing forms: GOI 147–150; CCCG 112–120

4.7. Aspiration: GOI 150–153; CCCG 120–122

5.2. Nouns and adjectives: gender: GOI 154; CCCG 158; SnaG 93–94

5.3. Nouns and adjectives: number: GOI 154–155; CCCG 160–161; SnaG 93

5.4. Nouns and adjectives: case: GOI 155–162; CCCG 162–165; SnaG 93

5.5. Adjectives: GOI 229–231; CCCG 180–181

5.6. The article: GOI 295–299; CCCG 219–220; SnaG 119–120

5.7. Word order: CCCG 267–268; SnaG 210; Pádraig MAC COISDEALBHA, *The Syntax of the Sentence in Old Irish. Selected Studies from a Descriptive, Historical and Comparative Point of View*, Tübingen 1998

6.4.–6.6. o-Stems: GOI 176–179; CCCG 165–167; SnaG 94–97; NWÄI 38–47

7.1.–7.3. The article: GOI 293–295; CCCG 217–218; SnaG 119–120

7.4. o-Stem adjectives: GOI 223–225; SnaG 118–121

8.4. Verbs of the W1-class (ā-verbs): GOI 336–337, 359; CCCG 276–277; EIV 27–28; SnaG 146

10.1.–10.2. ā-Stems: GOI 183–184; CCCG 168; SnaG 97–98; NWÄI 48–60; Liam BREATNACH, 'On the Flexion of the ā-stems in Irish,' in: *Dán do Oide. Essays in Memory of Conn R. Ó Cléirigh*, ed. Anders AHLQVIST and Věra ČAPKOVÁ, Dublin 1997, 49–57
10.3. *Ben* 'woman': OIG 184; CCCG 168–169; SnaG 100; NWÄI 39; J.A. HARĐARSON, 'Das uridg. Wort für Frau,' *MSS* 48 (1987), 115–37; Jay JASANOFF, 'Old Irish *bé* "woman",' *Ériu* 40 (1989), 135–141

11.4. The article after prepositions: GOI 293–295; CCCG 217–218; SnaG 119–120
11.5. ā-Stem adjectives: GOI 223–225; SnaG 118–121

12.1. Verbs of the W2-class (ī-verbs): GOI 336–337, 359; CCCG 276–277; EIV 27–28; SnaG 146
12.3. The prehistory of the W1 and W2 ending sets: OIG 360–365; CCCG 281–284; SnaG 135–147; Warren COWGILL, 'The Origins of the Insular Celtic Conjunct and Absolute Verbal Endings,' in: *Flexion und Wortbildung. Akten der V. Fachtagung der Indogermanischen Gesellschaft*, Regensburg, 9.–14. September 1973, ed. Helmut RIX, Wiesbaden 1973, 40–70; Kim MCCONE, 'From Indo-European to Old Irish: Conservation and Innovation in the Verbal System,' in: *Proceedings of the Seventh International Congress of Celtic Studies* (Oxford, 10th to 15th July, 1983), ed. D. ELLIS EVANS, John G. GRIFFITH and E. M. JOPE, Oxford 1986, 222–226; KP §8 and §10
12.4. Possessive pronouns: GOI 276–279, 495–534; CCCG 194–195; SnaG 188

14.1.–14.2. i̯o-Stems: GOI 179–180; CCCG 167; SnaG 98–99; NWÄI 201–211
14.3. i̯o-Stem adjectives: GOI 225–226; SnaG 121–122

15.1. Verbs: General remarks on compound verbs: GOI 495–531; CCCG 259–267; SnaG 176–177; KP §6
15.2. Verbs: Deuterotonic and prototonic verbal forms: GOI 351; SnaG 179–181; EIV 4–9
15.4. Adverbial compounds: GOI 240–241; various forms in CCCG 259–267

17.1. Nouns: Feminine i̯ā-stems: GOI 184–187; CCCG 169; SnaG 99; NWÄI 201–211
17.2. Adjectives: i̯ā- Stems: GOI 225–226; SnaG 121–122
17.3. Nouns: Feminine ī-stems: GOI 184–187; CCCG 169–170; SnaG 117–118; NWÄI 75–86

18.1. The conjugated prepositions: General remarks: GOI 272; SnaG 189–192
18.2. The conjugated prepositions 1: GOI 272–274; CCCG 199–201; OIPG 29–32
18.3.–18.4.: Verbs of the S1-class: EIV 29–31; GOI 353, 355–356 and 376–378 (note: GOI uses a different classification of the verbs); CCCG 276–278; SnaG 136–137, 141 and 147; OIPG 35; KP §5.1

20.1.–20.2. Nouns: i-Stems: GOI 190–192; CCCG 171–172; SnaG 116–117; NWÄI 61–74
20.3. i-Stem adjectives: GOI 226–227

21.1. The conjugated prepositions 2: GOI 275–276; CCCG 200–201; OIPG 32–33
21.3. Demonstrative particles: GOI 299–304; Peter SCHRIJVER, *Studies in the History of Celtic Pronouns and Particles*, Maynooth 1997, 9 ff.
21.4. Verbs of the S2-class: EIV 31; GOI 354–355 and 378; KP §5.1.4–5
21.5. Verbs of the S3-class: EIV 31; GOI 356–357 and 378–379; KP §5.1.8

23.1.–23.2. Nouns: u-Stems: GOI 194–197; CCCG 170–171; SnaG 114–116; NWÄI 87–98; David STIFTER, 'Celtiberian -*unei, Luguei*,' *Die Sprache* 39/2, 213–223

23.3. Adjectives: u-Stems: GOI 227–228; CCCG 182; SnaG 121

24.1. The cardinal numbers 1–19: GOI 242–246; CCCG 187–189; SnaG 200–205; Warren COWGILL, 'PIE *duwo* '2' in Germanic and Celtic,' *MSS* 46 (1985), 13–28; David GREENE, 'Celtic,' in: *Indo-European Numerals*, ed. J. GVOZDANOVIĆ, Berlin—New York 1992, 497–554; Kim MCCONE, 'Old Irish 'Three' and 'Four': a Question of Gender,' *Ériu* 44 (1993), 53–73; Peter SCHRIJVER, *Studies in British Celtic Historical Phonology*, Amsterdam 1995, 448–451; Heiner EICHNER, *Studien zu den indogermanischen Numeralia*, Regensburg 1982

24.2. The ordinal numbers 1–19: GOI 247–249; CCCG 192–193; SnaG 207–209

24.3. The copula: GOI 483–486 and 492–494; CCCG 317–319; OIPG 72–73; SnaG 138–139; EIV 18–19; Pádraic MAC COISDEALBHA, *The Syntax of the Sentence in Old Irish*, Tübingen 1998

25.1. Infixed pronouns class A: GOI 255–261; CCCG 193–195; SnaG 193–195; Peter SCHRIJVER, *Studies in the History of Celtic Pronouns and Particles*, Maynooth 1997

25.3. The conjugated prepositions 3: GOI 272–273; CCCG 200–201; OIPG 29 and 31–32

25.4. Emphasizing particles: GOI 252–253; CCCG 194–195; SnaG 189; Peter SCHRIJVER, *Studies in the History of Celtic Pronouns and Particles*, Maynooth 1997

27.1.–27.6. Hiatus verbs: GOI 352; CCCG 277; EIV 24–25 and 28–29; SnaG 149–150

27.7. The complete dependent forms at a glance: OIG 350–351 and 28–30

28.1. The substantive verb: GOI 475–479; CCCG 323–324; SnaG 139 and 149

28.2. The verbal noun: GOI 444–455; CCCG 312–317 (be careful: the verbal noun is called infinitive there!); SnaG 211; Jean GAGNEPAIN, *La syntaxe du nom verbal dans les langues celtiques. I. Irlandais*, Paris 1963; Jost GIPPERT, 'Ein keltischer Beitrag zur indogermanischen Morphosyntax: Das altirische Verbalnomen,' in: *Berthold Delbrück y la sintaxis indoeuropea hoy. Actas del Coloquio de la Indogermanische Gesellschaft. Madrid, 21–24 de septiembre de 194*, ed. Emilio CRESPO and José Luis GARCÍA RAMÓN, Madrid—Wiesbaden 1997, 143–164; Sabine ZIEGLER, 'Zur Syntax und Entwicklung des Verbalnomens in den keltischen Sprachen,' in: *Berthold Delbrück y la sintaxis indoeuropea hoy. Actas del Coloquio de la Indogermanische Gesellschaft. Madrid, 21–24 de septiembre de 1994*, ed. Emilio CRESPO and José Luis GARCÍA RAMÓN, Madrid—Wiesbaden 1997, 631–644

28.3. Infixed pronouns class B: GOI 257–262; CCCG 194–199; SnaG 193–194; Peter SCHRIJVER, *Studies in the History of Celtic Pronouns and Particles*, Maynooth 1997

28.5. The conjugated prepositions 4: GOI 274–275; CCCG 200–201; SnaG 189–191

30.1. Nouns: The consonant stems: GOI 199–202

30.2.–30.3. Guttural stems: GOI 202–204; CCCG 174–175; SnaG 113–114; NWÄI 29–30 and 177–184

30.5. The conjugated prepositions 5: GOI 273; CCCG 199–200; SnaG 190–191

31.1.–31.4. Deponent verbs: GOI 365–367; CCCG 301; EIV 74–77; SnaG 143–145

31.6.–31.7. Passive forms: GOI 367–370; CCCG 305–306; SnaG 145–146; EIV 79–85

33.1. Dental stems: Consonantal declension in t: GOI 205–207; CCCG 175–176; SnaG 112–113; NWÄI 155–169; Britta Sofie IRSLINGER, *Abstrakta mit Dentalsuffixen im Altirischen*, Heidelberg 2002

33.2. Dental stems: Consonantal declension in nt: GOI 207–209; CCCG 176; SnaG 113; NWÄI 170

33.3.–33.4. The numbers 20–1000: GOI 244–250; CCCG 189–193; SnaG 205–206; David GREENE, 'Celtic,' in: *Indo-European Numerals*, ed. J. GVOZDANOVIĆ, Berlin—New York 1992, 497–554

34.2. Absolute relative verbal endings: GOI 359–370; CCCG 236–237; EIV 14–15, 65–66 and 76–77; SnaG 196–197; Kim MCCONE, 'Der Präsens Indikativ der Kopula und die Relativendung -s im Altirischen,' in: *Verba et Structurae. Festschrift für Klaus Strunk zum 65. Geburtstag*, ed. Heinrich HETTRICH et al., Innsbruck 1995, 124–133; Jay JASANOFF, 'Some Relative Forms of the Verb in Old Irish,' in: *Compositiones Indogermanicae: in memoriam Jochem Schindler*, ed. Heiner EICHNER et al., Praha 1999, 205–221

34.3. Leniting relative clauses: GOI 313–316; CCCG 141–143; EIV 14–15; SnaG 197–198; Peter SCHRIJVER, *Studies in the History of Celtic Pronouns and Particles*, Maynooth 1997, 91 ff.

34.4. Negative leniting relative clauses: GOI 313 and 539–540; CCCG 248–250

34.5. Special relative forms: GOI 314

34.6. The prehistory of the relative endings: Kim MCCONE, 'Der Präsens Indikativ der Kopula und die Relativendung -s im Altirischen,' in: *Verba et Structurae. Festschrift für Klaus Strunk zum 65. Geburtstag*, ed. Heinrich HETTRICH et al., Innsbruck 1995

34.7. Independent personal pronouns: GOI 253–255, 279–280; CCCG 194–196; SnaG 186–189

36.1. Nouns: Consonantal declension in r: GOI 214–215; CCCG 176–177; SnaG 106–108; NWÄI 121–129; Kim MCCONE, 'Zum Ablaut der keltischen r-Stämme,' in: *In honorem Holger Pedersen. Kolloquium der Indogermanischen Gesellschaft vom 25. bis 28. März 1993 in Kopenhagen*, ed. Jens Elmegård RASMUSSEN et al., Wiesbaden 1994, 275–284

36.2. Nouns: Consonantal declension in s: GOI 215–216; CCCG 172–174; SnaG 102–104; NWÄI 140–154; KP §10.3.3

37.1. The habitual present of the substantive verb: GOI 331 and 480–481; CCCG 325

37.2. Relative forms of the substantive verb and the copula: GOI 479 and 484–485; CCCG 237, 318, 324; SnaG 196

37.3. The imperative: GOI 372–375, 481 and 487; CCCG 277–278; EIV 3 and 70–71; SnaG 161–162; DIL I 309.50–86

38.2. Infixed pronouns class C: GOI 259–260 and 262–264; CCCG 194–199; SnaG 194 and 199–200; P. SCHRIJVER, *Studies in the History of Celtic Pronouns and Particles*, Maynooth 1997, 138–139

38.3. Infixed pronouns after negative *ná*, *nád*: GOI 265–266; CCCG 197–198; SnaG 200

38.5. The deictic particle *í*: GOI 299 and 301; CCCG 220–221

38.6. Indefinite pronouns: GOI 309–310; CCCG 232–233; SnaG 189

38.7. The anaphoric pronoun *suide*: GOI 301–304; CCCG 195–196; SnaG 188

38.8. Interrogative pronouns: GOI 286–290; CCCG 226–230; SnaG 188

40.1. Nasal stems: neuter n-stems: GOI 210–214; CCCG 180; SnaG 105–106; NWÄI 100–120; Karin STÜBER, *The Historical Morphology of n-Stems in Celtic*, Maynooth 1998, 45–83

40.3. Comparison of adjectives: GOI 232–233; CCCG 186–187; SnaG 123–124

40.4. Comparison: The equative: GOI 233, 235 and 237–238; CCCG 182–183; SnaG 125

41.1. The preterite: GOI 332; CCCG 268; EIV 93–94

41.2.–41.3. The s-preterite: GOI 416–421; CCCG 292–295; SnaG 163–164; EIV 56–60; Calvert WATKINS, *The Indo-European Origins of the Celtic Verb — The Sigmatic Aorist*, Dublin 1962; KP §5.4.3

41.4. The t-preterite: GOI 421–424; CCCG 292–295; SnaG 164–165; EIV 54–56; Calvert WATKINS, *The Indo-European Origins of the Celtic Verb — The Sigmatic Aorist*, Dublin 1962; KP §5.4.2

43.1. Nasal stems: masculine and feminine n-stems: GOI 209–214; CCCG 177–180; SnaG 108–111; NWÄI 100–120; Karin STÜBER, *The Historical Morphology of n-Stems in Celtic*, Maynooth 1998, 65–176

43.3. Comparison: The superlative: GOI 234–236; CCCG 182–183; SnaG 123–126

44.1.–44.5. The suffixless preterite: GOI 424–437; CCCG 292–295 and 299–301; SnaG 166–171; EIV 51–54 and 72–74; KP §5.5

44.6. The preterite of the copula and the substantive verb: GOI 483 and 490–492; CCCG 327

44.7. Irregular preterite formations: GOI 483; KP §5.4.1

46.1. Irregular nouns: 46.1.1. *bó* 'cow': GOI 216–217; CCCG 171; SnaG 101–102; Kim MCCONE, 'The Inflection of Oir. *bó* »Cow« and the etymology of *Buchet*,' *Ériu* 42, 37–44; 46.1.2. *nó* 'boat': GOI 184; CCCG 171; 46.1.3. *dia* 'day': GOI 217; CCCG 171

46.2. Indeclinable words: GOI 217

46.3. Consonantal stem adjectives: GOI 228; CCCG 182; SnaG 122

46.4.–46.5. Comparison: The comparative: GOI 234–238 and 477–478; CCCG 183–184; SnaG 123–126

46.7. Additional degrees of comparison: GOI 232

47.1. Personal numerals and other numeral substantives: GOI 243–244; CCCG 193; SnaG 206–207 and 262; David GREENE, 'Celtic,' in: *Indo-European Numerals*, ed. J. GVOZDANOVIĆ, Berlin — New York 1992, 516–520

47.2. Possession in Irish: GOI 271, 279–280, 476–477 and 479; CCCG 199; SnaG 195; DIL *sub uocibus for, la, oc*

47.3.–47.4. The preterite passive: GOI 437–440; CCCG 305–306; SnaG 172–174; EIV 59–62; KP § 5.6

49.1. The imperfect: GOI 331 and 370–372; CCCG 268 and 277; SnaG 160–162; EIV 85–88

49.3. Nasalizing relative clauses: GOI 316–320; CCCG 115–117 and 236–238; Liam BREATNACH, 'Some Remarks on the Relative in Old Irish,' *Ériu* 31, 1–9; Kim MCCONE, 'The Nasalizing Relative Clause with Object Antecedent in the Glosses,' *Ériu* 31, 10–27; Ruairí Ó HUIGINN, 'The Old Irish Nasalizing Relative Clause,' *Ériu* 37, 33–87; Peter SCHRIJVER, *Studies in the History of Celtic Pronouns and Particles*, Maynooth 1997, 91–129

49.4. The marking of nasalization in nasalizing relative clauses: GOI 318–319; CCCG 116–117 and 197–198; SnaG 197–200

49.5. The *figura etymologica*: GOI 317; Ruairí Ó HUIGINN, 'On the Old Irish Figura Etymologica,' *Ériu* 34, 123–133

49.6. Conjunctions and dependent clauses: GOI 546–564

50.1. The augment (the particle *ro* etc.): GOI 341–343; CCCG 251–252; EIV 93–111

50.2. The choice of the correct augment: GOI 343–347; CCCG 252–255; EIV 127–147

50.3. The position of the augment: GOI 339–341; EIV 127–161

52.1. Prepositional relative constructions: GOI 312–313; CCCG 117–118; SnaG 198

52.2. Word order: GOI 326–327, 492–494 and 563–564; CCCG 116–117 and 238; SnaG 198 and 210–211; Pádraig MAC COISDEALBHA, *The Syntax of the Sentence in Old Irish. Selected Studies from a Descriptive, Historical and Comparative Point of View*, Tübingen 1996; Johan CORTHALS, 'Zur Entstehung der archaischen irischen Metrik und Syntax,' in: *Compositiones Indogermanicae in memoriam Jochem Schindler*, ed. Heiner EICHNER et al., Praha 1999, 19–46

53.1. The subjunctive: GOI 329–331 and 554–563; CCCG 269–272; SnaG 150; KP §5.2; Peter MCQUILLAN, *Modality and Grammar: A History of the Irish Subjunctive*, Maynooth 2002

53.2. The a-subjunctive: GOI 380–387; CCCG 284–289; SnaG 153–156; EIV 36–39 and 65–70; Kim MCCONE, *The Indo-European Origins of the Old Irish Nasal Presents, Subjunctives and Futures*, Innsbruck 1991, 11–54 and 85–113

53.3. The e-subjunctive: GOI 385–386, 481–482; CCCG 326; SnaG 156; EIV 35–36

53.4. The s-subjunctive: GOI 387–395; CCCG 284–286, 302–305; SnaG 151–153; EIV 33–35

53.5. The past subjunctive: GOI 333–335, 384–389, 395; CCCG 285–286, 302–306; EIV 85–88

53.8. The subjunctive of the copula: GOI 488–490; CCCG 326

55.1. The future tense: GOI 332; KP §5.3

55.2. The f-future: GOI 396–401; CCCG 289–290; SnaG 159–160; EIV 41–43

55.3. The s-future: GOI 407–413; CCCG 289–291; SnaG 157–159; EIV 43–45

55.4. The i-future: GOI 405–406; CCCG 291; SnaG 157; EIV 45–46

55.5. The a-future: GOI 401–405; CCCG 289–290; SnaG 157–158; EIV 46–49

55.6. Suppletive futures: GOI 403 and 406–407; EIV 48–49

56.1. The conditional: GOI 332–333, 400; CCCG 285–286, 302–306; EIV 85–88

56.2. Suffixed pronouns: GOI 270–271; CCCG 194–195 and 199; SnaG 194

58.1.–58.3. Old Irish Metrics: Gerard MURPHY, *Early Irish Metrics*, Dublin 1961; Eleanor KNOTT, *Irish Syllabic Poetry*, Dublin 1928; Kuno MEYER, *A Primer of Irish Metrics*, Dublin 1909; Rudolf THURNEYSEN, 'Mittelirische Verslehren,' in: *Irische Texte*, vol. 3.1, ed. Whitley STOKES and Ernst WINDISCH, Leipzig 1891, 1–182 (repr.: Rudolf THURNEYSEN, *Gesammelte Schriften. Band II. Keltische Sprachen und Literaturen*, ed. Patrizia DE BERNARDO STEMPEL and Rolf KÖDDERITZSCH, Tübingen 1991, 340–521); Calvert Watkins, '9. Ireland and the art of the syllable,' in: *How to Kill a Dragon. Aspects of Indo-European Poetry*, Oxford University Press, New York—Oxford 1995, 117–125; Johan CORTHALS, 'Zur Enststehung der archaischen irischen Metrik und Syntax,' in: ed. Heiner EICHNER et al., *Compositiones Indogermanicae: in memoriam Jochem Schindler*, Praha 1999, 19–45; Brian Ó CUÍV, 'The Phonetic Basis of Classical Modern Irish Rhyme,' *Ériu* 20 (1966), 94–103.

Appendix D — Solutions

In the declensions of nouns *do* 'to, for' has been used as the default preposition for the prepositional case, even if in some cases this doesn't make the best sense. The same is true for the use of the vocative and plural.

Exercise 3.5

The letters in brackets refer to the unmutated, underlying phonemes.

m'es'e ogus paŋguρ bāv,
k'eχtəρ naθəρ f'r'ia han'dāv;
b'ı̄θ' a [m']μ'enma-saμ f'r'i s'el'g',
mu [m']μ'enma k'ēv' im' hav'χ'er'd'.

kapəm'-s'e fos, f'er kaχ klū,
og mu [l']λ'eβρāv l'ēρ' iŋgnu.
n'ı̄ for'm'd'əχ f'r'im paŋguρ bāv,
kapəδ' k'es'əv a [m]μakδāv.

ō [r]ρu·b'iə̈μ (s'k'ēλ k'ev s'k'ı̄s')
inəρ [t']d'eγδəs' aρ voi̯nd'ı̄s',
tāθ'un (d'ıχ'ρ'ıχ'əδ'e k'l'iu̯s)
n'ı̄ f'r'is·taρdəμ aρ vāθ'us.

gnāθ uaρəβ' aρ [g'r']γ'ρ'esəβ' gaλ
g'l'evəδ' luχ ina [l']λ'ı̄v-saμ;
os m'ē, du·fud' im [l']λ'ı̄v χ'ēv'
d'l'iγ'əδ ndoρəδ' ku ndrovχ'ēl'.

fuaχəδ'-s'eμ f'r'i f'r'eγa fāλ
a [r]ρosk aŋ'g'l'ēs'e koμlāv.
fuaχəm' χ'ēv' f'r'i f'ēγ'i [f']β'is'
mu [r]ρosk r'ēλ', k'esu im'δ'əs'.

fai̯λ'əδ'-s'eμ ku n'd'ēv'e [d]δuλ,
i·ŋ'g'l'ev luχ ina [g']γ'ēρχρuβ;
i·[t]dugu χes'ť ndoρəδ' n'd'iλ',
os m'ē χ'ev'e am fai̯λ'əδ'.

k'ia b'em'i am'ı́v' naχ r'ē,
n'ı̄·d'eρβəv kāχ a χ'ēλ'e.
maθ' la k'eχtəρ nāρ a [d]δāv,
suβəγ'θ'us a oi̯vuρāv.

ē f'es'əv as χom'səδ' dau̯
in [m]μuδ' du·ŋ'g'n'ı̄ kaχ oi̯vλāu̯.
du θaβər'ť doρəδ' du [g'l']γ'λ'ē
foρ mu [m]μuδ k'ēv' am m'es'e.

Exercise 3.6

In this exercise I have not indicated the unmutated, underlying phonemes.

'alte-soμ ēμ,' oλ f'eργus, 'la māθəρ' ogus la haθəρ' ogənd ar'g'd'əγ' i maγ' μuρ'θ'əμ'v'i. aδ·f'esa dō aρ's'k'ēλe na makρəδ'e i v'eμəv'. aρ b'iəd' t'r'ı̄ koi̯gəd' mak and,' oλ f'eργus, 'oga gluχ'u. is saμλəδ' do·m'eλ' konχəβəρ a λaθ': t'r'iə̈v ind λai̯ og d'ēg's'ən' na makρəδ'e, a d'r'iə̈n nal' og im'b'ər'ť iδ'χ'əl'e, a d'r'iə̈n nal' og ōμλ χorme, kov'əδ·gaβ' kodλuδ d'e. k'ia b'em'i-n'i foρ loŋgəs' r'iə̈μ, n'ı̄·f'iλ' i v'ēρ'e ōgλəγ' bas aμρu,' oλ f'eργus.
'guδ'əδ' kū χuλən' d'iä μāθəρ' d'iδ'u a λ'ēg'uδ doχum na makρəδ'e. "n'ı̄·r'eγe," oλ a μāθəρ', "kond'əd·ρoβ' koi̯μ'θ'əχt d'i āvρəθəβ' uλəδ." "roχ'iav l'em-sa avəδ f'r'i soδəv'," oλ kū χuλən'. "inχos'k'-s'u daμ-sa k'eδ l'eθ ad·tā eμəv'." "faθúaδ' am'v'é," oλ a μāθəρ', "ogus is doρəδ' a vuδ'e," oλ s'i, "ad·tā s'l'iaβ βuad' edρuβ'." "do·b'ēρ indəs faρ'," oλ kū χuλən', "am'ı́v'."
t'ēd' as iaρuμ, ogus a s'k'iaθ s'l'is'əv las' ogus a βuvsəχ ogus a λorg āve ogus a λ'iaθρōd'. fo·k'er'd'əδ a βuvsəγ' r'iə̈μ konda·gaβ'əδ aρ λos r'es'ı́u̯ do·rotsəδ a buv foρ lāρ.

324

t'ēd' kosna maku iaꝑu꬇ k'en naδ'm' a oꬺs꬇a foru. aꝑ n'ɪ·t'ēɣ'əδ n'eχ kuku ina gluχ'ə꬇əɣ ko·vaꝑvəste a oꬺsə꬇. n'ɪ·f'id'əꝑ-so꬇ a v'ɪ-s'əv'. "non·sāꝑəɣ'əδəp in mak," oλ folə꬇əv mak konχəβuꝑ', "s'eχ ra·edə꬇əꝑ is d'i ultəβ' dō." argundəs' dō. maδ'əδ' foho.

fo·k'erdəd a d'r'ɪ koꬺgda buvsəχ faꝑ', ogus aꝑ·s'is'ədəꝑ is'ən s'k'iaθ s'l'is'əv uλ'i les'-s'o꬇. fo·k'erdəd davo a l'iaθꝑōd'i uλ'i faꝑ-s'o꬇. ogus vos·gaβ'-s'o꬇ kaχ voꬺv' l'iaθꝑōd' ina uχt. fo·k'erdəd davo a d'r'ɪ koꬺgda lorg vāve faꝑ'. aꝑa·k'l'iχ'-so꬇ konāχ·rāvgədəp, ogus ɣaβəs' arβ'əꝑ' d'iəβ' f'r'iha as'.

r'iastəꝑθe im'b'i-s'o꬇ i suδ'u. inda lat ba t'indərguv as·vort kaχ fol't've ina χ'en lasa go꬇'ēꝑ'ɣ'e kov·ēꝑəχt. inda lat ba oꬺβ'əl t'ev'əδ boꬺ foꝑ kaχ oꬺv'inu. iaδəs' indála sūλ' konāꝑβo l'eθa indáꬺs krō snāθəd'e. as·ol'g' aλáλ'i kombo mōꝑ' b'ēꭒλu f'iδχoꬽχ'. do·r'iɣ' d'iä ɣλav'ɪv'i ko·r'ig'i a āꭒ. as·ol'g' a β'ēꭒλu koha ivəꝑ'δ'ꝑ'uχ kombo egve a ivχꝑoꬺs. aδ·r'eχt in luav laθ' asa ꬇uluχ.

b'evəδ' fona maku iaꝑu꬇. do·skaꝑa koꬺgəd' mak d'iəβ' r'es'íꭒ r'ɪsdəs' doꝑus v'e꬇va. fo·ru꬇i novβəꝑ d'iəβ' toꝑəm-sa ogus χovχəβəꝑ; bāməꝑ og im'b'ər't' iδ'χ'əl'e. l'iŋ'g'əδ'-so꬇ davo tars'ən β'iδ'χ'əl' i n'd'eɣəδ' ind vonβuꝑ'.

gaβ'əδ' konχəβəꝑ a ꝑ'iɣ'əδ'. "n'ɪ maθ' ar·rāl't'əꝑ in ꬇akꝑəδ," oλ konχəβəꝑ. "d'eθ'β'əꝑ' daꭒ-sa, a φoba konχəβuꝑ'," oλ s'e. "dos·roꬽχt do χλuχ'u ōm θaɣ' ōm māθəꝑ' ogus ōm aθəꝑ', ogus v'ɪ maθ' ro·mbādəꝑ f'r'iꭒm." "k'ia θan'm'-s'u?" oλ konχəβəꝑ. "s'ēdənte mak sualtəꭒ' adəm·χoꭒvək'-s'e, ogus δ'eχ't'əꝑ'e do f'eθəꝑ-su. n'ɪβu doɣ' mo χov'f'ēꝑ'e sund." "k'eδ nāꝑo·vas do oꬺsə꬇-so davo forsna maku?" oλ konχəβəꝑ. "n'ɪ·f'edəꝑ-sa a v'ɪ-s'əv'," oλ kū χuλən'. "gaβ' it λāꭒ' mo oꬺsə꬇ ar'u d'iδ'u." "ad꬇u," oλ konχəβəꝑ.

la soδəv' do·ela-so꬇ fors'ən makꝑəδ' s'eχvōv in t'iɣ'e. "k'iδ no·daꬺ davo doβ' indósa?" oλ konχəβəꝑ. "ko·ro·vəstəꝑ a βoꬺsə꬇-so꬇ form-sa davo," oλ kū χuλən'. "gaβ' it λāꭒ' d'iδ'u," oλ konχəβəꝑ. "ad꬇u," oλ kū χuλən'.

lodəꝑ uλ'i isa gluχ'ə꬇əɣ iaꝑu꬇, ogus ada·reχtədəꝑ in ꬇ak'-ī ro·hλasa and. fos·rāθədəꝑ a mum'i ogus a vat'i.'

Exercise 4.8.1

a ainm /a han'm'/
a enech /a h'ev'əχ/
a indile /a h'in'd'əλ'e/
a oítiu /a hoꬺd'u/
a uball /a huβəl/

Exercise 4.8.2

mo phopul /mo φobuλ/
mo theine /mo θ'ev'e/
mo chú /mo χū/
mo bó /mo βō/
mo dét /mo δ'ēd/
mo gním /mo ɣ'v'í꬇/
mo muin /mo ꬇uv'/
mo nós /mo vōs/
mo lugbart /mo λuɣβərt/
mo ríge /mo ꝑ'íɣ'e/
mo serc /mo h'erk/
mo slúag /mo hλuaɣ/
mo smacht /mo smaχt/
mo ḟilidecht, m'ḟilidecht /mo iλ'əδ'əχt, m'iλ'əδ'əχt/
m' athair /maθəꝑ'/

Exercise 4.8.3

ar n-ainm /aρ van'm'/
ar n-enech /aρ v'ev'əχ/
ar n-indile /aρ v'in'd'əλ'e/
ar n-oítiu /aρ voịd'u/
ar n-uball /aρ vuβəl/
ar popul /aρ bobuλ/
ar teine /aρ d'ev'e/
ar cú /aρ gū/
ar mbó /aρ mbō/
ar ndét /aρ n'd'ēd/
ar ngním /aρ ŋ'g'n'īμ/
ar mmuin /aρ muv'/
ar nnós /aρ nōs/
ar llugbart /aρ luγβərt/
ar rríge /aρ r'īγ'e/
ar serc /aρ s'erk/
ar slúag /aρ sluaγ/
ar smacht /aρ smaχt/
ar filidecht /aρ β'iλ'əδ'əχt/
ar n-athair /aρ vaθəρ'/

Exercise 6.7

macc	dún	corp	ball	roth
maicc	dúin	cuirp	baill	roith
do macc	do dún	do churp	do baull	do routh
macc	dún	corp	ball	roth
á maicc	á dún	á choirp	á baill	á roith
maicc	dúna	cuirp	baill	roith
macc	dún	corp	ball	roth
do maccaib	do dúnaib	do chorpaib	do ballaib	do rothaib
maccu	dúna	curpu	baullu	routhu
á maccu	á dúna	á churpu	á baullu	á routhu
rosc	sorn	bech	bedg	leth
roisc	suirn	beich	bidg	leith
do rousc	do ṡurn	do beuch	do biudg	do leuth
rosc	sorn	bech	bedg	leth
á roisc	á ṡoirn	á beich	á bedg	á leth
rosca	soirn	beich	bidg	letha
rosc	sorn	bech	bedg	leth
do roscaib	do ṡornaib	do bechaib	do bedgaib	do lethaib
rosca	surnu	beuchu	biudgu	letha
á rosca	á ṡurnu	á beuchu	á biudgu	á letha

Exercise 7.5

in slóg mór	in tempul mór	in bél mór	in lóech becc
int ślóig móir	in tempuil móir	in béuil móir	ind loích bicc
dont ślóg mór	don tempul mór	dont béul mór	dond lóech biucc
in slóg mór	in tempul mór	in mbél mmór	in llóech mbecc
á ślóig móir	á thempuil móir	á béuil móir	á loích bicc

int ślóig móir	in tempuil móir	in béuil móir	ind loích bicc
inna slóg mór	inna tempul mmór	inna mbél mmór	inna llóech mbecc
donaib slógaib móraib	donaib templaib móraib	donaib bélaib móraib	donaib lóechaib beccaib
inna slógu móru/a	inna templu móru/a	inna béulu móru/a	inna lóechu biuccu/becca
á ślógu móru/a	á themplu móru/a	á béulu móru/móra	á lóechu biuccu/becca

a cenél mbecc	in cúan mór	a mbiad mbecc	a ndliged mór
in chenéuil bicc	in chúain mór	in biid bicc	in dligid móir
don chenéul biucc	don chúan mór	don biud biucc	don dligiud mór
a cenél mbecc	in cúan mmór	a mbiad mbecc	a ndliged mór
á chenél mbecc	á chúain móir	á biad becc	á dliged mór

inna cenél(a) becca	in chúain móir	inna biad(a) becca	inna dliged(a) móra
inna cenél mbecc	inna cúan mmór	inna mbiad mbecc	inna ndliged mór
donaib cenélaib beccaib	donaib cúanaib móraib	donaib bíadaib beccaib	donaib dligedaib móraib
inna cenél(a) becca	inna cúanu móru/a	inna biad(a) becca	inna dliged(a) móra
á chenéla becca	á chúanu móru/a	á bíada becca	á dligeda móra

in sacart becc	int íasc becc
int śacairt bicc	ind éisc bicc
dont śacurt biucc	dond íasc biucc
in sacart mbecc	in n-íasc mbecc
á śacairt bicc	á éisc bicc

int śacairt bicc	ind éisc bicc
inna sacart mbecc	inna n-íasc mbecc
donaib sacartaib beccaib	donaib íascaib beccaib
inna sacartu biuccu/becca	inna íascu biuccu/becca
á śacartu biuccu/becca	á íascu biuccu/becca

Exercise 8.5

móraimm, ·móraimm	légaimm, ·légaimm	glanaimm, ·glanaimm	berraimm, ·berraimm
mórai, ·mórai	légai, ·légai	glanai, ·glanai	berrai, ·berrai
móraid, ·móra	légaid, ·léga	glanaid, ·glana	berraid, ·berra
mórmai, ·móram	légmai, ·légam	glanmai, ·glanam	berrmai, ·berram
mórthae, ·móraid	légthae, ·légaid	glantae, ·glanaid	berrthae, ·berraid
mórait, ·mórat	légait, ·légat	glanait, ·glanat	berrait, ·berrat

Exercise 9.2

1. I love quietness, thou lovest good stories, the young boy loves swift horses. 2. We do not love psalm-books, you do not love the red cat, warriors do not love temples of priests. 3. The priests preach the story of God to the warriors, but the warriors kill the priests with the swords. 4. Does the nice boy shave the red hair of the small man? 5. Thou dost not praise stories of young men. 6. We love the holy quietness in God's temples. 7. Men, I do not clean the two swords for the young boy. 8. Strong warriors, you save the boys from bad men. 9. Men possess the big world, but God possesses the starry heaven. 10. Student, thou writest a story in a lined book. 11. Do you read good stories in old books? 12. We cut green grass for the swift horses. 13. I kill the small blue bird in the tree. 14. Do high trees grow in the green grass? You love the sounds of music, warriors. 16. The young warriors of the tribe shave the heads and clean the bodies. 17. The priests preach the laws of the true God. 18. Dost thou possess a big horse, small boy? 19. The man does not like the music of the birds in the trees. 20. Priests, you write in a big book and we read the story.

1. Ní·caraimm fos, in·carai degscél, ní·cara in macc oac ech ndían. 2. Carmai lebor salm, carthae cattu dergu (or. derga), carait loích templa sacart. 3. Pridchaid in sacart scéla Dé dond lóech, 7 ní·marba in lóech in sacart co claidiub. 4. Berraid in macc cóem folt nderg inna fer mbecc. 5. Mórmai scél inna fer n-oac. 6. Ní·carai fos nóeb i tempul Dé. 7. Á ḟir, ní·glanam in claideb arin macc ouc. 8. Á loích thréuin, sóerai macc ar drochḟiur. 9. Ní·techtat fir in domun mór, acht in·techta Día a rríched rrindach? 10. Á maccu léigind, scríbthae scéla i llibur línech. 11. Ní·légam degscél i senlebraib. 12. In·ngerraid fér nglas dond euch dían? 13. Ní·marbam in n-én mbecc ngorm isin chrunn. 14. Ásaid crann n-ard isind ḟéur glas. 15. In·carai son cíuil, á loích? 16. Ní·berra in lóech oac a cenn, acht glanaid in corp. 17. In·pridcha in cruimther dliged nDé ḟír? 18. Ní·techtai echu móru (or. móra), á maicc beicc. 19. In·carat ind ḟir céol inna n-én isin chrunn? 20. Á chruimthir, in·scríbai i senlibur? Ní·légaimm a scél.

Exercise 11.5

in grían gel	in chorr bán	ind ḟlesc chlóen
inna gréine gile	inna cuirre báine	inna fleisce cloíne
don gréin gil	don chuirr báin	dond ḟleisc chloín
in ngréin ngeil	in coirr mbáin	in fleisc cloín
á grían gel	á chorr bán	á ḟlesc chlóen
inna gríana gela	inna corra bána	inna flesca clóena
inna ngrían ngel	inna corr mbán	inna flesc clóen
donaib gríanaib gelaib	donaib corraib bánaib	donaib flescaib clóenaib
inna gríana gela	inna corra bána	inna flesca clóena
á gríana gela	á chorra bána	á ḟlesca clóena
ind lám ḟír	in ben chlóen	ind ires ḟír
inna lláime fíre	inna mná cloíne	inna irisse fíre
dond láim ḟír	don mnaí chloín	dond iris ḟír
in lláim fír	in mnaí (mbein) cloín	in n-iris fír
á lám ḟír	á ben chlóen	á ires ḟír
inna láma fíra	inna mná clóena	inna iressa fíra
inna llám fír	inna mban clóen	inna n-ires fír
donaib lámaib fíraib	donaib mnáib clóenaib	donaib iressaib fíraib
inna láma fíra	inna mná clóena	inna iressa fíra
á láma fíra	á mná clóena	á iressa fíra

int ślat bán
inna slaite báine
dont ślait báin
in slait mbáin
á ślat bán

inna slata bána
inna slat mbán
donaib slataib bánaib
inna slata bána
á ślata bána

in chloch gel
inna cluiche gile
don chluich gil
in cloich geil
á chloch gel

inna clocha gela
inna cloch ngel
donaib clochaib gelaib
inna clocha gela
á chlocha gela

Exercise 12.2

dáiliu/imm, ·dáiliu/imm
dáili, ·dáili
dáilid, ·dáili
dáilmi, ·dáilem
dáilte, ·dáilid
dáilit, ·dáilet

ráidiu/imm, ·ráidiu/imm
ráidi, ·ráidi
ráidid, ·ráidi
ráidmi, ·ráidem
ráitte, ·ráidid
ráidit, ·ráidet

guiriu/imm, ·guiriu/imm
guiri, ·guiri
guirid, ·guiri
guirmi, ·guirem
guirthe, ·guirid
guirit, ·guiret

roithiu/imm, ·roithiu/imm
roithi, ·roithi
roithid, ·roithi
roithmi, ·roithem
roitte, ·roithid
roithit, ·roithet

sluindiu/imm, ·sluindiu/imm
sluindi, ·sluindi
sluindid, ·sluindi
sluindmi, ·sluindem
sluindte, ·sluindid
sluindit, ·sluindet

Poem 13.1

I extend my little, wet pen
across the meeting of fair books;
without pause for the possession(s) of masters,
very tired (is) my paw from writing.

Exercise 13.3

1. I do not let the big pigs onto the grass. 2. My beautiful woman, dost thou relate the bad stories of thy tribe to the strong man under fierce tears? 3. Dost thou not believe in God, little man? 4. We distribute our food and our drink to the girls and boys. 5. Tribes of the big world, you do not believe in the true divinity of the living Christ, but you believe in your false gods. 6. The bad girls break the frame of the chariot with their swords. 7. I release sounds of music from my harp of gold and silver. 8. Thou enumeratest the numerous churches of thy tribe to the women, red-haired Émer. 9. The big troop believes the word of the priest. 10. We do not leave swords in the hands of the girls of the men. 11. Do you speak (about) the secret of the psalm book to the two beautiful daughters of the wise woman, priests? 12. The bright sun warms (the) bodies of men and women and (the) shapes of trees with might in the morning. 13. The strong wind breaks the mast of the ship. 14. Don't they kill troops of warriors? (or: Don't kill troops a warrior?) 15. You two old women, do you punish the young girls with hard rods on their sides? 16. Saint Colum Cille crucifies his body on the blue waves. 17. Colum Cille, the candel of Níall, sails his boat across the sea, safe and sound. 18. The saint breaks the high waves of the whales' sanctuary in a fragile boat. 19. The small bird, it releases (= gives) a whistle from the bright peak, the blackbird from the green branch. 20. A stag bellows, (the) wind (is) high (= strong) and cold, (the) sun (is) low.

1. Léicimm in mucc mór forsa fér. 2. Á mo mná lígacha, sluindte drochscél far thúath donaib feraib trénaib fo déraib díanaib. 3. Innád·creitid Día, á firu biccu? 4. In·dáilem ar mbiad 7 ar ndig forsna ingena 7 maccu? 5. Á thúatha in domuin, creitte fírdeacht Críst bíi, 7 ní·creitid far ngúdéu. 6. In·mbriset inna drochingena cretta inna carpat cona claidbib? 7. Ní·léicem son céoil asar crottaib di ór 7 argut. 8. Ní·sluindid cella lín-mara far túath don mnaí, á ingena rúada. 9. Innád·creiti in buiden mór bríathra int šacairt? 10. Léicmi claideb i lláim ingine ind fir. 11. Ráiti rúna ind libuir šalm dond ingin choím inna mná gaíthe, á chruim-thir. 12. In·nguiri in grían curpu fer 7 ban 7 delba crann co neurt isin maitin? 13. Ní·brisi in gáeth aicher cranna inna long. 14. In·mmarba buidin lóech? 15. Á šenben, in·cúrai in n-ingin óic co fleisc daingin tara tóeb? 16. In·crocha nóeb Colum Cille a chorp forsna tonna glassa? 17. Colum Cille, caindel Néill, innád·séola a luing tarsin sál, slán co céill? 18. Ní·brisi in nóeb tonna arda ind neimid bled i llongaib briscaib. 19. Int én becc, in·lléici feit din gup glan, in lon dinaib chráebaib glasaib? 20. Dordait daim.

Test 13.4

éoin: (o, m) gen. sg. or nom. pl.; *ind lám*: (ā, f) nom. sg.; *gaíth*: (ā, f) prep. sg. or acc. sg.; *in lláim*: (ā, f) acc. sg.; *in n-én*: (o, m) acc. sg.; *inna rosca*: (o, n) nom. pl. or acc. pl.; *claidbib*: (o, m) prep. pl.; *caindil*: (ā, f) prep. sg. or acc. sg.; *inna mban*: (ā, f) gen. pl.; *in macc mbecc*: (o, m) acc. sg.; *in macc becc*: (o, m) nom. sg. *inna macc mbecc*: (o, m) gen. pl.; *ech*: (o, m) nom. sg. or acc. sg. or gen. pl.; *inna rosc*: (o, n) nom. pl. or gen. pl. or acc. pl.; *inna mná*: (ā, f) gen. sg. or nom. pl. or acc. pl.; *á chenn*: (o, n) voc. sg.; *int én*: (o, m) nom. sg.; *ceill*: (ā, f) acc. sg.; *láim*: (ā, f) prep. sg. or acc. sg.; *ind leith*: (o, n) gen. sg.; *in chlaidib*: (o, m) gen. sg. or nom. pl.; *inna rún*: (ā, f) gen. pl.; *a cenn*: (o, n) nom. sg. or acc. sg.; *in bech*: (o, m) nom. sg.; *leth*: (o, n) nom. sg. or acc. sg. or nom. pl. or gen. pl. or acc. pl.

Exercise 14.4

in céile amrae	a cluiche foirbthe	in techtaire nue
in chéili amrai	in chluichi ḟoirbthi	in techtairi nui
don chéiliu amru	don chluichiu ḟoirbthiu	don techtairiu nuu
in céile n-amrae	a cluiche foirbthe	in techtaire nue
á chéili amrai	á chluiche foirbthe	á thechtairi nui

in chéili amrai	inna cluiche ḟoirbthi	in techtairi nui
inna céile n-amrae	inna cluiche foirbthe	inna techtaire nue
donaib céilib amraib	donaib cluichib foirbthib	donaib techtairib nuib
inna céiliu amrai	inna cluiche ḟoirbthi	inna techtairiu nui
á chéiliu amrai	á chluiche foirbthi	á thechtairiu nui

int ecnae dorchae	a fíadnaise n-amrae	int aite foirbthe
ind ecnai dorchai	ind ḟíadnaisi amrai	ind aiti ḟoirbthi
dond ecnu dorchu	dond ḟíadnaisiu amru	dond aitiu ḟoirbthiu
in n-ecnae ndorchae	a fíadnaise n-amrae	in n-aite foirbthe
á ecnai dorchai	á ḟíadnaise n-amrae	á aiti ḟoirbthi

ind ecnai dorchai	inna fíadnaise amrai	ind aiti ḟoirbthi
inna n-ecnae ndorchae	inna fíadnaise n-amrae	inna n-aite foirbthe
donaib ecnaib dorchaib	donaib fíadnaisib armaib	donaib aitib foirbthib
inna ecnu dorchi	inna fíadnaise amrai	inna aitiu foirbthi
á ecnu dorchai	á ḟíadnaise amrai	á aitiu foirbthi

Exercise 15.3

ad·suidiu, ·astu	con·tibiu, ·cuitbiu
ad·suidi, ·astai	con·tibi, ·cuitbi
ad·suidi, ·astai	con·tibi, ·cuitbi
ad·suidem, ·astam	con·tibem, ·cuitbem
ad·suidid, ·astaid	con·tibid, ·cuitbid
ad·suidet, ·astat	con·tibet, ·cuitbet

fo·gellaimm, ·foiglimm	con·scaraimm, ·coscraimm
fo·gellai, ·foigli	con·scarai, ·coscrai
fo·gella, ·foiglea	con·scara, ·coscra
fo·gellam, ·foiglem	con·scaram, ·coscram
fo·gellaid, ·foiglid	con·scaraid, ·coscraid
fo·gellat, ·foiglet	con·scarat, ·coscrat

Exercise 16.2

1. Young Cú Chulainn said: 'I overthrow the boys of the boygroup of the Ulaid alone.' 2. Thou refusest healing to the severely wounded man. 3. Great laughter ends the good story of the messenger. 4. Don't we overthrow the troop of strong warriors with our left hands? 5. You do not reject the words of the Gospel. 6. Do the messengers end the meeting of the clients with swords? 7. Do I not recount the clients of my family? 8. Dost thou visit the foster-sons of thy race? 9. Fear of God does not prevent the bold thief from stealing in the church. 10. We recount the last days of Conaire's grandson. 11. You visit the family of your client in a two-wheeled chariot. 12. The bold scribes stop the weak thieves in the ship. 13. Does the sun

light up the birds in the trees and the fish in the water? 14. Do you reject the belief in the resurrection of the bodies out of their grave and in the living man after his death? 15. The bright sun lights up the path of the yellow bee from a white blossom to a red blossom. 16. Oh unbearable person, thou preventest my two wonderful companions from playing fidchell. 17. Doesn't the horse-keeper distribute bread and water among the foster-sons? 18. God pours the water of all the clouds upon the wide world of the bad people. 19. I think of the fine people of the divine kingdom over the clouds, some over beautiful feast-days, some under strong tears. 20. Máel Rúain, the great sun of Mide, his grave heals the sigh of every heart.

1. Ní·tascraimm inna maccu di maccraid Ulad m'óenur. 2. In·díltai ícc donaib doínib athgoítib? 3. In-nád·foircnea gáire mór degscéla inna techtaire? 4. Do·scaram cuire llóech trén conar clélámaib. 5. Do·sluindid bréithir int šoiscélai. 6. For·cennat in techtairi dáil inna céile co claidbib. 7. Ad·rímiu céiliu do muintire. 8. Ad·ellai daltae mo cheníuil. 9. Ad·suidi omun Dé inna gataigiu dánu oc gait i cellaib. 10. In·náirmem laithe ndéidenach aui Chonairi? 11. Ní·aidlid muintir ar céile i cairptib. 12. Innád·n-astat ind notairi dánai in ngataige lobrae isind luing? 13. For·osnai in grían in n-én isin chrunn 7 inna íascu isind uisciu. 14. Do·sluindi creitim i n-eisséirgiu do chuirp asa ligiu 7 i nduiniu bíu íar do bás. 15. Innád·fursannai in grían gel uide inna mbech mbuide a bláth derg i mbláth find. 16. Ní·astai in duine nemfulachtae mo chéile n-amrae oc cluichiu fidchille. 17. Fo·dáili in daltae arán 7 uisce forsna echairiu. 18. In·dortai Día uisce inna n-uile nnél for domun llethan inna ndoíne n-olc? 19. Imm·ráidem poplu cáenu ind rígi díadai ós nélaib. 20. Innád·n-ícca a lige cneit cech cridi?

Exercise 17.4

in chomairle ḟoirbthe	int šoilse gel	ind labrae amrae
inna comairle foirbthe	inna soilse gile	inna labrae amrae
dond chomairli ḟoirbthi	dont šoilsi gil	dond labrai amrai
in comairli foirbthi	in soilsi ngeil	in llabrai n-amrai
á chomairle ḟoirbthe	á šoilse gel	á labrae amrae
inna comairli foirbthi	inna soilsi gela	inna labrai amrai
inna comairle foirbthe	inna soilse ngel	inna llabrae n-amrae
donaib comairlib foirbthib	donaib soilsib gelaib	donaib labraib amraib
inna comairli foirbthi	inna soilsi gela	inna labrai amrai
á chomairli foirbthi	á šoilsi gela	á labrai amrai

ind inis chían	Brigit ard	in blíadain aile
inna inse céine	Brigte ardae	inna blíadnae aile
dond insi chéin	Brigti aird	don blíadnai aili
in n-insi céin	Brigti n-aird	in mblíadnai n-aili
á inis chían	á Brigit ard	á blíadain aile
inna insi cíana		inna blíadnai aili
inna n-inse cían		inna mblíadne n-aile
donaib insib cíanaib		donaib blíadnaib ailib
inna insi cíana		inna blíadnai aili
á insi cíana		á blíadnai aili

in méit lán
inna méite láine
don méit láin
in mméit lláin
á meit lán

ind luib glas
inna lubae glaise
dond luib glais
in lluib nglais
á luib glas

inna lubai glasa
inna llubae nglas
donaib lubaib glasaib
inna lubai glasa
á lubai glasa

ind epistil śubae
inna epistle subae
dond epistil śubai
in n-epistil subai
á epistil śubae

inna epistli subai
inna n-epistle subae
donaib epistlib subaib
inna epistli subai
á epistli subai

Exercise 18.5

cilu, ·ciul
cili, ·cil
ceilid, ·ceil
celmai, ·celam
celte, ·ceilid
celait, ·celat

fedaimm (fidu), ·fedaimm (·fiud)
feidi (fidi), ·feid (·fid)
feidid, ·feid
fedmai, ·fedam
feitte, ·feidid
fedait, ·fedat

agu/aigimm, ·aug/aigimm
aigi, ·aig
aigid, ·aig
agmai, ·agam
aigthe, ·aigid
agait, ·agat

as·biur, ·eipiur
as·bir, ·eipir
as·beir, ·eipir
as·beram, ·eiprem
as·beirid, ·eiprid
as·berat, ·eipret

do·iccu, ·ticcu
do·icci, ·ticci
do·icc, ·ticc
do·eccam, ·teccam
do·iccid, ·ticcid
do·eccat, ·teccat

for·biur, ·forbur
for·bir, ·forbair
for·beir, ·forbair
for·beram, ·foirbrem
for·beirid, ·foirbrid
for·berat, ·foirbret

Poem 19.1

God's might to support me,
God's ear for me to hear,
God's word for me to speak,
God's hand to defend me,
God's path to go before me (…),
God's friendship to protect me
from the entrapments of the devil,
from the temptations of vice,
from the attacks of nature,
from every person (…)
alone and in a group.

Exercise 19.3

1. I say a word of welcome to thee, but thou dost not give welcome to me. 2. For the bringing (= infliction) of revenge thou carriest the sword with thee. 3. The light of the sun illuminates the whole world during the day, but the sun hides his (Olr. *her*!) face in the night. 4. We do not rear sons of poor women, but we rear foster-sons for queens. 5. Do you play fidchell with me, wives of the merchants? 6. The fish jump out of the sea in the light of the day. 7. I do not endure the darkness of the nights of Inis Fáil in the winter. 8. Thou goest (for) a day and two nights in thy curach to the big, high island. 9. The height of the snow does not hamper the swiftness of the brown horses. 10. Do we not go to heaven with its greatness of sanctity after our death? 11. For praying to Brigit you come into your meeting (= you meet) each night. 12. Do the wise priests teach the teaching of the New Testament to us? 13. Blessing from me on beautiful Eithne, the daughter of Domnall. 14. The sharp wind disturbs the white hair of the sea tonight. 15. Christ, thou blessest my speech, wonderful son of God. 16. God puts (= pours) without hesitance the lustre of red gold upon my speech. 17. The branch jumps from the hand of Bran into the hand of the woman. 18. The woman goes from them then and she carries the branch with her to the island. 19. The man in the chariot sings verses to him and to Bran's foster-brothers. 20. Does Bran send a man from his retinue into the Island of Joy?

1. Ní·eiprem bréithir faílte frib, acht do·beirid faílti frinn. 2. Ní·bir in claideb latt do thabairt díglae. 3. In·fursannai soilse inna gréine in n-uile ndomun isind lau, 7 in·díchil in grían a agaid isind aidchi? 4. Alait macc mná bochtae, acht ní·alat daltu do rígain. 5. Im·bir fidchill linn, á šéitig in chennaigi? 6. Lingid íasc asind ḟairrgi i soilsi ind laí. 7. Fo·longam dorchae n-aidche n-Inse Fáil isin gemriud. 8. In·tíagat lae 7 dí adaig inna curuch cosin n-insi móir n-aird? 9. Ad·suidi airde int šnechtai déini ind eich duinn. 10. Tíagu cosa rríched cona méit noíbe íarmo bás. 11. Do guidi do Brigti do·eccat inna ndáil cach n-aidchi. 12. For·cain in sacart gáeth forcetal ind Núḟiadnaisi dí. 13. Bendacht úainn for Eithni, ingen Domnaill. 14. Ní·fúasna in gáeth aicher findḟolt inna fairrge innocht. 15. Á Chríst, in·sénai mo labrai? 16. Fo·cerdat in dé cen dolmai néim n-óir deirg forar llabrai. 17. In·lengat inna cráeba di láim Brain i lláma inna mban? 18. Ní·tíagat inna mná úad íarum 7 ní·berat inna cráeba leo cosin n-insi. 19. Ní·cain in fer isin charput rann doib. 20. Foídid Bran firu dia muintir i n-Insi Subai.

Exercise 19.4

Then he goes away, and his shield of boards with him, and his toy javelin and his driving stick and his ball.

Exercise 20.4

a cuirm maith	in búachaill sochraid	ind ḟlaith šainemail
in chormo/a maith	in búachallo/a sochraid	inna flatho/a sainemlae
don chuirm maith	don búachaill šochraid	dond ḟlaith šainemail
a cuirm maith	in mbúachaill sochraid	in flaith sainemail
á chuirm maith	á búchaill šochraid	á ḟlaith šainemail

inna curmae maithi	in búachailli sochraidi	inna flaithi sainemlai
inna curmae maith(e)	inna mbúachaille sochraid(e)	inna flaithe sainemail/-mlae
donaib curmaib maithib	donaib búachaillib sochraidib	donaib flaithib sainemlaib
inna curmai maithi	inna búachailli sochraidi	inna flaithi sainemlai
á churmae maithi	á búachailli sochraidi	á ḟlaithi sainemlai

a ndruimm n-allaid
in drommo/a allaid
don druimm allaid
a ndruimm n-allaid
á druimm allaid

inna drummae alltai
inna ndrummae n-allaid/n-alltae
donaib drummaib alltaib
inna drummae alltai
á drummae alltai

in tailm śainemail
in telmo/a sainemlae
don tailm śainemail
in tailm sainemail
á thailm śainemail

inna talmai sainemlai
inna talmae sainemail/-mlae
donaib talmaib sainemlaib
inna talmai sainemlai
á thalmai sainemlai

Exercise 21.7

airiu, ·airiu
airi, ·airi
airid, ·air
airmi, ·airem
airthe, ·airid
airit, ·airet

guidiu/-imm, ·guidiu/-imm
guidi, ·guidi
guidid, ·guid
guidmi, ·guidem
guitte, ·guidid
guidit, ·guidet

fo·daimiu, ·fodmu
fo·daimi, ·fodmai
fo·daim, ·fodaim
fo·daimem, ·fodmam
fo·daimid, ·fodmaid
fo·daimet, ·fodmat

fris·gairiu, ·frecru
fris·gairi, ·frecrai
fris·gair, ·frecair
fris·gairem, ·frecram
fris·gairid, ·frecraid
fris·gairet, ·frecrat

ernaimm, ·ernaimm
ernai, ·ernai
ernaid, ·ern
ernmai, ·ernam
erntae, ·ernaid
ernait, ·ernat

renaimm, ·renaimm
renai, ·renai
renaid, ·ren
renmai, ·renam
rentae, ·renaid
renait, ·renat

fris·benaimm, ·freipnimm
fris·benai, ·freipni
fris·ben, ·freipen
fris·benam, ·freipnem
fris·benaid, ·freipnid
fris·benat, ·freipnet

for·fenaimm, ·foirbnimm
for·fenai, ·foirbni
for·fen, ·forban
for·fenam, ·foirbnem
for·fenaid, ·foirbnid
for·fenat, ·foirbnet

Exercise 22.1

Triad 66: Three prohibitions of the church: a nun for (= to ring) the bell, an ex-layman in abbacy, a drop on the altar.
Triad 156: Three qualities of clothes: fineness, protection, long life.

Exercise 22.2

Eating something of it from above does not put an end to a vine. People passing by visit the vine to take something for them from its fruit.

Exercise 22.4

1. I pray a prayer from my insignificant, hard heart to thee, Son of God. 2. Dost thou follow the stud of the horses to the meadow, lad? 3. He makes an assault on the boys after that. 4. Three signs of quality of glass: a look through it (= transparency), liquor in it, blood out of its fragments. 5. You ring the sweet-sounding bell of the church in a night of wind (= windy night), priests. I do not go in its meeting (= to meet it), however, but in a meeting of a wanton woman (= to meet a wanton woman). 6. The doctors answer the questions of the sick man. 7. I do not buy beer from the ugly merchant. 8. Thou sufferest a lot of pain and a lot of hunger alone on the sea. 9. My good ox does not plough that land for this price. 10. We do not spread gold and silver over the hands of the beautiful women. 11. Do you beat the head of the foreign prisoner against the wall, soldiers? 12. Thieves drive the pigs of the tribe from the meadow. The cowboys take victory from them (= defeat them) after that. 13. I do not pour good, sweet beer. 14. Cormac takes the rule of the men of Inis Fáil. 15. I break the bone of the back of the lad with a heavy stone. 16. Does not the messenger bring the son of the queen with him to school? 17. You see away from you to the North-East the glorious sea full of animals. 18. A wonderful beauty for Bran in his little boat over the clear sea. 19. Cold the night in the big bog, a storm, not weak, does pour. 20. In this way Conchobor spends his sovereignty: a third of the day playing fidchell, another third drinking beer.

1. Guidmi itche asar cridib deróilib dúraib duit, a maicc Dé. 2. Lenai graig inna n-ech cosin clúain, á búachailli? 3. In·mben fon macc íarum? 4. - 5. Benai clocán mbinn inna cille, á šacairt. Tíagu ina dáil, 7 ní·tíag i ndáil mná baíthe. 6. In·frecair in liaig ceisti ind fir thinn? 7. Crenmai cuirm dinaib cennaigib dochraidib. 8. Fo·daim mór péine 7 mór ngortae a óenur isin muir. 9. Airit mo daim in n-úir-sin arin llóg-so. 10. Sernai ór 7 argat for láim inna mná sochraide. 11. Benait loích cenna inna cimbide n-echtrainn frisin fraig. 12. Aigid gataige mucca inna túaithe ón chlúain. Gaibid búachaill búaid de íarum. 13. Fermai cuirm maith milis foraib. 14. In·ngaib Cormac flaith fer n-Inse Fáil? 15. In·mbrisem cnámai drommo in búachalla co cloich thruimm? 16. Berait in techtairi maccu inna rígnae leo dochum inna scoile. 17. Fégmai úainn sair fo·thúaid a muir múad mílach. 18. Caíne amrae lasna firu inna curchánaib tar muir nglan. 19. Úar ind adaig i mmóin móir, acht ní·fera dertan. 20. Is samlaid do·melat inna rígnai a flaith: trian ind laí oc imbirt fidchille, a trian n-aill oc óul chorma.

Test 22.5

foir: for, 3rd sg. m./n. acc.; *lib*: la, 2nd pl.; *dít*: di, 2nd sg.; *úainn*: ó, 1st pl.; *triit*: tre, 3rd sg. m./n.; *and*: i, 3rd sg. m./n. prep.; *fuiri*: for, 3rd sg. f. prep.; *ind*: i, 3rd sg. m./n. acc.; *foe*: fo, 3rd sg. f. acc.; *airium*: ar, 1st sg.; *dúnn*: do, 1st pl.; *inte*: i, 3rd sg. f. acc.; *indib*: i, 2nd pl. or 3rd pl. prep.; *fou*: fo, 3rd sg. m./n. prep.; *frie*: fri, 3rd sg. f.; *leis*: la, 3rd sg. m./n.; *form*: for, 1st sg.; *úadi*: ó, 3rd sg. f.; *friut*: fri, 2nd sg.; *foo*: fo, 3rd pl. acc.

Test 22.6

in·crenaid: (S3) 2nd pl. dep. (crentae); *ní·foircnet*: (W1) 3rd pl. dep. (for·cennat); *biri*: (S1) 2nd sg. indep. (·bir); *gairiu*: (S2) 1st sg. indep. (·gairiu); *in·díltai*: (W2b) 2nd sg dep. or 3rd sg. dep. (do·sluindi); *ní·eiprem*: (S1) 1st pl. dep. (as·beram); *ní·tascraid*: (W1) 2nd pl. dep. (do·scaraid); *for·cain*: (S1) 2nd sg. indep. or 3rd sg. indep. (·forcain); *ní·imbiur*: (S1) 1st sg. dep. (im·biur); *ráitte*: (W2a) 2nd pl. indep. (·ráidid); *imm·ráidem*: (W2a) 1st pl. indep. (·immráidem); *ní·frecrat*: (S2) 3rd pl. dep. (fris·gairet); *guidid*: (S2) 3rd sg. indep. (·guid); *for·fenam*: (S3) 1st pl. indep. (·foirbnem); *in·n-airem*: (S2) 1st pl. dep. (airmi); *rentae*: (S3) 2nd pl. indep. (renaid); *sernnai*: (S3) 1st pl. indep. (·sernam); *in·freipnid*: (S3) 2nd pl. dep. (fris·benaid); *ní·fodmam*: (S2) 1st pl. dep. (fo·daimem); *fo·gaibimm*: (S2) 1st sg. indep. (·fagbaimm); *gaibit*: (S2) 3rd pl. indep. (·gaibet)

Poem 22.7

Christ's cross across this face,
across the ear like this.
Christ's cross across this eye.
Christ's cross across this nose.

Christ's cross across this lip.
Christ's cross across this mouth.
Christ's cross across this back.
Christ's cross across this side.

(…) Christ's cross across this belly.
Christ's cross across this back.

Christ's cross across my hands (…)
Christ's cross across my hips.
Christ's cross across my legs.

Christ's cross with me before me.
Christ's cross with me behind me.
Christ's cross against every difficult thing
between valley and hill. (…)

Christ's cross across my sitting.
Christ's cross across my lying.
Christ's cross (is) all my force (…)

Christ's cross across my household.
Christ's cross across my temple.
Christ's cross in the hereafter.
Christ's cross in this world.

From the top of my crown
to the nail of my foot (…)

Until the day of my death,
before going into this soil, (…)

Exercise 23.5

a rrind ngel
ind rendo/a gil
dond rind giul
a rrind ngel
á rind gel

inna rind/renda gela
inna rendae ngel
donaib rendaib gelaib
inna rind/renda gela
á renda gela

in bith dorchae
in betho/a dorchai
don biuth dorchu
in mbith ndorchae
á bith dorchai

in bethae/ai/a dorchai
inna mbethae ndorchae
donaib bethaib dorchaib
inna bithu dorchu
á bithu dorchai

in molad clóen
in molto/a chloín
don molad chlóen
in mmolad clóen
á molad chlóen

in moltae/ai/a cloín
inna mmoltae clóen
donaib moltaib clóenaib
inna moltu clóenu/a
á moltu clóenu

337

a mbir n-aicher
in bero/a aichir
don biur aichiur
a mbir n-aicher
á bir aicher

inna bir/bera aichrea
inna mberae n-aicher
donaib beraib aichrib
inna bir/bera aichrea
á bera aichrea

int áes oac
ind áeso/a oic
dond áes ouc
in n-áes n-oac
á áes oic

ind áesae/ai/a oic
inna n-áesae n-oac
donaib áesaib ócaib
inna áesu ócu/a
á áesu ócu/a

in fid dorchae
ind ḟedo dorchai
dond ḟiud dorchu
in fid ndorchae
á ḟid dorchai

ind ḟedae/ai/a dorchai
inna fedae ndorchae
donaib fedaib dorchaib
inna fidu dorchu/a
á ḟidu dorchu/a

a mmind n-órdae
in mindo/a órdai
don mind órdu
a mmind n-órdae
á mind n-órdae

inna mind/minda órdae
inna mindae n-órdae
donaib mindaib órdaib
inna mind/minda órdae
á minda órdae

in foilsigiud clóen
ind ḟoilsigtheo/a cloín
dond ḟoilsigiud chlóen
in foilsigiud clóen
á ḟoilsigiud cloín

ind ḟoilsigthe/i/ea cloín
inna foilsigthe clóen
donaib foilsigthib clóenaib
inna foilsigthiu clóenu/a
á ḟoilsigthiu clóenu/a

Exercise 25.2

dom·chil, dot·chil, da·cil, dos·cil, da·chil, donn·cil, dob·cil, dos·cil
ním·léicet, nít·léicet, ní·lléicet, nís·lléicet, ní·léicet, nínn·léicet, níb·léicet, nís·lléicet
dom·scara, dot·scara, da·scara, dos·scara, da·scara, donn·scara, dob·scara, dos·scara
ním·thaibrem, nít·taibrem, ní·taibrem, nís·taibrem, ní·thaibrem, nínn·taibrem, níb·taibrem, nís·taibrem
nom·renaimm, not·renaimm, na·rrenaimm, nos·rrenaimm, na·renaimm, nonn·renaimm, nob·renaimm, nos·rrenaimm
nom·gairid, not·gairid, na·ngairid, nos·(n)gairid, na·gairid, nonn·gairid, nob·gairid, nos·(n)gairid

Test 26.1

immum: immum-sa; *cuicce*: cuicce-si; *etarru*: etarru-som; *friss*: fris-seom; *torunn*: torunn-ni; *dúib*: dúib-si; *latt*: latt-su; *fair*: fair-seom; *imbi*: imbi-seom; *leis*: leis-seom; *mo chos*: mo chos-sa; *do maicc*: do maicc-siu; *ar n-echu*: ar n-echu-ni; *a argat*: a argat-som or a argat-si; *for ngáire*: for ngaire-si; *a túath*: a túath-si or a túath-som; *a ḟir*: a fir-seom or a fir-si or a fir-seom; *nos·crenaimm*: nos·crenaimm-si or nos·crenaimm-seom or nos·crenaimm-se; *nínn·feid*: nínn·feid-ni or nínn·feid-seom or nínn·feid-si; *nít·glanat*: nít·glanat-som or nít·glanat-su; *na·mbenai*: na·mbenai-seom or na·mbenai-siu; *immum·agaid*: immum·agaid-se or immum·agaid-si; *níb·taibrem*: níb·taibrem-si or níb·taibrem-ni; *da·beirid*: da·beirid-seom or da·beirid-si; *fot·daimet*: fot·daimet-su or fot·daimet-som.

Exercise 26.3

1. Thou findest apples in the wood and I carry them to the queen. It is in the middle of the wood that thou findest them. 2. He strikes their four heads off them and he puts them on four points of the fork. 3. We do not love you, oh people of the war, and the power of your swords is a horror for us. 4. The clever merchant buys oak-wood for three *cumals*, and sells it to the queens for four *cumals*. 5. The temptations of the world are great, and we are captives to them. 6. It is not out of envy for you that I say that. 7. I am not like them. 8. The girls are joyful at the coming of *Beltaine*? 9. Sorrow is fitting for me, because I am miserable, I am an old woman. 10. My hair is short, is grey, a bad veil over it is no pity. 11. A pilgrimage to Rome (is) a lot of trouble and little profit. 12. Three streams of blood flow from the side of the warrior, and from his hand, and from his head after his wounding. 13. The whole world is dark and full of secrets in the night. 14. Envy for thee does not seize me, rich man, because great wealth is a heavy burden for thee. 15. He points his eye towards the enclosing wall (OIr.: enclosure of the wall), and I point my clear eye towards penetration of knowledge. 16. Five days and six nights they go over the back of the sea, and they come to a bright island full of birds on the seventh day. 17. They throw all their balls at him, and he catches them, every single ball, in his lap. 18. Then they throw all their driving sticks at him, but he wards them off and takes a bundle of them on his back. 19. 'I have not enough of my game yet, father Conchobar,' said the lad. 20. My hand is tired of writing, my pen pours fourth a stream of bright dark blue ink.

1. Fo·gaibiu-sa uball isind fid 7 na·bir-siu cosna rígnai. Is i mmedón ind feda fa·gaibem 2. Benait-seom a tri cenn diib 7 fos·cerdat for téora benna inna gablae. 3. Nob·caraimm-si, á áes catha, 7 ní úath dom-sa cumachtae for claideb. 4. Ní·crenat in chennaigi glicci fid ndarae ar chethéoraib cumalaib, 7 ní·rrenat frisna rrígnai ar théoraib cumalaib. 5. Innád móra aslacha in betha 7 inda chimbid-se doaib-sem? 6. Ní ar formut frit-su as·beram-ni in-so. 7. Am cummae-se frie-si. 8. In faílid ind ingen oc techt Beltaini? 9. Ní deithbir dún-ni brón, ar nítan tróig 7 nítan sentuinni. 10. Ní becc, ní líath mo thrilis, is líach drochcaille tarais. 11. In mór sáetho, becc torbai techt do Róim? 12. Do·lin óensruth folo a tóeb ind loích íarna guin. 13. Ní dorchae int uile bith. Acht in lán de rúnaib isind aidchi? 14. Nínn·gaib format frib-su, á firu saidbri, ar is aire tromm dúib indeb mór. 15. Innád·fúachat-som a rrosca fri fál inna frega, 7 innád·fúacham-ni ar rosca réili fri féigi ind fessa? 16. Sé lae 7 secht n-aidchi téit-sem tar druimm in mora, 7 do·tét co insi solais láin di énlaith isint ochtmad láu. 17. Fo·ceird a líathróiti uili forru-som 7 nos·gaibet-seom cach n-óenlíathróit inna n-ucht. 18. Fo·ceird dano a lorga ánae uili forru, acht nís·airchlichat-som 7 ní·gaibet airbir diib fria n-aiss. 19. 'Ammi sáithig diar cluichiu, á phopa Chonchobuir,' ol in gillai. 20. It scíth mo láma ón scríbund; ní·sceith mo phenn sruth di dub glégorm.

Exercise 26.4

Triad 223: A scholar after reading his psalm and a lad after laying off his load and a girl after making a woman out of her.

Exercise 27.5

ad·cíu, ·accu/accaim	im·soimm, ·impaimm	líuu, ·líu
ad·cí, ·accai	imm·soí, ·impai (?)	líi, ·lí
ad·cí, ·accai	im·soí, ·impai	liid, ·lí
ad·ciam, ·accam	im·soam, ·impam	límmi, ·liam
ad·ciid, ·accaid	im·soid, ·impaid	líthe, ·liid
ad·ciat, ·accat	im·soat, ·impat	liit, ·liat

Exercise 28.4

atom·fét, atot·fét, at·fét, ata·fét, at·fét, atonn·fét, atob·fét, ata·fét
cotom·gairi, cotot·gairi, cot·ngairi, cota·gairi, cot·gairi, cotonn·gairi, cotob·gairi, cota·gairi
fritom·benaimm, fritot·benaimm, frit·mbenaimm, frita·benaimm, frit·benaimm, fritonn·benaimm, fritob·benaimm, frita·benaimm
atom·chiat, atot·chiat, at·ciat, ata·ciat, at·chiat, atonn·ciat, atob·ciat, ata·ciat
atom·renam, atot·renam, at·rrenam, ata·renam, at·renam, atonn·renam, atob·renam, ata·renam
fortom·osnai, fortot·osnai, fort·n-osnai, forta·osnai, fort·osnai, fortonn·osnai, fortob·osnai, forta·osnai

Test 29.1

a cride: (i̯o, n) nom. sg. or acc. sg.; *inna umae*: (i̯o, n) nom. pl. or acc. pl.; *ingin n-allaid*: (ā, f; adj. i) acc. sg.; *srothae nglas*: (u, m; adj. o) gen. pl.; *inna céile*: (i̯o, m) gen. pl.; *cnámai báin*: (i, m; adj. o) nom. pl.; *súili*: (i, f) nom. pl. or acc. pl.; *inna rrígnae maith*: (long ī, f; adj. i) gen. pl.; *búaid amru*: (i, n; adj. i̯o) prep. sg.; *in soilsi follais*: (i̯ā, f; adj. u) acc. sg.; *in chathai*: (u, m) nom. pl.; *mindaib órdaib*: (u, n; adj. i̯o) prep. pl.; *liaig becc*: (i, m; adj. o) nom. sg.; *méit móir*: (short ī, f; adj. ā) prep. sg. or acc. sg.; *inna comairli*: (i̯ā, f) nom. pl. or acc. pl.; *búachaill rrígdae*: (i, m; adj. i̯o) acc. sg.; *muire n-ard*: (i, n; adj. o) gen. pl.; *áth chían*: (u, m; adj. o) prep. sg.; *ingin allaid*: (ā, f; adj. i) prep. sg.; *legai amrai*: (i, m; adj. i̯o) nom. pl. or acc. pl.; *int áesa oic*: (u, m; adj. o) gen. sg. or nom. pl.; *ungae*: (i̯ā, f) nom. sg. or gen. sg. or gen. pl.; *aidchi dorchai*: (long ī, f; adj. i̯ā) prep. sg. or nom. pl. or acc. pl.

Exercise 29.3

1. I do not do childish deeds. 2. You see us stealing the horses, and you tell it to the horse-keepers. 3. We drive them from the meadow across the ford. 4. Thou hidest thyself from the troop of bandits between the trees and the bushes in the middle of the forest, but they see thee and they find thee. 5. I gird myself today with great strength. 6. I call them to me to give me good advice, because they have a lot of knowledge. 7. Do you see Áed in the battle? We do not see him, but we see his shield protecting him. 8. It is therefore that they do it: they like to eat meat and to drink wine. 9. I am preaching the Gospel. 10. Thou art not here in the ford, but thou art in the middle of the forest making a glade in it. 11. God exists. 12. They row around it (the island, *lit.* her), and there is a large group gaping and laughing. 13. We are in exile from him, and our return is not likely for us. 14. You are not taking an apple from the apple-tree. Are there no apples in the trees? 15. There is no strength in Bran's hand to grab the branch. 16. We are without age from the beginning of creation,… sin touches us not. 17. It is in the person of Christ that I do that. 18. He sees a man before him with half his head on him and half of another man on his neck. 19. Cú Chulainn attacks him and strikes his head from him with the driving stick and he begins to drive the ball before him. 20. He sees a man at the cooking-pit in the middle of the forest, the one hand with his weapons on, the other hand roasting the boar. Great is the man's horror. He attacks him nevertheless and takes his head and his pig with him.

1. Do·gníu gním maccthae. 2. Atob·ciam-ni oc gait n-eich, 7 at·fíadam dond echairiu. 3. At·n-agaid-si ón chlúain tarsin n-áth. 4. Cotom·chiul-se etir cranna 7 dusu i mmedón ind feda for slóg inna mberg, acht atom·chiat-som 7 fom·gaibet. 5. Atonn·regam indíu co niurt tríun. 6. Atot·gair cuccai do thabairt chomairle maithe dó-som, ar at·tá mór fessa duit-siu. 7. In·n-accai inna firu isin chath? Nís·n-accu-som, acht ad·cíu a scíathu occa n-imdegail. 8. Is dó da·gní-si: ní maith lee ithe feola 7 ól fína. 9. Ní oc precept šoiscélai at·taam. 10. At·taam sund isind áth, 7 ninn·fil i mmedón inna caille oc dénum chlúana indi. 11. In·fil Día? 12. Imma·raam immacúairt, acht ní·fil slóg mór oc ginig 7 oc gáirechtaig. 13. Indob·fil-si for longais remi 7 in dóich far techt ar ais dúib? 14. At·taí oc tabairt uball dind abaill. At·taat (*or.* fil) ubla isnaib crannaib.

15. At·tá (*or.* fil) nert i lláim Brain do gabáil inna croíbe. 16. Ní·fil dúnn o thossuch inna ndúile cen áes, donn·aidlea in immarmus. 17. Is i persain Chríst da·gniam-ni sin. 18. Ata·cí 7 leth a cinn fuiri. 19. Fos·n-éirig Cú Chulainn 7 benaid a cenn di cosind luirg ánae. 20. Ata·cí ocond fulucht, a llám aile oc fuini inna torc. Fos·n-ópair-seom ar apu 7 do·beir a cenn 7 a muicc lais.

Exercise 30.4

in cháera dub	in chathair ard	in brí fliuch
inna cáerach duibe	inna cathrach ardae	inna breg fliche
don cháeraig duib	don chathraig aird	don brig flich
in cáeraig nduib	in cathraig n-aird	in mbrig flich
á cháera dub	á chathair ard	á brí fliuch
inna cáeraig dubai	inna cathraig arda	inna brig flichi
inna cáerach ndub	inna cathrach n-ard	inna mbreg fliuch
donaib cáerchaib dubaib	donaib cathrachaib ardaib	donaib bregaib flichib
inna cáercha dubai	inna cathracha arda	inna brega flichi
á cháercha dubai	á chathracha arda	á brega flichi
Lugaid trén	in choí glas	int aire oac
Luigdech tríuin	inna cuach glaise	ind airech oic
Luigdig thríun	don chuich glais	dond airig ouc
Luigdig trén	in cuich nglais	in n-airig n-oac
á Lugaid tríuin	á choí glas	á aire oic
Luigdig tríuin	inna cuich glasa	ind airig oic
Luigdech trén	inna cuach nglas	inna n-airech n-oac
Luigdechaib trénaib	donaib cuachaib glasaib	donaib airechaib ócaib
Luigdecha trénu/a	inna cuacha glasa	inna airecha ócu/a
á Luigdecha trénu/a	á chuacha glasa	á airecha ócu/a

ind nathair chlóen
inna nathrach cloíne
dond nathraig chloín
in nnathraig cloín
á nathair chlóen

inna nathraig clóena
inna nnathrach clóen
donaib nathrachaib clóenaib
inna nathracha clóena
á nathracha clóena

Exercise 31.6

foilsigiur, ·foilsigiur	béoaigiur, ·béoaigiur	samlur, ·samlur
foilsigther, ·foilsigther	béoaigther, ·béoaigther	samailter, ·samailter
foilsigidir, ·foilsigedar	béoaigidir, ·béoaigedar	samlaithir, ·samlathar
foilsigmir, ·foilsigmer	béoaigmir, ·béoaigmer	samlaimmir, ·samlammar
foilsigthe, ·foilsigid	béoaigthe, ·béoaigid	samaltae, ·samlaid
foilsigitir, ·foilsigetar	béoaigitir, ·béoaigetar	samlaitir, ·samlatar

airliur, ·airliur	labrur, ·labrur	ad·muiniur
airlither, ·airlither	labraither, ·labraither	ad·muinter
airlithir, ·airlethar	labraithir, ·labrathar	ad·muinethar
airlimmir, ·airlemmar	labraimmir, ·labrammar	ad·muinemmar
airlithe, ·airlid	labraithe, ·labraid	ad·muinid
airlitir, ·airletar	labraitir, ·labratar	ad·muinetar

Exercise 31.8

atom·rímther	dom·scarthar	ním·chuirther	nom·agar
atot·rímther	dot·scarthar	nít·chuirther	not·agar
ad·rímther	do·scarthar	ní·cuirther	agair
atonn·rímther	donn·scarthar	nínn·cuirther	nonn·agar
atob·rímther	dob·scarthar	níb·cuirther	non·agar
ad·rímter, ·rímiter	do·scartar, ·scaratar	ní·cuirter, ·cuiretar	agtair

nom·moltar	ním·chrenar	ním·gaibther
not·moltar	nít·chrenar	nít·gaibther
moltair	ní·crenar	ní·gaibther
nonn·moltar	nínn·crenar	nínn·gaibther
nob·moltar	níb·crenar	níb·gaibther
moltair, molaitir	ní·crentar	ní·gaibter, ·gaibiter

Exercise 32.2

1. I hear it: a sweet-sounding bell is struck in a windy night. 2. The rich noblemen do not fear the power of the tribal king. 3. Dost thou say words of welcome to the king and to his young queen at their coming to the town? 4. The spirit vivifies the body. 5. It is on the rear shafts of our chariot that we place the blood-red heads of the dead noblemen. 6. Do you not hear the whistling of the wind in the high willows at the bank of the Boyne? 7. Do the stupid scholars compare sheep to horses? They are not being compared to them. 8. The humans are shaped in the likeness of God. 9. There are no snakes in the green island, because Saint Patrick drives all of them from it. 10. The *rath*s and old cities of the pagans are not inhabited. 11. Divinity is revealed in Christ, but Christ reveals God's truth to the people of the world. 12. I am told thou hast a good son. 13. It is through the ruler's righteousness that great tribes and cities of the noble are judged. 14. The trilling of the blackbird and the lay of the cuckoo is sung around me in the middle of the wood. 15. Dad, dost thou no hear the king of the alder-tree speaking to me? 16. Son, this is not a king, but a cloud of fog and the wind stirring the leaves. 17. An Ogam inscription is being written on the side of a high stone and the stone is being placed at the top of a hill. 18. I am not being called to the battle, I am being left sleeping. 19. Thou art being seen driving the sheep from the meadow, thou art not being seen herding them. 20. Messengers are coming (= there is a going) from the king of the Ulaid to Tara to make a covenant between them.

1. Ra·chluinemmar: bentair clocáin binni i n-aidchi gaíthe. 2. Ad·ágathar in aire saidbre cumachtae ríg túath. 3. Ní·labraid bríathra faílte frisna rríga 7 fria rígnai óca oca techt don chathraig. 4. Innád·mbéoigedar in spirut inna curpu. 5. Is for feirt mo charpait suidigiur cenn cróderg ind airech mairb. 6. Ro·cluiniur feit inna gaíthe isnaib sailchib ardaib ar brú inna Bóinne. 7. Ní·samlathar in scolaire cáeraig fri ech. Ní·samaltar-si fris. 8. In·cruthaigter duine i cosmailius Dé? 9. At·taat (or. fil) nathraig isind insi glais, nís·n-aig nóeb Pátraic inna uili eissi. 10. Trebtair rátha 7 senchathraig inna ngeinte. 11. Innád·foilsigther deacht i Críst, 7 innád·foilsigethar Críst fírinni nDé do doínib domuin? 12. Ad·fíadar dún-ni at·taat maicc maithi lib-si. (FR 17 f.) 13. Is tre fír flatha miditir túath becc 7 a cathair. 14. Canair trírech inna lon 7 loíd inna cuach immut-su i mmedón ind fedo. 15. Á aiti, ro·cluinter-su ríga inna fern oc labrad frimm-sa. 16. Á maicc, indat ríg in-so? 17. Scríbtair oguim i tóebaib liacc n-ard 7 suidigtir ind liaicc-sin ar mullchaib tulach. 18. Nonn·gairther cosin cath, nínn·fácabar inar cotlud. 19. Indob·accastar oc áin inna cáerach ón chlúain? Atob·cíther oca n-airi. 20. Tíagair ó rígaib inna n-Ulad co Temair do dénum chairdessa etarro.

Exercise 33.3

in druí gáeth	in námae cumachtach	in fili dánae
in druad gaíth	ind námat cumachtaig	ind filed dánai
don druid gáeth	dond námait chumachtuch	dond filid dánu
in druid ngáeth	in nnámait cumachtach	in filid ndánae
á druí gaíth	á námae cumachtaig	á fili dánai
in druid gaíth	in námait cumachtaig	ind filid dánai
inna ndruad ngáeth	inna nnámat cumachtach	inna filed ndánae
donaib druídib gáethaib	donaib náimtib cumachtchaib	donaib filedaib dánaib
inna druída gáethu/a	inna náimtea cumachtcha	inna fileda dánu
á druída gáethu/a	á náimtea cumachtcha	á fileda dánu

in teine buide	in fíado fír	ind luch líath
in teined buidi	ind fíadat fír	inna lochad léithe
don teinid buidiu	dond fíadait fír	dond lochaid léith
in teinid mbuide	in fíadait fír	in llochaid lléith
á theine buidi	á fíado fír	á luch líath
in teinid buidi	ind fíadait fír	inna lochaid líatha
inna teined mbuide	inna fíadat fír	inna llochad llíath
donaib teintib buidib	donaib fíadtaib (?) fíraib	donaib lochthaib líathaib
inna teintea buidi	inna fíadta fíru/a	inna lochtha líatha
á theintea buidi	á fíadta fíru/a	á lochtha líatha

in traig sainemail
inna traiged sainemlae
don traigid sainemail
in traigid sainemail
á thraig sainemail
inna traigid sainemlai
inna traiged sainemail/-mlae
donaib traigthib sainemlaib
inna traigthea sainemlai
á thraigthea sainemlai

Exercise 35.2

1. This is it what I pray for. 2. (It is) thy royal household that I praise, because thou art my great king. 3. I swear by the god by which my tribe swears, you are the druids who say (= give, bring) charms on our enemies. 4. All run and it is one man who takes the victory from them at completing it. 5. It is he who puts without delay the lustre of red gold upon my speech. 6. A blessing from me upon the dear guest who brings news from our friends with him. 7. The death that we go to causes life to you, that means, it is for your life we go to death. 8. It is us who go into the wood and who hear the birds singing. 9. Do you not see the black sheep which the shepherd drives out of the middle of the white sheep? 10. She is the girl, who distributes food and who pours wine to the guests, and I call her to me. 11. The charioteers are sitting in front of the chariot-fighters, they are not sitting at their left. 12. They are poets of the first grade who sing 350 poems, that means seven times fifty poems. 13. I do not love the ill-omened water, which goes past my habitation. 14. It is riches that are being loved by you, it is not people. 15. O bright sun, which lightens up the heaven with its amount of sanctity, o king, who has power over the angels, o Lord of humans. 16. Three fools of the world: a young person who laughs about an old person, a healthy person, who laughs about a sick person, a wise person, who laughs about a stupid person. 17. Three dark places a woman is not entitled to go: the darkness of fog, the darkness of the night, the darkness of the forest. 18. Three (types of) blood(-shed) which do not entitle attendance: the blood of the battle, and of jealousy, and of interference. 19. Three free persons who make unfree persons of themselves: a lord who sells his prerogatives, a queen who goes to a peasant, a son of a poet who leaves his art. 20. Three inheritances which are divided in front of heirs: the inheritance of a fool and the inheritance of a lunatic and the inheritance of an old person.

1. Is ed in-so no·guidem. 2. Do rígrad no·molmar, ol is tú ar rruiri. 3. Tongmai do Día tongtae ar túatha, is tussu in druí beires brichtu forar nnámait-ni. 4. In·rrethat uili 7 in óenḟer gaibes búaid diib inna chomalnad? 5. It é fo·cherdat cen dolmai néim n-óir deirg forar labrai? 6. Bendacht úainn forsna oígetha dili bertae scéla diar carait leo. 7. A mbás no·tíag-sa do·áirci bethaid dúit-siu, .i. is ar bethaid dúit-siu tíagu-sa bás. 8. Is sib-si téite isin fid 7 ro·chluinethar inna éunu oc cétul. 9. Ad·ciam in cáeraig nduib agtae ind augairi a medón inna cáerach finn. 10. Is sí ind ingen nád·dáili biad 7 nád·dortai fín dond oígid, 7 nís·ngair cuccut. 11. At·tá int arae inna ṡuidiu ar bélaib ind eirred, ní·fil inna ṡuidiu fora chlíu. 12. Indat é filid prímgráid ind ḟir cantae cóecait ndúan ar thríb cétaib? 13. In·cara-si in n-uisce ndúabais imma·thét sech tóeb a árais? 14. Nídat moíni cartar linn, it doíni. 15. Á gelgrían nád·ḟursannai ríched, á Rí nád·chumaing aingliu! 16. Trí gaíth in betha: óc nád·chuitbi sen, slán nád·chuitbi galrach, gáeth nád·chuitbi báeth. 17. Trí dorchae dlegtae mnaí do imthecht. 18. Trí fuili dlegtae frecor. 19. Trí soír nád·dénat dóeru díb féin: tigernae nád·ren a déiss, rígain nád·tét co aithech, mac filed nád·léici a cheird. 20. Trí orbai nád·ranntar fíad chomarbaib.

Poem 35.3

The flour which the mill grinds,
it is not oats but red wheat;
it is from the choice of the great (family) tree,
the charge of Máelodrán's mill.

Poem 35.4

He is a heart,
a grove of nuts
he is young,
a kiss for him.

Exercise 36.3

int athair dil
ind athar dil
dond athair dil
in n-athair ndil
á athair dil

ind aithir dili
inna n-aithre ndil/e
donaib aithrib dilib
inna aithrea dili
á aithrea dili

a mmag llethan
in maige lethain
don maig lethun
a mmag llethan
á mag lethan

inna maige lethna
inna mmaige llethan
donaib maigib lethnaib
inna maige lethna
á maige lethna

in bráthair oac
in bráthar oic
don bráthair ouc
in mbráthair n-oac
á bráthair oic

in bráithir oic
inna mbráithre n-oac
donaib bráithrib ócaib
inna bráithrea óca
á bráithrea óca

a n-og tromm
ind uige truimm
dond uig thrumm
a n-og tromm
á og tromm

inna uige thromma
inna n-uige tromm
donaib uigib trommaib
inna uige thromma
á uige thromma

a nglenn nglas
in glinne glais
don glinn glas
a nglenn nglas
á glenn nglas

inna glinne glasa
inna nglinne nglas
donaib glinnib glasaib
inna glinne glasa
á glinne glasa

a lleth n-aill
ind leithe aili
dond leith ailiu
a lleth n-aill
á leth n-aill

inna leithe aili
inna lleithe n-aile
donaib lethaib ailib
inna leithe aili
á leithe aili

Exercise 37.5

-
(ná·)éiren
(ná·)éirned
(ná·)éirnem
(ná·)éirenar
(ná·)éirnid
(ná·)éirnet
(ná·)éirenatar

(ná·)glanaimm
(ná·)glan
(ná·)glanad
(ná·)glantar
(ná·)glanam
(ná·)glanaid
(ná·)glanat
(ná·)glanatar

(ná·)ciul
(ná·)ceil
(ná·)ceiled
(ná·)celar
(ná·)celam
(ná·)ceilid
(ná·)celat
(ná·)celtar

-
(ná·)finntae
(ná·)finnad
(ná·)finntar
(ná·)finnammar
(ná·)finnaid
(ná·)finnatar
-

-
(ná·)frecair
(ná·)frecrad
(ná·)frecrathar
(ná·)frecram
(ná·)frecraid
(ná·)frecrat
(ná·)frecratar

(ná·)midiur
(ná·)mitte
(ná·)mided
(ná·)mitter
(ná·)midem
(ná·)midid
(ná·)midetar
-

(ná·)foilsigiur
(ná·)foilsigthe
(ná·)foilsiged
(ná·)foilsigther
(ná·)foilsigmer
(ná·)foilsigid
(ná·)foilsigetar
-

Exercise 38.4

atom·ren, nacham·éiren
atot·ren, nachat·éiren
at·rren, nach·n-éiren
ata·ren, nacha·éiren
at·ren, nach(id)·éiren
atonn·ren, nachann·éiren
atob·ren, nachib·éiren
ata·ren, nacha·éiren

nom·glan, nacham·glan
not·glan, nachat·glan
na·nglan, nach·nglan
nos·(n)glan, nacha·glan
na·glan, nach(id)·glan
nonn·glan, nachann·glan
nob·glan, nachib·glan
nos·(n)glan, nacha·glan

nom·cheil, nacham·cheil
not·cheil, nachat·cheil
na·ceil, nach·ceil
nos·ceil, nacha·ceil
na·cheil, nach(id)·cheil
nonn·ceil, nachann·ceil
nob·ceil, nachib·ceil
nos·ceil, nacha·ceil

rom·finntae, nacham·finntae
rot·finntae, nachat·finntae
ra·finntae, nach·finntae
ros·finntae, nacha·finntae
ra·finntae, nach(id)·finntae
ronn·finntae, nachann·finntae
rob·finntae, nachib·finntae
ros·finntae, nacha·finntae

fritom·gair, nachat·frecair
fritot·gair, nachat·frecair
frit·ngair, nach·frecair
frita·gair, nacha·frecair
frit·gair, nach(id)·frecair
fritonn·gair, nachann·frecair
fritob·gair, nachib·frecair
frita·gair, nacha·frecair

nom·mitte, nacham·mitte
not·mitte, nachat·mitte
na·mmitte, nach·mmitte
nos·(m)mitte, nacha·mitte
na·mitte, nach(id)·mitte
nonn·mitte, nachann·mitte
nob·mitte, nachib·mitte
nos·(m)mitte, nacha·mitte

nom·foilsigthe, nacham·foilsigthe
not·foilsigthe, nachat·foilsigthe
na·foilsigthe, nach·foilsigthe
nos·foilsigthe, nacha·foilsigthe
na·foilsigthe, nach(id)·foilsigthe
nonn·foilsigthe, nachann·foilsigthe
nob·foilsigthe, nachib·foilsigthe
nos·foilsigthe, nacha·foilsigthe

Exercise 39.2

1. Protect (*sg.*) me! Don't be (*sg.*) patient (*lit.*: don't make patience)! 2. 'Help (*sg.*) me, Cú Chulainn! Carry (*sg.*) a while with me!' 3. Apply (*sg.*) the goad on the horses then! 4. 'Go, Conall, to the fort, and leave me here at the guard meanwhile!' 5. Don't let thy drunkenness overcome thee! 6. Don't let him judge you, that means don't let yourself be brought under the sway of the Old Law! 7. 'Let's go to our house!' said Conchobar. 8. Since we are sons of the day and of the light, let us not follow these (*things*)! 9. Be (*pl.*) fatherlike, that means take the heritage of your father and imitate his customs. 10. Let them not attempt (*it*)! 11. Let him be released from his chains, for the sake of our wealth and our cattle, and let the court be closed. 12. Three sisters of youth: desire, beauty, generosity. 13. Welcome to thee, little boy, for the sake of thy mother's heart! 14. Steadily therefore let Bran row, it is not long to the land of the women. 15. 'What is the mountain over there?' said Cú Chulainn, 'What is the bright mound over there on top of the mountain? What is the plain there? What is the herd, the wild one there?' 16. It is not thou who nourishes him, but it is he who nourishes thee. 17. The concern is great which I have for you. 18. If you are in communion with the body of Christ, you are children of Abraham like that, and it is you who are heirs of Abraham. 19. This then is a custom for him, reproval of the women in the beginning and giving her under the power of their men, so that it is afterwards that the men are reprimanded and are bent under the will of God. 20. 'This is its custom,' said Jesus, 'every anvil which is struck teaches everyone, who strikes it; and it is not it that is being taught.'

1. Donn·eimid-ni! Dénaid ainmnit! 2. Congnaid linn! Beirid síst linn! 3. Ná·indgaid brot forsin n-echraid! 4. Ná·eirg-siu trá, á Chonaill, don dún 7 nachan·léic-ni oc forairi sund colléic! 5. Nachib·tróethad far mescae! 6. Nachit·midetar, .i. nachit·berar i smachtu rechta fetarlaicce! 7. 'Ná·tíagam dom thaig!' ol Conchobar. 8. Seichem inna hí-siu! 9. Ban athramlai-ni .i. gaibem comarbus ar n-athrae 7 intamlam a mbéssu! 10. Nach·aimdithe! 11. Léicter dia slabradaib, dáig m'indile 7 mo chethrae, acht ná·dúntar in less! 12. Siur, dí phieir, trí seithir. 13. Fo chen dúib a maccánu, fo déig cride far máthrae! 14. Fossad air-sin imrat ind fir, ní cían co tír inna mban. 15. 'Citné sléibe in-so thall?' ol Cú Chulainn, 'Citné cairn gil in-so thall i n-úachtur inna sléibe? Citné maige a n-í thall? Citné slabrai, inna díscri-se thall?' 16. Ní sib nos·ail acht it é nob·ail. 17. Ní mór in deithiden file dún-ni duit-siu. 18. Má nodat·fil i n-ellug coirp Chríst, at mac/ingen *Abrache* amal sodin, 7 is tú as chomarbae *Abracham.* 19. Is bés trá diib-som a n-í-siu, cosc mná i tossug 7 a tabairt fo chumachtae a fir combi íarum coiscithir in fer 7 do·airberar fo réir Dé. 20. 'Is é a bés,' ol Ísu, 'inna indeona bentar ní·forcnat in cách noda·ben; ocus it é for·chantar.'

Test 39.3

eipred: (S1) 3rd sg. imp.; *comalnaithe*: (W1) dep. 2nd sg. imp.; *áirim*: (W2a) 2nd sg. imp.; *crochaid*: (W1) 2nd pl. imp.; *ná·crochaid*: (W1) neg. 2nd pl. imp.; *biur*: (S1) 1st sg. imp.; *immráidet*: (W2a) 3rd pl. imp.; *nach·ngairem*: (S2) 1st pl. imp. + neg. inf. pron. 3rd sg. masc.; *eiperr*: (S1) 3rd sg. pass. imp.; *foilsigid*: (W2b) 2nd pl. imp.; *rom·chluinter*: (S3) 1st sg. pass. imp.; *sóertar*: (W1) 3rd pl. imp.; *crochthar*: (W1) 3rd sg. pass. imp.; *ná·crochthar*: (W1) neg. 3rd sg. pass. imp.; *finntae*: (S3) 2nd pl. imp.; *áirmem*: (W2a) 1st pl. imp.; *cotob·ceilid*: (S1) 2nd pl. imp. + inf. pron. B 2nd pl.; *ná·déne*: (H2) neg. 2nd sg. imp.; *da·gniad*: (H2) 3rd sg. imp. + inf. pron. A 3rd sg. neutr.; *nach·chluined*: (S3) 3rd sg. imp. + neg. inf. pron. 3rd sg. neutr.; *eirg*: (S1) 2nd sg. imp. of téit; *dos·mbeir*: (S1) 2nd sg. imp. + inf. pron. A 3rd sg. f. or 3rd pl.; *ná·comalnatar*: (W1) neg. 3rd pl. imp.; *tair*: (S1) 2nd sg. imp. of do·tét

dáiles: (W2a) 3rd sg. rel.; *pridchimme*: (W1) 1st pl. rel.; *rímte*: (W2a) 3rd pl. rel.; *téite*: (S1) 3rd sg. rel.; *do·thíagat*: (S1) 3rd pl. len. rel.; *gattae*: (W1) 3rd pl. rel.; *crentar*: (S3) 3rd pl. pass. rel.; *fíriánaigemmar*: (W2b) 1st pl. rel; *nád·fil*: (subst. verb.) neg. len. rel.; *for·chaun*: (S1) 1st sg. len. rel.; *nád·fodmat*: (S2) neg. 3rd pl. len. rel.; *sernas*: (S3) 3rd sg. rel.; *nod·carat*: (W1) 3rd pl. len. rel. + inf. pron. C 3rd sg. masc.; *indat·chluinter*: (S3) interrog. 2nd sg. pass.; *adid·chí*: (H2) 3rd sg. len. rel. + inf. pron. C 3rd sg. neutr.

Test 39.4

inna traiged: (t, f) gen. sg. or gen. pl.; *ind fiadat*: (nt, m) gen. sg.; *Temraig*: (k, f) prep. sg. or acc. sg.; *aithir*: (r, m) nom. pl.; *cethrachat*: (nt, m) gen. sg. or gen. pl.; *tengthaib*: (t, f) prep. pl.; *ciach*: (k, m) gen. sg. or gen. pl.; *ind uige*: (s, n) gen. sg.; *sieir*: (r, f) prep. sg. or acc. sg.; *cathracha*: (k, f) acc. pl.; *cáera*: (k, f) nom. sg. or prep. sg.; *míledaib*: (t, m) prep. pl.; *slíab*: (s, n) nom. sg. or acc. sg.; *airecha*: (k, m) acc. pl.; *dét*: (nt, n) nom. sg. or gen. sg. or acc. sg. or nom. pl. or gen. pl. or acc. pl.; *int senduid*: (t, m) nom. pl.; *á ríga*: (g, m) voc. pl.; *ríga*: (g, m) acc. pl.

Exercise 40.2

a mbéimm n-aill	a n-imb mbuide	a lléimm n-ard
in béimme aili	ind imbe buidi	ind léimme aird
don béimmimm ailiu	dond imbimm buidiu	dond léimmimm ard
a mbéimm n-aill	a n-imb mbuide	a lléimm n-ard
á béimm n-aill	á imb mbuide	á léimm n-ard
inna béimmenn aili	inna imbenn buidi	inna léimmenn arda
inna mbéimmenn n-aile	inna n-imbenn mbuide	inna lléimmenn n-ard
donaib béimmennaib ailib	donaib imbennaib buidib	donaib léimmennaib ardaib
inna béimmenn aili	inna imbenn buidi	inna léimmenn arda
á béimmenn aili	á imbenn buidi	á léimmenn arda

a seinm mbinn	a n-ingrimm cróderg	a togairm mór
int šenmae binn	ind ingrimme cródeirg	in togarmae móir
dont šenmaimm binn	dond ingrimmimm chróderg	don togarmaimm mór
a seinm mbinn	a n-ingrimm cróderg	a togairm mór
á šeinm mbinn	á ingrimm cróderg	á thogairm mór
inna seinmenn binna	inna ingrimmenn chróderga	inna togarmann móra
inna seinmenn mbinn	inna n-ingrimmenn cróderg	inna togarmann mór
donaib seinmennaib binnaib	donaib ingrimmennaib cródergaib	donaib togarmannaib móraib
inna seinmenn binna	inna ingrimmenn chróderga	inna togarmann móra
á šeinmenn binna	á ingrimmenn chróderga	á thogarmann móra

Exercise 41.6

ansu, ·anus	do·sluindius, ·díltus	soísu, ·sous
ansai, ·anais	do·sluindis, ·díltais	soísi, ·soais
anais, ·an	do·sluind, ·dílt	soais, ·soí
ansaimmi, ·ansam	do·sluindsem, ·díltaisem	soísimmi, ·soísem
-, ·ansaid	do·sluindsid, ·díltaisid	-, ·soísid
ansait, ·ansat	do·sluindset, ·díltaiset	soísit, ·soíset

ad·ellus, ·aidlius	·cruthaigsiur	do·génus, ·dignius
ad·ellais, ·aidlis	·cruthaigser	do·génais, ·dignis
ad·ell, ·adall	·cruthaigestar	do·génai, ·digni
ad·ellsam, ·aidlisem	·cruthaigsemmar	do·génsam, ·digénsam (?)
ad·ellsaid, ·aidlisid	·cruthaigsid	do·génsaid, ·digénsaid (?)
ad·ellsat, ·aidliset	·cruthaigsetar	do·génsat, ·digénsat (?)

fo·ácbus, ·fácbus	imm·biurt, ·imbiurt	do·ét, ·dét
fo·ácbais, ·fácbais	imm·birt, ·imbirt	do·ét, ·dét
fo·ácab, ·fácab	imm·bert, ·imbert	do·ét, ·dét
fo·ácabsam, ·fácabsam	imm·bertammar, ·imbertammar	do·étammar, ·détammar
fo·ácabsaid, ·fácabsaid	imm·bertaid, ·imbertaid	do·étaid, ·détaid
fo·ácabsat, ·fácabsat	imm·bertatar, ·imbertatar	do·étatar, ·détatar

Poem 42.1

There is a woman in the land
—I do not say her name—
her fart breaks out of her
like a stone from a sling.

Exercise 42.3

1. Then his mound is dug. His (grave-)stone is set up. His name is written in Ogam (*lit.*: his Ogam-name is written). He is mourned (*lit.*: his mourning is done). 2. The two arms are as white as the snow of a single night and the two clean-beautiful cheeks are as red as the purple foxglove. 3. The two brows are as black as the back of a beetle. 4. The two eyes are as blue as a hyacinth. 5. This is another comparison with him, namely the comparison of a voice with a trumpet, because there are many sounds to the latter and each of them is separate, that means, the sound for war is separate, (the sound) for sleep (is) separate etc. 6. It is three cries that the cock made (*lit.*: shouted) in the morning. 7. Who is the mother who conceived this birth? 8. Jesus formed twelve little birds, 'sparrow' their names; on Saturday he made them from clay without breaking one. 9. Longing seized Connlae for the woman who spoke to him and who threw an apple to him. 10. I did not consume your food and your clothes, but it is you who consumed them. 11. Patrick settled in Druimm Daro after the offering (i.e., after it had been offered to him). Patrick left his foster-son there, *Benignus* his name. 12. This is the name of the island: Island of Pleasures. They left him then there. 13. The men called Judas to them; he received money from them for betraying the lord. 14. The Jews took hold of Jesus and flogged him and beat him across his cheeks. 15. A purple cloak was put around the king. 16. They gave him a 'parting drink' for his swift death's sake; they mixed for him gall with vinegar. 17. The sun hid its (*lit.*: her) light, the greatly thundering sea roared. 18. Jesus is the man who arose again in Israel; is it in his name that all peoples put their hope? 19. On a cruel Wednesday I parted from Máel Rúanaid. On Thursday I realized the loss of my father's son. 20. The chief poet of the king was called to the palace to play the harp. Were thou not called together with him?

1. Claittir a fertai íarom. Sáittir a lliaic. Scríbtair a n-anmann ogaim. Agair a ngubae. 2. Is gilithir snechtae a doe 7 is dergithir fuil a grúad. 3. Is duibithir aidchi a mala. 4. Is glaisithir muir a súil. 5. In·fil ilsenmann don tub? In sain seinm fri cath? In sain seinm fri súan ? 6. Is óengairm gartatar in chailig isin matain. 7. Is sí in máthair con·bert a ngein-se. 8. Delbais Ísu óenén, passir a ainm. Indid·ndigni dia Sabbait? (*or*: In dia Sabbait da·géni?) 9. In·ngab éulchaire inna firu immna mná ada·gládastar 7 do·chorastar ubla doib. 10. Do·meltammar-ni do biad 7 t'étach. Ní tussu doda·melt. 11. In·congab Pátraicc íarna aidbairt i nDruimm Daro? In·fácab Pátraicc a daltu and? 12. It é anmann inna n-inse-so. Fos·n-ácab and íarum. 13. Con·gart in fer Iudas cuci; ar·foet argat úaid ar mrath a choimded-som. 14. In·n-airgab int Iudaide Ísu 7 indid·sroigel 7 indid·n-essart tara grúaide? 15. In·ngabad tí chorcrae immna ríga? 16. Láthrais dí dig séto ar lainni a mochéco; con·mesc domblas dí ar fínacet. 17. Ní·dichelt grían a sollsi, ní·búirestar rían. 18. It é ind fir as·érachtatar; in inna n-anmannaib fris·accai uile cenél? 19. I Cétaín scarsaimmi-ni fri Máel Rúanaid. Dia Dardaín gabsaimmi-ni céill for ingnais maicc ar n-athar. 20. In·congartha prímfilid ind ríg cosa rrígthech do senmaimm a crott? Nínn·congrad-ni leo-som.

Exercise 43.2

int ollam tróg	Ériu álaind	in cú dían
ind ollamon tróig	Éirenn áilde	in chon déin
dond ollamuin thróg	do Éirinn/Ére álaind	don choin dían
in n-ollamuin tróg	Éirinn n-álaind	in coin dían
á ollam tróg	á Ériu álaind	á chú déin

ind ollamuin tróig		in choin déin
inna n-ollamon tróg		inna con dían
donaib ollamnaib trógaib		donaib conaib díanaib
inna ollamna trógu/a		inna cona díanu/a
á ollamna trógu/a		á chona díanu/e

ind rétglu gel	in menmae maith	in derucc nue
inna rétglann gile	in menman maith	inna dercon nue
dond rétglainn gil	don menmain maith	don dercoin nui
in rrétglainn ngeil	in mmenmain mmaith	in dercoin nnui
á rétglu gel	á menmae maith	á derucc nue

inna rétglainn gela	in menmain maithi	inna dercoin nui
inna rrétglann ngel	inna mmenman mmaith/e	inna ndercon nnue
donaib rétglannaib gelaib	donaib menmanaib maithib	donaib derconaib nuib
inna rétglanna gela	inna menmana maithi	inna dercona nui
á rétglanna gela	á menmana maithi	á dercona nui

in brú dorchae	ind aisndís follus
inna bronn dorchae	inna aisndísen foilse
don broinn dorchai	dond aisndís/in folluis
in mbroinn dorchai	in n-aisndísin folluis
á brú dorchae	á aisndís follus

inna broinn dorchai	inna aisndísin foillsi
inna mbronn dorchae	inna n-aisndísen follus
donaib bronnaib dorchaib	donaib aisndísenaib foillsib
inna bronna dorchai	inna aisndísena foillsi
á bronna dorchai	á aisndísena foillsi

Exercise 44.8

(·)tách	(·)rerag	ro·ánacc, ·ránacc	(·)lel
(·)tách	(·)rerag	ro·ánacc, ·ránacc	(·)lel
(·)táich	(·)reraig	ro·ánaicc, ·ránaicc	(·)lil
(·)táchammar	(·)rergammar	ro·áncammar, ·ráncammar	(·)lelmar
(·)táchaid	(·)rergaid	ro·áncaid, ·ráncaid	(·)lelaid
(·)táchatar	(·)rergatar	ro·áncatar, ·ráncatar	(·)leltar

(·)génar	(·)cér	for·cachan, ·forcachan
(·)génar	(·)cér	for·cachan, ·forcachan
(·)génair	(·)cíuir	for·cachain, ·forcachain
(·)génammar	(·)céorammar (?)	for·cachnammar, ·forcachnammar
(·)génaid	(·)céoraid (?)	for·cachnaid, ·forcachnaid
(·)génatar	(·)céoratar (?)	for·cachnatar, ·forcachnatar
		[the prototonic forms are hypothetic!]

Exercise 45.1

§1 How many ranks of poets are there? Not difficult: seven: the o., the á., the c., the d., the m., the f. They have three subgrades, namely the t., the d., the o.

§2 What are the poetical gift and the grade and the honor-price of each of them from small to great? Not difficult: the poetical gift of the ollam first: he has 350 literary compositions, namely, fifty of each rank; he is expert in every historical knowledge, and he is expert in judgements of Irish traditional law. His honor-price is forty *sét*s.

§6 How is rank conferred upon a poet? Not difficult, a presentation of his literary compositions (= he presents his…) to an ollam—and he must have the seven grades of knowledge—and the king receives him into his full rank…

§9 And a man from a family of poets who undertakes the labor (of becoming a poet) after his father and grandfather have parted from it (= poetry), what rank is conferred upon him? Not difficult, a rank according to his own poetical skill, because this is the one spark that kindles a flame.

Exercise 45.2

Triad 35: The three fairs of Ireland: the fair of Tailtiu, the fair of Crúachu, the fair of Colmán Elo.

Test 45.3

nád·eipert: (S1 as·beir) neg. 3rd sg. t-pret. rel.; *fo·lolgaid*: (S1 fo·loing) 2nd pl. red. pret.; *ro·cúalae*: (S3 ro·cluinethar) 3rd sg. red. pret.; *rersait*: (H1 raid) 3rd pl. s-pret.; *ná·dignius*: (H2 do·gní) neg. 1st sg. red. s-pret. rel.; *sirt*: (S3 sernaid) 3rd sg. t-pret.; *co·n-accae*: (H2 ad·cí) 3rd sg. pret.; *do·logsam*: (W2b do·luigi) 1st pl. s-pret.; *molaiser*: (W1 molaithir) 2nd sg. dep. s-pret.; *fo·caird*: (S1 fo·ceird) 3rd sg. a-pret.; *do·gádatar*: (S2 do·guid) 3rd pl. á-pret.; *sóerthai*: (W1 sóeraid) 3rd pl. pass. pret.; *ní·éracht*: (S1 at·reig) neg. 3rd sg. t-pret.; *do·fíchatar*: (S1 do·fich) 3rd pl. í-pret.; *cachnae*: (S1 canaid) 3rd sg. red. pret. rel.; *do·lod*: (S1 do·tét) 1st sg. or 2nd sg. pret.; *sephainn*: (S1 seinnid) 3rd sg. red. pret.; *at·gén*: (S3 ad·gnin) 1st sg. or 2nd sg. long vowel-pret. + inf. pron. B 3rd sg. neut.; *do·génais*: (H2 do·gní) 2nd sg. red. s-pret.; *génair*: (S2 gainithir) 3rd sg. dep. long vowel-pret.; *in·n-ibis*: (S1 ibid) interrog. 2nd sg. s-pret.; *fort·ndedgatar*: (S1 for·ding) 3rd pl. red. pret. + inf. pron. B 3rd sg. masc.; *boíe*: (H1 at·tá) 3rd sg. pret. rel.; *fo·cíuir*: (S3 fo·cren) 3rd sg. long vowel-pret.; *ní·phridchus*: (W1 pridchid) neg. 1st sg. s-pret. + inf. pron. A 3rd sg. neut.; *ráncatar*: (S1 ro·icc) 3rd pl. pret.; *cich*: (H2 ciid) 3rd sg. red. pret.; *fúarammar*: (S2 fo·gaib) 1st pl. pret.; *na·mbí*: (S3 benaid) 3rd sg. red. pret. + inf. pron. A 3rd sg. masc.; *ro·lámar*: (S2 ro·laimethar) 1st sg. á-pret. or 2nd sg. á-pret.; *ní·ded*: (S3 denaid) neg. 1st sg. red. pret.; *síasar-su*: (S1 saidid) 2nd sg. dep. long vowel pret. + emph. pron. 2nd sg.; *innád·fetar*: (S3 ro·finnadar) neg. interrog. 1st sg. pret. or 2nd sg. pret.; *·roacht*: (S1 ro·saig) 1st sg. t-pret. or 2nd sg. t-pret. or 3rd sg. t-pret.

Test 45.4

céimm: (n, n) nom. sg. or acc. sg.; *arbaimm*: (n, n) prep. sg.; *inna anmann*: (n, n) nom. pl. or acc. pl.; *ollomnaib*: (n, m) prep. pl.; *toimtin*: (n, f) prep. sg. or acc. sg. or nom. pl.; *seinmimm*: (n, n) prep. sg.; *abae*: (n, f) gen. sg.; *in chon*: (n, m) gen. sg.; *goibnea*: (n, m) acc. pl.; *Ére*: (n, f) prep. sg.; *bronna*: (n. f) acc. sg.; *Albain*: (n, f) prep. sg. or acc. sg.; *aisndís*: (n, f) nom.. sg.; *airmitin*: (n, f) prep. sg. or acc. sg. or nom. pl.; *talman*: (n, m) gen. sg. or gen. pl.; *airecha*: (k, m) acc. pl.; *noídin*: (n, m) prep. sg. or acc. sg. or nom. pl.; *suthainidir*: (i) equative; *ansam*: (i̯o, i̯ā) superlative; *toísigem*: (o, ā) superlative; *foilsithir*: (u) equative; *lir*: (u) equative; *messam*: irreg. superlative of *olc*.

Exercise 45.6

1. Thou art a debtor to me, I am not a debtor to thee. 2. The time of my offering came. 3. The axe fell off its handle into the sea and *Eliseus* threw his handle after it and the axe came back again onto the head of the handle, so that it was around it. 4. When David went into exile through a glenn, his enemies pelted him with stones while he was going (lit.: at his going) and they cursed him (lit.: gave curses upon him) from the top of the mountain. 5. One day Bran walked alone near (lit.: in the proximity of) his fort. He heard music behind his back. 6. The branch jumped from the hand of the woman, so that it was in Bran's hand, and there was no power in Bran's hand to take the branch. 7. It was not long afterwards until they reached the land of the women. 8. Bran did not dare to go into the land. 9. Bran put his hand on the clew. The clew stuck to his palm. 10. The clew's thread was in the hand of the woman. She pulled the boat towards the port. 11. Then they went into a large house. The found beds for each couple there, that means twenty-seven (lit.: thrice nine) beds. 12. They saw something, a flock of swans before them. Cú Chulainn placed (= shot) a small stone at the birds, so that he slew eight birds of them. 13. The waters, which were in the depths of the earth, were visible through the cleavings of that same earth. 14. That heaven did not fall upon their heads, that the fire did not burn them, that the sea did not drown them, that the earth did not swallow them! 15. A boy fell down a cliff, he did at once; all fled except Jesus, he waited for the host. 16. Three that are best for a ruler: truth, peace, an army. 17. He was the most beautiful warrior who was in Ireland and Scotland, but he did not live long. 18. This is the greatest love that we have, (for that) which we obtained through our own labor. 19. These are the three foremost things for a man, namely bread, wine and oil. 20. Three worst splendors: the splendor of a wave, the splendor of a wanton woman, the splendor of a dog at the jump.

1. Ammi féchemain dúib, nítad féchemain-si dúnn. 2. In·tánaicc aimser ar n-aidbairte-ni? 3. Do·certar in bélai dia samthachaib issa mmuir 7 fo·caird *Eliseus* a samthacha inna ndiaid 7 do·lotar in bélai arithissi ar chenna inna samthach, co·mbátar impu. 4. Dia·lotar in brithemain for longais tri glinne, dos·bidcset a nnámait di chlochaib oca techt 7 do·bertatar maldachta forru dano di mullchaib inna sléibe. 5. Im·lodmar lae n-and ar n-óenur i comocus diar ndún. In·cúalammar a céol íarnar cúl? 6. In·lleblaing in chróeb di láim inna mná co·mboí for láim Brain? Innád·mboí nert i lláim Brain do gabáil inna croíbe? 7. Ba cían íar-sin co·ránaicc tír inna mná. 8. Ro·lámatar techt isa tír. 9. Ní·corastar a lláma forsin ceirtli. Ní·lil in cheirtle dia ndernannaib. 10. Ní·boí in snáithe inna ceirtle i lláim inna mná. In·coisreng-si inna curchu dochum poirt? 11. Luid i tech mór. Ar·ánaicc imdai do-som and. 12. Co-n-accae-si ní, éill ngéisse ara ciunn. Látharsait cloich mbicc forsna éunu co·mbéotar cóic éonu deac díb. 13. Niba foidirc int uisce, boíe hi fudumnaib talman, tri indlacha inna talman. 14. Ní·tochair nem inna cenn, nís·lloisc in teine, nís·báid rían, nís·sloic in talam. 15. Do·certar maic fo aill, bebsait i n-óenúair. In·táchatar uili? Innád·n-an nech ar chiunn ṡlúaig? 16. Trí ata dech do ḟlaithemnaib: fír, síd, slóig. 17. Imbtar é loích batar áildem bátar i nÉrinn 7 i nAlbain? Acht níbtar suthaini. 18. In ed as moam serc lemm-sa ad·chotadus trem ṡáethar saindíles? 19. In ed tréide in-sin as toísigem do doínib? 20. Imbtar é trí luchra batar messam: luchair tonn, luchair mban mbáeth, luchair con fo léimmimm?

Exercise 46.6

cóir, córaithir, córu, córam
cosmail, cosmailidir, cosmailiu, cosmailem
deithbir, deithbiridir, deithbiriu, deithbirem
fírián, fíriánaidir, fíriánu, fíriánam
léir, léirithir, léiriu, léirem
sen, sinithir, siniu, sinem
sollus, soillsidir, soillsiu, soillsem
úasal, úaislithir, úaisliu, úaislem

Exercise 47.6

bendachthae, ·bendachad, bendachthai, ·bendachtha; bendachthae
fíriánaigthe, ·fíriánaiged, fíriánaigthi, ·fíriánaigthea; fíriánaigthe
críthe, ·críth, críthi, ·crítha; críthe
fo·críth, ·fochrith, fo·crítha, ·fochritha; fochrithe
as·breth, ·eipred, as·bretha, ·eipertha; eipirthe
ar·nass, ·arnas, ar·nassa, ·arnassa; airnisse
fo·cét, ·fochet, fo·céta, ·focheta; fochetae
fris·ort, ·frithort, fris·orta, ·frithorta; frithortae

Poem 48.1

Four groups of three, three groups of four,
harmonious in every matter;
two groups of six in the church,
between North and South.

Poem 48.2

More splendid his shape than any person,
more spiritful his vigorous blaze than any freeman,
wiser than any bosom under the sky,
more righteous than any judge.

Exercise 48.4

1. Cú Chulainn shut one of his two eyes so that it wasn't broader than the eye of a needle. He opened the other one so that it was as big as the mouth of a meadcup. 2. It is more certain to us what we see through the eyes than what hear through the ears. 3. This is what the heretics say, that the godliness of the son is lesser than the godliness of the father. 4. 'True,' said he, 'love by the Lord for those two men is greater than for me (*lit.*: than I am).' 5. I have a watch-dog. Three chains (are) on him and three men to every chain. 6. I had (= spent) a while with kings drinking mead and wine; today I drink whey-water. 7. The tender, good boys, they have joy in the eternal realm; but Herod, he has eternal sorrow and eternal hell. 8. His is every herd that he sees, his are the wild animals and the cattle. 9. Bran went on the sea. Three (times) nine men their number. One man for (= leading) the three (times) nine men from his foster-brothers and coevals. 10. There are twenty-four men (*sc.* allowed in company) for an ollam abroad, twelve men in legal action,

ten on festival feasts, eight on travels with a king. 11. His wanderings from this hour on are not known. 12. The music of the woods used to play around me with Cuirithir, with the sound of the blood-red sea. 13. A terrible warrior was brought by the Saxons for the death of Áedán in the battle. 14. This below is what was heard and seen in his manners and deeds. 15. A crown of thorns was given around his head. Nails were beaten through his feet, others through his palms. 16. The cries of the birds on their flight were heard. 17. 'God with thee, Mary,' said Gabriel. 'Thou art blessed from the head to the sole and the fruit of thy womb.' 18. He was reared by (his) mother and (his) father in the plain of Murthemne. Great stories of the boygroup in Emain were told to him. 19. Three rebirths of the world: the womb of a woman, the udder of a cow, the furnace of a smith. 20. Nine (times) twenty birds were seen, a silber chain between every two birds. Three birds of them were brought down.

1. In·n-íad Cú Chulainn a dí śúil dó connábtar letha in-dáte cruí śnáthat? 2. Ní demniu latt a n-ad·chí-siu húa śúilib ol-daas a rro·chluinter húa chlúasaib. 3. Is ed nád·eiper int heretec as moo deacht Maicc in-daas deacht Athar. 4. Is moo serc in triir-ucut la Tigernae in-daí-siu. 5. At·taat cethair árchoin lee-si. Cethéoir slabrada foraib 7 cethrar cacha slabraide. 6. Ronn·boí denus la ríg oc ól meda 7 ḟína; indíu ebmai medguisce 7. In macc móeth maith, táthai bithśubae i nim. 8. In lee cach alam ad·chiam, indat aí alltai 7 chethrai? 9. Lotar ind ḟir for muir. Noí triir a lín. 10. In·fil deichenbor do ollamnaib? 11. Fessae a n-imthecht ónd úair-sin. 12. Céol caille fob·canad lais-seom. 13. Do·bretha mílid úathmair la Saxanu dia bás isin chath. 14. It é in-so sís ro·chlossa 7 ad·chessa inna mbésaib 7 a ngnímaib. 15. In·taibred corann delgae timchell a chinn? In·mbítha cloi tria chossa, alaili tria bossa? 16. In·closs gairm ind éuin fora luamain? 17. Adib bendachtai ó chennaib co fonnu 7 toirthea for mbronn. 18. Altai-som lia mmáithrea 7 lia n-aithrea. Ad·fess doib airscél inna maccraide i nEmain. 19. Broinn ban, uith bó, neiss gobann. 20. In·n-accassa secht n-éuin deac? In·tascrad óenén díb?

Exercise 49.2

ad·ellainn, ·aidlinn	(no)·cinginn	ad·ciinn, ·accainn	(no)·renainn
ad·ellta, ·aidlithea	(no)·cingthea	ad·cíthea, ·accaithea	(no)·renta
ad·ellad, ·aidlid	(no)·cinged	ad·ciad, ·accad	(no)·renad
ad·ellmais, ·aidlimis	(no)·cingmis	ad·címis, ·accaimis	(no)·renmais
ad·ellte, ·aidlithe	(no)·cingthe	ad·cíthe, ·accaithe	(no)·rentae
ad·elltais, ·aidlitis	(no)·cingtis	ad·cítis, ·accaitis	(no)·rentais

(no)·midinn	fo·gaibinn, ·fagbainn	do·ceilinn, ·dichlinn
(no)·mittea	fo·gaibthea, ·fagbatha	do·ceiltea, ·dichlithea
(no)·mided	fo·gaibed, ·fagbad	do·ceiled, ·dichlid
(no)·midmis	fo·gaibmis, ·fagbaimis	do·ceilmis, ·dichlimis
(no)·mitte	fo·gaibthe, ·fagbathe	do·ceilte, ·dichlithe
(no)·mitis	fo·gaibtis, ·fagbaitis	do·ceiltis, ·dichlitis

Exercise 51.1

Conchobar then saw Cú Chulainn driving the ball against the three fifty boys, and he brought their defeat upon them (= defeated them). When they used to make (= play) 'driving of the hole,' he used to fill the hole with his balls and the boys were not able to ward him off. When it was they who used to hurl (at) the hole, he alone used to ward them off so that not even a single ball could go in. When they used to wrestle (lit.: make wrestling), he used to overthrow the three fifty boys alone and the number (necessary for) his overthrowing could not meet around him. When, however, they used to play 'mutual stripping,' he used to strip them all so that they were stark naked, and they could not even take only a pin out of his cloak.

Exercise 51.3

1. The bullfeast of the men of Ireland: A bull used to be kill by them, and one man used to eat his fill of it, and he used to drink its broth and a song of truthfulness used to be sung upon him lying. 2. He gave (= put) a noose around his own neck, so that he dies, since Abisolon did not make (= carry out) his piece of advice. 3. Every time you have done a good thing for the poor in my name, it is on me you have done it. 4. Every time you have not done a good thing for the poor in my name, it is on me you haven't done it. 5. My prayer has clung to me and has not gone from me. 6. Since it is in darkness of mind that I have said the words which I have said, it is therefore that thou hast heard the voice of my prayer. 7. I used to investigate, when I was in tribulations, whether God's friendship and his providence had departed, and I did not understand this, whether it had departed or not. 8. They have read the canon of the Old and New Testament as we have read it, but they have only perverted it. 9. This is the end which he has given (= put) to the great sins which his enemies had done against him, (namely) refusal of God's providence to him, because he had not given revenge to them who has done these things against him. 10. Why hasn't thy protection been bound on the boys? 11. It was not long after this deed, which Fergus has just related, that he had done another deed. 12. He had preserved (my) honor and (my) soul (= life) for me, the member of (my) household who has been taken from me, namely my dog. 13. 'Isn't it they who say,' said Cú Chulainn, 'that there are not more of the Ulaid who are alive than (those) whom they have slain of them?' 14. [...] it is to seek an encounter (= duel) with a man that this boy who is here has come. 15. 'I reached thee, Celtchar,' said Cet mac Mágach, 'by the door of thy house. Alarm was raised around me. Everybody came. Thou camest at last.' 16. 'Thou hast hurled a spear at me. I have cast another spear at thee, so that it came through thy thigh and through the upper part of thy testicles.' 17. 'I have brought this cow, then,' she said, 'from Síd Crúachan, so that the Donn Cúailnge has bulled her for me.' 18. The praises which I used to make in melody and choir, my voice has failed at them. 19. The men, the young warriors, the horses who used to be around Máel Fothertaig, they used to act without reproof outside, they used to prepare a horse-race (= horse-races). 20. A feat of Cú Chulainn's son: He would (= used) put (= give) a stone into his sling and he would cast (it) a stunning blow on the birds, so that it (= the blow) would take the conscience from them, and they still alive, so that he would release them from him into the air again.

1. No·marbtais tairb leo 7 no·ittis a sáith diib 7 no·ibtis a n-enbruithiu 7 no·cantae ór fírinne forru inna lligiu. 2. Do·bertatar goistiu imma mbráigtea, combtar mairb, húare nád·ndigensat a carait a comairli. 3. Cach tan do·rrignis maith arin bocht inar n-anmannaib-ni, is fornn-ni do·rignis. 4. Cach tan ná·ndergénais maith arin bocht inar n-anmannaib-ni, is fornn-ni ní·dergénais. 5. Ní·róeltar dínn ar n-ernaigdi acht do·cuatar úainn. 6. hÚare is hi foscud menman ro·ráidset-som inna bríathra as·rubartatar, is airi in-sin ro·cúalaid-si guthu a n-ernaigde-seom. 7. Ní·scrútad-si, in tan no·mbíth isnaib fochaidib, dús in·retarscar cairde nDé. Is airi ní·thuc-si in-sin. 8. Ro·légais canóin amal ronda·légus-sa, acht nís·rosáebais-siu. 9. Is hé forcenn du·ratsat-som forsna col du·rigénai mo námae frimm, húare nád·tartus dígail forsin n-í du·rigénai inna hí-sin frimm-sa. 10. Ro·nass far fóesam-si forsin macc. 11. Ba chían íarsna gnímu, ad·chuadmar indossa, co·ndergénsat-som bét n-aile. 12. Con·aggabsat enech dún-ni, ind fir muintire ructha úainn. 13. Is é-side as·berad as móo fil do feraib i mbethaid ol-dás ro·mbí-som díb. 14. Ní do chuingid chomraic fri firu do·dechutar in maicc fil and. 15. Níb·ráncammar-ni co doirsea far tige. Ní·réiged immunn. Ní·tánaicc cách. Ní·táncaid-si. 16. Ní·tairlecsid gau fornn-ni. Ní·reilcisem-ni gau aili cucuib-si co·ndechdatar trebar slíastai. 17. Do·uccsat inna bú conda·rodartatar tairb inna Laigen leo. 18. In molad, do·ngímis tri bindius 7 chlais, ara·rochíurtar ar ngothae occo. 19. In fer no·bíth im Maíl Fothertaig, in·dénad cen chosc i-mmaig, in·fóired grafaind? 20. Do·beirinn clocha imo chranntabaill 7 dos·léicinn táthbéimm forsin n-én, co·ngaibed inna airberta de, os é béo, condid·lléicinn úaimm in n-áer do-ridisi.

Test 51.4

·*torchar*: do·cer (3ʳᵈ sg. pret. S1 do·tuit); *ro·carus*: carsu (1ˢᵗ sg. pret. W1 caraid); *as·robair*: as·beir (S1 3ʳᵈ sg. pres.); ·*érbart*: ·eipert (3ʳᵈ sg. pret. S1 as·beir); *do·rónad*: do·gniad (3ʳᵈ sg. impf. H2 do·gní); ·*dergénsaid*: ·digénsaid (2ⁿᵈ pl. pret. H2 do·gní); *do·róet*: do·ét (3ʳᵈ sg. pret. S1 do·eim); *as·ib*: ibis (3ʳᵈ sg. pret. S1 ibid); *ro·suidigser*: suidigser (1ˢᵗ sg. pret. W2b suidigidir); *con·acab*: con·gab (3ʳᵈ sg. pret. S2 con·gaib); *do·raidled*: do·aidled (3ʳᵈ sg. pass. pret. W1 do·aidlea); *ad·ráigsetar*: ad·áigsetar (3ʳᵈ pl. pret. W2 ad·ágathar); *ro·laus*: fo·card (1ˢᵗ sg. pret. S1 fo·ceird); *con·acairt*: con·gairt (2ⁿᵈ sg. pret. S2 con·gair); *for·róechan*: for·cachan (3ʳᵈ sg. pret. S1 for·cain); *do·cuaid*: luid (3ʳᵈ sg. pret. S1 téit); *do·ratais*: do·birt (2ⁿᵈ sg. pret. S1 do·beir); *do·ruménar*: do·ménair (3ʳᵈ sg. pret. S2 do·moinethar); ·*tuidchid*: ·tulaid (3ʳᵈ sg. pret. S1 do·tét); *do·uccai*: do·bert (3ʳᵈ sg. pret. S1 do·beir); *con·ascrasat*: con·scarsat (3ʳᵈ pl. pret. W1 con·scara); ·*tartsam*: ·tubartammar (1ˢᵗ pl. pret. S1 do·beir); *tucsat*: do·bertatar (3ʳᵈ pl. pret. S1 do·beir); ·*fargabsat*: ·fácabsat (3ʳᵈ pl. pret. S2 fo·ácaib); *do·dechad*: do·lod (1ˢᵗ sg. pret. S1 do·tét) or (2ⁿᵈ sg. pret. S1 do·tét); *ad·cuadatar*: ad·fídatar (3ʳᵈ pl. pret. S1 ad·fét); ·*robae*: ·boí (3ʳᵈ sg. pret. H1 at·tá); *ro·nass*: naisse (3ʳᵈ sg. pass. pret. S1 naiscid); *ro·bátar*: bátar (3ʳᵈ pl. pret. H1 at·tá).

Exercise 53.5

scríba, ·scríb	millea, ·mill	ressu, ·ress
scríbae, ·scríbae	mille, ·mille	reissi, ·reiss
scríbaid, ·scríba	millid, ·millea	reiss, ·ré
scríbas, -	milles, -	ress, -
scríbthair, ·scríbthar	milltir, ·millter	ressair, ·ressar
scríbthar, -	millter, -	ressar, -
scríbmai, ·scríbam	millmi, ·millem	resmai, ·ressam
scríbmae, -	millme, -	resmae, -
scríbthae, ·scríbaid	millte, ·millid	reste, ·reissid
scríbait, ·scríbat	millit, ·millet	ressait, ·ressat
scríbtae, -	millte, -	restae, -
scríbtair, ·scríbtar	millitir, ·milliter	-, ·ressatar
scríbtar, -	milliter, -	-

-, ·léu	do·corar, ·tochrar	ar·messur, ·airmissur
lie, ·lie	do·coirther, ·tochraither	ar·meisser, ·airmisser
liaid, ·lia	do·corathar, ·tochrathar	ar·mestar, ·airmestar
-	do·coirther, ·tochairther	ar·messar, ·airmissar
lethir, ·lether	do·coirmer, ·tochrammar	ar·messammar, ·airmessammar
-	do·coraid, ·tochraid	ar·meissid, ·airmissid
-, ·liam	do·coratar, ·tochratar	ar·messatar, ·airmessatar
-	do·coirter, ·tochairter	ar·messatar, ·airmessatar
-, -		
-, ·liat		
lete, -		
letir, -		
-		

Exercise 53.7

do·melainn, ·toimlinn	fo·ressin, ·foirsinn	ad·ceinn, ·accainn
do·melta, ·toimletha	fo·resta, ·foirsetha	ad·cetha, ·accatha
do·melad, ·toimlid	fo·ressed, ·foirsed	ad·ced, ·accad
do·meltae, ·toimlethae	fo·resstae, ·foirsethe	ad·cethe, ·accathe
do·melmais, ·toimlemis	fo·resmais, ·foirsemis	ad·cemis, ·accaimis
do·meltae, ·toimlethae	fo·reste, ·foirsethe	ad·cethe, ·accathe
do·meltis, ·toimletis	fo·restais, ·foirsetais	ad·cetis, ·accaitis
do·meltis, ·toimletis	fo·restais, ·foirsetais	ad·cetis, ·accaitis

ro·ísainn, ·rísainn	do·corainn, ·tochrainn
ro·ísta, ·rísta	do·cortha, ·tochratha
ro·ísed, ·rísed	do·corad, ·tochrad
-	do·corthae, ·tochrathae
ro·ísmais, ·rísmais	do·cormais, ·tochramais
ro·íste, ·ríste	do·corthae, ·tochrathae
ro·ístais, ·rístais	do·corainn, ·tochrainn
-	do·cortais, ·tochratais

Poem 54.1

'Wilt thou lend me thy cart?'
'Yes, if thou break not my cart!
May my cart come back soon!'
'If thy cart break not, yes!'

Exercise 54.3

1. Though it be happiness which I should attain and which I should make, it is thou who causes it to me, God. 2. It is no grievance for me, provided it be Christ whom everybody preaches and thinks of. 3. Though it be that somebody should see the glorious things of this world, that it may not put him into amazement and wonder out of love of them and desire for them. 4. Though these two things should be in my speech, namely falsehood and truth, so that it may be different what I should say from my lips and what I should think in my heart. 5. It is therefore I used to do this, so that I might be similar to the innocent. 6. It were a fruit of labor for us if we consumed every food and if we did what our companions do. 7. It were no wonder that a god should be made from a stone by unbelieving pagans. 8. It is first (*OIr.* comparative) we see the throwing of the axe before we should hear its sound. 9. Even though He should go into a higher place, He is not higher from it. This is not this way with us, because we are higher by going into high places. 10. Every saint that was, that is, that will be until Judgement Day, may they be helping me! 11. May thou deliver me, Jesus with thy saints when they should come, as thou delivered Isaac from the hands of his father. 12. 'Though we be in exile before him, there is no warrior in Ireland who would be more wonderful,' said Fergus. 13. It was strange for Conn that Connlae would not give a reply to anyone provided that (= when) the woman would come. 14. He took him with him to his school in order that he might take up reading with him like every person. 15. I haven't found anything why (*lit.*: on account of which) thou should be feared by anybody. 16. This is the ogam inscription that had been written on the side of the tree, that no-one should go past it until a warrior of a single chariot should have jumped across it. 17. Another one/someone of the students asked the afore-mentioned for what this day would be good. 18. I desire a man with a single wife to whom should have been born but a single child.

19. There was no part of the parts of the world, into which they would not have been carried into captivity and out of which God would not have brought them. 20. There are three cleanings for every road, three times at which they are cleaned, three reasons for which they are cleaned.

1. Cid fáilte ad·cotam-ni 7 do·ngnem, it é-som immid·ḟolngat dúnn. 2. Ní imned linn, acht rop Día pridchite 7 imme·rádat uili doíni. 3. Cía beith ara·n-accaither rét n-inducbaide in betha-so, arnachat·chorathar i mmoth dia ṡeirc 7 dia accobur. 4. Combad sain a n-as·bertais óa mbélaib 7 a n-í imme·ráidtis óa cridib. 5. Is dó do·gniad-si a n-í-sin, combad cosmail-si fri encu. 6. Ba torad saíthir dam ce do·melainn cech túarai 7 ce do·gneinn a ndo·gní mo chéile. 7. Ba machthad nád·nderntais [too bad—an irregular form!] déi dinaib leccaib. 8. Innád toísigiu ad·ciat teilciud inna mbélae resíu ro·cloatar a nguth-side? 9. Cía théisi i loc bes ardu, níta ardu-su de. 10. Uili noíb batar, fil, innád·robat oconn cobair? 11. Ronn·sóeraid, á nóebu tan no·téisid, amal ro·sóersaid inna maccu de lámaib a n-aithre. 12. Cía béo-sa for longais remaib, ní·fil i nÉire óclacha bete amru ol-dáthae-si. 13. Nibu ingnad la Conn do·mberad taithesca acht ní·tístais inna mná. 14. Nob·bertammar linn dochum ar scuile ara·ngabthae léigend amal uili doíni. 15. In·fitid ní arndom·áigthe do neoch? 16. It é ind ogaim ro·scríbtha i tóebaib inna n-omnae arná·dechsatais seccu co·rribuilsitis eirrid carpat tairsiu. 17. Íarmi·foachtatar araili di ḟelmaccaib dó cid diambat maithi inna lae-sa. 18. Is toisc lee fir ilṡéitche dia·rructais iltuistin. 19. Ro·bátar ranna in domuin indom·ructhae i ndoíri 7 asnacham·tuccad Día. 20. In·fil óenglanad do róut, óenaimsir i·nglantar, óentucait ara·nglantar?

Exercise 54.4

cara: 1st sg. abs. a-subj. (W1 caraid); *·mille*: 2nd sg. conj. a-subj. (W2a millid); *·goram*: 1st pl. conj. a-subj. (W2b guirid); *rethir*: 3rd sg. pass. abs. a-subj. (S3 renaid); *do·gnetis*: 3rd pl. active or 3rd pl. pass. deuterot. past a-subj. (H2 do·gní); *con·melae*: 2nd sg. deuterot. a-subj. (S1 con·meil); *·messatar*: 3rd pl. deponent conj. s-subj. (S2 midithir); *sláiss*: 3rd sg. abs. s-subj. (S2 slaidid); *do·tías*: 1st sg. deuterot. s-subj. (S1 do·tét); *·folus*: 1st sg. protot. s-subj. (S1 fo·loing); *·seiss*: 2nd sg. conj. s-subj. (S1 saidid); *for·chana*: 3rd sg. protot. len.-rel. a-subj. (S1 for·cain); *ro·cloítis*: 3rd pl. deuterot. past a-subj. (S3 ro·cluinethar); *ad·fé*: 3rd sg. deuterot. s-subj. (S1 ad·fét); *imm·soa*: 3rd sg. deuterot. a-subj. (H3 imm·soí); *·tuidchissem*: 1st pl. protot. augm. s-subj. (S1 do·tét); *·lie*: 2nd sg. conj. a-subj. (S3 lenaid); *·coratar*: 3rd pl. dependent a-subj. (S1 fo·ceird); *·máissed*: 3rd sg. past s-subj. (S2 maidid); *bad*: 3rd sg. abs. past subj. (copula); *·tísmais*: 1st pl. protot. past s-subj. (S1 do·icc); *do·rónmais*: 1st pl. deuterot. augm. past a-subj. (H2 do·gní); *do·dig*: 3rd sg. deuterot. augm. s-subj. (S1 do·tét); *ar·menar*: 1st sg. deponent deuterot. a-subj. (S2 ar·moinethar); *fris·n-orratar*: 3rd pl. deuterot. nas.-rel. s-subj. (S1 fris·oirg); *nád·rrí*: 3rd sg. protot. neg. rel. s-subj. (S1 ro·icc); *as·roibre*: 2nd sg. deuterot. augm. a-subj. (S1 as·beir); *·accastar*: 3rd sg. protot. a/s-subj. (H2 ad·cí); *·criat*: 3rd pl. conj. a-subj. (S3 crenat); *·dernatar*: 3rd pl. pass. protot. augm. a-subj. (H2 do·gní); *do·rotsad*: 3rd sg. deuterot. augm. past s-subj. (S1 do·tuit); *fo·lóis*: 2nd sg. deuterot. s-subj. (S1 fo·loing); *ad·cetha*: 2nd sg. deuterot. past a-subj. (H2 ad·cí); *do·roilcea*: 3rd sg. deuterot. augm. a-subj. (W2a do·léici); *ro·sásam*: 1st pl. deuterot. s-subj. (S1 ro·saig); *·ré*: 3rd sg. conj. s-subj. (S1 reithid) or (S1 rigid); *·foir*: 3rd sg. protot. s-subj. (S1 fo·reith)

Exercise 55.7

rainnfea, ·rannub
rainnfe, ·rainnfe
rainnfid, ·rainnfea
rainnfes, -
rainnfidir, ·rainnfider
rainnfedar, -
rainnfimmi, ·rainnfem
rainnfimme, -
rainnfithe, ·rainnfid
rainnfit, ·rainnfet
rainnfite, -
rainnfitir, ·rainnfetar
rainnfetar, -

géra, ·gér
gérae, ·gérae
géraid, ·géra
géras, -
gérthair, ·gérthar
gérthar, -
gérmai, ·géram
gérmae, -
gérthae, ·géraid
gérait, ·gérat
gértae, -
gértair, ·gértar
gértar, -

selsa, ·selus
selsai, ·selais
selais, ·sela
selas, -
selaistir, ·selastar
selastar, -
selsammai, ·selsam
selsammae
selaste, ·selsaid
selsait, ·selsat
selsatae, -
selsatair, ·selsatar
selsatar, -

grádaigfer, ·grádaigfer
grádaigfider, ·grádaigfider
grádaigfidir, ·grádaigfedar
grádaigfedar, -
grádaigfidir, ·grádaigfedar
grádaigfedar, -
grádaigfimmir, ·grádaigfemmar
grádaigfemmar, -
grádaigfide, ·grádaigfid
grádaigfitir, ·grádaigfetar
grádaigfetar, -
grádaigfitir, ·grádaigfetar
grádaigfetar, -

do·sifius
do·sifis
do·sib
do·sifestar
do·sibsem
do·sibsid
do·sibset
do·sibsetar

Exercise 56.2

do·génainn, ·digénainn
do·génta, ·digénta
do·génad, ·digned
do·géntae, ·digénte
do·génmais, ·digénmais
do·géntae, ·digéntae
do·géntais, ·digéntais
do·géntais, ·digéntais

do·scérainn, ·tascérainn
do·scértha, ·tascértha
do·scérad, ·tascérad
do·scérthae, ·tascérthae
do·scérmais, ·tascérmais
do·scérthae, ·tascérthae
do·scértais, ·tascértais
do·scértais, ·tascértais

fo·lilsainn, ·fóelsainn
fo·lilsatha, ·fóelsatha
fo·lilsad, ·fóelsad
fo·lilsaithae, ·fóelsaithe
fo·lilsaimis, ·fóelsaimis
fo·lilsaithe, ·fóelsaithe
fo·lilsaitis, ·fóelsaitis
fo·lilsaitis, ·fóelsaitis

do·iccf(a)inn, ·ticcf(a)inn
do·iccf(a)ithea, ·ticcf(a)ithea
do·iccfa/ed, ·ticcfa/ed
do·iccf(a)imis, ·ticcf(a)imis
do·iccf(a)ithe, ·ticcf(a)ithe
do·iccf(a)itis, ·ticcf(a)itis

Exercise 57.1

Ninne mac Magach of the Féini went North into the territory of the Ulaid, altogether three riders, to visit friends there, and they unyoked their horses on a land which had belonged to the family of theirs before; (but) it was not to demand a piece (of the land) on it. And he whose the land was said to them: 'Take your horses out of the land!' The two who were with Ninne said then: 'The payment (due) to us is no greater even though we unyoke our horses here; it was not to demand a piece (of the land) here.' 'This is not very easy, it has been yours before. They (= the horses) will not be (= stay) here for that reason!' They had not known up till then that the land had been theirs before. They didn't take off their horses. Then the man whose the land was drives off their horses by force. After that they appealed on its account to Conchobar mac Nessa and he put a penalty for improper observation of the law of entry on the one who drove their horses from the land and a payment equal to that which he drove off, and he exacted (their) possessions for them in the same amount (they would have obtained) from legal entry.

Exercise 57.3

1. It is well-known, if you should not believe in the resurrection of Christ and of the dead, your faith will not sanctify you thus and will not separate you from your sins. 2. It will be a multitude that will dwell in thee and everyone who dwell in it (OIr.: it) will be happy. 3. We will compare ourselves with ourselves. 4. That which will follow the unbelieving, will be unbelieving. 5. That what I used to say so far, I will say it still. 6. And moreover this is the sign which God will give to anyone who will entrust himself to Him, and who will work through Him. 7. So that he should have said: 'I will do this holy thing and I will not do this prohibited thing, although I should wish it,' (but) he doesn't say it. 8. My confession will not be in vain to me, because whatever I will ask, God will give it. 9. You will pray (to) God for us that we may endure our tribulations. 10. If the head is not defeated, the members will not be defeated. (OIr.: If it breaks not upon the head, it will not break upon the members.) 11. A rebuilding of the temple will be undertaken by him, and he will preach the commands of the law of the Old Testament, and the Jews will receive him as lord (OIr.: abbot), and he will overthrow the law of the New Testament. 12. 'If only I had known it was (OIr.: would have been) thou, it wouldn't have been thus we (would have) parted,' said Cú Chulainn. 13. The mountain will be as high as a valley, […] the world will be like a board, so that an apple might run (across) it. 14. It is by thy son that a multitude will be struck down into the great fire, before the great king passes judgement on the deeds of every single person. 15. 'He has said,' said Cú Chulainn, 'that he would not go until he had taken my head or until he had left his head with me.' 16. He will shed the blood of every person who is in the enclosure, unless he be taken care of and stark naked women go against him. 17. 'Thou wilt not go,' said his mother, 'unless thou have accompaniment from the great warriors of the Ulaid.' 18. A puppy will be raised by me for thee and I will a dog to guard for thee meanwhile, until this dog has grown and is capable of action. And I will protect all Mag Murthemne. 19. Give food, give a drink to Máel Fothertaig's dog, the dog of a man who would have given food to everyone, though he had to buy it at a price. 20. Enemies will destroy Níall's plain, sentries will be fought around churches, every one will go out of his proper state, ruler will perish before usurpers, knowledge will be turned into perverted judgements.

1. Mani·creit esséirge inna mmarb, ním·noíbfea m'ires 7 ním·scairfea frim phecthu. 2. Imba sochaide ad·trefea and-som? Imbat fáilti uili doíni adid·trefet? 3. Indid·samlafadar fris féin? 4. Ind hí lilite dinaib ainchreitmechaib bit ainchreitmig. 5. A n-í as·beirmis co-sse, is ed as·béram beus. 6. Is airde són do·mbérat déi donaib hí nos·n-eirbfet intiu 7 génaite treu. 7. Do·génam a nnóeb-sa 7 ní·digénam a n-airgairthe-se, cid accobar linn. 8. Imba madae duit t'foísitiu? Na nní no·gigis, na·ebra Día? 9. Gigsea-sa Día leis ara·ful a fochaidi. 10. Ma·roma fora chenn, memais fora baullu. 11. Ní·digéntar aidchumtach tempuil leo, 7 ní·pridchibet smachtu rechto fetarlaicce, 7 nís·(n)gébat Iudaidi i n-aptha, 7 ní·coiscérat recht nufiadnaissi. 12. Acht ro·feissed roptis (or: beitis) é níbad samlaid no·scarfaitis. 13. Bit inna sléine comarda fri fánu. Imbe cosmail do chlár in domun conid·restais ubla? 14. Is lia maccu bethir sochaide isin teinid resíu

ro·messatar ruirig for gnímu inna n-uile ndoíne. 15. As·rubartatar ní·regtais co·rrucctais ar cenna-ni nó co·farcbatais-seom a cenna linn-ni. 16. Ar·dáilfet fuil inna n-uile ndoíne fil isind lius, mani·foichliter 7 mani·dig ben airnocht friu. 17. Ní·regam condonn·roib coimthecht di ánruth. 18. Eblaid culén dúnn 7 bid cú-som do imdegail dúnn. 7 im·dí Éirinn n-uili. 19. Tabair biad, tabair dig do chonaib fer do·bértais biad do neoch cid ar lúaig na·chretais. 20. Ní·cummélat námait Éirinn, ní·fessatar im chella cathaisi, ní·rega nech asa richt, ní·díbbet (?) flathai rén-anflathaib, ní·soífither ecnae i sóebbretha.

Test 57.4

glanfaid: 3rd sg. f-fut. abs. (W1 glanaid); *·glainfed*: 3rd sg. cond. f-fut. (W1 glanaid); *·ebrainn*: 1st sg. cond. irreg. a-fut. (S3 ernaid); *rires*: 3rd sg. rel. abs. red. i-fut. (S3 renaid); *·digéntais*: 3rd pl. or 3rd pl. pass. cond. protot. é-fut. (H2 do·gní); *fo·géram*: 1st pl. deuterot. é-fut. (S1 fo·geir); *·moilfithe*: 3rd sg. pass. cond. f-fut. (W1 molaithir); *do·lugub*: 1st sg. deuterot. f-fut. (W2b do·luigi); *cechnaite*: 3rd pl. abs. rel. red. a-fut. (S1 canaid); *do·gigius*: 1st sg. deuterot. red. s-fut. (S2 do·guid); *seiss*: 3rd sg. abs. unred. s-fut. (S1 saidid); *fo·didma*: 1st sg. deuterot. red. a-fut. (S2 fo·daim); *ro·chechlar*: 1st sg. deponent independent red. a-fut. (S3 ro·cluinethar); *at·ré*: 3rd sg. deuterot. unred. s-fut. (S1 at·raig); *regthae*: 2nd pl. abs. suppl. a-fut. (S1 téit); *·regtha*: 2nd sg. cond. suppl. a-fut. (S1 téit); *gérmae*: 1st pl. abs. rel. é-fut. (S2 gairid); *do·fí*: 3rd sg. deuterot. red. s-fut. (S1 do·fich); *·memsad*: 3rd sg. cond. red. s-fut. (S2 maidid); *lilid*: 3rd sg. abs. red. i-fut. (S3 lenaid); *·íssainn*: 1st sg. cond. red. s-fut. (S1 ithid); *lesstae*: 3rd pl. abs. rel. unred. s-fut. (S1 laigid); *bieid*: 3rd sg. abs. irreg. fut. (substantive verb); *fris·iurr*: 1st sg. deuterot. red. s-fut. (S1 fris·oirg); *·sáidfimmis*: 1st pl. cond. f-fut. (W2a sáidid); *ro·iccfe*: 2nd sg. deuterot. f-fut. (S1 ro·icc); *·tibértha*: 2nd sg. cond. protot. é-fut. (S1 do·beir); *fo·gébmais*: 1st pl. cond. deuterot. é-fut. (S2 fo·gaib); *fo·lilais*: 2nd sg. deuterot. red. s-fut. (S1 fo·loing); *gigner*: 1st sg. deponent abs. red. a-fut. (S2 gainithir); *for·fether*: 3rd sg. pass. red. i-fut. (S3 for·fen); *·tergad*: 3rd sg. cond. protot. suppl. a-fut. (S1 do·tét); *ad·cichset*: 3rd pl. deuterot. red. i/s-fut. (H2 ad·cí); *selsammai*: 1st pl. abs. red. s-fut. (S2 slaidid); *ro·sia*: 3rd sg. deuterot. red. s-fut. (S1 ro·saig); *·fessed*: 3rd sg. cond. of red. s-fut. (S3 ro·finnadar/ro·fitir) or of red. s-fut. (S1 fichid) or of unred. s-fut. (S1 feidid)

Test 57.5

mórsus: 3rd sg. f. or 3rd pl. suff. pron., 3rd sg. s-pret. (< mórais, W1 móraid); *comallaidi*: 3rd sg. m. or. n. suff. pron., 3rd sg. pres. ind. (< W1 comalnaithir); *táthut*: 2nd sg. suff. pron., 3rd sg. pres. ind. 'thou hast' (< H1 (ad·)tá, substantive verb); *bethum*: 1st sg. suff. pron., 3rd sg. pres. e-subj. 'may I have' (< H2 beith; substantive verb); *gegni*: 3rd sg. m. or n. suff. pron., 3rd sg. red. pret. (< geguin, S1 gonaid); *beirthi*: 3rd sg. m. or n. suff. pron., 3rd sg. pres. ind. (< S1 beirid); *filus*: 3rd sg. f. or 3rd pl. suff. pron., fil 'she is, they are' (substantive verb); *boíthunn*: 1st pl. suff. pron., 3rd sg. pret. 'we had' (< boí, substantive verb)

Exercise 58.3

1: *class*: rannaigecht; *syllabic count*: 8² 7¹ 8² 7¹ (*i* of *in* in line 1 elided); *rhyme*: ráith : cáich; *aicill*: dána : rátha; úasail : clúasaib; *internal rhyme*: none; *consonance*: none; *alliteration*: dúib : dagaisti : dána, ratha : ráith, ísil : úasail, clúasaib : cáich

2. *class*: rannaigecht; *syllabic count*: 8² 7¹ 8² 7¹; *rhyme*: déin : chéin; *aicill*: ríagla : clíara; *internal rhyme*: none; *consonance*: none; *alliteration*: fata : ferr : fégad, drumchla : dána : déin, robuicc : ríagla, clíara : chéin

3. *class*: rannaigecht; *syllabic count*: 8² 4¹ 8² 4¹ (suairc is disyllabic); *rhyme*: sorcha : ·molfa, dath : rath; *aicill*: ·molfa : romtha; *internal rhyme*: none; *consonance*: none; *alliteration*: gairit : gres, sáer : sorcha, romtha : rath; *fidrad freccomail*: rath : rannaigecht

4. *class*: rannaigecht; *syllabic count*: 7¹ 7¹ 7¹ 7¹; *rhyme*: úar : ndúan; *aicill*: áeb : cáem; *internal rhyme*: menmach : engach, fégaid : dénaim; *consonance*: mór : úar : áeb : ndúan; *alliteration*: menmach : mór, engach : úar, dénaim : ndúan

5. *class*: rannaigecht; *syllabic count*: 7^2 7^2 7^2 7^2; *rhyme*: mebail : dremain; *aiccill*: saigid : ndairib; *internal rhyme*: rannaigecht : mangairecht, ·gláma : dána; *consonance*: builid : mebail : saigid : dremain; *alliteration*: bec : builid, mangairecht : mebail, sund : saigid, ndairib : dána : dremain; *fidrad freccomail*: dremain : dechnad

6. *class*: rannaigecht; *syllabic count*: 8^2 6^2 8^2 6^2 (*a* in line 1 elided, *a* in *as* in line 4 elided); *rhyme*: gréine : nÉire; *aiccill*: none; *internal rhyme*: millsi : insi, gaiste : aiste, seng : ḟerr; *consonance*: laíde : gréine : síde : nÉire; *alliteration*: mór : millsi, gil : gréine, seng : síde, aiste : ḟerr : nÉire

7. *class*: rannaigecht; *syllabic count*: 8^2 4^2 8^2 4^2; *rhyme*: selba : ergna; *aiccill*: none; *internal rhyme*: cráeb : sáeb, laiste : aiste; *consonance*: chumra : selba : labra : ergna; *alliteration*: lethdechnad : lugbairt, cráeb : chumra, sáeb : selba, laiste : labra, aiste : ergna; *fidrad freccomail*: ergna : aiste

8. *class*: rannaigecht; *syllabic count*: 7^1 7^2 7^1 7^2; *rhyme*: rrind : bind, indlim : imrind; *rind-ardrind-rhyme*: rrind : indlim, bind : imrind; *aiccill*: none; *internal rhyme*: rathmar : athlam, bágaim : álaind; *consonance*: none; *alliteration*: rathmar : rrind, éicse : athlam : indlim, bágaim : bairdne : bind, álaind : imrind

9. *class*: deibide; *syllabic count*: 7^1 7^2 7^1 7^2 (*i* of *ind* in line 3 elided); *rind-ardrind-rhyme*: scél : ·aithgén, brass : senchas; *aiccill*: none; *internal rhyme*: none; *consonance*: none; *alliteration*: scáilte : scél, hí-side : ·aithgén, hí-seo : aiste, bláith : brass

10. *class*: rannaigecht; *syllabic count*: 8^2 7^3 8^2 7^3; *rhyme*: imníabthaig : milbríathraig; *aiccill*: rigim : midṡing; *internal rhyme*: réil : déin; *consonance*: none; *alliteration*: aiste : úallach : aile : ocum, hord : aicnid : imníabthaig, maith : maisse, raind : réil : rigim, midṡing : milbríathraig

11. *class*: rannaigecht; *syllabic count*: 7^3 7^3 7^1 7^3; *rhyme*: fungaire : cumraide; *aiccill*: gó : cnó; *internal rhyme*: dúas : chnúas; *consonance*: none; *alliteration*: snám : sebaicc : sluindébthair, firu : fungaire, chnúas : cnó : cumraide; *fidrad freccomail*: cumraide : cassbairdne

12. *class*: rannaigecht; *syllabic count*: 7^3 7^3 7^3 7^3; *rhyme*: ·binnige : indile; *aiccill*: none; *internal rhyme*: chas : brass, chóir : n-óir; *consonance*: chumaide : ·binnige : cammḟige : indile; *alliteration*: cassbairdne : chas : chumaide, brass : ·binnige, chóir : cammḟige, n-óir : indile; *fidrad freccomail*: indile : anamain

13. *class*: rannaigecht; *syllabic count*: 5^2 5^2 5^2 5^2; *rhyme*: slonnad : ollam; *aiccill*: duine : uile; *internal rhyme*: none; *consonance*: none; *alliteration*: anamain : irdairc, ·dénand : duine, uile : ollam; *fidrad freccomail*: ollam : íat-sain

14. *class*: rannaigecht; *syllabic count*: 8^2 7^1 8^2 7^1 (*i* of *in* in line 1 elided, *a* in *ar* in line 3 elided); *rhyme*: loing : ·sloind; *aiccill*: mbérla : ségda; *internal rhyme*: buide : duine; *consonance*: none; *alliteration*: íat-sain : ardaiste, llaíde : loing, beram : buide : mbérla, ségda : ·sloind; *dúnad*: ·sloind : sluindfet

Appendix E — Wordlist

This wordlist contains those words that are used in the exercises, poems and tests of this book. Words mentioned in the explanatory chapters are only included if they also appear in exercises and tests. After each word follows important grammatical information in parentheses. In the case of nouns, stem-class and gender are given. Where these are wanting, the relevant category is unknown or unclear. Where the inflection is somehow irregular, the genitive singular is cited. In the case of verbs, the class is given in parentheses. In the case of compound verbs, both deutero- and prototonic forms and the constituent elements are cited. Sometimes non-present stem forms are cited when these are irregular or difficult. Usually nominal and verbal forms that are not actually attested but can be set up with confidence have not been specifically marked.

This list has been specifically compiled for this book. It is not intended for outside use. The *Dictionary of the Irish Language* (DIL) has to be consulted for all other purposes.

A

1. a^H (+ prep.) – out of, from
2. a^H – her, 3.sg. f. poss. pron.
3. a^L – his, 3.sg. m. poss. pron.
4. a^N – their, 3.pl. poss. pron.
5. a^N – neutr. article
6. a^N – that which (+ len. rel.)
7. a^N – while, during (+ nas. rel.)
1. á^L, a^L – vocative particle
2. á (s, n?) – cart, wagon
ab, aub (n, f, g.sg. abann) – river
aball (ā, f) – apple-tree
accobor (o, n) – wish, desire (v.n. of ad·cobra)
acht – but; acht (+ subj.) – provided that
acrae (i̯o, n) – suing, legal action, process (v.n. of ad·gair)
ad·ágathar, ·ágathar (W2a; *ad-āg-*) – to fear (trans.); ad·áigestar pret.
adaig (ī, f, g.sg. aidche) – night
ad·aig, ·adaig (S1b; *ad-ag-*) – to drive, set in motion; ad·acht pret.
ad·annai, ·adnai (W2; *ad-and-*) – to kindle, light
adbar (o, n, g.sg. adbuir) – reason, cause, material
ad·cí, ·accai (H2; *ad-ci-*) – to see; co n·accae pret.; ad·condairc augm. pret.
ad·cobra, ·accobra (W1; *ad-cobar-*) – to wish, desire; ad·rochabair augm. pret.
ad·cota, ·éta (H1; *ad-cum-tā-* + *in-tā-*) – to get, attain; to be able
ad·ella, ·aidlea (W1; *ad-ell-*) – to visit
ad·fét (S1a; *ad-fēd-*; no prot. forms) – to tell, relate
ad·gair, ·acair (S2; *ad-gar-*) – to sue
ad·gládathar, ·acalldathar (W2; *ad-glād-*) – to talk to
ad·gnin, ·aithgnin (S3; *ate-gni-*) – to recognize; ad·géuin pret.
ad·midethar, ·aimdethar (S2; *ad-med-*) – to try, attempt

ad·muinethar (S2; *ad-man-*; no prototonic forms) – to remember
ad·rig, ·áraig (?) (S1a; *ad-rig-*) – to bind
ad·rími, ·áirmi (W2a; *ad-rīm-*) – to count
ad·suidi, ·astai (W2b; *ad-sod-*) – to hinder, stop, prevent
ad·treba, ·aitreba (W1; *ad-treb-*) – to dwell (in)
áe, aí – his, hers, theirs, 3rd person independent possessive pronoun
Áed (u, m) – male name
áer (o, m) – air
1. áes (o, n) – age
2. áes (u, m) – folk, people
agad (sg.: a-stem, pl.: i-stem, f) – face, surface
aí – see áe
aicher (o, ā) – sharp, bitter
aicned (o, n) – nature
aidbart (ā, f) – offering (v.n. of ad·opair)
aidchumtach (o, n) – rebuilding, reconstruction
aig (i, f, g.sg. ego) – ice
aigid (S1b) – to drive, impel; ·acht pret.
áilde, áille (i̯ā, f) – beauty
aile (i̯o, i̯ā; neut. aill) – other, another
ailid (S1b) – to rear, eblaid fut.
Ailill (i, m) – king of the Connachta
áilli – see álaind
aimser (ā, f) – time
áin (i, f g.sg. áno/-a, also án ā, f) – the driving (v.n. of aigid)
ainchreitmech (o, ā) – unbelieving
aingel (o, m) – angel
aingid (S1b) – to protect
ainm (n, n) – name
ainmne (nt, f?) – patience
airassae (i̯o, i̯ā) – very easy
airber (ā, f) – a handful, bundle
airbert (ā, f) – pl.: conscience, intelligence
airde (i̯o, n) – sign, token
1. aire (k, m) – nobleman

2. aire (i̯o, m) – burden, load

3. aire (i̯ā, f) – guarding

airgairthe (i̯o, n) – prohibited thing

airgart (ā, f) – prohibition

airid (S2) – to plough

airlithir (W2a) – to advise

airmitiu (n, f) – consideration, reverence

airnocht (o, ā) – stark naked

airrecht (?, ?) – attack

airscél (o, n) – great story

aisndís (n, f) – the telling, narration (v.n. of as·indet)

aiss (i, ?) – back

aithech (o, m) – vassal, servant

aithgin (n, n) – rebirth

aithis (short ı̆, f) – insult, reproach, disgrace

aitte (i̯o, m) – foster-father

alaile – araile

álaind, pl. áilli (i) – beautiful

alam (o, n) – herd, flock

Albu (n, f) – Scotland, Britain

all, aill (?) – cliff

allaid (i) – wild

alltar (o, n) – the Hereafter

altóir (short ı̆, f) – altar

amalᴸ (+ acc.) – like, as

ammait (short ı̆, f) – witch, imbecile woman

1. amrae (i̯o, i̯ā) – wonderful, marvellous

2. amrae (i̯o, n) – marvel, wonder

anaccul (o, n) – protection (v.n. of aingid)

anad (u, m, g.sg. anto/-a) – the staying, waiting (v.n. of anaid)

anaid (W1) – to stay, wait

and – there, then (3ʳᵈ sg. neut. of i)

anflaith (i, f) – improper ruler, usurper

anim (n, f) – soul

1. ánruth (o, m) – great warrior

2. ánruth (o, m) – a poetic grade, lit.: beautiful stream?

ansae (i̯o) – difficult

anúas – from above

ap (t, m) – abbot, lord

apdaine (i̯ā, f) – abbacy

apstal (o, m) – apostle

1. arᴸ (+ prep./acc.) – in front of, for, on account of

2. arᴺ – our, 1ˢᵗ pl. poss. pron.

3. ar, air – because

araᴴ (+ dep. subj.) – that, so that, in order that

ara·chrin, ·airchrin (S3; are-cri-) – to perish, fail

arae (t, m) – charioteer

ar agaid (nominal preposition) – in front of

araile, alaile (i̯o, i̯ā) – the other; pl.: some

ar ais (adv.) – back

arán (o, m) – bread

ar apu (adv.) – nevertheless

arbor (n, n. g.sg. arbae, d.sg. arbaimm) – grain, corn

ar chiunn – before, in front; awaiting

árchú (n, m) – war-hound, watch-dog

ar·clich, ·airchlich (S1a; are-clich-) – to ward off

ard (o, ā) – high

ardae (i̯o, n) – height

ar·dáili, ·airdáili (W2a; are-dāl-) – to pour forth, shed

ar·foím, ·eroím (S1; are-fo-em-) – to accept, receive

ar·gaib, ·airgaib (S2; are-gab-) – to seize, capture

argat (o, n) – silver, money

ar·icc, ·airicc (S1; are-icc-) – to find

arithissi – back again

ar·midethar, ·airmidethar (S2; are-med-) – to aim at

arná (+ dep. subj.) – in order that not

ar·naisc, ·arnaisc (S1; are-nad-) – to bind, guarantee

árus (o, n) – abode, dwelling

ásaid (W1) – to grow

as·beir, ·eipir (S1a; ess-ber-) – to say; as·bert pret.; as·rubart augm. pret.

as·éraig, ·esseirig (S1; ess-ess-reg-) – to rise again

aslach (o, n) – temptation

as·oilgi, ·oslaici (W2a; uss-od-lēc-) – to open

as·oirg, ·essairg (S1; ess-org-) – to cut down, beat

as·ren, ·éiren (S3; ess-rī-) – to sell, pay; as·rir pret.

at·baill, ·epil (S1c; ess-bel-) – to die; at·rubalt pret.

áth (u, m) – ford

athair (r, m) – father

athgoíte (i̯o, i̯ā) – severely wounded

athláech (o, m) – ex-layman

athramlae (i̯o, i̯ā) – father-like

at·reig, ·éirig (S1; ess-reg-) – to rise, get up

at·tá (H1; ad-tā-) – to be (substantive verb)

aue (i̯o, m) – grandson

augaire (i̯o, m) – shepherd

aurlabrae (i̯ā, f) – speech, gift of speech

B

báeth (o, ā) – stupid, foolish

baïd (H1) – to die

báidid (W2) – to drown, submerge

bainne (i̯o, n) – drop

bairgen (ā, f) – loaf, bread

baithis (short ı̆, f, gen. sg. baitse) – crown of the head

balc (o, ā) – stout, strong, vigorous

ball (o, m) – member

bán (o, ā) – white

bás (o, n) – natural death

bec, becc (o, ā) – small, little, short

bech (o, m) – bee

bedg (o, m) – leap

béimm (n, n) – the striking; blow, beat (v.n. of benaid)

beirid (S1a) – to carry; birt pret.; ro·uc augm. pret.

bél (o, m, g.sg. béoil) – lip; pl.: mouth

Beltaine (i̯o, n/m) – festival on the 1ˢᵗ May

ben (ā, f, g.sg. mna) – woman

benaid (S3) – to strike, beat; benaid fo + akk. – to attack

bendachaid (W1) – to bless

bendacht (ā, f) – blessing (v.n. of bendachaid)

benn (ā, f) – summit

béo (o, a, g. sg. masc. bii) – alive

béoigidir (W2 dep.) – to vivify, give life to

beos, beus (adv.) – still

berbad (u, m) – the cooking, boiling (v.n. of berbaid)

berg (ā, f) – brigand

berraid (W1) – to shave the head, shear

bés (u, m) – manner, custom

bét (u, m) – deed

bethu (t, m) – life; i mbethaid – alive

biäd (o, n, g.sg. biïd) – food

biáil, gen. bela (i, m) – axe

bind (i) – harmonious, sweet-sounding

bindius (u, m) – harmony

bir (u, n) – spit, spear

1. bith (u, m) – world

2. bith- – eternal, everlasting (in compounds)

bláth (o, m) – flower, bloom

bled (ā, f) – whale

blíadain (ī, f) – year

bó (irreg., f + m) – cow

Boand, gen Bóinne (ā, f) – the river Boyne

bocht (o, ā) – poor

borb (o, ā) – stupid, rude

bos (ā, f) – palm of the hand

brágae (nt, f) – neck, throat

Bran (o, m) – male name

bráth (u, m) – judgement; Judgement Day

bráthair (r, m) – brother

bratt (o, m) – cloak

bréc (ā, f) – lie

bréo (t, f) – flame

brestae (io, iā) – lively, spiritful

1. breth (ā, f) – the bringing (v.n. of beirid)

2. breth (ā, f) – judgement

brí (g, m, g.sg. breg) – hill

bríathar (ā, f, g.sg. bréithre) – word

bricht (u, m) – incantation, magical spell

Bricriu (n, m) – male name

bríg (ā, f) – strength, force

Brigit (ī, f) – female name, a saint

brisc (o, ā) – fragile

brisid (W2a) – to break (transitive)

brithem (n, m) – judge

brithemnacht (ā, f) – jurisprudence

bró (n, f) – mill

bróenach (o, ā) – wet

brón (o, m) – sorrow

brot (o, m) – goad

1. brú (n, f, g.sg. bronn) – womb

2. brú (?, ?) – edge, brink

brúach (o, n) – bank, shore, border

bruar (o, ?; singular!) – fragments, pieces, bits

bruiden (ā, f) – hostel

bruinne (io, m) – breast, bosom, chest

bruth (u, m) – heat, blaze

búachaill (i, m) – cowherd, cowboy, lad

búaid (i, n) – victory; feature of quality, characteristic

bugae (io, m) – hyacinth?

buide (io, iā) – yellow

buiden (ā, f) – troup

buirithir (W2) – to rage, roar

buith (short ī, f) – being, existing (v.n. of at·tá)

bunsach (ā, f) – toy javelin

C

cach (indecl. except g.sg.m. caich and g.sg.f. cacha) – each, every

cách – everybody

cáen (o, ā) – fair, beautiful

cáera (k, f) – sheep

cailech (o, m) – cock

caill (ī, f) – wood

caille (o, ?) – veil

caillech (ā, f) – nun, old woman

caindel (ā, f) – candle

caíne (iā, f) – beauty

caíned (u, m) – the reviling, slandering, reproach (v.n. of caínid)

caínid (S2) – to revile

cairde (io, n) – pact, covenant, peace

cairdes (u, m) – friendship, treaty, pact

cairdine (iā, f) – friendship, treaty

caite (interrogative) – what is

canaid (S1b) – to sing

cano (nt, m) – a poetic grade; lit.: whelp?, or: singer?

canóin (iā, f) – Bible, canon

carae (nt, m) – friend

caraid (W1) – to love

carcar (ā, f) – prison

carn (o, n) – heap of stones

carpat (o, m) – chariot

cartaid (W1) – to expel, drive off

cath (u, m) – battle, war

cathair (k, f) – city

cathais (short ī, f) – sentry, night-watch

catt (o, m) – cat

ce, cia (interrogative pronoun) – who, what, which

céL (indecl) – this here

cech – cach

céile (io, m) – client, companion

ceilid (S1a) – to hide, conceal; ·celt pret.

ceirtle (iā, f) – clew, ball of threads

ceist (short ī, f) – question (often used as an untranslatable interrogative marker)

cell (ā, f, g.sg. cille) – church, cell

Celtchar (o, m) – male name

cenL (+ acc.) – without

cenél (o, n, g.sg. cenéuil) – race, people

ceni (+ dep.) – although not

cenn (o, n) – head, end

cennaige (io, m) – merchant

cenntar (o, n) – the world here

céo (k, m, g.sg. ciäch) – fog, mist

céol (o, n, g.sg. cíuil) – music, song

cerd (ā, f) – art, skill

cerdchae (iā, f) – smithy

césaid (W1) – to suffer

cét (o, n) – hundred

Cetaín – Wednesday

cétal (o, n) – the singing (v. n. of canaid)

cethair (cethéora f.) – four

cethracha (t, m) – forty

cethrae (iā, f) – animal, cattle

cethramad (o, ā) – fourth

cethrar (o, n) – four men

Cet mac Magach (o, m) – male name

cétnae (i̯o, i̯ā) – (before a noun) first, (after a noun) the same

cétomus (adv.) – first, at first

1. cía (interrogative pronoun) – who

2. cía^L – although, even though

cíall (ā, f, g.sg. céille) – sense, meaning, reason

cían (o, ā) – far, distant

1. cid (neuter interrogative) – what is it

2. cid – even

cimbid (i, m) – prisoner

cin (t, m) – crime, sin

cing (t, m) – warrior

cingid (S1a) – to step; ·cechaing pret.

cis lir + nom. pl. (interrogative) – how many, lit.: what is the number

claideb (o, m) – sword

claidid, ·claid (S1) – to dig, construct

cland (ā, f) – children

clár (o, n) – board

clas (ā, f) – choir

clé (i̯o, i̯ā) – left

cless (u, m) – trick, feat

clí (?, m) – a poetic grade; lit.: pillar?

clithchae (i̯ā, f) – protection, shelter

cló (i̯o, m) – nail

cloc (o, m, g.sg. cluic) – bell

clocán (o, m) – little bell

cloch (ā, f) – stone

clóen (o, ā) – crooked, evil, bad

clú (s, n) – fame

clúain (i, m) – meadow

clúas (ā, f) – ear

cluiche (i̯o, n) – game

cnáim (i, m) – bone

cnet (ā, f) – sigh

cnú, gen. cnó (u, f) – nut

1. co^N (+ prep.) – with

2. co^H (+ acc.) – towards, up to

3. co^N (+ dep.) – (so) that

cobair (t, f, g.sg. cobrad) – help, assistance

cóem (o, ā) – nice

1. coí (i, f, g.sg. cuae) – coshering visit (= an annual journey by the king around his land during which the vassals had to provide food and quarter)

2. coí, cuach (k, f) – cuckoo

cóic^L – five

coimgne (i̯o, m) – historical knowledge

Coimmdiu (t, m) – the Lord

coimthecht (ā, f) – protection, escort, accompaniment

1. cóir (i) – right, correct

2. cóir (i, f) – correctness (fon cóir-se: this way)

coirce (i̯o, m) – oats

coiscid (S1) – to correct, reprimand, scold

col (o, n) – violation, sin

co-lléic, co-lléice – however, nevertheless, meanwhile

Colmán Ela – place-name

colum (o, m) – dove

Colum Cille – Irish name of Saint Columba (lit.: the dove of the church)

com- – prefix of the equative

comáes (o, m) – coeval, having the same age

comairle (i̯ā, f) – advice, counsel

comalnad (i̯o, m) – fulfillment (v. n. of comalnaithir)

comalnaithir (W1) – to fulfil, complete

comaltae (i̯o, m) – foster-brother

comarbae (i̯o, m) – heir

comarbus (u, m) – inheritance

comlóg (s, n) – equal payment

comocus (u, m) – proximity

comrac (o, n) – encounter (v.n. of con·ricc)

Conaire (i̯o, m) – male name

Conall (o, m) – male name

con·beir, ·coimbir (S1; cum-ber-) – to beget

con·ceil, ·coicil (S1a; cum-cel-) – to conceal

Conchobar mac Nessa (o, m) – male name, king of the Ulaid

con·dieig, ·condaig (S1a; cum-di-sag-) – to seek; con·aitecht augm. pret.

con·gaib, ·congaib (S2; cum-gab-) – to contain, preserve; settle down

con·gair, ·congair (S2; cum-gar-) – to call, summon, invite

con·gní, ·cungni (H2; cum-gní-) – to help, assist

con·icc, ·cumaic/·cumaing (S1a; cum-icc-) – can, to be able to; also: to have power over

con·meil, ·cummail (S1; cum-mel-) – to consume, destroy

con·mesca, ·cummasca (W1; cum-mesc-) – to mix

Conn (o, m) – male name

Connlae (i̯o, m) – male name

con·ricc, ·comraicc (S1; cum-ro-icc-) – to meet, join

con·rig, ·cuimrig (S1a; cum-rig-) – to bind together, tie

con·scara, ·coscra (W1; cum-scar-) – to destroy, overthrow

con·srenga, ·coisrenga (W1; cum-sreng-) – to pull

con·tibi, ·cuitbi (W2; cum-tib-) – to laugh about, make fun of

corann (ā, f) – crown

corcur (ā, f) – purple

Cormac (o, m) – male name; mythical Irish king

cornaire (i̯o, m) – horn-blower

corp (o, m) – body

corr (ā, f) – heron

cos (ā, f) – foot

cosc (o, n) – reproof, correction, punishment

co-se – up to this

cosmail (i) – similar

cosmailius (u, m) – similarity

cotlud (u,m) – sleep (v.n. of con·tulai)

cráeb (ā, f) – branch

cráes (o, m) – maw, mouth, gullet

crann (o, n) – tree, mast

cranntaball (ā, f) – sling

cré (t, f, g.sg. criäd) – clay, earth

creitem (ā, f) – belief (v.n. of creitid)

creitid (W2a) – to believe

crenaid (S3) – to buy; ·cíuir pret.

crett (ā, f) – frame, frame of a chariot

crích (ā, f) – boundary, territory

cride (i̯o, n) – heart

Críst (o, m) – Christ

cró (i̯o, m, pl. cruí) – eye of needle

crob (o, m) – paw

crochaid (W1) – to crucify

cródae (i̯o, i̯ā) – wild, brave

cróderg (o, ā) – bloodred

cróeb – cráeb

cros (ā, f) – cross

crott (ā, f, g.sg. cruitte) – harp

Cruachu (n, f) – place-name

cruimther (o, m) – priest

cruth (u, m) – shape; in chruth-so – thus, this way

cruthaigidir (W2a) – to shape

cú (n, m, g.sg. con) – dog

Cúailnge (i̯ā, f) – place-name

cúan (o, m) – harbor

cubaid (i) – harmonious, in accord

Cú Chulainn (only Cú (n, m) is inflected) – hero of the Ulaid

cuingid (i, f) – the requesting, the seeking (v.n. of con·dieig)

cuire (i̯o) – troup

·cuirethar – fo·ceird

cuirm (i, n, g. sg. corma) – beer

cuit (i, f, g.sg. cota) – share, portion, part

cúl (o, m) – back, backside

culén (o, m) – puppy

cumachtach (o, ā) – powerful, mighty

cumachtae (i̯o, n) – might, power

cumal (ā, f) – female slave, unit of currency (equal to three cows)

cumgabál (ā, f) – the raising up, lifting (v.n. of con·ocaib)

cummae (i̯o, n) – likeness, same amount (is X cummae fri Y – X is like Y)

cumrae (i̯o, i̯ā) – fragrant, sweet-smelling

curach (o, m) – boat

cúraid (W1) – to chastize, punish

curchán (o, m) – small boat

D

daL, dáL (+ dual) – two

daidbir (i) – poor, miserable

daig (i, f, g.sg. dego) – fire

dáig, déig (+ gen.) – because, on account of

dáilid (W2a) – to distribute

daingen (o, ā) – strong, hard

daire (i̯o, n) – oak wood

dairid (S2) – to bull

1. dál (ā, f) – meeting, council

2. dál (ā, f) – distribution (v.n. of dáilid)

daltae (i̯o, m) – foster-son

dam (o, m) – ox, stag

dán (u, n) – gift, skill, poetical skill

dánae (i̯o, i̯ā) – daring, fearless; dánu comp.

dano (adv.) – then

dar (+ acc.) – across; dar cenn (+ gen.) on account

Dardaín – Thursday

dásachtach (o, ā) – crazy

Dauid – David

daur (u, f, g.sg. daro) – oak

deacht (ā, f, gen. sg. deachtae) – deity, Godhead

dech – best, superl. of maith

deg-, dag- – good (in compounds)

degaid (i, f) – search, the seeking (v.n. of do·saig); i ndegaid: after

deichN – ten

déicsiu (n, f) – the looking (upon) (v.n. of do·écai)

deide (i̯o, n) – two things

déidenach (o, ā) – last, final

deilm (n, n) – loud noise, fart

deimin (i) – certain

déine (i̯ā, f) – swiftness

déis (short ī?, f) – vassalry, privileges of a lord

deithbir (i) – fitting, proper

deithiden (ā, f) – sorrow

delb (ā, f) – shape

delbaid (W1) – to form, shape

delg (s, n + o, m) – thorn, pin

demon (o, m) – demon, Devil

denaid (S3) – to suck

dénum (u, m) – the making, doing (v.n. of do·gní)

denus (u, m) – a while, a time

dér (o, m) – tear

derg (o, ā) – red

dernu (n, f) – palm of the hand, hand

deróil (i) – lowly, insignificant

dertan (o, m) – storm

derucc (n, f, g.sg. dercon) – acorn

dess (o, ā) – right, south

dét (nt, n) – tooth

deug (ā, f, g.sg. dige) – drink

diL, deL (+ prep.) – from, of

dí – fem. of dá

dia – day; dia mís – the end of a month

1. díaN (+ dep.) – if (+ subj.), when (+ ind.)

2. Día (o, m, g.sg. Dé) – God

díadae (i̯o, i̯ā) – divine

dían (o, ā) – swift, quick; eager

dias (ā, f) – two persons, pair

díbergach (o, m) – brigand, robber

didiu (particle) – then, now

dígal (ā, f) – revenge (v.n. of do·fich)

dil (i) – dear

díltud (u, m) – rejection, refusal (v.n. of do·sluindi)

dingid (S1) – to press, thrust, crush

díre (i̯o, n) – honor-price, penalty, mulct (v.n. of do·ren)

díscir (i) – wild

dliged (o, n) – law

dligid (S1) – to be entitled to

1. doL – thy, 2nd sg. poss. pron.

2. doL (+ prep.) – to, for

do·aidlea, ·taidlea (W1; *to-ad-ell-*) – to visit, touch

do·airbir, ·tairbir (S1; *to-are-ber-*) – to bend, lower, surrender

do·áirci, ·táirci (W2; *to-áirec-*?) – to cause, effect, bring about do·airicc, ·tairicc (S1; *to-are-icc-*) – to come back

do·bá, *·díba (H1; *dī-ba-*) – to perish

do·beir, ·tabair (S1a; *to-ber-*) – to give, bring; do·rat pret. gave; do·uc pret. brought

do·bidci, ·díbairgi (W2; *dī-bidc-*) – to hurl, cast, pelt (di – with)

do·boing, ·tobaing (S1; *to-bong-*) – to exact, levy

do·ceil, ·dichil (S1a; *dī-cel-*) – to hide

do·ceird (S1) – to throw to

dochraid (i) – ugly

dochum (+ gen.) – to, towards

do·coaid, ·dichid (S1; *di-cum-feth-*) – augm. stem of téit

do·cuirethar, ·tochraither (W2b; *to-cor-*) – to put, throw

doë (nt, f) – upper arm

do·écai, ·décci (H2; *di-in-ci-*) – to look at, behold

do·eim, ·dim (S1; *di-em-*) – to protect

dóel (o, m) – beetle

doér (o, m) – unfree person

do·fich, ·dích (S1; *dī-fich-*) – to avenge

do·formaig, ·tormaig (S1) – to increase

do·fortai, ·dórtai (W2b; *di-?-fort-*) – to pour

do·gní, ·dénai (H2; *di-gni-*) – to do, make; do·génai pret; do·rigéni augm. pret.

do grés – always

do·guid, ·digid (S2; *di-ged-*) – to entreat

do·icc, ·ticc (S1a; *to-icc-*) – to come

doich (i) – probable

doíni – pl. of duine

doíre (i̯ā, f) – captivity, state of being unfree

do·léici, ·teilci (W2a; *to-lēc-*) – to throw, cast

do·lin, ·tuilen (?) (S3b; *to-lin-*) – to flow

dolmae (i̯ā, f) – hesitation

do·luigi, ·dílgai (W2b; *dī-log-*) – to forgive

domblas (o, m) – gall

do·meil, ·tomail (S1; *to-mel-*) – to consume, use up

Domnall (o, m) – male name

do·moinethar, ·tomnathar (S2; *to-man-*) – to suppose, think

domun (o, m) – world

donn (o, ā) – brown, dark brown

doraid (i, n) – difficulty

1. dorchae (i̯o, i̯ā) – dark, gloomy

2. dorchae (i̯o, n) – darkness

dordaid (W1) – to make a humming, etc., sound

do·ridisi – again

do·rig, ·dírig (?) (S1; *dī-rig-*) – to strip

dorn (o, m) – fist

dorus (u, n) – door, i ndorus (+ gen.) in front of

1. dos (o, m) – bush

2. dos (o?, m?) – a poetic grade; lit.: bush, tall man?

do·scara, ·tascra (W1; *to-scar-*) – to destroy, bring down

do·seinn, ·tophainn (S1a; *to-s̯enn-*) – to hunt

do·sluindi, ·díltai (W2b; *dī-slund-*) – to deny, reject

do·tét, ·táet (S1a; *to-tēg-*) – to come; do·luid pret.; do·chuid augm. pret.

do·tuit, ·tuit (S2; *to-tud-*) – to fall, pret. do·cer, ·torchar

do·uccai, ·tuccai (W2b; *to-ucc-*) – augm. stem of do·beir; also: to understand

drécht (u, n) – literary composition

drisiuc (u? or n?, m) – a poetic grade

droch- – bad (in compounds)

druí (t, m, g.sg. druad) – druid, mage

druimm (i, n) – back, hill

druimne (i̯o, m) – back

drúth (o, m) – idiot

dúabais (i) – sad, unhappy

dúalaig (short ī, f) – vice, fault of character

dúan (ā, f) – song, poem

1. dub (u) – black

2. dub (u, n) – ink

duí (t, m) – idiot, fool

dúil (i, f) – element, creature; the creation, the universe

duille (i̯ā, f) – leaf

duine (i̯o, m, n.pl. doíni) – human being, person

dul – the going (v.n. of téit)

dún (o, n) – fort, hillfort

dúnaid (W1) – to close

dúr (o, ā) – hard, severe

dús – (to see) if

E

éc (u, m) – death

ech (o, m) – horse

echaire (i̯o, m) – stable boy

echrad (ā, f) – horses (yoked to a chariot)

echtrann (o, ā) – foreign

eclais (short ī, f) – the church

ecnae (i̯o, m) – knowledge, wisdom

éicen (ā, f) – necessity, force; ar éicin – by force

éigid (W2a) – to cry out, raise alarm

éim – particle of affirmation

eirr (t, m) – chariot fighter

eisséirge (i̯o, n) – resurrection

Eithne (i̯ā, f) – female name

ellach (o, m) – union, joining

Emain, Emain Machae (only Emain (short ī, f) is inflected) – royal seat of the Ulaid

Emer (ā, f) – female name

én (o, m, g.sg. éuin) – bird

énairt (i) – weak, powerless

enbruithe (i̯o, m) – broth

enech (ā, f) – face, honor

énlaith (i, f) – flock of birds, birds

ennac (o, ā) – innocent

éola (k?) – knowledgeable, skilled

epistil (short ī, f) – letter

erbaid, ·erbai (W2a) – to entrust

Ériu (n, f) – Ireland

ernaid (S3) – to bestow; ·ír pret.

ernaigde (i̯ā, f) – prayer

ersclaige (i̯ā, f) – the act of defending, warding off (v.n. of ar·clich)

·esser (2nd sg. dep. s-future) – will lend

ét (o, m) – jealousy

étach (o, n) – garment, clothing

etargaire (i̯o, n) – the intervening, interference

etar·scara, ·etarscara (W1; *eter-scar-*) – to separate, depart from

étsecht (ā, f) – the hearing (v.n. of in·túaisi)

éulchaire (i̯o, n) – longing, yearning, regret

F

fadeisin – féin

fáilid (i) – happy

fáilte (i̯ā, f) – happiness, welcome

fairrge (i̯ā, f) – sea

1. fál (o, m) – fence, enclosure

2. Fál (o, m) – poetical name for Ireland

fán (o, m) – valley, slope

fa naic – or not

féchem (n, m) – debtor

fégaid (W1) – to look at

feidid (S1a) – to lead

feidligidir (W2a) – to last

féige (i̯ā, f) – keenness, sharpness, penetration

féil (short ī, f) – festival

féile (i̯ā, f) – modesty, shamefulness

féin (pron.) – -self, own

Féini (i̯o) – old name for the Irish

feis (ā, f) – spending the night, feast

felmacc (o, m) – student, pupil

fénechas (o, m) – Irish customary law

feóil (i, f) – meat, flesh

fer (o, m) – man

fér (o, n, g.sg. féuir) – grass

feraid (W1) – to pour

fercaigidir (W2a) – to become angry

fern (ā, f) – alder-tree

ferr – better, compar. of maith

fert (ā, f) – shaft at the back of a chariot

fertae (i̯ā, f) – grave, mound, tumulus

fesine – féin

fet (ā, f) – whistle

fetarlaicce (i̯ā, f) – the Old Testament

fíad^L (+ prep.) – in the presence of

fíada (nt, m) – lord, The Lord

fíadnaise (i̯o, n) – witness, testimony

fiche (nt, m) – twenty

fichid (S1) – to fight, fut. fies-, fess-

fid (u, m) – wood

fidchell (ā, f) – a board-game (lit.: wood-sense)

·fil (+ acc. of the subject) – to be (rel. and dependent form of at·tá)

fili (t, m) – poet

filidecht (ā, f) – poetry

fín (u, n) – wine

fínacet (o, m) – vinegar

find (o, ā) – fair, white, blond

findfolt (o, m) – blond hair

fíne (i̯ā, f) – vine

1. fír (o, ā) – true

2. fír (o, n) – truth, correctness

fírián (o, ā) – just, truthful

fíriánaigidir (W2a) – to justify, make righteous

fírinne (i̯ā, f) – righteousness, truthfulness

fis (u, m + o, m) – knowledge

flaith (i, f) – rule, ruler

flaithem (n, m) – ruler

flann (o, ā) – red

fled (ā, f) – feast, banquet

flesc (ā, f) – rod

fo^L (+ prep., acc.) – under

fo·ácaib, ·fácaib (S2; *fo-ad-gab-*) – to leave

fo·cain, ·fochain (S1; *fo-can-*) – to sing around somebody

fo·ceird, ·cuirethar (S1a; *fo-cerd-*) – to put, throw; fo·caird pret.; ro·lá augm. pret.

fochaid (i, f) – tribulation, suffering

fochaide (i̯ā, f) – tribulation, sorrow

fo chen do (+ prep.) – welcome to

fo-chétóir – immediately

fochloc (o, m) – poet of the lowest grade

fo·cíallathar, ·foichlither (W1; *fo-cēll-*) – to pay heed to, take care of

fo·cren, ·foichren (S3; *fo-crī-*) – to hire

fo·dáili, ·fodlai (W2b; *fo-dāl-*) – to distribute

fo·daim, ·fodaim (S2; *fo-dam-*) – to suffer, endure

fodeisin – féin

fo·éirig, *·féirig (S1a; *fo-ess-reg-*) – to rise (to attack)

fóesam (o, m) – protection

fo·fera, ·foír(e)a (W1; *fo-fer-*) – to cause, prepare

fo·fúasna, ·fúasna (W1; *fo-od-uss-an-*) – to agitate, disturb

fo·gaib, ·fagaib (S2; *fo-gab-*) – to find, get

fo·geir, ·foigir (S1; *fo-ger-*) – to heat, warm

fo·gella, ·foiglea (W1; *fo-gell-*) – to appeal, submit to

fográd (o, n) – subgrade, inferior grade

fogur (o, m) – sound, noise

foídid (W2b) – to send

foidirc (i) – visible

foilsigidir (W2a) – to explain, reveal

foilsigiud (u, m) – revelation (v.n. of foilsigidir)

foirbthe (i̯o, i̯ā) – perfect

foirbthetu (t, m) – perfection

foísitiu (n, f) – confession

follamnaigid (W2a) – to rule

follamnugud (u, m) – the ruling (v.n. of follaimnigid)

follus (u) – bright, clear; foillsem superl.

fo·loing, ·fulaing (S1c; *fo-long-*) – to suffer, endure

folt (o, m) – hair

fonn (o, m) – sole, base

fo·ópair (fo·fúapair), ·fúapair (S1a; *fo-od-ber-*) – to attack

1. for (+ prep., acc.) – over, upon

2. for^N – your, 2nd pl. pers. pron.

foraire (i̯ā, f) – the guarding, guard

for·beir, ·forbair (S1; *for-ber-*) – to increase, grow

for·ben, ·forban (S3; *for-bī-*) – to complete

for·cain, ·forcain (S1b; *for-can-*) – to teach; for·cechain pret.; for·roíchan augm. pret.

forcenn (o, n) – end

for·cenna, ·foircnea (W1; *for-cenn-*) – to end, put an end to

forcetal (o, n) – teaching, instruction (v.n. of for·cain)

for·ding, ·fording (S1; *for-di(n)g-*) – to crush, oppress

fo·reith, *·foiret (S1a; *fo-reth-*) – to help, succour; fo·ráith pret.

for·fen, ·forban (S3; *for-fi-*) – to finish, complete

forglu (?) – choice (portion)

format (o, n) – jealousy

forngaire (i̯o, n) – order (v.n. of for·congair)

for·osnai, ·fursannai (W2b; *for-uss-and-*) – to light up

fortacht (ā, f) – help (v.n. of for·tét)

fos (o, n) – quietness

foscad (o, m) – darkness, shadow

fossad (o, ā) – firm, steadfast

fothae (o, m) – load

fo-thúaid – northward

fraig (i, f, g.sg. frego) – wall

frecor (o, m) – the care for, the attending to (v.n. of fris·cuirethar)

frecrae (i̯o, n) – answer (v.n. of fris·gair)

fri[H] (+ acc.) – towards, against

fris·accai, ·frescai (H2; *fris-ad-ci-*) – to expect, hope for

fris·ben, ·freipen (S3; *fris-bi-*) – to heal

fris·gair, ·frecair (S2; *fris-gar-*) – to answer

fris·oirg, ·frithoirg (S1b; *fris-org-*) – to hurt, offend

frithgnum (u, m) – labor, pain, effort, exertion (v.n. of fris·gní)

fúachaid (W1) – to point, direct

fudumain (i, ?) – depth, profundity

fuil (i, f, g.sg. folo) – blood

fuine (i̯ā, f) – the cooking, the roasting (v.n. of fo·noí)

fulacht (u, m) – cooking place

G

gabál (ā, f) – the taking (v.n. of gaibid)

gabul (ā, f) – fork

gáe (o, m) – spear

1. gáeth (ā, f) – wind

2. gáeth (o, ā) – wise, intelligent

gaibid (S2) – to take, begin, say; gaibid X búaid – X wins; gaibid X búaid de Y – X defeats Y; gaibid céill – to realize

gainithir (S2) – to be born

gáire (i̯o, m) – laughter

gáirechtach (ā, f) – laughter

gairid (S2) – to shout, call

gairm (n, n) – cry, shout (v.n. of gairid)

gaisced (o, m) – weapons (spear and shield)

galar (o, n) – illness

galrach (o, ā) – ill, sick, sad

gat (ā, f) – theft (v.n. of gataid)

gataid (W1) – to steal

gataige (i̯o, m) – thief

gáu (ā, f) – falseness

geilid (S1a) – to graze

gein (n, n) – birth (v.n. of gainithir)

geinti (i, m, pl.) – pagans

géis (ī, f) – swan

gel (o, ā) – bright

gemred (o, n) – winter

gér (o, ā) – sharp, pointed

gerraid (W1) – to cut, shave

gillae (i̯o, m) – lad, servant

gin (u, m) – mouth

ginach (ā, f) – gaping, laughing

glain (i, f) – glass

glan (o, ā) – clean

glanad (u, m) – the cleaning (v.n. of glanaid)

glanaid (W1) – to clean

glas (o, ā) – blue, green, grey

glégorm (o, ā) – dark blue

glenn (s, n) – valley

gléo (t, f, g.sg. gliäd) – fight

gleth (ā, f) – the grazing (v.n. of geilid)

glicc (i) – clever

glúasacht (ā, f) – motion, movement (v.n. of glúaisid)

glún (s, n) – knee

gniïd (H2) – to do, make

gním (u, m) – deed (v.n. of gniïd)

gnúis (i, f) – face

gobae (n, m) – smith

goiste (i̯o, m) – noose

gonaid (S1b) – to wound; geguin pret.

gop (o, m) – peak

gorm (o, ā) – blue, dark blue

gort (o, m) – field

gortae (i̯ā, f) – hunger

1. grád (o, n) – rank, grade, order

2. grád (u, n) – love, affection

grádaigidir (W2b) – to love

grafand (ā, f) – horse race

graig (i, n, g.sg. grego) – herd

grán (o, n) – corn

grés – do grés

grían (ā, f, g.sg. gréine) – sun

grúad (s, n) – cheek

gú- (first member of compound) – false

gubae (i̯o, n) – mourning, sighing

guide (i̯ā, f) – prayer, request (v.n. of guidid)

guidid (S2) – to pray, ask; gáid pret.

guin (i, n) – wound (v.n. of gonaid)

guirid (W2b) – to heat, warm

guth (u, m, g.sg. gotho) – voice

H

heretec (o, m) – heretic

Heroaid – Herod

hóre, húaire (+ dep.) – because

I

i[N] (+ prep., acc.) – in, into

í – deictic particle, see ch. 38.5.

íadaid (W1) – to close, shut

íall (ā, f) – a flock of birds

íar[N] (+ prep.) – after (temporal), according to

íarmi·foich, ·iarfoig (S1a; *iarmi-fo-sag-*) – to ask, seek

íarum (3rd sg. masc. of íar[N]) – then, afterwards

íasc (o, m, g.sg. éisc) – fish
ibid (S1a) – to drink
ícc (ā, f) – cure, healing (v.n. of íccaid)
íccaid (W1) – to heal, save; requit, pay
ídol (o, m) – idol
ifern (o, m) – hell
ifernach (o, ā) – infernal
il (u) – many; lir equative, lia compar.
imb (n, n) – butter
1. imdae (i̯ā, f) – bed, compartment
2. imdae (i̯o, i̯ā) – many, numerous
imdegal (ā, f) – protection (v.n. of imm·dích)
imdírech (o, n) – mutual stripping
immacúairt (adv.) – around, about
i-mmaig – outside, lit.: on the field
imm·aig, ·immaig (S1b; imbi-ag-) – to drive around
immáin (i, f, also -an á, f) – the driving (v.n. of imm·aig)
immarmus (u, m) – sin
imm·beir, ·imbir (S1a; imbi-ber-) – to play
imm·dích, ·imdig (S1; imbi-di-fich-) – to protect, guard; im·dís- fut.
imm·folngai, ·immfolngai (W2b; imbi-fo-long-) – to cause
imm·rá, ·immra (H1; imbi-rā-) – to row around
imm·ráidi, ·immráidi (W2a; imbi-rād-) – to think of, meditate
imm·soí, ·impai (H3; imbi-so-) – to turn
imm·téit, ·immthet (S1; imbi-tēg-) – to go around
imned (o, n) – sorrow, suffering
imram (u, m) – rowing (v.n. of imm·rá)
imthecht (ā, f) – the going around (v.n. of imm·téit)
imthrascrad (u, m) – wrestling (v.n. of imm·tascra)
1. in – article
2. inN (+ dep.) – interrogative particle
in·aig, ·indaig (S1; inde-ag-) – to apply
indala, indara – ind aile
indeb (o, n) – goods, possession
indéuin (i?, f) – anvil
i ndíaid (+ gen.) – after, behind
indile (i̯ā, f) – wealth, possession
indlach (o, n) – cleaving, cleavage
indmas (u/o, m) – wealth, treasure, goods
indossa – now
inducbaide (i̯o, ia) – glorious
in·fét, ·indid (S1; inde-fēd-) – to tell, relate
1. ingen (ā, f) – daughter, girl
2. ingen (ā, f) – fingernail, toenail
ingnad (o, ā) – strange
ingnas (ā, f) – absence, loss
ingnímae (i̯o, i̯ā) – capable of action
ingrimm (n, n) – persecution
inis (ī, f) – island
Inis Fáil – poetical name for Ireland
inmain (i) – dear
innádN (+ dep.) – negative interrogative particle
innocht – tonight
in·samlathar, ·intamlathar (W1; inde-samal-) – to imitate

in tanN, in tainN – when
intech (o, m) – path, way
intled (ā, f) – ambush
ires (ā, f) – belief, faith
1. is – to be (copula)
2. is – short form of ocus
ísel (o, ā) – low
is samlaid – thus, this way
Ísu – Jesus
itche (i̯o, m) – prayer
ithe (i̯ā, f) – the eating (v.n. of ithid)
ithid (S1a) – to eat
Iudaide (i̯o, m) – Jew

L

la (+ acc.) – with, by
lá, laa – lae
labrad (u, m) – the speaking (v.n. of labraithir)
labrae (i̯ā, f) – speech
labraithir (W1) – to speak
lae, laa, lá (i̯o, n) – day
laigid (S1a) – to lie
lainne (i̯ā, f) – eagerness; ar lainni – for the sake of
laith (i, ?) – liquor, intoxicating drink
laithe (i̯o, n) – day
lám (ā, f) – hand
lán (o, ā) – full
lánamain (i, f) – couple
lár (o, n) – floor, centre
lasseN – while
láthraid (W1) – to arrange, dispose
lebor (o, m, g.sg. libuir) – book
légad (u, m) – the reading (v.n. of légaid)
légaid (W1) – to read
légend (o, n) – the reading, the studying (v.n. of légaid)
léicid (W2a) – to let, leave
léiciud (u, m) – the letting, leaving (v.n. of léicid)
léimm (n, n) – the jumping, leap (v.n. of lingid)
léir (i) – eager, diligent
lenaid (S3) – to follow, stick to (+ de/di)
1. les (ā, f) – buttock, hip, haunch
2. les (o, m) – court, enclosed area around the house
3. les (u, m) – affair, matter; profit, advantage
leth (s/o, n) – half, side
lethan (o, ā) – broad; lethidir equativ
líach (o, n) – pain
liäig (i, m, g.sg. lego) – physician
líath (o, ā) – grey
líathróit (short ī, f) – ball
lië (nk, m, g.sg. liäcc) – stone
lígach (o, ā) – beautiful, fair
lígdae (i̯o, i̯ā) – brilliant, fair
lige (i̯o, n) – the lying, bed, grave (v.n. of laigid)
lígoll (o, ā) – very beautiful
liid (H2) – to accuse
lín (u, n + m) – full number
línaid (W1) – to fill, make full
línech (o, ā) – lined, with lines

lingid (S1a) – to jump; leblaing pret., ·ribuilsed
  augm. past. subj.
línmar (o, ā) – numerous
lobur (o, ā) – weak
loc (o, m) – place
lóech (o, m) – warrior
lóg, lúag (o, m + s, n) – price; ar lúaig – for a price
lóg n-enech – honor-price
loíd (short ī?, f) – song
loiscid (W2) – to burn, consume by fire
lon (o, m) – blackbird
long (ā, f, g.sg. luinge) – ship
longas (ā, f) – fleet; exile (longas re ᴺ – exile from)
lorg (ā, f) – stick
lorg ánae – hurling stick
lúag – lóg
luamain (short ī, f) – movement, flight
luch (t, f, g.sg. lochad) – mouse
luchair (i, n) – brightness, brilliance
Lugaid (k, m, g.sg. Luigdech) – male name
lugbart (o, m) – kitchen-garden
lugu – compar. of becc
luib (short ī, f) – herb, plant

M

maᴸ, máᴸ – if
macc (o, m) – boy, son
maccḟuirmid (?, m) – a poetic grade; lit.: son of effort?
macc léigind – student (lit.: son of learning)
maccrad (a f) – boygroup
maccthae (i̯o, i̯ā) – childish
machdath (m) – wonder
macrall (ā, f) – testicles
madae (i̯o, i̯ā) – vain
Máel Ḟothertaig (only the first element (ā, f!) is
  inflected) – male name
Máelodrán (o, m) – male name
Máel Rúain – saint, founder of Tamlacht
mag (s, n) – field, plain
Mag Muirthemne (s, n) – place-name
maidid (S2) – to break (intrans.); memaid pret.;
  memas- fut.; maidid for nech (acc.: vanquished)
  re neuch (prep.: victor) – to defeat;
  maidid aᴴ – to break out of
maidm (n, n) – breaking (v.n. of maidid)
maisse (i̯ā, f) – goodliness, fineness
maiten (ā, f) – morning
maith (i) – good; ferr compar., dech superl.
maithes (u, m) – goodness, excellence
mala (k, f) – eyebrow
maldacht (ā, f) – curse
mani (+ dep.) – if not
marb (o, ā) – dead
marbad (u, m) – the killing (v.n. of marbaid)
marbaid (W1) – to kill
marcach (o, m) – rider
marnaid (S3) – to betray; ro·mert pret.
máthair (r, f) – mother

medguisce (i̯o, m) – whey-water
medón (o, m) – middle
meilid (S1a) – to grind; ·melt pret.
méit (short ī, f) – size, amount
men (ā, f) – flour
menmae (n, m) – mind
mescae (i̯ā, f) – drunkenness
mess (u, m) – judgement (v.n. of midithir)
messa – worse, compar. of olc
mí (s, m, g.sg. mís) – month
míach (o, n, g.sg. méich) – sack
mid (u, m) – mead
midchuach (o, m) – meadcup
Mide (i̯o, n) – one of the five provinces of ancient Ireland
  (lit.: the middle)
midithir (S2) – to judge, estimate
míl (t, m) – warrior, soldier
mílach (o, ā) – full of animals
milis (i) – sweet
millid (W2a) – to ruin
mind (u, n) – crown, diadem
moᴸ – my, 1ˢᵗ sg. poss. pron.; m' before a vowel
mó – soon
moch- – fast, soon
móeth (o, ā) – tender
móin (short ī, f) – bog, turf
moín (i, f) – treasure, gift
molad (u, m) – praise (v.n. of molaithir)
molaithir (W1) – to praise
1. mór (o, ā) – big, great; móir equativ; móa, móo
  compar.; móam superl.
2. mór (o, n) – a lot of
móraid (W1) – to praise
moth (o, m) – amazement
mrath (u, m) – betrayal (v.n. of marnaid)
múad (o, ā) – glorious
mucc (ā, f) – pig
mug (u, m) – slave, serf
muilenn (o, m) – mill
muin (i, f) – neck
muinter (ā, f) – household, family, retinue
muir (i, n) – sea
mullach (o, m) – top, summit

N

ná – negation of the imperative
nach – any
nád (+ dep.) – negative relative particle
naiscid (S1) – to bind
námae (nt, m) – enemy
nammá – only
nathair (k, f) – snake
náthó – no
nech (o, m/f, no pl.) – anybody
neimed (o, m) – sacred place
nél (o, m, g.sg. níuil) – cloud
nem (s, n) – heaven, sky
nemdae (i̯o, i̯ā) – heavenly

nemḟulachtae (i̯o, i̯ā) – unbearable
nert (o, n) – power, strength
ness (o, m) – furnace
-ni – emphasizing particle 1st pl.
1. ní (+ dep.) – not
2. ní (gen. sg. neich) – anything, neutr. of nech
niäe (t, m), gen. niad – nephew
Níall (o, m) – male name; a mythical king of Ireland
níam (ā, f) – brightness, luster
nícon – ní
Ninne mac Magach (i̯o, m) – male name
no (+ conj.) – meaningless, grammatical particle
nó – or
noco(n) – nícon – ní
nóeb (o, ā) – holy, saint(ly)
nóebaid (W1) – to sanctify
noíN – nine
noídiu (n, m/f) – child, baby
nós (o, m) – custom, tradition
notaire (i̯o, m) – scribe
núall (o, n) – cry
nue (i̯o, i̯ā) – new
nuíadnaisse, nuḟíadnaisse (i̯o, n) – New Testament

O

óL (+ prep.) – from
1. oäc (o, ā) – young; óam superl.
2. oäc (o, m) – young man, warrior
oblaire (i̯o, m) – a poetic grade; lit.: juggler, trickster
oc (+ prep.) – at, by
óc – younger form of oäc
ócán (o, m) – little darling
ochtN – eight
óclach (ā, f) – warrior
ocusL – and
óen- – one (in compounds)
óenach (o, n) – assembly, fair
óenar (o, m) – one person; poss. pron. + óenur – alone
og (s, n) – egg
ogam (o, m) – ogam inscription
oíbell (ā, f) – spark
oíge, gen. oiged (t, m) – guest
oítiu, gen. oíted (t, m) – youth
1. ol – because
2. ol (defective verb) – (s)he said
ól (o, m) – the drinking (v.n. of ibid)
olae (i̯ā, f) – oil
olc (o, ā) – bad
oll (o, ā) – great, all
ollam (n, m) – poet of the highest grade
ollgorm (o, ā) – brilliant, famous (lit.: great blue)
omnae (i̯ā, f) – tree
omun (o, m) – fear; ar omun (+ gen.) for fear of
ór (o, n) – gold
orbae (i̯o, m) – inheritance
ord (o, m) – mallet
órdae (i̯o, i̯ā) – golden
ór fírinne – a truthful incantation

orgaid (S1b) – to slay; oirt pret.
os, ot + independent pers. pron. – and
ós (+ prep.) – over, above

P

passer (o, m) – Lat. passer, sparrow
Pátraic (m) – St. Patrick
peccad (u, m) – sin
penn (ā, f) – pen
persan (ā, f) – person
póc (ā, f) – kiss
pócán (o, m) – diminutive of póc, small kiss
poll (o, m) – hole
popa (m) – father, sir
popul (o, m) – people
port (o, m) – port
precept (ā, f) – preaching (v.n. of pridchid)
pridchid (W1) – to preach, teach
prím- – first- in compounds

R

rád (o, m) – the speaking, talk (v.n. of ráidid)
raïd (H1) – to row
ráidid (W2a) – to speak, talk
1. rann (o, m) – verse
2. rann (ā, f) – part
rannaid (W1) – to divide
ráth (ā, f) – a 'ráth' (round fort)
réN, ríaN (+ prep.) – before, in front of
recht (u, m) – law
rechtaire (i̯o, m) – steward
réil (i) – clear
reithid (S1a) – to run
remcaissiu (n, f) – providence, foresight (v.n. of *remi·ac-cai)
remdéicsiu (n, f) – providence (v.n. of remi·déci)
remthechtas (o, m) – the preceding (v.n. of remi·tét)
renaid (S3) – to sell; rir pret.
resíu (+ subj.) – before
rét (u, m) – thing
rétglu (n, f) – star
rí (g, m) – king
riam – before (3rd sg. n. of ré)
rían (o, m) – ocean
ríar (ā, f) – will
ríched (o, n) – heaven
richt (u, m) – form, shape, condition
rígain (ī, f) – queen
rígdae (i̯o, i̯ā) – royal, kingly
rígdún (o, n) – royal fort
ríge (i̯o, n) – kingdom
rigid (S1) – to stretch
rígrad (ā, f) – royal household
rímid (W2a) – to count
rind (u, n) – star
rindach (o, ā) – full of stars

ro· – grammatical particle
ro·cluinethar, ·cluinethar (S3; *ro-clun-*) – to hear; ro·cúa-
    lae pret.
rodarc (o, m) – sight, vision
róen (o, m) – way, path; here: defeat, rout
ro·finnadar, ·finnadar (S3; *ro-finn-*) – to find out
ro·fitir, ·fitir (S3, pret. of ro·finnadar) – to know
ro·icc, ·ricc (S1; *ro-icc-*) – to reach
roithid (W2b) – to make run
ro·laimethar, ·laimethar (S2; *ro-lam-*) – to dare
Róm, Rúam (ā, f) – Rome
rond (o, m) – chain
ro·saig, ·roich (S1; *ro-sāg-*) – to reach
rosc (o, n) – eye
rót (o, m) – road
roth (o, m) – wheel
ro·uccai, ·ruccai (W2b; *ro-ucc-*) – can carry, bear,
    bring (a suppletive stem of beirid)
rúad (o, ā) – red-haired
ruiri, gen. ruirech (g, m) – king
rún (ā, f) – a secret
rúndae (i̯o, i̯ā) – secret

S

1. –sa – demonstrative particle: this
2. –sa – emphasizing particle 1st sg.
Sabbait (i, f) – Saturday
sacart (o, m) – priest
sáebaid – sóebaid
sáer (o, m) – artisan, carpenter
sáeth (u, m) – trouble
sáethar (o, n) – labor, toil
saidbir (i) – rich
saidid (S1) – to sit, 3rd pl. sedait
sáidid (W2) – to fix, plant
1. saigid (S2) – to seek
2. saigid (i, f) – visit, the seeking (v.n. of saigid)
sail (k, f) – willow
sain (i) – special, separate, different
saindíles (o, ā) – special, peculiar, one's own
sainemail (i) – splendid, special
sair – eastward, forward
sáithech (o, ā) – saturated, satisfied (de + prep. – from)
sál (o, m) – sea
salm (o, m) – psalm
samlaid – thus, this way
samlaidir (W1) – to compare (fri + acc. with)
samthach (ā, f) – axe-handle
sáth (ā, f) – sufficiency, fill, appetite
scarad (u, m) – separation, the separating (v.n.
    of scaraid)
scaraid (W1) – to part, separate
scáth (o, m) – shadow
sceithid (S1?) – to vomit, spit out
scél (o, n, g.sg. scéuil) – story, tale, news
scíath (o, m) – shield
scíath slissen – shield made of boards
scíth (o, ā) – tired

scol (ā, f) – school
scolaire (i̯o, m) – student, scholar
scolóc (o, m) – student, scholar
scor (o, m) – the unyoking, rest (v.n. of scuirid)
scríbaid (W1) – to write
scríbend (o, n) – the writing (v.n. of scríbaid)
scríbndid (i, m) – scribe
scrútaid (W1) – to examine, investigate
scuirid (W2b) – to unyoke
-se – 1. + 2. -sa
séH – six
sech (conjuction) – and furthermore
sechmall (o, n) – the passing by
sechtN – seven
segonn (o, m) – master
seichithir (W2) – to follow
seinm (n, n) – the playing of an instrument (v.n.
    of seinnid)
seinnid (S1a) – to play an instrument
seir (t, f) – heel
seisser (o, n) – six men
séitig (ī, f) – wife
selb (ā, f) – possession
sen (o, ā) – old; siniu compar.
sénaid (W1) – to bless
sentuinne (i̯ā, f) – old woman
séolaid (W1) – to sail
-seom – -som
serc (ā, f) – love (v.n. of caraid)
sernaid (S3) – to arrange, dispose, order
1. sét (u, m) – way, path
2. sét (o, m) – object of value; a unit of value = ½ milch
    cow
1. –si – emphasizing particle 3rd sg. fem.
2. –si – emphasizing particle 2nd pl.
sian sléibe – purple foxglove (*digitalis purpurea*?)
síd (s, n) – burial mound, peace
sídamail (i) – peaceful
-side – anaphoric pronoun, see ch. 38.7.
-sin – demonstrative particle: that
sínid (W2) – to extend, stretch
sír (o, ā) – long, lasting; sía compar.
sís – below
síst (ā, f) – a while
-siu – 2. –so
-sium – -som
siur (r, f, g.sg. sethar) – sister
slabrad (ā, f) – chain
slabrae (i̯ā, f) – herd, cattle
slaidid (S2) – to strike
slán (o, ā) – sound, healthy
slat (ā, f) – rod, stick, twig
slíab (s, n) – mountain
slíasait (short ī, f) – thigh
slóg, slúag (o, m) – host, army
sloicid (W2) – to swallow
sluindid (W2b) – to mention, name
smacht (u, m) – institution, command
snáithe (i̯o, m) – thread
snáthat (ā, f) – needle

snechtae (i̯o, n) – snow
1. -so – demonstrative particle: this
2. -so – emphasizing particle 2nd sg.
sochaide (i̯ā, f) – multitude
sochraid (i) – beautiful
sochraite (i̯ā, f) – friendship
sóeb (o, ā) – perverted
sóebaid (W1) – to pervert
sóer (o, m) – free person
sóerad (u, m) – deliverance, the saving (v.n. of sóeraid)
sóeraid (W1) – to save, deliver
soïd, ·soí (H3) – to turn
soilse (i̯ā, f) – light, brightness
soinmige (i̯ā, f) – prosperity, affluence
soiscélae (i̯o, n) – Gospel
solus (u) – bright
-som – emphasizing particle 3rd sg. m. + n., 3rd pl.
son (o, m) – sound
són, ón – this
sonairt (i) – strong, firm
sorn (o, m) – oven
spirut (u, m) – the Holy Spirit
sroiglid (W1) – to scourge, flog
srón (ā, f) – nose
sruth (u, m) – stream
-su – 2. -so
súaichnid (i) – well-known, clear
súan (o, m) – sleep
subae (i̯o, n) – joy, pleasure
1. suide (i̯o, ia, neut. sodain) – this, that mentioned
2. suide (i̯o, n) – seat, the sitting (v.n. of saidid)
suidigidir (W2a) – to set up, place
súil (i, f) – eye
sund – here
suthain (i) – lasting
suthaine (i̯ā, f) – lastingness, long life

T

tabart (ā, f) – the giving, taking (v.n. of do·beir)
táeb – tóeb
tailm (i, f, g.sg. telmo) – sling
Tailtiu (n, f) – place-name, today: Teltown
tairr (i, m) – belly, stomach
taisbénad (u, m) – the showing, the demonstrating (v.n. of do·aisféna)
taithesc (o, n) – answer
talam (n, m) – earth
tall, thall – yonder
taman (o, m) – a poetic grade; lit.: trunk, blockhead?
tan – in tain
tánaise (i̯o, i̯ā) – second
tar (+ acc.) – across
tarb (o, m) – bull
táthbéimm (n, n) – a stunning blow
tech (s, n) – house
techt (ā, f) – the going (v.n. of téit)
techtaid (W1) – to possess
techtaire (i̯o, m) – messenger

teichid (S1a) – to flee; táich pret.
teilciud (u, m) – the throwing (v.n. of do·léici)
teine (t, m) – fire; benaid tenid – to make fire
téit (S1a) – to go (+ acc. – to); tíagair pass. messengers are sent; luid pret.; do·coïd augm. pret.
telach, tulach (ā, f) – hill
tellach (o, n) – legal entry on land
Temair (i, f + k, f) – spiritual centre of Ireland
tempul (o, m) – temple
tengae (t, m) – tongue, language
téora – f. of trí
tes (adv.) – the south
testimin (i, m) – text
tí (?, f) – cloak
tigernae (i̯o, m) – lord, ruler
timchell (+ gen.) – around
tinn (i) – ill
tír (s, n) – land
titul (o, m) – title, headlines
tó – yes
tob (o, m) – trumpet
tóeb (o, m) – side
tofonn (o, n) – the hunting (v.n. of do·seinn)
togairm (n, n) – the calling (v.n. of do·gair)
toimtiu (n, f) – opinion, act of thinking
toisc (i, f) – wish, desire
toísech (o, ā) – first; leader
tol (ā, f) – will, desire
tongaid, also toingid (S1c) – to swear
tonn (ā, f) – wave
torad (o, n) – fruit, profit
torbae (i̯o, n) – profit
torc (o, m) – boar
tornocht (o, ā) – stark naked
tossach (o, n) – begin
tothaimm (n, n) – the falling (v.n. of do·tuit)
trá (interjection) – then, now
traig (t, f) – foot, leg
trascrad (u, m) – down-throwing (v.n. of do·scara)
tre (+ acc.) – through
trebaid (W 1) – to inhabit
tréide (o, n) – three things (the OIr. word is singular!)
trén (o, ā) – strong; tressa compar.; tressam superl.
trénfer (o, m) – strong man
tress, triss (o, ā; usually not declined) – third
trethanbras (o, ā) – greatly thundering
tríH – three
trian (o, n) – third part
triar (o, n) – three men
trícha (nt, m) – thirty
trichem (?) – coughing
trilis (i, f) – hair
trírech (ā, f) – trilling of birds
trócaire (i̯ā, f) – mercy
trócairech (o, ā) – merciful
tróethaid (W1) – to subdue, abate
tróg, truag (o, ā) – sad, miserable
tromm (o, ā) – heavy; trummu compar.
trummae (i̯ā, f) – weight
túaid (adv.) – the north

túaire (i̯ā, f) – food

túath (ā, f) – people, kingdom (for túathaib – abroad)

tucait (short ī, f) – cause, reason

tuidecht (ā, f) – the coming, arrival (v.n. of do·tét)

tuirenn (ā, f) – wheat

tuistiu (n, f) – birth, offspring

tulach (ā, f) – hill

turcbál (ā, f) – the lifting (v.n. of do·furcaib)

U

úachtar (o, n) – upper part, surface

úair – úar

úallach (o, ā) – proud

1. úar (ā, f) – hour

2. úar (o, ā) – cold

úas (+ prep.) – over

úasal (o, á in sg., i in pl.) – noble; uaislem compar.

úath (o, n) – fear, horror, terror

úathad (o, n) – small number, singular (i n-úathad – alone)

úathmaire (i̯ā, f) – dreadfulness, horror

úathmar (o, ā) – terrible

uball (o, n) – apple

ucht (u, n) – breast, bosom

ucut – yonder

uide (i̯o, n) – path, way

uile (i̯o, i̯ā) – all, every, each

úir (short ī, f) – earth, clay

uisce (i̯o, m) – water

Ulad (o, m) – inhabitant of the province of Ulster

umae (i̯o, n) – copper, bronze

ungae (i̯ā, f) – ounce

úr (o, ā) – fresh, new

uth (u, m) – udder

Appendix F—Tables

F.1. Old Irish phonemes and their graphematic representation

phoneme	*anlaut*	example	*inlaut, auslaut*	example: *inlaut*	example: *auslaut*
a	a	anmann, ainm	a	daltae, dairid	dligeda, ·roilgea
e	e	ech, eich	e	cengait, ceilid	esséirge, daltae
i	i	inathar, indeb	i	bibdaid, cride	céili, do·uccai
o	o	orgaid, oirdnid	o	format, roithid	betho, doirseo
u	u	ungae, uile	u	·rubart, muilenn	sunu, cridiu
ä	ai, e, i, au, u	au-, i-, edbart	ai, e, i, au, u	tailaig, telaig, tilaig	
ə	-	-	a, e, i, o, u	See table F.2	
ā	á	ár, áin	á	fán, táin, gabáil	·tá
ē	é, ǽ	ét, éisc, ǽssi	é, ǽ	fér, gréin, cenél, ·bǽr	cré, dǽ
ī	í	íccaid, ísel	í	síl, fírinne	sí
ō	ó	óg, óig	ó	slóg, cétóir	bó
ū	ú	únach, úire	ú	dún, dúilem	cú
ai̯	áe, aí	áes, aíne	áe, aí	máel, maíl	·taí
au̯	au	auraicept	au	baullu	-
āu̯	áu, áo	áu, áo	áu, áo	?	gáu, gáo
oi̯	oí, óe	oín, óen	oí, óe (aí, áe)	toísech, clóen	boí, bóe
eu̯	eu	euch	eu	neurt	-
ēu̯	éo, éu	éoin, éula	éu, éo	cenéuil	béo, béu
ui̯	-	-	uí	-	druí
iu̯	iu	iubar	iu	fiur	-
ī̯u̯	?	?	íu	·cíuir	·bíu
ia	ía	íasc	ía	fíadnisse	día
ua	úa	úan	úa	túaithe	-
m	m, mb	maith, a mbó	m, mm, mb	marbm(m)ai	form, lomm, camb
n	n, nd	nall, a ndún	n, nn, nd	mná, cenna	Éirenn, dín, find
ŋ(g)	ng	ar ngothae	ng	ingor, tengae	cumang
r	r, rr	rann, a rrann	r, rr	sruth, carrac	ferr
l	l, ll	lóg, for llóg	l, ll	slond, búachalla	ball
m'	m	méit	m, mm, mb	imbi	ainm(m), caimb
n'	n, nd	ní, a ndígal	nn, nd	tinne, ind í	Érinn, bind
ŋ'	ng	ar nglenn	ng	lingid	fo·loing
r'	r, rr	rind, a rríagol	r, rr	bríathar	eirr
l'	l, ll	léimm, i lleth	l, ll	clérech, cille	céill
μ	m	mo macc	m	brithemon	coém

Table F.1.1: Old Irish phonemes and their graphematic representation

phoneme	anlaut	example	inlaut, auslaut	example: inlaut	example: auslaut
ν	n	do *n*ámae	n	dé*n*um, se*n*-	bu*n*
ρ	r	mo *r*ún	r	a*r*athar	aratha*r*
λ	l	do *l*ubgort	l	a*l*aile	scé*l*
μ'	m	mo *m*enma	m	ni*m*e	nei*m*
ν'	n	do *n*ert	n	si*n*iu	ingi*n*
ρ'	r	mo *r*echt	r	fí*r*ián	athai*r*
λ'	l	do *l*ibuir	l	fi*l*i	béoi*l*
b	b, p	*b*ás, ar *p*opul	p, b, (bb)	po*p*ul, Al*b*u	cer*b*, a*p*, a*bb*
d	d, t	*d*áil, for *t*orbae	t, d, (dd)	e*t*ar, car*d*ae	·bera*t*, ar*d(d)*
g	g, c	*g*alar, for *c*uit	c, g, (gg), cc	é*c*en	der*c*, der*g(g)*, be*cc*
p	p	*P*átraic	p, pp	·im*p*ai	so*pp*
t	t	*t*ol	t, tt	a*tt*ach, dal*t*ae	och*t*, bra*t(t)*
k	c	*c*oimdiu	c, cc	cu*c(c)*u	ma*c(c)*
b'	b, p	*b*eirid, ar *p*íana	p, b, (bb)	·e*p*ir	cei*r*b
d'	d, t	*d*íabul, ar *t*ige	d, t, (dd)	cai*r*t/*d(d)*ea	bai*r*d, téi*t*
g'	g, c	*g*lenaid, ar *c*inn	c, g, (gg), cc	léi*c*id, ·roil*g*ea	dei*r*g(g), bi*cc*
p'	p	*p*ridchid	p, pp	im*p*i	sui*pp*
t'	t	*t*ír	t, tt	ei*tt*i	brai*t(t)*
k'	c	*c*íall	c, cc	cui*c(c)*e	mai*c(c)*
β	b, f	mo *b*oc, ar *f*uil	b	le*b*or	claide*b*, Med*b*
δ	d	do *d*án	d	Me*d*b	nípa*d*
γ	g	no·*g*uidimm	g	ad·á*g*athar	Lu*g*
f φ	f, ph	*f*ormat, a *ph*opul	f, ph	to*f*unn, ne*ph*-	-
θ	th	mo *th*abairt	th	ber*th*air	ca*th*
χ	ch	do *ch*lann	ch	a*ch*t	imma*ch*
β'	b, f	mo *b*reth, in·*f*il	b	noí*b*e	tigi*b*
δ'	d	do *d*elb	d	dei*d*bir	marbai*d*
γ'	g	mo *g*illae	g	té*g*i	·téi*g*
f' φ	f, ph	*f*ír, a *ph*recept	f, ph	ní·léic*f*ea, ne*ph*is	-
θ'	th	mo *th*ech	th	túai*th*e	túai*th*
χ'	ch	a *Ch*ríst	ch	fi*ch*e	ei*ch*
s	s	*s*úil	s, ss	ne*s*sam	marba*s*
s'	s	*s*íl	s, ss	éi*c*se, fei*ss*in	lei*s*
h	Ø, s, ṡ	a ainm, mo súil/ṡúil	-	-	-
h'	Ø, s, ṡ	a én, mo serc/ṡerc	-	-	-

Table F.1.2: Old Irish phonemes and their graphematic representation

F.2. Unaccented *inlauting* short vowels

phoneme	normal	example	adjacent to labial sounds	example: *inlaut*
CəC	a	car*a*t	o, u	Conch*o*bor, brithem*u*n
C'əC	e	fil*e*da	e	·gaib*e*m
CəC'	ai, i	ber*ai*t, ber*i*t	ai, i, ui	menm*ai*n, menm*i*n, menm*ui*n
C'əC'	i	beir*i*d	i	claidb*i*b
CuC	u	carp*u*t	-	-
C'uC	iu	léic*iu*d	-	-
CuC'	ui	Conchob*ui*r	-	-
C'uC'	-	-	-	-

Table F.2: The spelling of unaccented *inlauting* short vowels

F.3. The complete article at a glance

case	masculine; neuter				feminine		
	basic pattern	*anlauting* s	*anl.* f, l, r, n	*anl.* vowel	basic pattern	*anlauting* s	*anl.* f, l, r, n,V
nom.sg	*in; a^N*		*int; a^N*		*in^L*	*int^L*	*ind^L*
gen.	*in^L*	*int^L*	*ind^L*		*(in)na^H*		
prep.	*-(s)in^L* etc. (*auslaut* as in gen.sg.)				*-(s)in^L* etc. (*auslaut* as in nom.sg.)		
acc.	m. *in^N*, n. *a^N*; m. *-(s)in^N*, n. *-(s)a^N*				*in^N*; *-(s)in^N*		
nom.pl.	*in^L; (in)na^H*	*int^L; (in)na^H*	*ind^L; (in)na^H*		*(in)na^H*		
gen.	*(in)na^N*						
prep.	*-(s)naib*						
acc.	*(in)na^H; -(s)na^H*						
n.-a. du.	m. *in dá^L*, n. *in dá^N*; acc. m. *-(s)in da^L*, n. *-(s)in da^N*				*in dí^L*; acc. *-(s)in dí^L*		
gen.	*in dá^L; in dá^N*				*in dá^L*		
prep.	*-(s)naib dib^N*						

Table F.3: The article at a glance

F.4. The infixed pronouns at a glance

The table below gives an overview of all infixed pronoun classes side by side. I have simplified the presentation: note that in class B the internal vowel may also be *a* and *u* (-*dam*^{L}, -*tum*^{L} etc.), that in class C it may also be *a, u* and *i*, and that with *nach°* it also may be *i* (*nachim*^{L}).

person	class A	class B	class C	*nach°*
	after preverbs ending in a vowel	after preverbs ending in a consonant	in dependent clauses and after *in*^{N}	instead of negative *ná·* and *nád·*
1ˢᵗ sg.	-*m*^{L}, -*mm*^{L}	-*dom*^{L}, -*tom*^{L}	-*dom*^{L}	*nacham*^{L}·
2ⁿᵈ sg.	-*t*^{L}	-*tot*^{L}, -*t*^{L}	-*dat*^{L}	*nachat*^{L}·
3ʳᵈ sg. m.	-*a*^{N}	-*t*^{N}	-*id*^{N}, -*did*^{N}, -*d*^{N}, (-*da*^{N})	*nach*^{N}·
3ʳᵈ sg. f.	-*s*$^{(N)}$	-*da*^{H}, -*ta*^{H}	-*da*^{H}	*nacha*^{H}·
3ʳᵈ sg. n.	-*a*^{L}	-*t*^{L}	-*id*^{L}, -*did*^{L}, -*d*^{L}	*nach*^{L}·, *nachid*^{L}·
1ˢᵗ pl.	-*n*, -*nn*	-*don*, -*ton*	-*don*	*nachan·*
2ⁿᵈ pl.	-*b*	-*dob*, -*tob*	-*dob*	*nachab·*
3ʳᵈ pl.	-*s*$^{(N)}$	-*da*^{H}, -*ta*^{H}	-*da*^{H}	*nacha*^{H}·

Table F.4: Overview of the infixed pronouns

F.5. Irregular comparison at a glance

positive	equative	comparative	superlative
accus, ocus 'near'	n/a	*nessa*	*nessam*
becc 'small, few'	n/a	*laugu, lugu, laigiu*	*lugam (lugimem)*
il 'many'	*lir*	*lia*	n/a
lethan 'broad'	*leithir, lethithir*	*letha*	n/a
maith, dag- 'good'	n/a	*ferr*	*dech, deg*
már, mór 'much, big'	*móir*	*mó, móu, moo* etc.	*máam, moam*
oac, óc 'young'	n/a	*óa*	*óam*
olc, droch- 'bad'	n/a	*messam*	*messam*
remor 'thick'	*reimithir, reimir*	*reime*	n/a
sír 'long'	*sithir, sithithir*	*sia, sía*	*síam*
trén 'strong'	*treisithir*	*tressa*	*tressam*

Table F.5: Irregular comparison at a glance

F.6. Synopsis of the different verbal classifications

In section 8.2 I mentioned that there exist three different classifications of the present stems of OIr. verbs. I have followed Kim MCCONE's classification (EIV 23–25) with the one difference of introducing a subdivision of S3 verbs. Widely used among scholars is Rudolf THURNEYSEN's classification (GOI 352–358); John STRACHAN's system from *Old Irish Paradigms and Glosses* (OIPG 34) is hardly used. To a large extent these variant classifications are just different labels for the same contents, so that it is generally easy to change from one system into the other. The following table will help you in this task.

EIV	GOI	OIPG
W1	AI	B(1)
W2	AII	B(2)
H1	AIII -a-	-
H2	AIII -i-	-
H3	AIII -o/u/e-	-
S1	BI/III	A(1)
S2	BII	A(3)
S3a	BIV	A(2)
S3b	BV	-

Table F.6: Synopsis of verbal classes

F.7. The complete Old Irish verbal classes at a glance

The following table gives an overview of Old Irish verbal classes, including those sub-classes that I did not explain in detail in the lessons. This subtle classification is based on the 1st edition of Kim MCCONE's *Early Irish Verb* (Maynooth 1987). In his 2nd edition from 1997 he produced a simplified classification of S1 verbs, which is also the basis of my own teaching in 18.3. Thus the following table has a kind of historical touch.

verbal class			short description	examples
W1			n.pal. √fin. C; 3rd sg. conj. -*a*	*marbaid, ·marba*
W2			pal. √fin. C; 3rd sg. conj. -*i*	
	W2a			*léicid, ·léici*
	W2b		√V *u* or *o*	*do·luigi, ·dílgai; roithid*
H1			√V *a*	*raid; at·tá; ad·cota*
H2			√V *i*	*gniid; do·gní, ·déni*
H3			√V *e/o/u*	*sceid, ·scé; soaid, ·soí, ·intai; as·luí, ·élai*
S1			alternation in palatalization of √fin. C	
	S1a		pal. in 2nd, 3rd sg. and 2nd pl.	
		S1a i	*ĕ* in stressed √ (*i* in 2nd sg.)	*beirid, ·beir;* 2nd sg *biri, ·bir*
		S1a ii	*ĕ* + *d/th* in √; *t* as √fin. in unstressed position	*reithid, ·reith,* but *du·etarrat; ·réid,* but *ríadait;*
		S1a iii	*ĕ* > *a* before pal. *d/g*	*laigid; ·laig;* but *legait, ·legat*
		S1a iv	*i* > *e* before n.pal. C	*ibid, ·ib,* but *ebait, ·ebat*
	S1b		√V *a, o*; n.pal. √fin. C except 3rd sg. conj.	*canaid, ·cain*
	S1c		*n* disappears ouside of pr.stem	
		S1c i	like S1a iv	*for·ding,* but *for·dengat*
		S1c ii	like S1b	*fo·loing, fo·longat*
S2			pal. √fin. C; √V *a* or *u*	*gaibid, ·gaib*
S3			n.pal. √fin. *n*; *n* disappears outside of pr.stem	
	S3a		√V *e*	*benaid, ·ben*
	S3b		√V *i*	*do·lin; ro·cluinethar*

Table F.7: The classification of OIr. verbs

Legend:

pal.= palatalized, n.pal.= non-palatalized, √= root, √fin. C= root-final consonant, √V= root vowel, conj.= conjunct ending, pr.stem= present stem.

S1a i, iii, iv = S1a in EIV²; S1a ii = S1b in EIV²; S1b = S1c in EIV²; S1c = S1d in EIV²

F.8. The preterite stem formations at a glance

pret.	type	subtype	class	remarks
s	redupl.		W1	√fin. C n.-pal.
			W2	√fin. C pal.
			W2b	pres. stem *u* > pret. *o*; √fin. C n.-pal., exc. 3rd sg. conj.
			H3	exc. *foaid* 'to sleep' and *do·goa* 'to choose'
			S	*gaibid* 'to take,' *ibid* 'to drink'
			H1	
			H2	exc. *ciid* 'to weep' and compounds of *·cí* 'to see'
t				√ ends in *r, l* (exc. *ernaid* 'to bestow')
				*em- 'to take', **sem-* 'to pour'
				some verbs with √ ending in *g*
suffixless	reduplicated	e	strong	basically √structure C(R)e(i̯)/aC
		a		*canaid* 'to sing'
		o		S1c verbs with √V *o* < **u*
		i		S3 verbs with √structure C₁ī, *ciid* 'to weep'
		special		*·icc, ad·cí* 'to see'
	long vowel	ē		*gainithir* 'to be born,' *·moinethar* 'to think,' *·gnin* 'to know,'
		ī		*fichid* 'to fight,' *in·fét* 'to tell,' *midithir* 'to judge,' *ernaid* 'to grant,' *fenaid* 'to fence,' *sichid* 'to declare'
		ā		√structure CeT, *daimid* 'to suffer,' *ro·laimethar* 'to dare'
		a		*fo·ceird* 'to put,' *sceirdid* 'to strip'
		iu		S3 verbs with √structure CRī
		eo		*benaid* 'to beat,' *foaid* 'to sleep'
		iə/ia		*saidid* 'to sit' has *siasair* /siə̯səρ'/ with three syllables
		ua		*·cluinethar* 'to hear'
		special		substantive verb *at·tá*, copula *is*
	irreg.			*téit, ·finnadar, fo·gaib, do·tuit, at·bath*

Table F.8: The preterite formations at a glance

Legend:

pal.= palatalized, n.pal.= nonpalatalized, √= root, √fin. C= root-final consonant, √V= root vowel, pres. stem= present stem, pret. = preterite stem

F.9. The subjunctive at a glance

verbal class	subjunctive	remarks
W1		
W2a	a-subj.	present stem u > o
W2b		
H1		
H2	e-subj.	*ad·cí, ·accai*: mixture of a- and s-subj.
H3	a-subj.	*luid + do·goa*: mixture of a- and s-subj.
S1	s-subj./ a-subj.	roots ending in gutturals (except *aigid*),
S2		dentals or -*nn* have s-subj., all others a-subj.
S3	a-subj.	

Table F.9: The subjunctive formations at a glance

F.10. The future at a glance

class	future	remarks
W1	f-fut.	*caraid*: redupl. a-fut.; *gataid* & comp. of *scaraid*: é-fut.
W2a	f-fut.	*ad·gládathar*: redupl. a-fut.
W2b	f-fut.	
H1	redupl. a-fut.	*at·tá*: suppletive
H2	i-fut.	*ad·roilli*: f-fut.; *·cí*: traces of s-fut.; *·gní* & *·sní*: é-fut.
H3	f-fut.	*do·goa*: redupl. a-fut.
S1	s-fut./a-fut.	*·icc*: f-fut.; *téit* & *agaid*: suppletive
S2	s-fut./a-fut.	*·moinethar*: f-fut.
S3	i-fut.	*·gnin*: é-fut.; *·cluinethar*: redupl. a-fut.; *·fitir*: s-future

Table F.10.1: The complete future at a glance

The following table tells you which future formation uses which inflection:

future	inflection/ending set
f	like a-subj. (except 1st sg. conj.)
s	like s-subj. (except 1st sg. conj.)
i	like W2 (except 2nd sg.)
a	like a-subj.
suppl.	like a-subj.

Table F.10.2: The inflection of the various future formations

F.11. The complete substantive verb

	1st sg.	2nd sg.	3rd sg.	impers.	1st pl.	2nd pl.	3rd pl.
pres.	at·táu, at·tó ·táu, ·tó	at·taí ·taí	at·tá rel. fil, file ·tá, ·fil	- ·táthar	at·taam ·taam	at·taid ·taid	at·taat ·taat
cons.	biuu ·bíu	- ·bí	biid rel. biis, bís ·bí, ·rubai	bíthir ·bíther, ·rubthar	bímmi rel. bímme ·biam	- -	biit rel. bíte ·biat, ·rubat
imperf.	·biinn	-	·bíth	·bíthe	·bimmis	-	·bítis
pret.	(·)bá	(·)bá	(·)boí rel. boíe	bothae ·both	(·)bámmar	·báid	(·)bátar
augm. pret.	ro·bá ·ro/aba	ro·bá ·raba	ro·boí ·ro/abae	ro·both ·robad	ro·bámmar ·robammar	ro·báid ·robaid	ro·bátar ·ro/abatar
fut.	bia -	bie -	bieid, bied rel. bias ·bia	bethir -	bemmi ·biam	bethe ·bieid, ·bied	bieit rel. bete ·biat
cond.	·beinn	-	·biad	-	·bemmis	-	·betis
imper.	-	bí	biid, bíth	-	-	biid, bíth	biat
pres. subj.	béo, béu ·béo	bé, bee ·bé	beith, beid rel. bes ·bé, roib	bethir -	bemmi ·bem, ·robam	bethe ·beid, ·robith	beit rel. bete ·bet, ·robat
past subj.	·beinn	·betha	·beth, ·bed ·robad	·bethe	·bemmis	·bethe	·betis ·roibtis

Table F.11.1: The complete substantive verb at a glance

person		present tense	preterite
1st sg.	I have, I had etc.	táthum	baíthum, baíthium
2nd sg.	thou hast etc.	táthut	baíthut
3rd sg. m. n.	he/it has etc.	táithi, táthai	baíthi
3rd sg. f.	she has etc.	táthus	boíthus
1st pl.	we have etc.	táthunn, táithiunn	n/a
2nd pl.	you have etc.	táthuib	n/a
3rd pl.	they have etc.	*táthus	*boíthus

Table F.11.2: The substantive verb with suffixed pronouns

F.12. The complete copula

	1st sg.	2nd sg.	3rd sg.	1st pl.	2nd pl.	3rd pl.
pres.	*am* / -ta^L, -da^L	*at, it* / -ta^L, -da^L	*is* rel. *as* special[1]	*ammi, ammin* / -tan^L, -dan^L	*adi, adib* / -tad^L, -dad^L	*it* rel. *ata, at* / -tat^L, -dat^L
cons.	-	-	-bi, -pi	-	-	-
past	*basa* ·psa	- / -	*ba* / -bu^L, -pu^L, -bo^L, -po^L	- / -	- / -	*batir, batar* / -btar
augm. past.	*ropsa, robsa* ·rbsa	*ropsa* / -	*rop/bo^L, rop/bu^L* / -rbo^L, -rbu^L	*robummar* / -rbommar	- / -	*roptar, robtar* / -rbtar
fut.	*be* / -	*be* / -	*bid* rel. *bes^L, bas^L* / -ba, -pa	*bimmi, bemmi* / -	- / -	*bit* rel. *beta^L, bat^L* / -bat
cond.	- / -	- / -	*bed^L, robad^L* / -bad^L	- / -	- / -	*beitis* roptis
imper.	-	*ba^L*	*bed^L, bad^L* / -bad^L	*baan^L, ban^L*	*bed^L, bad^L* / -bad^L	*bat^L* / -bat^L
pres. subj.	*ba* / -ba^L	*ba, be* / -ba	*ba* rel. *bes, bas* special[2] / -ban	-	*bede* / -bad	*ropat^L* rel. *bete, beta* / -pat^L, -bat^L
past subj.	- / -benn, -bin	- / -ptha	*bed^L, bad^L, bid^L* / -bed^L, -bad^L	*bemmis* / -bimmis	- / -	*betis, bitis* / -btis, -ptis

Table F.12: The complete copula at a glance

Legend:

[1]= *ní; nád, nand, nant, nách; (co)ndid, (co)nid; connách; cesu^L, ceso^L, ciasu^L, ciaso^L; maso^L, masu^L; cenid; manid.*

[2]= *-dib, -dip; cid, ced; mad.*

Index

The numbers refer to the paragraphs in which the relevant topics are discussed.